OF THE PEOPLE

Four score and seven years ago our fathers brought
forth, on this continent, a new nation, conceived in
Liberty, and dedicated to the proposition that all
men are created equal.

Now we are engaged in a great civil war, testing
whether that nation, or any nation so conceived, and
so dedicated, can long endure. We are met on a
great battle-field of that war. We have come to
dedicate a portion of that field, as a final resting-
place for those who here gave their lives, that
that nation might live. It is altogether fitting
and proper that we should do this.

But, in a larger sense, we can not dedicate—
we can not consecrate— we can not hallow— this
ground. The brave men, living and dead, who struggled here, have consecrated it far above our poor
power to add or detract. The world will little
note, nor long remember what we say here, but
it can never forget what they did here. It is
for us the living, rather, to be dedicated here to the
unfinished work which they who fought here have thus
far so nobly advanced. It is rather for us to be
here dedicated to the great task remaining before us— that from these honored dead we take increased devotion to that cause for which they here gave
the last full measure of devotion— that we here highly resolve that these dead shall not have died in
vain— that this nation, under God, shall have
a new birth of freedom— and that government
of the people, by the people, for the people, shall
not perish from the earth.

GETTYSBURG ADDRESS

Of the People

EDITED BY

HARRY R. WARFEL

PROFESSOR OF ENGLISH, UNIVERSITY OF MARYLAND

AND

ELIZABETH W. MANWARING

PROFESSOR OF RHETORIC AND ENGLISH COMPOSITION
WELLESLEY COLLEGE

New York

OXFORD UNIVERSITY PRESS

1942

PREFACE

THE COMPILERS of *Of the People* believe that this book of readings differs from any that has yet been made. It presents for consideration, with emphasis on the concrete instance, evidence that the American student in these years of uncertainty and anxiety is not only highly privileged as heir to a great past, but is also, whatever the perils now threatening us and whatever our dark places of inequality, prejudice, injustice, the possessor of a rich estate in the present. Along with honest recognition of imperfection, the compilers have tried to present affirmations of achievement and of faith and have subordinated abstract discussion to living examples of democracy in action. They have defined 'democracy' and 'freedom' as touchstones against which to measure American activities in politics, in social striving, in religious idealism, in education, in science, and in the arts. The radio and the film, two important modes of communication with new techniques, are here joined with the older arts of communication to indicate the most popular methods of shaping and transferring ideas and feelings, and to emphasize the importance of a knowledge of these techniques in preserving our pattern of society.

Because idiom is of time as well as of place, most of the selections have been chosen from recent writing, and many of them are examples of good journalism. Enough older material has been included to make interesting connections in thought and to provide basis for comparison of expression. Grouping has been by idea rather than by type of discourse, but a table of contents by types has been prepared for those who wish to use it. Notes, Questions, and Exercises are given in an appendix. The Notes aim to unify the whole volume, to invite discussion of the principles illustrated, and to place certain selections against the background necessary for their proper interpretation. The Questions are suggestive rather than complete; their

v

number varies with the difficulty of the selections. The Exercises are designed for oral and written composition; numerous brief commentaries on types of writing or speaking are given with a view to stimulating a variety of classroom activities.

Unusual emphasis is placed upon the source or term paper and upon reviews. More research papers, with full apparatus of scholarship, are given here than in any similar work. Although these papers are by experienced authorities, each is a model of simplicity in statement and organization.

Acknowledgments of permission to use material are made elsewhere, but the compilers wish to thank here the colleagues, authors, editors, and publishers, who have given so much advice and assistance.

H. R. W.
E. W. M.

April 1942.

CONTENTS

III

'FROM AN UNCHALLENGEABLE EMINENCE'

IV

DEMOCRACY IN ACTION

V

EDUCATION FOR FREEDOM

VI

'THE PURSUIT OF HAPPINESS'

VII
TIMES THAT TRY MEN'S SOULS

I

The Voice of the People

THE AMERICAN'S CREED

I BELIEVE in the United States of America as a government of the people, by the people, for the people; whose just powers are derived from the consent of the governed; a democracy in a Republic; a sovereign Nation of many sovereign States; a perfect Union, one and inseparable; established upon those principles of freedom, equality, justice, and humanity for which American patriots sacrificed their lives and fortunes.

I therefore believe it is my duty to my country to love it; to support its Constitution; to obey its laws; to respect its flag; and to defend it against all enemies.

WILLIAM TYLER PAGE

DEMOCRACY, A TRAINING-SCHOOL

POLITICAL democracy, as it exists and practically works in America, with all its threatening evils, supplies a training-school for making first-class men. It is life's gymnasium, not of good only, but of all. We try often, though we fall back often. A brave delight, fit for freedom's athletes, fills these arenas . . . Whatever we do not attain, we at any rate attain the experiences of the fight, the hardening of the strong campaign, and throb with currents of attempt at least. Time is ample. Let the victors come after us. Not for nothing does evil play its part among us. Judging from the main portions of the history of the world, so far, justice is always in jeopardy, peace walks amid hourly pitfalls, and of slavery, misery, meanness, the craft of tyrants and the credulity of the populace, in some of their protean forms, no voice can at any time say, They are not. The clouds break a little, and the sun shines out—but soon and certain the lowering darkness falls again, as if to last forever. Yet there is an immortal courage and prophecy in every sane soul that cannot, must not, under any circumstances, capitulate. *Vive,* the attack—the perennial assault! *Vive,* the unpopular cause—the spirit that audaciously aims—the never-abandon'd efforts, pursued the same amid opposing proofs and precedents.

WALT WHITMAN, *Democratic Vistas,* 1871

YOUNG MAN IN SEARCH OF A FAITH

By Alvin M. Josephy, Jr.

Music:

NARRATOR: We have come to a black night in the history of man's destinies.

Music:

YOUNG MAN: I am a young man. I was brought up in this country. My father before me and his father before him also. The realism of a changing world has frightened me. For some reason, I feel there is nothing solid to set my feet on . . . nothing firm for my hands to grasp, no ideal to champion . . .
My father and his father also.

Music:

NARRATOR: Foolish boy! Foolish American!

YOUNG MAN: Foolish American, did you say? What has the fact that I'm an American got to do with it?

NARRATOR: Everything!

YOUNG MAN: Everything? And why am I foolish? Who are you? What do you mean?

NARRATOR: I can explain what I mean . . .

Music:

NARRATOR: For a century and a half, men have known a stirring faith. For a century and a half, men have lived that faith. Between those years, a world has changed, old idols fell, new tyrants rose, weird dreams were born and died again, strange shadows dimmed the skies. For a century and a half men have kept alive a faith, and that faith is still alive, and will always be alive, despite the changing idols, wars and dreams of ruthless worlds, as long as men still know and live that faith.

Now why do you despair?

BOY: You mean there is a faith which may yet give me hope for the future?

NARRATOR: Yes. So long as it breathes and kicks with the struggle for life, there is a faith to move all men.

BOY: Will you tell me what it is?

NARRATOR: It is a single word—America.

BOY: How can that be a faith? I've heard men say that before, but I never really understood what they meant. What is there about America that can give you such a faith?

NARRATOR: If you knew America, you wouldn't be asking such a question.

BOY: But I do know America! I told you, I was born here.

NARRATOR: Maybe you've never *seen* America. Why don't you go out and look for it?

BOY: I've seen America. I've been in thirty-four of the States. Once I drove to the coast and back.

NARRATOR: You still don't know America. You still haven't seen it. Why don't you look for it?

BOY: But—what am I supposed to look for? What am I supposed to find?

NARRATOR: Look for America. You'll find it.

BOY: Look for America—*look* for America? People will think I'm crazy.

Music:

BOY: Pardon me. Are you a tourist guide?

WOMAN: [*Low woman's voice*] Yes, sir, at your service.

BOY: I think you can help me. I'm looking for America. Can you show it to me?

WOMAN:	Certainly. What part of America? East? West? North? South?
BOY:	The whole thing. All of it.
WOMAN:	I see. Well, showing people America is my business. I guess I can take care of you. Just step over this way, please. Over to this map. Now here is America. America is a map, high and broad, with its face to the sky and its back to the ground. America is a land, bounded by oceans and borders and veined with rivers. America is a country of green, yellow, and brown, depending on its varying physical elevations and depressions. America is a country of differing frost, sunshine, annual precipitation, wind velocity, temperature, evaporation, drought, population, wealth, farm produce, manufactures, mineral output. It is also a country of different kinds of dirt, rock, water, vegetation—
BOY:	Just a minute. That's not what I'm looking for. What is it that makes America a *great* country?
WOMAN:	I was coming to that. You interrupted me. Let me go on. America is a total output of much wealth and a storehouse of great resources. America is tobacco growing in the brown dirt of Carolina, sheep grazing near the snowy rocks of Montana, coal blackening the water in the Lehigh Valley, corn waving on the prairies of Iowa, trout swimming in the rapids of Maine, oil gushing from the hills of California, cattle on the plains of the Panhandle, wheat over the swells of Kansas, copper making red mountains in Arizona—
BOY:	But excuse me. That still isn't what I'm looking for. Those products of the earth can be found in other parts of the world. What is it that is purely America?

WOMAN: Names are purely America. Names of mountains, like the curving hills of the Blue Ridge, Ozark, Catskills; the tall humps of the Alleghenies; the snow-capped Rockies. Names of rivers like the proud, rolling Mississippi, Ohio, Colorado, the Columbia.

Names of cities, like the English Jamestown, Portsmouth, and New York; like the French Detroit, Vincennes, and Laramie. Like the Spanish La Junta and San Luis Obispo. Like the Indian Kalamazoo, Walla Walla, Tallahassee, and Pocatello.

BOY: You're just reading a map. That isn't what I want.

WOMAN: Why not? That map is America. Those names are America. They all have the sounds of America.

BOY: There's something in what you say. But I still don't think it's exactly what I'm looking for.

WOMAN: Then I can't help you. Why don't you try a historian?

BOY: That's a good idea. Thanks.

Music:

BOY: I'm looking for a historian. Are you a historian?

HISTORIAN: [*Oldish man*] Yes, in a way. I'm a man who's proud of my country's history. When I close my eyes and try to see what has gone before, I can hear sounds of men struggling, of great deeds being accomplished, of victories being won.

BOY: Do you think America is the story of these occurrences?

HISTORIAN: Yes, I do. America is each one of them, and America is all of them.

BOY: Well, I'm searching for America. I wish you'd explain.

HISTORIAN: Certainly. I'll be glad to.

Music:

HISTORIAN: America is a continuity of men and deeds. America is the Boston Massacre, men spilling their blood on the cobblestones before the Old State House. America is the rising up, the anger, the men singing. America is Bunker Hill and men running out of ammunition. America is snow and freezing cold and soldiers dragging their bloody way through a Christmas Eve, to attack at Trenton. America is rags and dirt and hunger at Valley Forge. America is Morgan's riflemen, George Rogers Clark, Herkimer at Oriskany, Francis Marion and guns on the Yorktown Peninsula.

And then, America is the Declaration of Independence coming true.

BOY: [*Deprecating it all*] Now listen. I remember all that when I was in school. I had to learn the Declaration of Independence by heart. [*He runs through it like a schoolboy going through a memory lesson*] 'When in the course of human events we hold these truths to be self-evident that all men are created equal, that they are endowed by their Creator with certain *unalienable* rights, that among these are life liberty and the pursuit of happiness.

HISTORIAN: If that's the way you say it, young man, then you haven't found America.

America is a quest for government, a search for a state that shall rule by the consent of the governed. America is the pursuit of that search by one of the greatest groups of men that ever came together at one time in all history. America is a convention and one of its members, Dr. Benjamin Franklin, telling the people of his country: 'We have given you a republic, if you can keep it.'

The War of 1812. The Constitution and the Guerrière. The smoke of battle on the rolling sea and the crash of fore- and mainmast. The clearing of the smoke and the victory of Old Ironsides, her drummers coming to attention on the blackened decks and striking up Yankee Doodle Dandy!

[*Loud*] Oh; this is America, proud, proud America!

Music:

But America is not all war, for when the fight is over, America is another march to the westward. Pioneer families in covered wagons, swinging along to the old drummer song—

Music:

HISTORIAN: Trappers, hunters, traders, swindlers, and men of the clergy. Kit Carson, Bonneville, Jim Bridger, and the Reverend Timothy Flint bringing religion to the Mississippi. Yankee peddlers talking through their noses in log-cabin towns; Springfield, the frontier, Brigham Young, Independence, and on to Oregon!

BOY: Say, listen. That's old stuff. I've seen it in a hundred movies. It's history, old history. I'm looking for America in this year. This year of 1941.

HISTORIAN: I'm afraid I can't help you. I think you should see someone who knows the present-day scene. Perhaps a poet.

Music:

BOY: A poet! That's a good idea. Poets are supposed to see things other people don't. Maybe a poet can help me.

Music:

BOY: Say, do you think you can help me? You're a poet. I'm trying to find America. No one seems to know exactly what it is; at least they can't tell *me* what it is. Do you think you can?

POET: [*Very lyric*] Certainly I can. I spend my life writing about America. America is the people who inhabit it. We the people—

BOY: Yes, I heard that before.

POET: Let me explain—

Ever since the country began, the people have been America, and America has been the people. Look there in the center of a crowded city, a ball park, a theater. The unformed ranks of people overwhelm you with their complete, individual human-beingness.

BOY: What?

POET: Look at them. Each is America. Each and all together. Their life, their emotions, their physical and mental actions. Their births and first frightened days at school. Their struggles to exist, to find jobs, marry, raise families, buy cars, pay the grocer, go to the movies, win at bridge, take a vacation—and avoid death. All that is America.

BOY: I don't understand. Why is all that America?

POET: Look at them! Department store clerks with aching feet and tightened nerves. Bricklayers with lunchboxes spread on their laps; Indians selling baskets and blankets along New Mexican roads; traffic cops blowing whistles and holding up white-gloved hands; steam shovel operators pushing levers and digging in the earth; telephone clerks speaking into seven telephones at once, in Wall Street; automobile salesmen being very 'folksy' to prospective clients; dirt farmers looking up at the skies for rain; trolley-car motormen clanging their bells in traffic; unemployed crying on their pillows at night. All of these are America because all of them are individualistic human beings.

Music:

BOY: Can't you help me any better? Other countries have people who are certainly human beings.

POET: I don't think I can make myself any clearer. It is something I feel. I go among these people and I watch them and listen to them, and I know they are America.

BOY: I'm sorry, but I still haven't found what I'm looking for.

NARRATOR: Foolish boy! Foolish American! You still don't understand, do you?

BOY: What?

NARRATOR: Here, you have seen what you have been looking for, and you still don't recognize it.

BOY: Who are you? Where are you?

NARRATOR: Why, I'm you, feeling in your own way these things that others have been feeling. I am the one who first started you off on this search. I am the one who first told you there is still a faith. Remember?

Music:

NARRATOR: Look with me now, over there across the seas— a little, ruined town in Europe. Huddled in darkness in a silent refuge, an old man is scrawling on a piece of tattered paper. Around him a world has retreated in terror. In the gloom there is nothing left save the rats and the flickering, dripping candle, by which he writes. Look, do you see him? Read what he is writing.

BOY: [*As though reading*] 'In this terrible world, we miserable, frightened folk must retain the feeling that some day, somewhere, man will yet know a nation of right and justice, a nation in which the humble prayers of all the common people will find sanctuary. It will be a land founded on kindliness, where the weak and the poor may not be trod on, but will be sought after for the best that is in them.'

[*Interrupting his reading*] Say. What does he mean?

NARRATOR: Don't talk. Read as he writes.

BOY: [*Reading*] 'What we see is a land of great wealth and pride, a land where men will exult at the mere sound and thought of what is theirs.'

WOMAN: Tobacco, sheep, coal, copper, oil—

BOY: 'It will be a nation where men will worship the very names of the cities they have builded.'

WOMAN: Kalamazoo, Baton Rouge, Albuquerque—

BOY: 'And the mountains beneath which they live.'

WOMAN: Blue Ridge, Ozark, Big Horn—

BOY: [*Crying out*] I know! He's writing about America.

NARRATOR: Ssshh. Read on!

BOY: [*Reading*] 'I see this land, even now, in this most awful night of our suffering. It is a land of people, each in himself a part of the nation, but also, each an important, all-powerful entity—'

POET: We, the people.

BOY: 'I see it as a nation, happy and bright, filled with a peace that has come because of a faith—'

HISTORIAN: Bunker Hill, Trenton—

BOY: I see this faith, founded on the blood and flesh of men who would be free—

HISTORIAN: Valley Forge—

BOY: 'Of men who would keep this freedom and hand it on to others.'

HISTORIAN: Adams, Franklin, Jefferson—

BOY: 'This I see as a triumph of man.'

POET: Four score and seven years ago . . .

BOY: 'To be free!'

POET: Our fathers brought forth . . .

BOY: 'To be alive!'

POET: On this continent . . . a new nation . . .

BOY: 'God, as we die in these smoking ruins, let someone, somewhere, have that which we do not!'
            But we do . . . we do. We have it! It's here. It's America! America!

Music:

NARRATOR: Now you have found America. You have found

a faith in which to believe . . . a faith to defend and keep alive in these terrible days.

Music:

VOICE: . . . that from these honored dead we take increased devotion

. . . to that cause for which they gave the last full measure of devotion

. . . that we here highly resolve that these dead shall not have died in vain

. . . that this nation, under God, shall have a new birth of freedom

. . . and that government of the people, by the people and for the people

. . . shall not perish from the earth.

Music:

AMERICA THE BEAUTIFUL

By Katharine Lee Bates

O BEAUTIFUL for spacious skies,
  For amber waves of grain,
For purple mountain majesties
  Above the fruited plain!
    America! America!
  God shed his grace on thee
And crown thy good with brotherhood
  from sea to shining sea!

O beautiful for pilgrim feet,
  Whose stern, impassioned stress
A thoroughfare for freedom beat
  Across the wilderness!
    America! America!
  God mend thine every flaw,
Confirm thy soul in self-control,
  Thy liberty in law!

O beautiful for heroes proved
  In liberating strife,
Who more than self their country loved,
  And mercy more than life!
    America! America!
  May God thy gold refine
Till all success be nobleness
  And every gain divine!

O beautiful for patriot dream
  That sees beyond the years
Thine alabaster cities gleam
  Undimmed by human tears!
    America! America!
  God shed his grace on thee
And crown thy good with brotherhood
  from sea to shining sea!

By permission of Mrs. George Sargent Burgess.

U.S.A.: THE LAND, THE PEOPLE, AND THE GOVERNMENT

By D. W. Brogan

THE area of the continental United States is just over 3,000,000 square miles (3,026,789). This area is less than that of Europe (including European Russia), Canada, or Brazil. But in population, resources, and unity of government, the only rival of the United States is Soviet Russia.

In variety of climate and, so, of ways of life, the territory of the continental United States resembles Europe more than it does such less varied masses as Brazil, Canada, or Australia. Regions as unlike as Norway and Andalusia are united under one government, speak a common language, regard themselves as part of one nation. This unity is reinforced by the most elaborate transportation system in the world, a system the elaboration of which has been made possible by the political unity. Thus a system of air-navigation, aided by beacons, direction-beams, airports, has been created which political divisions would make impossible in Europe, even were Europe less ridden by war and fear of war.

But if the first thing to emphasize is unity, the second is sectionalism. Although the United States is less varied for its size than Europe, it is varied. It is possible to bathe out of doors with comfort in one part of the United States, while temperatures of 50° below zero are prevalent in another. These great climatic differences are reinforced by general geographic differences. Thus the United States can be divided into the great central valley of the Missouri-Mississippi system, with the coastal mountains and plains on the Atlantic and Pacific. But that is a

From D. W. Brogan, *U.S.A.*, An Outline of the Country, Its People, and Institutions, Oxford University Press, London, 1941. By courtesy of the publishers.

very crude division. More helpful are the great regions that geographers have discovered—regions ranging in number from half-a-dozen to forty or fifty, according to the standards used. These regions, though mainly based on obvious geographical features, are, in fact, modified by history, by economic development, by the racial origin of the population. Thus a very important dividing line—that between the long grass and the short grass [1]—cuts off Minnesota and eastern North Dakota from the plains west of the Missouri. But the common Scandinavian origin of the population and the common interest in world wheat prices unite these regions. Louisiana is not merely a state of the 'Deep South,' and not merely the only cane-sugar region of the continental United States, it is a state of French origin and still largely of 'non-Anglo-Saxon' character.

The difficulty of accurately delimiting a natural region can be illustrated from the case of the South. Historically speaking, the South is either the sixteen states in which slavery was legal in 1860, or the eleven which attempted to leave the union in 1861. But Dr. Odum has shown good reason for excluding from the South, Texas (and its child, Oklahoma), for adding Kentucky, which did not secede, but excluding the other non-seceding slave states, Maryland, Delaware, Missouri. The South has the highest proportion of Negroes, of members of evangelical churches, of illiterates, of murders, of drinkers of coca-cola, of tenant-farmers. It has the smallest number of income-tax payers, of Jews, of Catholics. All or almost all of these characteristics are explicable in terms of the others, even the coca-cola drinking, but, in addition, the South is a region that has had a common and binding historical experience—that of being on the losing side in a civil war.

New England is not merely a region of barren soil, of water-power, of hard winters, it is a region unified for three centuries by common educational, religious, and political experiences; and the Polish immigrants, working the farms abandoned by the Yankees, are profoundly affected by the social organization set up by the people whose descendants are now farming land in

[1] Roughly west of 100° W., the rainfall is too uncertain to make cereal farming anything but a gamble.

Ohio or Nebraska, or are settled in the cities, or have simply vanished like the Indian. And even across the comparative uniformity of the Middle West, historical accident has differentiated Kansas from Nebraska, northern Ohio from southern Ohio.

But, primarily, these geographical regions have, in common, their economic interests. The South is the 'land of cotton,' as it was when 'Dixie' was written. It is dependent on world markets; it is sensitive to the change in women's taste in dress from cotton to artificial silk. But the Middle Western farmer, though he is less conscious of it, is united by varied economic misfortunes arising from the slowing down of population increase and the growth of economic nationalism in the United States and in the rest of the world. His industry of turning maize into fats via the pig, the basis of the 'corn-hog cycle,' is affected by a change in tastes in food—and by the fact that tropical areas can produce the equivalent of his lard without the intermediate stage of the pig. The mountain states are united by the variations in the price of silver, and to the Pacific Slope the Japanese are both potential enemies and actual customers.

Climate unites regions in other ways. A drought that kills all the crops west of the Missouri may merely serve to raise the price of cereals east of the Mississippi, to the profit of the Indiana farmer. Frost does not necessarily attack the citrus crops of Florida and California simultaneously, nor does the boll-weevil or the corn-borer attack the cotton or corn crops over all the United States at the same time. Sectionalism—the habit of working as one political unit—is thus imposed by a variety of forces on groups of states, and the legal units, the states, are only convenient weapons for the sections to use in the endless battle of pressure groups for the favor of the Government of the United States. It is these six or seven sections, not the forty-eight states, that are the realities underlying the American federal structure, the internal obstacles to the more perfect union promised by the preamble to the Constitution.

II

The population of the United States according to the census of 1940 is 131,409,881, an increase of just under 9,000,000 since

1930, *which is the smallest percentage increase in American history*. But even in the decade 1920-1930, which showed a growth of 17,000,000 in total population, the greatest absolute increase in any decade in American history, the proportionate rate of increase had already fallen off. The increase of American population had been one of the wonders of the world; from 2,500,000 in 1776 to 122,000,000 in 1932, but the days of multiplication were passing and experts were estimating a rapid decline in increase, a speedy stabilization and a possible absolute decline, all within the life-span of persons now living. Not only has the population increase begun to taper off rapidly, but the character of the population has begun to change. A most striking change has been the relative and absolute decline of the farm population. Between 1920 and 1930 urban population rose by 14,600,000, and farm population (as apart from nominal rural population) fell by 1,200,000.

Ideally, America is a farmer's republic, but farmers are now only a quarter of the population. Ideally, America is a country the population of which doubles in every generation; actually the population increase is rapidly approaching zero. It was assumed that the value of land, except in certain ill-favored regions, was bound to rise, substantially if agricultural land was in question, perhaps spectacularly if urban land was concerned. It is only just beginning to be realized that these beliefs are possibly baseless, that the great uncontrolled and exuberant growth of American population and home market is over.

It is apparently paradoxical that the American farmer should have been one of the strongest supporters of the restriction on immigration that accounts in part for the decline in population growth. Before 1914, apart from limitations on contract labor and some health regulations, immigration was unlimited, and often reached the figure of 1,000,000 a year. There had long been agitation for a reduction in the number of immigrants, but in the optimistic years it was ill-received. The war of 1914-1918 changed that. Alarm, not wholly baseless, was evoked by the spectre of what was called 'hyphenization.' The German-Americans were accused of being 'hyphenated,' i.e. of not being Americans unconditionally. The reaction from Europe which followed the end of the war, the panic caused by the Russian Revolution, the more legitimate panic bred by the thought of ruined Europe pouring her derelicts into America, combined with an intolerant nationalism to make possible the introduction, for the first time, of the idea of *numerical* limitation of immigration. Temporary laws arbitrarily reduced the number of immigrants from certain countries. Quotas were fixed first on the basis of the census of 1910, then on that of the census of 1890, then on a figure which was said to represent the proportions of various 'races' in the American population of 1790. The object of these regulations was not merely to cut down the total immigration, but to change its character. A distinction was made between the 'old' and 'new' immigrations. The old immigration was mainly British, Irish, German, and Scandinavian. The new was mainly Italian, Jewish, Polish, Greek, etc. What was not stated openly was that the old immigration, with some important exceptions, like the Irish and a large part of the Germans, was Protestant, and the United States in 1920 was desperately trying by law to preserve the ethos of rural America, the weak position of which was made evident by each new census. The same forces that imposed the religious taboo of rural America by the prohibition amendment were behind the new immigration policy, as they were behind the passing of state laws barring the teaching of evolution in public schools, state laws attempting to suppress Catholic 'parochial' (private) schools, denunciations of cigarette advertisements that suggested that good women could smoke, and so on.

The new immigration policy had a good deal to commend it from the point of view of a citizen of the United States, if not of a citizen of the world. It was a natural extension to the labor field of the doctrine of high tariffs and it gave ground for hope that, with a more racially homogeneous labor force, trade union organization would be easier. Nor was that all. As most immigrants now settled in industrial areas and largely in racial enclaves, the problem of assimilation became more difficult and it had in any case been easier to assimilate literate North European Protestants than illiterate South and East European Catholics, Greek Orthodox, and Jews. But to assert, what was palpably true, that America was a Protestant nation anxious to preserve its fundamental character, anxious to turn away from a Europe that had made such a mess of things, was to deny the official dogma of religious neutrality and the public conviction that the United States was the Good Samaritan of nations. So the new policy, a natural result of the movement that produced prohibition and the revived Ku Klux Klan, was provided with a scientific fig-leaf. Bogus science was called in, and it was asserted that 'the English, Dutch, Swedes, Germans, and even the Scotch-Irish who constituted practically the entire immigration prior to 1890, were less than two thousand years ago one Germanic race in the forests surrounding the North Sea.' [2] This fable quieted professorial and congressional consciences, but it did not alter the fact that what Congress wanted to do was to exclude Catholics and Jews, and non-English-speaking immigrants in general, even though their anthropological classification might be the same as George Washington's and their blood group identical with that of the passengers in the *Mayflower* . . .

A century ago, the American people was young, prolific, mainly British, overwhelmingly Protestant, and (Negroes apart) remarkably unified. Today the population is middle-aged,[3] moving rapidly towards stability if not sterility, certainly a good deal less than half British in origin, with a very great Catholic and large Jewish and Greek Orthodox minorities.

America is not likely to have any large new elements added to its population; the free distribution of public lands, long ended as an effective economic safety-valve, was formally ended in 1935, and the census of 1930 revealed that, for the first time since the white man landed on North America, the area of forest had increased. When the size of the country is considered, when the variety of the racial origins of the people is considered, the degree of unity attained is marvelous, and the national motto, *e pluribus unum,* if still a prophecy, seems a plausible prophecy.

[2] Roy L. Garis, *Immigration Restriction, A Study of the Opposition to and Regulation of Immigration into the United States,* p. 203.
[3] In 1850, the age of the average American was just under 20; in 1930, it was just under 40.

III

The United States is a federation, governed according to a written Constitution as interpreted by the Supreme Court. Each of the forty-eight states is theoretically sovereign and equal. What rights and powers have not been delegated to the federation remain to the states—or the people. But, not only have amendments to the original Constitution of 1787 increased federal power, but the permanent trend of judicial interpretation of the Constitution has been towards its extension, and as modern government grows more complex and more expensive, the Federal Government, by making grants of money—on conditions—has induced states to accept its lead, even in departments in which they are still nominally sovereign. It is, in fact, a fiction that the desert plateau of Nevada, with a population of less than 100,000, is a sovereign state in the sense that New York is. Nevada was invented as a state to give extra electoral votes to Lincoln in 1864, and it lives off dear silver and easy divorce, the price of both being, in fact, regulated by the legal activities of the Union and of less liberal states. Federalism still has meaning. It permits variations in domestic law. It permits far greater variations in the efficiency of public services than would be possible in a unitary country. It makes the enforcement of criminal law difficult, and thus justifies the increasing police activities of the Federal Government, of which the G men are the best publicized example. It produces such absurd situations as that which divides the sovereignty over the lands round New York harbor among three states, a situation the inconvenience of which co-operation between New York and New Jersey only partly removes: but the average American state has more formal than real power, is the decreasingly important partner in the federal relationship.

The Constitution of the United States is the oldest written constitution in the world, and, in form, is still very like that which went into effect in 1789. In the 150 years that have elapsed, the territory of the United States has increased more than threefold, the population more than fiftyfold, and the Constitution has stood this strain only by developing astonishing elasticity. The chief agent in this stretching process has been the Supreme

Court, the most remarkable judicial body in the world. The experience of Switzerland and of other countries shows that a federation with a written constitution does not necessitate a court with power to determine the limits of federal power, or the meaning of the constitution. And the frequent English assumption that the Supreme Court only decides whether a power belongs to a state or to the union is absurdly wrong. The most important constitutional cases in modern times have nothing to do with a federal system as such. The Court decides the present meaning of terms like 'due process of law' or 'person,' and as it refuses to treat these words merely in their legal technical sense, it is forced to give them a political, indeed, a philosophical, meaning. The Court scrutinizes state and federal legislation not to determine whether there are clauses in the Constitution justifying the power claimed, but in accordance with what it calls 'the rule of reason,' and the rule of reason means what any five justices out of nine think reasonable. 'The Constitution is what the judges say it is.' So declared Chief Justice Charles Evans Hughes before he mounted the Bench.

One consequence of the power of the Supreme Court to decide what state or federal statutes are 'reasonable,' and so constitutional, is to make it very uncertain at any given moment what the law is. For until the Supreme Court has ruled on it, any statute may plausibly be asserted to be unconstitutional. Thus the Wagner Labor Act of 1935 was boldly asserted to be unconstitutional and it was ignored, until the Supreme Court decided in its favor in 1937. What had been very doubtful law became undoubted law overnight, and a body (the National Labor Relations Board) which had been of the mildest academic importance suddenly became central in New Deal policy.[4]

In most matters an irreverent people, the Americans are the most reverent people in the world in political matters. They re-

---

[4] More startling still, a local statute passed by Congress in its capacity as legislator for the District of Columbia (the City of Washington), and held to be unconstitutional in the case of *Adkins* v. *Children's Hospital* in 1923, suddenly came alive, and overnight became law, though no machinery now existed for putting it into effect. The Supreme Court, in the spirit of Emerson and Whitman, showed its contempt for consistency and its readiness to contradict itself. In America the law is not only occasionally an ass, as in all countries, it is even more than in other countries a lottery.

gard the Constitution as sacred, as a national talisman, and, as President Roosevelt discovered when he attacked the Supreme Court in 1937, even the most popular politicians assail the sacred priesthood of the constitutional temple at their peril. That he was soon after given a chance to appoint a majority of the Court, and that the infallible interpreter of the Constitution promptly began to contradict its recent self, do not seem to have shaken the popular faith.

The Constitution provides for the distribution of the federal power between the judicial, the executive, and the legislative powers, or so it is held. The judicial power is vested in the Supreme Court, whose membership and most of whose duties are defined by Congress, and in such subsidiary federal courts as Congress may determine. But all state courts are bound to enforce the 'supreme law of the land,' i.e. valid federal legislation and treaties. The executive power is vested solely in one man, the President, elected for a term of four years, in form indirectly, in fact directly by popular vote in each state. The legislative power is vested in a Congress of two Houses, of which no member may accept federal office and retain his seat.

The position of the President of the United States is double. He is the formal head of the nation, embodying the national sovereignty as a constitutional monarch does; he is also effective head of the executive. Indeed, since he can veto any bill that cannot muster the support of two-thirds of each House of Congress, he has an important part in the legislative function too. His executive duties and powers are general and specific. Thus he is, by precise constitutional grant, commander-in-chief of the Army and Navy, a power of vast importance in war time. But, in addition to these specific powers, he has been held by the Courts to have rights arising from the fact that the executive power of the United States is entrusted to him. All federal officials, with very few exceptions, owe him implicit obedience, and can be dismissed by him should they fail in their duty to the President. And these powers he exercises, for the four years of his term, with few or no customary limitations. He has a right to do as he likes, within his wide powers, as long as he is President. Congress can hamper him by refusing money, for instance, but it cannot get rid of him except by impeachment, and that remedy has only been tried once, in the case of Andrew Johnson, and then failed.

The President's 'Cabinet' is unknown to the law. The President appoints, removes, and controls the 'principal officers' of the executive departments and has a right to demand their advice in writing or orally. But it is only custom that decrees that the President shall meet every week, or at other fixed times, the ten chief executive officers. There is no legal means of enforcing this custom and an American Cabinet, unlike a British, is purely the creation and creature of its chief. The President usually includes in it some eminent political leaders of his own party, but most of the Cabinet members may be chosen quite outside the usual political organizations.[5] An American Cabinet has no independent life or authority of its own, and the administration stands or falls by the success of its chief. There is no possibility of such a transfer of power as that which replaced Mr. Chamberlain by Mr. Churchill. And it is important to remember that since 1900 no congressional leader has been elected President.

In national politics, the President is always something of a new-comer compared with the congressional leaders. The proposal to let members of the Cabinet address either House of Congress has much to commend it, but the American system opposes great obstacles to any open and regular liaison between the President and Congress; there is a constant tug-of-war between the two powers, and closer unity can only be achieved to the loss of one party to the contest—usually the President.

The official residence of the President is an attractive though not a very large building, but 'the White House'[6] occupies a place in the hearts of the American people that no other residence, however splendid, could do. The President's salary ($75,-000 a year) and a handsome allowance for entertainment make possible a dignified way of life for the head of the nation, but there is no possibility of such a parody of court life as was at-

[5] In 1940, only one member of the Cabinet, the Secretary of State, Mr. Hull, had ever been a member of Congress.

[6] The White House acquired this name after it had been burned by the British troops who occupied Washington in 1814. The walls were painted white to cover the marks of burning.

tempted in France under the Third Republic. The dignity of the greatest office in the world (as almost all Americans think the presidency to be) would not be added to by an Elysée or Rambouillet, any more than it would be by honorific titles. Except in the neighborhood of Boston (where it means the head of Harvard University), 'the President' means always the President of the United States—and it is title enough.

In the federal Congress, prestige and, to some extent, power, is very unevenly divided between the two Houses. The Lower House, with its short term of office (two years), its large membership, and its rigid rules, cannot compete for popular interest either with the Senate or with the President. As there is no Front Bench of Cabinet Ministers controlling the time of the House, that has to be done by an elaborate system of committees which decide what bills or motions shall be considered at all, and what killed off. But this decision is made in private and by men who have risen to power in the committee system mainly by seniority, by surviving many elections, and that means, in the American system, by representing the most party-ridden constituencies, the Solid South, the rural North, regions where winds of controversy seldom blow. Congressional leaders tend, that is to say, to be out of touch with public opinion in the nation when any great issue is being debated, and congressional leaders know that, to borrow a phrase from a former member, 'the world will little note nor long remember' what they say or do. The dramatic possibilities of parliamentary life are almost entirely concentrated in the Senate. The House often does very useful work; it takes its duties as a law-making body more seriously than does the House of Commons; and it has no room for the mere passengers so numerous in the Mother of Parliaments; but the House never gives the nation a lead and is not often even a good sounding-board.

The Senate is a very different body. It is small; its ninety-six members know each other well; they are elected for six years, retiring in thirds every two years, so that two-thirds of the Senate at any moment is above vulgar preoccupation with re-election. The Senate, too, by its right to confirm treaties (by a two-thirds majority) and to confirm important presidential appointments, has duties that can be dramatized. As a body which never dies, it can set up those committees of enquiry which have no parallel in other parliaments, and which have done so much to expose abuses and reveal the *arcana* of government to the people. Small, long-lived, the Senate gets along with very elastic rules indeed. The rules of the House practically condemn to silence the new and unimportant representative, but in the Senate the youngest senator (as Mr. Smith [7] discovered) has a chance to make a name of some kind. The kind depends on himself, not on the favor of the senior members. So in the perpetual conflict between the executive and the legislature, it is almost always the Senate that fights the battle against the White House, often with success, especially as the Senate usually only wishes to stop something being done.

The power and prestige of the Senate are, at first sight, hard to understand. That body is fantastically unrepresentative of the numerical majority of the American people, and yet it is more powerful than the House of Representatives, which is elected on a reasonably just proportional basis. Each state has the same number of senators—two—so that Nevada, with less than 100,000 permanent inhabitants, has the same representation in the Senate as New York, with over 12,000,000. The western plains and mountain states, representing cattle and mining, are far more powerful in Congress than they should be, since they command as many Senate votes as the six most populous states. On the one hand are New York, Pennsylvania, Illinois, Ohio, California, Michigan, with 40,000,000 inhabitants—about a third of the population—on the other, Colorado, Idaho, Montana, Arizona, New Mexico, Nevada with only 3,000,000 inhabitants but the same number of senators. Such an over-representation of one area accounts, for example, for the absurdly important role played by silver in American monetary policy. The silver states are rich in senators, and the United States as a whole has to pay for that fact. There are occasional revolts against the sectionalism of the Senate; heated Eastern protests against the cost of this

[7] The hero in the motion picture, 'Mr. Smith Goes to Washington.'

formal equality between New York and Nevada; but they are less frequent than one would expect.

Not only do the American people, from their reverence for the Constitution, display a great tolerance of such anomalies, but the Western senators are often very eminent persons. Borah of Idaho, Walsh of Montana, Cutting of New Mexico, to name only the dead, were among the most respected senators of recent times. Points of view and interests in great regions ill-represented in the Senate may find their spokesmen in the Western senators. The locality rule which effectively bars from active politics the minority party over great areas, makes it natural that the minority should look for its spokesmen in the senators or representatives of other regions. New York or Pennsylvania are not such homogeneous blocks of interest or sentiment that all their inhabitants regret the existence of the 'acreage states.' And in so vast an area as the United States, minorities are fearful of arguments that may lead to too close an identification of the numerical with the political majority. There *are* possibilities of grave abuse. A small minority could prevent a needed amendment of the Constitution, and the nightmare of the prohibition amendment being maintained over the opposition of a great majority of the population was plausible before 1933; but, in fact, there was no attempt by the sparsely inhabited and arid regions to oppose their will to that of the whole country . . .

The American political scene is dominated by the two major parties, Democratic and Republican. The United States is a republic and a democracy, and whatever meaning ingenious political commentators have managed to read into these words, they mean the same thing to the average man. The Republican party is so called because it is the party to which Republicans belong, and so with the Democratic party and the Democrats.

Historically, there *were* differences between the parties. The Democratic party was the party of low tariffs and states' rights. It was overwhelmingly strong in the old slavery states, not only because the Republicans were the party which had defeated and in part ruined those states, but because, as producers of cotton and tobacco for export, they had nothing to gain by high tariffs and had reason to fear that extensions of federal power would be at the expense of the class and race structure built up in the generation that followed the Civil War.

The Republican party believed in high tariffs much more firmly than did the Democratic party in free trade, but the old issue of a 'tariff for revenue only' is dead. Today all American parties are protectionist and, where local products are concerned, there is nothing to choose between a Democrat and a Republican, but on general questions of this type the completely credulous and uncritical protectionist is commoner in the Republican than in the Democratic ranks. It is probable that if a Republican Secretary of State, say Mr. Stimson, had tried to put through Mr. Hull's trade-treaty program, he would have been more opposed by a large and important section of his own party than Mr. Hull has been hampered by dissidence among Democrats.

The states' rights issue is even more artificial. When the federal power has been in other and possibly hostile hands, all parties and sections, under varying pretexts, have been in favor of limiting federal power; when federal power has been theirs to use, they have been in favor of using it. On the whole, the Democrats have in the past been in favor of states' rights because they have been the opposition party for most of the time since 1860, and because their stronghold, the South, had more to fear (or its ruling class had more to fear) from federal action than it had to hope. But some of the boldest extensions of federal authority have been the work of Democratic Presidents like Cleveland and Wilson, and Mr. Roosevelt is a spiritual heir of Jackson, if not of Jefferson, in his bold attacks on constitutional formality.

If American parties are not based on doctrine, what are they based on? On *sectional* interest and on *sentiment*. For three or four generations there has not been available in America the raw materials of politics as it is understood in other countries. No party like the old German Social Democratic party could arise in America, since all were democrats and none were socialists. But Americans in textile regions like New England who had been profoundly influenced by the New England moral attitude, naturally differed from Americans in cotton-growing regions like Georgia, whose religious tradition was more violently

emotional and less intellectual. Even before the Civil War, various forces, slavery, disputes over foreign policy and over land
policy had created the system which still functions, i.e. a system
whereby one national party predominates in one area, no matter what the social structure of the area may be. In England
wealthy suburbs are invariably Conservative and mining districts almost invariably Labor, but in America both suburbanites
and miners in one region will belong to one party—or at any
rate did so before the upheaval of Mr. Roosevelt's 'New Deal.'
The most striking example of this complete local predominance
is 'the Solid South.' Until 1928 it was axiomatic that at least
ten states in the South always voted the Democratic ticket, no
matter who was the candidate or what the 'issue.' Slavery, the
Civil War and its sequel 'Reconstruction,' made the theme of
southern politics 'white supremacy' and made the Democratic
party the instrument of that supremacy. All classes in the South
(excluding Negroes) voted Democratic; party conflict was within
the party, but, except for a brief period in the 'nineties when
the 'Populists' threatened the old order, no party but the Democratic had any but the most formal existence.

Less obvious than the 'Solid South' was the 'Solid North.' No
region was quite as completely one party as Georgia or Mississippi, but over most of the rural North and Middle West the
average man was, except in moments of extreme economic irritation, a good Republican. There were exceptions, but these
were explicable on historical grounds. In most big cities the proletariat had a weakness for the Democratic party. But the proletariat in Philadelphia was as firmly riveted to the Republican
party by the local Republican machine as was the proletariat of
New York to the Democratic party by the slightly less corrupt
local Democratic machine, commonly known as Tammany Hall.
American citizens, by birth or adoption, voted according to the
local political history of their city or state. Thus, in Indiana and
Illinois, the southern parts of the states, peopled from the South,
were the strongholds of the Democratic party in these states.
Blocks of immigrants tended to have their own party affiliations.
The Irish were overwhelmingly Democratic, and even today,
though eminent Irish Republicans are not unknown, they are

uncommon. To find a Danaher or a Donovan high in the ranks of the Republicans, locally or nationally, is slightly surprising, if not shocking. Italians and French-Canadians were, on the whole, Republicans, as were, of course, the Negroes, while the Germans were fairly evenly divided. One consequence is that when the Democratic party has been in national office, those groups, mainly Irish and Southern, who clung to the party in dark and evil days, have reaped their reward. A Tennessee lawyer settled in North Dakota, an Irish lawyer practicing in Wisconsin, found themselves in important federal office and in a position of real power because, until the landslide of 1932, few voters, not either Irish or Southern, wasted their time in the ranks of the hopeless Democratic party in these states.

The complete domination of American politics by two major parties based on historical, not contemporary, issues has many odd results. But the fact that the great prize of American politics, the presidency, can only be won by one man, forces formal unity on the party every four years. The Republican and Democratic parties may, indeed, be defined as groups of persons united to choose presidential candidates . . .

American political history is littered with the wrecks of parties which were based on 'rational' plans of political organization, but no third party has succeeded in becoming a rival of the two dominant parties. Third parties serve a useful purpose in stimulating the old parties; they sometimes serve local interests or sentiments effectually, and they give comfort to the too systematically-minded, but that is all. They fall into two classes: parties making an ineffective national appeal on behalf of some panacea, and local parties, with perhaps a pretense of national appeal, but fundamentally expressing some local idiosyncrasy which even the extraordinarily elastic national parties have not been able to cater for . . .

Haunting the minds of critics of the American party system is the vision of an American equivalent of the British Labour party. That vision has never been embodied in any concrete shape that need worry the professional politician. For one thing, the indispensable trade-union basis is lacking. The American trade-union movement has never attained the strength and unity of the British, and it is at present divided into two bitterly hostile groups, with some neutral unions watching the issue of the battle.

The older group is the American Federation of Labor (A.F.L.). The A.F.L. is a very loose federation; its main business is to safeguard the interests of the skilled workers. Its basic philosophy is completely untainted by socialism, and far from wishing to extinguish private property, it extends the idea of private property to the worker's job. The skilled worker has a right to be sure that he will not be undercut in wages, hours, or conditions by other workers—and that the right of a skilled man, e.g. a carpenter, to do the work of a carpenter, shall not be made less valuable by the competition of a less-skilled man or a man of a different craft. So the main business of the A.F.L. is to decide what unions, in what industries, shall do what work, to issue 'charters,' and to decide jurisdictional disputes. It is not an instrument of class conflict.

Given this bias, the A.F.L. was necessarily slow and incompetent in its efforts to unionize the great mass-production industries, where its ideal of the skilled worker's right to the specialized job had no place. It made an attempt to unionize steel in 1919 and failed; it made fresh attempts to unionize steel, automobiles, and other great mass-production industries in 1933 and 1934, when the coming of the Roosevelt administration gave political support to the trade-union movement. Its efforts were successful in only a small degree, and the leadership in the movement was taken over by the head of the only great industrial union in the federation, the United Mine Workers' chief, Mr. John L. Lewis. At first the C.I.O. (Committee for Industrial Organization) worked from within the A.F.L., but a clash between the interests and bias of the old craft unions and the new mass unions was certain to come. The C.I.O. became the 'Congress of Industrial Organization,' a rival federation of unions, and became associated in the public mind with the Roosevelt administration. Funds from the C.I.O., or from the United Mine Workers, helped to fill the Democratic war-chest in the presidential election of 1936, and the triumphant return of Mr. Roosevelt was followed by the great sit-down strikes in the automobile plants in Detroit and by the validation, by the Supreme Court, of the Wagner Act, setting up the N.L.R.B. (National Labor Relations Board). F.D.R., C.I.O., N.L.R.B. were linked in the public mind. But the C.I.O. victories in Detroit did not extend to the Ford plants, and although United States Steel, Jones and Laughlin, and others recognized C.I.O. unions, it was defeated in its attack on 'Little Steel,' and Mr. Ford's agents continued to persuade his workmen, by the traditional means of spies, thugs, blackjacks, and blacklists, that they had no need of unions in their relations with their paternal employer. The war between the C.I.O. and the A.F.L. took on more and more the appearance of a personal feud between Mr. Lewis and Mr. William Green, head of the A.F.L. There was general approval of Mr. Roosevelt's 'plague-on-both-your-houses' speech, and the reaction towards the Republican party, marked by the congressional and local elections of 1938, was also a reaction against the C.I.O. In Michigan, Governor Frank Murphy, who had refused to use force to expel the strikers from the plants, was defeated, as were many Left-wing candidates elsewhere. The relations between the Roosevelt administration and the C.I.O. grew cooler, especially after the outbreak of war in Europe and the Communist *volte-face*. Many C.I.O. unions were susceptible to Communist or semi-Communist influence—far more, indeed, than the mere number of Communist members made plausible, and the party turned from its active foreign policy to preaching indifference to all the issues involved in the 'imperialist war.' As the Roosevelt administration more and more leaned towards aid to the Allies, the extreme Left of the C.I.O. found itself in open opposition to the President, in uneasy alliance with the Nazi and Fascist organizations. It became evident, however, that the mass of the workers followed Mr. Roosevelt rather than Messrs. Lewis, Quill, and Bridges, and the dream of a union-dominated Democratic party was over. And there was more and more reason to expect some kind of reunion between the old A.F.L. and the C.I.O., the members of both bodies being far more ready to make peace than were the leaders.

In fact, American public opinion is still suspicious of trade unions, still suspicious of forms of social legislation that deny the tacit rural premise that unemployment and poverty are normally the fruit of personal ill-doing and to be dealt with in terms of charity, not of right. But the New Deal innovations, the deliberate fostering of trade unions, the introduction of unemployment insurance, the acceptance of the idea of 'social security' are here to stay. They have been provided by one of the two great capitalist parties and reluctantly accepted by the other, and the American worker is not as yet asking for more than the great capitalist parties will, if forced, give.

For generations the problems of an urban society were met, if at all, by the work of the great city 'machines.' These organizations gave, as charity, substitutes for the social services of the modern State, substitutes paid for by money raised by taxation or by corrupt sale of public assets and valuable favors to all kinds of buyers, from great businesses to cheap prostitutes and petty gamblers. In return for coal and blankets and picnics, the machines asked only for votes, which they transformed into vendible power. The growth of social services in the last ten years has made it harder for the machines to win popular support merely by occasional hand-outs. In the same way, the 'voluntary' taxation of the prosperous to supply 'community chests' and the like has given way to formally more coercive taxation designed to minimize the effects of unemployment, disease, and other misfortunes. More and more, unofficial instruments of social relief have become official, and as Government servants become more a professional class, and as the 'spoils system'—the rewarding of political service by jobs on the public pay roll—has become less and less important, the character of American Government, local and central, has become more sharply contrasted with the picture of it painted by national tradition, but the discrepancy is not yet obvious enough for the American people to insist on a recasting of the American party system.

DEMOCRACY

de·moc′ra·cy . . . **1.** Government by the people; a form of government in which the supreme power is retained by the people and exercised either directly **(absolute,** or **pure, democracy)** or indirectly **(representative democracy)** through a system of representation and delegated authority periodically renewed, as in a constitutional representative government, or republic (which see). An *absolute democracy* is a government in which the sovereign powers are exercised theoretically by all the people, actually only by the electorate (voters). Even in the primitive forms, such as the Athenian democracy, where the governing powers were directly exercised by the assembled people, children and slaves, and usually women, were excluded. Specifically, and commonly in modern use, a *democracy* is a representative government where there is equality of rights without hereditary or arbitrary differences in rank or privilege, and is distinguished from *aristocracy*. In modern representative democracies, as the United States and France, the governing body, that is, the electorate, is a minority of the total population, but the principle on which the government is based is popular sovereignty.

By permission. From *Webster's New International Dictionary,* Second Edition, copyright, 1934, 1939, by G. & C. Merriam Co.

DEMOCRACY AS DEFINED BY HISTORY

By Carl Becker

DEMOCRACY, like liberty or science or progress, is a word with which we are all so familiar that we rarely take the trouble to ask what we mean by it. It is a term, as the devotees of semantics say, which has no 'referent'—there is no precise or palpable thing or object which we all think of when the word is pronounced. On the contrary, it is a word which connotes different things to different people, a kind of conceptual Gladstone bag, which, with a little manipulation, can be made to accommodate almost any collection of social facts we may wish to carry about in it. In it we can as easily pack a dictatorship as any other form of government. We have only to stretch the concept to include any form of government supported by a majority of the people, for whatever reasons and by whatever means of expressing assent, and before we know it the empire of Napoleon, the Soviet regime of Stalin, and the fascist systems of Mussolini and Hitler are all safely in the bag. But if this is what we mean by democracy, then virtually all forms of government are democratic, since virtually all governments, except in times of revolution, rest upon the explicit or implicit consent of the people. In order to discuss democracy intelligently it will be necessary, therefore, to define it, to attach to the word a sufficiently precise meaning to avoid the confusion which is not infrequently the chief result of such discussions.

All human institutions, we are told, have their ideal forms laid away in heaven, and we do not need to be told that the actual institutions conform but indifferently to these ideal counterparts. It would be possible then to define democracy either in

From Carl Becker, *Modern Democracy*, 1940. By permission of Yale University Press.

terms of the ideal or in terms of the real form—to define it as government of the people, by the people, for the people; or to define it as government of the people, by the politicians, for whatever pressure groups can get their interests taken care of. But as a historian I am naturally disposed to be satisfied with the meaning which, in the history of politics, men have commonly attributed to the word—a meaning, needless to say, which derives partly from the experience and partly from the aspirations of mankind. So regarded, the term democracy refers primarily to a form of government by the many as opposed to government by the one—government by the people as opposed to government by a tyrant, a dictator, or an absolute monarch. This is the most general meaning of the word as men have commonly understood it.

In this antithesis there are, however, certain implications, always tacitly understood, which give a more precise meaning to the term. Peisistratus, for example, was supported by a majority of the people, but his government was never regarded as a democracy for all that. Caesar's power derived from a popular mandate, conveyed through established republican forms, but that did not make his government any the less a dictatorship. Napoleon called his government a democratic empire, but no one, least of all Napoleon himself, doubted that he had destroyed the last vestiges of the democratic republic. Since the Greeks first used the term, the essential test of democratic government has always been this: the source of political authority must be and remain in the people and not in the ruler. A democratic government has always meant one in which the citizens, or a sufficient number of them to represent more or less effectively the common will, freely act from time to time, and according to established forms, to appoint or recall the magistrates and to enact or revoke the laws by which the community is governed. This I take to be the meaning which history has impressed upon the term democracy as a form of government.

ESSENTIALS OF DEMOCRACY

By Charles A. Beard

In the early days of this nation, the term democracy, when used, was generally applied to direct popular rule in small communities, such as the city states of antiquity; and by a study of history leaders among the founders of the republic reached the conclusion that this type of government led inexorably to tumults, to ruthless attacks on persons and properties, and finally to the triumph of despotism. Scarcely less did they fear indirect popular rule through the representative assemblies of the American states, and especially the possibilities of full manhood suffrage. 'Give the votes to the people who have no property,' exclaimed Gouverneur Morris in the constitutional convention of 1787, 'and they will sell them to the rich who will be able to buy them.' Broadly speaking, these founders of the republic were as much alarmed by the specter of democracy in either form, direct or representative, as they were by the menace of monarch or the dictatorial propensities of a military caste.

Only by slow and halting processes have Americans arrived at the application of the word democracy to the government and society of the United States. Nothing like official sanction was given to this usage until 1917, when President Wilson declared that the war on the Central Powers of Europe was a war for democracy. Even now, said all the prolix eloquence about it, the term has no seal of national resolve and awaits both comprehensive statement and formal adoption.

Whence came the idea of democracy, so vaunted and so celebrated in our day? For an answer we must search; and our search carries us far back in time. Beyond the Declaration of Independ-

Charles A. Beard, *Public Policy and the General Welfare*, New York: Farrar & Rinehart, Inc., 1941. By permission of the author and publisher.

ence into colonial and English history. Beyond England to the continent of Europe, through the Protestant Reformation, the renaissance, and medieval civilization. Beyond the Christian doctrine of universal brotherhood, through the natural law of the Romans, to the social ideals of the stoics. Far beyond stoicism into the very origins of primitive society, with man as the hunter and fighter and woman as the mother, originator of domestic arts, conservator of the humane spirit in mutual aid. And when we can scan the horizon of the future, contemplate the coming fortunes of democracy, we find ourselves caught in the toils of this historical sweep. If we are bold enough and insistent enough our search will carry us into a consideration of the nature of all things human—the ultimate design of the universe.

When, however, we concentrate our thought upon experience in the United States, we find six enduring elements now intertwined under the prevalent conception of democracy: popular government within a span of time, efficiency in function, sustaining economy, civil liberty, appropriate education and the spirit of humanity and enlightenment which lifts men and women above the beasts of the field and confers upon them moral rights and social duties. These six elements are closely related, are aspects of the same thing, are inseparable parts of the whole. The neglect or failure of one imperils the fortunes of all. Any conception of democracy in America less comprehensive would not correspond to irreducible facts in the case.

It is true that democracy is often defined narrowly as the 'form of government in which the sovereign power resides in the people as a whole and is exercised either directly by them . . . or by officers elected by them.' But this definition is both exclusive and superficial. It fails to specify the concrete practices necessarily associated with the exercise of popular sovereignty in a span of time. Under this definition the despotism of Napoleon III might be called a democracy, for his elevation as emperor was approved by a popular vote of adult males, by a majority of ten to one. The definition omits all reference to society, in which every form of government must operate. In other words, it leaves out of account specific conditions of life and economy indispensable to the existence and functioning of democracy. It disregards the eternal oppositions of power and life, authority and liberty, public spirit and private interest, brute force and humanity, with which the institutions of democracy must cope if they are to endure.

Both in conception and practice popular government in the United States transcends any superficial definition of form at a given moment. It is democratic in the sense that all high public authorities endowed with political power over lives and properties are chosen directly or indirectly by popular vote, and in the long run the sustained and matured will of the duly constituted majority is allowed to prevail. Here popular sovereignty and the time span are combined. Under this system, no mere majority of men and women at any momentary election of public authorities or in any given legislative assembly can immediately compel the enaction and enforcement of any law they are pleased to demand amid the heats and tumults of a single campaign. If such immediacy is an essential element of democracy, then America has never been and is not now a democracy. Only in limited matters do simple majorities or pluralities control the decisions and actions of government. In all sovereign matters, as the Constitution of the United States prescribes, extraordinary majorities are required and a due process calling for an extension of actions in time must be followed. In no sovereign matter does the snap judgment of a majority or a plurality given at a mere moment have the force of law. Our system, in respect of great issues, allows for the time element and guarantees that prudence and daring, conservatism and radicalism, may each have its day in court, that discussion and education may intervene, that pleas and counter-pleas may be heard, and that decision may be matured.

The declaration of popular will, even if matured, is only the beginning of democratic government; in action its function is the discharge of concrete duties. Government in action deals with issues of finance, economy, health, utilities, conservation of resources, human relations, national defense, foreign affairs, and the general welfare broadly and realistically conceived. If it is to endure, government must grapple with these issues competently, efficiently. Is popular government a guarantee that a democratic government can and will display this competence, this efficiency? If it were, then surely the elected parliaments of so many nations would not have vanished in our own time. Unless the agencies of popular will can legislate appropriately and administer efficiently, then democratic forms will perish, no matter what oceans of ink are spilt and what flowers of eloquence bloom in their defense. In ancient Rome men mouthed the grand phrase *Senatus Populusque Romanus* long after the assembly had degenerated into a farce and the senate had become the home of gibbering ghosts. The wrecks of monarchies, tyrannies, aristocracies, dictatorships, and democracies scattered through fifty centuries are solemn demonstrations that varied forms of government have failed at their tasks, in the discharge of their functions, under their symbols, in their times and places.

When, therefore, the test of efficiency is applied to democracy in the United States, an inescapable question arises: Is popular government, as now constituted, really competent to deal effectively with the general functions common to all governments, and more especially with the specific issues forced upon this government by giant technology, by the power of enormous private corporations, by huge urban aggregations unlike the cities of earlier times, by organized labor, by the decline in freehold agriculture, by periodic crises in economy, by the complications of internal rivalries? Here is a question of the hour which challenges all talents and powers. Can popular government come to grips with these issues, overcome them and efficiently administer its decisions?

Already in our smaller laboratories of popular experimentation—cities and states—has appeared a profound conviction that many of our inherited institutions are not adapted to the requirements of the age, are in fact inefficient. In all our great cities the double chamber council has been abolished, a single chamber installed, and the mayor endowed with broad powers in his own right. In 650 cities the mayor-and-council system has been discarded and the city-manager plan substituted for it. In a majority of the states the inherited scheme of administration has recently been abrogated, in whole or in part, and the power of the governor over finance and the conduct of public business has been materially increased. In several states an attack has been made on the weaknesses of legislatures, and a legislative council has been instituted for the purpose of concentrating research, knowledge and imagination on public questions. More and more, the technical literature of competence in the field of state and local government is filled with doubt, inquiry, and a searching for constructive proposals.

This quest for efficiency in government extends to national affairs. Already critics are saying that in the Congress of the United States a zeal for spending borrowed money, placating special interests, and framing bills against dissident minorities outruns the capacity to concentrate powers of mind upon the supreme issues of the time. Already critics are saying that democracy cannot really act effectively in great matters, that party bickerings defeat the preparation, discussion, enactment, and administration of measures necessary to evoke creative energies, allay alarms, and bring our moral, industrial, and natural resources into wise and full use.

In allowing some validity to these criticisms no aid and comfort need be given to the carping censors who fondly imagine that they can set the clock back to 1928 or 1898, or any other year in the past, and thus find instantaneous solutions of our pressing problems of efficiency in government. Most of the measures now urged upon the federal administration by its detractors are the identical measures which were in full force during the regime of golden prosperity, so-called, which exploded with such a devastating crash in 1929. Why repeat the very origins of our present calamity? Both experience and reason suggest that the search for efficiency in government be turned to the invention of new devices for concentrating talents and wills on needs now clearly before us. The recitation of old phrases by a thousand specialists in propaganda will only add to the nation's confusion and delay the application of its abilities and energies to the attainment of efficiency in government.

Bound up with popular government and its functioning is the economy of the people who are supposed to control the form and process. Nothing is truer than the old adage: An empty meal sack cannot stand up. All governments have economic foundations. This axiom of politics does not come from armchair philosophers or demagogues or agitators. It comes from the founders of the nation, builders of our institutions, from leaders of large vision, wide experience and demonstrated capacity in great affairs. They made a revolution, waged a continental war for independence, offered their lives and property in defense of their cause, established the republic, and steered it through perilous times. As against the weight of their authority and achievement, the axioms of private men pursuing private interests and of all petty phrase-makers in public affairs are as dust in the balance. Let those speak whose public accomplishments display the depth of their insight, the precision of their knowledge, the suppleness of their minds, the invincibility of their courage.

In words that admit of no equivocation these great of old who instruct us from their tombs declare that politics and economics are forever united. Ringing through utterances like the tones of a clear bell is the warning thesis: A wide diffusion of property and a general equality of condition are the very foundation stones of popular government; a high concentration of wealth is incompatible with universal suffrage; a broad distribution of opportunity and assurance to labor is necessary to the security of republican institutions; the revolutions which have shaken other societies to pieces have sprung from the antagonism of private interests and popular power, fired by ambitious leaders. These findings, wrought out of hard experience, are set forth in many places by American statesmen of early times—nowhere more trenchantly than in the writings of James Madison, justly called the Father of the Constitution.

Near the close of his long life, devoted to public services, Madison reviewed his rich experience and sought to lift the veil on the future of his country. He estimated that by 1930 the population of the United States would probably be 192,000,000 and that a majority of the people would then be 'without property or the hope of acquiring it.' What is to be done? he asked anxiously.

Upon due deliberation, Madison confessed that he was unable to answer his own question. He thought that it would be unsafe to admit this 'unfavored class . . . to a full share of political power,' but the alternative of exclusion, he quickly added, 'would lead to a standing military force, dangerous to all parties and to liberty itself.'

Having arrived at this dilemma, Madison remarked with diffidence that 'republican laws of descent in equalizing the property of the citizens' might divert the course of the events he predicted. But he forecast the necessity of great alterations in public policy to meet the exigencies which he had divided. 'To the effect of these changes, intellectual, moral, and social,' he insisted, 'the institutions and laws of the country must be adapted; and it will require for the task all the wisdom of the wisest patriots.'

Although Madison overestimated the population of 1930, he did with amazing vision forecast the primary features of the economic scene as they appeared one hundred years later, in 1930. The proportion of farmers who are tenants has increased rapidly until it is now more than 40 per cent of the total number; and at least one third of the nominal owners are heavily burdened by debts. In the great cities the major portion of the inhabitants are without property sufficient for assurance if not entirely without hope of acquiring it. About ten million workers are unemployed and losing faith in the possibilities of employment. There have been grand gestures in the direction of economic security, but grave doubts are entertained respecting the underlying strength of that assurance. Our economic machine, on which all the people rely for sustenance and the government depends for its very existence, rumbles along in uncertainty at about one half of its full capacity.

Such are the axioms of experienced statesmen. Such are glaring economic facts of our present situation. The crisis in national life forecast long ago has arrived. This is the age in which the wisdom of the wisest patriots, as Madison warned us, is required for the resolution of the dilemma. Not curtailment but expansion of production is now a primary need of American democracy. Our output of wealth must be materially increased, and there must be a distribution of employments, goods, and services wide enough to afford those opportunities and assurances upon which popular government rests and must ever rest. If the wisdom is lacking, force may be offered as a substitute. Nay, if history is any guide, force will be offered and democracy may be started swiftly spinning on a downward spiral.

In the light of this imperative, the policy of reduction applied generally to agriculture, however defensible as a temporary expedient in respect of certain commodities, is, in the long run, a peril to the economy of a democratic society. No less perilous is the apparent inability of leadership in business enterprise to prevent those periodical and drastic curtailments of production in industry, which harrow the hearts and minds of men and women with fear and despair. No less perilous is the apparent inability of that leadership to force or guarantee the expansion of industrial production toward the very borders of the capacity indicated by our plants, skills, and resources. Nor is the strife of organized labor over crumbs that fall from a diminishing table any contribution to bringing about the economic arrangements necessary to perpetuity of democratic institutions.

If we are to learn from the instructions bequeathed to us by the founders and builders of the republic, it is idle gossip to speak of the long-term promise of democracy unless leaders in government, business enterprise, agriculture, and labor can cast off their hate-born formulas, rise to the occasion as did the creators of the republic, unite upon methods and measures that will expand production, enlarge and steady the domestic market, and assure the wide distribution of employments, goods, and services essential to the stability and progress of a democratic society.

But at a given moment government may be popular in form, efficient in administration, competent to provide the condition necessary for a wide economic security, and yet by its conduct of affairs undermine those civil liberties upon which democracy depends for its long-run existence. It may destroy that freedom which brings knowledge and wisdom to bear upon its operations, supplies criticism, and furnishes constructive thought for new occasions and measures. In operation popular government is government by public opinion and decision, enlightened by discussions that permit all causes and parties to be duly heard, even those hateful to the majority. Without freedom of press, speech, and person from arbitrary power, popular election becomes a farce, government a tyranny, and administration an agency of personal vengeance.

Hence indispensable to the functioning of a democratic system on its own principles are those constitutional safeguards which place restraints upon the regular operations of majorities and upon the irregular insolence of mobs. Safeguards against press censorship, against interference with free speech, against arbitrary arrest, against secret trial and condemnation. Safeguards against the enactment of *ex post facto* laws making crimes out of actions that are not crimes when committed. Safeguards against depriving persons of life, liberty, and property without due process of law, against cruel and unusual punishments, against the suspension of the writ of habeas corpus, against the introduction of martial law, against assaults upon the whole structure of civil rights so painfully built up through centuries of conflict and sacrifice. To permit the suppression of civil liberties by public agencies or private mobs is to cut away the intellectual and moral foundations on which popular government rests in the long run, and to open the way for government by prescription and the firing squad, perhaps in the very name of the people.

It is not enough that the maxims of civil liberty be spread upon paper and celebrated by sunshine patriots. They are futile unless made dynamic in government itself. They are mere trash unless supported by citizens in daily conduct. Again and again they have been flouted by the Congress of the United States, by state legislatures, by prosecuting attorneys, by judges sworn to administer justice under law and by lawless crowds of rich and poor.

Indeed so flagrant have been violations in recent years that the danger has become obvious even to careless and indifferent citizens, and a counter-movement has been well launched. Defenders of liberty have come to its support. The Supreme Court, long heedless, has at length spoken out clearly and strongly against infractions. Once negligent, indeed apparently hostile, the American Bar Association has at last recovered the grand tradition of Erskine and Mackintosh, established a powerful committee on civil liberty, and offered aid and counsel in the trial of causes involving personal rights. But more is needed:

systematic instruction in the subject by the public schools and a deep-rooted respect for the tolerances of civil liberty among the people in whose hands rests the fate of their own government.

In connection with the functioning of democracy, in its public and private aspects, education may point the way upward or downward. It may prepare the people for the fulfillment of a great mission or for subjection to sheer force. If education is to be effective in strengthening all phases of democracy, it must be appropriate to the exigencies of American civilization. While it has a precious heritage to guard, education has a duty to assemble and diffuse the knowledge required by citizens and their leaders in operating popular institutions, in making them effective in every sphere, and in preserving civil liberties. No longer can education proceed safely on the assumption that, by training youth for the successful pursuit of private interests, it will automatically insure the general welfare and the perpetuity of democracy. Like other alluring illusions, that is highly dangerous. It is even now too widely cherished. Other conceptions of purpose and action are needed to counterbalance it. Only by a program of instruction that deals resolutely and realistically with the processes of democracy, with questions of sustaining economy and culture, and with the protection of civil rights can American education 'defy powers that seem omnipotent' and span the full measure of its opportunity.

Universal suffrage, efficient government, material foundations, declarations of rights, and education alone cannot guarantee the safety of civilization against the storms of passion and the lust of men for power. Behind all beneficent institutions of society, ever helping to sustain them, is that elusive but potent force known as the humane spirit. This spirit has ever been affiliated with and expressed in the noblest philosophies that have commanded the allegiance of hearts and minds since the beginnings of civilization. It has been associated with all great religions. Trampled upon by power, crushed by the organization of interests, the humane spirit endures in many forms, under varied professions of faith, and offers the strength of justice and mercy against the effronteries of tyranny and the angers of brute destruction. Without it even democratic government is an empty shell—a numerical counting of heads that may be farcical in procedure and cruel in outcome.

If our powers are to be effectively applied in sustaining the forms and achieving the ends of popular government, this humane spirit must be cherished and quickened, and ever brought to bear as a dynamic element in the enrichment of life. Knowledge is not enough. Science is not enough. Both may be employed to kill as well as to heal. Accumulated facts, though high as mountains, give us no instruction in human values and the choices of application. It is the humane spirit that points the way to the good life. To reiterate the maxims of this spirit, to restate them in terms of new times, to spread them through education and daily intercourse, to exemplify them in private conduct, to incorporate them in public practice, to cling to them despite our infirmities and hypocrisies—this too is a task of all who fain would make government by the people and for the people endure upon the earth.

Such are the components of American democracy—all essential to its perpetuity and development. They are not figments of an imagination, fashioned in a philosopher's alcove. They are realities of experience, tried and tested in the fires of centuries.

Such too are the challenges of dissolution and sheer might which threaten the existence and unfolding of all that is best in this democracy. Despite the weakness of my presentation, open as it may be to many criticisms, here are the central points for our consideration; here is the conflict that engages our contemplation.

Facing this antithesis, nay, caught in the turmoil of these contending forces, it will not do for us, as Carlyle warned America long ago, to sit idly caucusing and ballot-boxing upon the graves of our ancestors, saying, 'It is well, it is well.' Rather it is for us to look with clear eyes upon the welter before us, to curb our hates and passions, to forget our trivial slogans and party distempers, to clarify and purify our hearts and minds, to discover or invent, by concerted effort, the best means for coping now with the central issues raised amid indubitable facts. It is for us to find the common denominators of faith, interest, and action necessary to success in applying the conclusions of our earnest searching, and, equipped with all the strong instruments of civilization, march upon the goal we have set before us, remembering that those who labor thoughtfully in this undertaking labor under the eye of eternity in a cause worthy of the greatest talents and the noblest wisdom.

THE BLACK COTTAGE

By Robert Frost

WE chanced in passing by that afternoon
To catch it in a sort of special picture
Among tar-banded ancient cherry trees,
Set well back from the road in rank lodged grass,
The little cottage we were speaking of,
A front with just a door between two windows,
Fresh painted by the shower a velvet black.
We paused, the minister and I, to look.
He made as if to hold it at arm's length
Or put the leaves aside that framed it in.
'Pretty,' he said. 'Come in. No one will care.'
The path was a vague parting in the grass
That led us to a weathered window-sill.
We pressed our faces to the pane. 'You see,' he said,
'Everything's as she left it when she died.
Her sons won't sell the house or the things in it.
They say they mean to come and summer here
Where they were boys. They haven't come this year.
They live so far away—one is out west—
It will be hard for them to keep their word.
Anyway they won't have the place disturbed.'
A buttoned hair-cloth lounge spread scrolling arms
Under a crayon portrait on the wall
Done sadly from an old daguerreotype.
'That was the father as he went to war.
She always, when she talked about the war,
Sooner or later came and leaned, half knelt

From *The Collected Poems of Robert Frost,* 1939. By permission of the author and publisher, Henry Holt and Company.

Against the lounge beside it, though I doubt
If such unlifelike lines kept power to stir
Anything in her after all the years.
He fell at Gettysburg or Fredericksburg,
I ought to know—it makes a difference which:
Fredericksburg wasn't Gettysburg, of course.
But what I'm getting to is how forsaken
A little cottage this has always seemed;
Since she went more than ever, but before—
I don't mean altogether by the lives
That had gone out of it, the father first,
Then the two sons, till she was left alone.
(Nothing could draw her after those two sons.
She valued the considerate neglect
She had at some cost taught them after years.)
I mean by the world's having passed it by—
As we almost got by this afternoon.
It always seems to me a sort of mark
To measure how far fifty years have brought us.
Why not sit down if you are in no haste?
These doorsteps seldom have a visitor.
The warping boards pull out their own old nails
With none to tread and put them in their place.
She had her own idea of things, the old lady.
And she liked talk. She had seen Garrison
And Whittier, and had her story of them.
One wasn't long in learning that she thought
Whatever else the Civil War was for
It wasn't just to keep the States together,
Nor just to free the slaves, though it did both.
She wouldn't have believed those ends enough
To have given outright for them all she gave.
Her giving somehow touched the principle
That all men are created free and equal.
And to hear her quaint phrases—so removed
From the world's view to-day of all those things.
That's a hard mystery of Jefferson's.
What did he mean? Of course the easy way

Is to decide it simply isn't true.
It may not be. I heard a fellow say so.
But never mind, the Welshman got it planted
Where it will trouble us a thousand years.
Each age will have to reconsider it.
You couldn't tell her what the West was saying,
And what the South to her serene belief.
She had some art of hearing and yet not
Hearing the latter wisdom of the world.
White was the only race she ever knew.
Black she had scarcely seen, and yellow never.
But how could they be made so very unlike
By the same hand working in the same stuff?
She had supposed the war decided that.
What are you going to do with such a person?
Strange how such innocence gets its own way.
I shouldn't be surprised if in this world
It were the force that would at last prevail.
Do you know but for her there was a time
When to please younger members of the church,
Or rather say non-members in the church,
Whom we all have to think of nowadays,
I would have changed the Creed a very little?
Not that she ever had to ask me not to;
It never got so far as that; but the bare thought
Of her old tremulous bonnet in the pew,
And of her half asleep was too much for me.
Why, I might wake her up and startle her.
It was the words 'descended into Hades'
That seemed too pagan to our liberal youth.
You know they suffered from a general onslaught.
And well, if they weren't true why keep right on
Saying them like the heathen? We could drop them.
Only—there was the bonnet in the pew.
Such a phrase couldn't have meant much to her.
But suppose she had missed it from the Creed
As a child misses the unsaid Good-night,
And falls asleep with heartache—how should *I* feel?

I'm just as glad she made me keep hands off,
For, dear me, why abandon a belief
Merely because it ceases to be true.
Cling to it long enough, and not a doubt
It will turn true again, for so it goes.
Most of the change we think we see in life
Is due to truths being in and out of favor.
As I sit here, and oftentimes, I wish
I could be monarch of a desert land
I could devote and dedicate forever
To the truths we keep coming back and back to.
So desert it would have to be, so walled
By mountain ranges half in summer snow,
No one would covet it or think it worth
The pains of conquering to force change on.
Scattered oases where men dwelt, but mostly
Sand dunes held loosely in tamarisk
Blown over and over themselves in idleness.
Sand grains should sugar in the natal dew
The babe born to the desert, the sand storm
Retard mid-waste my cowering caravans—
'There are bees in this wall.' He struck the clapboards,
Fierce heads looked out; small bodies pivoted.
We rose to go. Sunset blazed on the windows.

II

'That All Men Are Created Free'

WE want a state of things which allows every man the largest liberty compatible with the liberty of every other man.

RALPH WALDO EMERSON,
The Fortune of the Republic, 1879

AT every moment some one country more than any other represents the sentiment and the future of mankind. None will doubt that America occupies this place in the opinion of nations.

RALPH WALDO EMERSON,
The Fortune of the Republic, 1879

THE purpose of democracy . . . is . . . to illustrate, at all hazards, this doctrine or theory that man, properly train'd in sanest, highest freedom, may and must become a law, and series of laws, unto himself.

WALT WHITMAN, *Democratic Vistas,* 1871

DECLARATION OF INDEPENDENCE

WHEN, in the Course of human events, it becomes necessary for one people to dissolve the political bands which have connected them with another, and to assume among the powers of the earth, the separate and equal station to which the Laws of Nature and of Nature's God entitle them, a decent respect to the opinions of mankind requires that they should declare the causes which impel them to the separation.

We hold these truths to be self-evident, that all men are created equal, that they are endowed by their Creator with certain unalienable Rights, that among these are Life, Liberty and the pursuit of Happiness. That to secure these rights, Governments are instituted among Men, deriving their just powers from the consent of the governed. That whenever any Form of Government becomes destructive of these ends, it is the Right of the People to alter or to abolish it, and to institute new Government, laying its foundation on such principles and organizing its powers in such form, as to them shall seem most likely to effect their Safety and Happiness. Prudence, indeed, will dictate that Governments long established should not be changed for light and transient causes; and accordingly all experience hath shewn, that mankind are more disposed to suffer, while evils are sufferable, than to right themselves by abolishing the forms to which they are accustomed. But when a long train of abuses and usurpations, pursuing invariably the same object, evidence a design to reduce them under absolute Despotism, it is their right, it is their duty, to throw off such Government, and to provide new Guards for their future security. Such has been the patient sufferance of these Colonies; and such is now the necessity which constrains them to alter their former Systems of Government. . . .

ON THE BILL OF RIGHTS

15 December 1941

By Franklin D. Roosevelt

No date in the long history of freedom means more to liberty-loving men in all liberty-loving countries than the fifteenth day of December 1791. On that day, one hundred and fifty years ago, a new nation, through an elected Congress, adopted a declaration of human rights which has influenced the thinking of all mankind from one end of the world to the other.

There is not a single republic of this hemisphere which has not adopted in its fundamental law the basic principles of freedom of man and freedom of mind enacted in the American Bill of Rights.

There is not a country, large or small, on this continent which has not felt the influence of that document, directly or indirectly.

Indeed, prior to the year 1933, the essential validity of the American bill of rights was accepted at least in principle. Even today, with the exception of Germany, Italy, and Japan, the peoples of the world—in all probability four-fifths of them—support its principles, its teachings and its glorious results.

But, in the year 1933, there came to power in Germany a political clique which did not accept the declarations of the American bill of human rights as valid: a small clique of ambitious and unscrupulous politicians whose announced and admitted platform was precisely the destruction of the rights that instrument declared. Indeed the entire program and goal of these political and moral tigers was nothing more than the overthrow, throughout the earth, of the great revolution of human liberty of which our American bill of rights is the mother charter.

The truths which were self-evident to Thomas Jefferson—which have been self-evident to the six generations of Americans who followed him—were to these men hateful. The rights to life, liberty, and the pursuit of happiness which seemed to Jefferson, and which seem to us, inalienable, were, to Hitler and his fellows, empty words which they proposed to cancel forever.

The propositions they advanced to take the place of Jefferson's inalienable rights were these:

That the individual human being has no rights whatever in himself and by virtue of his humanity;

That the individual human being has no right to a soul of his own, or a mind of his own, or a trade of his own; or even to live where he pleases or to marry the woman he loves;

That his only duty is the duty of obedience, not to his God, and not to his conscience, but to Adolf Hitler; and that his only value is his value not as a man, but as a unit of the Nazi State.

To Hitler the ideal of the people, as we conceive it—the free, self-governing, and responsible people—is incomprehensible. The people, to Hitler, are 'the masses,' and the highest human idealism is, in his own words, that a man should wish to become 'a dust particle' of the order 'of force' which is to shape the universe.

To Hitler, the government, as we conceive it, is an impossible conception. The government to him is not the servant and the instrument of the people but their absolute master and the dictator of their every act.

To Hitler the church, as we conceive it, is a monstrosity to be destroyed by every means at his command. The Nazi church is to be the 'national church,' 'absolutely and exclusively in the service of but one doctrine, race, and nation.'

To Hitler, the freedom of men to think as they please and speak as they please and worship as they please is, of all things imaginable, most hateful and most desperately to be feared.

The issue of our time, the issue of the war in which we are engaged, is the issue forced upon the decent, self-respecting peoples of the earth by the aggressive dogmas of this attempted revival of barbarism; this proposed return to tyranny; this effort to impose again upon the peoples of the world doctrines of absolute obedience, and of dictatorial rule, and of the suppression of truth, and of the oppression of conscience, which the free nations of the earth have long ago rejected.

What we face is nothing more or less than an attempt to overthrow and to cancel out the great upsurge of human liberty of which the American Bill of Rights is the fundamental document: to force the peoples of the earth, and among them the peoples of this continent, to accept again the absolute authority and despotic rule from which the courage and the resolution and the sacrifices of their ancestors liberated them many, many years ago.

It is an attempt which could succeed only if those who have inherited the gift of liberty had lost the manhood to preserve it. But we Americans know that the determination of this generation of our people to preserve liberty is as fixed and certain as the determination of that earlier generation of Americans to win it.

We will not, under any threat, or in the face of any danger, surrender the guaranties of liberty our forefathers framed for us in our Bill of Rights.

We hold with all the passion of our hearts and minds to those commitments of the human spirit.

We are solemnly determined that no power or combination of powers of this earth shall shake our hold upon them.

We covenant with each other before all the world that, having taken up arms in the defense of liberty, we will not lay them down before liberty is once again secure in the world we live in. For that security we pray; for that security we act—now and evermore.

THE BILL OF RIGHTS: A NEW ARRANGEMENT

HEREIN is presented a typographical re-arrangement showing not 10, not 14, but 74 separate personal guaranties of right in these fundamental documents of American liberty. The 10 original amendments to the Constitution of the United States, plus the four later amendments embodying guarantees, have simply been re-set typographically to show each guarantee as a separate provision. Thus, for example, the first amendment is not one guarantee but six distinct guarantees. Note, too, the extreme precision of language as in the first amendment where Congress may make laws respecting the press but not *abridging the freedom* of the press. This re-arrangement was devised for *The Christian Science Monitor* by Denys P. Myers, whose discovery that Massachusetts had never ratified the 10 original amendments led to ratification in 1939.

AMENDMENT I

Congress shall make no law
  respecting an establishment of religion, or
  prohibiting the free exercise thereof; or
  abridging
    the freedom of
      speech or of the
      press; or
    the right of the people peaceably
      to assemble, and
      to petition the Government for a redress of grievances.

AMENDMENT II

A well regulated Militia, being necessary to the security of a free State, the right of the people to
  keep and
  bear
    Arms, shall not be infringed.

This arrangement of the Bill of Rights and the following article are from *The Christian Science Monitor*, 13 December 1941. By permission of Denys P. Myers and the Christian Science Publishing Society.

58

Amendment III

No Soldier shall,
>in time of peace be quartered in any house, without the
>consent of the Owner, nor
>in time of war, but in a manner to be prescribed by law.

Amendment IV

The right of the people to be secure in their
>persons,
>houses,
>papers, and
>effects,
>>against unreasonable searches and
>>seizures,
>>>shall not be violated, and

no Warrants shall issue, but upon probable cause, supported by
Oath or affirmation, and particularly describing
>the place to be searched, and
>the persons or things to be seized.

Amendment V

No person shall be held to answer for a
>capital, or
>otherwise infamous
>>crime, unless on a presentment or indictment of a Grand Jury,
>>>except in cases arising in the
>>>>land or
>>>>naval forces, or in the
>>>>Militia, when in actual service in time of war, or public
>>>>danger;

nor shall any person be subject for the same offence to be twice put
in jeopardy of life or limb;

nor shall be compelled in any criminal case to be a witness against
himself,

nor be deprived of
>life,
>liberty, or
>property,
>>without due process of law;

nor shall private property be taken for public use, without just compensation.

AMENDMENT VI

In all criminal prosecutions, the accused shall enjoy the right to a
   speedy and
   public
   trial, by an impartial jury of the State and district wherein the
   crime shall have been committed, which district shall have been
   previously ascertained by law, and
to be informed of the nature and cause of the accusation;
to be confronted with the witnesses against him;
to have compulsory process for obtaining witnesses in his favor, and
to have the Assistance of Counsel for his defence.

AMENDMENT VII

In suits at common law, where the value in controversy shall exceed
twenty dollars, the
   right of trial by jury shall be preserved, and
   no fact tried by jury, shall be otherwise reexamined in
   any Court of the United States, than according to the rules
   of the common law.

AMENDMENT VIII

Excessive bail shall not be required,
nor excessive fines imposed,
nor cruel and unusual punishments inflicted.

AMENDMENT IX

The enumeration in the Constitution, of certain rights, shall not be
construed to
   deny or
   disparage
      others retained by the people.

AMENDMENT X

The powers
   not delegated to the United States by the Constitution,
   nor prohibited by it to the States,
     are reserved

to the States respectively, or
to the people.

Amendment XIII

Neither slavery
nor involuntary servitude, except as a punishment for crime where-
of the party shall have been duly convicted,
  shall exist
    within the United States, or
    any place subject to their jurisdiction.

Amendment XIV

All persons
  born or
  naturalized
    in the United States, and subject to the jurisdiction thereof,
      are citizens
        of the United States and
        of the State wherein they reside.
No State shall
  make or
  enforce
    any law which shall abridge the
      privileges or
      immunities
      of citizens of the United States;
nor shall any State
  deprive any person of
    life,
    liberty, or
    property,
      without due process of law;
nor deny to any person within its jurisdiction the equal protection
of the laws.

Amendment XV

The right of citizens of the United States to vote shall not be
  denied or
  abridged
    by the United States or
    by any State

on account of
    race,
    color, or
    previous condition of servitude.

Amendment XIX

The right of citizens of the United States to vote shall not be
    denied or
    abridged
        by the United States or
        by any State
        on account of
            sex.

THE BILL OF RIGHTS TODAY

By Denys P. Myers

'MAN shall not live by bread alone,' but the world bears witness today that he has not yet found out what else he does live by. Painfully in war and tumult through ages of political experiment we have learned much of what successful living requires, only to find that gangsters can destroy human rights by the very instruments civilization has made for their service. Never has it been more important for living Americans to know which of all values are to them most precious.

The Bill of Rights forms and molds the American spirit that makes the United States what it is. From the guaranties to which we are born has come a people in whose blood run instincts of self-respect, of respect for others, of personal improvement, of open opportunity, of fair play, of reciprocal justice. These many rights guaranteed to every citizen just because he exists are axiomatic to us all, though none of us could recite more than a few of them by rote. But we do not need to 'know' our rights, for we live them. Ponder the unconscious way you give vent to your opinions, or go and come, or revise your household affairs, and you come to appreciate that the Bill of Rights is not a set of words but a pattern of life.

The Bill of Rights was in the American blood before it was in the Constitution. The colonists stemmed from generations of Englishmen who had been establishing civil rights for a thousand years. The Mayflower Compact of 1620, the Connecticut Bill of Rights of 1650, the half dozen similar bills of pre-Revolutionary decades, that of December 5, 1774, the Declaration of Independence carried on the disposition that gave their forebears Magna Carta in 1215.

In Massachusetts a constitution was disapproved in 1778 because it contained no bill of rights. The Massachusetts Constitution of 1780, which remains to this day, begins with a declaration of 30 rights, the last of which originated the typical American separation of powers, 'to the end it may be a government of laws and not of men.' The first Congress was so full of such ideas that the resolution finally adopted as the Bill of Rights was the 297th proposal submitted in six months.

The part which the Bill of Rights has played in molding political character is phenomenal. It has created for all American institutions a legal ceiling and a moral floor, above which it is not permitted for American society to go and below which American society does not allow itself to fall. Within such limits man's most perfect freedom is attainable. On sundry occasions the United States has acted as reprehensibly as any country you may name, but the spirit of the Bill of Rights has always impelled us to re-establish standards of decency and fair play. The guaranties of the American national are the guidons of the American nation. They insure that we are a self-correcting body of human beings.

Crystal clear, the war that now engages us is a conflict to confirm and establish civil liberties in a world where our Bill of Rights is in jeopardy unless other peoples can also preserve theirs. For our Bill of Rights, in the oldest Constitution of the world, has gone around the globe. It appears in substance in practically all written national constitutions, with one distinction. Our Constitution records rights inalienably possessed by the people; it does not grant them. That direct ownership of our guaranties is the most precious thing about them, the thing we are fighting to keep. When you examine the world's constitutions, you discover that in the gangster states human rights are not owned by the people, but are just rented out to the docile. And you find the equally striking fact that all the peoples who have flocked and are flocking to the standard we uphold because our civil nature says we must, have constitutions under which they possess their civil rights directly and thereby control their governments.

WHAT IS FREEDOM?

By David Cushman Coyle

WE the people of the United States have been working on our democracy since long before the American Revolution, trying to keep ahead of the new problems that have come up. Our ideas have grown too. First the main point was political freedom, because red-blooded people will choose freedom before security or prosperity when they have a clear choice. So first our ancestors had to have freedom of speech and religion, which in our modern language means no gestapo to spy on them.

Afterward, their descendants realized they also had to have economic freedom. Everyone must have a chance to make a living. We have been working on that, and the job is not finished.

Now, we are also beginning to see that democracy will not satisfy us until everybody in our country belongs. It isn't enough to be free to talk, or even to have a job; people also have to stand together as friends. There has always been a lot of comradeship and good feeling among Americans, and now it must be enlarged until there are no forgotten men, women or children. We have to build up a democracy of responsibility in which everyone of us will have the satisfaction of doing his share to promote the general welfare.

The first words of our Constitution lay down the line that Americans have tried to follow.

'We the people of the United States, in order to form a more perfect union, establish justice, insure domestic tranquility, provide for the common defense, promote the general welfare, and secure the blessings of liberty to ourselves and our posterity, do

From David Cushman Coyle, *America*, 1941, published at 25¢ a copy by The National Home Library Foundation, Washington, D. C. By permission of the publisher.

ordain and establish this Constitution for the United States of America.'

The difference between a dictatorship and a democracy is plain, and should never be forgotten. In a dictatorship, the men who are in the government can be thrown out in only one way, by staging a rebellion and killing them. In a political democracy, we the people have a regular system of elections when our political candidates have to come before us and ask our permission to hold office. Nobody doubts that on November 5, 1940, if Willkie had won by even the slimmest margin, President Roosevelt would have bowed to the will of his master, the people, and on January 20, 1941, he would have peacefully handed over the job to the new man.

That is the first point of difference between democracy and dictatorship, and on that point the United States is a democracy.

The second point of difference is that we the people have the right to criticize our President, our Governors, our Senators, and all our other public servants. We can go to almost any limit, considerably farther than the law will let you go in criticizing a private citizen.

Nobody doubts that the American people can criticize President Roosevelt. They do it all the time. The Washington newspaper men have a club called the Gridiron Club, that holds a dinner twice a year. The Gridiron Club puts on a show, and the President is invited to sit right in front of the stage, while they roast him. Foreign diplomats are also invited to come and see our President take his medicine. What do you suppose would happen if German newspaper men wanted to roast Hitler on a gridiron?

Hitler's feelings may be represented by his comment on the attitude of the German Congress or Reichstag toward Emperor William. He says in *Mein Kampf:*

'I was indignant at the fact that in a State where every halfwit not only claimed the right to criticize, but where in the Reichstag he was let loose on the nation as a "legislator," the bearer of the imperial crown could be given "reprimands" by the greatest babbling institution of all time.'

We not only choose our public servants by voting, we can also discuss their qualifications in any way we please. Moreover, we can tell them what we think of them.

This is the second point of difference between democracy and dictatorship, and on this point the United States scores 100 per cent.

We the people are the masters of this country. If we elect good public servants, we have a good government. If we elect bad ones or stupid ones, we have a bad government. If we are not interested, and don't give our government a mandate for the protection of our interests, of course the people with private axes to grind will take advantage of our carelessness. It is all up to us. We the people are slow. We kick and growl and argue, and take a long time making up our minds, but when we decide, there is no power in this country that can tell us to lie down.

We the people are good sports about our politics. In a campaign we go at each other hammer and tongs, until election day. Then the majority takes the victory, and the losers come forward and shake hands. We go on having our own opinion but we let the majority rule. Next time, the loser may build up a majority. That is our way of getting things settled without having to kill people. The majority can be wrong, but we believe it is better to let the majority make mistakes and learn from experience.

This political system is entirely different from the Nazi system where the little gang around Hitler is the master of the people. Our way may be slow and blundering, but it gives us a chance to work toward the gradual improvement of our laws and government. Most of our attempts at improvement in the past few years have had to do with the problems of unemployment.

Where the shoe pinches, the pain takes up all the attention, and properly so if the question is only where to stretch the shoe. But if it is a question of throwing away the shoes, we have to consider how other shoes might pinch. Our democracy pinches lately at the point of economic freedom. You are not free if you can't get a job or if you have a job and would starve if you lost it. So of course the chief attention of public policy in America, until the war crisis came on, has been to stretch employment and relieve the pinch that gave the greatest pain.

But this war brings up the possibility of throwing the whole system away and getting a new one guaranteed to give jobs to all. The Nazis will give us jobs, sure enough, if we let them take charge, and let them write their own ticket about our wages and our working conditions. But the Nazi shoe would pinch in certain other places so painfully that we would long to go back to the happy days of the Great Depression. Americans easily forget the civil liberties that are commonplace here, and sometimes we wonder why our ancestors were excited about such dull matters as habeas corpus or trial by jury. Why should any American want to die for a municipal police court?

There are millions of Europeans who could tell you in burning words why they would risk their lives to win for their children the high privilege of having a municipal police court, even a somewhat corrupt one. The Europeans of today who have lost all their civil liberties are as eager about them as our respected forefathers who had suffered under the European laws of their time.

Freedom of worship may seem a small matter to anyone who seldom goes to church. But those who live day and night under the shadow of the German police know that religion is a strong rock of defense against the danger of going insane under the reign of terror. Religion for many is a desperate adventure in the New Order of Europe, an adventure where people risk their lives to keep their spiritual light burning through the darkness. Christian martyrs are not confined to stories of 1800 years ago. Would you rather live in a country where religion is still open to men and women and children, or in one where people are killed because of their beliefs?

It is true that we have had some religious persecution here. But in the main our religious freedom is so nearly universal we take it for granted. We forget it took centuries to win, but would be lost in a moment if we have to bow to the Fuehrer— 'the soul of Germany made flesh.' You don't miss the air you breathe until you can't get it.

We also take our legal freedom too much for granted. Most Americans are impatient with our courts of law. The court is slow and cumbersome. Criminals sometimes escape the 'rap' although everyone knows they are guilty. Once in a while a juryman is 'reached,' though everyone who has ever sat on a jury must acknowledge the high average integrity of his fellow citizens as they argue their verdict in the secrecy of the jury room.

In Italy, if you are accused of a crime, your lawyer must begin his argument by admitting that you are guilty. That simplifies the legal technicalities greatly. In Germany, if you are allowed a trial, the judge is bound to 'protect the safety of the State' against you, which also simplifies the process of liquidating you. What we think of as justice is not allowed in those countries to interfere with political persecution. But the net result is that if someone with a grudge has turned you in, or if circumstantial evidence has pointed to you in a crime you did not commit, the law is not concerned with finding the true facts. And if you are not quite enthusiastic in support of the Fuehrer or of the local *gauleiter,* any charge is good enough to use as a stick to beat a dog like you.

Our ancestors have handed down a system of law, designed first of all to protect the life and liberty of the individual, and second to protect the public as well as possible. From the ancient Jewish law we have inherited the principle that a man is entitled to an open trial, with the public looking on. From Greek and Roman law have come other great principles that are now a part of our standards of a fair trial. An accused man is entitled to meet his accuser face to face in open court. He is entitled to have a lawyer to see that he is not tricked by his own ignorance of the processes of law. If he cannot pay, the court provides him a lawyer without charge. Above all, he is entitled to a jury trial. If you are accused of murder or any other crime, you can reject from your jury anyone who is your enemy, or an enemy of your race or creed, or who in any way is known to be prejudiced against you. The jury represents the decent respect for the opinions of mankind, which, with all its faults, is the best guarantee of fair treatment we know how to find.

Finally, you may never have had to use a habeas corpus, but you would soon learn to miss it if you had to live in Europe. This is how the right of habeas corpus works. Down through the centuries our ancestors learned that the first guarantee of liberty was the right of not being arrested by the police without some show of cause. In our country, you can drag any lawyer out of bed at three o'clock in the morning and demand that he get you a habeas corpus for someone who has been arrested. He will wake up a judge, any judge he can find—even a Justice of the U.S. Supreme Court—in the same way a doctor can be called for an emergency operation. The judge will issue a habeas corpus, which is an order to a warden or a sheriff to produce the prisoner without delay and explain why he was arrested. If the arrest was not justified, the prisoner must immediately be set free and may sue the police for damages.

All this elaborate precaution has just one purpose, to prevent any system of police terror being established among a free people. The system of protection does not always work. Men are sometimes arrested without legal reason, and even given the third degree although they may be innocent. Here, as in every other way, we are human and imperfect. But it is worth noting that with all the faults of our law, it protects freedom in a sense that the Nazi system does not. Nazi Europe has the gestapo and we do not. There is a difference—the difference between an imperfect system that aims to protect our life and safety, and an almost perfect system of brutality and terror.

The danger to our country has waked us up to the fact that democracy is not all made up of rights. Democracy is also made up of duties. We have to stand together and support our country, if we want to have a country and keep our rights. We have to pay taxes, and serve in national defense. We have to help protect the health and security of all Americans. We have to work to build unity and good feeling among ourselves. These duties are a necessary price that must be paid for freedom either in peace or war. The threat of Nazi aggression has shown us new reasons for paying that price.

We have our troubles with liberty, especially on the economic side. We have troubles with legal 'civil liberties.' The shoe pinches here and there, sometimes pretty hard. But if we carelessly lose these old shoes that we have inherited, and that sometimes seem a bit shabby, we shall regret it, when we find ourselves squeezed by the Nazi boot.

THE TRADITION OF LIBERTY IN ENGLAND AND AMERICA

By Stanley Pargellis

THOUGH most people shy away from talk of liberty, fearing, amid the confused uses of the term, that whatever they hear will be somebody's propaganda, they all know at what point liberty begins. It is the point at which they resent being shoved about. Simply, then, liberty can be defined in biological terms: 'All living organisms abhor restraint,' or, 'Whenever any situation or any force stops an organism from doing what it has convinced will and ability to do, it does not feel free until the restraint is removed.' There are by this definition as many forms of liberty for the individual as there are possible situations which he thinks restrain him, or possible objectives which he may wish to attain. In this broad sense there can be no one particular thing which is liberty, no state of affairs which represents the absolute and true liberty, no mystic reservoir of liberty which we must try to keep full. Nor is liberty something to be defined and caught by someone within a formula and imposed upon the rest of us. Liberty is an abstract term standing for the sum of all separate liberties, just as Man is an abstract term standing for the sum of all separate men. There is no one man who is Man; there is no one liberty which is Liberty. In this sense liberty has been one of the driving forces in history, and history's persistent conflicts have always been between your liberty and mine.[1]

From *The Pennsylvania Magazine of History and Biography*, October 1941. By permission of the Historical Society of Pennsylvania and the author.

[1] Dorothy Fosdick, *What is Liberty* (1939), analyzes the term in this biological sense. A recent symposium, edited by Ruth Nanda Anshen, *Freedom: Its Meaning* (1940), gives definitions by some of our ablest living writers and scholars. Benedetto Croce, *History as the Story of Liberty* (1941), magnificently argues for another meaning of liberty in history than the biological one alone.

In America and England one widely held interpretation of liberty, in the course of the last three centuries, can be said to have conformed fairly closely to that broad definition. We have more and more tended to call only that state a free one where as many individual liberties as possible are permitted expression, where every individual has reasonably wide scope to define and work out his particular form of liberty. That tradition is the child of the seventeenth century. In the course of the seventeenth century, in pain and in fumbling and largely by accident, we found a solution to its social conflict, embodied it in institutional form, and managed to retain it. What men did during that century was to boil down all possible liberties into four that were considered essential. Customarily we define these four liberties thus: (1) liberty to acquire and hold private property; (2) liberty of conscience, to worship, speak, write, and believe as each chooses; (3) liberty to have some voice in the management of political affairs; (4) liberty of the person, to act under a law which lays the same impartial restraints upon everyone, governors and governed alike. Not one of these specific liberties implies that the only true liberty is belief in a Catholic or an Anglican or a Presbyterian God, though to many people such belief does really constitute true liberty; not one of them avows that true liberty consists in following a ruler best fitted, by God or by nature, to rule, though many people find their true liberty in uncritical service to a man or an institution. None of these liberties states explicitly that the reason why preference is allowed the individual to choose his way of life is that he may arm himself with moral armor, though it is perfectly true that this concept of individual self-growth, in the varying expressions of it by the most gifted of American and British writers, has ever furnished a chief inspiration for the continuance of our belief in the capacity of the individual to choose well.[2] These four liberties, as such, say nothing about choosing well; they allow wide latitude to a great many forms of individual liberty; they have had as object the creating and maintaining of a situa-

[2] In the last war Robert Bridges edited a famous little anthology, *The Spirit of Man* (1916); the equivalent volume today is Bruce L. Richmond, *The Pattern of Freedom in Prose and Verse* (1940).

tion where individual preferences have opportunity for expression.

These four liberties are man-made. They grew as compromise from the conflict both of organized groups and of individuals with the authoritarian bodies which professed, being especially entrusted by God with the mission, to impose a rule, that is a definition of liberty, of their own. The parliamentarians of the 1620's wanted freedom from certain restraints. They objected to the divine-right concepts of Stuart kings because they did not want their property endangered by taxation without consent; because they did not want to be led into a war they disapproved; because they wanted, as a group, management of their own affairs; because, being Protestants, they feared the re-establishment of Catholicism. Innovators, even revolutionists, they were, but they had to couch the arguments by which they supported their fight in terms that conformed to the accepted arguments of the times, to tradition, and to God. They therefore discovered new interpretations of precedents to justify their efforts to control the administration, and later in the century, when the lawyers had given way to divines and political theorists, these latter found sweeping philosophical sanction in the word 'nature.' Man has natural rights, they said, to his property, to his life, to a fair trial, to his opinions. They appealed to that vague term 'nature' because they needed something as divine and as authoritative as the law of God, to which their opponents, with the books and evidence well in hand, were appealing.

In the same way those Separatists who founded Massachusetts to be a theocracy of the elect, and attempted to turn the colony into a sovereign commonwealth, were seeking liberty in no wide sense, but as a group appealing to the Bible against the church, and to the saints against the king. The merchants who wanted to make money either urged that the state utilize its powers, in the laying of tariffs and bounties, so that the trading groups would profit, and invoked the idea of the nation against the local and traditional interests of guild or feudal survivals; or they urged that the trading privileges reserved by patent to the great companies be thrown open to all, and brought as witness the law of nature to justify this early form of 'free trade.'

Out of the clash of these more or less well-organized groups, the court, the church of England, the country gentry, the merchants, and the sects—some of them surviving from feudal times, some the product of the commercial revolution and the Reformation—there came by the end of the century a definition of the liberties which were to safeguard the particular form of liberty which each group desired. The bill of rights and the revolution settlement wrote into law the concept that the government itself was bound by laws which propertied groups had a share in making. The act of toleration guaranteed that no punishment would be imposed on men because they were members of a Protestant faith other than the Anglican. The failure to reimpose censorship, largely because no censor could be found whom all would accept, began a free press. The crop of statutes relating to trade widened the avenues within which the individual merchant could seek his markets. By such acts the interests of every group powerful enough to make its weight felt were protected, and in every case the arguments justifying such protection were couched in terms which embraced more than the group itself, in terms of the nation, as in mercantilism or the theory of balanced government, or in terms of mankind. And for every group the final working settlement meant something less than it had hoped.

Up to this point the biological definition of liberty serves adequately to let us understand the seventeenth century. Put in this way, as the result of a compromise between conflicting groups, no one of which was strong enough to dominate all the others, these four liberties seem no more heroic than expediency usually seems.

But the biological interpretation, by itself, misses an essential feature of this settlement and these liberties. To the men who engineered the settlement, who could, like Halifax, call themselves trimmers, these liberties did in point of fact rest upon the conviction that the groups to which they were extended would choose, if not well, at least not badly. Anglicans and non-conformists were safe; Catholics, atheists, and Jews were not. Propertied groups could be entrusted with government; unpropertied ones were dangerous. Businessmen were safe, but they had to be kept from too much meddling in statecraft. Free speech could be checked by the laws of libel from becoming too extravagant. In the colonies, too, similar limitations of these liberties existed, perhaps to a lesser degree, and to a lesser degree in some than in others, but for the same reasons. The point is worth emphasizing, that while the public arguments for them were couched in universal terms, these liberties were in reality confined to those groups who had more or less agreed, however reluctantly, to live together and to share power.

At the same time there was a handful of men in the seventeenth century who took the arguments about universals at their face value. When Roger Williams or William Penn or William Chillingworth or even Lord Baltimore talked about religious toleration, they considered all religious opinion to be safe. When the men in Cromwell's army, like Colonel Rainborow, used the argument from nature, they thought of all men as having a right to share in government and to make a living. To John Pym justice was a principle to be followed wherever it led, and not to be invoked in any interest less than that of the whole of mankind. Milton believed in free speech because he believed that only through free speech would truth emerge. Such men provided the emotional and intellectual food for the future. They thought that under the right conditions all men might be trusted to choose well.

The history of liberty in the next two hundred years, from the end of the seventeenth century to the end of the nineteenth, from Penn, say, to the time Carnegie sold out to U.S. Steel, has been the broadening of the base upon which the four liberties rested to approach the universal speculations concerning them. Two great economic forces in England and America, having the same social effects, were at work in these two centuries. The expanding frontier and the expanding forces of the industrial revolution were alike in this, that they altered the social structure of a comparatively static, agrarian society molded in feudal forms. Today in both countries we have a society mainly composed of entrepreneurs, rentiers, professional and salaried men, workers, and farmers. Yet in spite of the shifting social complexion, we have managed in both countries to continue and to enlarge the successful compromise of 1689, which, in all its essentials, not basically altered by a federal republican form, the American constitution of 1787 repeated.

Each liberty of the four broadened. All men who have property, said Locke, have a natural right to its protection, and therefore to a voice in government; all men, said Paine, have that right; all men, said the Populists and the Socialists, have a right to make that voice effective in economic matters where alone it counts. The wealth of England will be enhanced, said the mercantilist, if the economy is put on a national basis; the Wealth of Nations, said Adam Smith, will be enhanced if every man is allowed to dig for gold in the hills of an expanding economy; wealth will increase, echoed everyone on the make in mid-nineteenth-century America, pioneer and industrialist alike, if we all are permitted to exploit the country as quickly as our skills and energies let us. Liberty of conscience, except for the limitations which the social conventions of Victorian morality in England, and even more in frontier America, imposed upon it, was undeniably broadened. The religious outcasts of 1689 were freed from all liabilities by the end of the nineteenth century, and there was no question and no point of view which one could not discuss, in print or aloud. The scope of the law widened, as it extended the concept of impartiality to larger groups.

Likewise there sprawled on into the nineteenth century that grand but woefully incomplete assumption of the seventeenth, the notion that there is a law of nature in political matters and that men have natural rights under it. Of all the well-known political thinkers of his time, Hobbes alone avoided the pitfall. Hobbes said that where every man seeks his own liberty without regard for the liberties of others, he actually has no liberty and is wretched. If he is to have any measure of liberty, he must set some limits to his pursuit of it. Hobbes advocated compromise, therefore, and the adherent to the biological definition of liberty can rightly say that its history in England and America since his time has been pure Hobbes. He took no truck in a law of nature or natural rights, any more than in any morality not built on expediency. But belief in a law of nature continued; it led in the next century to the concept of the great chain of being, with all life keeping its appointed place in the God-given order of things; and in the nineteenth century to the doctrine of progress, as irresistibly ordained by God and nature.

Those seventeenth-century men who interpreted liberties in universal terms had so increased in numbers by the nineteenth that they could take to themselves the name of Liberals, and give that name to the century. A nineteenth-century liberal not only believed in change; he believed in change towards a goal. The goal was the eventual making flesh of all the universals, so that every man should be as free as possible. But so obsessed was the liberal with the effort to make men free to choose, that, as his many critics pointed out, he spent little time in teaching them to choose well. He either forgot or took for granted the second essential feature of these four liberties, that they work only when a common morality underlies them.

By the end of the nineteenth century a few observers saw that, as its earlier critics had prophesied, something had actually gone wrong with liberalism. Some saw that the organized workers, instead of merely sharing in government, might gain enough voting strength to overbalance the rest. Democracy seemed to be marching towards dictatorship. Others saw that the broadening of the liberty to accumulate property without any very marked restrictions had led through *laissez-faire* to the modern corporation. The corporation seemed to be well on the way to accumulating all the property which meant power, and therefore effectually to be destroying the liberty to accumulate property. Liberty of conscience, which for Mill as for Milton meant that truth need not fear the test of the market-place, had been so broadened through the spread of semi-education that the wildest and most half-baked statement often seemed to contend, having equal credence and equal effect, with those which had the sanction of experience and disciplined thought. In a welter where all values become equal, the notion of value itself, even the value of liberty, must be lost. The disintegrating attack upon the keystone of these four liberties, the supremacy of the law, had not begun by the end of the century, but it began in America some fifteen years later. By such processes liberty seemed to be about to kill liberty.

It is a black enough picture, blacker than any we have ever faced as a nation, but perhaps not more dark than the seventeenth century seemed to Sir Thomas Browne: 'the uncertainty and ignorance of things to come.' When to Hoover the only true liberty is economic individualism, and to Philip Murray the right of the worker to a secure means of livelihood—both definitions resulting from the broadening of the old mercantilist argument—the difference between them is not greater than between Cavalier and Roundhead, court and parliament, Massachusetts 'saint' and Catholic. Compromise between one freedom and another, in which lies all the merit of our English and American heritage, between the organized groups of government, managers, professionals, workers, and farmers, is as possible as not. Yet, if it is to be compromise, its precise form hidden in the future, to every group that has power must be left something satisfying as well as something less than each had hoped. The biological definition of liberty shows us that. While the external forms of our institutions may change beyond our recognition, if compromise is the eventual outcome, it is difficult to see how it can be on any ground other than those of the four liberties. All groups will want a share in government; all will want to argue their own case; all will want economic security; and all will see that only an impartial law can save each's particular desire. The biological definition of liberty shows us that, also. And perhaps, for it is equally necessary in any compromise, we are on the way to redefining the liberty which underlay the seventeenth-century one, which the nineteenth-century liberals overlooked, the liberty not only to choose, but to choose not too badly. If, as is perfectly possible, not compromise, but the victory of one dominant group, whether of government, managers, labor, or Nazis, proves to be the outcome, then we return to the authority from which we once escaped. In an economy that has ceased to expand rapidly, it will be an authority much more unpleasant and much less human than that either of church or of king.

There would still be liberty under it, the rare kind of liberty which the philosopher and the religious mystic know, or the liberty to use one's capacities in deliberate serving of the new order, but it will be less than that which we have had, liberty to exercise an individual preference in the choice of a group or a life.

THE GRAY CHAMPION

By Nathaniel Hawthorne

THERE was once a time when New England groaned under the actual pressure of heavier wrongs than those threatened ones which brought on the Revolution. James II, the bigoted successor of Charles the Voluptuous, had annulled the charters of all the colonies, and sent a harsh and unprincipled soldier to take away our liberties and endanger our religion. The administration of Sir Edmund Andros lacked scarcely a single characteristic of tyranny: a governor and council, holding office from the king, and wholly independent of the country; laws made and taxes levied without concurrence of the people, immediate or by their representatives; the rights of private citizens violated, and the titles of all landed property declared void; the voice of complaint stifled by restrictions on the press; and, finally, disaffection overawed by the first band of mercenary troops that ever marched on our free soil. For two years our ancestors were kept in sullen submission by that filial love which had invariably secured their allegiance to the mother country, whether its head chanced to be a parliament, protector, or popish monarch. Till these evil times, however, such allegiance had been merely nominal, and the colonists had ruled themselves, enjoying far more freedom than is even yet the privilege of the native subjects of Great Britain.

At length a rumor reached our shores that the Prince of Orange had ventured on an enterprise, the success of which would be the triumph of civil and religious rights, and the salvation of New England. It was but a doubtful whisper; it might be false, or the attempt might fail; and, in either case, the man that stirred against King James would lose his head. Still the intelligence produced a marked effect. The people smiled mys-

81

teriously in the streets, and threw bold glances at their oppressors; while, far and wide, there was a subdued and silent agitation, as if the slightest signal would rouse the whole land from its sluggish despondency. Aware of their danger, the rulers resolved to avert it by an imposing display of strength, and perhaps to confirm their despotism by yet harsher measures. One afternoon in April 1689, Sir Edmund Andros and his favorite councilors, being warm with wine, assembled the red-coats of the governor's guard and made their appearance in the streets of Boston. The sun was near setting when the march commenced.

The roll of the drum, at that unquiet crisis, seemed to go through the streets less as the martial music of the soldiers than as a muster-call to the inhabitants themselves. A multitude, by various avenues, assembled in King Street, which was destined to be the scene, nearly a century afterwards, of another encounter between the troops of Britain and a people struggling against her tyranny. Though more than sixty years had elapsed since the Pilgrims came, this crowd of their descendants still showed the strong and somber features of their character, perhaps more strikingly in such a stern emergency than on happier occasions. There was the sober garb, the general severity of mien, the gloomy but undismayed expression, the scriptural forms of speech, and the confidence in Heaven's blessing on a righteous cause, which would have marked a band of the original Puritans when threatened by some peril of the wilderness. Indeed, it was not yet time for the old spirit to be extinct; since there were men in the street, that day, who had worshiped there beneath the trees before a house was reared to the God for whom they had become exiles. Old soldiers of the parliament were here too, smiling grimly at the thought that their aged arms might strike another blow against the house of Stuart. Here, also, were the veterans of King Philip's war, who had burned villages and slaughtered young and old with pious fierceness, while the godly souls throughout the land were helping them with prayer. Several ministers were scattered among the crowd, which, unlike all other mobs, regarded them with such reverence as if there were sanctity in their very garments. These holy men exerted their influence to quiet the people, but not to disperse them. Meantime, the purpose of the governor, in disturbing the peace of the town at a period when the slightest commotion might throw the country into a ferment, was almost the universal subject of inquiry, and variously explained.

'Satan will strike his master-stroke presently,' cried some, 'because he knoweth that his time is short. All our godly pastors are to be dragged to prison! We shall see them at a Smithfield fire in King Street!'

Hereupon the people of each parish gathered closer round their minister, who looked calmly upwards and assumed a more apostolic dignity, as well befitted a candidate for the highest honor of his profession, the crown of martyrdom. It was actually fancied, at that period, that New England might have a John Rogers of her own, to take the place of that worthy in the primer.

'The pope of Rome has given orders for a new St. Bartholomew!' cried others. 'We are to be massacred, man and male child!'

Neither was this rumor wholly discredited, although the wiser class believed the governor's object somewhat less atrocious. His predecessor under the old charter, Bradstreet, a venerable companion of the first settlers, was known to be in town. There were grounds for conjecturing that Sir Edmund Andros intended, at once, to strike terror by a parade of military force, and to confound the opposite faction, by possessing himself of their chief.

'Stand firm for the old charter, governor!' shouted the crowd, seizing upon the idea. 'The good old Governor Bradstreet!'

While this cry was at the loudest, the people were surprised by the well-known figure of Governor Bradstreet himself, a patriarch of nearly ninety, who appeared on the elevated steps of a door, and with characteristic mildness besought them to submit to the constituted authorities.

'My children,' concluded this venerable person, 'do nothing rashly. Cry not aloud, but pray for the welfare of New England, and expect patiently what the Lord will do in this matter.'

The event was soon to be decided. All this time the roll of the drum had been approaching through Cornhill, louder and deeper, till with reverberations from house to house, and the regular tramp of martial footsteps, it burst into the street. A double rank of soldiers made their appearance, occupying the whole breadth of the passage, with shouldered matchlocks, and matches burning, so as to present a row of fires in the dusk. Their steady march was like the progress of a machine that would roll irresistibly over everything in its way. Next, moving slowly, with a confused clatter of hoofs on the pavement, rode a party of mounted gentlemen, the central figure being Sir Edmund Andros, elderly, but erect and soldier-like. Those around him were his favorite councilors, and the bitterest foes of New England. At his right hand rode Edward Randolph, our arch-enemy, that 'blasted wretch,' as Cotton Mather calls him, who achieved the downfall of our ancient government, and was fol-lowed with a sensible curse through life and to his grave. On the other side was Bullivant, scattering jests and mockery as he rode along. Dudley came behind, with a downcast look, dread-ing, as well he might, to meet the indignant gaze of the people, who beheld him, their only countryman by birth, among the oppressors of his native land. The captain of a frigate in the harbor, and two or three civil officers under the crown, were also there. But the figure which most attracted the public eye, and stirred up the deepest feeling, was the Episcopal clergyman of King's Chapel, riding haughtily among the magistrates in his priestly vestments, the fitting representative of prelacy and per-secution, the union of Church and State, and all those abomina-tions which had driven the Puritans to the wilderness. Another guard of soldiers, in double rank, brought up the rear.

The whole scene was a picture of the condition of New Eng-land, and its moral, the deformity of any government that does not grow out of the nature of things and the character of the people. On one side, the religious multitude, with their sad visages and dark attire, and on the other, the group of despotic rulers, with the high churchman in the midst, and here and there a crucifix at their bosoms, all magnificently clad, flushed with wine, proud of unjust authority, and scoffing at the uni-versal groan. And the mercenary soldiers, waiting but the word to deluge the street with blood, showed the only means by which obedience could be secured.

'Oh! Lord of Hosts,' cried a voice among the crowd, 'provide a champion for thy people!'

This ejaculation was loudly uttered, and served as a herald's cry to introduce a remarkable personage. The crowd had rolled back, and were now huddled together nearly at the extremity of the street, while the soldiers had advanced no more than a third of its length. The intervening space was empty—a paved solitude between lofty edifices, which threw almost a twilight shadow over it. Suddenly there was seen the figure of an ancient man, who seemed to have emerged from among the people, and was walking by himself along the center of the street, to confront the armed band. He wore the old Puritan dress, a dark cloak and a steeple-crowned hat, in the fashion of at least fifty years before, with a heavy sword upon his thigh, but a staff in his hand, to assist the tremulous gait of age.

When at some distance from the multitude, the old man turned slowly round, displaying a face of antique majesty, rendered doubly venerable by the hoary beard that descended on his breast. He made a gesture at once of encouragement and warning, then turned again and resumed his way.

'Who is this gray patriarch?' asked the young men of their sires.

'Who is this venerable brother?' asked the old men among themselves.

But none could reply. The fathers of the people, those of fourscore years and upwards, were disturbed, deeming it strange that they should forget one of such evident authority, whom they must have known in their early days, the associate of Winthrop, and all the old councilors, giving laws, and making prayers, and leading them against the savage. The elderly men ought to have remembered him, too, with locks as gray in their youth as their own were now. And the young! How could he have passed so utterly from their memories—that hoary sire, the relic of long departed times, whose awful benediction had surely been bestowed on their uncovered heads in childhood?

'Whence did he come? What is his purpose? Who can this old man be?' whispered the wondering crowd.

Meanwhile, the venerable stranger, staff in hand, was pursuing his solitary walk along the center of the street. As he drew near the advancing soldiers, and as the roll of their drum came full upon his ear, the old man raised himself to a loftier mien, while the decrepitude of age seemed to fall from his shoulders, leaving him in gray but unbroken dignity. Now, he marched onward with a warrior's step, keeping time to the military music. Thus the aged form advanced on one side, and the whole parade of soldiers and magistrates on the other, till, when scarcely twenty yards remained between, the old man grasped his staff by the middle, and held it before him like a leader's truncheon.

'Stand!' cried he.

The eye, the face, and attitude of command; the solemn yet warlike peal of that voice, fit either to rule a host in the battlefield or be raised to God in prayer, were irresistible. At the old man's word and outstretched arm the roll of the drum was hushed at once, and the advancing line stood still. A tremulous enthusiasm seized upon the multitude. That stately form, combining the leader and the saint, so gray, so dimly seen, in such an ancient garb, could only belong to some old champion of the righteous cause, whom the oppressor's drum had summoned from his grave. They raised a shout of awe and exultation, and looked for the deliverance of New England.

The governor, and the gentlemen of his party, perceiving themselves brought to an unexpected stand, rode hastily forward, as if they would have pressed their snorting and affrighted horses right against the hoary apparition. He, however, blenched not a step, but glancing his severe eye round the group, which half encompassed him, at last bent it sternly on Sir Edmund Andros. One would have thought that the dark old man was chief ruler there, and that the governor and council, with soldiers at their back, representing the whole power and authority of the crown, had no alternative but obedience.

'What does this old fellow here?' cried Edward Randolph, fiercely. 'On, Sir Edmund! Bid the soldiers forward, and give the dotard the same choice that you give all his countrymen —to stand aside or be trampled on!'

'Nay, nay, let us show respect to the good grandsire,' said Bullivant, laughing. 'See you not he is some old round-headed dignitary who hath lain asleep these thirty years, and knows nothing of the change of times? Doubtless he thinks to put us down with a proclamation in Old Noll's name!'

'Are you mad, old man?' demanded Sir Edmund Andros, in loud and harsh tones. 'How dare you stay the march of King James's governor?'

'I have stayed the march of a king himself ere now,' replied the gray figure, with stern composure. 'I am here, sir governor, because the cry of an oppressed people hath disturbed me in my secret place; and beseeching this favor earnestly of the Lord, it was vouchsafed me to appear once again on earth in the good old cause of his saints. And what speak ye of James? There is no longer a popish tyrant on the throne of England, and by tomorrow noon his name shall be a byword in this very street, where ye would make it a word of terror. Back, thou that wast a governor, back! With this night thy power is ended—tomorrow the prison!—back, lest I foretell the scaffold!'

The people had been drawing nearer and nearer, and drinking in the words of their champion, who spoke in accents long disused, like one unaccustomed to converse, except with the dead of many years ago. But his voice stirred their souls. They confronted the soldiers, not wholly without arms, and ready to convert the very stones of the street into deadly weapons. Sir Edmund Andros looked at the old man; then he cast his hard and cruel eye over the multitude, and beheld them burning with that lurid wrath so difficult to kindle or to quench; and again he fixed his gaze on the aged form, which stood obscurely in an open space, where neither friend nor foe had thrust himself. What were his thoughts he uttered no word which might discover. But whether the oppressor were overawed by the Gray Champion's look, or perceived his peril in the threatening attitude of the people, it is certain that he gave back, and ordered his soldiers to commence a slow and guarded retreat. Before another sunset, the governor, and all that rode so proudly with him, were prisoners, and long ere it was known that James had abdicated, King William was proclaimed throughout New England.

But where was the Gray Champion? Some reported that when

the troops had gone from King Street, and the people were thronging tumultuously in their rear, Bradstreet, the aged governor, was seen to embrace a form more aged than his own. Others soberly affirmed, that while they marveled at the venerable grandeur of his aspect, the old man had faded from their eyes, melting slowly into the hues of twilight, till where he stood there was an empty space. But all agreed that the hoary shape was gone. The men of that generation watched for his reappearance, in sunshine and in twilight, but never saw him more, nor knew when his funeral passed, nor where his gravestone was.

And who was the Gray Champion? Perhaps his name might be found in the records of that stern Court of Justice which passed a sentence, too mighty for the age, but glorious in all after-times, for its humbling lesson to the monarch and its high example to the subject. I have heard that, whenever the descendants of the Puritans are to show the spirit of their sires, the old man appears again. When eighty years had passed, he walked once more in King Street. Five years later, in the twilight of an April morning, he stood on the green, beside the meeting-house, at Lexington, where now the obelisk of granite, with a slab of slate inlaid, commemorates the first fallen of the Revolution. And when our fathers were toiling at the breastwork on Bunker's Hill, all through that night the old warrior walked his rounds. Long, long may it be ere he comes again! His hour is one of darkness, and adversity, and peril. But should domestic tyranny oppress us, or the invader's step pollute our soil, still may the Gray Champion come, for he is the type of New England's hereditary spirit; and his shadowy march, on the eve of danger, must ever be the pledge that New England's sons will vindicate their ancestry.

THE SOURCES OF 'THE GRAY CHAMPION'

By G. Harrison Orians

A BOWDOIN lad with Hawthorne's temperament, curiosity, and magisterial lineage, in a time absorbed with the glories of by-gone ages, could scarcely have failed to develop his scholarly interests or to study colonial antiquities. He turned, even during his later college years, to the New England scene as the subject of fictional prose. Before 1825 he had ready 'Seven Tales of My Native Land,' a series he consigned to the flames, but in the fourteen years succeeding graduation he continued with sketch after sketch to cultivate New England legends and characters, contributing the best of these to *The Token* and *The Salem Gazette*. To his tales he brought a mind already filled with antiquarian lore from his extensive reading in local and general histories and his wide observation of various localities in his own section of the Union.

In 1835, after seven years of anonymous publication, came 'The Gray Champion,' [1] the sources of which were once considered by Elizabeth Chandler in a monograph on Hawthorne's tales and romances.[2] She merely grouped it with 'Young Goodman Brown' and 'The Maypole of Merry Mount' as having a 'common origin in Hawthorne's feeling for history.' That it owes something to the histories of colonial New England is perhaps clear. Extensive use Hawthorne had already made—in 'My Kinsman, Major Molineux,' 'Dr. Bullivant,' and 'The Gentle Boy' [3]—of Hutchinson's *History of Massachusetts*.[4] The description of the

---

[1] Published in the *New England Magazine*, January 1835. Reprinted in *Twice-Told Tales*, Boston: American Stationers Co., 1837.

[2] *Smith College Studies in Modern Languages*, Northampton, 1926.

[3] For the indebtedness to Hutchinson, Sewel, and others, see *The New England Quarterly*, xiv, 664-78, December 1941.

[4] The first two volumes were originally published in 1764; the third volume appeared in 1828. For other details of the oppression under Andros see

colonial distresses at the hands of a tyrant, the disquietude about houses and lands, the sustained love of freedom in the face of the abridgment of former charter rights, the suppressed excitement at the rumor of the Prince of Orange's expedition may all be referred to this same work. Snow's *History of Boston*,[5] Trumbull's *General History of the United States*,[6] Morse and Parish's *Compendious History of New England*,[7] and Neal's *History of New England*[8] could have supplied additional details. For his description of the temper of the crowd and the mention of words of caution by Ex-Governor Bradstreet, Hawthorne had adequate historical warrant. Andros's reliance upon mercenary troops to impress the people found source in Hutchinson[9] and in the April 18, 1689, declaration of the Boston citizens, who charged that 'several companies of soldiers were now brought from Europe to support what was imposed upon us, not without repeated menaces, that some hundreds more were intended for us.'[10]

Although he thus exercised considerable arbitrary power, Andros really did nothing at the end which furnished that climactic note desired by tellers of historical tales. Harmonizer of fact and fiction that he was, however, Hawthorne needed no actual occurrence. He transferred a popular legend from the Con-

a work familiar to Hawthorne: Cotton Mather's *Magnalia Christi Americana*, Book II, Appendix: 'Pietas in Patriam, or the Life of His Excellency, Sir William Phips, Late Governor of New-England,' Section 8, London, 1702.

[5] Boston, 1825. Chapter XXXI briefly summarizes the governorship of Sir Edmund Andros and reprints the account of the April Resolution sent to the governor of Plymouth on April 22, 1689.

[6] New York, 1810. Trumbull's account leans heavily upon Hutchinson. See especially pages 172-8.

[7] Charlestown, 1804. Brief as this history is, pages 284-6 are devoted to showing that Massachusetts was the principal seat of this despotism and suffering between 1686 and 1689.

[8] London, 1720, II, 433-41. Daniel Neal reprinted 'The Declaration of the Gentlemen, Merchants, and Inhabitants of Boston and the Country Adjacent' upon the overthrow of Andros, a document of utmost importance in fathoming the emotions of 1689.

[9] Mayo Edition: Cambridge, 1936, I, 304. The passage reads as follows: 'Several churches had agreed to set apart days of thanksgiving for his Majesty's [King James II] gracious declaration of liberty of conscience. The governor forbade them . . . He told them that they should meet at their peril, and that he would send soldiers to guard their meeting-houses.'

[10] Neal, op. cit. II, 434-5.

necticut Valley to Massachusetts, shifting the emphasis from the defense of frontier towns to a defiance of arbitrary power. That the gray champion, so dramatically introduced, was regarded as one of the Hadley regicides [11] is apparent in the phrase that he had 'stayed the march of a King himself.' To determine what Hawthorne owed to his predecessors in the use of this theme, it will be necessary to examine briefly the whole tradition of the Angel of Hadley before 1835. The legend may be summarized from the account by President Stiles in his *History of the Judges of Charles I* (1794): [12]

During the abode in Hadley, the famous and most memorable Indian War that ever was in New-England, called King Philip's War, took place . . . The northern tribes were in agitation and attacked the new frontier towns along through New-England, and Hadley among the rest . . . That pious congregation . . . being at public worship in the meeting-house there, on a fast day, September 1, 1675, were suddenly surrounded and surprised by a body of Indians . . . The people immediately took to their arms, but were thrown into great consternation and confusion . . . Suddenly, and in the midst of the people there appeared a man of very venerable aspect, and different from the inhabitants in his apparel, who took the command, arranged and ordered them in the best military manner, and under his direction they repelled and routed the Indians, and the town was saved. He immediately vanished, and the inhabitants could not account for the phenomenon

---

[11] Judgment against Charles I was given on January 26, 1649, and there were fifty-nine signers of the death warrant, among whom were Major-General Whalley, Major-General William Goffe, son-in-law of General Whalley, and Colonel John Dixwell. Fearful that the Restoration Parliament might except them from the pardon promised in the Declaration of Breda, a number of the regicides fled from England, some to Holland and some to Switzerland. Two of the number sailed for Boston on the *Prudent Mary*, even before the action of Parliament was taken. Dixwell, less active than the others in Commonwealth activities, fled to Hanau in Germany, and five years later appeared in New England. The wisdom of their flight was apparent upon the passage of the Act of Indemnity of August 29, 1660, which excepted from pardon a number of the regicides, including the three herein named. From 1661 to their decease, Goffe and Whalley lived in hiding in New England, removing from one haven to another as their safety seemed jeopardized. They were in Guilford, New Haven, Hartford, and Hadley. In all there were six searches for the regicides and at least four search warrants were issued in New England in an attempt to take them, but in the Puritans of that day they found able protectors.

[12] Hartford, 1794, pp. 109-10.

but by considering that person as an Angel sent of God upon that special occasion for their deliverance . . . The mystery was unriddled after the revolution (in England in 1688) when it became not so very dangerous to have it known that the Judges had received an asylum here, and that Goffe was actually at Hadley at that time. The Angel was certainly General Goffe, for Whalley [13] was superannuated in 1675.

Before Stiles, this story of the concealment of the Judges at Hadley and of Goffe's timely leadership had received written notice only in an anecdote printed in Hutchinson's *History of Massachusetts*.[14] The first extended treatment after 1794 was in Timothy Dwight's *Travels in New England* (1821).[15] Three years later Epaphras Hoyt included the incident in his *Antiquarian Researches*,[16] but his account apparently derived from Dwight and Stiles. The last redaction of the story pertinent to this study appeared in *The Worcester Magazine* for October 1826.

Authors, not as greatly concerned over the historicity of this matter as local historians, were not long in appropriating the regicide theme for works of imagination; and subsequent to its first use by Scott, in 1822, it became a minor feature in fiction for years. With the exception of H. W. Herbert's *Ruth Whalley*,[17] Coggeshall's *The Regicides*,[18] *The Salem Belle*,[19] and short tales by Bacon and Stone, fictional treatments of the Judges of

[13] Whalley died in Hadley either late in 1674 (after August 6) or early in 1675. See Stiles, op. cit. p. 113; Sylvester Judd, *History of Hadley*, Springfield: Hunting and Co., 1905, p. 222.

[14] London edition, 1765, I, 218. Hutchinson relied on Hadley traditions as handed down in Governor Leverett's family. See Timothy Dwight, *Travels in New England and New York*, New Haven, 1821, I, 353. Dwight declared: 'The following story has been traditionally conveyed down among the inhabitants of Hadley.' For traditions of Goffe see also an Address by Rev. F. D. Huntington for the *Celebration of the Two Hundredth Anniversary of the Settlement at Hadley, June 8, 1859*, Northampton: Bridgman and Childs, 1859, p. 42. A contemporary hint of the 'Angel of Hadley' episode is offered in a letter to Increase Mather from Rev. John Russell, bearing date of April 18, 1677. See *Collections of Massachusetts Historical Society*, Fourth Series, VIII, 81. The historicity of the tradition was examined by George Sheldon in *The Historical and Genealogical Register*, XXVIII, 379, October 1874.

[15] Letter xxxv. The work was published posthumously. It is of interest to note, as explanatory of Dwight's interest in this tradition, that he was born in Northampton, a few miles from Hadley.

[16] Greenfield: A. Phelps, 1824, pp. 83-5; 135-7.

[17] Boston: Henry L. Williams, 1844.

[18] New York: The Baker & Taylor Co., 1896.

[19] Boston: Tappan & Dennet, 1842.

Charles I included the picturesque episode of the Angel of Hadley.[20]

Hawthorne's use of the regicide theme has been noted by Quinn[21] and Musser[22] with the vague implication that the source of inspiration in his case, as in Cooper's, was Barker's *Superstition* (1826), but a study of the use of the Hadley motif will make clear that the matter of Hawthorne's antecedents can scarcely be referred to a stage-piece alone when so many fictional models were available.

The first literary use of the regicide theme occurred in *Peveril of the Peak* (1822). There is a tradition often told that Scott had once planned a poem with New England scenes and incidents, and Indians figuring prominently in the action. This interest led him to collect Americana which might prove useful in such a literary venture and to peruse with more than casual interest the American publications which came to hand. One of the most interesting volumes of his collection[23] was *Increase Mather's Brief History of the War with the Indians in New England*,[24] for from this he could have found the roots of the story of the 'Alarm' at Hadley. With the work of Hutchinson he was doubtless familiar, but Stiles's *History of the Judges* he seems not to have discovered, for he identified the Angel of Hadley with Whalley, as no careful student of Stiles was likely to do, and he further confused Edward Whalley with Richard, his father. Exactly where Scott found the materials which he incorporated into the Amer-

20 Utilization of the Hadley tradition along with other aspects of regicide activity or King Philip's War may be found in the following novels after Hawthorne: J. K. Paulding, *The Puritan and his Daughter*, New York, 1849; G. H. Hollister, *Mount Hope*, New York, 1851; D. P. Thompson, *The Doomed Chief*, New York, 1860; and Margaret Sidney [Mrs. Harriet Mulford Lothrop], *The Judges' Cave*, New York, 1900.

21 *A History of the American Drama*, New York, 1923, p. 147; also, *Representative American Plays*, New York, 1917, p. 111.

22 *James Nelson Barker*, Philadelphia, 1929, p. 95.

23 Scott's collection was described by Hugh Wynne, *Private Libraries of New York*, New York, 1860, p. 106.

24 London, 1676. In this passage I cite the title as given by Wynne. The remarks of Mather, possibly communicated to him by Stoddard, are as follows: 'On the first of September one of the churches in Boston was seeking the face of God by fasting and prayer before him. Also that very day, the church in Hadley was before the Lord in the same way, but were driven from the holy service by a most sudden and violent alarm, which routed them the whole day after.' See Sylvester Judd, op. cit. p. 137.

ican reminiscences of Major Bridgenorth [25] is not therefore clear, for in referring to the fate of the regicides in the notes to the 1831 edition of *Peveril of the Peak,* he spoke of the story of the regicide's issuance from concealment during an Indian attack as a remarkable and beautiful story and as a common tradition which was 'in all probability true.' [26] The story may have reached him through some secondary English reference, or have been related by some of his numerous American visitors to Abbotsford before 1822—Irving, Ticknor, Bigelow, Cogswell, or Everett. Or he may have enlarged upon the story in Hutchinson, since it was there presented as anecdote, not history. But whatever his source, Scott seems to have relied more upon his memory than on historical documents, though Major Bridgenorth's relation differs from the traditional account only in such minor matters as the addition of a woman with 'disordered locks and disheveled hair,' who brings the news of the Indian advance, and the placing of Hadley thirty miles from Boston.

There is little in Scott's version not to be found in prior accounts, but his use of the tradition in the popular Waverley series undoubtedly aroused widespread interest. His elaboration of the story and his effective descriptive touches, moreover, were such as might easily stimulate imaginative writers. First, the description of the regicide: 'I never saw anything more august than his features, overshadowed by locks of gray hair, which mingled with a long beard of the same color.' Or again: 'His gray eye retained all its lustre, and though the grizzled beard covered the lower part of his face, it prevented me not from recognizing him.' Second, the conjecture of the populace regarding the character of the mysterious stranger: 'The prevailing opinion was, notwithstanding his own disclamation, that the stranger was really a supernatural being; others believed him *an inspired champion,*[27] transported in the body from some distant climate, to show us the way to safety; others, again, concluded that he was a recluse who, either from motives of piety, or some other cogent reasons, had become a dweller in the wilderness.' [28] From these

---

25 *Peveril of the Peak*, Edinburgh, 1831, Vol. I, Chap. xiv, pp. 198 ff.
26 Ibid. 201 n; in Centenary Edition, note 11, p. 158.
27 The italics are mine. G. H. O.
28 Scott, op. cit. p. 198.

two passages Hawthorne might easily have found the title for his story, 'The Gray Champion,' and also precedent for a crowd vocal with conflicting opinions on the mysterious character and disappearance of the venerable visitor.

The second use of the regicide theme was in *The Spectre of the Forest*.[29] I need not hesitate to ascribe the appearance of Goffe in this novel to Scott's influence, for the book appeared the year after *Peveril of the Peak* and was written by one of Scott's most ardent American disciples, James McHenry.[30] He did not make Scott's mistake about the identity of the Unknown, but his account of the regicide's activities, though impressive in its handling, is scarcely historical at all. Goffe's appearance in this novel was in the *deus ex machina* role of freeing George Parnall and Amos Settle, who had been imprisoned for sympathetic demonstrations toward those accused of witchcraft. The specter's oracular words effected their release:

Men of Connecticut, one of you has this night invoked me to your presence. I have obeyed the call, for he whom ye wish to serve, but whose will ye often mistake, has permitted me to tell you the error into which you are now fallen, and to command you to correct and forsake that error, if you would avoid the wrath to come . . . Unbind these men, thou Abishai Ironheart . . . or tremble at the incensed justice of Heaven.[31]

Thus Goffe, both in his rescue of Amos Settle and in his active ministrations in favor of Esther Devenart, was definitely presented as a champion of the right, though his prophetic mission was a long cry from the military activity at Hadley which tradition assigned to him. All that later writers could have derived from McHenry's spectacular pictures, aside from the employment of an ubiquitous rescuer, was the idea of transferring the sphere of his movements and of spanning his life until the Salem Delusion in 1692. Such lengthened life for the regicide was employed in Hawthorne and hinted in Cooper, who says of the

29 New York: E. Bliss and E. White, 1823.
30 See my forthcoming volume, *Scott in America*, for the influence of Scott on McHenry.
31 II, 99.

tombstone inscription of Submission that it 'was impossible to ascertain whether the date was 1680 or 1690.'

Barker's use of the story of the Judges in *Superstition* (1826) [32] presents certain parallels to *The Spectre of the Forest,* but unlike McHenry he clung to the essential facts of the Indian attack on the village, except that there was no congregational service in progress when the warning came. The Unknown, as in the traditional account, arrived when the villagers were on the verge of flight and with seasoned experience wisely disposed the forces and led them to victory.

Cooper, in his use of the theme,[33] seized upon the essential features suggested by Stiles and elaborated on by Scott. Something he also owed to Barker's play, for both visualized the regicide as dwelling in a hill-side fastness not far removed from the assailed village; but he went beyond his contemporaries in his imaginative elaboration of the episode. Submission, never in the novel given his true name of Goffe, was represented both in purely imaginary and in legendary roles. Thus his first appearance at the Blockhouse in the Connecticut Valley was pure fabrication. His second coming, in Volume II, to the village church (when the single household had become a community), bearing warning of what he has observed from his hilltop eyrie and taking charge of the defense, was a free handling of already familiar legend. In order to integrate the three-strand plot, Cooper linked the attack upon Hadley with the fortunes of King Philip's War and at the same time heightened the singularly picturesque puritanism of the Heathcote family with which Submission had unexplained connections. In making use of the staunch devotion to principle on the part of the recluse, Cooper featured the sterling qualities of the Puritan leaders whose intrepidity made the Commonwealth glorious. Willing, however, that the leadership of Submission should not be the sole factor in the repulse of the savages (as it had been in prior accounts), Cooper supplied convincing superstition on the part of Conanchet, who was awe-stricken

[32] *Superstition* was first acted March 12, 1824, in Philadelphia, but not printed until the Lopez and Wemyss Edition in 1826. See Quinn, *Representative American Plays,* p. 112.

[33] *The Wept of Wish-ton-Wish: A Tale,* Philadelphia: Carey, Lea & Carey, 1829.

at the seeming resurrection of those whom he had thought burned years before, as a potent motive for the redmen's withdrawal. In this way a respite from further bloodshed and the Narragansett break with Metacom was effected.

Thus, exclusive of stories by Delia Bacon [34] and William Leete Stone,[35] there were four literary works which employed the Hadley tradition before Hawthorne, and all of these are of particular interest as having given positive direction to Hawthorne's treatment in 'The Gray Champion.' From Scott he may have secured the title of the story as well as the force of the first literary use of the episode. The suggestion of a symbolical ending, a note discoverable in Scott and Hawthorne, may have been found in a sentence of Bridgenorth: concluding his notice of the regicide he declared that 'perhaps his voice may be heard in the field once more, should England need one of her noblest hearts.' This is a key to the prophetic passage with which Hawthorne's tale concludes: 'should domestic tyranny oppress us, or the invader's step pollute our soil, still may the Gray Champion come.'

In McHenry, Hawthorne could have found the use of Goffe as a general utility agent whose activities were totally removed from the village of Hadley, and also the idea of a significant role for a regicide beyond the year 1679. Here also was the invocation for the regicide which Hawthorne deftly turned into both a petition and a herald's cry. And from Scott, Barker, and Cooper, the emergence of an old man from his seclusion to become a leader of the people could have suggested Hawthorne's

[34] To historical themes she turned in her *Tales of the Puritans,* New Haven: A. H. Maltby, 1831, particularly in 'The Regicides,' the first piece in the volume. She presented a highly romantic and entertaining account of the activities of Goffe and Whalley at New Haven and Guilford, relied strongly upon Stiles, *The Worcester Magazine,* I, 208, October 1826, and source material such as the report of Kellond and Kirk to the Governor of Massachusetts, but upon the story of the 'Angel of Hadley' she did not touch.

[35] Before the publication of Hawthorne's 'The Gray Champion,' though probably not more than a month or so in advance, William Leete Stone published 'Mercy Disborough,' a story in which Goffe and Whalley were again introduced, but only to provide spectral effects by the introduction of a mysterious barn in which he and his associates hid during their stay in New Haven. But this and other stories made the theme attractive for contributors to gift-books, in which Hawthorne's tales were appearing. For 'Mercy Disborough,' see *Tales and Sketches,* New York: Harper & Brothers, 1834, I, 1-75. This same tale was published anonymously under the title of *The Witches; a Tale of New England,* Bath, 1837.

conception of an ancient man clad in old-time raiment, who appeared at a time of great public danger and who vanished with the dangers which summoned him. But even these items might conceivably have been gleaned from the phrases of Hutchinson, whose posthumous third volume, published in 1828, might easily have directed attention to the account in the 1765 volume:

Suddenly a grave, elderly person appeared in the midst of them. In his mien and dress he differed from the rest of the people. He not only encouraged them to defend themselves; but put himself at their head, rallied, instructed and led them on to encounter the enemy, who by this means were repulsed. As suddenly, the deliverer of Hadley disappeared. The people were left in consternation, utterly unable to account for this strange phenomenon.[36]

And from the original tradition, or any of the redactions, he could have gained the details about the mysterious appearance of the old man, his proud bearing even under the weight of years, his old Puritan dress and his heavy sword, and the general mystery regarding his disappearance.

Neither models nor historical considerations, however, imposed restrictions upon Hawthorne's imagination. For him to have related the tale in its legendary outlines would have been to retell the story of Scott or Cooper in gift-book compass. He accordingly transferred the regicide from Hadley to Boston, introduced him as participating in events of 1689, ten years beyond his last reputed appearance, and challenging, not the force of howling Indians, but the advancing soldiery of the tyrannous Andros. Since there was nothing in the happenings of April 18, 1689, which provided him with the kind of heightened moment for which he was seeking, unless the demand that Andros surrender the fort and frigate be regarded as one, Hawthorne secured proper incident by imbuing the actual with the imaginary until the scene not only took on a very life-like character but surpassed history itself in its dramatic force. Into the spirit of one man he fused the protests of the entire Boston citizenry against illegal taxation by the Governor and his Council; and though Hawthorne was free in his handling of some details, he was true

[36] I, 215. Quoted in Stiles, op. cit. pp. 22-4.

to the central and significant fact in the events of that Revolution, the refusal of the people to keep silence in the face of oppressive measures.

Thus, though 'The Gray Champion' is based ostensibly upon historical materials and owes something undoubtedly to Scott and to others, it has definitely Hawthornesque features. It is historical in atmosphere, if only partly so in incident. It affords a tableau of characteristic order: at a startlingly dramatic moment when the governor's desire to impress his authority upon the multitude seems likely to conflict with the mounting anger and scarcely concealed hatred of freedom-loving citizens, an upraised staff and a commanding voice halt a column of soldiery. A withering piece of news, uttered with the assurance of knowledge not rumor, and an intrepidity of manner unite to force a withdrawal of troops and to prevent a probable bloody affair. Hawthorne made Goffe as history and literary tradition combined to present him: a man of vigorous stamp, worthy leader in the army of Old Noll, fearless, independent, intimidated by no show of royalty, no rattle of musketry. And though his end, as in true history, was shrouded with mystery, Hawthorne did not suffer him to disappear forever. He imparted to him, in his own characteristic way, a symbolic force, in heralding him as the type of colonial independence, and sent him on a stately but shadowy march into a spiritual seclusion whence he emerged at Lexington and Bunker Hill and might again emerge should great danger again threaten the land. Thus 'The Gray Champion' joins in spirit with 'Howe's Masquerade,' 'Endicott and the Red Cross,' and 'My Kinsman, Major Molineux' and other stories in which Hawthorne celebrates *con amore* the emergence of the New England spirit of freedom.

CONCORD HYMN

Sung at the Completion of the
Battle Monument, July 4, 1837

By Ralph Waldo Emerson

By the rude bridge that arched the flood,
   Their flag to April's breeze unfurled,
Here once the embattled farmers stood
   And fired the shot heard round the world.

The foe long since in silence slept;
   Alike the conqueror silent sleeps;
And Time the ruined bridge has swept
   Down the dark stream which seaward creeps.

On this green bank, by this soft stream,
   We set to-day a votive stone;
That memory may their deed redeem,
   When, like our sires, our sons are gone.

Spirit, that made those heroes dare
   To die, and leave their children free,
Bid Time and Nature gently spare
   The shaft we raise to them and thee.

LIBERTY AND GOVERNMENT

By Benjamin N. Cardozo

LIBERTY as a legal concept contains an underlying paradox. Liberty in the most literal sense is the negation of law, for law is restraint, and the absence of restraint is anarchy. On the other hand, anarchy by destroying restraint would leave liberty the exclusive possession of the strong or the unscrupulous. 'This is a world of compensation,' said Lincoln,[1] 'and he who would be no slave must consent to have no slave.'

The paradox was long ago perceived by Locke who gave expression to it in terms that have not been bettered since his day.[2] 'For law in its true notion,' he said, 'is not so much the limitation as the direction of a free and intelligent agent to his proper interest, and prescribed no farther than is for the general good of those under that law . . . That ill deserves the name of confinement which hedges us in only from bogs and precipices. So that however it may be mistaken, the end of law is not to abolish or restrain, but to preserve and enlarge freedom. For in all the states of created beings, capable of laws, where there is no law there is no freedom. For liberty is to be free from restraint and violence from others, which cannot be where there is no law; and is not, as we are told, "liberty for every man to do what he lists." For who could be free, when every other man's humor might domineer over him? But a liberty to dispose and order freely as he lists his person, actions, possessions, and his whole property within the allowance of those laws under which he is, and therein not to be subject to the arbitrary will of another, but freely follow his own.' Modern research in social science

Reprinted from Cardozo, *Paradoxes of Legal Science*, 1928. By permission of Columbia University Press.
[1] Sandburg, *Abraham Lincoln: The Prairie Years*, II, 182.
[2] *Treatises on Civil Government*, Book 2, sec. 57.

has amplified the thought of Locke, but without changing its essentials.

'If liberty is a social conception,' says Hobhouse,[3] 'there can be no liberty without social restraint. For any one person, indeed, there might be a maximum of liberty if all social restraints were removed. Where physical strength alone prevails, the strongest man has unlimited liberty to do what he likes with the weaker; but clearly the greater the freedom of the strong man, the less the freedom of the weaker. What we mean by liberty as a social conception is a right to be shared by all members of society, and very little consideration suffices to show that, in the absence of restraints enforced on or accepted by all members of a society, the liberty of some must involve the oppression of others . . . Excess of liberty contradicts itself. In short there is no such thing; there is only liberty for one and restraint for another.' [4]

Is there then no path of compromise except such as may be marked by the opportunism of the hour? We find in state and national constitutions a pledge of individual liberty. By common consent this means at least immunity from slavery or serfdom. In so far as it seems to promise more, are we restricted to a choice between a rhetorical flourish and a canonization of what is? Is there no criterion of rationality to enlighten decision with the inspiration of a principle?

In delimiting the field of liberty, courts have professed for the most part to go about their work empirically and have rather prided themselves on doing so. They have said, we will not define due process of law. We will leave it to be 'pricked out' by a process of inclusion and exclusion in individual cases.[5] That was to play safely, and very likely at the beginning to play wisely. The question is how long we are to be satisfied with a series of *ad hoc* conclusions. It is all very well to go on pricking the lines, but the time must come when we shall do prudently to look them over, and see whether they make a pattern or a

[3] *Social Evolution and Political Theory*, p. 189.
[4] Cf. the same author's *Liberalism*, Home University Library, pp. 23, 139, 140, 144, 145.
[5] Davidson *v.* New Orleans, 1877, 96 U.S. 97, 104; cf. Village of Euclid *v.* Ambler Realty Co., 1926, 272 U.S. 365.

medley of scraps and patches. I do not suggest that political or social science has formulated a conception of liberty so precise and accurate that, applied as a touchstone by the courts, it will mechanically disclose the truth. I do suggest and believe that empirical solutions will be saner and sounder if in the background of the empiricism there is the study and the knowledge of what men have thought and written in the anxious search and groping for a co-ordinating principle.

Bills of rights give assurance to the individual of the preservation of his liberty. They do not define the liberty they promise. In the beginnings of constitutional government, the freedom that was uppermost in the minds of men was freedom of the body. The subject was not to be tortured or imprisoned at the mere pleasure of the ruler. There went along with this, or grew from it, a conception of a liberty that was broader than the physical. Liberty became identified with the reign of law. 'Freedom of men under government,' says Locke,[6] 'is to have a standing rule to live by, common to every one of that society and made by the legislative power erected in it.' The individual may not be singled out from among his fellows, and made the victim of the shafts of malice. Those who are put over him 'are to govern by promulgated established law, not to be varied in particular cases, but to have one rule for rich and poor, for the favorite at court and the countryman at plough.' [7]

Up to this, there is no restraint upon the scope or force of law so long as it be law, i.e. so long as it be general or equal, a rule as contrasted with an 'extemporary decree.' [8] Liberty means more than this, however, as a concept of social science. It has come to mean more, at least in our own system, as a concept of constitutional law. The concept in our constitutional development has undergone a steady and highly significant development. The individual may not only insist that the law which limits him in his activities shall impose like limits upon others in like circumstances. He will also be heard to say that there is a domain of free activity that may not be touched by government or law

6 *Treatises on Civil Government,* Book 2, sec. 21.
7 Ibid. Book 2, sec. 142.
8 Ibid. Book 2, secs. 131, 136.

at all, whether the command be special against him or general against him and others. By express provision of the Constitution, he is assured freedom of speech and freedom of conscience or religion. These latter immunities have thus the sanctions of a specific pledge, but they are merely phases of a larger immunity which finds expression in the comprehensive declaration that no one shall be deprived of liberty without due process of law. Such at least appears to be the more recent doctrine of the court that speaks the final word.[9] Apart from any enumerated phase of liberty and beyond it, this declaration gives immunity against 'the play and action of purely personal and arbitrary power.'[10] What is personal and arbitrary in mandate and restraint does not gain rationality and coherence because it takes the form of statute. The legislature does not speak with finality as to the measure of its own powers. The final word is for the courts.

Time does not permit, and my aim does not require, that I should catalogue the cases in which statutes have been condemned as founded on no other basis than malice or caprice. A few typical instances will serve to point my meaning. The government may not prohibit the teaching of a foreign language in private schools and colleges.[11] For the same reason, we can safely say, it may not prohibit the teaching in such places of other branches of human learning. It may not take unto itself exclusively the instruction of the young and mould their minds to its own model by forbidding them to be taught in any schools except its own.[12] Restraints such as these are encroachments upon the free development of personality in a society that is organized on the basis of the family. We reach the penetralia of liberty when we throttle the mental life of a group so fundamental . . .[13]

History and reason unite in the warning that 'liberty' is im-

[9] N. Y. v. Gitlow, 1925, 268 U.S. 652; Pierce v. Society of the Sisters of the Holy Name of Jesus and Mary, 1925, 268 U.S. 510; Whitney v. Cal., 1927, 274 U.S. 357; Warren, 'The New "Liberty" under the Fourteenth Amendment,' 39 Harvard Law Review, p. 431.
[10] Yick Wu v. Hopkins, 1886, 118 U.S. 35, 369.
[11] Meyer v. Nebraska, 1923, 262 U.S. 390; Bartels v. Iowa, 1923, 262 U.S. 404.
[12] Pierce v. Society, etc., 1925, 268 U.S. 510.
[13] Cf. Spinoza, Tractatus Politicus, ch. 8.

paired by statutes clogging or diverting the free development of personality, or, in other words, of mind or spirit. By history, I have in mind specifically our own history, our own institutional origins; by reason, the scientific interpretation of the ideal of social welfare in the light of universal history, psychology, and ethics. Our own institutional origins give the angle of departure. 'I have sworn upon the altar of the living God eternal hostility against every form of tyranny over the mind of man.' The words are those of Jefferson, but the spirit was in the air. In that faith was organized what Professor Beard has called the great American tradition.[14] To the minds of the fathers of the nation repression of thought and speech, and above all repression of conscience, were vivid and portentous evils.[15] Liberty in its other phases was guaranteed in generalities that were pregnant with uncertainty. The deliverance of the soul was proclaimed in the forefront of our bill of rights, where all might know it as a cornerstone of our political philosophy. Some doubtless there were even in those days who lost their hold upon these verities of the spirit when theory met the test of practice. Witness the Sedition Act of 1798.[16] Yet deeper and more overwhelming than the passing inroad upon principle was the backwash of the returning wave. True, indeed, it is that the tide was to ebb and flow thereafter. The article of the Constitution which proclaimed the emancipation of the spirit was not phrased, nor could it be, in terms so definite and certain as to avoid the opportunity for conflicting interpretations when specific measures from time to time were subjected to its test. With all these allowances the underlying principle of our political philosophy—the great American tradition—has been for the life of the mind the principle of liberty. 'Ye shall know the truth, and the truth shall make you free.'

[14] Beard, 'The Great American Tradition,' *The Nation*, vol. 123, no. 3183, p. 7, 7 July 1926; cf. Beard, *The Rise of American Civilization*, 1, 151, 152, 160, 185, 379, 449, 487.

[15] See e.g. Jefferson's *Bill for the Introduction of Religious Freedom in Virginia;* also his 'Notes on Virginia,' quoted by Hirst, *Life and Letters of Thomas Jefferson,* pp. 136, 138; Franklin, and the questions put to new members of his Academy, Beard, op. cit. 1, 169; Chafee, *Freedom of Speech in War Time,* pp. 4, 21, 23.

[16] Cf. Whipple, *The History of Civil Liberty in the United States;* also address by Judge Irving Lehman on 'Religious Liberty in New York,' printed in N.Y.L.J. of 6 May 1927; Beard, op. cit. 1, 543.

In unison with the voice of history as it spoke at our national beginnings is the deeper voice of science, the science of social life, interpreting universal history and the fundamental needs of man. Personal liberty is a poor and shrunken thing, incapable of satisfying our aspirations or our wants, if it does not exact as its minimal requirement that there shall be the maintenance of opportunity for the growth of personality.[17] 'He is the free man,' said Spinoza, 'who lives according to the dictates of reason alone.'[18] We are free only if we know, and so in proportion to our knowledge. There is no freedom without choice, and there is no choice without knowledge—or none that is not illusory. Implicit, therefore, in the very notion of liberty is the liberty of the mind to absorb and to beget. Here is the fundamental privilege to be maintained in Lord Acton's words, 'against the influence of authority and majorities, customs and opinion.'[19] 'His own belief,' says Dr. Figgis, in summarizing Acton's character, 'his one belief was the right of every man not to have but to be his best.'[20] The mind is in chains when it is without the opportunity to choose. One may argue, if one please, that opportunity to choose is more an evil than a good. One is guilty of a contradiction if one says that the opportunity can be denied, and liberty subsist. At the root of all liberty is the liberty to know.

This freedom of the soul in some of its major postulates, the freedom to speak and write, had its classic vindication by Milton nearly three centuries ago.[21] The vindication was aimed at a particular form of encroachment upon the free development of mind, but it has implications not to be confined to its immediate occasion. What is true of restrictions upon printing must be true of other restrictions upon the movement of ideas. They are all condemned by the same curse. The difficulty about them is that they presuppose a gift of prophecy in fields where history makes it plain that prophecy is futile. Galileo and Copernicus and Bruno have taught us many lessons, yet not the least is the

17 Cf. Hobhouse, *Social Evolution and Political Theory*, p. 199.
18 Spinoza, *Ethics*, p. 187, Everyman's ed., also p. 158.
19 Lord Acton, *The History of Freedom and other Essays*, p. 3.
20 Ibid. Introduction, p. xxvii.
21 *The Areopagitica*, a plea for the liberty of unlicensed printing, 1644.

lesson of intellectual humility. 'Raised to Giordano Bruno by the generation which he foresaw,'—the inscription that commemorates his glory and his torment,[22] has disquieting reminders. It tells us that the burning of books, the holocaust of ideas, is likely to be as ineffective as the burning of bodies, and almost as odious for those who light the fires. Experimentation there may be in many things of deep concern, for thought freely communicated is the indispensable condition of intelligent experimentation, the one test of its validity [23] . . . If political philosophy has any message to impart, the right of the individual, 'not to have but to be his best,' has been accredited by the voice of wisdom as an inexpugnable inheritance, the good that it secures one of the accepted treasures of mankind.

We begin with Spinoza whose *Tractatus Theologico-Politicus* was published anonymously in 1670, contemporaneously almost with Milton's plea for liberty. 'The more obstinate freedom of speech has been denied the more resolutely have mankind striven against the restraint,—not flatterers and sycophants indeed, . . . but those whom a liberal education and integrity of life have made more free . . . Men in general are so constituted that they bear nothing more impatiently than to see opinions which they hold for true regarded as crimes, and all that moves them to piety towards God and charity towards man accounted for wickedness; whence it comes that laws are detested, and whatever can be adventured against authority is held to be not base and reprehensible, but brave and praiseworthy . . . They . . . are the true disturbers of the state who in a free commonwealth refuse that liberty of opinion which cannot be repressed.'

Modern speculation in sociology and ethics has been able to do little more than elaborate and fortify this triumphant declaration of the explosive power of mind.

'The value of liberty,' says Hobhouse,[24] 'is to build up the life of the mind while the value of state control lies in securing the external conditions, including the mutual restraint, whereby the

[22] Robinson, *The Mind in the Making*, p. 219; White, *History of the Warfare of Science with Theology*, 1, 57; cf. MacDonnell, *Historical Trials*, pp. 66, 83.

[23] Cf. Bury, *A History of Freedom of Thought*, pp. 233, 239.

[24] *Social Evolution and Political Theory*, p. 202.

life of the mind is rendered secure. In the former sphere, compulsion only defeats itself. In the latter, liberty defeats itself. Hence in the main the extension of control does not impair liberty, but on the contrary is itself the means of extending liberty and may and should be conceived with that very object in view. Thus it is that upon the whole we see a tendency to the removal of restraints in the sphere in which whatever there is of value to mankind depends on spontaneity of impulse, free interchange of ideas, and voluntary co-operation going along with the tendency to draw tighter the bonds which restrain men from acting directly or indirectly to the injury of their fellows and to enlarge the borders of the action of the state in response to a developing sense of collective responsibility. We are dealing with two conditions of harmonious development apparently opposed and requiring themselves to be rendered harmonious by careful appreciation of their respective functions, and the general direction in which harmony is to be sought may be expressed by saying that the further development of the state lies in such an extension of public control as makes for the fuller development of the life of the mind.'

Says Laski in his *Grammar of Politics:* 'What seems to be of the permanent essence of freedom is that the personality of each individual should be so unhampered in its development, whether by authority or by custom, that it can make for itself a satisfactory harmonisation of its impulses.' [25] 'Where restraint becomes an invasion of liberty is where the given prohibition acts so as to destroy that harmony of impulses which comes when a man knows that he is doing something it is worth while to do. Restraint is felt as evil when it frustrates the life of spiritual enrichment.' [26] 'The freedoms I must possess to enjoy a general liberty are those which, in their sum, will constitute the path through which my best self is capable of attainment. That is not to say it will be attained. It is to say only that I alone can make that best self, and that without those freedoms I have not the means of manufacture at my disposal.' [27] 'Freedoms are there-

---

[25] Cf. Maitland, *Collected Papers,* Liberty, III, 102.
[26] Ibid. III, 143.
[27] Ibid. III, 144.

fore opportunities which history has shown to be essential to the development of personality.' [28]

Quotation may close with the words of a great apostle of liberty who foresaw that his plea for the free development of the spirit would be likely to survive when his other contributions to our knowledge of the life of the mind should be distanced in the march of thought.

'If all mankind,' says Mill in his essay on *Liberty*,[29] 'if all mankind minus one were of one opinion and only one person were of the contrary opinion, mankind would be no more justified in silencing that person than he, if he had the power, would be justified in silencing mankind. Were an opinion a personal possession of no value except to the owner; if to be obstructed in the enjoyment of it were simply a private injury, it would make some difference whether the injury was inflicted only on a few persons or on many. But the peculiar evil of silencing the expression of an opinion is, that it is robbing the human race; posterity as well as the existing generation; those who dissent from the opinion still more than those who hold it. If the opinion is right, they are deprived of the opportunity of exchanging error for truth; if wrong, they lose, what is almost as great a benefit, the clearer perception and livelier impression of truth, produced by its collision with error.' [30]

The acceptance of this principle, like that of any other so general or abstract, does not mean, of course, that application to particular cases is without the opportunity for error . . . The right of free development does not exclude the right of government to insure for the young a minimum of knowledge. There is, of course, an opportunity even here for illegitimate encroachment. The state under the guise of paternal supervision may attempt covertly and gradually to mould its members to its will. The difference as so often is a difference of degree. The world has a certain stock of knowledge which has been garnered through the toil of centuries. The value of this stock has been so tested and verified by successive generations that to shut the

28 Ibid. III, 144; cf. Dewey, *The Public and its Problems*, p. 150.
29 P. 79, Everyman's ed.
30 Cf. MacIver, *The Modern State*, p. 153.

young out from the opportunity of sharing in it would be to shut them out from the opportunity of pushing the bounds of knowledge farther. If private schools do not reach a level of reasonable competence, the state may insist that the young shall be trained in its own schools till this level is attained. That is a very different exercise of power from the suppression of private schools altogether, irrespective of their merit, in furtherance of a purpose to give to all within the state a cast and mode of thought established by itself. We may ask how we are to know when the required level has been reached. There is no other standard save the judgment of skill and experience, the judgment of those trained in pedagogics. To this the courts will refer, and by this, when ascertained, they will be bound, though the function of ascertaining it will, of course, be theirs. Like difficulties may be encountered in precincts not judicial, as, for example, in the universities with their ever recurring problem of academic freedom. There is general agreement that a teacher is not to be dismissed unless for some better reason than the fact that he has inculcated novel or heterodox or unpopular doctrine, yet novelty or heterodoxy or unpopularity may be so extreme as to be other names for ignorance. The stream of principle will seem to lose itself at times in all the maze of varying circumstances, yet it emerges in the end and pursues its shining course.

Troublesome, too, at times are the distinctions between thought and conduct. The liberty that is assured to us is not liberty to act. It is liberty to think and speak. Thought and speech in certain contexts may be equivalent to acts. When this boundary is reached, we reach the limit of immunity. 'No one pretends,' says Mill, 'that acts should be as free as opinions. On the contrary, even opinions lose their immunity where the circumstances in which they are expressed are such as to constitute their expression a positive instigation to some mischievous act. An opinion that corn-dealers are starvers of the poor, or that private property is robbery, ought to be unmolested when simply circulated through the press, but may justly incur punishment when delivered orally to an excited mob assembled before the house of a corn-dealer, or when handed about among the same mob in the form of a placard. Acts, of whatever kind, which, without justifiable cause, do harm to others may be, and in the more important cases, absolutely require to be, controlled by unfavorable sentiments, and, when needful by the active interference of mankind.' [31] So Hobhouse: [32] 'Even in regard to matter of opinion it is only opinion and persuasion that can be absolutely free, and even here it must be admitted that there are forms of persuasion that are in fact coercive, and it is fair for the state to consider how far the liberty of the younger or weaker must be protected against forms of temptation which overcome the will. Apart from this when opinion leads, however conscientiously, to action, such action may coerce others, and this would bring the state into play in the name of liberty itself.' [33]

One will find it instructive to apply these pronouncements to some of the rulings of the courts. We may apply them, e.g. to the ruling that the institution of polygamy is not protected by the Constitution against abolition by the legislature because the supposed virtue of the practice is a tenet of a church.[34] We may apply them again to limitations upon freedom of utterance that have been held to be permissible in the emergency of war, or, for the preservation of the state, in times of peace as well. Here restraint and immunity have troublesome gradations. 'There may indeed be breaches of the peace,' says Stephen in his *History of the Criminal Law*,[35] 'which may destroy or endanger life, limb, or property, and there may be incitements to such offenses. But no imaginable censure of the government, short of a censure which has an immediate tendency to produce such a breach of the peace, ought to be regarded as criminal.' [36] We may say the same of expressions of opinion generally. Yet the test is one that it is easier to state than to apply. There are rulings in recent cases as, e.g. in Abrams v. U. S., 1919, 240 U.S. 616, and N. Y. v.

[31] 'The most stringent protection of free speech would not protect a man in falsely shouting fire in a theatre and causing a panic.'—Holmes, J., in Scheneck v. U. S., 1916, 249 U.S. 47, 52.

[32] *Social Evolution and Political Theory*, p. 200; cf. the same author's *Liberalism*, p. 148.

[33] See the same author's *Liberalism*, p. 148, and his *Elements of Social Justice*, pp. 73, 74; but cf. Laski, *A Grammar of Politics*, p. 120, and the same author's *Authority in the Modern State*, p. 56.

[34] Reynolds v. U. S., 1878, 98 U.S. 145.

[35] II, 300.

[36] See also Holdsworth, *History of English Law*, VIII, 338.

Gitlow, 1925, 268 U.S. 652, that have provoked a sharp division of opinion among the judges of our highest court.[37] The division is a warning that delicate must be the scales for the weighing of the interactions between behavior and belief. If the reading of the balance is doubtful, the presumption in favor of liberty should serve to tilt the beam. That lesson, if no other, stands out from the surrounding darkness. Aglow even yet, after the cooling time of a century and more, is the coal from the fire that was the mind of Voltaire: 'I do not believe in a word that you say, but I will defend to the death your right to say it.'

[37] Cf. Brandeis, J., in Whitney v. Cal., 1927, 274 U.S. 357, 372.

EMBATTLED FARMERS

By Walter A. Dyer

My name is Shays; in former days
In Pelham I did dwell, sir;
But now I'm forced to leave that place
Because I did rebel, sir.

Within the state I live of late,
By Satan's foul invention,
In Pluto's cause, against the laws,
I raised an insurrection.

THUS begins a somewhat lengthy doggerel ballad that was chanted in the taverns of New England and sung at political gatherings during the closing years of the eighteenth century. Captain Daniel Shays, held a self-seeking adventurer, a braggart, and a rascal generally, became a social outcast and, for a time, a legal outlaw. A fugitive in Vermont with a price on his head, and later a hapless wanderer, he died in poverty and obscurity in a little village in western New York long after the bitterness in Massachusetts had died out and the things he had fought for had come to pass. Only recently have truth-seeking historians discovered adequate reasons for revising the traditional estimate of his character.[1]

For the facts concerning the so-called Shays' Rebellion, all subsequent historians have been indebted to George Richards Minot, whose book, *The History of the Insurrections in Massachusetts, in the year 1786, and the Rebellion Consequent Thereon,* was published in Worcester, Massachusetts, in 1788. So far as narra-

From *The New England Quarterly*, July 1931. By permission of the author and publisher.

[1] James Truslow Adams, *New England in the Republic* (Boston, 1926), ch. VI, especially pp. 148-50; Allan Nevins, *The American States During and After the Revolution* (New York, 1924), pp. 536-7.

tion of the leading incidents is concerned, Minot would seem to have been fair and reliable, but writing as he did so soon after the turmoil, he would have been rather more than human if he had not reflected the feelings and opinions of one side or the other, and his side was that of the constituted Government. J. G. Holland, whose *History of Western Massachusetts* appeared in 1855, further emphasized the infamy of the rebel Shays and helped to perpetuate the adverse opinion concerning him.[2]

Nor did his followers escape this opprobrium, though the State found it politic to grant a general amnesty and even pardoned, eventually, the ring-leaders. They have been pictured in history, fiction, oratory, and song as a rabble of cowardly ne'er-do-wells taking advantage of a weak young Government to further their own ends, or, at best, as dull-witted rustics misled by ambitious demagogues. This is rather curious when it is realized that contemporary estimates state that at one time nearly one-third of the able-bodied men of the State were under arms and fully half of the citizens were in active or passive sympathy with the insurgent movement.[3] They could not all have been tavern roisterers and lawless loafers. It is a matter of record that of the delegates who met on January 9, 1788, to vote on the question of ratifying the Federal Constitution, eighteen had borne arms under Shays.

The story of the actual rebellion—the forcible closing of the courts of law, the Battle of Armory Hill, the Siege of Pelham, and the surrender at Petersham—is stirring and romantic enough, in spite of an element of absurdity; but thoroughly to understand these events, and properly to estimate their importance, one must take a glance at the political and economic causes of the unrest that led up to them.

Not to probe into these causes too minutely, it may be stated as a generalization that a state of penury and apprehension

[2] Cf. also Alden Bradford, *History of Massachusetts* (Boston, 1825), ch. II, and John Stetson Barry, *The History of Massachusetts: the Commonwealth Period* (Boston, 1857).

[3] Doubtless an overstatement. Adams, *New England* (pp. 150 and 159), quotes General Knox as stating in letters to Washington that the numbers of insurgents amounted to 'one-fifth part of several populous counties,' and that 'twelve or fifteen thousand desperate men' were involved.

existed as the normal aftermath of an exhausting war. The Revolution was over and America had won her independence, but at a terrific cost. Hard times inevitably followed, especially for the country people. Work was scarce, and the wages of mechanics and laborers remained unpaid owing to the scarcity of currency. The state and federal governments found themselves saddled with huge debts which they could not pay. Land taxation was burdensome, real estate values declined, trade was at a low ebb, farms were run down, interest rates were usurious, and money was so scarce that many people had literally none at all. The profiteers in the eastern cities, indeed, had accumulated most of the real money, and feeling was bitter against the merchant class and the politicians. The paper currency issued during the war had depreciated until it was practically worthless.

Revolutionary soldiers returned to their farms, after the long years of privation and fighting, to find their homes mortgaged and their families in debt. There was no bankruptcy law in those days, and a poor man had no protection against grasping creditors. When a judgment was obtained against a debtor in court, the sheriff could sell his roof over his head or drive off his cattle, or put him in prison. Throughout a large part of Massachusetts, from Middlesex to Berkshire, feeling ran high against the lawyers, whose fees for defense were exorbitant, as well as against the rich merchants of Boston and Salem and the politicians who failed to represent their constituents.

The law courts were choked with civil suits. Cases were rushed through and debtors were locked up. In Worcester County alone, with a total population of less than fifty thousand, there were more than two thousand of these actions in the year 1784. In the same county in 1785, of one hundred and four persons committed to prison, ninety-four were jailed for debt. There were three hundred and thirty-three cases on the calendar of the February term of the Court of General Sessions in Hampshire County in 1786.[4]

The citizens of the western counties began to organize for re-

[4] Barry, *History of Massachusetts*, p. 218; William Lincoln, *The History of Worcester* (Worcester, 1837), p. 131; Mason A. Green, *Springfield, 1636-1886* (Springfield, 1888), p. 316; Adams, p. 144.

lief as early as 1782, and during the following two or three years conventions were held in Westfield, Hatfield, Hadley, and elsewhere. Lengthy resolutions were adopted setting forth the grievances of the citizens and demanding such reforms as a revision of the Constitution of the Commonwealth, the issuance of more paper money, the removal of the General Court from Boston, and some that were even more fantastic, reflecting the desperation of the people. But none of these petitions was effective, and Governor James Bowdoin turned a deaf ear to all pleas.

By 1786 the situation had become acute. Impatient with the failure of their legislators to enact relief measures, men all over the state, and particularly in Hampshire County, began to talk sedition. Gathering in the rural taverns, they aired their grievances and demanded whether this was the liberty and justice for which they had fought and which had been guaranteed to them in the Declaration of Independence. They began organizing semi-military bodies, to call themselves 'Regulators,' and to wear in their hats a sprig of hemlock. In the clearing before the Conkey Tavern in Pelham Hollow, Captain Daniel Shays, the Town Warden, was drilling a desperate little company of Pelham and Shutesbury men.

Daniel Shays was born in Hopkinton, Massachusetts, in 1747, of poor and obscure parents. He is said to have been uneducated, but he probably spent the average amount of time in the district schools. At least he wrote a good hand, as shown by existing documents.[5] He was a man of pleasing address and an industrious worker, so that he seems to have had no trouble in getting work as a farm hand. He lived for a time in Framingham, and in 1770 he was in Brookfield, earning good wages for that day—fifty-three dollars a month. In 1772, he married Abigail Gilbert, daughter of Jonathan Gilbert, one of the leading citizens of Brookfield. He took his bride first to Great Barrington and then to Pelham. The exact dates of these moves are not known, but in 1775, he had a farm of his own on the slope of Pelham East Hill, now the town of Prescott. Not far away in

---

[5] Shays Collection, Jones Library, Amherst, Massachusetts.

the Hollow was the old Conkey Tavern, the social center for the region. Shays and William Conkey, Jr., were fast friends.[6]

Shays was one of the first to enlist from Pelham at the time of the Lexington alarm, joining a company of Minute-Men under Captain Reuben Dickinson of Amherst for eleven days. On May 1, 1775, Captain Dickinson organized another company and Shays enlisted for three months and was made an ensign. They marched to Boston, and Shays won his promotion for bravery at Bunker Hill, becoming a sergeant. With the same company he took part in the expedition against Ticonderoga in 1776.

He was then transferred to Colonel Varnum's Rhode Island regiment, was made a lieutenant, and because of his special talents was assigned to the recruiting service. He returned to Massachusetts and raised a company which he took to West Point. He failed, however, to obtain his captain's commission until 1779. He was present at Burgoyne's surrender at Saratoga and was with Mad Anthony Wayne at Stony Point. He served five years in all, was wounded at least once, and his war record was admittedly excellent. He was with Rufus Putnam's regiment in Newark, New Jersey, when mustered out in 1780.[7]

Just one incident has been used to darken his reputation as a soldier. Shays was one of a number of officers who received ornamental swords from General Lafayette at Saratoga and, being desperately poor, he sold his for cash. For this act he was socially ostracized by some of his fellow officers and his father-in-law never forgave him.[8]

This seems not to have damaged his standing in his home town, however. He returned to Pelham in 1780 and began to take an active part in the affairs of the town. His name appears annually in the town reports from 1781 to 1786. He was elected to the Committee of Safety in 1781 and 1782, was a delegate to the county convention in 1782, and was elected town warden in 1786. Daniel Shays and his wife, Abigail, were recorded as mem-

[6] Carpenter and Morehouse, *History of Amherst* (Amherst, 1896), p. 124; C. O. Parmenter, *The History of Pelham* (Amherst, 1898), p. 391, *et seq.;* James Russell Trumbull, *The History of Northampton* (Northampton, 1898), II, 494.

[7] Records, U.S. Bureau of Pensions.

[8] Trumbull, *Northampton*, p. 494.

bers of the Second Parish Church of Pelham when it was incorporated in 1786. Such was the man who, a year or two later,
was being vilified and held up before the youth of Massachusetts
as the worst of all possible bad examples.

But Shays, like many others, was feeling the pinch of poverty
and injustice of repression. His soldier's pay was in arrears, he
owed money to his friend Conkey, and his farm was heavily
mortgaged. He shared the common feeling of apprehension and
insecurity. In February 1784, he was sued in the Court of Common Pleas in Hadley for twelve dollars which he could not pay.
In Conkey's Tavern he met and argued with other disaffected
citizens—over the flip glasses, no doubt—and the seed of rebellion was sowed in his heart by rural orators.

It would appear from the records that Captain Shays was
not a leader in the insurgent movement at the beginning but
was drawn into it by reason of his accomplishments as a drill-
master. Not only in Pelham but elsewhere he was called upon to
whip raw recruits into shape, and little by little the 'Regulators'
came to look upon him as one of their military leaders.

On August 15, 1786, a dignified and orderly meeting of delegates from thirty-seven towns in Worcester County was held at
Leicester, and a week later a similar meeting of representatives
of fifty Hampshire County towns was held in Hatfield. Resolutions citing a long list of grievances were adopted and forwarded
to Boston, demanding, among other things, the abolition of the
Court of Common Pleas, the cessation of payments to the federal Congress, and a new issue of paper money. It was the final
attempt to move the state administration by constitutional
means, and it failed. No word of hope came out of Boston.
Then a committee was appointed, of which Daniel Gray of
Pelham was chairman, to set forth these grievances and the general situation for the better understanding of the people at
large. Their statement was significantly addressed 'To the people of the several Towns in the County of Hampshire, *now under arms.*' 9

It was now determined to prevent by force the sitting of the
law courts, so that no more judgments could be taken against

9 For full text, see Minot, *History of the Insurrections*, pp. 82-3.

debtors. This movement spread east and west, and courthouses from Concord to Great Barrington were guarded by armed insurgents. To counteract this move, Governor Bowdoin called out the militia, placing the troops in western Massachusetts under the command of General William Shepard of Westfield.

On August 29 some fifteen hundred insurgents, of whom about one-third were armed—Shays was not among them, by the way—took possession of the courthouse in Northampton and prevented a sitting of the Court of General Sessions. A few days later similar action was taken in Concord and also in Great Barrington, where the jail was thrown open and the imprisoned debtors set free. Early in September the court session was broken up in Worcester, and Chief Justice Artemas Ward was threatened with bayonets.

Two days after the Worcester affair a mass meeting of citizens of near-by towns was held on Pelham Hill, presided over by Colonel John Powers of Shutesbury, and Shays was appointed to represent Pelham on a Committee of Seventeen to raise and equip a force of 'Regulators' in Hampshire County. He found himself thrust into the forefront of the movement, but apparently he did not flinch, for he proceeded at once to organize the recruiting in co-operation with Captain Luke Day of West Springfield, Eli Parsons of Adams, Captain Joel Billings of Amherst, and others. General Shepard, taking alarm, proceeded to muster his militia, many of whom were friends and neighbors of the insurgents.

The Supreme Court of the State was scheduled to sit in Springfield on September 27. It was expected that indictments would be found against members of the Committee of Seventeen and other insurgent leaders, and as they would then become outlaws and greatly hampered in their operations, it seemed particularly important that this court should not be allowed to sit. General Shepard, with a force of eight hundred men, surrounded the courthouse to insure non-interference with the proceedings.

Captain Shays arrived in Springfield on September 26, joined Luke Day, and with him marched down Main Street at the head of a force of six hundred armed men wearing, in lieu of a uniform, sprigs of hemlock in their hats. It began to look as though a serious conflict were impending, but there was manifest a reluctance on both sides to fight against friends and neighbors. A parley was held, and Shays withdrew his men from the immediate vicinity of the courthouse and waited to see what would happen. The court was allowed to sit, but as it was totally unable to secure a meeting of the grand jury, the judges decided that discretion was the better part of valor and soon adjourned, having finished very little business. Shays marched his men away, and each side claimed the victory.

The insurgents continued to intimidate the courts of Massachusetts, and practically none sat outside of Essex County. In October, another sitting of the Supreme Court was scheduled in Great Barrington, but the Berkshire 'Regulators' gathered in large numbers, and the justices decided to leave without making any attempt to open court.

Shays was now in supreme command of the insurgent forces, which numbered altogether several thousands. Sure of success, he issued the following orders from Pelham on October 23, 1786:

GENTLEMEN:—By information from the General Court they are determined to call all those who appeared to stop the court to condign punishment. Therefore I request you to assemble your men together to see that they are Well armed and equipped with sixty rounds each man, and be ready to turn out at a Minute's warning; likewise be properly organized with officers.

DANIEL SHAYS [10]

This order was approved by the action of a convention held in Worcester a few days later.

The first bloodshed of the rebellion took place in Middlesex County, where the insurgents had succeeded in closing the Concord courthouse and had intimidated the wealthier inhabitants. Late in November, the militia captured Job Shattuck and other leaders after a brisk fight near Groton. The insurgents were dispersed, and the backbone of the rebellion was broken in that county.

To the west, however, the movement grew apace. On November 21, armed 'Regulators' filled the courthouse of General Ses-

[10] Josiah G. Holland, *The History of Western Massachusetts* (Springfield, 1855), p. 250, *et al.*

sions in Worcester, and again in Springfield early in December
a sitting of the Court of Common Pleas was prevented by three
hundred men under Day. Governor Bowdoin called for more
militia and ordered the arrest of some of the ring-leaders. Shays
retired to Rutland, where he opened headquarters for the winter campaign. Concentrating there a force of some twelve hundred men, he kept them occupied and made a show of force by
marching them about Worcester, Shrewsbury, Holden, and
Grafton. Not all went well with him, however, for the commis-
sary department was poorly organized, provisions were difficult
to obtain, and the men suffered many hardships, several dying
from frost-bite.

Evidence exists which seems to show that Shays was at this
time in low spirits and that he would have deserted the cause
if he could have got a promise of immunity.[11] This promise,
however, was not forthcoming, and there was nothing for him
to do but pursue the course he had mapped out and seek to
deliver some telling blow. On January 10, Governor Bowdoin
ordered the arrest of all the members of the Committee of Seventeen for treason, as an act of war, including Shays, Day, Billings, and Powers. Their backs were now to the wall; they had to
fight or hang.

Bowdoin, now thoroughly alarmed, sent orders to General
Shepard to co-operate with the county sheriffs in apprehending
the leaders and to take steps to break up the insurrection. He
called for a special mobilization of the state militia for sixty
days' service, to include horse, foot, and artillery—some 4,400
men in all—and placed at their head the Revolutionary general,
Benjamin Lincoln of Hingham. Lincoln ordered this force, gathered from all sections of the state, to assemble in Boston,
Worcester, and Springfield on January 18 and 19.

By this time the alarm had spread to Philadelphia, and Washington wrote, 'It was but the other day that we were shedding
our blood to obtain the Constitutions under which we now live
—Constitutions of our own choice and making—and now we are

[11] Minot, *History of the Insurrections*, p. 89; Parmenter, *Pelham*, pp.
395-8.

unsheathing the sword to overturn them.' [12] He sent his Secretary of War, General Henry Knox, post-haste to Massachusetts. Knox found Shepard's force weak and poorly equipped and, cutting the red tape, allowed him to withdraw cannon and munitions from the federal arsenal in Springfield. Then he hurried on to Boston to strengthen the hands of Bowdoin and Lincoln.

There was insufficient money in the state treasury to pay and equip the little army, and Bowdoin and Lincoln were forced to go to the wealthy men of Boston for private loans, arguing that otherwise they might lose all. They raised in this way over twenty thousand dollars. Lincoln mobilized a force of 2,500 men in Boston, including cavalry, artillery, and supply trains, equipped for a six-months campaign, and started west to join the militia in Worcester and Springfield.

Lincoln reached Worcester January 22, 1787, and under his protection court was held there on the next day. Shays, learning of the approach of this formidable force, was desperate. Above all he needed better arms and equipment, and he hit upon the bold plan of capturing the federal arsenal in Springfield. He would need to move rapidly, however, in order to attack Shepard's detachment before Lincoln arrived. He set out from Rutland on January 22 with about a thousand men, variously armed, and gathered a hundred more in Palmer on January 23. The next day he appeared in Wilbraham, two days ahead of Lincoln.

The weather was cold and the snow deep. Sheriff Asaph King of Wilbraham, learning what was afoot, leaped on his horse and dashed to Springfield to warn Shepard. He arrived with his horse's legs red with blood, cut by the sharp crust. Shepard, cut off from the relief force on the east, sent an urgent call to Lincoln and took up a position with about a thousand men on the level ground east of the armory.

Shays now had 1,200 men. Eli Parsons was at Chicopee with four hundred Berkshire insurgents and Luke Day in West Springfield with four hundred more. Shays sent orders to Day to attack with him on January 25, coming up on Shepard's rear. This strategy might well have succeeded, but Day was unready.

[12] John Marshall, *The Life of George Washington* (Philadelphia, 1804-7), v, 116.

He requested Shays to postpone the attack until the twenty-sixth, but his message was intercepted by Shepard, and Shays never received it. Day, therefore, remained inactive with his four hundred men in West Springfield during the engagement, though the Connecticut River was frozen and passage was easy.

At about four o'clock on the afternoon of the twenty-fifth, Shays appeared with his army on the Boston Road—the old Bay Path. The 'Regulators' marched steadily along in open columns formed in platoons. Shepard's force was drawn up in readiness for the attack. The insurgents advanced blithely, with their hemlock sprigs in their hats, until they were some two hundred and fifty yards away. Then they halted to prepare for the rush. Shepard, riding out in front, shouted an order to disperse. He received an insolent reply.

'What do you want?' he demanded.

'Barracks,' cried Shays, 'barracks we would have, and stores.'

'You shall purchase them dear, then,' said Shepard.[13]

Shays ordered his men to advance. At a distance of two hundred yards, Shepard fired a howitzer over their heads. Still they came. Then he fired a shot to the right of the advancing column and one to the left. Still the 'Regulators' maintained an unbroken front.

Then he ordered a shot fired point-blank into the approaching ranks at a distance of fifty yards. Not a musket was fired during the entire episode, but that one cannon shot was instantly effective. The troops which Shays had so patiently drilled were nevertheless an independent, undisciplined lot, and Day's better-trained company was not there. The entire army of 1,200, without firing a shot in reply, turned and fled toward Ludlow, leaving three dead on the field and one mortally wounded. Thus ended the Battle of Armory Hill. Shays tried in vain to rally his men and at length was forced to retire to the Chapin Tavern, about five miles east, for the night. Shepard, observing the demoralization of the insurgents, decided to remain on guard at the arsenal rather than waste his energies in pursuit.

The next day, the twenty-sixth, Shays managed to reform at

---

[13] Parmenter, *Pelham*, p. 377, *et al.*

Ludlow such of his army as had not deserted. He marched them through the snow to South Hadley, where he was joined by Parsons, and thence over Mt. Holyoke Notch to Amherst. Shepard, meanwhile, had sent a force against Day, who moved on up the river to Northampton and joined Shays in Amherst on the twenty-seventh with about two hundred and forty of his men. More desertions had occurred along the line of march, and the original force of 2,000 had dwindled to about 1,100.

Learning that Lincoln had taken up the pursuit, Shays decided to move on to the snow-bound Pelham Hills. On January 28, a thousand men, weary and disheartened, marched to Pelham. Half of them camped in front of the Pelham meeting-house and the rest on the East Hill, now Prescott. Here they must have starved had it not been for the arrival of seven sleigh-loads of provisions sent by Berkshire sympathizers and hurriedly forwarded from Amherst by Landlord Oliver Clapp a few minutes before the militia arrived.[14] Shays took up his headquarters in the Conkey Tavern in Pelham Hollow.

Lincoln had arrived in Springfield on the twenty-seventh, and after reforming his forces and sending a detachment after Day, he started for Amherst at 2 A.M. on the twenty-eighth. Finding Amherst deserted and the roads choked with snow, he decided not to follow Shays into Pelham. He withdrew his men to Hadley and Hatfield, taking up his headquarters in Hadley. Pelham was held in a state of siege.

Shays, finding his provisions dwindling and his men discontented and suffering from cold, realized that this state of affairs could not go on indefinitely. On January 30, he opened parleys with Lincoln, seeking pardon as the price of laying down arms. Lincoln replied that he had no authority to grant pardon and demanded unconditional surrender. Shays sparred for time. A conference was arranged for February 3, but Shays was only preparing to move to better quarters. On that day he mustered his entire force at Prescott and marched on a dozen miles, through North Dana, to Petersham. When Lincoln received word of this

[14] For an amusing account of this episode, see Carpenter and Morehouse, *Amherst*, pp. 136-7.

move, he was angry and determined to follow Shays into the hills.

There followed a forced march scarcely equalled in the annals of the Revolution. Lincoln got the news at six in the evening. Two hours later his force was in motion, cannon and all, marching through North Amherst to Shutesbury. The day had been relatively mild, but the temperature dropped below zero after nightfall, and about two o'clock in the morning the militiamen ran into a biting northeast wind and a raging blizzard at New Salem. The snow was deep and the road led up hill and down, through wilderness. They had to push on or freeze. At nine o'clock in the morning, according to Minot's almost incredible account, the advance guard—Colonel Haskell with a company of men and two cannon—entered Petersham, having covered thirty miles of all but impassable roads in thirteen hours. The rear guard came up an hour or so later.

Lincoln was a better strategist than Shays, and the 'Regulators,' out foraging for their Sunday morning breakfast, were taken completely by surprise. Scarcely a shot was fired. The insurgents gathered as quickly as they could and most of them fled in a disorderly body toward Athol and Northfield. About one hundred and fifty were captured and released after giving up their arms and taking the oath of allegiance. A tablet on the Athol-Petersham road now marks the spot. Some escaped and managed to get home. Shays himself, with about three hundred of his followers, reached Winchester, New Hampshire, where the remnant soon disbanded. Day was arrested soon afterward and the Shays Rebellion came to an ignoble end, save for a month of guerrilla warfare in Berkshire County. On February 26, Captain Hamlin and several hundred men attacked Stockbridge and captured hostages in the hope of thus being able to make better terms of surrender. They were pursued by the militia and were defeated in a skirmish at Sheffield, suffering casualties of thirty killed and wounded. The rest of the band dispersed.

The insurgent leaders began petitioning for pardon. There was a demand in the eastern part of the state for drastic punishment, but Lincoln's counsels prevailed [15] and a general amnesty

[15] Barry, *History of Massachusetts*, pp. 251-3; Adams, p. 163.

was at last proclaimed for all save the ringleaders. The towns
chiefly involved hastened to assert their loyalty to the Commonwealth, fearing confiscation. Most of the insurgents were pardoned and restored to citizenship after giving up their arms and
taking the oath of allegiance, and justices of the peace were busy
for weeks. Fourteen of the leaders were tried and sentenced, six
of them to death. Pressure was brought to bear on the Governor for their release, and one by one they were pardoned.
At least two of them, Henry McCulloch of Pelham and Jason
Parmenter of Bernardston, received their reprieves literally at
the foot of the gallows.[16] Their final pardons were signed by
Governor Hancock in September. Shays and Parsons, however,
who had fled from justice, were not pardoned till a year later.
It may well be that the 'Regulators' deserved all that they got
of the ignominy of defeat, and yet one cannot help feeling that
they have been maligned. Their grievances were real, their case
desperate. They were fighting for their rights just as surely as
were those other embattled farmers at Concord bridge.

Historians have commonly agreed that the chief result of the
Shays Rebellion was to impress upon the federal Congress and
the General Court of Massachusetts the need for a stronger centralized government, with power and means to deal with such
uprisings. Doubtless it had its effect on the growing sentiment
in favor of ratifying the federal Constitution; it may even have
caused some changes in that document before it was adopted in
Philadelphia in May 1787. The more important outcome, however, has seldom been emphasized. Following this revolt, the state
laws were modified and reforms were undertaken which resulted
in the abolition of imprisonment for debt and other oppressive
practices—together with measures which included a complete
overhauling of the unjust tax system, with the purpose of re-
lieving the towns and polls of some of the burden and placing it
on trade. The immediate sequel was a bloodless revolution, for
in the 1787 elections John Hancock, running on a platform of
leniency and reform, defeated James Bowdoin for the governorship of Massachusetts by a vote of nearly three to one, and only

[16] For dramatic accounts of this incident, see Parmenter, *Pelham*, pp. 384-9;
Trumbull, *Northampton*, pp. 514-16.

one-fourth of the members of the House of Representatives were returned.[17] Victory for the cause; defeat for poor Dan Shays.

Lonely, friendless, for a time a hunted outlaw, and spending the remainder of his life under a cloud of opprobrium, Shays had done more than any other one man to free his fellow-citizens from the shackles of unjust discrimination and oppression. Governor Bowdoin offered seven hundred and fifty dollars for his capture, but he succeeded in escaping from New Hampshire into Vermont, where he remained for a time in hiding and where interesting but probably apocryphal legends have grown up about him. In February 1788, he or his friends petitioned for pardon, and it was granted the following summer. That he was still in Vermont in 1791 is proved by a dated document in his hand that has recently come to light.[18] His subsequent movements are not certainly known. It is said that he returned to Pelham for a time in 1792, but apparently Massachusetts had no place for him. He never prospered. He moved westward into New York State, and eventually to Sparta in Ontario (now Livingston) County, where there are records of his residence in 1814.

The following is taken from the records of the United States Bureau of Pensions:

Captain Shays was allowed pension on his application executed April 22, 1818, at the rate of $20 a month, at which time he was aged seventy years and a resident at Sparta, Ontario County, N. Y. He died September 15, 1824, or September 25, 1825. He married April 1, 1815, at Sparta, N. Y., Rhoda, her maiden name not given. They were both then residents of Sparta, where they resided thirteen years. She was allowed a pension on her application executed April 2, 1853, at which time she was aged eighty-two years and resided in Springwater, Livingston County, N. Y. She died January 14, 1858, place not stated.

According to Holland, his estate, at the time of his application for a pension, amounted to only $40.62. What became of his first wife, Abigail, is not known. The date of his death is usually

---

17 Adams, *New England*, p. 165; Nevins, *The American States*, p. 219.

18 A paper granting the power of attorney to one Jonathan Danforth of Hardwick, Massachusetts, and signed by Daniel Shays at 'Allington' (Arlington), Bennington County, Vermont, April 25, 1791, at the present writing in the possession of Mr. J. V. Malone of Granby, Massachusetts.

given as September 29, 1825. He was buried in what is now the
Union Cemetery at Conesus, New York. A small, simple head-
stone of slate, roughly marked 'Da. Shays,' was placed on his
grave by a friend, but for nearly a century his burial place was
neglected and forgotten. A few years ago, however, it was cleared
and a more suitable marker erected by the Livingston County
Historical Society.

By sifting the available testimony, friendly and unfriendly, it
is possible to gain a somewhat clearer conception of the character
of Daniel Shays than has been current hitherto. He had his obvious weaknesses. He was not an educated man, not a competent
leader or a man of great military talent. He drank; on one or
two occasions he displayed a streak of moral cowardice. But he
was not the shabby vagabond or the criminal that he has been
often pictured. There is ample evidence that he was brave under
fire and possessed a magnetic personality. When he was at the
height of his brief power he commanded admiration and loyalty. He was an actual sufferer from the inequities of the times,
and his heart was unquestionably in his cause. And though
Luke Day and one or two others have often been called his
superiors in ability, the fact remains that Daniel Shays was the
leader of the wide-spread insurrection that bears his name—an
insurrection that was not wholly without its justification at a
time of great economic stress, when the republican form of government was still in an experimental stage, and revolution, as a
means of securing tardy justice, was the political fashion. It may
be over-dramatizing the situation, but it is difficult to escape the
conviction that a fitting epitaph might well read as follows:

Here lies the body of Captain Daniel Shays, a 'village Hampden'
who fought bravely in the War for Independence and who, in January 1787, led the embattled farmers of western Massachusetts on a
desperate adventure which ended in ignominious defeat but which
resulted eventually in juster laws and happier living.

BIBLIOGRAPHY

Adams, James Truslow. *New England in the Republic, 1776-1850.* Boston, 1926.

Barry, John Stetson. *The History of Massachusetts.* 3 vols. Boston, 1855-7. Vol. III, *The Commonwealth Period.*

Bradford, Alden. *History of Massachusetts.* 3 vols. Boston, 1822-9.

Carpenter [E. W.] and Morehouse [C. F.], compilers. *The History of Amherst, Massachusetts.* Part I.—*General History of the Town.* Part II.—*Town Meeting Records.* Complete in One Volume. Amherst, 1896.

Green, Mason A. *Springfield, 1636-1836; History of the Town and City* . . . Springfield, Mass., 1888.

Holland, Josiah G. *The History of Western Massachusetts. The Counties of Hampden, Hampshire, Franklin and Berkshire.* . . . Springfield, Mass., 1855.

Lincoln, William. *The History of Worcester, Massachusetts, from its Earliest Settlement to September, 1836* . . . Worcester, 1837.

Marshall, John. *The Life of George Washington, Commander in Chief of the American Forces . . . and First President of the United States . . .* 5 vols. and atlas. Philadelphia, 1804-7.

Minot, George Richards. *The History of the Insurrections in Massachusetts, in the Year* MDCCLXXXVI, *and the Rebellion Consequent Thereon.* Worcester, Mass., 1788.

Nevins, Allan. *The American States During and After the Revolution, 1775-89.* New York, 1924.

Parmenter, C. O. *The History of Pelham, Mass., from 1738-1898, including the Early History of Prescott.* Amherst, Mass., 1898.

Trumbull, James Russell. *The History of Northampton, Massachusetts, from Its Settlement in 1654.* 2 vols. Northampton, 1898-1902.

Shays Collection, Jones Library, Amherst, Massachusetts.
United States Bureau of Pensions, Records.

COLONEL SHAYS

By Dorothy Canfield Fisher

I DARE say when you studied American history you read about
Shays' Rebellion, in Massachusetts, and duly learned that it was
put down, and the instigators punished. But I am sure that you
never knew, and never wondered, what became of Colonel Shays
himself, of whom the history books says succinctly, 'the leader
himself escaped.'

I have never seen in print anything about the latter part of
his life beyond one or two scanty and inaccurate references in
one or two out-of-date books of reference; but all the older people in our town were brought up on stories about him, for it
was to the valley just over the mountain from us that he fled
after his last defeat. And later on, as an old man, he lived for
some years in our town, in a house still standing, and told many
people what I am going to set down here.

At the time when he made his escape from the officers of the
State in Massachusetts, Vermont was, quaintly enough, an independent republic, all by itself, and hence a sufficient refuge for
men fleeing from the officers of any state in the Union. Further-
more it was still rather wild, sparsely settled, none too respectful
of any authority, and distinctly sympathetic to strangers who
came from the east, south, or west over the mountains on the
run, with the manner of men escaping from sheriffs. Sheriffs were
not popular persons in Vermont in 1787.

But all this did not seem to make it a safe enough refuge to
the man with a price set on his head, the man who had risked
everything on the boldest of enterprises, and had lost everything.
He passed by the rough scattered little hamlets and went into a

From Dorothy Canfield Fisher, *Raw Material,* 1923. By permission of Harcourt, Brace and Company, Inc., publisher.

remote, narrow, dark, high valley, which is to this day a place where a man might hide for years and never be seen. Colonel Shays, traveling at night, on foot, through the forests, came down into the Sandgate valley through the Beartown notch, over the mountains, and not a soul knew that he had come.

He made his first camp, which was also his permanent and last one, since he was never disturbed, high up on a shoulder of the mountain, overlooking the trail for a great distance, and densely surrounded with a thick growth of pine trees. Very cautiously, making no noise, using the ax and knife which were his only tools, he put up a rough shelter, and building a fire only at night in a hollow where rocks masked its flame, began cooking some of the game he caught. He lived in this way, all alone for years and years. Game was abundant; like most men of that time he was an adroit trapper, a good pioneer, and knew how to smoke and preserve the flesh of animals and to save their skins. For the first year he did not dare to let any one know that a man was living there, and literally saw not one soul.

Then one day about a year after he began this life, a little boy going fishing saw a tall, strong, black-haired stranger standing in the trail and holding a large packet of furs. He told the child to take the packet and ask his father for a bushel of seed-corn and a bag of salt. He specified that the man who brought it was to leave it just where they then stood and go away without waiting.

The child's father was a rough, half-civilized, good-natured trapper, who had had troubles of his own with unreasonable officers of the law in York State. When the child told his story, the father laughed knowingly, took the skins, got the seed-corn and the salt, left them in the place indicated, and kept a neighborly shut mouth. He could not read or write, had never heard of Shays' Rebellion, and supposed the man in hiding to be in the same situation as himself. Living as he did, it seemed no awful fate to make one's living out of the woods, and he thought little of the fact that he had a new neighbor.

After this, Colonel Shays began a little cultivation of the ground, in scattered places, hidden behind screens of thick trees, in a few natural clearings in the forest. He used to say that life was infinitely more tolerable to him after the addition to his diet of salt and cereals. After some months he risked a little more, and, buying them with furs worthy forty times their value, he secured a few tools and some gunpowder. The transactions were always carried on through the child, the only one to see the fugitive.

Nothing has come down to me of what this terrible dead halt in mid-career, and this grim isolation from the world meant to the active, intelligent, ambitious man at the height of his powers. None of the old people who heard him talk seem to have asked him about this, or to have had any curiosity on the subject. Only the bare facts are known, that he lived thus for many years, till the little boy grew up, till his own hair turned gray and then white, till the few families in that valley were quite used to the knowledge that a queer, harmless old man was living up in the woods near the northern pass of the mountains, miles from any neighbor. Once in a great while, now, some one saw him—a boy fishing, a hunter far on the trail of a deer, or a group of women picking berries. He occasionally exchanged a few words with his neighbors at such times, but he had almost forgotten how to speak aloud. All the stories about him mention the rough, deep hoarseness of his unused voice.

One day his nearest neighbor, meaning to do him a kindness, told him with a rough good-will that he might as well quit hiding now, 'Whatever 'tis you done, 'tis so long past now! And up here . . . nobody from your part of the country, wherever 'tis, would ever be coming up here. And if they did they wouldn't know you. Why, your own mother wouldn't know you in them clothes, and with that white beard.'

It is said that Colonel Shays on hearing this, drew back and looked down at himself with a strange air of astonishment.

Apparently the advice stuck in his mind, for, some weeks after this, he decided to risk it, and to make the trip to Cambridge, the nearest town to those mountain settlements. Early one morning the people of the Sandgate valley were astonished to see the old man going down the trail of the valley which led into the

State road going to Cambridge. Well, that was something to talk about! He was going to town at last like anybody else.

Now, this happened a good many years after Shays' Rebellion had failed, and the bitterness of the feeling about it had died down. Although Colonel Shays could not know this, most people had even forgotten all about him, and as for looking for him to arrest him, nobody would have dreamed of doing it. There were many other things in the world to think of by that time and although to himself Colonel Shays was still the dramatically hunted fugitive with every man's hand against him, to other people he had begun to sink into the history-book paragraph, which he has since remained. His family and friends in Massachusetts had waited till the occasion seemed favorable, and then petitioned for his pardon, on the ground that he must be, if still living, an old man now, quite harmless, and that it would be only decent to let him come back to spend his last days in his own home; and if he were dead, his pardon would clear his family name, and straighten out certain complications about his property. At first they had not succeeded. People still remembered too vividly the treasonable attempt to overturn the authority of the state, only just established and none too strong. But by and by, the pertinacity of the petitioners wore out the fading hostility to his name. He was proclaimed pardoned, and notices were sent to all American newspapers informing him that he could now return. This had happened a year before Colonel Shays had started down to Cambridge, but you may be sure that at that period no newspapers found their way to the Sandgate valley.

After a year had gone by, and no sign came from the fugitive, people generally thought him dead. But a fellow-townsman who had known him well by sight and who, some years after his flight, had married his youngest sister, volunteered to try to spread the news more widely than by newspaper. There had been a faint notion among his kinspeople that he had fled to Vermont, although they had taken care to keep this to themselves as long as he was an outlaw, and had now almost forgotten about it. Acting on this notion, Shays' brother-in-law took the long journey on horseback up into Vermont. He entered the state at Bennington and slowly worked his way north, branching off at every practicable road. But nowhere did he find any one who had ever heard of any such man as his wife's brother. Colonel Shays had hidden himself only too well.

The Massachusetts man began to think his errand a futile one, and prepared to turn back. But on a chance he rode down to Cambridge, just over the New York line. Cambridge was the nearest town to a number of small valley settlements in Vermont. He would ask there if any one had seen or heard of the man he was seeking. He knew that men from the remote outlying settlements came to Cambridge to do their trading. He arrived rather late one evening and as he was no longer young, and very much tired by his long and fruitless journey, he slept that night in the Cambridge Inn.

For the rest of the story there are plenty of details, for Colonel Shays told over and over exactly what happened and just how he felt, and why he acted as he did. It seared deep into him, and to the end of his days, he always showed a consuming agitation in speaking of it.

He walked along the road, the first road he had seen since the night so many years ago when he had fled along the roads in Massachusetts. It seemed like iron to his buckskin-shod feet. He walked slowly for this and other reasons. Every house which came into view along the road brought him up short with a jerk like a frightened horse. The instinct to hide, to trust himself in no man's sight, had deformed his whole nature so that the bold leader of men halted, trembling and white-faced, at the sight of an ordinary farm-house. He forced himself to go on, to pass those sleeping homes, but after he had passed each one with his silent, stealthy wood-dweller's tread, he quickened his pace and looked fearfully over his shoulder, expecting to see men run out after him with warrants for his arrest.

By the time he approached Cambridge, the nervous strain was telling on him. He was wet with sweat, and as tired as though he had been four times over the mountains. Only a few people were abroad, as it was the breakfast hour. Partly from the old fear of years, partly from the mere habit of total isolation, every strange face was startling to him. He felt his knees weak under him and sat down on a bench in front of the kitchen door of the Cambridge Inn to get his breath. He had been a man of powerful will and strong self-control or he never could have lived through those terrible years of being buried alive, and he now angrily told himself there was nothing to fear in this remote little hamlet, where everybody was used to the sight of men in buckskins coming down to trade their furs for gunpowder and salt. At the sight of all those human faces taking him back to the days of his human life, a deep yearning had come upon him to get back into the world of living men. He could have wept aloud and taken them into his arms like brothers. He was determined to master his tense nerves, to learn to move about among his fellow-men once more. In a moment, just a moment, he decided he would stand up and move casually over to the general store across the street where a lad was then unlocking the door. He would go in and make a purchase—the first in so many years!

He turned his head to glance into the kitchen of the Inn, and as he did so, the door opened, and a man came in, a traveler with a face familiar to him in spite of gray hair and wrinkles, a man he had known in Massachusetts, who knew him, and no friend of his, a man who had been on the other side in the Rebellion.

Colonel Shays' heart gave a staggering leap. He caught at the doorjamb and shrank out of sight. He heard the other voice say, 'I stepped in to ask if any of you know whether Colonel Shays was ever heard of in this . . .'

And then the old man, running madly for his life, fled back to his den in the woods.

A whole decade passed after this, before he happened to learn in a conversation overheard between two trappers, that for eleven priceless, irreplaceable years, he had been a free man.

FREE

By Jack Yeaman Bryan

As the service ended, Daniel sent another look across the pews. Sophia was rising beside her mother. This time her gaze was not down. It was waiting for his. Her expression did not change much, if at all. But he could tell what she was thinking, and he guessed she could tell as much about him.

He sidled lankily out of the pew, and his long, awkward stride carried him out the aisle as naturally as if there had been no shakiness and stir and worry beneath his calm. He went out to a shaded place under the wall, where the steeple poked a warped point of shadow into the noon sunlight. He waited there.

To everyone who went by toward a buggy or wagon or automobile he spoke a grave, 'Ha-do, sir,' or 'Ha-do, ma'm.' Most people returned the greeting, but none came over to talk with him, as they would have in the past. Their faces were as familiar to him as the lean Georgia hills that squatted with senile infertility on the horizons all around. Under the bygone friendliness of these faces he had grown from infancy through boyhood and youth as he had under the vanishing and returning sun. But what smiles he saw today were only a quick nod at old times. One woman, as she passed, muttered, 'Linthead!'

Sophia came around the corner alone. Being accustomed to go barefoot on week days, like most women hereabout, she walked uncertainly in her battered shoes. Still, every sign of hurry or tension was hidden deep within the slow strength of her movements.

He said gently, 'Where's your ma?'

'In there talking to Miz Hindley. Just walk off like we aint thinking nothing.'

From *American Prefaces,* Summer, 1939. By permission of the author and publisher.

They headed toward his father's rusty sedan. People stared after them and whispered. Daniel, swaying from one long shank to the next, pondered far-off things. Sophia, her eyes always down, let one browned hand touch here and there the wilting fringe of her Sunday curls. They drove away, never hurrying, never looking back.

As they jostled along he said, 'Far as I can see there aint a thing wrong with it. Nary a thing.'

'No, there aint.'

'We'll go down to Hillford and get us some ice cream. We'll get some for your folks, too.'

'It'll be most melted again we get back,' she said. 'But they'll like it mighty well.'

The day was hot for spring. For more than a week the winds had been lazy and the sun close. In fields on both sides of the road, where there was any strength left in the soil, the crops had already begun to show.

He said, 'Like I told you in that letter, Sophy, this man at the mill is fixing to loan the folks a hundred dollars for seed and fertilize. So we're going to McGinnis right after dinner to sign the papers. I sure would like it a heap if you'd come along.'

'It skeers me, Dan'l.'

'You could just come along and ride right back with Henry and the folks. It wouldn't hurt ary a thing.'

'I mean you signing—it skeers me.'

'Me, too. But reckon I got to do it. It'll be many's the month before I get back, Sophy. Maybe when your daddy knows about the loan and the ice cream, he'll let you come. Maybe just for the once.'

'He'll be plumb mad on account of me running off like this. Besides, he don't think a heap of no loans.'

'Lintheads neither,' he added.

She said nothing. He jockeyed the car along between the lines of dried ruts that stretched away before them. As they turned onto the highway to Hillford, he slowed down to peel off his church-going coat, then drove on. Sophia folded it carefully. A faint masculine smell came from it. Her nostrils drew at this smell. She laid the coat along the length of her lap, where it would not wrinkle. After a while she began talking again, but only to pass on the paltry oddities of local news.

Near the outskirts of Hillford they stopped at Tipton's Place, a combination store, pop stand, and gas station. Inside, a hatless young fellow was sitting with his back to the counter, licking an ice cream cone. There was a suitcase near his feet. He nodded just as any plain folk here in Georgia would do, but his 'Hello!' was Yankee. Joe Tipton, son to the owner of the place, was shoving dust across the floor with a push broom. He stopped and gawked comically.

'Morning, Sophy! And Dan'l! You old scoun'el, you! Where in sam you been?'

'Howdy, Joe. We just come for some ice cream.'

'Lord he'p us, I aint seen you for—well, since way last fall. And you're looking poorly, Dan'l. Sort of pekid. Say, where you been, anyhow?'

'Up to McGinnis.' Daniel glanced at Sophia. She studied the floor. He took a breath and added quietly, 'In the mill.'

'Oh.' The cheer sagged off Joe's features. He put the broom aside and drifted around the counter. 'I didn't hear nothing about that. Nobody told me. I was down to my uncle's most all winter. Maybe that's why.'

Daniel ordered a pint of chocolate. The Yankee had stopped eating his cone. He looked puzzled.

'Pardon,' he said to Daniel. 'What kind of a mill?'

'Textile.'

Sophia spoke for the first time. In her voice was a slow, dogged energy. 'He done it because he figured it was right,' she said. 'Dan'l likes farming. He do like it a heap. But his folks is having a mighty hard time. So, quick as he become free, he went off and got him a job of work at McGinnis. He figured he could help his folks and maybe him and me could get married by and by. That's how come he done it.'

'Did what?' said the Yankee.

'Become a linthead.'

'Oh . . .'

Joe handed the package across the counter, using a curious

mixture of sympathy and restraint. 'I put it in two sacks, Dan'l,' he said, 'so's it won't melt so fast.'

When Daniel and Sophia went outdoors, the Yankee followed. He was nearly as tall as Daniel, but not stooped and not so dark.

'By the way, you going up the road north?'

Daniel said, 'Yessir, a fair piece—seven-eight mile before we turn off. You're mighty welcome to ride along, if you're a mind to.'

'Thanks—you bet!'

Bringing his suitcase, he climbed into the back seat of the lame old sedan. Daniel steered back to the highway and on toward home. The hitch-hiker explained about his travels. He had been everywhere and was now headed for some place an amazing way north—up in Pennsylvania. At last he broke off.

He said, 'I can't help being curious. What the heck's wrong with work in a mill?'

'You see,' said Daniel, 'it's this way. There's a mill four-five-miles over the hills. The lintheads there is the lowdownest white-folks you ever did see. Nobody around here won't have nothing to do with them—thinks lintheads is some kind of a slave. But, come last fall, they had a strike at McGinnis. That's about sixty mile across the state. The mill there was taking on green hands at eleven dollars a week, cash money. It looked to me like I'd ought to go. At first the folks says no—says I couldn't become no linthead. Still and all, I figured I could pay some debts and help keep the rest of the land. A heap of folks around here lost theirs already. We don't want to be next. So come November I was free, and I went.'

The Yankee said, 'I've heard about these mills. But a fellow hears about share-cropping, too. If you lost the land and had to farm on shares it looks like you'd be as much a slave *any* day as in a good cotton mill.'

'See there, Sophy! That's exactly what I told you.' But she did not cease gazing at the road ahead, and his look of conviction was brief. 'Still and all,' he added, 'seems like folks don't figure that-a way. Any kind of work in the country is supposed to be different. And when you own the land, you're independent. You probably don't really own it—the only thing you own is the pay-ing end of a mortgage. And you might not make nothing at all, nary a cent. But on a farm they claim you're independent.' Bit-terness twisted his face. Then a colorless melancholy settled over it as before. 'Fact is,' he admitted, 'a mill *is* worse, some ways. It's tiresome work, especially if a man don't like machines. And that cussed lint—it's always thick everywhere, like a mist. Some folks that's been there a good spell take to coughing. Many's the man and woman dies of a cough around a mill.'

'Well, why not quit?—quit and go back to farming or get another job?'

Daniel blew out a sigh. 'First place there aint no other jobs. Might be for a man like you that's got some education and knows his way around. Not for green hands from the hills. But I caint quit noway. When I first went up there we worked steady, and I sent home two-three dollars a week. The folks sure was glad to get that cash money. They forgot all about not wanting me to be a linthead. Before long, though, we'd work some weeks, and some we wouldn't. First thing I knew I was owing the com-pany for room and board, seeing they own the houses and all. But the folks still couldn't pay for the seed and fertilize this spring, let alone the interest and taxes. So I aim to borrow us a hundred dollars from a new man they got in to kind of work along with the company. If I do, he gets two-forty a week out of my pay. That's all I can spare. He gets it for one year. Any weeks we don't work has to be made up next year. So I caint quit. Not now.'

'Let's see, two-forty for fifty-two weeks—that's about a hun-dred and twenty-five dollars. Holy mack, that's about twenty-five per cent interest! And what if you quit before it's paid?'

'Well sir, then he gets the crop. If I'd quit after the crop was sold, he'd get everything loose on the farm. Henry—he's my brother—he come up and brung me home yesterday evening to talk it over with the folks.'

The Yankee's words came out sharp and quick. They were not cold, as some think Northern words are. He had the air of trying to argue a friend out of jumping over a cliff.

'If your farm,' he pointed out, 'is anything like the others a man sees in the hills around here, it can't be worth killing your-self over. It never will pay out again, good years or bad, till the soil is built up. So you might as well let it go this year as next. Anything is better than selling yourself off for a lousy hundred bucks.'

When they came to the corner where Daniel had to turn off the main road, the hitch-hiker thanked his way out the rear door. Daniel and Sophia, alone again, drove on into the back-country.

He observed, 'That boy do talk a sight. He could talk up a storm.'

'Reckon so. But he had sense, too, Dan'l. For a Yankee he had a heap of sense.' She lifted and refolded the coat she held. Once more she laid it with care along her thighs. 'Maybe you'd ought to tell them, Dan'l.'

'It wouldn't do no good. The only thing it'd do is raise a ruckus.'

'Still and all, you'd ought to tell them like he said. It'll be a long, long time again we get married if you don't. Maybe never. Right off they won't like it, but maybe by and by they'll take to seeing how it is.' She looked at his knee. 'You going to tell them?'

'Maybe.'

She settled back against the seat. Daniel turned off toward a house, squat, paintless, and shabby, like others in the neighbor-hood. Children were idling about the yard. On the porch sat a muscular, overalled man who was paring out his pipe with a pocket-knife.

'Your daddy's been watching for us,' Daniel whispered. Sophia nodded. They both made a show of not looking toward the house.

'It's Sophy and Dan'l!' shouted a girl of about ten.

The other children began clamoring, 'Sophy and Dan'l, papa!' Their father said, 'Y'all hush!'

They fell silent. He pulled his shoes over his bare feet and came toward the car. In motionless awe the children watched him. His eyes flashed under the sagging brim of his hat.

Daniel turned off the ignition and climbed out. With the

sack of ice cream in one hand he began to squire Sophia toward the back door.

'Sophy,' her father rasped, 'I got half a mind to give you a skinning. What in sam you been up to?'

'Nothing, sir. After church me and Dan'l just went down to Tipton's to get some ice cream for y'all.'

The peace offering was well chosen. The children sprang up and down, shouting at every jump.

'Hush!' said their father. 'Damn it to hell, *hush!*' It was clear, though, that the ice cream had somewhat cooled his anger. To Sophia he merely said, 'Get on in the house.'

Daniel handed her the bag, but she did not leave him. She stood looking at the ground and said, 'There warn't no harm in it, sir.'

Her father blazed again. 'None of your mouth!'

She tried a second time. 'Dan'l aint et a thing yet.'

Her father shook in exasperation. 'Great Godda-Mighty!'

Sophia walked away toward the back door. Her shoulders and arms were slack, and her run-down shoes scuffed heavily across the dusty, grassless yard.

More calmly her father said, 'Dan'l, you better go, before me and you take to fighting.'

'Yessir, I—'

'Again you went up to McGinnis I told you to stay plumb away from Sophy, long as you was a linthead. But you keep sending her them damn letters, and then you sneak back and take her riding off from church when her ma aint looking. That's exactly what you done.'

'Yessir, but I got a chance to get money for seed, and—'

'Money for seed! Yeah, Sophy told about that from your letters. But I allow you aint quitting the mill. Nosir, you caint. I don't aim to be onreasonable, Dan'l, but this is how it is: Folks says, "Once a linthead, always a linthead." And it's a fact. Supposing you and Sophy was to marry like you was studying to do. You caint feed no family on pay from the mill, aint that so?'

'Yessir, but—'

'She'd have to work in the mill, too. She'd be a linthead same as you.'

'Still and all, a farm's no easy life for women neither. On a farm women got to work hard as men.'

'Sure—naturally! But it don't hurt them none. Take Sophy now. You know yourself, Dan'l, she's about as good a hand on a farm as a man could find. She's nigh the best hand with a hoe I ever did see. And she's healthy, aint she?'

All his life Daniel had seen farm women broken and warped before they reached thirty. Somehow, though, he could find no words for this fact that everyone here knew well.

'Yessir, she's healthy and all, but—'

' 'Taint no use arguing no more, Dan'l. I don't want none of you lintheads messing around my gals. Go on, git! Don't be coming back here neither.'

Daniel went slowly to the car. While he was backing around, Sophia came out to wave from the kitchen steps.

'Sophy!' her father called. 'Get back in there, gal, before I whup your contrary hide plumb off of you!'

She turned away. She was not crying, but she looked as though it would be a good thing for her if she did.

In a moment Daniel was again jostling over the narrow road. Hunching above the steering wheel, he frowned at the slow revolving of his thoughts. From the road, he followed a lane that led toward a paintless house built upon props of stone. A few sparsely leafing apple trees stood about the yard. Beneath the greenest his father, Robert Martin, and brother Henry drowsed in rocking chairs. Both were wearing Sunday best. Henry was a loose-jointed tobacco chewer of seventeen. Mr. Martin was stooped and gray. Through the drag of year after year his energies had been drained away by failure as if by the long, slow wasting of some chronic disease.

As Daniel came up, Henry said, 'How's Sophy?'

'All right.' Daniel switched to talk of how they gave a ride to a Yankee. 'Funny thing,' he remarked, 'he had a little sense, too, Yankee or no Yankee. Fact!'

Mr. Martin snorted. The loose skin around his eyes screwed up. '*You* picking up with *Yankees!* See that?' He pointed to a brush-grown spot near the chicken coop. A stone chimney rose out of the thicket. Henry winked at Daniel, then gawked up into the apple tree. But their father would not be denied this chance to display his antique and corroding hatred. 'That there,' he went on, 'was your granddaddy's house—the only two floor house hereabout anywheres, except on Mr. Watkins' plantation. But the Union Army burned it. They ruined every cussed thing they come near. Back in them times this farm would grow cotton up to a man's belly. Now look at it!'

He flourished a hand at the surrounding fields. Most were over-run with briars or a feeble scatter of weeds. Except for a plot of garden truck near the house, only one patch had been planted, and that to corn. Cotton, tobacco, corn—the same draining crops had been raised year after year. This and unchecked erosion had knifed and skinned and gutted the soil everywhere until it would no longer grow a crop without heavy fertilizing.

'Yessir,' Mr. Martin concluded, 'the Union Army ruined every-thing—them and the damned carpetbaggers that came after the War. And *you*, dad blast it, Dan'l, you go picking up with Yankees!'

Henry sighed and wagged a hand at his father. 'General Lee hisself!'

'You lay everything to the Yankees,' said Daniel, 'including flies, boll weevils, the itch, and chillsinfever.'

His mother, even more stooped and withered than Mr. Martin, called from the back door. 'Dan'l, you have dinner up to Sophy's?'

'No'm.'

'Well, come in and get you some before we go.'

His father followed him into the kitchen. In preparation for the trip to McGinnis, Henry stopped at the pump to soak his hair, then came in to comb it at the kitchen mirror. Meanwhile, Mr. Martin slouched at the table, droning to Daniel about the crops he and Henry were going to plant once they got the loan.

'How come so much cotton and corn?' said Daniel. 'Looks like you'd ought to put in some cowpeas and soya beans.'

'For what? No money in that. We got to have us a sight of cash money.'

'Put in some for hay, but mostly for plowing under, like Mr.

Watkins done last year. We got to put some strength in the ground.'

'For plowing *under!*' Mr. Martin stared as if disbelieving that his own son could be tripped by such ideas.

They began to argue, the father heatedly, Daniel with grave insistence. His mother became nervous. She did not like cross words in the house, especially on Sunday. She worried around the table, pushing bowls of food toward Daniel and watching for a chance to change the topic.

'I reckon, Dan'l,' she said, 'I reckon it took Sophy's pa down right smart, finding out about the money!'

She smiled. At once her husband, dropping his scowl, smiled, too. Their smiles were like a glitter of light passing over the depths of a hopelessness chronic and incurable in them both.

'No'm, he just says to git. And don't come back. Looks like he figures getting the money will only make things worse.'

There was an indignant, staring pause. Daniel tried to go on and speak his mind, as Sophia had asked him to, but he couldn't. The pause grew. Finally Mr. Martin broke it by scoffing at a man too ignorant to see what a fine thing it was for a boy to help his family out of trouble. Daniel ceased to listen. He sat looking at his plate.

A loose board on the kitchen stoop rattled. Sophia was at the door. Daniel was so astonished that his legs pushed him from his chair. She was still wearing her Sunday dress. On it were nettles and beggar burrs, such as come from a walk through the woods. A leaf clung to the bedraggled remains of her curls. With all eyes upon her, she bent to one side and plucked at the burrs. Sunlight gleamed on her tanned neck. Daniel noticed a trickle of sweat run down it where a muscle rose under her softly feminine skin.

Mrs. Martin hurried to the door. 'Sophy! Come in, gal! Do come in and set awhile.'

'Yes'm.' She went quietly to a chair near Daniel. 'I went off from the house like to hunt for a setting hen in the jackpines,' she said. Her eyes were on her lap, but her words were for him. 'I figured I'd ought to come.'

He nodded. For a moment he ate hastily, as if trying to force

into himself by knife and fork the courage to say what she expected him to say.

Swallowing hard, he began, 'I reckon we oughtn't to get no
loan at all!'

Again consternation hushed the room. A heavy-bellied cat
strutted across the floor with sleepy daintiness and stroked her
back against Sophia's leg. Her purring, an asthmatic sort of
wheeze, rattled in the silence.

Daniel tried again. His words hurried out, to get the whole
thing said.

'It sure looks like we oughtn't. On the way home the Yankee
told a sight of things about loans. That loan man is just a blood
sucker. He acts friendly and smiles nice and when he hands you
the money he snaps a chain on your leg. If I borrow the money,
the Yankee says, I'll be a slave sure enough. Farming on shares,
y'all couldn't be much worse off than now. The only difference
is I wouldn't have to work indoors all the time, breathing up
that lint. And me and Sophy might could get married and share-
crop another place. If I borrow the money we won't never have
a chance to marry.'

His father glared at him. Daniel, nervous and flushing, kept his
eyes on his plate. Sophia had her fingers locked together in her
lap. Mrs. Martin nursed one bony hand with the other, and
began to cry. Through the mirror Henry stared at one, then
another.

'Now *there*,' said Mr. Martin at last, 'there's what comes of
picking up with a damn Yankee!'

Henry came from the mirror and flourished his comb. 'Lord
God, Dan'l, that's—why, that's selfish!'

Mrs. Martin murmured tearfully, 'Dan'l, you was always such
a *good* boy! Always—'

Her husband ranted at Yankee notions. He pictured what it
would mean to lose the homestead, where for generations the
family had been born, reared, and buried. Henry and Mrs.
Martin added helter-skelter pleas. The pressure of their entreaties bore heavily upon Daniel. And Sophia, too, slackened
and relaxed. Daniel at last agreed to get the loan on condition
they clear off two fields that were going to briars and sow them

to restorative cover crops. His parents and brother went limp in relief.

During a pause Sophia remarked, 'If I could I'd like mighty well to go up to McGinnis and back with y'all. Again I go home I'll get a skinning sure. I'd get it if I'd go now or if I'd go this evening. So—well, Dan'l asked me, and if I could—'

Soon afterward, the five of them were riding away together, Sophia and Daniel in back with Mrs. Martin. Mr. Martin was with Henry, who was driving. As he herded the sedan up the road, he kept throwing lazy, genial remarks over his shoulder to Daniel. On reaching the highway he turned the talk back to the hitch-hiker.

'You say that Yankee was going clear on up to Pennsylvania? Pennsylvania, Lord ha' mercy! Cleveland Hindley was up there on that trip he took again he was free. He seen Philadelphia and the Liberty Bell. Cleveland, he seen him some powerful sights.'

'He did that,' said Daniel wryly. 'But I recollect the scoun'el was mighty glad to sit down to a plate of victuals again he got back.'

His father said, 'Yessir, his ma tells how he ate a whole loaf of cornbread quick as he got in the house, and sopped up a sight of molasses. He was plumb wore out from looking for work, and didn't have a penny. 'Taint no wonder he's been staying right close to the farm ever since.'

'Well,' said Henry, 'I aint studying about going off like him, free or not free. I got too much sense.'

The sedan clattered steadily. Mile on mile, Sophia said nothing unless questioned. But Daniel knew she was thinking toward some idea. Her thoughts were working patiently, slowly forward, like the hoofs of a plow mare. This time he couldn't tell what she was thinking, and maybe she couldn't either.

In about two hours they came to McGinnis. A hundred more towns like it might be seen here and there about the southeastern states. On one side of the road stood the mill. On the other spread many gray cottages—or, more accurately, gray boxes. They were set close together and each was exactly like the next.

On the front stoops men and women, lounging in Sunday ease, gaped after the car with the motionless fixity of children. They were much the same as country people, but paler and more apathetic. They looked inwardly flat—two-dimensional.

Near the center of town, where the stores were, Henry stopped in front of a large house, part of which had been made into an office. Loans were advertised in gilt letters on the windows. A Negro girl tending a baby on the front walk told them the proprietor was not home, but would be back soon.

A thin man and a woman came strolling toward the car. The man was chewing tobacco, the woman snuff. They and Daniel lived in the same house. Cocking a foot on the running board, the man turned the talk to the loan and to planting. Thought of spring in the country brought glints of worn, faded nostalgia to his eyes. His brown teeth appeared in tobaccoy smiles, and he hacked often.

'Some of these days,' he declared, 'I'm going back to farming. Sure am. I used to farm up the other side of Toccoa. But things got bad so we come here for a while. Seems a long time— five-six years, I reckon. Lula,' he said to the woman, 'how long we been here?'

She had been standing listlessly on the sidewalk behind him. At his question she pursued an itch around her side, digging her fingers into her shapeless cotton dress.

'I don't rightly know. Been so long I most forgot. Eight years, I reckon. Eight years come next month.'

'Lord ha' mercy, eight years!' He gaped into space with un-hinged jaw. 'But some of these days I aim to farm again.' He talked awhile, and then his cough seized him again by the throat. He and the woman trailed away, his gaunt shoulders quivering as he gasped for breath.

An imposing section of the mill stood behind a fence along the opposite side of the street. Occasionally Daniel's bony face turned in that direction. A Sunday quiet enshrouded the building. The windows were closed. In each one the rows of panes reflected the lowering sun, and the lines of leading between the panes stood out at darkly as iron bars. The fence was topped with barbed wire. A gate not far away was locked, and there was an armed guard behind it.

A brisk little man who wore a ready smile, a tweed suit, a blue shirt with a white collar, and a fancy silk tie came down the street. Recognizing Daniel, he stopped before turning up the walk. As he showed the way to his office, he chattered in amiable quickness of tongue. He threw out his remarks as a jaunty gambler throws out dice. Mr. Martin, his wife, and Henry responded to this friendliness in grateful country warmth. The man's accent was decidedly Northern; in fact he had been here less than a month. But Mr. Martin jovially overlooked the point so as to get the cash without a hitch.

Daniel and Sophia followed in silence. In the office she took a chair off to one side. She sat heavily, feet apart, toes pointing inward, and each knee leaned against the other. As she often had before during the day, she kept Daniel's coat folded in her lap. She moved but once, and then only to brush prickles of sweat and wilted curls away from her face. On his part Daniel listened with blank expression while the conditions of the loan were rehearsed. When his turn came to use the pen, he signed with a grave and cramped exactness.

Then Sophia went to the brisk man and stood looking at his feet. She was taller than he was, but she looked only at his feet. All the while she clutched Daniel's coat.

'Mister, could I get a job of work here? I'm a good hand at hard work.'

'Sophy!' Mrs. Martin gasped. 'You caint do that, gal! You aint free. Your daddy'd come up here and—oh, lord ha' mercy!'

Mr. Martin remarked, 'He'd raise sam sure enough! He'd raise sam every *which*-a way!'

'No—now, look here,' said the loan broker hastily, 'we don't want any trouble. We simply can't have it.'

Sophia went on, 'I'll be free next year—next year come May. And when I *am* free, can I get a job of work so's Dan'l and me can—'

'Free? Say, what do you people mean, "free"?'

Henry grinned lazily at this ignorance. 'Why,' he said, 'of age!

You know, twenty-one for us and eighteen for gals. What did you figure it meant?'

'Oh—nothing, nothing.' The man's smiles came back. He turned benignly to Sophia. 'Oh, so you and Daniel—hm!' It pleased him to fancy himself an agent of romance and wedded happiness. 'Well, miss, when you're "free," you come up here and I'll take you to the employment manager myself. Maybe he'll find something for you.'

Daniel did not beam with the others. Neither did Sophia. But the broker gave him a genial pat on the shoulder.

'You know how the mill is, Dan,' he went on. 'We like to take care of our own people.'

THE PRICE OF YOUR FREEDOM

By Henry A. Wallace

WORLD affairs have now taken such a turn that all of us must begin to think about the basis of our democracy, the price of our freedom. Even before the Nazi peril grew great, it was becoming obvious that our citizens, and our boys and girls, must be taught that every right carries with it a corresponding duty, every privilege a responsibility; that we must talk more and more about individual success in terms of service to the general welfare. If we could have jogged along as we did in the nineteenth century, with an abundance of new, rich land, and without any threats from the outside world, such ideas might have amounted to little more than pleasant philosophizing. But now, with our lands fully occupied to our ocean frontiers, and with totalitarian dangers facing us across both of those oceans, we have no alternative but to develop a Bill of Duties, a bill which will maintain, revivify, and fulfill the Bill of Rights.

The Bill of Rights consists of the first ten amendments to the Constitution. It was adopted just 150 years ago. These rights guarantee the great freedoms of religion, speech, press, and person. Their essence is respect for the dignity of the individual human soul. We take these freedoms for granted. We forget that it has been only in the last 160 years that they have had any real vitality and place in the world. And now, as we see the march of nations in which the State is everything, the individual nothing, we realize that it is possible for liberty in the modern sense to disappear from the world as suddenly as it came. We see that the time has come when our Bill of Rights must be defended by a Bill of Duties. While the danger from abroad may spur us to

From *The American Magazine*, July 1941. By permission of the publisher and the author.

this, the need for such a Bill of Duties may be even greater after the peace comes. The tremendous power of modern machinery, large corporations, strong labor organizations, and aggressive pressure groups makes it absolutely essential that there exist some effective counterbalance on behalf of the general welfare . . .

The Bill of Rights was the product of long thought and discussion by many men and many minds. So must be the Bill of Duties. I hope that the question will come to the front in the forums and discussion groups, in the high schools and colleges, among our citizens everywhere. Because it is vitally important to us all, and in the hope that I may help to stimulate such discussion, I venture to put forth a tentative Bill of Duties, followed by some comment on their meaning:

1. The duty to think, every day, how I can best serve the general welfare; to put it ahead of the welfare of my party, of my group, of my region, and of myself.

2. The duty to make democracy efficient by working harder and more harmoniously every day to produce the products most needed.

3. The duty to provide government mechanisms to enable our power of consumption to equal our power of production.

4. The duty to work for an economic democracy to match our political democracy, where the right to a job will be as definite as the right to a vote.

5. The duty to study and know our country, and to see it as an interdependent whole.

6. The duty of order, not imposed from above, but coming from the individual human heart.

7. The duty of observing the spirit as well as the letter of the Bill of Rights.

Article 1, with its emphasis on the public welfare, contains the essence of the Bill of Duties, just as Amendment One of the Constitution, which grants the freedoms of speech, press, and assemblage, contains the very spirit of the Bill of Rights.

The time is ripe in the United States today for a practical yet religious acceptance of the doctrine of the public welfare in a more complete and understanding manner by each individual than has ever been the case with any nation in any previous time in the world.

All must catch the vision. Workers must learn to look beyond their objective of shorter hours and higher pay to the problem of how best to produce more goods in a balanced way for all workers, and not merely for those who are organized. Farmers must look beyond parity prices to the problem of how best to balance agricultural production and income with city production, so as to bring about the greatest welfare of all in the long run. Businessmen must look beyond the problem of obtaining maximum profits on their invested capital to the job of bringing about a stable increased outflow of goods year after year on a basis which will best serve the welfare of all.

This allegiance to the general good must take the form of a widespread passionate conviction.

But now, I know the readers are beginning to ask me, 'Just what would you have us do?' In reply, I want to give you a formula which has in it more power for the individual's success and the country's success than you will believe until you have tried it. If you are a young person it will prepare channels for you in a manner which will influence your entire future for the better.

Day after day, say to yourself as a kind of prayer, morning, noon, and night: 'My purpose is to do everything possible for the general welfare, for the long-time good of all mankind.'

This may seem vague and general, but, if you really believe it and make it a part of your very being, you will begin to see the results. You will find persons of like mind to work with you; you will find new opportunities opening for service to your fellows; you will be amazed at how much happier, more useful, and more joyous your life will be.

Article 2, the duty to make democracy efficient, has at this moment a special urgency and meaning: production. Production for defense; production to carry out our resolve to aid nations resisting aggression.

Boys who have given up good jobs and are serving in our camps at a fraction of the pay they formerly received are complying with the Bill of Duties. Anyone, whether in business, labor, or agriculture, who interferes with the increased supplies of products so vitally needed, is violating the Bill of Duties.

In the long run, however, making democracy efficient has a wider meaning. I am certain that the best type of administration is to give as many people as possible the feeling that they belong, that they are really wanted, and that they are *participants* in their own right in serving something enormously bigger than they are. Poverty in the midst of plenty, unemployment for men who are able and eager to work—these are deadly enemies of the efficiency as well as the spirit of democracy.

But efficient production is not enough. In peacetime, a central dilemma of modern democratic capitalism is to get the goods we make into the hands of the people who use those goods. Hence, the imperative duty, in Article 3, to use all our intelligence, ingenuity, and good will, in devising government mechanisms to enable our power of consumption to equal our power of production.

Article 4 is the duty to work for an economic democracy to match our political democracy. The Bill of Rights 150 years ago granted individual liberty. It meant much in those days when, if hard times came, men could always strike out for rich lands and broadening frontiers.

But can these rights mean what they should to a modern citizen who, entangled in our complex industrial system, finds himself jobless, hungry, in despair at being unable to provide for his family? You cannot eat the Bill of Rights. And we cannot permit unbalances in the economic structure which make liberty meaningless for millions. Capitalism, with its emphasis on thrift, hard work, and new methods of production, has a great contribution to make to the future. But it must be humanized and geared to the public welfare, until we have economic as well as political democracy.

To aid in this we have the further duty, in Article 5, to study and know our varied people; to know all regions and their vast resources; to appreciate the mighty inheritance which comes from the toil of our forefathers; and to understand the interdependence which bids us all to work together.

This is not easy to do. But if you approach life as I have suggested, with a prayerful daily resolve directed toward the general welfare, you will find yourself curious about everything. You will attract information as a magnet attracts iron. Workers, business-men, and farmers will all tell you how they look at life. If you travel, it will become education. And the hard, dry facts of eco-nomics will come alive to you as you see how they affect the good of your fellow men.

You will see the country as a whole. You will see that every eroded acre, every jobless man, every idle factory, every unused talent, is sinful waste of our inheritance, damaging not only to the individuals involved, but to all of us. And thus a responsi-bility to all of us.

Article 6 is the duty of order. Modern civilization, if it is to continue at all, must have order. In the totalitarian scheme, it is imposed from above. In a democracy, most of the order must and should come from the human heart. The most perfect order in the world will be obtained when the citizens of democracy recognize, instinctively and fully in all of its implications, the fatherhood of God, the brotherhood of man, and the dignity of the individual human soul.

The Bill of Rights guarantees us our rights. But it also clearly implies a duty, Article 7, to observe the spirit as well as the let-ter of these freedoms. It obligates us to use these fairly and wisely, so as not to injure the general welfare. The forefathers who established our rights knew this. Look back at their debates and see their temperate tone, their attitude of fairness.

Too many, today, have forgotten this obligation. They use our precious freedom of speech as a license for wholesale attack against religions, or races, or classes of other good American citi-zens. Others distort fact, misplace emphasis, or stir up dissension and controversy for the mere sake of sensationalism.

Not only the freedom of speech and press, but their purity, accuracy, temperance, and fairness are vital to the information and unity of our democracy.

The above, then, are seven tentative suggestions for a Bill of Duties. I do not ask you to agree with them. I do ask your de-vout thought as to what our duties should be.

For the first time in the history of the world, we have here in the United States the possibility of combining into a harmonious whole all the prerequisites of the good life. The opportunity is ours, but it may not linger. Events abroad or selfishness at home can wreck our dream of building a Kingdom of Heaven here on earth—unless we, every last one of us, look to our duties.

We can't run away. The time of responsibility is upon us.

LIGHT AROUND THE CORNER

By Francis J. Curtis

Man becomes civilized in the measure by which he controls his surroundings. The savage, as is the wild animal of today, was at the mercy of chance at every point of his existence. The slow climb up has been due to the gradual gain of more control over the thousands of variables of living. At an infinitely slow rate, hunting gave way to animal husbandry, the collection of wild grains and fruits to agriculture. Surprisingly, fishing has remained largely in the same uncontrolled state. Though the means of catching fish have been vastly improved, we do not grow fish as we do cattle.

When we look into the future, therefore, we can take this principle as our guide and expect that as some super-ape first picked up a stone, threw it at an animal to kill it, and thereby achieved more than he could with his bare hands, so at some future date some scientist will tie up the last variable and control will be complete.

The savage believed that his world was controlled by thousands of outside influences and spirits, and at times we are inclined to pity his faith. Consider the faith of the farmer; he sows a seed whose requirements he does not know, in a soil of whose suitability he has no idea, to be grown under conditions of chance rain or sun over which he has no control, and he competes for his products with a host of insects, fungi, and animals which have no sense of property rights. He has faith. Slowly we may expect to know the requirements of every type of seed, the hormones and soil constituents, and probably other things that we have never heard of which are necessary for the best life cycle of each plant. We will no longer look at a field and judge

From *News Edition*, 25 February 1941. By permission of the editor.

it by its color and the consistency of its soil but will know exactly what the constituents are and be able to plan for what they should be used. Constantly better insecticides and fungicides are being developed and will be, always becoming more particularized, so that they injure only that for which th y are intended.

An unprejudiced look at a plant would show us that it is not a particularly efficient piece of apparatus for our purposes, however satisfactory it may be for its own. We may conceive of the development of newer varieties with greater yield and the tying down of the factors of taste, ripening, and quality as well as quantity. If true figures on efficiency were applied to agriculture as they are, for instance, to the manufacture of sulfuric acid, the results would be startling. Time was when industry operated with almost as little control as agriculture does now. Are we to visualize, as one by one the controlling factors are discovered and handled properly, the output of the individual plant increased, the necessity for soil as such diminished, that agriculture will gradually pass into a factory stage where there will be no guess and no fourteen-hour day? The infant science of hydroponics is a straw in that direction, even though it is still only pointing.

Did we choose the animals to be domesticated from any other standpoint than chance? Largely no, although it is quite probable that there has been some weeding out by evolution. It would be very surprising if, during the long course of man's history, other animals than those we have now had not been domesticated, but gradually reverted to the wild state. As domesticated animals differ widely from their wild ancestors, it is quite conceivable that other species might have been more satisfactory. Much of the work being done on human health will be applied to animals. They also have their endocrines and vitamin necessities. Like the plants, they have been submitted to too many variables in the way of food and the catching of it, living conditions, and exercise. We may expect controlled feeding and controlled exercise to give maximum yield of the best qualities. At best the efficiency on sirloin steaks is low.

Animal foods are rarely consumed immediately. Much will be done to control the processes of preservation and flavoring.

Much is done to change the properties of cotton on the way from the cotton plant to the afternoon gown. Why should we not, therefore, expect to enhance the flavor and palatability of meats to a degree greater than what chance enzymes or bacteria will perform for reasons and in ways out of our control?

The element of chance has equipped many foods with valuable constituents but sporadically. Man in his processing has oftentimes removed some of those that were there. We hedge on the problem by attempting to achieve the so-called balanced diet, but we must realize that for very large numbers the balanced diet is impossible. We can conceive, therefore, in the future of controlling the necessary constituents of foods, adding those which are needed, and replacing those removed. I can remember at one time trying to sell to ceramic manufacturers who were making cream-colored dishes a clay which when burnt gave a cream color itself, but I found that they would much rather purchase the more expensive white clay and add the necessary coloring matter because thereby they achieved control. So we will be better off by having the health-giving elements added to our foods than by taking a chance that they may be present. Under war conditions in England now, vitamin B and calcium are added to flour by government decree—the straw in the wind is pointing the way. Many people do not really get any pleasure out of eating. This has always appalled me as I have never belonged to that class. We have taken our flavors as we found them, but in the future new and unheard-of flavors will be created. We cannot blandly assume that only those exist which are found in the chance combinations of Nature. We know now that natural dyestuffs were not 10 per cent of the story.

The chemical control of disease is in everyone's consciousness, and now that we expect to be able to see inside the bacteria and watch their reactions under the electron microscope we may expect an even greater extension of control by chemical means. Even if we extrapolate the idea to the nth power and find a specific for each virus or pathological bacterium, we still will have the problem of conditioning our natural defenders, the white corpuscles. The bacterial world also has its evolution and the sudden springing up of a new species might wreak havoc on degen-

erated natural defenders. After all, to some extent, vaccination
is exercise for the white corpuscles, so we may expect that the
chemists will not quite have it all their own way. All of this indicates that medicine will be far more preventative than curative. The tendency has been greatly in that direction and will
be increased until to be sick will be something of a social disgrace like poor teeth. The act of Fate idea will be demoted.

We have some funny quirks and one of them is on standardization. Maybe we are in an intermediate stage of evolution but
the man who would not think of asking the Ford Motor Co. to
give him a special car, separate and distinct in all but the bare
essentials from every other Ford car, will see red if he is expected to inhabit a house which has any identity with another.
If he were asked to wear a toga instead of a business suit he
would go wild. His idea of clothing is that it should be exactly
the same in all but the most minor points as what other men
wear. This, of course, does not apply to women. The individually built house is as much an anachronism as the shoemaker
going to the slaughterhouse to get a piece of skin to make a
single pair of shoes.

Whatever psychological advantages they may have, windows
are inefficient lighting and ventilating equipment. We may expect far greater control along these lines in the future and can
conceive of the elimination even of dusting. Focused lighting
will be decreased; we can conceive of fluorescent panels spreading a diffused sufficient light in all parts of the room with no
excess in any one spot. Power may be obtained directly by transmission through the air; one electrical company is already ex-
perimenting with such apparatus. The materials of construction
will be lighter and stronger. The piling up of brick and concrete
will be outmoded. Houses and buildings will be fitted together
by standard sections. Interiors will be of plastic, washable and
even exchangeable. All intricate shapes, carvings, etc., will be
made by plastic processes, even if they are of metals, through the
powder technique. We may even conceive that the glass industry
may solve its problem of plasticization, even as has the plastics
industry. Glass fabrics and other fireproof and mothproof textiles may be expected to play a greater part in interior decora-

tion. Corrosion will be eliminated by metal treatment, new alloys, or coatings, and even inorganic paints may be expected. There is an astonishing lack of use of roofs, particularly for summer living. Buildings should not reduce the amount of available surface area of a city.

The main sources of clothing, cotton and wool, are now variable within wide limits. There are over a dozen grades of wool on an individual sheep's back, and even these vary with the breed and history of the animal. Such basic variations cannot be tolerated in the future. We will see the inevitable growth of controlled fibers of standard sizes, grades, and strengths. The complicated plaiting process, called 'weaving,' goes back to prehistoric baskets. We may expect the problems of softness, strength, pliability, and porosity of fabrics made by sheeting and matting methods to be brought to a point where such fabrics will compete. New finishes for textiles, modifying their properties profoundly, are in existence and will give us a control over the wear, feel, and handle of textiles which we have never before experienced. Leather is even more variable than wool and is another example of the race having been forced to be satisfied with what was on hand. Plastics are moving into the shoe industry and their controlled qualities may give them an advantage over the aleatory process of leather making. The use of wool and skins will not be eliminated, but the competition from something that is better will force greater control and standardization. We might even conceive of their utilization to replace cotton linters in the viscose process for rayon. Many complicated chemicals could be made at the cost per pound of a pair of shoes.

Feet protected by some type of shoe were once the only means of traveling. We have progressed far from that, but traveling is still a very uncomfortable process. Too many things are out of control. We have bumps, whirls, sways, bangs, and accidents. Stratosphere flying may solve many of these problems, and we may conceive of trains at 100 miles an hour running as smoothly as moving stairways. Train ennui will be eliminated. Is there anything more discouraging-looking than the row of passengers in a Pullman car? The automobile is a masterpiece of gadgetry.

The trend is already toward simplification. Plastic unbreakable bodies and undentable fenders will contribute to safety of person and purse.

Communication between individuals may be freed from dependence upon wires, and it may be possible to talk to anyone at any time, anywhere. We will look back on the telephone as we do on the early radios with their complications of A, B, and C batteries. Television will change habits profoundly. For most people great crowded spectacles will be eliminated. Newspapers will become more and more commentators rather than reporters. There should be a great increase in sports since there seems to a principle that necessities when eliminated are apotheosized into sports. This has happened with hunting, fishing, running, rowing, archery, and horse racing. May we expect the next candidate to be farming, carpentering, and masonry?

Entertainment will be one of our largest businesses. We will complete the full cycle back to individual listening to radio, particularly in public places. The Pullman lounge car will be no longer filled with the raucous noises particularly pleasing to porters. Books will be written for reproduction for sight corresponding to radio for sound rather than for printing and binding between covers. Most of our pleasures are now concerned with these two senses. We have an almost untouched field for developing entertainment for taste, touch, and smell.

The means of control will be known, but who will control the controllers? Through all history the world has been run largely by the men of action—the warriors. From time to time and for short periods the thinkers, until recently only the priests, have exercised authority. The more controls are achieved over living the more possible is absolute rule and the better it can paint its picture, yet once let absolutism be in operation for an appreciable length of time it will sow the seeds of its own destruction and that of the controls it has wielded. This is the research problem of the future.

A BROADER BASE FOR SCIENCE

By Anton J. Carlson

THE mysteries of the starry heavens and the urgency of human pain appear to have been among the earliest incentives to man's venture into the realm of science. At any rate, the earliest written records of man's experimental and rational gropings toward understanding are in astronomy and human disease. An engineer may challenge this statement. It is likely that primitive man felled a tree across a stream for a footbridge long before he gave rational attention to the machinery of his body in health and in disease. But such primitive engineering feats are probably on the level with today's monkeys' using any available box or stool to reach a banana.

The men of the later Stone Age had acquired not a little engineering skill, if not engineering science, in the making of tools, in the construction of conveyances for water transport, in the erection of buildings for their leaders and temples to their gods. But these achievements seem to have been a mere flotsam on the current of life. At any rate, these tools and these buildings are now mere fossils. What these ancient engineers knew, and how they acquired their understanding, and why their early science failed to be perpetuated—all of this knowledge is gone with the wind, though the race endures.

The same comments can be made about the greater and more recent achievements in applied science of the ancient Babylonians, Egyptians, and Aztecs. Some men among these peoples must have had a respectable amount of understanding and skill in mechanical engineering, some grasp of the forces of nature. All this knowledge was lost. Nothing but ruins, like the fossils of earlier times, and the mummies of the ancient dead remain to

From *The Technology Review*, July 1941. By permission of the editor.

stir the curiosity of the archaeologist. The reason for the total disappearance of understandings of nature and the loss of skills in modifying the environment does not seem to be lack of written records, or the complete destruction or dispersion of the people themselves. We find instances of the same total failure of acquired scientific understandings to survive in more recent times, when written records were made. I may cite one example from ancient Egypt and one from the China of but yesterday.

The Smith papyrus, translated by the Egyptologist, James H. Breasted, is estimated by him to date back some five thousand to seven thousand years before Christ. The original and ancient side of this remarkable script deals with medicine—with injuries of various parts of the body and how to treat them. The description of the symptoms of the injuries, as well as the recommendations for treatment, discloses a remarkable amount of knowledge of human anatomy and human physiology. To be sure, on the reverse side of this papyrus are recipes for quack medical remedies of all sorts, formulas for sorcery, incantation against disease, and so on. But I am concerned here with the original truly scientific medical document. As far as we know now, this early knowledge of anatomy and physiology as applied to human injuries was completely lost. It therefore had apparently no effect on the subsequent development of science and medicine in Greece or in Egypt. We may presume that the knowledge was confined to the few. It was in the ivory tower, with no broad base in the life stream of the people of Egypt.

No surprise should be registered at the medical quackery and the religio-medical superstitions recorded on the reverse side of the Smith papyrus. Possibly this ancient period of relative medical understanding was followed by a longer period of medical dark ages in ancient Egypt. But, even if this was the case, medical superstition and quackery are as tenacious of life as are other customs of the jungle: Witness the persistence and flourishing of similar practices in our own day side by side with the results of three hundred years of medical science, medical research, and scientific medical practice. Indeed, misconceptions, frauds, and quackery may flourish in the realms of medicine for a thousand years because of human hope and human credulity, as is instanced by the taking of powdered tiger bone for heart disease by countless generations in the Orient. The mistaken or fraudulent claim of the chemist that he has synthesized a new compound, or similar baseless claims of the engineer that he has devised a new and sure method of smoke control are, in the nature of things, more quickly deleted from the human scene.

My next example may cause surprise, since some may not be aware that vaccination against smallpox was discovered by the Chinese several hundred years before Jenner and the milkmaid in the then Merry England. The Chinese vaccinated effectively against smallpox by taking the dried pox scale with its attenuated virus from a patient and rubbing this powdered scale on the mucous membrane of the nose or mouth. A mild case of smallpox develops, which gives immunity. In the same way, somehow, they had discovered the efficacy of dried, or powdered, seaweed—or even fresh seaweed—and its iodine against simple goiter. Certainly these discoveries did not spread to any extent even in China, though recorded in the Chinese books on drugs and therapy. The discoveries, really scientific discoveries, remained in the ivory tower and for all practical purposes were lost to the world.

These examples from the past do seem to show that, for the endurance and the effective value of science, a broader base than the ivory tower is indicated. The next question is this: Is such a broad base possible? Is the average man or woman—the common man—capable of understanding, of being conditioned to, the spirit and the method of science? The fact that to date the significant contributions to science, the important new discoveries in science, the great generalizations in science, are the work of the relatively few conspicuous leaders in science, has led to the easily accepted view that the rank and file of mankind are either not able or not sufficiently interested in science to understand and follow its spirit and method.

To my way of thinking, nothing about the scientific method is so abstruse or mystical that it cannot be understood and mastered by every man and woman of average mentality. Conspicuous use of the scientific method in securing new understanding is a different matter. For some time to come, that function, that privilege, will probably be only for the few with sufficient curiosity, ingenuity, and drive to defy all obstacles.

As things seem to me, it is going to be more difficult to condition society to the spirit of science, that is, to absolute truthfulness. The primitive thalamus has as yet too much influence on the conspicuously human part of the brain: the cerebral cortex. Armchair dicta, social and political dogmatism, pretense at knowledge and understanding, call for less work and less worry than does the establishment of facts by adequately controlled experiments and rechecked observations.

I am a physiologist, not a prophet. According to William James there are, still untapped, 'lakelets of energy' in the human brain machinery, ready for more intense, if not more intelligent or better, human behavior. Maybe so, but I doubt it as a universal proposition. We can, however, grasp the scientific method without tapping these hypothetical lakelets. Wherever we go, the *going forward* will not be speedy, judging from the rate of man's evolution. It may be too speedy if the path leads down. As a Roman poet put it long, long ago, *'Facilis descensus Averno,'*—easy the road down unto hell. Our esteemed colleagues, the philosophers, have a perennial debate on the question: 'Is man a *rational* animal?' Is there, as yet, any evidence of any activity of any man that can be labeled 'pure reason'? Strict definition of terms and a small dose of the theory of relativity would in all probability terminate this debate, with the following conclusion: The behavior of the average normal man, including the man of science, is relatively rational in the sense of awareness of facts, motives, and choice, during varying parts of his hours awake. But probably nothing like pure reason (that is, behavior machinery free from conditioning and from affective mental states) is found in any human action.

If our citizens understood the scientific way of establishing facts and the identity of the scientific spirit with honesty and truth, our leaders would not get to first base by promising us complete freedom from want and complete freedom from fear, through any political, social, or economic order. The dreamers of the past put that goal in heaven. It can be approached but never reached on earth by providing freedom to work and to enjoy in full the fruits of one's labor. For it is certain that such calamities in nature as earthquakes, tornadoes, floods, droughts, consuming fires, and killing frosts will create both want and fear among men in the coming years. Some accidents, disease, and pain, some greed, hate, and violence will be with us to the end of time. It is the duty and the privilege of science to decrease the want and fear created by man. It is the duty and the privilege of science to inject understanding, reason, and approximate justice as factors in the social evolution of tomorrow. To do so, I think science must descend from its ivory tower and reach the understanding of the common man.

Since science and scientific research are calling for more and more financial and moral support from society, it would seem to go without saying that in return science owes society the service of education in science so that such support may be given with joy and intelligence. To my way of thinking, a broader base for science in society is urgent and needed: (a) for the persistence and progress of science itself, and (b) for the advancement, safety, and happiness of man. The first point is of no consequence if the second is not true. But obviously if science does contribute to the advancement, safety, and happiness of man, the persistence and progress of science itself become highly desirable. My second proposition is challenged by many people who confuse the primary function of science, which is the increasing of human understanding, with the misuse by stupid man of the practical inventions derived from our increasing scientific knowledge. In the minds of some people, this misuse has reached the state of calling for a moratorium on science for the welfare of man. These people charge science with the following misdemeanors, if not actual major crimes: (1) Science facilitates violence, robbery, and murder. (2) Science promotes and brutalizes war. (3) Science promotes or intensifies unemployment. (4) Science speeds the depletion of some of our natural resources. (5) Science creates or promotes industrial disease of man.

Needless to say, the gun, the knife, the automobile, and some modern drugs do give the individual bent on crime a wider range, a wider scope. With regard to science and war, however, neither science itself, its method or its spirit, nor scientists as a class can be held responsible for war, ancient or modern. No one denies that modern gadgets, developed out of our scientific understanding, render war more destructive and brutal today. But let me call your attention to the attitude of most of the men of science on this issue by quoting from the minute adopted in 1939 by the American Association for the Advancement of Science. This declaration reads as follows: '. . . *Science is wholly independent of national boundaries and races and creeds and can flourish permanently only where there is peace and intellectual freedom. . . .*'

As to unemployment, I think President Karl Compton made clear not very long ago that, while some inventions may produce temporary unemployment or dislodgment of labor, the total effect of new inventions is to increase employment of labor. Certainly, the growth of cities, inhabited by people not directly engaged in securing sustenance from the soil, would have been absolutely impossible without the inventions stemming from science, both industrial and transportational.

I think the last two charges against science are the most serious, though they reflect less on science and more on man, more on human nature, human selfishness, and human myopia. I think there is no doubt that some gadgets developed through practical applications of scientific knowledge render it possible for myopic man to deplete and waste natural resources at a rate that could not occur by the aid of the bare hands, the crowbar, the spade, the ox, the horse, or the mule. As an example I am thinking of the strip mining of soft coal in my own state of Illinois, where tens of thousands of acres of fertile soil, soil rendered fertile by the processes of nature during perchance more than 100,000 years, are ruined for agriculture, for the production of food and clothing for man, in order to get a few tons of soft coal mined at less expense, for a few pennies of profit for a few individuals. To me, this is not an indictment of science or the application of science; it is an indictment of individual myopia and of social and economic statesmanship in our democracy.

That the applications of science in the growth of modern industries have created a serious individual public health problem under the head of industrial disease, is known to all. Our modern science of medicine is effectively combating this menace, although it is not entirely under control as yet. A sobering thought is the fact that, in the development of industries due to our expanding understanding of nature, man is increasingly and suddenly exposed to chemical substances formerly unknown to him in the whole history of the race or is exposed to substances of injurious potentialities in larger and larger amounts. If we could really establish a broader base for science in society, and by science I include the science of modern medicine and modern preventive medicine, we should soon effectively control this growing hazard. At present we go at things too blindly and we (society and the medical profession) assume that as long as the individual exposed to industrial hazards is not actually sick enough to call a doctor, he is not really injured. Frequently we have discovered, and we shall probably increasingly discover, that this is not the true situation.

To refer again to the charge that science makes war or makes war more violent, I think we may admit that, unless the spirit of science—honesty coupled with the sense of justice and fair play —manages to keep pace with our expanding scientific knowledge and its practical applications, man may destroy himself in days not so very far away, and the insects will rule the world without having to fight man for its possession.

Science is still in the ivory tower to the extent that our laborers, our farmers, and even our leaders in politics, trade, and industry do not understand or at least do not follow the scientific method. Hence I insist that ours is not yet an age of science, for the character of the age is writ by man's behavior. Men are still driven by greed and confused by guile, rather than guilded by reason and justice based on our expanding scientific knowledge. I said on another occasion, but the thought bears repeating here, that science has greatly enlarged man's understanding, conquered many of his diseases, lengthened his life, multiplied his joys, decreased his fears, and added much to his physical comforts and powers. Man may use these and other achievements for a greater social injury instead of for a further social advance. Science is specifically human, in that it stems from the innate curiosity of all men and the conspicuously plastic brains of the ablest, if not the noblest, of our fellows. If this be so, then the scientific method and its products cannot be, in any fundamental and permanent sense, in conflict with human nature, though our present human society, product of a past dominated by greed, force, and fear, may be and is in conflict with the scientific method. Whether science and the scientific method, even on the broader social base for which I plead, can contrive survival values equal if not superior to the blind forces of nature which shaped man's past, is as yet in the laps of the gods. Still, we cannot deny the possibility, and we *will* nurse the hope, that the hairy ape who somehow lost his tail, who grew a brain worth having, who built speech and song out of a hiss and a roar, and who stepped out of the cave to explore and master the universe, may some day conquer his own irrational and myopic behavior toward his kin.

I think we can say, even in the face of current fear and pessimism, that during the ups and downs of past ages, man has through science gradually acquired more understanding and hence more freedom from fear, more dignity, greater kindness, and a clearer conception of justice. Despite the fact that for the moment 'the bird of sorrow' is not only flying over our heads but is actually nesting in our hair—to borrow a Chinese proverb —that bird will not nest in our hair forever, even though a blackout on the light of science is decreed in every land. When we have achieved the broader base for science in the understanding of the common man, the method of science will slowly but surely help to make life more intelligent, toil more cheerful, fear, hatred, pain, and tears less prevalent in our lives. If in any place or time the insane violence of war renders the pursuit of science impossible and the scientific method submerged and forgotten, it will be rediscovered in better days by better men. At least up till now man has demonstrated his ability to survive and to reassert his manhood and his intelligence.

The establishment of a broader base for science is too great a task for the handful of scientists in our universities and in our institutions for scientific research, even were these men agreed that this is both an important and a desirable goal. What is called for is the co-operative effort of all men and women with sufficient training in science to comprehend and follow the scientific method. These are principally the large armies of physicians, industrial chemists, and engineers, and the scattering of competent teachers of science in our secondary schools. Perchance the newly born Association of Scientific Workers will lend a hand. All teachers in our secondary schools, were they themselves conditioned in the spirit of science and aware of the scientific method, could be the spearhead of this advance. The scientific method, the achievement of understanding by controlled experience, has not yet had much of a chance in our formal education, on any level.

We pride ourselves, I think without good grounds, that our age is the 'age of science.' As Arthur H. Compton recently put it, ours is an age of science only in the sense that the applications of science, the fruits of science, influence our external mode of living, both in peace and in war, to a much greater extent than they have at any other period in human history. But even today guile and deceit, violence and war, hate and vanity—the very antithesis of science, the very negations of the method and the spirit of science—are just as rampant as in the days of the cave man and the saber-toothed tiger.

When the twilight beckons men of my years, we still have our children, we still have our dreams. I dream of a day when through social experience in science and justice we shall actually put the principles of democracy to work within our land—in politics, in industry, in trade, in education; when understanding and kindness will more than hold their own against guile and greed; when force and violence are replaced by conference, compromise, and approximate justice in all our domestic relations. When that day is at hand in our own land, our example will be a greater impetus to science, peace, and justice in other lands than are our present speeches and our lend and lease of the implements of violence and war to all present and potential democracies of the world. For then we at least will be strong enough to fear no ill wind from across any ocean, strong enough to maintain our own ways of life, a life worth living for a million years.

III

'From an Unchallengeable Eminence'

A GREAT style of hero draws equally all classes, all the extremes of society, till we say the very dogs believe in him. We have had such examples in this country . . . Abraham Lincoln is perhaps the most remarkable example of this class that we have seen,—a man who was at home and welcome with the humblest, and with a spirit and a practical vein in the times of error that commanded the admiration of the wisest. His heart was as great as the world, but there was no room in it to hold the memory of a wrong.

RALPH WALDO EMERSON, *Greatness*, 1875

BECAUSE he has cared so much, he has made others care too. That quality, it is important to note, has been characteristic of every significant President in the record. It is true of Jefferson, of Jackson, of Lincoln, of Theodore Roosevelt, of Woodrow Wilson. They were all positive Presidents. They had a policy to recommend which seemed to their generation a challenge . . . The leader's passion has communicated itself to his followers. He has aroused the dynamic of democracy, an energy when it is aroused, more powerful and pervasive than the dynamic of any other form of state.

HAROLD J. LASKI, *The American Presidency*, 1940

THE PRESIDENT AS LEADER

A CONSTITUTION works well when men are in large agreement over the ends it should achieve; but their minds must be directed to the definition of those ends. And that there may be clarity in the direction, it is essential that there be leadership of a kind that no one but the President is in a position to supply. If he has the gift of leadership, if he has imagination, if, not least, he has the power, so supremely possessed by Lincoln, of understanding his fellowmen, he speaks in America from an unchallengeable eminence. Whatever voice is drowned amid the babel of tongues, his, granted these qualities, can always be heard. Even today there are phrases of Washington and Jefferson that remain a constant part of the national tradition; and some of the more vital of their gestures shape the habits to which all Americans must conform. Lincoln's brief utterance at Gettysburg has transcended all national boundaries; and wherever a civilized tradition remains, its echo still lives in the minds and hearts of men.

HAROLD J. LASKI, *The American Presidency*, 1940
By permission of Harper and Brothers, publishers.

HOW AMERICANS CHOOSE THEIR HEROES

By Dixon Wecter

HERO-WORSHIP answers an urgent American need. The fan and
the autograph hunter, now imitated elsewhere, are as native to
the United States as the catbird and the Catawba grape. To fix
our relation with greatness by means of a signature in an album,
a lock of hair, a photograph, or a baseball that has scored a
home run; to haunt stage doors and entries to locker-rooms; to
pursue our favorites with candid cameras and sound recorders,
invading their meditations and their honeymoons—this passion
has made us the premier nation of hero-worshippers. Others, of
course, have like impulses. The phlegmatic Cockney collects
Famous Cricketers from the coupons in cigarette packets; the
Spaniard helps to carry off a great matador on his shoulder.
But only in the United States has the greeter become a profession and the ovation a fine art.

Homage to heroes is a vital part of our patriotism. Patriotism
springs traditionally from love of place; it is a filial relation toward mother country or fatherland. The earth upon which our
feet are planted, from which we draw our livelihood, becomes an
over-soul, the greatest hero of our national loyalties. The 'patria'
of the ancient Romans, 'this precious stone set in the silver sea'
of Shakespeare's England, and 'la belle France' of many generations, sprang from this piety of place. Even the 'blood and soil'
of current Nazi mythology and the 'magnetic mountain' of Communist mysticism are attempts to build on the old foundation;
while these new masters of Europe, on the negative side, seek to
destroy the folk integrity of those whom they have conquered by
uprooting whole populations. But with us, in the New World,

From Dixon Wecter, *The Hero in America*, 1941. By permission of Charles
Scribner's Sons, publishers.

there are certain differences. We love the broad span of America, and sing of our affection for its rocks and rills, its woods and templed hills. But we are a restless people, moving from New York to San Francisco as our job demands, and in old age deserting the windswept homestead for a sunny bungalow in Florida. We have lost something of that warm devotion to the soil which stirred the embattled farmers of 1776, or even the agrarian days of Andrew Jackson and young Lincoln.

In 1820 about 93 per cent of all Americans lived in the country, 60 per cent as late as 1900, but only 43 per cent a generation later. Even in 1838 Francis Grund, a visitor from overseas, remarked that an American does not love his birthplace with the ardor of a Frenchman or an Englishman: 'an American's country is his understanding; he carries it with him wherever he goes, whether he emigrates to the shores of the Pacific or the Gulf of Mexico; his home is wherever he finds minds congenial to his own.' His patriotism is apt to be curiously abstract. Save for old-fashioned groups in New England and in the South, American loyalty in the pure geographical sense is a trifle cold and bloodless. Even the majority of our forty-eight states, as a Frenchman lately observed, are bounded by rectangles that suggest plane geometry more than *esprit de corps*. However much we love and would fight for America, as a concept and a way of life, our feeling for place is hardly more than a booster's slogan—such a one as used to hang, in electric lights, over the main street of a Texas town known to the writer: 'Greenville—The Blackest Land, The Whitest People.' With the passing of time, the floods of immigration and migration, the rise of cities and railroads and highways, our ancient roots into the earth of America have had an anchorage less firm. To many, the United States as geography means many interchangeable places where one may hang his hat. It is a continent and civilization too vast for the warm immediate embrace possible to the patriot of Patrick Henry's day, when one's farm stood well enough for America, and its defense brought to mind the squirrel rifle that lived beside the chimney.

Because of these things, our collective symbols—the Flag, the Declaration of Independence, the Constitution, and the touchstone of our heroes—are more precious than such institutions are

in the Old World. They nourish our sense of national continuity. Not even Englishmen appeal to their Magna Charta
with the fervor that we—conservatives, liberals, radicals alike—
appeal to the Constitution. With a faith not untouched by
pathos, we accept its framers, as Thomas Jefferson described
them, as 'demigods,' and their work as without flaw. Its guarantees, in a sense, mean America to us. In an earlier day, when
political oratory flourished in the barbecue era, and the defiance of tyranny seemed more glorious than the unity symbolized by the Constitution, our most prized document was the
Declaration of Independence. Likewise, the Supreme Court,
standing for a 'fundamental law' conceded to be more stable
than the fickle will of the people, is another sacred symbol of
government—as Theodore Roosevelt in 1912, after advocating a
popular referendum on judicial decisions, and the second Roosevelt in 1937, by proposing to pack the Court, discovered to their
surprise. Recent scholars, ranging from the playfully cynical
Thurman Arnold to the soberly sympathetic Ralph Gabriel,
have written about these symbols. Emblems even more homely,
like Uncle Sam, have had a great influence upon our national
character. Lincoln's Secretary of State, Seward, told of a man
just after the Revolution who had put up a Liberty pole in his
village. Neighbors asked him why, wasn't he free enough now?
And he answered, 'What is liberty without a pole?' . . .

The people's choice of heroes for America has been prevail-
ingly sound; our major favorites are those any nation might be
proud of. They go toward vindicating the whole democratic
theory of careers open to talents. We believe that character is
more important than brains. Hard work, tenacity, enterprise,
and firmness in the face of odds are the qualities that Americans
most admire, rather than originality or eloquence of tongue and
pen.

The hero must be a man of good will and also a good neighbor, preferably something of a joiner. Of the solitudes and
lonely isolations of a great man like Lincoln the public has little
conception. It likes to think of its idol as simple in greatness.
Love of the soil, of dogs and horses and manual hobbies and fishing, is better understood than absorption in art, literature, and

music. (The public distrusts Presidents who are photographed fishing in their store clothes.) The hero must not lose touch with his birthplace and origins, however humble; the atmosphere of small towns and front-porch campaigns, cultivated by so many candidates for President, pays tribute to this demand. 'I really believe there are more attempts at flattering the farmers than any other class,' Lincoln as candidate for President remarked at the Wisconsin State Fair, 'the reason for which I cannot perceive, unless it be that they cast more votes than any other.' Also, the touch of versatility and homely skill is applauded in a hero. Thomas Jefferson is remembered less as the eighteenth-century virtuoso than as an inventor of gadgets from which he plainly got a great deal of fun. 'Tinkering' is American. European lads —like Henrich Steffens growing up in Denmark, and Michael Pupin in a Serbian village—have testified to the fascination that Franklin, 'wiser than all the wise men of Idvor,' held for them. The hero must do things better than the common folk, but his achievements (unlike those of the artist, philosopher, and pure scientist) must lie open to everyman's comprehension. It is well, too, that the labels of the hero conform to those of the group, so that identification between him and the majority can more easily be made: for example, all of our major idols have been both Anglo-Saxon and Protestant.

Bravery, honesty, strength of character are the stuff for hero-worship. At the boy's level, this worship gravitates toward the doer of spectacular deeds; on the average adult level, toward the wielder of power; and in the eyes of a more critical judgment, toward idealism and moral qualities. The most universal hero is he who can fill all these specifications. This, by the many shapes of their courage, integrity, and strength, Washington and Lincoln and Lee are able to do. But Jefferson the sedentary man, Franklin the opportunist, and Andrew Jackson the rough-hewn soldier fail to satisfy everybody. Upon a still lower rank, men like Daniel Boone and Crockett and Buffalo Bill and Edison remain almost juvenile heroes. They do not have all the dimensions of our few supreme symbols. Was it not Emerson who suggested that we Americans were the shattered pieces of a great mould?

Our most powerful hero epics center about our leaders. What, then, in the final analysis do Washington, Franklin, Jefferson, Jackson, Lincoln, and in a provisional verdict Wilson and the Roosevelts have in common? Among them lie many differences. In heredity, economic origins, training, skill, temperament, party affiliations, and attachment to specific policies they may seem as diverse as we could find by sifting the nation from Atlantic to Pacific. All save perhaps Washington were 'liberals' by the gauge of their times—and Washington, one must not forget, was an arch political rebel, who even in old age sought to balance his conservatism by an honest effort to be nonpartisan. (And even Washington has slowly waned before the warmer humanity of Lincoln.) What is their common denominator?

All of them, the people believe, loved America more deeply than any selfish consideration. The hero as made in America is a man who has the power and yet does not abuse it. He is the practical demonstration of romantic democracy. Washington is most sublime because, after winning our freedom, he refused a crown, military dictatorship, and every personal reward. Lee is grandest because he did what he thought was his duty, failed under heartbreaking odds, and then with gentleness did his best to repair all hate and malice. Lincoln is most appealing because, in the conduct of that same desperate war which gave him the power of a czar, he never forgot his love for the common people of North and South. More clearly than the great heroes of Europe, military and political, ours stand for a progress concept. They spring from stock that has bred schemes both wise and foolish—with its talk about the pursuit of happiness, the more abundant life, and the American Dream. None of these epic leaders left the Republic as he found it—although to avoid disturbing a single stick or stone seems to have been the policy of men like James Buchanan, Chester A. Arthur, William McKinley, and Calvin Coolidge. At times, to be sure, the people themselves have wanted no change, felt no urge to take on fresh responsibility in the national sphere. In eras like theirs, nothing is added to the stature of American ideals—such as civil liberty, equality of opportunity, faith in the average man, social justice, respect for the rights of weaker nations and for the good

estate of democracy throughout the earth. A Chief Executive
may then be called to office who rules as a minor Augustus over
a gilded age, or serves as the genial host at a great barbecue. But
ten years hence he is not likely to be remembered as a great
man, or even as a symbol worth keeping.

Our heroes, we believe, are cast in a different mould. Their
ruling passion, as we see it, is a sense of duty, alert to the best
among the stirring impulses of their time, and able to make
that impulse effective. They translate the dream into act. The
supreme leader is he who can hitch the great bandwagon to the
star of American idealism.

Men become tribal heroes when the voice of a nation says to
them, 'Well done, thou good and faithful servant.' Usually this
happens in a man's lifetime, though an occasional minor figure
like Paul Revere owes his fame to the postscripts of poets, orators, or biographers. In general, futurity concerns itself not with
discovering new heroes but with seeing old ones in a more symbolic aspect or hewing them to new requirements. Of the major
symbol, the Lincoln or the Washington, it may be said—as the
skeptic said of God—that he is the noblest work of man.

In a democracy, where the favorite should rightly be the people's choice—and not the elect of hereditary honors or of a myth-
making 'party' leadership—he is an index to the collective mind
and heart. His deeds and qualities are those which millions en-
dorse. He speaks words that multitudes want said; he stands for
things that they are often willing to spill their blood for. The
hero is he whom every American should wish to be. His legend
is the mirror of the folk soul. Of course that mirror is sometimes clouded by the breath of fame, by sheer publicity. In this
age, above all others, newspapers and newsreels and radio and
the mechanisms of ovation have such power, in making or breaking the idol of the moment, that fresh irony has been given the
old saying, 'Heroes are not born but made.' Yet, in the long
run, their power is less than is often supposed. The tumult and
the shouting dies, the captains and the kings depart—and posterity, across the dusty valleys of time, will probably deal out
fair justice to those who served their day with honesty and

strength, along with those who served only themselves and the baser instincts of their time. Lincoln fares better than Napoleon, in satisfying the eternal human hunger for a man to admire. Over the centuries, the Galilean is far greater than Caesar.

The foreground of our history is still shifting, uncertain. Washington and Franklin and Jefferson and Lincoln remain giants, symbols so durable that they could be broken only by an America which deliberately renounced its great past, its independence and democratic faith, in favor of alien mythologies like those of Marx and Hitler. The approval of these American symbols is clear. What hero-worship of the future will say about Woodrow Wilson and Edison and Lindbergh, about Theodore and Franklin Roosevelt, is far less certain. In the changing skies of our republic some stars will set, while other lights seen to be planets will glow more brightly as the heavens become bare around them. Meanwhile, today seems always less heroic than yesterday. 'In those days there were giants,' men keep saying, curiously blind to the fact that human potentiality remains much the same, and that so long as a nation has faith worth fighting for, new crises will breed new champions. Carlyle, sweeping the sky of history for great men ancient and medieval, overlooked the nearer phenomenon of Abraham Lincoln. The Scottish sage's American friend, Emerson, another philosopher of hero-worship a little dazzled by Napoleon, did not begin to take the measure of Lincoln's greatness until it had been given perspective by a martyr's death. It usually happens thus.

Also, over the longer reaches of our history, there are visible changes of taste and spirit in our hero-worship as well as in our patriotism. In the era of oratory from Patrick Henry to Webster, and of biography from John Marshall's *Washington* to Randall's *Jefferson,* our heroes were treated with grandiosity. This was the Silver Age of our patriotism. Forum and pulpit, Fourth of July and school declamation, poetry and fiction, the art of battle-scenes and equestrian statues and pioneer memorials, enshrined them in a vaguely classical and nebulous respect. One could hardly see the hero for the incense. Then came the age of sentiment, anticipated early by Weems but not reaching its flower until the 1840's and after—'the sentimental years,' as

Douglas Branch called them. The Lincoln cult, sprouting after the Civil War, drew much sustenance from it. The mothers and the infancy of heroes, their domestic lives and their tender hearts, supplanted the old accent on grandeur. Patriotism as taught by the McGuffey readers and by children's lives of the great, stressed homely simple goodness. This idealization marched abreast of the humanitarian spirit in Victorian times: heroes were good to the poor, they cherished children and dumb animals. The great man entered, not to the fanfare of trumpets, but to the still sad music of humanity. Love of country and its traditions blended into the love of home. Longfellow became our greatest patriotic bard, while across the pages of Josiah Gilbert Holland and other Lincoln biographers sometimes one could not see the hero for the tears.

Meanwhile, in the workaday world, in the long fat years of peace that followed Appomattox, the high inspiration of patriotism and hero-worship began to ebb. Politicians and schoolmasters continued to pay it lip-service, but there were too many distractions to keep it at the pitch of intensity a new nation had maintained for a generation after the Revolution. Our frontier was gone, and our expansion completed; of the international scene we were not yet aware. Jefferson's 'choice country, with room enough,' occupied us rather than Jefferson's idealism. A nation building railways and dams and factories tended to forget its heroic temper. We neglected even to idealize the White House and its prerogatives of leadership; in this era Lord Bryce, writing his *American Commonwealth,* penned a chapter called 'Why Great Men Are Not Chosen Presidents.' Our most exalted soldier, General Grant, was drowned in materialism. At the end of the century the Spanish-American War, a kind of military *fête champêtre,* gave us a few easy heroes but stirred no more than a ripple on the surface of our national life. Here and there, in the first decade of a new century, the torpor was broken by the demands of a rather naive imperialism and of an equally naive (though more lastingly significant) crusade toward social justice. Then the World War I brought back a breath of our strenuous past, and for two or three years we tried to remember the idiom of a nobler language. Song-writers and poets and 'four-minute men' called for high endeavor. Many Americans, like Rupert Brooke in England, thanked God that the old smugness was gone, and with T. E. Hulme thrilled to 'the long note of the bugle.'

But more quickly than ever before, under the post-war disillusion, we renounced all that we had fought for. Turning to normalcy, we felt ashamed of a tingle in the spine at the invocation of Washington and Lincoln or a catch at the throat upon seeing the Stars and Stripes. Justifying ourselves for deserting a world not yet made safe for democracy, we began to debunk our heroes and their traditions. Some followed the path of sheer cynicism. Others—led by social historians, explaining that there were no great men but only movements, and by 'progressive educators' filled with what Professor George S. Counts has lately and ruefully called 'irrational optimism'—eased us away from the concept of patriotism. Patriotism was nothing but a conditioned reflex. 'O beautiful my Country' was nothing but a form of 'institutional behavior.' It had been taught us, subtly, by various groups—chiefly the patrioteers who were buttressing the capitalist system. Patriotism was class propaganda, or, as Ambrose Bierce had defined it in the days when he worked for Hearst, 'combustible rubbish ready to the torch of any one ambitious to illuminate his name.' Any one who gave an arm or leg for his country was, as a nationally spread poster proclaimed, 'a sucker.' Heroes were bunk. There was no glamour in American history, only class struggle. These teachings had a powerful effect upon at least two groups. The first were immigrants, or the children of immigrants, whose feeling for American heroes and American tradition was naturally undernourished. The second were boys and girls of high school and college age, who decided they would never fall for the bait of nationalism as their fathers had fallen. If the world in general, and America in particular, came to grief, it was no skin off their backs. Today a new phase of the cycle has begun. Many of the elder social historians are growing aware, as Walter Lippmann observes, that they have been sentimentalists, 'men who wanted to enjoy the good life without earning it.' Their hope in the Soviet experiment, for example, has been utterly destroyed. They are beginning to grope for the traditions of our great past. They are about to decide that the heroes bred by that tradition are not jingoist symbols. They wonder if something is not to be said for the bitter, but tonic, taste of sacrifice. The prophets of intellectual youth have done some recanting: Walter Millis has concluded that there are roads to war not paved by Morgan dollars, while overseas John Strachey has enlisted in the R.A.F. in the coming struggle for power. Youth is still critical of war hysteria—and indeed would one wish to exchange youth's new sense of realism for the provincial innocence of 1914? But, if sacrifice is needed for democratic liberty, youth will probably die just as certainly as it did a generation ago. England has demonstrated that fact. And one who dies for his cause in cooler blood is a greater hero than one who dies intoxicated by hysteria.

In his day Walt Whitman saw the United States as a citadel 'invincible to the attacks of the whole of the rest of the earth,' because it was 'the new city of friends.' A nation of good will and brotherhood, seeking neither territory nor sovereignty over its neighbors, it was also the land of Washington and Lincoln —its 'saints,' as the poet called them. Such memories were a vital part of its great tradition, its moorings of idealism that he believed would strengthen in tautness and hold fast in any storm.

WASHINGTON

By James Russell Lowell

WHAT figure more immovably august
Than that grave strength so patient and so pure;
Calm in good fortune; when it wavered, sure;
That mind serene, impenetrably just . . .
Soldier and statesman, rarest unison;
High-poised example of great duties done
Simply as breathing, a world's honors worn
As life's indifferent gifts to all men born;
Dumb for himself, unless it were to God,
But for his barefoot soldiers eloquent;
Tramping the snow to coral here they trod,
Held by his awe in hollow-eyed content;
Modest, yet firm as Nature's self; unblamed
Save by the men his nobler temper shamed; . . .
Rigid, but with himself first, grasping still
In swerveless poise the wave-beat helm of will;
Not honored then or now because he wooed
The popular voice, but that he still withstood;
Broad-minded, higher-souled, there is but one
Who was all this and ours, and all men's—WASHINGTON.

From 'Under the Old Elm.'

THE YOUNG MAN WASHINGTON

By Samuel Eliot Morison

WASHINGTON is the last person you would ever suspect of having been a young man, with all the bright hopes and black despairs to which young men are subject. In American folklore he is known only as a child or a general or an old, old man: priggish hero of the cherry-tree episode, commander-in-chief, or the Father of his Country, writing a farewell address. By some freak of fate, Stuart's 'Athenæum' portrait of an ideal and imposing, but solemn and weary, Washington at the age of sixty-four has become the most popular. This year it has been reproduced as the 'official' portrait, and placed in every school in the country; so we may expect that new generations of American school-children will be brought up with the idea that Washington was a solemn old bore. If only Charles Willson Peale's portrait of him as a handsome and gallant soldier could have been used instead! Or one of the charming miniatures that shows him as a young man exulting in his strength! His older biographers, too, have conspired to create the legend; and the recent efforts to 'popularize' Washington have taken the unfortunate line of try-ing to make him out something that he was not: a churchman, politician, engineer, business man, realtor, or even 'traveling man.' These attempts to degrade a hero to a 'go-getter,' an aristo-crat to a vulgarian, remind one of the epitaph that Aristotle wished to have carved on the tomb of Plato: *Hic jacet homo, quem non licet, non decet, impiis vel ignorantibus laudare* ('Here lies a man whom it is neither permissible nor proper for the irreverent or the ignorant to *praise*') .

Perhaps it is not the fault of the painters and biographers that we think of Washington as an old man, but because his out-

From *The Young Man Washington*, Cambridge: Harvard University Press, 1932. Reprinted by permission of the President and Fellows of Harvard College.

standing qualities—wisdom, poise, and serenity—are not the qualities usually associated with youth. He seemed to have absorbed, wrote Emerson, 'all the serenity of America, and left none for his restless, rickety, hysterical countrymen.' The Comte de Chastellux, one of the French officers in the war, said that Washington's most characteristic feature was balance: 'the perfect harmony existing between the physical and moral attributes of which he is made up.' Yet Gilbert Stuart, after painting his first portrait of Washington, said that 'all his features were indicative of the most ungovernable passions, and had he been born in the forests, it was his opinion that he would have been the fiercest man among the savage tribes.' Both men were right. Washington's qualities were so balanced that his talents, which were great but nothing extraordinary, were more effective in the long run than those of greater generals like Napoleon, or of bolder and more original statesmen like Hamilton and Jefferson. Yet as a young man Washington was impatient and passionate, eager for glory in war, wealth in land, and success in love. Even in maturity his fierce temper would sometimes get the better of him. In Cambridge, at his headquarters in the Craigie House, he once became so exasperated at the squabbling of drunken soldiers in the front yard that, forgetting the dignity of a general, he rushed forth and 'laid out' a few of the brawlers with his own fists; and then, much relieved, returned to his study. Under great provocation he would break out with a torrent of Olympian oaths that terrified the younger men on his staff. Tobias Lear, the smooth young Harvard graduate who became Washington's private secretary, admitted that the most dreadful experience in his life was hearing the General swear!

It was only through the severest self-discipline that Washington attained his characteristic poise and serenity. Discipline is not a popular word nowadays, for we associate it with schoolmasters, drill-sergeants, and dictators; and it was certainly not discipline of that sort that made the passionate young Washington into an effective man. His discipline came in a very small part from parents, masters, or superiors; and in no respect from institutions. It came from environment, from a philosophy of life that he imbibed at an impressionable age; but most of all from his own will. He apprehended the great truth that man can only be free through mastery of himself. Instead of allowing his passions to spend themselves, he restrained them. Instead of indulging himself in a life of pleasure,—for which he had ample means at the age of twenty,—he placed duty first. In fact he followed exactly that course of conduct which, according to the second-hand popularizers of Freud, makes a person 'thwarted,' 'inhibited,' and 'repressed.' Yet Washington became a liberated, successful, and serene man. The process can hardly fail to interest young men who are struggling with the same difficulties as Washington—although, I am bound to say, under the far more difficult conditions of depression and mechanization.

Whence came this impulse to self-discipline? We can find nothing to account for it in the little we know of Washington's heredity. His family was gentle but undistinguished. George knew little of his forbears and cared less, although he used the family coat of arms. Lawrence Washington, sometime Fellow of Brasenose College, Oxford, was ejected from his living by the Roundheads as a 'malignant Royalist.' His son John came to Virginia by way of Barbados as mate of a tobacco-ship, settled there, and became an Indian fighter, so undisciplined as to embarrass the Governor of Virginia as much as the Indians. His son Lawrence, father of Augustine, George's father, earned a competence in the merchant marine and settled down to planting. Love of the land was a trait which all Washingtons had in common: they might seek wealth at sea or glory in war, but happiness they found only in the work and sport that came from owning and cultivating land.

Usually the Washingtons married their social betters, but the second marriage of George's father was an exception. Mary Ball, the mother of Washington, has been the object of much sentimental writing; but the cold record of her own and her sons' letters shows her to have been grasping, querulous, and vulgar. She was a selfish and exacting mother, whom most of her children avoided as soon and as early as they could; to whom they did their duty, but rendered little love. It was this sainted mother of Washington who opposed almost everything that he did for the public good, who wished his sense of duty to end with his duty to her, who pestered him in his campaigns by complaining letters, and who at a dark moment of the Revolutionary War increased his anxieties by strident complaints of neglect and starvation. Yet for one thing Americans may well be grateful to Mary Ball: her selfishness lost George an opportunity to become midshipman in the Royal Navy, a school whence few Americans emerged other than as loyal subjects of the King.

There is only one other subject connected with Washington upon which there has been more false sentiment, misrepresentation, and mendacity than on that of his mother, and that is his religion. Washington's religion was that of an eighteenth-century gentleman. Baptized in the Church of England, he attended service occasionally as a young man, and more regularly in middle age, as one of the duties of his station. He believed in God: the eighteenth-century Supreme Being, a Divine Philosopher who ruled all things for the best. He was certain of a Providence in the affairs of men. By the same token, he was completely tolerant of other people's beliefs, more so than the American democracy of today; for in a letter to the Swedenborgian church of Baltimore he wrote, 'In this enlightened age and in the land of equal liberty it is our boast that a man's religious tenets will not forfeit the protection of the law, nor deprive him of the right of attaining and holding the highest offices that are known in the United States.' But Washington never became an active member of any Christian church. Even after his marriage to a devout churchwoman, and when as President of the United States the eyes of all men were upon him, he never joined Martha in the beautiful and comfortable sacrament of the body and blood of Christ. The story of the 'prayer at Valley Forge' is pure fable, and 'George Washington's Prayer' is a pious fabrication. Christianity had little or no part in that discipline which made Washington more humble and gentle than any of the great captains, less proud and ambitious than most of the statesmen who have proclaimed themselves disciples of the Nazarene. His inspiration, as we shall see, came from an entirely different source.

Washington gained little discipline from book-learning; but like all young Virginians of the day he led an active outdoor life which gave him a magnificent physique. When fully grown he stood a little over six feet, and weighed from 175 to 200 pounds. Broad-shouldered and straight-backed, he carried his head erect and his chin up, and showed a good leg on horseback. There is no reason to doubt the tradition of his prowess at running, leaping, wrestling, and horsemanship. The handling of horses, in which Washington was skilled at an early age, is one of the best means of discipline that a youngster can have: for he who cannot control himself can never handle a spirited horse; and, for the same reason fox-hunting on horseback, which was Washington's favorite sport, is the making or the breaking of a courageous and considerate gentleman. George may not have actually thrown a dollar across the Rappahannock (though as one elderly punster remarked, 'a dollar went farther in those days!') ; but his amazing physical vitality is proved by an incident of his reconnaissance to the Ohio. At the close of December, 1753, he and the scout Christopher Gist attempted to cross the river just above the site of Pittsburgh, on a raft of their own making. The river was full of floating ice, and George, while trying to shove the raft away from an ice-floe with his setting-pole, fell overboard, but managed to climb aboard again. They were forced to land on an island and spend the night there without fire or dry clothing. Gist, the professional woodsman, who had not been in the water, froze all his fingers and some of his toes; but Washington suffered no ill effects from the exposure. For that, his healthy Virginia boyhood may be thanked.

His formal education was scanty. The colonial colleges provided a classical discipline more severe and selective than that of their successors,—for higher education had to become painless in America before it could be popular,—but George had none of these 'advantages.' There were no means to prepare him for William and Mary, the college of the Virginia gentry; his father died when he was eleven years old; and his only schoolmasters were chosen haphazardly, as was natural for a younger son in a land-poor family. Endowed with the blood and the instincts of a gentleman, he was not given a gentleman's education, as he became painfully aware when at adolescence he went to live with his half-brother at Mount Vernon.

In modern phrase, George was 'parked' on the estate which would one day be his. Evidently there had been some sort of family consultation about what to do with him; and Lawrence good-naturedly offered to take him in hand, if only to get him away from the exigent mother. Lawrence Washington, his father's principal heir and hope, had been sent to England for his schooling, had served under Admiral Vernon in the War of Jenkins's Ear, and had inherited the bulk of his father's property, to the exclusion of George and the four younger brothers and sisters. The proximity of Mount Vernon to the vast estates of the Fairfax family in the Northern Neck of Virginia gave Lawrence his opportunity. He married a Fairfax, and was admitted to the gay charmed circle of the First Families of Virginia. He was already a well-established gentleman of thirty when his hobble-de-hoy half-brother came to stay.

George was then a tall, gangling lad of sixteen years, with enormous hands and feet that were continually getting in his way. Young girls giggled when he entered a room, and burst out laughing at his awkward attempts to court them. He was conscious that he did not 'belong,' and made every effort to improve his manners. About three years before, a schoolmaster had made him copy out 110 'Rules of Civility' from a famous handbook by one Hawkins—a popular guide to good manners already a century and a half old; and George was probably glad to have this manuscript manual of social etiquette ready to consult. One of the most touching and human pictures of Washington is that of the overgrown schoolboy solemnly conning old Hawkins's warnings against scratching oneself at table, picking one's teeth with a fork, or cracking fleas in company, lest he commit serious 'breaks' in the houses of the great.

These problems of social behavior no doubt occupied considerable space in Washington's adolescent thoughts. But he was also preparing to be a man of action. At school he had cared only for mathematics. He procured books, progressed farther than his schoolmaster could take him, and so qualified to be surveyor to Lord Fairfax. This great gentleman and landowner had much surveying to be done in the Shenandoah Valley, and it was difficult to find men with enough mathematics to qualify as

surveyors, or with sufficient sobriety to run a line straight and
see a job through. So George at sixteen earned as Lord Fairfax's
surveyor the high salary of a doubloon (about $7.50) a day,
most of which he saved up and invested in land. For he had
early decided that in the fresh lands of the Virginian Valley and
the West lay the road to position, competence, and happiness.
His personality as well as his excellent surveying earned him
the friendship of the Fairfaxes, liberal and intelligent gentlemen; and this, as we shall see, was of first importance in Washington's moral and intellectual development.

That friendship, not the doubloon a day, was the first and
most fortunate gain from his surveying job; the second was the
contact which it gave young Washington with frontiersmen, with
Indians, and with that great teacher of self-reliance, the wilderness. He had the advantage of a discipline that few of us can
get today. We are born in crowded cities, and attend crowded
schools and colleges; we take our pleasure along crowded highways and in crowded places of amusement; we are tempted to
assert ourselves by voice rather than deed, to advertise, to watch
the clock, escape responsibility, and leave decisions to others.
But a hungry woodsman could not afford to lose patience with a
deer he was trying to shoot, or with a trout he was trying to
catch; and it did not help him much to 'bawl out' an Indian. If
you cannot discipline yourself to quiet and caution in the wilderness, you won't get far; and if you make the wrong decision in
woods infested with savages, you will probably have no opportunity to make another. What our New England forbears learned
from the sea—that tough old nurse who plays no favorites and
suffers no weaklings—Washington learned from the wilderness.

His life from sixteen to twenty was not all spent on forest
trails. This was the golden age of the Old Dominion, the fifteen
years from 1740 to the French and Indian War. The old rough-
ness and crudeness were passing away. Peace reigned over the
land, high prices ruled for tobacco, immigrants were pouring
into the back country; the traditional Virginia of Thackeray
and Vachel Lindsay—'Land of the gauntlet and the glove'—came
into being. Living in Virginia at that time was like riding on
the sparkling crest of a great wave just before it breaks and

spreads into dull, shallow pools. At Mount Vernon, on the verge of the wilderness, you felt the zest of sharp contrasts, and received the discipline that comes from life. On the one side were mansion houses where young Washington could learn manners and philosophy from gentlefolk. He took part in all the sports and pastimes of his social equals: dancing and card-playing and flirting with the girls. When visiting a town like Williamsburg he never missed a show; and later as President he was a patron of the new American drama. He loved gunning, foxhunting, horse-racing, and all the gentleman's field sports of the day; he bet small sums at cards, and larger sums on the ponies —and was a good loser. He liked to make an impression by fine new clothes, and by riding unruly steeds when girls were looking on; for though a graceful figure on horseback he was ungainly afoot. He belonged to clubs of men who dined at taverns and drank like gentlemen; that is to say, they drank as much wine as they could hold without getting drunk—the opposite of modern drinking, the object of which appears to be to get 'as drunk as a lord' on as little liquor as possible. Tobacco, curiously enough, made George's head swim; but he learned to smoke the peace-pipe with Indians when necessary without disgracing himself.

On the other side of Mount Vernon were log cabins, and all the crude elements of American life: Scotch and 'Pennsylvania Dutch,' and other poor whites who as insubordinate soldiers would prove the severest test of Washington's indefatigable patience, and proof of his power over men. The incidents of roughing it, such as the 'one thread bear blanket with double its weight of vermin, such as lice, fleas, etc.,' which he records in the journal of his first surveying trip, were not very pleasant at first, but he took it all with good humor and good sportsmanship. A little town called Alexandria sprang up about a tobacco warehouse and wharf, and young Washington made the first survey of it. A Masonic Lodge was formed at Fredericksburg, and George, who was a good 'joiner,' became brother to all the rising journalists and lawyers of the northern colonies. The deep Potomac flowed past Mount Vernon, bearing ships of heavy burthen to the Chesapeake and overseas; you sent your orders to England every year with your tobacco, and ships returned with the latest modes and manners, books and gazettes, and letters full of coffee-house gossip. London did not seem very far away, and young George confessed in a letter that he hoped to visit that 'gay Matrapolis' before long.

It was probably just as well that he did not visit London, for he had the best and purest English tradition in Virginia. When Washington was in his later teens, just when a young man is fumbling for a philosophy of life, he came into intimate contact with several members of the Fairfax family. They were of that eighteenth-century Whig gentry which conformed outwardly to Christianity, but derived their real inspiration from Marcus Aurelius, Plutarch, and the Stoic philosophers. Thomas, sixth Lord Fairfax, was a nobleman devoted to 'Revolution Principles' —the 'Glorious Revolution' of 1688, in which his father had taken an active part. Of the same line was that General Lord Fairfax, commander-in-chief of the New Model Army, who of all great soldiers in English history most resembles Washington. The ideal of this family was a noble simplicity of living, and a calm acceptance of life: duty to the Commonwealth, generosity to fellow-men, unfaltering courage and enduring virtue; in a word, the Stoic philosophy which overlaps Christian ethics more than any other discipline of the ancients. A Stoic never evaded life: he faced it. A Stoic never avoided responsibility: he accepted it. A Stoic not only believed in liberty: he practiced it.

It is not necessary to suppose that young Washington read much Stoic philosophy, for he was no great reader at any time; but he must have absorbed it from constant social intercourse with the Fairfaxes of Belvoir, neighbors whom he saw constantly. At Belvoir lived George William Fairfax, eight years Washington's senior, and his companion in surveying expeditions. Anne, the widow of Lawrence Washington, was Fairfax's sister, and Sally, the lady with whom George Washington was so happy—and so miserable—as to fall in love, was his wife. Books were there, if he wanted them. North's Plutarch was in every gentleman's library, and it was Plutarch who wrote the popular life of Cato, Washington's favorite character in history —not crabbed Cato the Censor, but Cato of pent-up Utica. At the age of seventeen, Washington himself owned an outline, in English, of the principal Dialogues of Seneca the younger, 'sharpest of all the Stoicks.' The mere chapter headings are the moral axioms that Washington followed through life:

A Sensual Life is a Miserable Life
Hope and Fear are the Bane of Human Life
And Honest Man can never be outdone in Courtesy
A Good man can never be Miserable, nor a Wicked man Happy
The Contempt of Death makes all the Miseries of Life Easy to us

And of the many passages that young Washington evidently took to heart, one may select this:

No man is born wise: but Wisdom and Virtue require a Tutor; though we can easily learn to be Vicious without a Master. It is Philosophy that gives us a Veneration for God; a Charity for our Neighbor; that teaches us our Duty to Heaven, and Exhorts us to an Agreement one with another. It unmasks things that are terrible to us, asswages our Lusts, refutes our Errors, restrains our Luxury, Reproves our avarice, and works strangely on tender Natures.

Washington read Addison's tragedy *Cato* in company with his beloved; and if they did not act it together in private theatricals, George expressed the wish that they might. At Valley Forge, when the morale of the army needed a stimulus, Washington caused *Cato* to be performed, and attended the performance. It was his favorite play, written, as Pope's prologue says,

To make mankind in conscious virtue bold,
Live o'er each scene, and be what they behold.

Portius, Cato's son, whose 'steddy temper'

Can look on guilt, rebellion, fraud, and Caesar
In the calm lights of mild Philosophy

declares (I, ii, 40-45):

I'll animate the soldiers' drooping courage
With love of freedom, and contempt of Life:
I'll thunder in their ears their country's cause
And try to rouse up all that's Roman in 'em.
'Tis not in Mortals to Command Success
But we'll do more, Sempronius, we'll Deserve it.

These last two lines sound the note that runs through all Washington's correspondence in the dark hours of the Revolutionary struggle; and these same lines are almost the only literary quotations found in the vast body of Washington's writings. Many years after, when perplexed and wearied by the political squabbles of his presidency and longing to retire to Mount Vernon, Washington quoted the last lines of Cato's advice to Portius (IV, iv, 146-154):

> Let me advise thee to retreat betimes
> To thy paternal seat, the Sabine field,
> Where the great Censor toil'd with his own hands,
> And all our frugal Ancestors were blest
> In humble virtues, and a rural life.
> There live retired, pray for the peace of Rome:
> Content thy self to be obscurely good.
> When vice prevails, and impious men bear sway,
> The post of honour is a private station.

From his camp with General Forbes's army in the wilderness Washington wrote to Sally Fairfax, September 25, 1758:

> I should think our time more agreeably spent, believe me, in playing a part in Cato with the Company you mention, and myself doubly happy in being the Juba to such a Marcia as you must make.

Marcia was the worthy daughter of Cato, and Juba her lover, the young Numidian prince to whom Syphax says

> You have not read mankind; your youth admires
> The throws and swellings of a Roman soul;
> Cato's bold flights, th' extravagance of Virtue.

To which Juba replies (II, iv, 49-58) :

> Turn up thy eyes to Cato!
> There may'st thou see to what a godlike height
> The Roman virtues lift up mortal man,
> While good, and just, and anxious for his friends,
> He's still severely bent against himself;
> Renouncing sleep, and rest, and food, and ease,
> He strives with thirst and hunger, toil and heat;
> And when his fortune sets before him all
> The pomps and pleasures that his soul can wish,
> His rigid virtue will accept of none.

Given this combination—a young man of innate noble qualities, seeking a philosophy of life, thrown in contact during his
most impressionable years with a great gentleman whom he admired, a young gentleman who was his best friend, and a young
lady whom he loved, all three steeped in the Stoical tradition—
and what would you expect? Can it be a mere coincidence that
this characterization of the Emperor Antoninus Pius by his
adopted son Marcus Aurelius, the imperial Stoic, so perfectly
fits the character of Washington?

Take heed lest thou become a Caesar indeed; lest the purple stain
thy soul. For such things have been. Then keep thyself simple, good,
pure, and serious; a friend to justice and the fear of God; kindly, affectionate, and strong to do the right. Reverence Heaven and succour man.
Life is short; and earthly existence yields but one harvest, holiness of
character and altruism of action. Be in everything a true disciple of
Antoninus. Emulate his constancy in all rational activity, his unvarying
equability, his purity, his cheerfulness of countenance, his sweetness, his
contempt for notoriety, and his eagerness to come at the root of the
matter.

Remember how he would never dismiss any subject until he had
gained a clear insight into it and grasped it thoroughly; how he bore
with the injustice of his detractors and never retorted in kind; how he
did nothing in haste, turned a deaf ear to the professional tale-bearers,
and showed himself an acute judge of characters and actions, devoid of
all reproachfulness, timidity, suspiciousness, and sophistry; how easily
he was satisfied,—for instance, with lodging, bed, clothing, food, and
servants,—how fond of work and how patient; capable, thanks to his
frugal diet, of remaining at his post from morning till night, having
apparently subjected even the operations of nature to his will; firm and
constant in friendship, tolerant of the most outspoken criticism of his
opinions, delighted if any one could make a better suggestion than himself, and, finally, deeply religious without any trace of superstition.

LETTERS OF JOHN AND ABIGAIL ADAMS

['THE experience of writing letters,' said Emerson in 'Inspiration,' 'is one of the keys of the *modus* of inspiration. When we have ceased for a long time to have any fulness of thoughts that once made a diary a joy as well as a necessity, and have come to believe that an image or happy turn of expression is no longer at our command, in writing a letter to a friend we may find that we rise to thought and to a cordial power of expression that costs no effort, and it seems to us that this facility may be indefinitely applied and resumed. The wealth of the mind in this respect of seeing is like that of a looking glass, which is never tired or worn by any multitude of objects which it reflects.'

From the following letters, in which the writers expressed frankly their sentiments, we have a better idea than from any other one correspondence of the part played by the women whose husbands and sons engaged in public efforts, political and military, to achieve independence. John Adams is seen as a man of courage and high character, worthy indeed of the responsibilities with which he was entrusted, as member of the Assembly which drew up the Declaration of Independence, as Joint Commissioner of the new nation to France, and as signer of the Treaty of Peace with Great Britain. It may be questioned whether he could have carried the burden of cares and anxieties so well without the support he received in his wife's courage and affection, good humor, and firm patriotism.

Abigail Adams is a brilliant example of the important contribution of women to the moral sense of a people. She represents the height of cultivation to which some women reached in times when the education of women passed little beyond the three R's. While her husband was absent from home in governmental service, Abigail managed the farm, sold its produce, and brought up the children. In our day of almost instantaneous communication, it is hard to conceive the agonies of suspense which taxed her courage when she waited to know whether her husband and son had escaped the British fleet and the February seas, after they sailed for France in the little ship *Boston* in 1778. Abigail joined her husband in London when he was the first Minister to the Court of St. James's, and she lived in Philadelphia during the term of John Adams as second President. From these high stations she returned serenely to her home in Quincy, Massachusetts, to live a quiet country life until her death, fifty-four years after her marriage, 28 October 1818. John Adams died on the fiftieth anniversary of the Declaration he had helped to frame, 4 July 1826.

See the following books:

C. F. Adams, ed., *Familiar Letters of John Adams and His Wife* (1875)
J. T. Morse, Jr., *John Adams* (American Statesman Series) (1884)
Mellen Chamberlain, *John Adams, the Statesman of the Revolution* (1898)
Gamaliel Bradford, *Portraits of American Women* (1919)
Laura E. Richards, *Abigail Adams and Her Times* (1917)
Dorothy Bobbe, *Abigail Adams, the Second First Lady* (1929)]

I

A Vow

From JOHN ADAMS   YORK, 1 July, 1774

I am so idle that I have not an easy moment without my pen in my hand. My time might have been improved to some purpose in mowing grass, raking hay, or hoeing corn, weeding carrots, picking or shelling peas. Much better should I have been employed in schooling my children, in teaching them to write, cipher, Latin, French, English, and Greek.

I sometimes think I must come to this—to be the foreman upon my own farm and the schoolmaster to my own children. I confess myself to be full of fears that the ministry and their friends and instruments will prevail, and crush the cause and friends of liberty. The minds of that party are so filled with prejudices against me that they will take all advantages, and do me all the damage they can. These thoughts have their turns in my mind, but in general my hopes are predominant.

Dr. Gardiner, arrived here today from Boston, brings us news of a battle at the town meeting, between Whigs and Tories, in which the Whigs, after a day and a half's obstinate engagement, were finally victorious by two to one. He says the Tories are preparing a flaming protest.

I am determined to be cool, if I can. I have suffered such torments in my mind heretofore, as have almost over-powered my constitution, without any advantage. And now I will laugh and be easy if I can, let the contest of parties terminate as it will, nay, whether I stand high or low in the estimation of the world, so long as I keep a conscience void of offense towards God and man. And this I am determined by the will of God to do, let what will become of me or mine, my country or the world.

I shall arouse myself ere long, I believe, and exert an industry, a frugality, a hard labor, that will serve my family, if I can't serve my country. I will not lie down in despair. If I cannot serve my children by the law, I will serve them by agriculture, by trade, by some way or other. I thank God I have a head, and heart, and hands, which, if once fully exerted altogether, will succeed in the world as well as those of the mean-spirited, low-minded, fawning, obsequious scoundrels who have long hoped that my integrity would be an obstacle in my way, and enable them to outstrip me in the race.

But what I want in comparison of them of villainy and servility, I will make up in industry and capacity. If I don't, they shall laugh and triumph. I will not willingly see blockheads, whom I have a right to despise, elevated above me and insolently triumphing over me. Nor shall knavery, through any negligence of mine, get the better of honesty, nor ignorance of knowledge, nor folly of wisdom, nor vice of virtue.

I must entreat you, my dear partner in all the joys and sorrows, prosperity and adversity of my life, to take a part with me in the struggle. I pray God for your health—entreat you to rouse your whole attention to the family, the stock, the farm, the dairy. Let every article of expense which can possibly be spared be retrenched; keep the hands attentive to their business, and [let] the most prudent measures of every kind be adopted and pursued with alacrity and spirit.

II

A Caution

From JOHN ADAMS   YORK, 2 July, 1774

. . . I write you this tittle-tattle, my dear, in confidence. You must keep these letters to yourself, and communicate them with great caution and reserve. I should advise you to put them up safe and preserve them. They may exhibit to our posterity a kind of picture of the manners, opinions, and principles of these times of perplexity, danger, and distress . . .

III

Provocation to Revolution

From JOHN ADAMS   FALMOUTH, 5 July, 1774

. . . I spent an hour last evening at Mr. Wyer's, with Judge Cushing. Wyer's father, who has a little place in the customs, came in. He began upon politics, and told us that Mr. Smith had a fast last week which he attended. Mr. Gilman preached, he said, part of the day, and told them that the judgments of God upon the land were in consequence of the mobs and riots which had prevailed in the country; and then turning to me old Wyer said, 'What do you think of that, Mr. Adams?'

I answered, 'I can't say but mobs and violence may have been one cause of our calamities. I am inclined to think that they do come in for a share; but there are many other causes. Did not Mr. Gilman mention bribery and corruption as another cause? He ought to have been impartial, and pointed out the venality which prevails in the land as a cause, as well as tumults.' 'I think he did,' says Wyer. I might have pursued my inquiry, whether he did not mention universal pilfering, robbery, and picking of pockets which prevails in the land,—as every man's pocket upon the continent is picked every day by taking from him duties without his consent. I might have inquired whether he mentioned the universal spirit of debauchery, dissipation, luxury, effeminacy, and gaming, which the late ministerial measures are introducing, etc., etc., etc., but I forbore.

How much profaneness, lewdness, intemperance, etc., have been introduced by the army and navy and revenue; how much servility, venality, artifice, and hypocrisy have been introduced among the ambitious and avaricious by the British politics of the last ten years. In short the original faulty causes of all the vices which have been introduced are the political innovations of the last ten years. This is no justification and a poor excuse for the girls who have been debauched, and for the injustice which has been committed in some riots; but surely the soldiers, sailors, and excisemen who have occasioned these vices ought not to reproach those they have corrupted. These Tories act the part of the devil. They tempt the women into sin and then reproach them for it, and become soon their tormentors for it. A tempter and tormentor is the character of the devil. Hutchinson, Oliver, and others of their circle, who for their own ends of ambition and avarice have pursued, promoted, encouraged, counseled, aided, and abetted the taxation of America, have been the real tempters of their countrymen and women into all the vices, sins, crimes, and follies which that taxation has occasioned. And now by themselves and their friends, dependents, and votaries, they are reproaching those very men and women with those vices and follies, sins and crimes.

There is not a sin which prevails more universally and has prevailed longer than prodigality in furniture, equipage, apparel, and diet. And I believe that this vice, this sin, has as large a share in drawing down the judgments of Heaven as any. And perhaps the punishment that is inflicted may work medicinally and cure the disease.

IV

On Mobs

From JOHN ADAMS   FALMOUTH, 7 July, 1774

. . . I am engaged in a famous cause,—the cause of King, of Scarborough, *versus* a mob that broke into his house and rifled his papers and terrified him, his wife, children and servants in the night. The terror and distress, the distraction and horror of his family cannot be described by words or painted upon canvas. It is enough to move a statue, to melt a heart of stone, to read the story. A mind susceptible of the feelings of humanity, a heart which can be touched with sensibility for human misery and wretchedness, must reluct, must burn with resentment and indignation at such outrageous injuries. These private mobs I do and will detest. If popular commotions can be justified in opposition to attacks upon the Constitution, it can be only when fundamentals are invaded, nor then unless for absolute necessity, and with great caution. But these tarrings and featherings, this breaking open houses by rude and insolent rabble in resentment for private wrongs, or in pursuance of private prejudices and passions, must be discountenanced. It cannot be even excused upon any principle which can be entertained by a good citizen, a worthy member of society . . .

I go mourning in my heart all the day long, though I say nothing. I am melancholy for the public and anxious for my family. As for myself, a frock and trousers, a hoe and a spade would do for my remaining days.

For God's sake make your children *hardy, active,* and *industrious;* for strength, activity and industry will be their only resource and dependence.

V

Love, Faith and Hope

From ABIGAIL ADAMS   BRAINTREE, 16 October, 1774

My much loved Friend,—I dare not express to you, at three hundred miles' distance, how ardently I long for your return. I have some very miserly wishes, and cannot consent to your spending one hour in town, till, at least, I have had you twelve. The idea plays about my heart, unnerves my hand, whilst I write; awakens all the tender sentiments that years have increased and matured, and which, when with me, every day was dispensing to you. The whole collected stock of ten weeks' absence knows not how to brook any longer restraint, but will break forth and flow through my pen. May the like sensations enter thy breast, and (spite of all the weighty cares of state) mingle themselves with those I wish to communicate; for, in giving them utterance, I have felt more sincere pleasure than I have known since the 10th of August. Many have been the anxious hours I have spent since that day; the threatening aspect of our public affairs, the complicated distress of this province, the arduous and perplexed business in which you are engaged, have all conspired to agitate my bosom with fears and apprehensions to which I have heretofore been a stranger; and, far from thinking the scene closed, it looks as though the curtain was but just drawn, and only the first scene of the infernal plot disclosed. And whether the end will be tragical, Heaven alone knows. You cannot be, I know, nor do I wish to see you, an inactive spectator; but if the sword be drawn, I bid adieu to all domestic felicity, and look forward to that country where there are neither wars nor rumors of war, in a firm belief, that through the mercy of its King we shall both rejoice there together.

I greatly fear that the arm of treachery and violence is lifted over us, as a scourge and heavy punishment from Heaven for our numerous offenses, and for the misimprovement of our great advantages. If we expect to inherit the blessings of our fathers, we should return a little more to their primitive simplicity of manners, and not sink into inglorious ease. We have too many high-sounding words, and too few actions that correspond with them. I have spent one Sabbath in town since you left. I saw no difference in respect to ornament, etc.; but in the country you must look for that virtue, of which you find but small glimmerings in the metropolis. Indeed, they have not the advantages, nor the resolution, to encourage our own manufactories, which people in the country have. To the mercantile part, it is considered as throwing away their own bread; but they must retrench their expenses, and be content with a small share of gain, for they will find but few who will wear their livery. As for me, I will seek wool and flax, and work willingly with my hands; and indeed there is occasion for all our industry and economy . . .

VI

General George Washington

From JOHN ADAMS   PHILADELPHIA, 11 June, 1775

I have been this morning to hear Mr. Duffield, a preacher in this city, whose principles, prayers, and sermons more nearly resemble those of our New England clergy than any that I have heard. His discourse was a kind of exposition on the thirty-fifth chapter of Isaiah. America was the wilderness, and the solitary place, and he said it would be glad, 'rejoice and blossom as the rose.' He labored 'to strengthen the weak hands and confirm the feeble knees.' He 'said to them that were of a fearful heart, Be strong, fear not. Behold, your God will come with vengeance, even God with a recompense; he will come and save you,' 'No lion shall be there, nor any ravenous beast shall go up thereon, but the redeemed shall walk there,' etc. He applied the whole prophecy to this country, and gave us as animating an entertainment as I ever heard. He filled and swelled the bosom of every hearer. I hope you have received a letter, in which I inclosed you a pastoral letter from the synod of New York and Philadelphia; by this you will see, that the clergy this way are but now beginning to engage in politics, and they engage with a fervor that will produce wonderful effects.

17 June

I can now inform you that the Congress have made choice of the modest and virtuous, the amiable, generous, and brave George Washington, Esquire, to be General of the American army, and that he is to repair, as soon as possible, to the camp before Boston. This appointment will have a great effect in cementing and securing the union of these colonies. The continent is really in earnest, in defending the country. They have voted ten companies of riflemen to be sent from Pennsylvania, Maryland, and Virginia, to join the army before Boston. These are an excellent species of light infantry. They use a peculiar kind of musket, called a rifle. It . . . carries a ball with great exactness to great distances. They are the most accurate marksmen in the world.

I begin to hope we shall not sit all summer. I hope the people of our province will treat the General with all that confidence and affection, that politeness and respect, which is due to one of the most important characters in the world. The liberties of America depend upon him, in a great degree . . .

I have found this Congress like the last. When we first came together, I found a strong jealousy of us from New England,

and the Massachusetts in particular; suspicions entertained of designs of independency; an American republic; Presbyterian principles, and twenty other things. Our sentiments were heard in Congress with great caution, and seemed to make but little impression; but the longer we sat, the more clearly they saw the necessity of pushing vigorous measures. It has been so now. Every day we sit, the more we are convinced that the designs against us are hostile and sanguinary, and that nothing but fortitude, vigor, and perseverance can save us.

But America is a great, unwieldy body. Its progress must be slow. It is like a large fleet sailing under convoy. The fleetest sailers must wait for the dullest and slowest. Like a coach and six, the swiftest horses must be slackened, and the slowest quickened, that all may keep an even pace . . .

VII

Benjamin Franklin

From JOHN ADAMS   PHILADELPHIA, 23 July, 1775

You have more than once in your letters mentioned Dr. Franklin, and in one intimated a desire that I should write you something concerning him.

Dr. Franklin has been very constant in his attendance on Congress from the beginning. His conduct has been composed and grave, and, in the opinion of many gentlemen, very reserved. He has not assumed anything, nor affected to take the lead; but has seemed to choose that the Congress should pursue their own principles and sentiments, and adopt their own plans. Yet he has not been backward; has been very useful on many occasions, and discovered a disposition entirely American. He does not hesitate at our boldest measures, but rather seems to think us too irresolute and backward. He thinks us at present in an odd state, neither in peace nor war, neither dependent nor independent; but he thinks that we shall soon assume a character more decisive. He thinks that we have the power of preserving ourselves; and that even if we should be driven to the disagreeable neces-

sity of assuming a total independency, and set up a separate
state, we can maintain it. The people of England have thought
that the opposition in America was wholly owing to Dr. Franklin; and I suppose their scribblers will attribute the temper
and proceedings of Congress to him; but there cannot be a greater
mistake. He has had but little share, further than to co-operate
and to assist. He is, however, a great and good man . . .

VIII

Liberty or Death

From JOHN ADAMS   7 October, 1775

. . . The situation of things is so alarming, that it is our duty
to prepare our minds and hearts for every event, even the worst.
From my earliest entrance into life, I have been engaged in the
public cause of America; and from first to last I have had upon
my mind a strong impression that things would be wrought up
to their present crisis. I saw from the beginning that the controversy was of such a nature that it never would be settled, and
every day convinces me more and more. This has been the source
of all the disquietude of my life. It has lain down and risen up
with me these twelve years. The thought that we might be driven
to the sad necessity of breaking our connection with Great
Britain, exclusive of the carnage and destruction, which it was
easy to see must attend the separation, always gave me a great
deal of grief. And even now I would cheerfully retire from public life forever, renounce all chance for profits or honors from
the public, nay, I would cheerfully contribute my little property,
to obtain peace and liberty. But all these must go, and my life,
too, before I can surrender the right of my country to a free
Constitution. I dare not consent to it. I should be the most miserable of mortals ever after, whatever honors or emoluments might
surround me.

IX

Women's Rights

From ABIGAIL ADAMS   BRAINTREE, 31 March, 1776

. . . I long to hear that you have declared an independency. And, by the way, in the new code of laws which I suppose it will be necessary for you to make, I desire you would remember the ladies and be more generous and favorable to them than your ancestors. Do not put such unlimited power into the hands of the husbands. Remember, all men would be tyrants if they could. If particular care and attention is not paid to the ladies, we are determined to foment a rebellion, and will not hold ourselves bound by any laws in which we have no voice or representation.

That your sex are naturally tyrannical is a truth so thoroughly established as to admit of no dispute; but such of you as wish to be happy willingly give up the harsh title of master for the tender and endearing one of friend. Why, then, not put it out of the power of the vicious and the lawless to use us with cruelty and indignity with impunity? Men of sense in all ages abhor those customs which treat us only as the vassals of your sex; regard us then as beings placed by Providence under your protection, and in imitation of the Supreme Being make use of that power only for our happiness . . .

X

Our Country

From ABIGAIL ADAMS   BRAINTREE, 7 May, 1776

How many are the solitary hours I spend ruminating upon the past and anticipating the future, whilst you, overwhelmed with the cares of state, have but a few moments you can devote to any individual. All domestic pleasures and enjoyments are absorbed in the great and important duty you owe your country, 'for our country is, as it were, a secondary god, and the first and greatest parent. It is to be preferred to parents, wives, children, friends, and all things,—the gods only excepted; for, if our country perishes, it is as impossible to save an individual as to preserve one of the fingers of a mortified hand.' Thus do I suppress every wish, and silence every murmur, acquiescing in a painful separation from the companion of my youth and the friend of my heart . . .

XI

The Declaration

From JOHN ADAMS   PHILADELPHIA, 3 July, 1776

. . . Yesterday, the greatest question was decided which ever was debated in America, and a greater, perhaps, never was nor will be decided among men. A Resolution was passed without one dissenting Colony 'that these United Colonies are, and of right ought to be, free and independent States, and as such they have, and of right ought to have, full power to make war, conclude peace, establish commerce, and to do all other acts and things which other States may rightfully do.' You will see, in a few days, a Declaration setting forth the causes which have impelled us to this mighty revolution, and the reasons which will justify it in the sight of God and man. A plan of confederation will be taken up in a few days.

When I look back to the year 1761, and recollect the argument concerning writs of assistance in the superior court, which I have hitherto considered as the commencement of this controversy between Great Britain and America, and run through the whole period from that time to this, and recollect the series of political events, the chain of causes and effects, I am surprised at the suddenness as well as greatness of this revolution. Britain has been filled with folly, and America with wisdom; at least, this is my judgment. Time must determine. It is the will of Heaven that the two countries should be sundered forever. It may be the will of Heaven that America shall suffer calamities still more wasting, and distresses yet more dreadful. If this is to be the case, it will have this good effect at least. It will inspire us with many virtues which we have not, and correct many errors, follies, and vices which threaten to disturb, dishonor, and destroy us. The furnace of affliction produces refinement in states as well as individuals. And the new Governments we are assuming in every part will require a purification from our vices, and an augmentation of our virtues, or they will be no blessings. The people will have unbounded power, and the people are extremely addicted to corruption and venality, as well as the great. But I must submit all my hopes and fears to an overruling Providence, in which, unfashionable as the faith may be, I firmly believe.

Had a Declaration of Independency been made even months ago, it would have been attended with many great and glorious effects. We might, before this hour, have formed alliances with foreign states. We should have mastered Quebec, and been in possession of Canada. You will perhaps wonder how such a declaration would have influenced our affairs in Canada, but if I could write with freedom, I could easily convince you that it would, and explain to you the manner how. Many gentlemen in high stations, and of great influence, have been duped by the ministerial bubble of Commissioners to treat. And in real, sincere expectation of this event, which they so fondly wished, they have been slow and languid in promoting measures for the reduction of that province. Others there are in the Colonies who really wished that our enterprise in Canada would be defeated, that the Colonies might be brought into danger and distress between two fires, and be thus induced to submit. Others really wished to defeat the expedition to Canada, lest the conquest of it should elevate the minds of the people too much to hearken to those terms of reconciliation which, they believed, would be offered us. These jarring views, wishes, and designs occasioned an opposition to many salutary measures which were proposed for the support of that expedition, and caused obstructions, embarrassments, and studied delays, which have finally lost us the province.

All these causes, however, in conjunction would not have disappointed us, if it had not been for a misfortune which could not be foreseen, and perhaps could not have been prevented; I mean the prevalence of the small-pox among our troops. This fatal pestilence completed our destruction. It is a frown of Providence upon us, which we ought to lay to heart.

But, on the other hand, the delay of this Declaration to this time has many great advantages attending it. The hopes of reconciliation which were fondly entertained by multitudes of honest and well-meaning, though weak and mistaken people, have been gradually, and at last totally extinguished. Time has been given for the whole people maturely to consider the great question of independence, and to ripen their judgment, dissipate their fears, and allure their hopes, by discussing it in newspapers and pamphlets, by debating it in assemblies, conventions, committees of safety and inspection, in town and county meetings, as well as in private conversations, so that the whole people, in every colony of the thirteen, have now adopted it as their own act. This will cement the union, and avoid those heats, and perhaps convulsions, which might have been occasioned by such a Declaration six months ago.

But the day is past. The second day of July, 1776, will be the most memorable epoch in the history of America. I am apt to believe that it will be celebrated by succeeding generations as the great anniversary festival. It ought to be commemorated as the day of deliverance, by solemn acts of devotion to God Almighty. It ought to be solemnized with pomp and parade, with shows, games, sports, guns, bells, bonfires, and illuminations, from one end of this continent to the other, from this time forward forevermore.

You will think me transported with enthusiasm, but I am not. I am well aware of the toil and blood and treasure that it will cost us to maintain this Declaration and support and defend these States. Yet, through all the gloom, I can see the rays of ravishing light and glory. I can see that the end is more than worth all the means. And that posterity will triumph in that day's transaction, even although we should rue it, which I trust in God we shall not.

XII

Education of Women

From ABIGAIL ADAMS   14 August, 1776

Your letter of August 3 came by this day's post. I find it very convenient to be so handy. I can receive a letter at night, sit down and reply to it, and send it off in the morning.

You remark upon the deficiency of education in your countrymen. It never, I believe, was in a worse state, at least for many years. The college is not in the state one could wish. The scholars complain that their professor in philosophy is taken off by public business, to their great detriment. In this town I never saw so great a neglect of education. The poorer sort of children are wholly neglected, and left to range the streets, without schools, without business, given up to all evil. The town is not, as formerly, divided into wards. There is either too much business left upon the hands of a few, or too little care to do it. We daily see the necessity of a regular government . . .

If you complain of neglect of education in sons, what shall I say with regard to daughters, who every day experience the want of it? With regard to the education of my own children, I find myself soon out of my depth, destitute and deficient in every part of education.

I most sincerely wish that some more liberal plan might be laid and executed for the benefit of the rising generation, and that our new Constitution may be distinguished for encouraging learning and virtue. If we mean to have heroes, statesmen, and philosophers, we should have learned women. The world perhaps would laugh at me and accuse me of vanity, but you, I know, have a mind too enlarged and liberal to disregard the sentiment. If much depends, as is allowed, upon the early education of youth, and the first principles which are instilled take the deepest root, great benefit must arise from literary accomplishments in women.

XIII

Country versus City

From JOHN ADAMS   18 August, 1776

My letters to you are an odd mixture. They would appear to a stranger like the dish which is sometimes called *omnium gatherum*. This is the first time, I believe, that these two words were ever put together in writing. The literal interpretation I take to be 'a collection of all things.' But, as I said before, the words having never before been written, it is not possible to be very learned in telling you what the Arabic, Syriac, Chaldaic, Greek, and Roman commentators say upon the subject. Amidst all the rubbish that constitutes the heap, you will see a proportion of affection for my friends, my family, and country, that gives a complexion to the whole. I have a very tender, feeling heart. This country knows not, and never can know, the torments I have endured for its sake. I am glad it never can know, for it would give more pain to the benevolent and humane than I could wish even the wicked and malicious to feel.

I have seen in this world but a little of that pure flame of patriotism which certainly burns in some breasts. There is much of the ostentation and affectation of it. I have known a few who could not bear to entertain a selfish design, nor to be suspected by others of such a meanness; but these are not the most respected by the world. A man must be selfish, even to acquire great popularity. He must grasp for himself, under specious pretenses for the public good, and he must attach himself to his relations, connections, and friends, by becoming a champion for their interests, in order to form a phalanx about him for his own defense, to make them trumpeters of his praise, and sticklers for his fame, fortune, and honor.

My friend Warren, the late Governor Ward, and Mr. Gadsden are three characters in which I have seen the most generous disdain of every species of such meanness. The two last had not great abilities, but they had pure hearts. Yet they had less influence than many others, who had neither so considerable parts nor any share at all of their purity of intention. Warren has both talents and virtues beyond most men in this world, yet his character has never been in proportion. Thus it always is and has been and will be. Nothing has ever given me more mortification than a suspicion that has been propagated of me, that I am actuated by private views and have been aiming at high places. The office of Chief Justice has occasioned this jealousy, and it never will be allayed until I resign it. Let me have my farm, family, and goosequill, and all the honors and offices this world has to bestow may go to those who deserve them better and desire them more. I court them not. There are very few people in this world with whom I can bear to converse. I can treat all with decency and civility, and converse with them, when it is necessary, on points of business. But I am never happy in their company. This has made me a recluse and will one day make me a hermit. I had rather build stone wall upon Penn's hill, than to be the first Prince in Europe, or the first General or first Senator in America.

XIV

The Cost of Freedom

From JOHN ADAMS   PHILADELPHIA, Saturday Evening,
26 April, 1777

. . . I am wearied out with expectations that the Massachusetts troops would have arrived, ere now, at Headquarters. Do our people intend to leave the continent in the lurch? Do they mean to submit? or what fatality attends them? With the noblest prize in view that ever mortals contended for, and with the fairest prospect of obtaining it upon easy terms, the people of the Massachusetts Bay are dead. Does our State intend to send only half or a third of their quota? Do they wish to see another crippled, disastrous, and disgraceful campaign, for want of an army? I am more sick and more ashamed of my own countrymen than ever I was before. The spleen, the vapors, the dismals, the horrors seemed to have seized our whole State. More wrath than terror has seized me. I am very mad. The gloomy cowardice of the times is intolerable in New England. Indeed, I feel not a little out of humor from indisposition of body. You know I cannot pass a spring or fall without an ill turn, and I have had one these four or five weeks; a cold, as usual. Warm weather and a little exercise, with a little medicine, I suppose, will cure me, as usual. I am not confined, but mope about and drudge, as usual, like a galley-slave. I am a fool, if ever there was one, to be such a slave. I won't be much longer. I will be more free in some world or other. Is it not intolerable, that the opening spring, which I should enjoy with my wife and children, upon my little farm, should pass away, and laugh at me for laboring, day after day and month after month, in a conclave where neither taste, nor fancy, nor reason, nor passion, nor appetite can be gratified?

Posterity! you will never know how much it cost the present generation to preserve your freedom! I hope you will make a good use of it. If you do not, I shall repent it in heaven that I ever took half the pains to preserve it.

XV

'I Can Glory in Any Sacrifice'

From ABIGAIL ADAMS   18 May, 1778

I have waited with great patience, restraining as much as possible every anxious idea, for three months . . . Difficult as the day is, cruel as this war has been, separated as I am, on account of it, from the dearest connection in life, I would not exchange my country for the wealth of the Indies, or be any other than an American, though I might be queen or empress of any nation upon the globe. My soul is unambitious of pomp or power. Beneath my humble roof, blessed with the society and tenderest affection of my dear partner, I have enjoyed as much felicity and as exquisite happiness as falls to the share of mortals. And, though I have been called to sacrifice to my country, I can glory in my sacrifice and derive pleasure from my intimate connection with one who is esteemed worthy of the important trust devolved upon him . . .

23 December, 1782

. . . 'If you had known,' said a person to me the other day, 'that Mr. Adams would have remained so long abroad, would you have consented that he should have gone?' I recollected myself a moment, and then spoke the real dictates of my heart: 'If I had known, sir, that Mr. Adams could have effected what he has done, I would not only have submitted to the absence I have endured, painful as it has been, but I would not have opposed it, even though three years more should be added to the number (which Heaven avert!) I feel a pleasure in being able to sacrifice my selfish passions to the general good, and in imitating the example which has taught me to consider myself and family but as the small dust of the balance, when compared with the great community.'

HE DEDICATED US TO LIBERTY

By Dumas Malone

MORE than a century after his death and almost two centuries after his birth, 13 April 1743, Thomas Jefferson remains our greatest personal symbol of the spirit of liberty. The cause of national independence was more perfectly embodied in George Washington, Andrew Jackson is probably more representative of American democracy, and Abraham Lincoln is our major symbol of the Union of States; but, while Lincoln freed the slaves, Jefferson is our most conspicuous apostle of liberty in general. In the present hour of mechanized despotism in other lands he stands forth as the complete antithesis of Adolf Hitler. In these two men, faith and fear, reason and prejudice, freedom and tyranny confront each other in timeless antagonism.

It would be quite improper, however, to carry the contrast so far as to say that the Fuehrer is positive and active, while the author of the Declaration of Independence was essentially negative and passive. Most people, when they think of Jefferson, will recall his famous statement that human beings are endowed by their Creator with the unalienable right of liberty, and some of them have assumed the meaning of this to be that they don't need to do anything about it. There was nothing in his philosophy or practice, however, which should lead any one to suppose that freedom comes to any man or any people as a painless inheritance.

Said he to the Marquis de Lafayette a century and a half ago: 'We are not to expect to be translated from despotism to liberty in a feather bed.' Freedom, as he and his colleagues knew full well in 1776, is something that men must fight for; otherwise there would have been no need for them to pledge to each other

From *The New York Times Magazine*, 13 April 1941. By permission of the author and *The New York Times*.

their lives, their fortunes, and their sacred honor. What they regarded as priceless was not peace but liberty.

The facile penman of the most noted of American political documents had no personal liking for the clash of arms. Indeed, above all things, he found delight in the tranquillity of his book-lined study and in the peaceful pursuit of science. Yet he had no thought, in 1776 or afterward, of taking his ease in Zion. He was no apostle of negation. 'The tree of liberty,' he said in 1787, 'must be refreshed from time to time with the blood of patriots and tyrants. It is its natural manure.'

In later years, especially when he was bearing the responsibilities of executive office, his utterances were more restrained, and he preferred to employ peaceful measures as long as there was hope that these would prove effective; but there never was a time when he countenanced complacency in the face of tyranny, or when he thought that freedom could be won or maintained without pain or cost.

He and the comrades of his early manhood, as they struggled to overthrow ancient tyrannies, thought of themselves as living in an age of beginnings from which more just governments would emerge. Many of these comrades fell away from him when the storm in France was gathering fury, but he wrote to one of his friends there:

'I continue eternally attached to the principles of your revolution. I hope it will end in the establishment of some firm government, friendly to liberty, and capable of maintaining it. If it does, the world will become inevitably free.'

Without condoning excesses, he regarded the violence of that era as an incident in the struggle for new freedoms. If he were here now, no one would be quicker to perceive that the far greater violence of our time is an incident in the struggle to destroy freedoms and to make men slaves.

Viewed in its world setting, the struggle of Jefferson's own presidency was for the maintenance of such liberty as the feeble American Republic had already won, at a time when new tyrannies had arisen in Europe to replace the old. Two years after his retirement, in the midst of world conflict and threats of American disunion, he said:

'The last hope of human liberty in this world rests on us. We ought, for so dear a stake, to sacrifice every attachment and every enmity.'

In a time like ours, when American strength is so much greater and isolation is so much less complete, it is unlikely that he would have much patience with those who speak complacently or timorously of the sunset of freedom and the coming of the night.

The eternal elements in Jefferson are the spirit of liberty that burned within his breast as an undying flame, and the faith that by free intelligence the problems of humanity can at last be solved. But there is no eternal validity in the specific means that he advocated or employed. Some of these now seem as antiquated as the clothes he wore.

As he said toward the end of his life, the dead have no rights, the world always belongs to the living, and every generation has to be trusted to manage its own affairs. Obviously, he did not expect the Republic to be directed from the graveyard at Monticello; but the inscription on his tombstone in which he described himself as 'Author of the Declaration of Independence, of the Statute of Virginia for Religious Freedom, and Father of the University of Virginia' reveals the hope within him that he would be remembered as an implacable foe of tyranny.

A list of specific tyrannies that Jefferson opposed would be interesting but relatively unimportant, for many of these have changed their form and others have disappeared. The important thing to remember is this: he attacked those that seemed most menacing in his own time. At the outset of his career he spoke much of the despotism of kings, but it would be utterly absurd to apply to King George VI the charges that he made against King George III. It would be equally absurd to apply to the American Republic today his fearful statements of a century and a half ago about the encroachments of the Federal Government upon the States. Most of his strongest language dates from the period when he was leader of the opposition. When he was President he was fully convinced of the need for united action against threats of disunion emanating from New England.

He was rarely permitted to be a closet-philosopher for long;

during most of his life he was a practicing statesman, and as such he did not succeed in establishing a record of unvarying consistency. When he was President he made compromises, as responsible officers so generally have to do, and upon occasion he assumed powers that he might easily have described as danerous if wielded by another hand at another time. When he imposed his well-known embargo he was compelled to infringe upon the economic freedom of individuals, in behalf of the larger interest as he perceived it.

It is grossly unjust to his memory to attribute to him such a preposterous doctrine as that government should be weak under any and all circumstances, but it is correct to say that he valued power only as a means and not as an end. 'The freedom and happiness of man . . . are the sole objects of all legitimate government,' he said. To those persons in the world today who value power for its own sake he would be unalterably opposed.

No one has any right to say that if Jefferson were living now he would favor or oppose any specific measure in either domestic or foreign policy. But we can say this, and it is enough: he would oppose with all his might what he regarded as the greatest tyrannies of this age and the chief obstacles to the free life of the human spirit; and he would do all within his power to establish the rule of free intelligence upon the earth. 'Light and liberty go together,' as he perceived.

He was never a defender of an imperfect and unjust status quo, either in his own country or in the world, but always believed in the necessity of change and the possibility of vast improvement. The road to human perfection has proved longer than he thought, showing that it needs to be recharted; and some men have employed his language of individualism as a cloak for selfishness, indolence, and greed; but never has it been more important than it is now to reassert his faith in light and freedom.

With entire appropriateness, therefore, we may cite the famous words he wrote shortly before his election to the presidency. 'I have sworn upon the altar of God eternal hostility against every form of tyranny over the mind of man.' We may likewise invoke the declaration of faith he penned at the beginning of his career: 'The God who gave us life, gave us liberty at the same time: the hand of force may destroy, but it cannot disjoin them.'

One of the most challenging of all his practical admonitions was uttered privately in 1811, at a time when this country was being drawn into the maelstrom of world war and was threatened by internal dissension. Perhaps it represents, as well as any quotation from another period can ever do, the attitude that he would take if he were living now, amid perils that are greater than any we have faced since he was gathered to his fathers:

'When we reflect that the eyes of the virtuous all over the earth are turned with anxiety on us, as the only depositories of the sacred fire of liberty, and that our falling into anarchy would decide forever the destinies of mankind, and seal the political heresy that man is incapable of self-government, the only contest between divided friends should be who will dare farthest into the ranks of the common enemy.'

He would expect us to designate the common enemy and the divided friends and to determine the precise form of our own daring.

FAITH IN THE PEOPLE

By Thomas Jefferson

AT the first session of our Legislature [in Virginia] after the Declaration of Independence, we passed a law abolishing entails. And this was followed by one abolishing the privilege of primogeniture, and dividing the lands of intestates equally among all their children, or other representatives. These laws, drawn by myself, laid the axe to the foot of pseudo-aristocracy. And had another which I prepared been adopted by the legislature, our work would have been complete. It was a bill for the more general diffusion of learning. This proposed to divide every county into wards of five or six miles square, like your townships; to establish in each ward a free school for reading, writing, and common arithmetic; to provide for the annual selection of the best subjects from these schools, who might receive, at the public expense, a higher degree of education at a district school; and from these district schools to select a certain number of the most promising subjects, to be completed at an University, where all the useful sciences should be taught. Worth and genius would thus have been sought out from every condition of life, and completely prepared by education for defeating the competition of wealth and birth for public trusts.

My proposition had, for a further object, to impart to these wards those portions of self-government for which they are best qualified, by confiding to them the care of their poor, their roads, police, elections, the nomination of jurors, administration of justice in small cases, elementary exercises of militia; in short, to have made them little republics, with a warden at the head of each, for all those concerns which, being under their eye, they would better manage than the larger republics of the county or

From A Letter to John Adams, 28 October 1813.

State. A general call of ward meetings by their wardens on the same day through the State, would at any time produce the genuine sense of the people on any required point, and would enable the State to act in mass, as your people [in New England] have so often done, and with so much effect by their town meetings. The law for religious freedom, which made a part of this system, having put down the aristocracy of the clergy, and restored to the citizen the freedom of the mind, and those of entails and descents nurturing an equality of condition among them, this on education would have raised the mass of the people to the high ground of moral respectability necessary to their own safety, and to orderly government; and would have completed the great object of qualifying them to select the veritable aristoi, for the trusts of government, to the exclusion of the pseudalists . . .

With respect to aristocracy, we should further consider, that before the establishment of the American States, nothing was known to history but the man of the Old World, crowded within limits either small or overcharged, and steeped in the vices which that situation generates. A government adapted to such men would be one thing; but a very different one, that for the man of these States. Here every one may have land to labor for himself, if he chooses; or, preferring the exercise of any other industry, may exact for it such compensation as not only to afford a comfortable subsistence, but wherewith to provide for a cessation from labor in old age. Every one, by his property, or by his satisfactory situation, is interested in the support of law and order. And such men may safely and advantageously reserve to themselves a wholesome control over their public affairs, and a degree of freedom, which, in the hands of the *canaille* of the cities of Europe, would be instantly perverted to the demolition and destruction of everything public and private. The history of the last twenty-five years of France, and of the last forty years in America, nay of its last two hundred years, proves the truth of both parts of this observation.

But even in Europe a change has sensibly taken place in the mind of man. Science had liberated the ideas of those who read and reflect, and the American example had kindled feelings of right in the people. An insurrection has consequently begun,

of science, talents, and courage, against rank and birth, which
have fallen into contempt. It has failed in its first effort, because
the mobs of the cities, the instrument used for its accomplishment, debased by ignorance, poverty, and vice, could not be restrained to rational action. But the world will recover from the
panic of this first catastrophe. Science is progressive, and talents
and enterprise on the alert. Resort may be had to the people
of the country, a more governable power from their principles
and subordination; and rank, and birth, and tinsel-aristocracy
will finally shrink into insignificance, even there. This, however,
we have no right to meddle with. It suffices for us, if the moral
and physical condition of our own citizens qualifies them to
select the able and good for the direction of their government,
with a recurrence of elections at such short periods as will enable them to displace an unfaithful servant, before the mischief
he meditates may be irremediable.

I have thus stated my opinion on a point on which we differ,
not with a view to controversy, for we are both too old to change
opinions which are the result of a long life of inquiry and reflection; but on the suggestions of a former letter of yours, that
we ought not to die before we have explained ourselves to each
other. We acted in perfect harmony, through a long and perilous
contest for our liberty and independence. A constitution has
been acquired, which, though neither of us thinks perfect, yet
both consider as competent to render our fellow citizens the happiest and the securest on whom the sun has ever shone. If we do
not think exactly alike as to its imperfections, it matters little to
our country, which, after devoting to it long lives of disinterested labor, we have delivered over to our successors in life, who
will be able to take care of it and of themselves . . .

LINCOLN

By James Russell Lowell

His was no lonely mountain-peak of mind,
Thrusting to thin air o'er our cloudy bars,
A sea-mark now, now lost in vapors blind;
Broad prairie rather, genial, level-lined,
Fruitful and friendly for all human kind,
Yet also nigh to heaven and loved of loftiest stars . . .
Here was a type of the true elder race,
And one of Plutarch's men talked with us face to face . . .
He knew to bide his time,
And can his fame abide,
Still patient in his simple faith sublime,
Till the wise years decide.
Great captains, with their guns and drums,
Disturb our judgment for the hour,
But at last silence comes;
These all are gone, and, standing like a tower,
Our children shall behold his fame.
The kindly-earnest, brave, foreseeing man,
Sagacious, patient, dreading praise, not blame,
New birth of our new soil, the first American.

From Ode Recited at the Harvard Commemoration 21 July 1865.

AUTOBIOGRAPHY

By Abraham Lincoln

I WAS born February 12, 1809, in Hardin County, Kentucky. My parents were both born in Virginia, of undistinguished families —second families, perhaps I should say. My mother, who died in my tenth year, was of a family of the name of Hanks, some of whom now reside in Adams, and others in Macon County, Illinois. My paternal grandfather, Abraham Lincoln, emigrated from Rockingham County, Virginia, to Kentucky about 1781 or 1782, where a year or two later he was killed by the Indians, not in battle, but by stealth, when he was laboring to open a farm in the forest. His ancestors, who were Quakers, went to Virginia from Berks County, Pennsylvania. An effort to identify them with the New England family of the same name ended in nothing more definite than a similarity of Christian names in both families, such as Enoch, Levi, Mordecai, Solomon, Abraham, and the like.

My father, at the death of his father, was but six years of age, and he grew up literally without education. He removed from Kentucky to what is now Spencer County, Indiana, in my eighth year. We reached our new home about the time the state came into the Union. It was a wild region, with many bears and other wild animals still in the woods. There I grew up. There were some schools, so called, but no qualification was ever required of a teacher beyond 'readin', writin', and cipherin',' to the rule of three. If a straggler supposed to understand Latin happened to sojourn in the neighborhood, he was looked upon as a wizard. There was absolutely nothing to excite ambition for education. Of course, when I came of age I did not know much. Still, somehow, I could read, write, and cipher to the rule of three, but that was all. I have not been to school since. The little advance

I now have upon this store of education, I have picked up from time to time under the pressure of necessity.

I was raised to farm work, which I continued till I was twenty-two. At twenty-one I came to Illinois, Macon County. Then I got to New Salem, at that time in Sangamon, now in Menard County, where I remained a year as a sort of clerk in a store. Then came the Black Hawk War; and I was elected a captain of volunteers, a success which gave me more pleasure than any I have had since. I went the campaign, was elated, ran for the legislature the same year (1832), and was beaten—the only time I ever have been beaten by the people. The next and three succeeding biennial elections I was elected to the legislature. I was not a candidate afterward. During this legislative period I had studied law, and removed to Springfield to practice it. In 1846 I was once elected to the lower House of Congress. Was not a candidate for re-election. From 1849 to 1854, both inclusive, practiced law more assiduously than ever before. Always a Whig, in politics; and generally on the Whig electoral tickets, making active canvasses. I was losing interest in politics when the repeal of the Missouri Compromise aroused me again. What I have done since that is pretty well known.

If any personal description of me is thought desirable, it may be said I am, in height, six feet four inches, nearly; lean in flesh, weighing on an average one hundred and eighty pounds; dark complexion, with coarse black hair and gray eyes. No other marks or brands recollected.

1859

OPEN LETTER TO HORACE GREELEY

Executive Mansion,
Washington, August 22, 1862

HON. HORACE GREELEY.

DEAR SIR: I have just read yours of the 19th, addressed to myself through the New York *Tribune*. If there be in it any statements or assumptions of fact which I may know to be erroneous, I do not, now and here, controvert them. If there be in it any inferences which I may believe to be falsely drawn, I do not, now and here, argue against them. If there be perceptible in it an impatient and dictatorial tone, I waive it in deference to an old friend whose heart I have always supposed to be right.

As to the policy I 'seem to be pursuing,' as you say, I have not meant to leave any one in doubt.

I would save the Union. I would save it the shortest way under the Constitution. The sooner the national authority can be restored, the nearer the Union will be 'the Union as it was.' If there be those who would not save the Union unless they could at the same time save slavery, I do not agree with them. If there be those who would not save the Union unless they could at the same time destroy slavery, I do not agree with them. My paramount object in this struggle is to save the Union, and is not either to save or to destroy slavery. If I could save the Union without freeing any slave, I would do it; and if I could save it by freeing all the slaves, I would do it; and if I could save it by freeing some and leaving others alone, I would also do that. What I do about slavery and the colored race, I do because I believe it helps to save the Union; and what I forbear, I forbear because I do not believe it would help to save the Union. I shall do less whenever I shall believe what I am doing hurts the cause, and I shall do more whenever I shall believe doing more will help the cause. I shall try to correct errors when shown to be errors, and I shall adopt new views so fast as they shall appear to be true views.

I have here stated my purpose according to my view of official duty; and I intend no modification of my oft-expressed personal wish that all men everywhere could be free.

Yours,

A. Lincoln.

SECOND INAUGURAL ADDRESS

4 March 1865

By Abraham Lincoln

FELLOW COUNTRYMEN: At this second appearing to take the oath of the presidential office, there is less occasion for an extended address than there was at the first. Then a statement, somewhat in detail, of a course to be pursued, seemed fitting and proper. Now, at the expiration of four years, during which public declarations have been constantly called forth on every point and phase of the great contest which still absorbs the attention and engrosses the energies of the nation, little that is new could be presented. The progress of our arms, upon which all else chiefly depends, is as well known to the public as to myself; and it is, I trust, reasonably satisfactory and encouraging to all. With high hope for the future, no prediction in regard to it is ventured.

On the occasion corresponding to this four years ago, all thoughts were anxiously directed to an impending civil war. All dreaded it—all sought to avert it. While the inaugural address was being delivered from this place, devoted altogether to saving the Union without war, insurgent agents were in the city seeking to destroy it without war—seeking to dissolve the Union, and divide effects, by negotiation. Both parties deprecated war; but one of them would make war rather than let the nation survive; and the other would accept war rather than let it perish. And the war came.

One-eighth of the whole population were colored slaves, not distributed generally over the Union, but localized in the southern part of it. These slaves constituted a peculiar and powerful interest. All knew that this interest was, somehow, the cause of the war. To strengthen, perpetuate, and extend this interest was the object for which the insurgents would rend the Union, even by war; while the government claimed no right to do more than to restrict the territorial enlargement of it.

Neither party expected for the war the magnitude or the duration which it has already attained. Neither anticipated that the cause of the conflict might cease with, or even before, the conflict itself should cease. Each looked for an easier triumph, and a result less fundamental and astounding. Both read the same Bible, and pray to the same God; and each invokes His aid against the other. It may seem strange that any men should dare to ask a just God's assistance in wringing their bread from the sweat of other men's faces; but let us judge not, that we be not judged. The prayers of both could not be answered—that of neither has been answered fully.

The Almighty has his own purposes. 'Woe unto the world because of offenses! for it must needs be that offenses come; but woe to that man by whom the offense cometh.' If we shall suppose that American slavery is one of those offenses which, in the providence of God, must needs come, but which, having continued through His appointed time, He now wills to remove, and that He gives to both North and South this terrible war, as the woe due to those by whom the offense came, shall we discern therein any departure from those divine attributes which the believers in a living God always ascribe to Him? Fondly do we hope—fervently do we pray—that this mighty scourge of war may speedily pass away. Yet, if God wills that it continue until all the wealth piled by the bondman's two hundred and fifty years of unrequited toil shall be sunk, and until every drop of blood drawn with the lash shall be paid by another drawn with the sword, as was three thousand years ago, so still it must be said, 'The judgments of the Lord are true and righteous altogether.'

With malice toward none; with charity for all; with firmness in the right, as God gives us to see the right, let us strive on to finish the work we are in; to bind up the nation's wounds; to care for him who shall have borne the battle, and for his widow, and his orphan—to do all which may achieve and cherish a just and lasting peace among ourselves, and with all nations.

THE NEW AMERICAN SYMBOLISM

By Ralph Henry Gabriel

PERHAPS the most striking phenomenon in the post-Appomattox history of the democratic faith is the evolution of its symbolism. It has paced evenly with the intensification of the sentiment of American nationalism. After 1865 the symbolic significance of the Declaration of Independence declined relatively and the glorious Fourth degenerated. The Fourth of July address was replaced by the oration pronounced on Memorial Day. Similarly Washington went into relative eclipse. He was not, however, forgotten. And his cult underwent a revival in 1932 when Americans celebrated with becoming piety and ceremony the two hundredth anniversary of his birth. After Appomattox and particularly after 1900 the place once held in the American democratic symbolism by the Declaration was taken by the Constitution, and the figure of Washington was replaced by that of Lincoln. After Lenin's triumph in Russia in October 1917, Americans were less inclined to emphasize with Jefferson the natural right of revolution.

One of the reasons for the relative decline of the older symbols was that they were both associated too closely with the eighteenth century. They belonged to the period of Georgian architecture, of Revere silver, and of Sheraton chairs. They depended as symbols for their emotional power upon the imaginative re-creation of eighteenth-century issues and scenes. The changing perspective of time affected each symbol adversely. When the twentieth century opened upon a United States of continental proportions in possession of an empire stretching half-way around the world, it was difficult for the average American to imagine that fear of and hostility to monarchy which was the theme of the Declaration and of which Washington was the personification.

In the case of the Washington symbol other factors militated against the perpetuation of that universal appeal which the living hero had for his own generation. The image was lost of that dynamic young rebel leader who gathered a ragged army about himself, held it together through every discouragement, and finally brought it to triumph. It was the elderly Washington, the Father of his Country, who became the symbol of national unity to mid-nineteenth century Americans. Gilbert Stuart's portrait, whose sternness was partly the result of the first President's iron false teeth, became the universally accepted effigy. The generation which tried to avoid the tragedy begun at Sumter when they made use of the memory of Washington, suppressed the potential symbol of the right of rebellion and built up that of nationalism. Unconsciously Washington was dehumanized. The clumsy sculptors who dressed him in Roman togas assisted in the process. The majestic obelisk, pointing in chaste and solitary beauty toward the sky, is the perfect artistic representation of the symbolism which was useful before 1861—and which remains useful today. But it meant that for symbolic purposes Washington had ceased to be a man of flesh and blood and had become almost an abstraction. The dignified, self-disciplined, austere first President remains today an important national symbol, but he is no longer first in the hearts of his countrymen. Lincoln holds that place, with the exception of the South where Lee is enshrined. Yet in the modern age of tyrants the memory of the chieftain who, after leading his people to freedom, put away the sword and gave their government to the people takes on a new significance.

The preservation of the Union—and of the Constitution—by the Civil War prepared the way for that reverence of the document of 1787 now so important in the twentieth century. The doctrine of states' rights, in the old Southern sense, was dead. Nationalism triumphed over sectionalism, the supremacy of the federal Constitution over those of the states was established.

The saving of the Union and the freeing of the Negroes were, moreover, emotionally related. The ogres of secession and of slavery were exorcised from American culture at the same time. To the victors the Constitution had been on the side of righteousness. For the men and women of the North the outcome of the Civil War fitted into a larger pattern, that of the ultimate triumph of good over evil, of God over Satan. Lieutenant Oliver Wendell Holmes, on leave from the front, read at the first reunion of his Harvard class a poem of his own composition that expressed the crusading mood dominating the war years and that, in time, came to serve as the background (though not for Associate Justice Holmes) of the cult of the Constitution.

> Let others celebrate our high endeavor
> When peace once more her starry flag shall fling
> Wide o'er the land our arms made free forever;
> We do in silence what the world shall sing.[1]

The Supreme Court, which functioned without fanfare but in a physical and ceremonial setting which emphasized dignity, became, in an age of developing nationalism, the living symbol of the old American ideal of a government by law. The Court symbolized the faith that man can find fixed and certain principles upon which to build his social structure.

The Court, moreover, grew in importance as the social significance of religion declined. Churches do not dominate urban America as they once did the countryside and the rural village. As the religious interpretation of the fundamental law declined in prestige, the influence of other interpreters increased. And of these secular expounders of the basic laws of nature and of society the two most important classes were the men of the laboratory and of the robe. It is true that the Supreme Court before the Wagner decision in 1937 followed often a narrow and reactionary policy in apparent support of corporate wealth, and the power of management over its employees. For this reason it enjoyed the active support of big business. But it is an error to assume that such a fact is an adequate explanation of the phenomenon either of the rise of judicial supremacy or of its

[1] T. V. Smith, *Creative Skeptics*, 1934, p. 187.

acceptance by the citizens of the Republic. Institutions, like social beliefs, are to be explained in terms of all their utilities. In an age of change when the legislature, which the Revolutionary fathers had trusted, was under suspicion and when the Church had lost much of its mid-nineteenth century authority, the Supreme Court emerged as an institution which enabled men to believe that they could establish their social structures upon the rock of fundamental principles. Judicial supremacy is, then, but another aspect of man's age-old search for security. The Supreme Court has replaced the Church as the American symbol of social stability.

The Lincoln cult rose with that of the Constitution. The two are inseparable. Neither can be understood without the other. Together they represent the most significant development in the post-Appomattox social beliefs of the American people.

Before the end of the Civil War Lincoln's contemporaries had discovered that the frontier lawyer, untrained for executive responsibility, was a great man. The common blindness of the 1860's to his genius seems, often, inexplicable to generations taught from earliest childhood to revere his memory. Yet it is understandable. The war was a vast disaster. Defeats followed victories with disheartening swiftness. Until near the end, the outcome remained uncertain. The attention of those men who were not soldiers was taken from the battle just lost to the campaign just begun. In the confusion and clamor inevitable when a democracy wages war, the presidential figure at Washington did not stand out like a sentinel pine. The generals, particularly Sherman and Grant, commanded the headlines. Lincoln's momentary prestige, moreover, was lowered by a campaign of ridicule and of vilification. John Wilkes Booth suddenly directed the thought and the emotions of the nation toward one bier.

Twentieth-century readers are not surprised that Whitman, while the assassination was still fresh in the minds of men, could write 'O Captain, My Captain' and, not long after, that immortal hymn to death, 'When Lilacs Last in the Dooryard Bloom'd.' These two poems are timeless. That they could have been produced in 1865, however, is almost incredible; they suggest the transcendent quality of Whitman's genius. Emerson reflected more truly the attitude of a generation who knew the man, Lincoln, and who lived with him through the tragedy of war.

Asked by his fellow townsmen to speak at the memorial service held at Concord on April 19, 1865, Emerson described Lincoln as a unique product of his native land. 'He was thoroughly American,' said the great transcendentalist, 'had never crossed the sea, had never been spoiled by English insularity or French dissipation; a quiet, native, aboriginal man, as an acorn from the oak; no aping of foreigners, no frivolous accomplishments, Kentuckian born, working on a farm, a flatboatman, a captain in the Black Hawk War, a country lawyer, a representative in the rural legislature of Illinois;—on such modest foundations the broad structure of his fame was laid.' [2]

The fame of Lincoln grew as the nineteenth century hurried to its close. Yet the martyred President remained an intimate hero. Thousands lived who had known or, at least, had seen him. A bulging sheaf of Lincoln stories, authentic and apocryphal, was collected. Legends grew up about him. Emerson, in a eulogy of Lincoln after the excitement of his death had passed, concluded that, had it not been for the printing press, Lincoln would 'have become mythological in a very few years.' [3]

It is strange that the mystical Emerson should so misjudge the temper of the scientific age into which he had come in his declining years. He thought that telegraphs and newspapers, that books of history and of biography, that scientific historical criticism and doctrines of evolution had put an end to such folk mythology as had transformed Odin into a god. Emerson's contemporaries agreed with him in this conclusion. Yet twentieth-century generations, who never saw Lincoln in the flesh, who thought they were scientific, and who were sure they were sophisticated, elevated the dead Lincoln to the status of a demigod.

The evidence is on every hand. It consists primarily of the use of Lincoln's words as an argument for the validity of a position or the soundness of a principle. The implication always is

2 R. P. Basler, *The Lincoln Legend*, 1935, pp. 236-7.
3 Ibid. p. 307.

that, if Lincoln so believed, the matter is closed. No man can guess the number of times since 1900 references have been made to Lincoln, the authority, in the political and social literature of the nation. His name has been called upon to support causes as widely different as those of Calvin Coolidge and of Earl Browder. Two illustrations will suffice. On February 12, 1938, *The Saturday Evening Post* entitled its leading editorial, 'With Malice Toward None.' No 'words of Lincoln,' said the editorial writer, 'have worn so well as his appeal to the American people to be firm in the right, as God has given them to see the right, with malice toward none, with charity for all . . . But there is a letter of his to Cuthbert Bullitt, written nearly three years earlier, not long after the capture of New Orleans, and dealing with reconstruction in Louisiana. His concluding words are: "I shall do nothing in malice. What I deal with is too vast for malicious feeling." . . . The responsibilities of government are at all times too vast a thing for malice, or for the appearance of malice . . . It does not promote national confidence or national discipline when Administration spokesmen rail against aristocratic anarchists unlashing their bulldogs of the press as part of a general conspiracy against the nation's well-being. It does not promote domestic peace if legitimate democratic criticism of government policy is always to be denounced as Fascism—and a straightforward, open, democratic protest becomes Sabotage.'

A little more than four months later the President of the United States spoke, on July 3, from that same Gettysburg battlefield which had called forth Lincoln's most famous address. 'It seldom helps to wonder how a statesman of one generation would surmount the crisis of another,' said the second Roosevelt. 'But the fullness of the stature of Lincoln's nature and the fundamental conflict which events forced upon his presidency, invite us ever to turn to him for help.' [4]

American poets have been more explicit in their homage to the shade of Lincoln. Edwin Markham published in 1901 his *Lincoln, the Man of the People*. It was the last great poem which, in the tradition of Emerson's memorial address, presented the

[4] New York *Times*, 4 July 1938.

war President as a product of the culture of the young Republic.
Nine years later Edwin Arlington Robinson's 'The Master' suggested the shift toward apotheosis.

> For he to whom we had applied
> Our shopman's test of age and worth,
> Was elemental when he died,
> As he was ancient at his birth:
> The saddest among kings of earth,
> Bowed with a galling crown, this man
> Met rancor with a cryptic mirth,
> Laconic—and Olympian.

During the dark days of the World War, when democracy seemed
at stake and Americans gave their lives that freedom might not
perish from the earth, Vachel Lindsay wrote 'Abraham Lincoln
Walks at Midnight.' Its theme was the return of the troubled
spirit of Lincoln to his old home where

> On the well-worn stones
> He walks until the dawn-stars burn away . . .

> He cannot rest until a spirit-dawn
> Shall come;—the shining hope of Europe free;
> The league of sober folk, the Worker's Earth,
> Bringing long peace to Cornland, Alp and Sea.

> It breaks his heart that kings must murder still,
> That all his hours of travail here for men
> Seem yet in vain. And who will bring white peace
> That he may sleep upon his hill again?

Lindsay's poem inspired Oswald Villard's *Nation* to comment
editorially on 'The Poetical Cult of Lincoln.' 'Our poets,' said
the editorial writer, 'have a folk-hero who to the common folk-
virtues of shrewdness and kindness adds essential wit and eloquence and loftiness of soul. Perhaps the disposition just now
to purge him of all rankness and make him out a saint and a
mystic may not last forever, but obviously it is a step in his
poetical history analogous to those steps which ennobled Charle-
magne and Arthur and canonized Joan of Arc.' [5]

[5] 17 May 1919.

The *Nation's* staff writer obviously thought that the celebration of folk-heroes was a part of the license allowed to poets. Even as he wrote, however, John Drinkwater, Englishman, finished his play, *Abraham Lincoln*. It opened in New York in 1919, and achieved a triumph. In 1920 the playwright published a little book, *Lincoln, the World Emancipator*. It began: 'Lincoln, the world emancipator. It is a significant phrase, having surely an air of reality for those who know the story of the man . . . Intimately of the world, yet unsoiled by it; vividly in contact with every emotion of his fellows and aware always of the practical design of their lives; always lonely, brooding apart from all, yet alienated from none—Abraham Lincoln, pioneer, citizen, country lawyer, astute politician, and incorruptible statesman, stands readily enough in the alert imagination as a new symbol of regenerative power. Already, half a century after his death, the mind of man perceives in this single-hearted champion of a moral idea a figure to whom all sorrows and ambitions may be brought, a touch-stone by which every ideal of conduct may be tried, a witness for the encouragement of the forlornest hope.' [6]

Drinkwater's religious implications are unmistakable. How much he meant by his words is obscure. They probably should not be taken literally. Their significance, however, lies in the fact that they were not looked upon as funny. His, however, was not the only rhetoric concerning Lincoln to use the language of worship. In February 1931, in the midst of a gaunt and despairing winter when rumors of revolution were whispered about, Dr. John Wesley Hill lifted his hands in supplication. 'Oh, Lincoln,' he prayed, 'Arise! Stand forth that we may gaze as thou didst at Gettysburg; stretch forth thy hand; point the way of destiny and duty that America may be thy living monument down to the end of time. Oh, Lincoln, come down from thy summit of bronze and march!' [7]

The opening weeks of 1937 saw shadows deepen in America as news of calamities and of strife filled the press. Vast floods brought destruction and death to New England and the Ohio

---

[6] John Drinkwater, *Lincoln, the World Emancipator*, 1920, pp. 3-4.
[7] *National Republic*, February 1931.

Valley. Industrial war raged in the automobile and the steel industries. Abroad England sought to repair the damage caused by the constitutional crisis ending in the abdication of Edward VIII. Franco shelled the defenses of Madrid, and seemed about to enter the city. Mussolini, conqueror of Ethiopia, in imitation of the Caesars, prepared a triumphant tour to Tripoli and to Libya to proclaim Italy a Moslem power. Hitler, standing on January 30 before a wildly cheering Reichstag, repudiated the Treaty of Versailles and brought an epoch of European history to an end. On February 12, 1937, a sonnet led the *New York Herald Tribune's* 'Conning Tower' and was signed by the initials **G. A.** The poet used Whitman's title, 'O Captain, My Captain!'

> Lincoln, thou shouldst be living at this hour,
> Son of the soil, brother of poverty,
> Those hard sharers of great destiny;
> Exemplar of humility in power,
> Walking alone to meet thy waiting fate
> Whose shadow was reflected on thy brow,
> Lincoln, thy people invoke thy spirit now—
> Preserve, protect, defend our sovereign state!
> Lover of justice and the common good,
> Despiser of lies, from thy yonder solitude
> Consider the land of thine and freedom's birth—
> Cry out: It shall not perish from the earth!
> Engrave upon our hearts that holy vow.
> Spirit of Lincoln, thy country needs thee now.

A cult has a ritual. Ritual is the expression of reverence through symbolic and repeated behavior patterns. The Lincoln ritual is performed each year on February 12. On that day or on the nearest possible day the press and the popular magazines publish again the familiar stories and portraits. Editorial writers discuss Lincoln once more and often seek to judge current happenings against the eternal verities which guided his life. Children in the public schools pronounce the Gettysburg oration or the Second Inaugural.

A developed cult produces unbelievers. Edgar Lee Masters is one of these. Masters' book, entitled *Lincoln, the Man,* was published in 1931 and produced a violent though not universal storm. The diligent editors of *The Literary Digest* compiled the comments upon the book. Among them were the following. 'It is far too late in the day for any small confectioner of acidulated antisocial epigrams to attempt the destruction of the fame of Abraham Lincoln.' 'Lincoln belongs to the ages; Edgar Lee Masters, in this instance, to but a fleeting and nasty moment.' 'We are thus reminded now that we must revere Lincoln with greater sanctity. This latest abuse will accomplish good if it awakens all of us, as it should, to our duty to give expression to our love of Lincoln by applying to our lives the ideals of human service which governed his career and assure for him immortality.' [8]

A developed cult requires a sanctuary. That of Lincoln has three—the birthplace in Kentucky, the grave in Illinois, and the great Memorial at Washington. Of these the last is the most important. Analysis reveals significant characteristics. It is a Greek temple. Within it is a graven image. Daniel Chester French's figure is a romanticized Lincoln. Three devices enhance the religious atmosphere; on the walls in bronze are the words of the hero; a light falls from the ceiling upon his forehead; and above the brooding figure is an inscription. It reads: 'In this temple as in the hearts of the people for whom he saved the Union the memory of Abraham Lincoln is enshrined forever.' Hubert Work, Secretary of the Interior, called the Memorial in 1926 holy ground. In such temples and with similar inscriptions the citizens of ancient Greece placed statues of Apollo. By so little is the twentieth century after Christ separated from the fifth before His coming.

What is it that Americans worship when they stand, uncovered, before that great, silent figure? For worship they do, more sincerely many of them, than when they occupy their pews in church. They do reverence, if one may hazard an analysis of those inarticulate emotions which put an end to loud talk and to boisterous conduct, to a personification of the American democratic faith. The phenomenon of Lincoln, Woodrow Wilson once remarked, makes it possible to believe in democracy.

[8] 28 February 1931.

He rose, without the aid of a patron, from the poverty of the open-faced camp on Pidgeon Creek to more than the White House. He wielded such power as no previous President had ever known. Mighty armies of volunteers marched at his command to fight for the Union and for the freedom of men. He led his people to a righteous victory. But triumph did not make of him a Caesar. Through all the years in which he sat in the seats of the mighty he remained the sincere, humane, and humble democrat. His career was the fulfillment of the romantic democratic vision; it was Aladdin's dream come true. He founded his life on the Constitution and on its fundamental moral law. In striking the irons from the slave he gave new meaning to the doctrine of the free individual. He not only saved the Union; he expressed in unforgettable words the mission of democracy and of America. They are written on the walls of his temple: 'With malice toward none; with charity for all; with firmness in the right as God gives us to see the right, let us strive to finish the work we are in; to bind up the nation's wounds; to care for him who shall have borne the battle and for his widow and his orphan, to do all which may achieve a just and lasting peace among ourselves, and with all nations.'

The brooding Lincoln who sits in the Memorial at Washington is first among the folk-heroes of the American people. He personifies that faith upon which the Republic rests.

THE FAITH OF WOODROW WILSON

By William Langer

THE dedication of Woodrow Wilson's birthplace as a national memorial, coming as it does in the midst of a great international crisis, should serve not only to recall and refresh the memory of a truly great American but to remind us of his message to his country and to mankind, confronted with a highly organized, unbelievably efficient and utterly ruthless dictatorship, the few democracies remaining in the world today see before them the fate of Europe. On many sides may be heard the question whether democracy can be saved and whether it is worth saving.

Wilson's reply in the crisis of the World War was unequivocal: he spoke for democracy and was unshakable in his conviction of its superiority over any other system of government or life; he had boundless faith in the ultimate victory of democracy over autocracy, imperialism and militarism; he believed that men have the right to govern themselves, that small nations are entitled to respect along with the large, and that the world must be organized to prevent the ruthless exploitation or complete extermination of the weak by the strong.

What is going on in Europe today is the complete negation of everything that Wilson stood for: tyranny is the order of the day and the terrible power of Nazism, scoffing at ideas of liberty, equality, and international co-operation, rolls like a juggernaut over one free nation after another, reducing millions to a state of servitude. Now, indeed, is the time to recall the teaching of Wilson and to draw fresh inspiration from his message.

We know how Wilson viewed the great conflict of his time. We recall the circumstances under which we associated our-

From *The New York Times Magazine*, 4 May 1941. By permission of *The New York Times* and the author.

selves with the opponents of Germany; we appreciate the part
played by this country in bringing about the final victory and
drafting the terms of the peace settlements. It may be very instructive, however, to review and reconsider the policies and
objectives of our World War President, and to raise the question of their applicability to the present crisis.

One ought to begin, I think, by stressing Wilson's intense and
unswerving faith in democracy, his profound conviction that the
democratic way of life and the democratic system had proved
themselves in this country and that from the experience of the
American colonies something useful might be derived for the
world at large.

Woodrow Wilson had no use for 'governments clothed with
the strange trappings and the primitive authority of an age that
is altogether alien and hostile to our own,' he called them. Already in the Autumn of 1914 he saw that if Germany won, 'it
would change the course of our civilization and make the United
States a military nation,' whence it followed that 'England is
fighting our fight' and that we should put no obstacles in her
way.

To be sure, it was almost three years after the beginning of
the war before Wilson took this country into the fray. But this
was not because the President was an isolationist. Quite the contrary; like many other prominent Americans he realized that
the conditions of the modern world make isolation an illusion.

Addressing the League to Enforce Peace in May 1916, he declared: 'We are participants, whether we would or not, in the
life of the world. The interests of all nations are our own also.
We are partners with the rest.' And similarly in a speech at
Long Branch in September 1916: 'We can no longer indulge
our traditional provincialism. We are to play a leading part in
the world drama whether we like it or not.' And finally, in his
address at Shadow Lawn in November 1916: 'It does not suffice
to look, as some gentlemen are looking, back over their shoulders, to suggest that we do again what we did when we were
provincial and isolated and unconnected with the great forces
of the world, for now we are in the great drift of humanity
which is to determine the politics of every country in the world.'

Despite the Lusitania and other provocations, Wilson kept us out of war because he believed that we had a mission to fulfill toward mankind at large. As a great power standing aside, we could at the crucial moment step in as disinterested mediators, perhaps influence the terms of peace in the direction of moderation and justice, and certainly see to it that provision should be made for some type of international organization and action that would prevent the recurrence of such a catastrophe.

In the end this policy proved impossible; the German submarine campaign landed us in the war. But Wilson was more intent than ever on the organization of collective security after victory had been attained. He envisaged a league of democratic States: 'A steadfast concert for peace can never be maintained except by a partnership of democratic nations. No autocratic government should be trusted to keep faith with it or observe its covenants.'

He wanted self-determination for nations, and insisted that the rights of small States should be respected as are those of the great powers: 'Shall there be a common standard of right and privilege for all peoples and nations, or shall the strong do as they will and the weak suffer without redress?' The new world order, he held, must guarantee the political independence and territorial integrity of all States and must make provision for common action against aggressors.

Nor did he shun the eventual application of military force to attain this end: 'If you say, "We shall not have any war" you have got to have the force to make that "shall" bite'; 'If the peace presently made is to endure, it must be a peace made secure by the organized major force of mankind'; 'If the moral force of the world will not suffice, the physical force of the world shall.'

There is no need to analyze here the way in which these ideas were translated into the Covenant of the League of Nations, nor even to recall Wilson's insistence that the Covenant be made an integral and inextricable part of the peace settlements. The Covenant was essentially the expression of Anglo-American views and was a great disappointment to the French, who had thought in terms of a league of victors to hold down the vanquished and had advocated an international army which would have ignored accepted ideas of national sovereignty.

As a matter of fact, the Covenant as it stood proved to be too much for the American digestion. Plain ignorance on the part of many, slavish adherence to outworn slogans on the part of others, the let-up in crusading fervor on the part of most, and the exploitation of the situation by Wilson's political enemies resulted in rejection of the treaty and the Covenant.

Whether the American people in 1919-20 were really opposed to the League is still a moot question. Whether Wilson was maladroit in his handling of the situation can be debated *ad nauseam*. The fact of the matter is that the United States did not join the League. The President, who had suspected and distrusted the greed and wrongheadedness of the Europeans, was let down by his own people, in whom he had had boundless confidence and of whom he could never have dreamed that they would fling his Covenant into the gutter to rot, as Lloyd George puts it.

Of the League but little is heard in these hectic days. That it turned out a failure is a widely held opinion, and there are not a few Americans who have thanked Providence that we did not allow ourselves to be implicated. But a few points perhaps require consideration.

In the first place it is clear that the League with the United States as a member would have been a very different thing from what it became as a result of our defection. Our relative disinterestedness, our power, our prestige would have made all the difference in the world. Instead of the dynamic, creative force which Wilson had envisaged, it tended to become a mere method of preserving the status quo.

We who thought once more to wash our hands of responsibility and to stand aloof from the European mess may well in these cataclysmic days return to Woodrow Wilson. He had a vision and he had a message. Within the League, we might have helped to forestall disaster. We refused to play the role which Wilson regarded not only as desirable in the cause of humanity, but necessary in the interest of our own country.

Of course international collaboration means sacrifices, involves contributions. Wilson knew that too, but he was convinced that the game was well worth the candle, that for the good of the world and for our own good we would have to shoulder the burden. 'The League is dead; long live the League.' Wilson can still guide us, for it becomes more and more obvious that if the future of mankind is once more in jeopardy, the trouble has lain not with too much international organization and activity, but with too little.

contributions, Wilson knew that too, but he was convinced that the game was well worth the candle, that for the good of the world and for our own good we would have to shoulder the burden. The League is dead, long live the League, Wilson can still guide us, for it becomes more and more obvious that, if the future of mankind is once more in jeopardy, the trouble has lain not with too much international organization and activity, but with too little.

IV

Democracy in Action

MEN of character are the conscience of the society to which they belong.
RALPH WALDO EMERSON, 'Character,'
Essays, Second Series, 1844.

THERE is no trade or employment but the young man following it may become a hero.
WALT WHITMAN, *Song of Myself,* 1855.

THE main enterprise of the world for splendor, for extent, is the upbuilding of a man. The private life of one man shall be a more illustrious monarchy than any kingdom in history.
RALPH WALDO EMERSON, *The American Scholar,* 1837.

THE American democracy I have always loved is a different creature, appearing in many disguises. Sometimes she takes the form of a young labor organizer, sometimes of a farm wife, and sometimes of an old woman at an auction, telling the stranger how she plans to send her grandsons to college. She inspires the farmers sending instructions to their Senator in Washington—'He's our hired man, ain't he?'—and the travelers striking sudden friendships in a transcontinental bus, and the garageman in Tennessee who ends a long discussion by saying, 'Your car is good, mister, but I like my car,' as if to summarize in ten words Emerson's essay on self-reliance. Her manners are bad by European standards, but she makes this country a pleasant place to live in, and worth keeping that way. She deserves a book of her own, a treasury not of opinions but of people.
MALCOLM COWLEY, 'Americans All,'
The New Republic, 29 September 1941. By permission.

GOOD MEN—GOOD COUNTRY

In America, the necessity of clearing the forest, laying out town and street, and building every house and barn and fence, then church and town house, exhausted such means as the Pilgrims brought, and made the whole population poor; and the like necessity is still found in each new settlement . . . These needs gave their character to the public debates in every village and state. I have often been impressed at our country meetings with the accumulated virility, in each village, of five or six or eight or ten men, who speak so well, and so easily handle the affairs of the town. I often hear the business of a little town (with which I am most familiar) discussed with a clearness and thoroughness, and with a generosity too, that would have satisfied me had it been in one of the larger capitals . . .

And every one knows that in every town or city is always to be found a certain number of public-spirited men who perform, unpaid, a great amount of hard work in the interest of the churches, of schools, of public grounds, works of taste and refinement . . . With all our haste, and slipshod ways, and flippant self-assertion, I have seen examples of new grace and power in address that honor the country. It was my fortune not long ago, with my eyes directed on this subject, to fall in with an American to be proud of. I said never was there such force, good meaning, good sense, good action, combined with such domestic lovely behavior, such modesty and persistent preference for others. It is of course that he should ride well, shoot well, sail well, keep house well, administer affairs well; but he was the best talker, also, in the company: what with a perpetual practical wisdom, with an eye always to the working of the thing, what with the multitude and distinction of his facts (and one detected continually that he had a hand in everything that has been done), and in the temperance with which he parried all offense and opened the eyes of the person he talked with without contradicting him. Yet I said to myself, How little this man suspects, with his sympathy for men and his respect for lettered and scientific people, that he is not likely, in any company, to meet a man superior to himself. And I think this is a good country that can bear such a creature as he is.

RALPH WALDO EMERSON, 'Social Aims,' *Letters and Social Aims*, 1875.

Glad and Proud To Be American, He Writes To Tell Roosevelt Why

From the Herald Tribune Bureau

WASHINGTON, July 8.—President Roosevelt read to his press conference today a letter he had received from an unidentified resident of Missouri—a letter he thought appealing and an example of what an American should feel. In it the writer, a citizen of Czechoslovakian ancestry, outlined the reasons he was pleased with his citizenship.

The text of the letter, read by the President without further comment, follows:

'Dear President Roosevelt:

'I am a married man twenty-eight year old; a boy, three, and a girl, one. Here's how I feel about being an American.

'My ancestors were Czechoslovakians, my wife's English; but we're Americans.

'I look at my refrigerator, my oil heater and my radio. I'm glad I'm an American.

'My children get cod liver oil, nourishing food and a doctor's watchful care. They'll be glad they're Americans.

'This morning I went to church. Amongst my neighbors, unafraid and unmolested, I thanked God for giving us America.

'I went home to my wife and kiddies. My little boy, Douglas, came running and said, "Hi, pop. You gonna take me to see the ribber?" and I said, "Sure, Doug, I'll take you to see the river." "And we'll stand on the bridge and see the car cars, pop?" "Sure, Doug." "Pop, see the sun. Look, see, pop. It shine in the car car's window." "Yes, Doug, the sun's shining on all America."

'After our walk we came home and sat down to veal chops, baked potatoes, fresh green beans and corn on the cob. I said grace with tears in my eyes. I'm so happy I'm an American.

'This afternoon we listened to a radio rebroadcast of British children, here in America, talking to their parents in England, and I was proud to be an American.

'Tomorrow I'll go to work. I work in an electrotype foundry, and I love my job. I made it, in fact, from errand boy to production manager in two years. I had ideas and I told the boss about them. He's an American.

'Tonight, before going to bed, I told my wife, "Honey, I'm going to buy a large flag and hang it out the window Friday. The President wants every one to pledge allegiance to a new and united America. And honey, I'm going to do my part, because I'd rather be an American than anything else on earth." '

It was, the President said when he had finished reading, a nice letter. He refused to make the writer's name public.

From *New York Herald Tribune*, 9 July 1941. By permission of the publisher.

AN AMERICAN HOME

By Della T. Lutes

TIMES there have been and many, in the years that lie between my youth in southern Michigan and now, when memories of the homes I knew so intimately have seemed the only safe and sane anchor to cling to in a muddled world. One of these stands out with special clarity, not because it differed greatly from a hundred others, but because, thinking of it often as I have, it has become to me a symbol of what the American Home then was; of what, in spirit, it should be now; and what, if we could once get and cling to the vision, it might become again. That was the house where the Mason family lived—Uncle Jed, Aunt M'ri', and their flock of children, with an ever-fluctuating occupancy of hired men, visiting seamstresses, transient book-agents, school-teachers, tin-peddlers, and comp'ny. A plain, homely, squat old house it was—but what a home!

I can see it clear as day, brooding there beside the country road, close to the ground, a wing to the north, where the spare bedroom opened off the front room, and another to the south, which held kitchen and woodshed with a loft overhead where boys and hired men slept. I recall the doorstep over which gay wedding guests and faltering pallbearers' feet trod, the frost-thickened windows, and the soap-stones, salt-bags, and stone jugs heated to guard against a frigid night. Warm and glowing in the raw Michigan winters, it was yet a simple house, lacking not only the elegance, but also the actual space of many of its neighbors. There was just the front room, large and square, and another—long and wide, used for eating, sewing, and sitting. The front room was for comp'ny and for the girls' beaux. In this dining-sitting room were a dilapidated old lounge where

From the *American Mercury*, May 1936. By permission of the publisher and the author.

Uncle Jed stretched himself of a winter's evening, and Aunt M'ri's rocking chair where she sat to knit mittens, wristlets, and scarves for the boys, and petticoats for the girls. Also, of course, the chunk stove, an unconscionably long dining table, and innumerable chairs of all sizes and shapes.

Uncle Jed's was a large family—five girls and two boys, appallingly large according to the present average, but no larger than most families in that day and community. When people married they expected to have families and built their houses accordingly. The two boys—one in his early twenties and the other several years older and bordering upon the ludicrous state of bachelorhood—having finished with school, worked with their father on the farm. That was what boys expected to do until they came of age and were able to set up for themselves, either on the same farm (but in a separate house) or on a rented one until they could buy. The girls went to school as long as they cared to and then stayed at home until they married. Occasionally one more valorous than the rest cut loose from the parent branch and went out to teach 'deestrick' school, but there were very few other vocations open, and girls looked upon marriage and the making of a home as the natural—and desirable—consummation of life, and prepared themselves accordingly for this estate.

And that was what a home was for. That was the obligation a man took upon himself when he married—to build a refuge for those for whom he was responsible, a harbor of safety during all their youth, a sure retreat in case of later need, a haven of comfort and welcome in time of trouble. That was why homes had front rooms—to provide a place for courtings, for weddings, for reunions, for the honoring of guests, for all the essential rites and ceremonies attendant upon and necessary to family life.

Uncle Jed was a pretty well-to-do farmer, and so when the older girls reached the courting age, he bought a new Brussels carpet for the front room (huge, over-running urns of roses with ivy trailing), window shades of green paper with gaudy peacocks trailing their gay tails across the bottom, and lace curtains. He had bought a melodeon some years before, and Cordelia, the eldest, had taken lessons. She played the *Battle of Waterloo* (with variations) and *Moonlight on Killarney*. A younger sister, Flora, took singing and elocution. She often recited for company and was in demand at school exhibitions and church affairs. Together the sisters sang *Whispering Hope, Juanita,* and *Listen to the Mocking Bird*—the boys whistling the refrain. They had even learned one musical duet together in which they crossed hands. The girls worked happily about the home, sewed, pieced quilts (still hoping, the gossips said), gathered and preserved fruits, even went into the fields to help in times of stress, attended church, went visiting, sang, played games, danced.

Uncle Jed and Aunt M'ri' were getting along in years. Uncle Jed had turned most of the hard work over to the two boys and the hired man, and the girls did the housework. Cordelia, besides being a musician, was something of an artist and spent considerable time at her easel; Flora had her elocution to master and was often heard declaiming from some upper room. In spite of this there was never any confusion, never, seemingly, any work left undone, and always an amazing quantity of food on hand. Only a thorough knowledge of the necessary routine and a technique resultant upon training and experience could have accomplished such apparent wonders. The law of the house, as of all other houses of that day, was order. The woman who did not manage her housework according to a system was stamped as a poor manager if, indeed, she did not fall to the lower estate of slattern. There had to be order to accomplish the necessary ends of housekeeping.

Aunt M'ri' had rheumatism and took it easy. There were, however, certain household rituals wherein she still remained supreme, as in the making of sausage and mincemeat at butchering time, the making of the pudding for Christmas, and the dyeing of rags for a new carpet in spring. No one else could reach the acme of perfection in the seasoning of sausage—that exact proportion of sage to rose-and-ivory flesh—or that transcendent flavor upon which the complete success of mince pies depends. Neither were the girls able, try as they might, so to mingle butternut shuck and sumac bud as to get that lovely shade of reddish brown which their mother could get. So, Aunt

M'ri' was still supreme house-mistress in her own right, although she nodded in the sun of a winter's day, and pottered about in her garden during the summer.

II

Uncle Jed often drove to town. He liked to saunter into the grocery store, help himself to a link of boloney or a piece of cheese, a fist-full of crackers from the barrel, a pickle from a keg by the door, and, comfortably munching, join a group about the pot-bellied stove with a wooden spittoon at one side and a checkerboard lying athwart a cask on the other. Uncle Jed did not play checkers, but he liked to look on for a while. The action, however, was too slow for a man with errands to do; so, after he had exchanged views on the weather, the price of hogs and wheat, picked up any stray advertising matter that might lie around the counters, and filled his pockets with purchases of candy, peanuts, and oranges, he would go his way.

He usually took to town with him a small load of grain, apples, potatoes, crocks of butter, and baskets of eggs, to exchange for a piece of beef or what groceries were needed, or possibly some spools of thread or a yard of cambric for the girls. They went themselves to do more personal trading. And quite often he carried someone home with him. It might be a friend of the family, or it might be an utter stranger. Uncle Jed's hospitality did not stop at known quantities. There was always a spare bed (according to the standards of homemaking and hospitality) and plenty to eat. There was always an invitation to the chance guest to pull up and have some dinner. 'Aw—come on, no matter if you have et, you can put down a piece o' pie!' Or 'Put up yo' ho'ses and stay all night.' A far more common form of hospitality than is the mendacious 'Drop in and see us sometime' of today, and infinitely more sincere.

Uncle Jed loved bringing someone home, especially on Saturday nights. And, as a matter of fact, the family also loved it. Along about dark they would begin to watch for him. As the piebald team hove in sight down by the cross-roads, their jogging pace quickened by the sight of home, eager faces would peer from window and door. 'Has he got anybody?' 'Can you tell who it is?'

He liked best to bring someone who was in need of good food and strong nourishment. Someone half ill, run down, or low in spirits. Let such a one—butcher or candlestick-maker—so much as mention a depressed state of mind or a questionable condition of health and Uncle Jed was upon him. 'You come along home 'th me. Some good fried salt-pork gravy and taters'll put flesh on yer bones.'

Once, having occasion to consult a lawyer—an unusual occurrence in his life—he called upon the son of an old acquaintance, a young man, unmarried, and with a shingle still swinging rather listlessly in the legal wind. The man had been ill with a bad cold, and looked wretched. He apologized for frequent use of his handkerchief, and immediately Uncle Jed forgot all former reason for his visit. Nothing would do but the young man must go home with him. The lawyer demurred, made a feeble argument for business, could not think of thus thrusting himself, a stranger—

'Fiddlesticks!' Arguments fell before Uncle Jed's forceful insistence. 'I'm goin' home about four o'clock. You be to Green's store—I got to get some cheese and things—'

Bundled in muffler, ear-laps, arctics, overcoat, and mittens, for this particular incident happened in winter, the young man was at Green's store at four o'clock, bag in hand, looking rather wan and sheepish, but wistful and eager as well. Arrived at the Mason Farm, the guest, a stranger to everyone in the house, was welcomed as if he had been expected for the last six months and fate hung upon his arrival. One divested him of wraps. Another drew a chair up to the stove—a fire would be laid in the front room as soon as the boys came in. Aunt M'ri' assured him that supper was all ready, just waiting for them to come. So there he sat, drowsily lolling in the downy lap of warmth and content, voices flowing melodiously about and over him, occasionally addressed to him. Was he getting warm? Wouldn't he like a drink of fresh milk? The boys were just in with it—some people who came there loved it—others couldn't bear it. Supper was all but on the table.

Uncle Jed came in, drew his old arm-chair to the other side of the stove, and took from his pocket the weekly paper. He had no need to talk. They had talked all the way home. He had learned from his young guest all that he felt concerned to know about the city's and the nation's problems. He had inquired regarding his family relations, manner of living, state of health, and business. He had brought him safely into the bosom of his family; now he would, for the time being at least, feel no further responsibility toward him. A man who couldn't take care of himself, once delivered into a home like this, was poor timber for visiting.

The guest was grateful for the consideration. All he wanted, at the present time, was just this good warm fire, this old comfortable chair, the sight of these friendly faces, the smell of hot, odorous food wafting in from the kitchen.

In the meantime the boys had come in—and the hired man as well—scrubbed to luminosity, their hair sleeked, pants pulled down over boots, clean wam'uses over sweaty shirts. They were introduced. They shook hands vigorously and assured the city feller that they were pleased to meet him, accompanied by shy glances that almost convinced him of their sincerity. One of them built the fire in the front room. Another helped, fetching kindling and wood to fill the box. The eldest son stood about making awkward inquiries as to the guest's health, greatly to his embarrassment. He was beginning to feel that just a place at that already bountifully laid table would immediately put him amongst the halest of the hale; that even to speak of noisome disease would be repulsive to a lusty man—like him. Eagerly, hungrily, he awaited the call to supper.

III

In a family the size of Uncle Jed's, where there were never less than nine at the table and usually from one to three extra, preparing any meal was a considerable undertaking. Some of the others set the table. Amongst them all there was a constant passing to and fro from kitchen to dining room, from there to the front room to watch the fire, to the spare room to see that it was heating, and down cellar. It was like a pageant, a moving, stirring spectacle of homely family life.

With so large and so hearty a family there must of necessity be quantities of food at every meal, although supper was counted a slight one. Choice of food depended largely upon the season, but with a richly stocked cellar in which were a variety of winter vegetables, countless jars of preserves and pickles, rows of smoked hams sewed into white-washed bags, the ubiquitous pork barrel, with a large butt'ry in which were stored dry groceries, flour, crackers, and sugar, there was never any lack in either quantity or quality, even though diversity might be wanting.

The guest from the city, finally invited to draw up, was by this time in so febrile a state from aggravation of eye and ear and nose that he was barely able to wedge himself, a mere vacuum of human propensities, into the place reserved. Well-accustomed though he may have been in his own home to a not unplentiful supply of food, his eye was gorged, his digestion barely able to wait on appetite. But, Christian man though he may have been, it was many years since his head had lowered in acknowledged gratitude for the food he was about to eat, and he was suddenly abashed in his own ardor as Uncle Jed stood with hoary head bowed before his plate, and, lifting his hand for silence, raised his benign voice in simple supplication for a blessing on the food before them.

The guest lifted his eyes to rest with renewed deference upon his patriarchal host. His greed subsided. Food took its proper place in the category of human needs. Hospitality, friendliness, beneficence, kindliness—where, when, had he last heard these words? Appreciatively, thoughtfully, he took in the scene before him. A snow-white cloth with napkins; lustrous china, banded with gold. In the center of the table the caster—a customary accessory to table furnishing of that day—dignified, even elegant in its gleaming coat of silver, with the usual five bottles—vinegar, hot-sauce, mustard, salt, and pepper—in the revolving rack. At one end of the table a huge platter of thinly sliced cold corned beef, wine-red, ivory-edged; and at the other a great tureen, the lifted cover of which revealed creamy cubes of potatoes drenched in golden butter; plates of hot bronze-cheeked biscuits napkin-covered, and bread as well—generous slices of salt-risin' bread, freshly-baked.

Neither Uncle Jed nor the hired man held much barter with biscuits. Uncle Jed's brief was not so much against biscuits as for bread. He liked salt-risin' bread because it had body to it. 'So'thin' to clamp onto,' he said as with evident relish he set his seventy-year-old teeth into a crusty slice. 'Biscuits is all right for wimmen,' conceded the hired man generously, 'and children. But you take a man 'at's been out in the wood-lot on one end of a cross-cut saw all day, and he's got to have fodder 't's substantial.' And so great loaves of bread came fresh from the oven on baking days—Wednesdays and Saturdays—with biscuits almost daily for the less manually employed.

Butter was put at both ends of the table, pound pats of butter, stamped with an ear of corn or a sheaf of wheat. Three times a week thick layers of cream were skimmed from long rows of tin pans into the stone churn, and from the churn, after due agitation on the part of the wooden dasher, came great lumps of yellow butter, ladled into a huge wooden bowl where it was 'worked' over and over to free it from milk, then salted and moulded into pats for the table or crocks for trade. Butter, with ten or fifteen cows on the farm, was one of the most abundant of foods, and buttermilk served as fattening matter for the hogs.

Uncle Jed also kept bees, and so there was on this munificently abundant table a handsome glass dish in which lay a perfect comb filmed with transparent wax, ready to drip ambrosia at the touch of a knife. On the cover of the dish the word HONEY was stamped in fine embossed lettering. Another dish, also of glass (what would not a collector give for those things today!) held pickled pears, red-chestnut in color, glazed with syrup of nectar, and indented here and there with cloves—Aunt M'ri's pickled pears, the receipt for which has traveled down along the years. And for dessert, hot gingerbread fresh from the oven and preceded by such a heavenly aroma of molasses, cinnamon, allspice, and ginger as would start the sweat from a man's tongue. Gingerbread and whipped cream—a huge bowl, blue, with a weeping-willow beside a little bridge on its fat side, filled with it, heaped to capacity and more, its surface roughened into tiny peaks and minarets where the last few precious spherules dropped from the spoon. And even this godly dish not unaccompanied, for there was sauce. Sauce in a crystal compote upheld by lovely crystal hands, with small sauce-dishes each to receive its quota of royal damson plums and their rich red-purple syrup, tart and sweet together like the sun and rain which had brought them to perfection. And tea. Farmer folk had tea for supper. Coffee for breakfast, yes—coffee boiled in a tin pot and 'settled' with a broken egg. But tea for dinner and tea for supper. Green tea, hot and strong, reduced to reason with milk and to a state of amiability with sugar.

After supper the guest, in a state of mellowed somnolence, was escorted to the front room, and further honored. The family hearth, though it was but a sheet-iron chunk stove, had been lit for him. He was given the best chair. One of the girls (the eldest as being more seemly, since he was an unmarried man), showed him the newest pictures for the stereoscope. The eldest son, who had once broken loose from parental discipline and traveled as far west as Nebraska, brought forth a trophy—a buffalo's horns, polished and mounted in plush—a hatrack!

But Uncle Jed did not come in. His duties as host done, he had flopped down upon the lounge in the dining room to snooze. Neither did Aunt M'ri'. Her knitting in her hands, she drew her rocking chair a little nearer the stove, a little nearer Uncle Jed. The front room was for young folks and comp'ny. For her the comfort of the older fire, older things—each other. The hired man slid unobtrusively to a chair in full view of the front room, tilted it against the wall, and occupied himself with a toothpick.

The dishes had been washed. The girls came in. Cordelia went to the melodeon. Flora stood beside her. They all sang—a few old hymns, a few old songs. The boys replenished the fire. It was going to be a cold night. Finally the guest was asked if he would like to retire. They bade him good-night and hoped he would rest. They would call him in the morning. The eldest daughter preceded him into the bedroom, drew the shade, fussed around. One of the boys brought in a soapstone wrapped in a towel. The guest protested. He was never so pampered in all his life. As a boy he had slept in a room where snow blew in about the windows. They laughed, made friendly little remarks, bade him good-night again. Told him to leave the door into the front room open for better air and the remaining warmth . . .

And now he sinks into the ethereal depths of a feather bed. Lord! He had forgotten the heavenly softness of a feather bed! He draws a soft, light comfortable over his shoulders. He sniffs the odor from the sheets—lavender, as I live and breathe! And so white, so crisp, so clean, lace-trimmed (the lace tickles his nose). He sighs and burrows his face into the pillow. He is warm, content, happy. He has forgotten the strife of little men, their petty quarrels, their animosities, their greed, envy, enmity, their everlasting 'lawin'.' Before he left the office today he had been sunk in dejection. Partly due to illness, of course. But there had seemed so little to live for. He had not realized his own loneliness. Now he recognizes it as a cloud that has brooded over his spirits, hampered his thoughts.

But now—throughout this house—in this room and that, sleep people who are his friends. Almost, he feels—his family. They have welcomed him as one of themselves. They like him. Smiling a bit at his own sentiment he murmurs, 'God bless Uncle Jed.' And his last conscious thought is, 'As long as there are Uncle Jeds in the world, and Aunt M'ri's—and grace before meat—'

IV

I have a neighbor today whose family numbers four. If all goes reasonably well, the man and his wife will continue to reproduce themselves for better or for worse. The eldest child, a girl, has finished with school and is working in an office. The boy is still in high school, his tenure hanging by a thread. The mother, not content with the limited income of her husband, has a part-time job outside. Their apartment consists of a living room, a small dining room, two bedrooms, a bath, and small kitchen. The boy sleeps on a cot set up each night in one place or another.

'Why don't you bring your young man in?' I have heard the father querulously ask his daughter. 'I don't like the idea of you being out in a car till all hours of the night—or morning. When

I was young I used to have to face the old man and all the family. And go home at ten. Hey, Mama?'

The mother sighs. The daughter sneers.

'Yeah? And did they all stick around in one room with a radio goin' and a smart-aleck kid makin' wisecracks? Not on your life.'

'Well,' the father regretfully admits, 'we have no place to go —unless it's to bed.'

'And I s'pose I can take to the street,' the young smart-aleck derides. 'Okay with me. I'd rather go, anyway.'

Meals at this house are seldom on time, due to the irregularity of the mother's hours, and when ready they are sketchy and unappetizing. A can of salmon, potato salad from the store, tasteless bread, and a still more tasteless baker's cake. The children eat, not for pleasure, but to appease youthful hunger. Filled but never satisfied. The father eats—his inner eye envisioning the meals that graced the table of his boyhood home. Then they are off—the movies, the car, the street, or the living room and the radio.

Sometimes I think the living room, that interloper which in a moment of mad modernity ousted the good old parlor and sitting room at one and the same time, has done more to cause the disintegration of family life and hospitality than any other one factor, except the complete rout of the spare bedroom. In the too-small kitchen with the unstocked cupboards which have replaced the good old butt'ry, there is neither room nor food for the impromptu guest. As for a casual overnight visitor, there is not the slightest chance. And where there were once a hundred homes like Uncle Jed's to one feeble imitation like my neighbor's, the opposite is now true. Uncle Jed's home is almost extinct; the other is found at every turn.

If America does need any one thing more than another it is a million homes based upon a modernized version of Uncle Jed's. A pantry well stocked is a more self-respecting device any day than a cabinet furnished with a sugar bowl and spice rack. A cellar provisioned against the fangs of winter will in reality save time, energy, and money. An extra chair in the dining room, an extra bed in the house, a heart for hospitality, might do more for the peace of the world than armored cruisers or a league of something that does nothing. You cannot hate a man whom you have invited to sit at your table, and you cannot help feeling an interest in the welfare of one who has slept in your house.

No one would have us go back to the actuality of Uncle Jed's house, to its discomforts, inconveniences, and restrictions. Science and invention have brought us freedom from much that was unpleasant, from much that was actual suffering. But they have also driven out of our homes that gentle spirit of contentment in simplicity, of beneficence, of hospitality, which once made the American home.

THE FOURTH OF JULY

By Lucy Furman

On Tuesday noon, Uncle Lot announced to Aunt Ailsie that he would go to the quare women's Fourth-of-July picnic the following day, and would take her along.

'Hit appears to be my duty, as a law-loving man, like they said, to be thar on the hill in case of trouble, which is nigh-about sartain to come, there not being hardly a gethering in two year, be hit election or court or funeral-meeting or what not, that hain't been shot up, and sometimes broke up, generally by Fult and his crowd.'

'O paw, you allus a-faulting Fulty, and him your own grand-child, and the picter of you when you was young!'

'Picter or no picter, I hain't proud of daddying no sech, and don't uphold none of his doings. And if Darcy's crowd is there, too, which hit will be, with all the county a-mustering, then hit's unknowing what the day may bring forth.'

About eight o'clock Wednesday morning, the two started down the branch—Uncle Lot, a tall, grizzled figure in dark home-spun and black slouch hat, leading, on Tom-mule; Aunt Ailsie following on old flat flea-bitten Darb. Profiting by the quare women's example, she had discarded the hot brown-linsey dress in favor of an everyday one of blue cotton; but she still clung to the black sunbonnet and light-print apron—inevitable badges of the respectable married woman.

When they arrived at The Forks, the one street was lined with nags,—they could scarcely find two palings to which to tie Tom and Darb,—and a stream of people was zigzagging up the steep hill behind the courthouse. Uncle Lot went on up, while Aunt Ailsie stopped at the hotel for her daughter, Cynthy Fal-

From Lucy Furman, *The Quare Women*, 1923. By permission of Little, Brown & Company and the Atlantic Monthly Press.

lon, whom she found in the kitchen frying chicken, while three or four of the girls packed baskets. Cynthy was complaining:—

'Fulty, he allus has so many to feed, jest pine-blank like his paw—all them boys that runs with him, and then a big gang more he's sartain to ax to eat. I allow to feed anyhow fifty.'

'You go wash and dress and I'll fry what's left,' insisted Aunt Ailsie.

Half an hour later, the two started up with their heavy baskets. Cynthy, too, wore a black sunbonnet and print apron; and from their appearance it would have been impossible to say which was mother, which daughter. If anything, Aunt Ailsie looked the younger, Cynthy's face being so lined and drawn from the troubles she had had as Fighting Fult's wife and widow.

The first thing they saw, as they toiled up past the deserted tents, was a tall pole, with the great flag which usually hung in the large tent flying before the breeze. It was set beside the flat rock, just at the top of the ascent, which the women had named Pulpit Rock. Beyond, on the level top of the spur, were numbers of seats made by laying saplings across logs; and here elderly folk and mothers with babies were tightly packed, while hundreds wandered about, or sat under the trees, or against the small, latticed grave-houses; for the spur-top was also a burying-ground.

The two women, Virginia and Amy, who sat on a puncheon-bench beside the rock, with Uncle Ephraim Kent between them, beckoned for Aunt Ailsie and Cynthy to join them. A phalanx of young people, whom Aunt Ailsie recognized as the singing class, stood beneath the flag, all wearing sashes of red, white, and blue across shoulders and breasts. Fult was in the front line, beside Lethie.

Aunt Ailsie leaned forward and said anxiously: 'Lot, he's sartain there'll be trouble; he says some of the boys will get liquor, shore, and then—'

'I'm not very much afraid,' replied Amy. She turned to little John Wes, Cynthy's four-year-old, who was perched on the rock behind her. 'Tell Fult to step here,' she said.

He came forward, looking very handsome, his dark beauty set off by the bright colors of his sash.

'Your grandparents fear drinking and trouble here today,' Amy said.

Fult drew himself up. 'I have give my word,' he said, 'not only that there won't be no drinking and trouble on the hill today by me and my friends, but that nary drap of liquor shall be fotched up here by nobody. Me and t'other boys have been scouting around all morning, meeting folks as they rid in, and going into saddlebags and coat-pockets, and warning all hands that we aim to have peace on the hill today if hit takes cold steel to get hit. And Charlie Lee and two more boys air still spying around for hit, whilst I sing.'

This astonishing transformation of peace-breakers into peace-compellers laid Aunt Ailsie's fears. A little later, however, when she saw Darcy Kent, Fult's arch-enemy, come up with the pretty young woman who presided over the cooking-tent, and sit down not twenty feet from Fult, anxiety again awoke.

'Hit gives me a spell to see them two so nigh together,' she whispered to Cynthy.

The latter cast a glance of cold, withering hatred at Darcy. ' 'Pears like he's trying to get him a fotched-on gal,' she sneered.

But the program was already beginning, with the singing of the 'Star-Spangled Banner' by the class, Fult's rich voice leading. Then followed a prayer by Uncle Lemmy Logan, an Old Primitive preacher. Then the reading of the Declaration of Independence by Giles Kent, the schoolteacher, and a song and march by fifty little kindergartners, who aroused more enthusiasm than any of the performers; then Lincoln's Gettysburg Address, read, somewhat haltingly but most impressively, by Uncle Lot. Then more patriotic songs by the class, and an oration, 'The Founding of Our Nation,' by Lawyer Nathe Gentry.

All had gone finely so far. Everybody was reassured by seeing Fult and Darcy in such conspicuous and peaceable proximity, and attention was rapt, even the scores of babies being quiet. Then, when everybody hung breathless upon the orator's words, and he was just launching into his peroration, three loud pistol-shots were fired in the immediate rear of the crowd. Instant panic fell. Women, without a word, seized their smaller children and scuttled down the hill like rabbits; men sought the shelter

of trees, all save a compact group, headed by Darcy and Uncle
Lot, which made for the scene of the trouble. Aunt Ailsie wrung
her hands.

'I seed Fulty leave the singers a little grain ago,' she said;
'I'll warrant hit's him!'

It was. They found Fult bending, pistol in hand, over a pros-
trate young man. 'Hit's Charlie Lee, my best friend,' he said.
'He holped me sarch all comers for liquor this morning, and
then I left him and two more to patrol the hill whilst I sang.
First thing I knowed, I seed him behind a tree tipping a bottle,
and gethered that he was drinking some he had tuck off of
somebody, and, knowing his weakness, I felt sartain he'd never
stop till he was crazy drunk. I had give my hand to the women
there would be no drinking on the hill, and there wasn't but
one thing to do—take hit away from him. When I come back
to do so, he already had enough in him to be mean, and refused to give hit up; and when I tried to take it anyhow, he
drawed on me. I seed then the onliest thing to do was to shoot
the pistol out of his hand, which I done, scaring him pretty
bad, and maybe grazing two-three of his fingers, but not hurting
him none to speak of. Hit was the only way.'

Sure enough, while Charlie's hand was bleeding profusely, it
was found that there was not even a bone broken.

'Where's the fotched-on nurse-woman?' was the cry.

But she was already at hand, with a small first-aid outfit; the
fingers were quickly bandaged, and Charlie, sobered by the shock
and extremely shamefaced, was soundly berated by Fult for his
faithlessness.

And now arose a dilemma. By rights Darcy, being sheriff,
should have placed both disturbers of the peace under arrest.
He made no move, however. A hand was placed upon his arm,
and Uncle Ephraim whispered:—

'Don't do nothing at all; hit would start a battle that would
never eend.'

Then the old man stepped forward, and spoke authoritatively.

'Fult here desarves a vote of thanks from the citizens of this
county for keeping the peace here on this hill today, and not

having hit broke up by even his best friend. In the name of the people, and the women, I thank him.'

He solemnly offered a hand to the boy, who took it, flushing.

Uncle Lot also stepped forward. 'I hain't never in life seed you do nothing I tuck pride in afore,' he said to his grandson, 'but you done hit today when you went pine-blank again' your feelings and your friendship to maintain the peace.'

He also put forth his hand, which Fult accepted as one in a daze.

In fifteen minutes the women and children were all back, relieved and smiling, and the lawyer was completing his peroration. There was then a slight pause in the proceedings, while everybody talked of the panic and its happy ending.

Then, very slowly, Uncle Ephraim Kent, a notable figure, with his mane of white hair, his crimson hunting-jacket, his linen trousers and moccasins, his tall, lean body, very little bent by the passing of eighty-two years, mounted the pulpit-rock and faced the audience.

'Citizens and offsprings,' he began, 'hit were not in my thoughts to speak here in this gethering today, even though the women axed and even begged me so to do. I never follered speaking, nor enjoyed listening at the sound of my own voice, the weight of no-larning allus laying too heavy upon me. But sarcumstances has riz and sot up lines of thought that calls for the opening of my mind to you, and I will therefore do the best I am able.

'And firstways I will say how I rej'ice that them shots that brung fear to our hearts today was good shots, and not bad ones, fired to keep the peace by one that has too often follered breaking hit. And I'll say furder that, in my opinions, he never would have broke hit that first time but for old, ancient wrongs, done afore he seed the light: sins of the fathers, visited down on the children, and ketching 'em in a quile they can't hardly on-ravel.'

The audience, well knowing that the old man referred to the killing of his son, Rafe, by Fult, and to the previous warfare between Kents and Fallons, listened breathless.

'But,' continued Uncle Ephraim, 'let me leave that sorrowful tale for a spell, and go back to the good old days when there

wa'n't no sech things as wars betwixt friends and neighbors—
the days when our forbears first rid acrost the high ridges from
Old Virginny or North Cyar'liny and along these rocky creeks,
and tuck up land in these norrow valleys. A rude race they was,
but a strong, with the blood of old England and bonny Scotland
in their veins, and in their hearts the fear of naught; a rude
race, but a free, chasing the deer and the b'ar and the wild
turkey and the Indian, tending their craps with a hoe in one
hand and a gun in t'other; a rude race, but a friendly, banding
together again' all foes, helping one another in all undertakings. Some of 'em, like my grandsir, the old cap'n, come in to
live on land that was granted 'em because they had fit under
Washington; t'others jest wandered in and tuck up what pleased
'em.

'Well, atter they settled theirselves in this rugged, penned-in
land, then what happened to 'em? Well, right there was the
trouble—*nothing* never happened. Here they was, shut in for
uppards of a hunderd year, multiplying fast, spreading up from
the main creeks to the branches and hollows, but never bettering their condition—you might say, worsening hit. For before
long the game was all kilt off, and life become the turrible struggle hit still is, jest to keep food in our mouths—raising craps on
land that's nigh straight-up-and-down, like we have to. And
while a many of the first settlers, like my grandsir, had been
knowledgeable men, with larning, their offsprings growed up in
the wilderness without none, because there wa'n't no money to
send the young-uns out to school, or to fotch larning in to 'em.
And the second crap, of which I was one, was wusser and ig-
noranter still, being raised up maybe, like me, eighty mile from
a schoolhouse or church-house; and the third was wusser and
meaner yet; and so on down to now, when they hain't no better, though there is a few pindling deestrict schools here and
yan.

'And about the onliest times in all them years our folks found
out there was a world outside these mountains was when the
country sont in a call to fight hits battles. Then we allus poured
forth, rej'icing—like when there was trouble again with the
British, and we mustered under Old Hickory behind them cot-

ton-bales and palmetty-logs at New Orleens; and then later, when Mexico got sassy; and then when the States tuck sides and lined up, you know how we fit through them four year—mostly for the Union; this here stiff right arm I fotched back remembers me of hit; then there's this here leetle war in Cuby, too, not long finished.

'All of which proves we air a brave and fighting race. And if the fighting had stopped with wars for our country, all would have been well. But, citizens and offsprings, hit never stopped there. You all know how, when there wa'n't no outside wars to keep us peaceified, there was allus them amongst us, for thirty year and more, that couldn't take no satisfaction in life onless they was starting wars amongst theirselves.

'And right here you will say to me, "Uncle Ephraim, begin at home." Which is but true and just. For well I know the part my offsprings has bore in the troubles of this country, and that the Kents, which used to be a peaceable gineration, has come down to be a mean one. But, friends, hit never was with my counsel or consent. I have loved peace and pursued hit. But all in vain. War hit raged hither and yan; battles was fit all over the county; and here at The Forks many was kilt—three of my sons amongst 'em—and many a more wounded, and sorrow was brung to many hearts. Hit was not until Fighting Fult and my son Rafe was both kilt, that we had a taste of peace. Then, for a spell, whilst young Fult was down at Frankfort, and fighting in Cuby, we rested; and oh, what a joyful rest hit was!

'Then young Fult come back, and sad times begun again— not that I am faulting him for hit, for Darcy, being older, ought to have knowed better than to sarve them warrants on him in the first place. Hit was like throwing fire in gunpowder. In my opinion, if the boy had been let alone a spell, to kindly work off his youth and sperrits, he'd 'a' soon settled down. But he wa'n't, and the war hit flamed up again, and for nigh two year we have seed trials on top of tribulations. As I said afore, I hain't blaming neither boy—both was bitter-hearted from the family hate which they had drawed in, you might say, with their mothers' milk; both had loved their paws; both had lost them; revenge was naetural. But if ever a people was wore out with

wars and troubles, we air them people; if ever folks yearned
and pined and prayed for peace, we air them folks.

'Yes, many's the time, walking the ridge-tops, standing up
yander on the high rocks, I have looked down on the valley
of Troublesome and agonized in sperrit over hit, calling upon
the God of Israel to send us help and peace. Many's the time,
too, up there, I have dreamed dreams and seed visions.

'People under the shadow of my voice—all you that the mountains has give birth and suck to,—you know what I mean. Though
we air ignorant folk, not able to get much acquainted with God
through his written Word, yet He hain't never left us without a
witness; He hain't never failed to speak to our minds and our
hearts. In the high, lifted-up places, gazing out over the green
mountain-tops, with maybe the sun-ball drapping low in the
west, and the clouds and the elements all a-praising Him in their
beauty; or maybe of a cold winter's day, with the whole world
white and the snow a-sparkling and the shadows deep-blue in
the hollows; He talks to us, He shows us things that no level-
lander don't know nothing about, or get no inkling of—visions,
and dreams, and things to come. You have all, even the mean-
est, kotched a glimp of 'em. For we air a seeing people.

'And several times in sech visions, friends, I have beheld down
there below, in the valley of Troublesome, all manner of peaceful and happy homes, where every man had his mind made up
to let liquor and guns alone, and the women-folks tended their
offsprings in the fear of the Lord, and even the young was too
busy getting larning to be briggaty and feisty.

'I allow, moreover, that there is but few here that, in their
better hours, hain't beheld and wished for the same. But how
hit was to come about didn't appear. We wa'n't able to help
ourselves, or bring about a change; hit was like a landslip:
things had got too much headway to be turnt back. We needed
outside help, but where hit was to come from, nobody knowed.
But from the time I were a leetle shirt-tail boy, hoeing corn on
yon hillsides, I have had faith to believe the Lord would send
hit in some time, from somewheres, and have never ceased a-pray-
ing for hit.

'And in the weeks past, friends, sence these here women tuck up their abode with us, hit has appeared like my prayers was answered, my visions a-coming true. I hain't heared a gun fired off sence that first night they come in; I have seed the boys that ginerally drinks and fights and shoots (because they hain't got nothing better to do) all a-gethered in, happy and peaceable, singing and playing, and even sewing; and the gals, that is apt to idle and squander their time, taking joy in larning how to cook right vittles and dig out dirt; and the older folks likewise waking up to things they never heared of before; and me myself,—which hit don't seem noways possible, but yet hit is true,—me, that nigh a lifetime ago had give up all hope of ever being knowledgeable; me, with you might say both feet in the grave, becoming a man of larning. For the women here has already teached me my letters, and I'm a-studying on page three of my primer; and before the summer passes I'll be a-reading in my grandsir's old yaller Bible I have churrished so long, praise the Lord!

'In all which, friends, I see the hand of the Almighty. Hit is Him that has sont these women in to us; hit is Him that has led 'em along the rough way to our help; hit is Him that has answered my long-raised prayers.

'Now, the Lord having done his part so complete, and these here women a-doing theirn, what about ourn? Deep down in our hearts, don't we feel to do something, too, to help along the good work and bring the visions to pass?

'There is several things, citizens and offsprings, we can do if we so feel to. One is to treat these women kind and friendly, and incourage 'em to keep on; another is to send our young-uns in to take the benefits of what they can get. But the most demand-ingest thing of all for us to do, 'pears like, is to patch up our differences and troubles for the time the women air amongst us, and publicly agree on hit. I hain't got no differences or troubles with nobody nowhere, thank God! but some of my off-springs has, and this is what I am getting down to, right now. I ax my grandson, Darcy Kent, and likewise my young friend, Fult Fallon, that has already showed sech a fine sperrit here to-day, to step forrard here, whilst I lay the matter before 'em.'

The two young men, startled, flushed, reluctant, came slowly forward, avoiding one another's eyes, and stood, some distance

apart, in front of Uncle Ephraim, at the foot of the rock. The
audience held its breath.

'I praise and thank you, boys,' began the old man, 'that in
these past few days, for the sake of these women and the work
they are doing for us, you have turnt aside from follering your
feelings and have sunk your troubles out of sight. I was glad
a-Saturday, when I seed you playing in the same set. I was glad
when I seed you, and all the boys that follers you both, a-keep-
ing peace on the hill here today. Hit is fine and honorable in
both of you; and the only trouble is, we hain't got no assurance
hit will last, and that your innard feelings won't bust out in
death and destruction maybe the next minute. Hit is, therefore,
my desire to counsel you two boys—being the leaders in the war
—to declare here and now a truce, a solemn truce, in the presence
of this county, for the full time the women stays with us.

'Hatred is long and lasty, boys—you have got a lifetime before
you to work hit out in. The folks of this county is plumb wore
to a frazzle with fighting and fear. What they need is a spell
of rest. I allow you would have kept the peace anyhow for these
few weeks, out of respect to the women; but everybody'll feel
better if hit's agreed on in public. Now I don't ax you to take
one another's hands—hit would be hy-pocrisy, your feelings being what they air; but I do ax you both to jine hands with me,
and give your solemn word not to take up the war again in no
way, or let it be tuck up by your friends, while these women
stays with us. Ponder hit, boys,—study on hit,—take all the time
you need; be plumb satisfied in your minds.'

Silence fell, while Uncle Ephraim and all the audience gazed
upon the two tall young men, one so fair, one so dark, both so
handsome, and both standing as if turned to stone.

Uncle Ephraim's voice again broke the intense stillness.

'As I look upon you two boys,' he said, 'both so pretty, both
so upstanding and brave, both orphants through this war that
has been handed down to you, both honest as the day, both feeling hit your bounden duty to kill each other off if you can,
both knowing that, if either one had his way, t'other's fair body
would be laying under the sod, hit does seem like sorrow plumb
swallows me up, and my heart swells too big for hits socket, like

I would gladly pour out my life here before you, if hit could only bring you together in right feeling.

'Boys, when Amy here was a-reading Scripter to me a-Sunday, she read where hit said, "Give place to wrath—vengeance is mine, saith the Lord"; and another, and better, read: "Love your enemies, pray for them that despitefully use you." I ax you to meditate on them words in days to come, to open up your hearts and your minds to 'em. Not now,—the day is still far off when you can accept sech idees,—love being a puny-growing and easy-killed plant. I don't ax for nothing of that kind now. All I request is your word calling a truce while the women stays. All I ax is for you to think about the county and forget yourselves. Do you, Darcy, my offspring, and the oldest of the two, feel to give me your hand on hit?'

Darcy, flushed and then pale, reached up and slowly laid a hand in his grandfather's. 'I do,' he said, firmly.

Fult did not wait to be asked. 'Me, too,' he said, taking Uncle Ephraim's other hand. Then, impulsively, 'And I'll say furder, Uncle Ephraim, that if all the Kents was like you there never would have been no war.'

'There would not,' repeated Uncle Ephraim, emphatically, clasping the hands of the two.

He looked out over the assembly. 'Citizens of this county,' he said, 'you have witnessed this solemn covenant this day made and sealed in your presence. And I call upon all here that has ever tuck sides or had hard feelings, to see to hit that they keep the truce their leaders has agreed on, and make hit stand. And I hereby declare peace in this county for the time these women stays with us. And now, may the Lord dig round our hearts with the mattock of his love, till the roots goes to spreading, and the sap goes to rising, and the leaves bud out, and the blossoms of love and righteousness shoots forth and abounds in all our lives!'

'WHAT DID IT GET YOU?'

A RUMPLED, bulky, droop-mustached man stood beside the white dazzle of the Unknown Soldier's marble tomb in Arlington Cemetery. He too had been a soldier—Sergeant Alvin C. York, the Tennessee mountaineer who, 23 years ago, single-handed, disabled a German machine-gun battery and with seven privates killed or captured 152 of its defenders. He spoke:

'Liberty is not merely something the veterans inherited. Liberty is something they fought to keep . . .

'There are those in our country today who ask me and the other veterans who fought in World War No. 1: "What did it get you?" Let me answer them now. It got me twenty-three years of living in America where a humble citizen from the mountains of Tennessee can stand on the same platform with the President of the United States. It got me twenty-three years of living in a country where the Goddess of Liberty is printed on men's hearts, and not only on the coins in their pockets.

'People who ask us that question, "What did it get you?" forget one thing. True, we fought the last war to make the world safe for democracy, and we did for a while.

'The thing they forget is that liberty and freedom and democracy are so very precious that you do not fight to win them once —and then stop. Liberty and freedom and democracy are prizes awarded only to those peoples who fight to win them and then keep fighting eternally to hold them.'

From *Time: The Weekly Newsmagazine,* 9 June 1941. By permission of the publisher.

AMERICA IN MY BLOOD

By Leon Z. Surmelian

HOPE had returned with the spring. After the bewilderment, the loneliness of my first winter in America, I began to live again when I saw the lawns turning green and dandelions growing exactly as in Trebizond and Constantinople. The old familiar dandelions—they were with me again, hundreds and thousands of them, smiling at me in the streets. I felt a personal triumph in them like a convalescent who has defeated death after a long illness. I picked them with trembling fingers, to make sure they *were* dandelions.

Yet now, on the train hurtling across the Kansas countryside in the summer night, the renewed pain of my being in a strange land became a sharp physical anguish. The farm where I was to get the practical experience required for my degree in agriculture was more than a hundred miles away. Always I was going farther from Europe. The college town of Manhattan, however unhappy I had been there during the winter, now seemed a place of civilized security, a sort of European oasis in the wilderness of America. Outside in the darkness was the terror of the unknown, as the great train thundered on with cataclysmic force. Now and then, looking anxiously out of the window, I caught glimpses of weird gaunt silos rising like wooden minarets in the gloom. They might have been primitive tombs inhabited by lonely Indian ghosts. Somehow these wooden towers of Kansas made me think of Turkestan and filled me with the dread of Moslem Asia.

When I got off at the little country station where Harry, my college friend, was waiting for me in the family Ford, I felt like a man deposited by a rocket on the moon. His presence in this strangely unreal world had comforting substance.

From *Common Ground*, Summer 1941. By permission of the publisher.

We drove through the streets of a small town and then across open country. Fields and woods shone phosphorescent in the moonlight. I smelled June-in-the-country, the familiar fragrance of moon-drenched earth when the wheat is almost ready to be harvested and red poppies are knee high. Was this really Kansas, really America?

In vain I looked for a village. Everywhere was open country, though we drove past isolated houses now and then. 'No villages in Kansas?' I asked Harry, who piloted the Ford on the rutty road with marvelous skill.

'Sure we have villages. Just passed through one. Where you came in on the train. Knox Springs is classified as a village by the census.'

But it hadn't looked like one to me. It was a town, with banks, barber shops, stores, filling stations.

'I guess your villages are different,' Harry said after a silence.

'Well, you see in ours, farmers live together,' I explained. 'Not one house here, another house there, a mile away, behind that hill. You can see our farmers walking to their fields in the morning and coming back in the evening, though there are fields also in the villages. On Sundays the people gather on the green and the young folks dance, all together, hand in hand, not two by two. The musicians play wooden flutes attached to sacks of calf skin—what do you call them—bagpipes? Also little violins, which they hold like violoncellos. They play very well. Our farmers are poor, but happy. They sing when they plow or sow'— (which I pronounced *sau*)—'or harvest their crops. Folk songs, you know. Everybody in my country knows them.'

'Sing me one,' said Harry.

'But you will not understand.'

'Sing it just the same.'

I cleared my throat and broke into a gay peasant song, addressed to birds. But the words sounded strange. I had not heard Armenian for so long I felt as if somebody else were singing. I was so deeply moved by what I sang—or rather heard—I could have cried.

At the Schultz farm, Harry's mother, a short chubby woman, and his two very attractive sisters, met us in the yard. I wondered what they thought of me. My heart was thumping with deep hammer blows and I felt like running away.

'Where's Dad?' asked Harry.

'Gone to bed,' his mother answered.

As we entered the house, I noticed the radio, phonograph, sewing machine, and book shelves in the living room. To my intense surprise there was nothing rural about this house except that it was lighted by kerosene lamps. This delighted me. I hadn't seen a kerosene lamp in America.

The two girls were friendly enough, but I scarcely dared to look at them! One was a milk-white blonde, with hair the color of yellow corn. I took her to be about eighteen, my age. The other, a brunette, was younger, and looked like a Greek or Armenian girl to me, so that I was more attracted to her than to her fair sister, though the latter was obviously the beauty of the family. Both were dressed simply, like two neat city girls. This was like any middle-class city family, and I realized that the American urban and rural populations were substantially on the same economic and cultural level. It was so different in the old country, where villages were a thousand years behind the cities.

We talked for a while, and I had to answer the usual questions: How did I like America? Were the houses in my country like American houses? Did people over there wear the same type of clothes?

'Harry, you'd better show him to his room,' Mrs. Schultz said, after I had told them nearly my whole life story.

'Yes, you'd better get all the rest you can tonight. We have to get up mighty early in the morning,' Harry chuckled. 'Four-thirty. That too early for you?'

'No, not at all,' I said, eager to please.

'It's early to bed, early to rise with us,' Mrs. Schultz said. ' "Early to bed, early to rise, makes a man healthy, wealthy, and wise," ' she added, smiling. 'I'll have a pair of overalls ready for you in the morning. You're just about Harry's height.'

Harry took me upstairs to a large airy bedroom, with a wide double bed, a writing desk, a dresser, and a framed religious motto hanging on the wall. The windows had shutters like the village houses in Trebizond. The room was flooded with moon-light and the good smell of the cooling earth on a summer night.

'How do you like it?' Harry asked, putting down the kerosene lamp.

'I like it very much,' I said gratefully. I had wondered if I was to live in the same house with them, or be treated like a servant.

Alone in my room, I touched the window shutters caressingly and looked out to see the environs of the farm. In the yard, a water pail by the pump cast a shadow just like a water pail in the old country—an exciting detail in this nocturnal phantasy of Kansas-Trebizond. I filled my lungs with the intoxicating odor rising from a freshly mown alfalfa field, and listened to the thrill-ing night sounds of my childhood; for, amazingly enough, the crickets and frogs of Kansas sounded just like the crickets and frogs of Trebizond. It was the same resonant silence of the night that I was hearing again, the same sweet summertime music of the earth's dreams.

I looked up at the sky. It had sprouted and bloomed with stars, like dark-green fields covered with dandelions and the little golden flowers, the holy yellow flowers of Trebizond we called the Tears of the Virgin. Like a girl reaper with a white kerchief around her head, the moon moved across these flower-fields of the sky. All about me was the quivering, lyric translucence of an enchanted world that was dearly familiar to me. What miracle was this, what magic transfiguration? For the first time in Amer-ica I did not feel a stranger. I had discovered the earth I had lost, the stars and the moon of my childhood: my exile was over.

Early the next morning I began my apprenticeship on an American farm, wearing overalls. In them I felt like an Ameri-can. Harry and I went to the pasture to bring in the cows. It was a golden June morning. The young corn crackled in the breeze, and the orchard was ablaze with ripe sour cherries. I was in secret raptures over those cherry trees.

'Do you know,' I said to Harry, who majored in horticulture, 'cherries come from a place near my home town, from Cerasus, or Kerasund, on the Black Sea. That's why they're called cherries.'

He was surprised.

'And do you know the scientific name of the apricot?'

'I'll be damned if I do,' he said.

'*Prunus armeniaca*. Armenian prune. Oh, a lot of other fruits come from my country! Chestnuts, for example. The English word chestnut is derived from the Armenian word *kaskeni*, which means chestnut tree.'

A little brook ran through the pasture, where I saw blackberry and gooseberry bushes, and even loquat trees. To complete this miraculous picture, a spring flowed from under a rock through a narrow wooden trough, with a leaf dangling at its end! I wondered if I was dreaming, if this would vanish like an hallucination.

The sleepy cows struggled to their feet, heavy with milk, their big udders tight and full. We drove them to the barn, where Harry's father was waiting. He was a man of dignity, given to few words, tall, impressive, with keen blue 'eyes. But he looked ridiculous when he sat on a small stool, put a pail between his knees, and proceeded to milk, just like a woman. Yes, preposterous as it seemed, we three men had to do the milking. Mrs. Schultz and the girls were nowhere near the barn.

They were busy preparing breakfast and setting the table. It was an excellent breakfast they served when we finished milking—grapefruit, bran flakes and cream, home-cured ham and eggs, fresh country butter, home-made bread, good hot coffee. Mr. Schultz said Grace, thanking God for His many blessings —the God of America. Yes, America seemed to have a different God, a more generous one.

My first efforts as a milker supplied the conversation at the table. Of course I was clumsy and nervous, but in a week I could milk as well as Harry.

After breakfast we put two full ten-gallon milk cans in the Ford and drove to a collection point on the highway where they were picked up by a truck. That drive was another thrilling experience. The road, with its startlingly familiar bends, the bushes and trees that bordered it, the chip-chip of the sparrows, the tufts of wool caught on the wire fences—all these might have been in a village of Trebizond, and were infinitely dear to me. I felt that at any moment my childhood playmates, Vahe, Nikolaki, Anthula, Penelope, would come running down a field with bows and arrows, sling shots and sticks, wearing wreaths and baldrics of wild flowers. 'Hey, where have you been?' they would ask. 'Come on, we're going to pick wild strawberries and have a picnic lunch.'

The real toil began after these preliminary morning chores. A field had to be plowed, and I begged Harry to let me do it. Plowing was the fundamental art in agriculture I had to learn, and I had very romantic conceptions about it. What a thing of beauty and precision the modern steel plow was! Harry showed me how to cut furrows of uniform depth and width, turning the surface completely under.

A no less heroic task was pitching hay in the afternoon. This was sheer poetry. True, my hands became blistered, my face, neck, and shoulders sunburned, and the blue shirt on my back wringing wet with perspiration. The mighty Indian sun blazed down upon the immense fertility of the Missouri Valley. But I exulted in the powerful heat of the earth, in the dust and odor of alfalfa hay.

By nightfall I was dead tired, with a fine fatigue.

Something important had happened to me, but I did not know how to word it, not even to myself. Somehow I felt as if the earth and sun of Kansas flowed through my veins, that I had suddenly become an American, that I had been born again and wedded to the American soil.

This kind of Americanization has nothing to do with speaking English, taking out first and second papers, and swearing allegiance to the Constitution. Those are comparatively insignificant and superficial processes.

When, three months later, I returned to college, I was not only thoroughly Americanized, but, paradoxical as it may seem, was my former Old World self again. The nightmare of the previous winter was over. I could laugh and clown. I was happy, a boastful, rabid Kansan. If anybody said our college wasn't the greatest and best in the world, I felt insulted. I yelled myself hoarse at football games, avidly read the sport pages of newspapers, which had meant nothing to me before. I wrote two poems about Kansas which I sent to the Topeka Capital, and to my utter astonishment and joy they were published. I joined organizations, was invited to speak before various clubs, dined in some of the best homes in Manhattan, learned how to use finger bowls, and dated pretty co-eds—but that is another story!

What is it soldiers fight and die for? What is it that makes nations? Language, history, traditions, political organizations? These are contributing factors, yes; but, fundamentally, it is the land, a common identity with the earth—with dandelions and moonlight and crickets and the crackling of young corn in the morning breeze.

That summer I saw how the sun made love to the earth in the Missouri Valley, and how from that love poured forth rivers of golden grains. I heard the droning of bees among wild flowers in the stillness of the noon, the sound of the woodpecker. I listened to the song of bread sung by millions of invisible lips in miles of scented wheatfields at night.

America flowed into my blood; the earth and the sun, the wind and the rain, the moon and the stars of America were within me.

FOREIGNER

By Fred D. Wieck

I WAS seven when the idea of some people being foreigners
entered my thoughts. That was in the fall of 1917 on a large farm
in Germany. A number of French war prisoners were working
there, among them a tall, powerful young peasant from the
Provence, named Viala. He had a broad brown face that flashed
when he talked, and big brown hands that moulded his thoughts
in the air until you could touch them.

By and by I took to him. I was short, pale, fattish, and sullen;
but Viala did not mind. He taught me to ride, sought me out
to give me a specially beautiful apple, and hid a big glass of
milk for me in the cow-shed every day. The taste of cow-warm
milk still brings back to me the smile in his eyes, and the feeling
of safety they gave me. After work, he used to sit on the ground
behind the tool-shed, brooding, his hands stroking the tips of
the grass. But when I joined him, he always changed quickly
and began to talk to me or sing in French, or use some other
of the many ways he had to make me happy.

One night I was out late, against orders, and therefore moving with stealth. Behind the barn I came upon Viala and a
maid. I stopped, and since I had not been seen, hid behind a
walnut tree and watched. I could hear Viala's breathing and
see the girl's eyes shimmer in the reflection of a kitchen light.
They were facing each other in silence.

Viala said, 'Marie!' in a voice low and pleading. She cocked
her head and gave a throaty giggle. He repeated, 'Marie!' and
reached for her shoulder. With a quick twist she brushed his
hands off and slapped his face. Then she spoke. She said neither
'Don't!' nor 'Take your dirty paws off me!' Tossing her chin

From *Common Ground*, Spring 1941. By permission of the publisher.

high, with an inflection of infinite disgust, she said, *'Ausländer!'*
—'Foreigner!'

Swinging her shoulders proudly, she walked away. Viala stared
after her, hunched with humiliation, silent but for one painful
intake of breath.

For a second I stayed behind my tree, wondering if Marie
with her outcry had not appealed to something to which I, a
native like her, must be loyal. But I caught a glimpse of Viala's
face. It was terrible, dead. I thought of the way he could laugh
with me. I hated Marie. I tiptoed over to him, tugged his sleeve,
and said softly, 'Viala?'

He turned but did not seem to see me. I smiled. He lifted his
hand and gently ruffled my hair. The pressure of his fingers bade
me stay where I was; without a word he walked away into the
dark.

I did not dare to follow. I was moved and frightened by his
face, which was limp and loose with desperate loneliness.

The next time *I* was the foreigner, in 1934. I had left Germany. My name was on the waiting list for a U.S. visa.

While waiting, I had gone to France. I had been abroad before, as a visitor, but this was different. Though politically free
to return to the country of my birth, I loathed the idea. Should
I not obtain a U.S. visa (and it seemed too good to come true),
I wanted to stay in France and grow roots there. For I realized
a man must have a place where he belongs.

France is fascinating to discover; so it may be I took my quest
somewhat as an adventure. After two years of traveling as a
salesman throughout the country, I had learned the language
and the ways of the people. And I believed I was well on my
way toward the identification with the whole that is called 'being at home.' Up to the day I called on Master Tinel-Haese, I
failed to see that this was one-sided.

Tinel-Haese—'master' by virtue of being a lawyer—lived in
Epernay, a small township in the champagne country surrounding Reims. The traditional golden plaque over his door caught
my eye, and I rang the bell to sell my wares.

A little boy let me in and asked me to wait. The room in

which I found myself was bright with flower pots in the open windows. What gave it spirit were the pictures it held, delicate watercolors, an oil painting, and, on a wall by itself, a large charcoal portrait.

This showed the face of a man about fifty—unmistakably a French face, with eyebrows, eyes, mustache, and mouth ascending toward the center like a Gothic arch, chin beard and widow's peak giving the counterpoint. The somber eyes stared at me with an almost physical impact. I was still studying it when the original entered.

He was very tall, with wide, hanging shoulders. His temples and beard were gray, his complexion sallow. Beads of sweat stood on his forehead. He was in shirt-sleeves, without a collar. As he stood in the door, glowering at me out of gloomy eyes, I was frightened. And then, of the two of us, he was the one to be shy.

After learning my name, he addressed me in uncertain German, using the familiar *du*—'thou'—a language he may have learned in a war prisoners' camp. Occasionally he gave me a shy side-glance, as if aware of his mistake but unable to correct it. Then I, too, changed to 'thou,' which seemed to reassure him. He apologized for the disorder in the room. There were, indeed, toys and a picture book lying on the floor, and a silk hair-ribbon hanging over a chair. 'Three children, you understand, small ones, and my wife is not well . . .' I assured him that traces of children were something endearing, and began to compliment him on the pictures.

They were exquisite, he agreed. Obviously I was a connoisseur . . . Weren't they beautiful? His wife had done them. And others, too, even better. But did I know the delicacy of health that so often goes with genius? She wasn't well at all. In fact, consumption. So one worked hard, hard indeed, to save enough to send her to Tetuan. And Tetuan, as everyone knew, would absolutely cure her.

Master Tinel-Haese gave this information in bits and fragments, surreptitiously, as if ashamed to trouble me with the things that were breaking his heart. Meanwhile he went through my sample case, ordering some of all the over-expensive office supplies I had for sale. He kept asking my forgiveness for not ordering more, and for this and that, until I understood his humble manner was only a plea to be kind and bear with him in his foolish hope that the inevitable would not happen, to help him deny that his wife whom he loved would die.

Other men in France had talked to me without reserve: Hegedusch, the Hungarian; Arno, from Vienna; Simon and Solanas, Spaniards; Billy, the Englishman. And a few others. But all of them had been foreigners like myself. In this country full of Frenchmen, Tinel-Haese was the first Frenchman who had spoken with me as to an equal.

It came to me with a shock. Only tragedy and extreme loneliness had forced him to accept me as a fellow man. I suddenly became aware of the invisible wall that separated me from the people who I had hoped would admit me as their countryman. Tinel-Haese's distress had forced him to let down the barrier, and, in so doing, had showed me it was there.

Centuries ago, when distance meant isolation, the ancestors of France had conceived a culture and nursed it through the generations into something shining, all their own. Its highest artistic articulation I could understand and love; but its essence had filtered down into the soul and minds and bodies of Frenchmen so deep that I, in my one lifetime, would hardly catch up to it. They would always feel it and set me apart. In France I was lost.

I knew of only one country where my relations with my fellows would be based not on these intangible traditions but on reasoned effort to share all that is common to those who hold themselves free-born, to respect the complicated differences history, race, and culture have created. And to that country I had not yet been allowed to go.

In 1935 I obtained my U.S. immigration visa.

The first two weeks in New York, I stayed with German-born relatives. They assured me I was an 'immigrant'—a word new but of familiar melody—and that I would never be a real American. At first I took their word for it and was downhearted. But I began to suspect they had imported an attitude common abroad; that the America I had dreamed of in France was here in spite of them; and that they had not bothered to find it.

I got a job and took a room by myself. My English improved, and I went to take out first papers. With my heart in my shoes, I presented myself to the Immigration Service, for any contact with governmental agencies abroad had meant trouble and disaster. This official smiled. 'Lift your right hand, folks!' We huddled together, frightened. 'O.K. That's all. Good luck. I'll be seeing you!'

It couldn't be! It couldn't be that easy. One doesn't just walk into America and make a reservation like that in the world's most splendid hotel, without fame or fortune for deposit, with nothing but oneself. It just couldn't be.

Yet the boys and girls at the shop treated me from the first like a new club member. They helped me all they could, in every way. But I am most grateful for something they did unknowingly: they kept on being as they had always been, regardless of my presence.

Soon I had a position with a firm sporting a Mayflower on its stationery. It was owned by an elderly man of patrician air, with the narrow-templed face and tall lean body of the thoroughbred. Once the company had made much money, in a genteel way; but now little was left but memories and innumerable steel files crowding a meager staff. The 'old man,' who indulged in nostalgic sighs, ruled with whispering voice and iron fist. It was depressing, and I began to look for something else almost immediately. In a short while I found it and gave notice.

The 'old man' turned purple. I, a 'foreigner,' a 'charity case,' had double-crossed him!

Choking with rage and humiliation I went to my rooming house, where I knew Johnny Webster, a truck-driver from Pennsylvania, with the gentle ways of those who are very strong.

'And you didn't even talk back?'

I found I had not acted the way Johnny expected.

'Look here, Johnny,' I apologized. 'You see, he—well, he's an old-stock American, and I'm just a newcomer. Maybe I did something I shouldn't, just because I didn't know any better.'

Johnny was completely puzzled. 'What's the matter with you?

You're payin' your own way, ain't you? You're doin' yours? He ain't no better than you—he can't call you no names!'

Johnny's lack of comprehension was sweet. My name, my accent, my origin—to him they did not matter. As long as I did mine, I was as good as anybody else and, what's more, good enough to be the friend of Johnny Webster from Pennsylvania.

Then there was Collins, called the night watchman because of the late hours he kept, who, through the partition between our rooms, one night addressed me as 'You damn' foreigner!'

I sat up in bed with a start. I resented the word fiercely. I thought of Viala's face. I got up and went to his room. He had heard me coming and was awaiting me in the middle of the room, under the light. I stepped up close to him. 'What did you just say?'

'Gee, Fred,' he said, 'I didn't mean nothin' special—just one of them words you use . . .'

I went to bed happy. I, technically still a foreigner, could protest when I was called an intruder. I was here by rights, among equals. True, I had bullied him into apology. But it was important he had known exactly why I was furious. He had understood that I didn't mind being 'cussed,' but being called an intruder.

A few months ago I volunteered for military service under the Selective Service Act, and am now, as I write, in the reception camp at Fort Dix. Thousands of boys pass through here on their way to a permanent station with some Army unit. They are all volunteers representing a cross-section of the three Eastern states from which they come.

My tent holds six men. The cots are numbered clockwise; mine is No. 1, by the door. In cot No. 2 there is Eddy Green, Jewish, former bell-hop in one of New York's largest hotels. He tells me that whenever he called a Jewish name in the lobby, he had to add a Gentile name—Webster, for instance—'to clear the air.' Yet he is a volunteer. Our company commander is Jewish. Why, then, should Eddy worry about being Jewish? Doesn't he belong to the Army of America?

In cot No. 3 is Jack Csezak. One night after tattoo, I came

upon him alone in a dark part of our company street, singing a song his mother had taught him on an upstate New York farm. We talked awhile. 'Freddie,' he said suddenly, 'you're German; I'm Polish. Let's write a letter to the President, you and I!'

'What about?'

'About us being here. Well . . . about being in the Army . . . It's swell.' Then, I assume, he blushed in the darkness, embarrassed by his own emotion and impulse, and said, 'Oh, hell with it! Just an idea I had. He's too busy to read our letter anyhow.'

There is, of course, no little growling and bellyaching (marvelous word! with a long tradition, I am told) in this Army, but the chances are Jack Csezak is not alone in feeling and thinking as he does. The Grabiecs and Websters and Hunzingers and Mockapetris and Sicilianos in the camp probably have similar thoughts.

In cot No. 4 is Joe Lanzilotta. 'Must be a funny feeling, Joe,' one of the others said to him one day, 'you being in the Army and thinking all the time, "Some day I may have to kill my own countrymen." ' But Joe doesn't see it that way. He said, 'That's just my name—Lanzilotta—doesn't mean a thing.' I look at him and envy his Latin ease in living his life. But put Joe into any crowd anywhere in Europe, and you will be able to single him out as American by the unmistakable air about him, by something for which I have no name.

In cot No. 5 is Hans Rumpler, born an Austrian. 'I've emigrated three times—Czechoslovakia, Switzerland, the States,' he said to me one day. 'Now I'm going to stay put. I'm through running. This is my last stand. You can't emigrate to the moon!' In this last ditch, he and I became friends. In New York he used to engage in futile arguments about the world situation; now he has a feeling he is doing something about it; something positive. I feel the same way. In my own mind I could not condone what was happening in Germany. But doing nothing about the situation was, I felt, condoning it. Now, a German American in the U.S. Army, I know a personal purging and satisfaction.

In cot No. 6 is Isidro Rivera, from Porto Rico. He came over only two months ago to volunteer, and his English is still young and awkward. One day I ran into him, raging and in tears. 'If the people not like how I speak, why ask me questions always, and laugh? Why people have so little shame? Why they kid me all the time?' . . . But I have an idea he will be all right, by and by.

In another tent is Slim, from Brooklyn, of negroid features. He escaped being classified as 'colored,' only because Jim Keane, an Irish American who had met him twenty minutes before the examination, assured the physician he had known Slim for years and that Slim was as white as he, Jim. But for a lie, and a scientist accepting it as proof, Slim would be in a segregated company for his year of service in the Army and, probably, for the rest of his life.

Jim, who is in another company, comes to visit us often. He has opaque, smoke-blue eyes and is full of manly stories about women, poker, beer, and money spent freely. I don't remember seeing him serious except on one occasion when somebody drifted into our tent and made a remark about there being too damn' many kikes and wops and foreigners in this man's Army. Joe Lanzilotta lay still on his bunk, his eyes glittering. Eddy Green, who is small, began to unbutton his blouse.

Jim spoke calmly: 'Listen, bud—that kinda talk don't go 'round here. Beat it!'

'And suppose I don't?'

'In that case,' said Jim, 'I'll have to ask you to come behind the butts and I'll try to knock the living hell outa you.'

The intruder left, muttering.

For several minutes we sat silent. Then Jack Csezak started to whistle the tune of his Polish song.

NEIGHBOUR ROSICKY

By Willa Cather

WHEN Doctor Burleigh told neighbour Rosicky he had a bad heart, Rosicky protested.

'So? No, I guess my heart was always pretty good. I got a little asthma, maybe. Just a awful short breath when I was pitchin' hay last summer, dat's all.'

'Well now, Rosicky, if you know more about it than I do, what did you come to me for? It's your heart that makes you short of breath, I tell you. You're sixty-five years old, and you've always worked hard, and your heart's tired. You've got to be careful from now on, and you can't do heavy work any more. You've got five boys at home to do it for you.'

The old farmer looked up at the Doctor with a gleam of amusement in his queer triangular-shaped eyes. His eyes were large and lively, but the lids were caught up in the middle in a curious way, so that they formed a triangle. He did not look like a sick man. His brown face was creased but not wrinkled, he had a ruddy colour in his smooth-shaven cheeks and in his lips, under his long brown moustache. His hair was thin and ragged around his ears, but very little grey. His forehead, naturally high and crossed by deep parallel lines, now ran all the way up to his pointed crown. Rosicky's face had the habit of looking interested,—suggested a contented disposition and a reflective quality that was gay rather than grave. This gave him a certain detachment, the easy manner of an onlooker and observer.

'Well, I guess you ain't got no pills fur a bad heart, Doctor Ed. I guess the only thing is fur me to git me a new one.'

Doctor Burleigh swung round in his desk-chair and frowned

Reprinted from Willa Cather, *Obscure Destinies*, 1932. By permission and special arrangement with Alfred A Knopf, Inc., authorized publishers.

at the old farmer. 'I think if I were you I'd take a little care of the old one, Rosicky.'

Rosicky shrugged. 'Maybe I don't know how. I expect you mean fur me not to drink my coffee no more.'

'I wouldn't, in your place. But you'll do as you choose about that. I've never yet been able to separate a Bohemian from his coffee or his pipe. I've quit trying. But the sure thing is you've got to cut out farm work. You can feed the stock and do chores about the barn, but you can't do anything in the fields that makes you short of breath.'

'How about shelling corn?'

'Of course not!'

Rosicky considered with puckered brows.

'I can't make my heart go no longer'n it wants to, can I, Doctor Ed?'

'I think it's good for five or six years yet, maybe more, if you'll take the strain off it. Sit around the house and help Mary. If I had a good wife like yours, I'd want to stay around the house.'

His patient chuckled. 'It ain't no place fur a man. I don't like no old man hanging round the kitchen too much. An' my wife, she's a awful hard worker her own self.'

'That's it; you can help her a little. My Lord, Rosicky, you are one of the few men I know who has a family he can get some comfort out of; happy dispositions, never quarrel among themselves, and they treat you right. I want to see you live a few years and enjoy them.'

'Oh, they're good kids, all right,' Rosicky assented.

The Doctor wrote him a prescription and asked him how his oldest son, Rudolph, who had married in the spring, was getting on. Rudolph had struck out for himself, on rented land. 'And how's Polly? I was afraid Mary mightn't like an American daughter-in-law, but it seems to be working out all right.'

'Yes, she's a fine girl. Dat widder woman bring her daughters up very nice. Polly got lots of spunk, an' she got some style, too. Da's nice, for young folks to have some style.' Rosicky inclined his head gallantly. His voice and his twinkly smile were an affectionate compliment to his daughter-in-law.

'It looks like a storm, and you'd better be getting home before it comes. In town in the car?' Doctor Burleigh rose.

'No, I'm in de wagon. When you got five boys, you ain't got much chance to ride round in de Ford. I ain't much for cars, noway.'

'Well, it's a good road out to your place; but I don't want you bumping around in a wagon much. And never again on a hay-rake, remember!'

Rosicky placed the Doctor's fee delicately behind the desk-telephone, looking the other way, as if this were an absent-minded gesture. He put on his plush cap and his corduroy jacket with a sheepskin collar, and went out.

The Doctor picked up his stethoscope and frowned at it as if he were seriously annoyed with the instrument. He wished it had been telling tales about some other man's heart, some old man who didn't look the Doctor in the eye so knowingly, or hold out such a warm brown hand when he said good-bye. Doctor Burleigh had been a poor boy in the country before he went away to medical school; he had known Rosicky almost ever since he could remember, and he had a deep affection for Mrs. Rosicky.

Only last winter he had had such a good breakfast at Rosicky's, and that when he needed it. He had been out all night on a long, hard confinement case at Tom Marshall's,—a big rich farm where there was plenty of stock and plenty of feed and a great deal of expensive farm machinery of the newest model, and no comfort whatever. The woman had too many children and too much work, and she was no manager. When the baby was born at last, and handed over to the assisting neighbour woman, and the mother was properly attended to, Burleigh refused any breakfast in that slovenly house, and drove his buggy—the snow was too deep for a car—eight miles to Anton Rosicky's place. He didn't know another farm-house where a man could get such a warm welcome, and such good strong coffee with rich cream. No wonder the old chap didn't want to give up his coffee.

He had driven in just when the boys had come back from the barn and were washing up for breakfast. The long table, covered with a bright oilcloth, was set out with dishes waiting for them, and the warm kitchen was full of the smell of coffee and hot biscuit and sausage. Five big handsome boys, running from twenty to twelve, all with what Burleigh called natural good manners,—they hadn't a bit of the painful self-consciousness he himself had to struggle with when he was a lad. One ran to put his horse away, another helped him off with his fur coat and hung it up, and Josephine, the youngest child and the only daughter, quickly set another place under her mother's direction.

With Mary, to feed creatures was the natural expression of affection,—her chickens, the calves, her big hungry boys. It was a rare pleasure to feed a young man whom she seldom saw and of whom she was as proud as if he belonged to her. Some country housekeepers would have stopped to spread a white cloth over the oilcloth, to change the thick cups and plates for their best china, and the wooden-handled knives for plated ones. But not Mary.

'You must take us as you find us, Doctor Ed. I'd be glad to put out my good things for you if you was expected, but I'm glad to get you any way at all.'

He knew she was glad,—she threw back her head and spoke out as if she were announcing him to the whole prairie. Rosicky hadn't said anything at all; he merely smiled his twinkling smile, put some more coal on the fire, and went into his own room to pour the Doctor a little drink in a medicine glass. When they were all seated, he watched his wife's face from his end of the table and spoke to her in Czech. Then, with the instinct of politeness which seldom failed him, he turned to the Doctor and said slyly: 'I was just tellin' her not to ask you no questions about Mrs. Marshall till you eat some breakfast. My wife, she's terrible fur to ask questions.'

The boys laughed, and so did Mary. She watched the Doctor devour her biscuit and sausage, too much excited to eat anything herself. She drank her coffee and sat taking in everything about her visitor. She had known him when he was a poor country boy, and was boastfully proud of his success, always saying: 'What do people go to Omaha for, to see a doctor, when we got the best one in the State right here?' If Mary liked people at all, she felt physical pleasure in the sight of them, personal

exultation in any good fortune that came to them. Burleigh
didn't know many women like that, but he knew she was like
that.

When his hunger was satisfied, he did, of course, have to tell
them about Mrs. Marshall, and he noticed what a friendly interest the boys took in the matter.

Rudolph, the oldest one (he was still living at home then)
said: 'The last time I was over there, she was lifting them big
heavy milkcans, and I knew she oughtn't to be doing it.'

'Yes, Rudolph told me about that when he come home, and
I said it wasn't right,' Mary put in warmly. 'It was all right for
me to do them things up to the last, for I was terrible strong,
but that woman's weakly. And do you think she'll be able to
nurse it, Ed?' She sometimes forgot to give him the title she
was so proud of. 'And to think of your being up all night and
then not able to get a decent breakfast! I don't know what's
the matter with such people.'

'Why, Mother,' said one of the boys, 'if Doctor Ed had got
breakfast there, we wouldn't have him here. So you ought to be
glad.'

'He knows I'm glad to have him, John, any time. But I'm
sorry for that poor woman, how bad she'll feel the Doctor had
to go away in the cold without his breakfast.'

'I wish I'd been in practice when these were getting born.'
The Doctor looked down the row of close-clipped heads. 'I missed
some good breakfasts by not being.'

The boys began to laugh at their mother because she flushed so
red, but she stood her ground and threw up her head. 'I don't
care, you wouldn't have got away from this house without breakfast. No doctor ever did. I'd have had something ready fixed that
Anton could warm up for you.'

The boys laughed harder than ever, and exclaimed at her:
'I'll bet you would!' 'She would, that!'

'Father, did you get breakfast for the doctor when we were
born?'

'Yes, and he used to bring me my breakfast, too, mighty nice.
I was always awful hungry!' Mary admitted with a guilty laugh.

While the boys were getting the Doctor's horse, he went to

the window to examine the house plants. 'What do you do to your geraniums to keep them blooming all winter, Mary? I never pass this house that from the road I don't see your windows full of flowers.'

She snapped off a dark red one, and a ruffled green leaf, and put them in his button-hole. 'There, that looks better. You look too solemn for a young man, Ed. Why don't you git married? I'm worried about you. Settin' at breakfast, I looked at you real hard, and I seen you've got some grey hairs already.'

'Oh, yes! They're coming. Maybe they'd come faster if I married.'

'Don't talk so. You'll ruin your health eating at the hotel. I could send your wife a nice loaf of nut bread, if you only had one. I don't like to see a young man getting grey. I'll tell you something, Ed; you make some strong black tea and keep it handy in a bowl, and every morning just brush it into your hair, an' it'll keep the grey from showin' much. That's the way I do!'

Sometimes the Doctor heard the gossipers in the drug-store wondering why Rosicky didn't get on faster. He was industrious, and so were his boys, but they were rather free and easy, weren't pushers, and they didn't always show good judgment. They were comfortable, they were out of debt, but they didn't get much ahead. Maybe, Doctor Burleigh reflected, people as generous and warm-hearted and affectionate as the Rosickys never got ahead much; maybe you couldn't enjoy your life and put it into the bank, too.

II

When Rosicky left Doctor Burleigh's office he went into the farm-implement store to light his pipe and put on his glasses and read over the list Mary had given him. Then he went into the general merchandise place next door and stood about until the pretty girl with the plucked eyebrows, who always waited on him, was free. Those eyebrows, two thin India-ink strokes, amused him, because he remembered how they used to be. Rosicky always prolonged his shopping by a little joking; the girl knew the old fellow admired her, and she liked to chaff with him.

'Seems to me about every other week you buy ticking, Mr. Rosicky, and always the best quality,' she remarked as she measured off the heavy bolt with red stripes.

'You see, my wife is always makin' goosefedder pillows, an' de thin stuff don't hold in dem little down-fedders.'

'You must have lots of pillows at your house.'

'Sure. She makes quilts of dem, too. We sleeps easy. Now she's makin' a fedder quilt for my son's wife. You know Polly, that married my Rudolph. How much my bill, Miss Pearl?'

"Eight eighty-five.'

'Chust make it nine, and put in some candy fur de women.'

'As usual. I never did see a man buy so much candy for his wife. First thing you know, she'll be getting too fat.'

'I'd like dat. I ain't much fur all dem slim women like what de style is now.'

'That's one for me, I suppose, Mr. Rosicky!' Pearl sniffed and elevated her India-ink strokes.

When Rosicky went out to his wagon, it was beginning to snow,—the first snow of the season, and he was glad to see it. He rattled out of town and along the highway through a wonderfully rich stretch of country, the finest farms in the county. He admired this High Prairie, as it was called, and always liked to drive through it. His own place lay in a rougher territory, where there was some clay in the soil and it was not so productive. When he bought his land, he hadn't the money to buy on High Prairie; so he told his boys, when they grumbled, that if their land hadn't some clay in it, they wouldn't own it at all. All the same, he enjoyed looking at these fine farms, as he enjoyed looking at a prize bull.

After he had gone eight miles, he came to the graveyard, which lay just at the edge of his own hay-land. There he stopped his horses and sat still on his wagon seat, looking about at the snow-fall. Over yonder on the hill he could see his own house, crouching low, with the clump of orchard behind and the windmill before, and all down the gentle hill-slope the rows of pale gold cornstalks stood out against the white field. The snow was falling over the cornfield and the pasture and the hay-land, steadily, with very little wind,—a nice dry snow. The graveyard had only a light wire fence about it and was all overgrown with long red grass. The fine snow, settling into this red grass and upon the few little evergreens and the headstones, looked very pretty.

It was a nice graveyard, Rosicky reflected, sort of snug and homelike, not cramped or mournful,—a big sweep all round it. A man could lie down in the long grass and see the complete arch of the sky over him, hear the wagons go by; in summer the mowing-machine rattled right up to the wire fence. And it was so near home. Over there across the cornstalks his own roof and windmill looked so good to him that he promised himself to mind the Doctor and take care of himself. He was awful fond of his place, he admitted. He wasn't anxious to leave it. And it was a comfort to think that he would never have to go farther than the edge of his own hayfield. The snow, falling over his barnyard and the graveyard, seemed to draw things together like. And they were all old neighbours in the graveyard, most of them friends; there was nothing to feel awkward or embarrassed about. Embarrassment was the most disagreeable feeling Rosicky knew. He didn't often have it,—only with certain people whom he didn't understand at all.

Well, it was a nice snowstorm; a fine sight to see the snow falling so quietly and graciously over so much open country. On his cap and shoulders, on the horses' backs and manes, light, delicate, mysterious it fell; and with it a dry cool fragrance was released into the air. It meant rest for vegetation and men and beasts, for the ground itself; a season of long nights for sleep, leisurely breakfasts, peace by the fire. This and much more went through Rosicky's mind, but he merely told himself that winter was coming, clucked to his horses, and drove on.

When he reached home, John, the youngest boy, ran out to put away his team for him, and he met Mary coming up from the outside cellar with her apron full of carrots. They went into the house together. On the table, covered with oilcloth figured with clusters of blue grapes, a place was set, and he smelled hot coffee-cake of some kind. Anton never lunched in town; he thought that extravagant, and anyhow he didn't like the food.

So Mary always had something ready for him when he got home.

After he was settled in his chair, stirring his coffee in a big cup, Mary took out of the oven a pan of *kolache* stuffed with apricots, examined them anxiously to see whether they had got too dry, put them beside his plate, and then sat down opposite him.

Rosicky asked her in Czech if she wasn't going to have any coffee.

She replied in English, as being somehow the right language for transacting business: 'Now what did Doctor Ed say, Anton? You tell me just what.'

'He said I was to tell you some compliments, but I forgot 'em.' Rosicky's eyes twinkled.

'About you, I mean. What did he say about your asthma?'

'He says I ain't got no asthma.' Rosicky took one of the little rolls in his broad brown fingers. The thickened nail of his right thumb told the story of his past.

'Well, what is the matter? And don't try to put me off.'

'He don't say nothing much, only I'm a little older, and my heart ain't so good like it used to be.'

Mary started and brushed her hair back from her temples with both hands as if she were a little out of her mind. From the way she glared, she might have been in a rage with him.

'He says there's something the matter with your heart? Doctor Ed says so?'

'Now don't yell at me like I was a hog in de garden, Mary. You know I always did like to hear a woman talk soft. He didn't say anything de matter wid my heart, only it ain't so young like it used to be, an' he tell me not to pitch hay or run de cornsheller.'

Mary wanted to jump up, but she sat still. She admired the way he never under any circumstances raised his voice or spoke roughly. He was city-bred, and she was country-bred; she often said she wanted her boys to have their papa's nice ways.

'You never have no pain there, do you? It's your breathing and your stomach that's been wrong. I wouldn't believe nobody but Doctor Ed about it. I guess I'll go see him myself. Didn't he give you no advice?'

'Chust to take it easy like, an' stay round de house dis winter. I guess you got some carpenter work for me to do. I kin make some new shelves for you, and I want dis long time to build a chest in de boys' room and make dem two little fellers keep dere clo'es hung up.'

Rosicky drank his coffee from time to time, while he considered. His moustache was of the soft long variety and came down over his mouth like the teeth of a buggy-rake over a bundle of hay. Each time he put down his cup, he ran his blue handkerchief over his lips. When he took a drink of water, he managed very neatly with the back of his hand.

Mary sat watching him intently, trying to find any change in his face. It is hard to see anyone who has become like your own body to you. Yes, his hair had got thin, and his high forehead had deep lines running from left to right. But his neck, always clean shaved except in the busiest seasons, was not loose or baggy. It was burned a dark reddish brown, and there were deep creases in it, but it looked firm and full of blood. His cheeks had a good colour. On either side of his mouth there was a half-moon down the length of his cheek, not wrinkles, but two lines that had come there from his habitual expression. He was shorter and broader than when she married him; his back had grown broad and curved, a good deal like the shell of an old turtle, and his arms and legs were short.

He was fifteen years older than Mary, but she had hardly ever thought about it before. He was her man, and the kind of man she liked. She was rough, and he was gentle,—city-bred, as she always said. They had been shipmates on a rough voyage and had stood by each other in trying times. Life had gone well with them because, at bottom, they had the same ideas about life. They agreed, without discussion, as to what was most important and what was secondary. They didn't often exchange opinions, even in Czech,—it was as if they had thought the same thought together. A good deal had to be sacrificed and thrown overboard in a hard life like theirs, and they had never disagreed as to the things that could go. It had been a hard life, and a soft life, too. There wasn't anything brutal in the short, broad-backed man with the three-cornered eyes and the forehead that went on to the top of his skull. He was a city man, a gentle man, and though he had married a rough farm girl, he had never touched her without gentleness.

They had been at one accord not to hurry through life, not to be always skimping and saving. They saw their neighbours buy more land and feed more stock than they did, without discontent. Once when the creamery agent came to the Rosickys to persuade them to sell him their cream, he told them how much money the Fasslers, their nearest neighbours, had made on their cream last year.

'Yes,' said Mary, 'and look at them Fassler children! Pale, pinched little things, they look like skimmed milk. I'd rather put some colour into my children's faces than put money into the bank.'

The agent shrugged and turned to Anton.

'I guess we'll do like she says,' said Rosicky.

III

Mary very soon got into town to see Doctor Ed, and then she had a talk with her boys and set a guard over Rosicky. Even John, the youngest, had his father on his mind. If Rosicky went to throw hay down from the loft, one of the boys ran up the ladder and took the fork from him. He sometimes complained that though he was getting to be an old man, he wasn't an old woman yet.

That winter he stayed in the house in the afternoons and carpentered, or sat in the chair between the window full of plants and the wooden bench where the two pails of drinking-water stood. This spot was called 'Father's corner,' though it was not a corner at all. He had a shelf there, where he kept his Bohemian papers and his pipes and tobacco, and his shears and needles and thread and tailor's thimble. Having been a tailor in his youth, he couldn't bear to see a woman patching at his clothes, or at the boys'. He liked tailoring, and always patched all the overalls and jackets and work shirts. Occasionally he made over a pair of pants one of the older boys had outgrown, for the little fellow.

While he sewed, he let his mind run back over his life. He had a good deal to remember, really; life in three countries. The only part of his youth he didn't like to remember was the two years he had spent in London, in Cheapside, working for a German tailor who was wretchedly poor. Those days, when he was nearly always hungry, when his clothes were dropping off him for dirt, and the sound of a strange language kept him in continual bewilderment, had left a sore spot in his mind that wouldn't bear touching.

He was twenty when he landed at Castle Garden in New York, and he had a protector who got him work in a tailor shop in Vesey Street, down near the Washington Market. He looked upon that part of his life as very happy. He became a good workman, he was industrious, and his wages were increased from time to time. He minded his own business and envied nobody's good fortune. He went to night school and learned to read English. He often did overtime work and was well paid for it, but somehow he never saved anything. He couldn't refuse a loan to a friend, and he was self-indulgent. He liked a good dinner, and a little went for beer, a little for tobacco; a good deal went to the girls. He often stood through an opera on Saturday nights; he could get standing-room for a dollar. Those were the great days of opera in New York, and it gave a fellow something to think about for the rest of the week. Rosicky had a quick ear, and a childish love of all the stage splendour; the scenery, the costumes, the ballet. He usually went with a chum, and after the performance they had beer and maybe some oysters somewhere. It was a fine life; for the first five years or so it satisfied him completely. He was never hungry or cold or dirty, and everything amused him: a fire, a dog fight, a parade, a storm, a ferry ride. He thought New York the finest, richest, friendliest city in the world.

Moreover, he had what he called a happy home life. Very near the tailor shop was a small furniture-factory, where an old Austrian, Loeffler, employed a few skilled men and made unusual furniture, most of it to order, for the rich German housewives up-town. The top floor of Loeffler's five-story factory was a loft, where he kept his choice lumber and stored the odd pieces of furniture left on his hands. One of the young workmen he employed was a Czech, and he and Rosicky became fast friends. They persuaded Loeffler to let them have a sleeping-room in one corner of the loft. They bought good beds and bedding and had their pick of the furniture kept up there. The loft was low-pitched, but light and airy, full of windows, and good-smelling by reason of the fine lumber put up there to season. Old Loeffler used to go down to the docks and buy wood from South America and the East from the sea captains. The young men were as foolish about their house as a bridal pair. Zichee, the young cabinet-maker, devised every sort of convenience, and Rosicky kept their clothes in order. At night and on Sundays, when the quiver of machinery underneath was still, it was the quietest place in the world, and on summer nights all the sea winds blew in. Zichee often practised on his flute in the evening. They were both fond of music and went to the opera together. Rosicky thought he wanted to live like that for ever.

But as the years passed, all alike, he began to get a little restless. When spring came round, he would begin to feel fretted, and he got to drinking. He was likely to drink too much of a Saturday night. On Sunday he was languid and heavy, getting over his spree. On Monday he plunged into work again. So he never had time to figure out what ailed him, though he knew something did. When the grass turned green in Park Place, and the lilac hedge at the back of Trinity churchyard put out its blossoms, he was tormented by a longing to run away. That was why he drank too much; to get a temporary illusion of freedom and wide horizons.

Rosicky, the old Rosicky, could remember as if it were yesterday the day when the young Rosicky found out what was the matter with him. It was on a Fourth of July afternoon, and he was sitting in Park Place in the sun. The lower part of New York was empty. Wall Street, Liberty Street, Broadway, all empty. So much stone and asphalt with nothing going on, so many empty windows. The emptiness was intense, like the stillness in a great factory when the machinery stops and the belts and bands cease running. It was too great a change, it took all the strength out of one. Those blank buildings, without the stream of life pouring through them, were like empty jails. It struck young Rosicky that this was the trouble with big cities; they built you in from the earth itself, cemented you away from any contact with the ground. You lived in an unnatural world, like the fish in an aquarium, who were probably much more comfortable than they ever were in the sea.

On that very day he began to think seriously about the articles he had read in the Bohemian papers, describing prosperous Czech farming communities in the West. He believed he would like to go out there as a farm hand; it was hardly possible that he could ever have land of his own. His people had always been workmen; his father and grandfather had worked in shops. His mother's parents had lived in the country, but had rented their farm and had a hard time to get along. Nobody in his family had ever owned any land,—that belonged to a different station of life, altogether. Anton's mother died when he was little, and he was sent into the country to her parents. He stayed with them until he was twelve, and formed those ties with the earth and the farm animals and growing things which are never made at all unless they are made early. After his grandfather died, he went back to live with his father and stepmother, but she was very hard on him, and his father helped him to get passage to London.

After that Fourth of July day in Park Place, the desire to return to the country never left him. To work on another man's farm would be all he asked; to see the sun rise and set and to plant things and watch them grow. He was a very simple man. He was like a tree that has not many roots, but one tap-root that goes down deep. He subscribed for a Bohemian paper printed in Chicago, then for one printed in Omaha. His mind got farther and farther west. He began to save a little money to buy his liberty. When he was thirty-five, there was a great meeting in New York of Bohemian athletic societies, and Rosicky left the tailor shop and went home with the Omaha delegates to try his fortune in another part of the world.

IV

Perhaps the fact that his own youth was well over before he began to have a family was one reason why Rosicky was so fond of his boys. He had almost a grandfather's indulgence for them. He had never had to worry about any of them—except, just now, a little about Rudolph.

On Saturday night the boys always piled into the Ford, took little Josephine, and went to town to the moving-picture show. One Saturday morning they were talking at the breakfast table about starting early that evening, so that they would have an hour or so to see the Christmas things in the stores before the show began. Rosicky looked down the table.

'I hope you boys ain't disappointed, but I want you to let me have de car tonight. Maybe some of you can go in with de neighbours.'

Their faces fell. They worked hard all week, and they were still like children. A new jack-knife or a box of candy pleased the older ones as much as the little fellow.

'If you and Mother are going to town,' Frank said, 'maybe you could take a couple of us along with you, anyway.'

'No, I want to take de car down to Rudolph's, and let him an' Polly go in to de show. She don't git into town enough, an' I'm afraid she's gettin' lonesome, an' he can't afford no car yet.'

That settled it. The boys were a good deal dashed. Their father took another piece of apple-cake and went on: 'Maybe next Saturday night de two little fellers can go along wid dem.'

'Oh, is Rudolph going to have the car every Saturday night?'

Rosicky did not reply at once; then he began to speak seriously: 'Listen, boys; Polly ain't lookin' so good. I don't like to see nobody lookin' sad. It comes hard fur a town girl to be a farmer's wife. I don't want no trouble to start in Rudolph's family. When it starts, it ain't so easy to stop. An American girl don't git used to our ways all at once. I like to tell Polly she and Rudolph can have the car every Saturday night till after New Year's, if it's all right with you boys.'

'Sure it's all right, Papa,' Mary cut in. 'And it's good you thought about that. Town girls is used to more than country girls. I lay awake nights, scared she'll make Rudolph discontented with the farm.'

The boys put as good a face on it as they could. They surely looked forward to their Saturday nights in town. That evening

Rosicky drove the car the half-mile down to Rudolph's new, bare little house.

Polly was in a short-sleeved gingham dress, clearing away the supper dishes. She was a trim, slim little thing, with blue eyes and shingled yellow hair, and her eyebrows were reduced to a mere brush-stroke, like Miss Pearl's.

'Good evening, Mr. Rosicky. Rudolph's at the barn, I guess.' She never called him father, or Mary mother. She was sensitive about having married a foreigner. She never in the world would have done it if Rudolph hadn't been such a handsome, persuasive fellow and such a gallant lover. He had graduated in her class in the high school in town, and their friendship began in the ninth grade.

Rosicky went in, though he wasn't exactly asked. 'My boys ain't goin' to town tonight, an' I brought de car over fur you two to go in to de picture show.'

Polly, carrying dishes to the sink, looked over her shoulder at him. 'Thank you. But I'm late with my work tonight, and pretty tired. Maybe Rudolph would like to go in with you.'

'Oh, I don't go to de shows! I'm too old-fashioned. You won't feel so tired after you ride in de air a ways. It's a nice clear night, an' it ain't cold. You go an' fix yourself up, Polly, an' I'll wash de dishes an' leave everything nice fur you.'

Polly blushed and tossed her bob. 'I couldn't let you do that, Mr. Rosicky. I wouldn't think of it.'

Rosicky said nothing. He found a bib apron on a nail behind the kitchen door. He slipped it over his head and then took Polly by her two elbows and pushed her gently toward the door of her own room. 'I washed up de kitchen many times for my wife, when de babies was sick or somethin'. You go an' make yourself look nice. I like you to look prettier'n any of dem town girls when you go in. De young folks must have some fun, an' I'm goin' to look out fur you, Polly.'

That kind, reassuring grip on her elbows, the old man's funny bright eyes, made Polly want to drop her head on his shoulder for a second. She restrained herself, but she lingered in his grasp at the door of her room, murmuring tearfully: 'You always lived in the city when you were young, didn't you? Don't you ever get lonesome out here?'

As she turned round to him her hand fell naturally into his, and he stood holding it and smiling into her face with his peculiar, knowing, indulgent smile without a shadow of reproach in it. 'Dem big cities is all right fur de rich, but dey is terrible hard fur de poor.'

'I don't know. Sometimes I think I'd like to take a chance. You lived in New York, didn't you?'

'An' London. Da's bigger still. I learned my trade dere. Here's Rudolph comin', you better hurry.'

'Will you tell me about London some time?'

'Maybe. Only I ain't no talker, Polly. Run an' dress yourself up.'

The bedroom door closed behind her, and Rudolph came in from the outside, looking anxious. He had seen the car and was sorry any of his family had come just then. Supper hadn't been a very pleasant occasion. Halting in the doorway, he saw his father in a kitchen apron, carrying dishes to the sink. He flushed crimson and something flashed in his eye. Rosicky held up a warning finger.

'I brought de car over fur you an' Polly to go to de picture show, an' I made her let me finish here so you won't be late. You go put on a clean shirt, quick!'

'But don't the boys want the car, Father?'

'Not tonight dey don't.' Rosicky fumbled under his apron and found his pants pocket. He took out a silver dollar and said in a hurried whisper: 'You go an' buy dat girl some ice cream an' candy tonight, like you was courtin'. She's awful good friends wid me.'

Rudolph was very short of cash, but he took the money as if it hurt him. There had been a crop failure all over the country. He had more than once been sorry he'd married this year.

In a few minutes the young people came out, looking clean and a little stiff. Rosicky hurried them off, and then he took his own time with the dishes. He scoured the pots and pans and put away the milk and swept the kitchen. He put some coal in the stove and shut off the draughts, so the place would be warm for them when they got home late at night. Then he sat down and had a pipe and listened to the clock tick.

Generally speaking, marrying an American girl was certainly a risk. A Czech should marry a Czech. It was lucky that Polly was the daughter of a poor widow woman; Rudolph was proud, and if she had a prosperous family to throw up at him, they could never make it go. Polly was one of four sisters, and they all worked; one was book-keeper in the bank, one taught music, and Polly and her younger sister had been clerks, like Miss Pearl. All four of them were musical, had pretty voices, and sang in the Methodist choir, which the eldest sister directed.

Polly missed the sociability of a store position. She missed the choir, and the company of her sisters. She didn't dislike house-work, but she disliked so much of it. Rosicky was a little anxious about this pair. He was afraid Polly would grow so discontented that Rudy would quit the farm and take a factory job in Omaha. He had worked for a winter up there, two years ago, to get money to marry on. He had done very well, and they would always take him back at the stockyards. But to Rosicky that meant the end of everything for his son. To be a landless man was to be a wage-earner, a slave, all your life; to have nothing, to be nothing.

Rosicky thought he would come over and do a little carpenter-ing for Polly after the New Year. He guessed she needed jolly-ing. Rudolph was a serious sort of chap, serious in love and serious about his work.

Rosicky shook out his pipe and walked home across the fields. Ahead of him the lamplight shone from his kitchen windows. Suppose he were still in a tailor shop on Vesey Street, with a bunch of pale, narrow-chested sons working on machines, all coming home tired and sullen to eat supper in a kitchen that was a parlour also; with another crowded, angry family quarrel-ling just across the dumb-waiter shaft, and squeaking pulleys at the windows where dirty washings hung on dirty lines above a court full of old brooms and mops and ash-cans . . .

He stopped by the windmill to look up at the frosty winter stars and draw a long breath before he went inside. That kitchen

with the shining windows was dear to him; but the sleeping
fields and bright stars and the noble darkness were dearer still.

v

On the day before Christmas the weather set in very cold; no
snow, but a bitter, biting wind that whistled and sang over the
flat land and lashed one's face like fine wires. There was baking
going on in the Rosicky kitchen all day, and Rosicky sat inside,
making over a coat that Albert had outgrown into an overcoat
for John. Mary had a big red geranium in bloom for Christmas,
and a row of Jerusalem cherry trees, full of berries. It was the
first year she had ever grown these; Doctor Ed brought her the
seeds from Omaha when he went to some medical convention.
They reminded Rosicky of plants he had seen in England; and
all afternoon, as he stitched, he sat thinking about those two
years in London, which his mind usually shrank from even
after all this while.

He was a lad of eighteen when he dropped down into London,
with no money and no connexions except the address of a cousin
who was supposed to be working at a confectioner's. When he
went to the pastry shop, however, he found that the cousin had
gone to America. Anton tramped the streets for several days,
sleeping in doorways and on the Embankment, until he was in
utter despair. He knew no English, and the sound of the strange
language all about him confused him. By chance he met a poor
German tailor who had learned his trade in Vienna, and could
speak a little Czech. This tailor, Lifschnitz, kept a repair shop
in a Cheapside basement, underneath a cobbler. He didn't much
need an apprentice, but he was sorry for the boy and took him
in for no wages but his keep and what he could pick up. The
pickings were supposed to be coppers given you when you took
work home to a customer. But most of the customers called for
their clothes themselves, and the coppers that came Anton's way
were very few. He had, however, a place to sleep. The tailor's
family lived upstairs in three rooms; a kitchen, a bedroom, where
Lifschnitz and his wife and five children slept, and a living-room.
Two corners of this living-room were curtained off for lodgers;
in one Rosicky slept on an old horsehair sofa, with a feather

quilt to wrap himself in. The other corner was rented to a wretched, dirty boy, who was studying the violin. He actually practised there. Rosicky was dirty, too. There was no way to be anything else. Mrs. Lifschnitz got the water she cooked and washed with from a pump in a brick court, four flights down. There were bugs in the place, and multitudes of fleas, though the poor woman did the best she could. Rosicky knew she often went empty to give another potato or a spoonful of dripping to the two hungry, sad-eyed boys who lodged with her. He used to think he would never get out of there, never get a clean shirt to his back again. What would he do, he wondered, when his clothes actually dropped to pieces and the worn cloth wouldn't hold patches any longer?

It was still early when the old farmer put aside his sewing and his recollections. The sky had been a dark grey all day, with not a gleam of sun, and the light failed at four o'clock. He went to shave and change his shirt while the turkey was roasting. Rudolph and Polly were coming over for supper.

After supper they sat round in the kitchen, and the younger boys were saying how sorry they were it hadn't snowed. Everybody was sorry. They wanted a deep snow that would lie long and keep the wheat warm, and leave the ground soaked when it melted.

'Yes, sir!' Rudolph broke out fiercely; 'if we have another dry year like last year, there's going to be hard times in this country.'

Rosicky filled his pipe. 'You boys don't know what hard times is. You don't owe nobody, you got plenty to eat an' keep warm, an' plenty water to keep clean. When you got them, you can't have it very hard.'

Rudolph frowned, opened and shut his big right hand, and dropped it clenched upon his knee. 'I've got to have a good deal more than that, Father, or I'll quit this farming gamble. I can always make good wages railroading, or at the packing house, and be sure of my money.'

'Maybe so,' his father answered dryly.

Mary, who had just come in from the pantry was wiping her

hands on the roller towel, thought Rudy and his father were getting too serious. She brought her darning-basket and sat down in the middle of the group.

'I ain't much afraid of hard times, Rudy,' she said heartily. 'We've had a plenty, but we've always come through. Your father wouldn't never take nothing very hard, not even hard times. I got a mind to tell you a story on him. Maybe you boys can't hardly remember the year we had that terrible hot wind, that burned everything up on the Fourth of July? All the corn an' the gardens. An' that was in the days when we didn't have alfalfa yet,—I guess it wasn't invented.

'Well, that very day your father was out cultivatin' corn, and I was here in the kitchen makin' plum preserves. We had bushels of plums that year. I noticed it was terrible hot, but it's always hot in the kitchen when you're preservin', an' I was too busy with my plums to mind. Anton came in from the field about three o'clock, an' I asked him what was the matter.

' "Nothin'," he says, "but it's pretty hot, an' I think I won't work no more today." He stood round for a few minutes, an' then he says: "Ain't you near through? I want you should git up a nice supper for us tonight. It's Fourth of July."

'I told him to git along, that I was right in the middle of preservin', but the plums would taste good on hot biscuit. "I'm goin' to have fried chicken, too," he says, and he went off an' killed a couple. You three oldest boys was little fellers, playin' round outside, real hot an' sweaty, an' your father took you to the horse tank down by the windmill an' took off your clothes an' put you in. Them two box-elder trees was little then, but they made shade over the tank. Then he took off all his own clothes, an' got in with you. While he was playin' in the water with you, the Methodist preacher drove into our place to say how all the neighbours was goin' to meet at the schoolhouse that night, to pray for rain. He drove right to the windmill, of course, and there was your father and you three with no clothes on. I was in the kitchen door, an' I had to laugh, for the preacher acted like he ain't never seen a naked man before. He surely was embarrassed, an' your father couldn't git to his clothes; they was all hangin' up on the windmill to let the sweat dry out of 'em.

So he laid in the tank where he was, an' put one of you boys on top of him to cover him up a little, an' talked to the preacher.

'When you got through playin' in the water, he put clean clothes on you and a clean shirt on himself, an' by that time I'd begun to get supper. He says: "It's too hot in here to eat comfortable. Let's have a picnic in the orchard. We'll eat our supper behind the mulberry hedge, under them linden trees."

'So he carried our supper down, an' a bottle of my wild-grape wine, an' everything tasted good, I can tell you. The wind got cooler as the sun was goin' down, and it turned out pleasant, only I noticed how the leaves was curled up on the linden trees. That made me think, an' I asked your father if that hot wind all day hadn't been terrible hard on the gardens an' the corn.

' "Corn," he says, "there ain't no corn."

' "What you talkin' about?" I said. "Ain't we got forty acres?"

' "We ain't got an ear," he says, "nor nobody else ain't got none. All the corn in this country was cooked by three o'clock today, like you'd roasted it in an oven."

' "You mean you won't get no crop at all?" I asked him. I couldn't believe it, after he'd worked so hard.

' "No crop this year," he says. "That's why we're havin' a picnic. We might as well enjoy what we got."

'An' that's how your father behaved, when all the neighbours was so discouraged they couldn't look you in the face. An' we enjoyed ourselves that year, poor as we was, an' our neighbours wasn't a bit better off for bein' miserable. Some of 'em grieved till they got poor digestions and couldn't relish what they did have.'

The younger boys said they thought their father had the best of it. But Rudolph was thinking that, all the same, the neighbours had managed to get ahead more in the fifteen years since that time. There must be something wrong about his father's way of doing things. He wished he knew what was going on in the back of Polly's mind. He knew she liked his father, but he knew, too, that she was afraid of something. When his mother sent over coffee-cake or prune tarts or a loaf of fresh bread, Polly seemed to regard them with a certain suspicion. When she observed to him that his brothers had nice manners, her tone implied that it was remarkable they should have. With his mother she was stiff and on her guard. Mary's hearty frankness and gusts of good humour irritated her. Polly was afraid of being unusual or conspicuous in any way, of being 'ordinary,' as she said!

When Mary had finished her story, Rosicky laid aside his pipe.

'You boys like me to tell you about some of dem hard times I been through in London?' Warmly encouraged, he sat rubbing his forehead along the deep creases. It was bothersome to tell a long story in English (he nearly always talked to the boys in Czech), but he wanted Polly to hear this one.

'Well, you know about dat tailor shop I worked in in London? I had one Christmas dere I ain't never forgot. Times was awful bad before Christmas; de boss ain't got much work, an' have it awful hard to pay his rent. It ain't so much fun, bein' poor in a big city like London, I'll say! All de windows is full of good t'ings to eat, an' all de pushcarts in de streets is full, an' you smell 'em all de time, an' you ain't got no money,—not a damn bit. I didn't mind de cold so much, though I didn't have no overcoat, chust a short jacket I'd outgrowed so it wouldn't meet on me, an' my hands was chapped raw. But I always had a good appetite, like you all know, an' de sight of dem pork pies in de windows was awful fur me!

'Day before Christmas was terrible foggy dat year, an' dat fog gits into your bones and makes you all damp like. Mrs. Lifschnitz didn't give us nothin' but a little bread an' drippin' for supper, because she was savin' to try for to give us a good dinner on Christmas Day. After supper de boss say I can go an' enjoy myself, so I went into de streets to listen to de Christmas singers. Dey sing old songs an' make very nice music, an' I run round after dem a good ways, till I got awful hungry. I t'ink maybe if I go home, I can sleep till morning an' forget my belly.

'I went into my corner real quiet, and roll up in my fedder quilt. But I ain't got my head down, till I smell somet'ing good. Seem like it git stronger an' stronger, an' I can't git to sleep noway. I can't understand dat smell. Dere was a gas light in a hall across de court, dat always shine in at my window a little. I got up an' look round. I got a little wooden box in my corner fur a stool, 'cause I ain't got no chair. I picks up dat box, and under it dere is a roast goose on a platter! I can't believe my eyes. I carry it to de window where de light comes in, an' touch it and smell it to find out, an' den I taste it to be sure. I say, I will eat chust one little bite of dat goose, so I can go to sleep, and to-morrow I won't eat none at all. But I tell you, boys, when I stop, one half of dat goose was gone!'

The narrator bowed his head, and the boys shouted. But little Josephine slipped behind his chair and kissed him on the neck beneath his ear.

'Poor little Papa, I don't want him to be hungry!'

'Da's long ago, child. I ain't never been hungry since I had your mudder to cook fur me.'

'Go on and tell us the rest, please,' said Polly.

'Well, when I come to realize what I done, of course, I felt terrible. I felt better in de stomach, but very bad in de heart. I set on my bed wid dat platter on my knees, an' it all come to me; how hard dat poor woman save to buy dat goose, and how she get some neighbour to cook it dat got more fire, an' how she put it in my corner to keep it away from dem hungry children. Dey was a old carpet hung up to shut my corner off, an' de children wasn't allowed to go in dere. An' I know she put it in my corner because she trust me more'n she did de violin boy. I can't stand it to face her after I spoil de Christmas. So I put on my shoes and go out into de city. I tell myself I better throw myself in de river; but I guess I ain't dat kind of a boy.

'It was after twelve o'clock, an' terrible cold, an' I start out to walk about London all night. I walk along de river awhile, but dey was lots of drunks all along; men, and women too. I chust move along to keep away from de police. I git onto de Strand, an' den over to New Oxford Street, where dere was a big German restaurant on de ground floor, wid big windows all fixed up fine, an' I could see de people havin' parties inside. While I was lookin' in, two men and two ladies come out, laughin' and talkin' and feelin' happy about all dey been eatin' an' drinkin', and dey was speakin' Czech,—not like de Austrians, but like de home folks talk it.

'I guess I went crazy, an' I done what I ain't never done be-

fore nor since. I went right up to dem gay people an' begun
to beg dem: "Fellow-countrymen, for God's sake give me money
enough to buy a goose!"

'Dey laugh, of course, but de ladies speak awful kind to me,
an' dey take me back into de restaurant and give me hot coffee
and cakes, an' make me tell all about how I happened to come
to London, an' what I was doin' dere. Dey take my name and
where I work down on paper, an' both of dem ladies give me ten
shillings.

'De big market at Covent Garden ain't very far away, an' by
dat time it was open. I go dere an' buy a big goose an' some
pork pies, an' potatoes and onions, an' cakes an' oranges fur de
children,—all I could carry! When I git home, everybody is still
asleep. I pile all I bought on de kitchen table, an' go in an' lay
down on my bed, an' I ain't waken up till I hear dat woman
scream when she comes out into her kitchen. My goodness, but
she was surprise! She laugh an' cry at de same time, an' hug me
and waken all de children. She ain't stop fur no breakfast; she
git de Christmas dinner ready dat morning, and we all sit down
an' eat all we can hold. I ain't never seen dat violin boy have
all he can hold before.

'Two three days after that, de two men come to hunt me up,
an' dey ask my boss, and he give me a good report an' tell dem
I was a steady boy all right. One of dem Bohemians was very
smart an' run a Bohemian newspaper in New York, an' de
odder was a rich man, in de importing business, an' dey been
travelling togedder. Dey told me how t'ings was easier in New
York, an' offered to pay my passage when dey was goin' home
soon on a boat. My boss say to me: "You go. You ain't got no
chance here, an' I like to see you git ahead, fur you always been
a good boy to my woman, and fur dat fine Christmas dinner
you give us all." An' da's how I got to New York.'

That night when Rudolph and Polly, arm in arm, were running home across the fields with the bitter wind at their backs,
his heart leaped for joy when she said she thought they might
have his family come over for supper on New Year's Eve. 'Let's
get up a nice supper, and not let your mother help at all; make
her be company for once.'

'That would be lovely of you, Polly,' he said humbly. He was a very simple, modest boy, and he, too, felt vaguely that Polly and her sisters were more experienced and worldly than his people.

VI

The winter turned out badly for farmers. It was bitterly cold, and after the first light snows before Christmas there was no snow at all,—and no rain. March was as bitter as February. On those days when the wind fairly punished the country, Rosicky sat by his window. In the fall he and the boys had put in a big wheat planting, and now the seed had frozen in the ground. All that land would have to be ploughed up and planted over again, planted in corn. It had happened before, but he was younger then, and he never worried about what had to be. He was sure of himself and of Mary; he knew they could bear what they had to bear, that they would always pull through somehow. But he was not so sure about the young ones, and he felt troubled because Rudolph and Polly were having such a hard start.

Sitting beside his flowering window while the panes rattled and the wind blew in under the door, Rosicky gave himself to reflection as he had not done since those Sundays in the loft of the furniture-factory in New York, long ago. Then he was trying to find what he wanted in life for himself; now he was trying to find what he wanted for his boys, and why it was he so hungered to feel sure they would be here, working this very land, after he was gone.

They would have to work hard on the farm, and probably they would never do much more than make a living. But if he could think of them as staying here on the land, he wouldn't have to fear any great unkindness for them. Hardships, certainly; it was a hardship to have the wheat freeze in the ground when seed was so high; and to have to sell your stock because you had no feed. But there would be other years when everything came along right, and you caught up. And what you had was your own. You didn't have to choose between bosses and strikers, and go wrong either way. You didn't have to do with dishonest and cruel people. They were the only things in his experience he had found terrifying and horrible; the look in the eyes of a dishonest and crafty man, of a scheming and rapacious woman.

In the country, if you had a mean neighbour, you could keep off his land and make him keep off yours. But in the city, all the foulness and misery and brutality of your neighbours was part of your life. The worst things he had come upon in his journey through the world were human,—depraved and poisonous specimens of man. To this day he could recall certain terrible faces in the London streets. There were mean people everywhere, to be sure, even in their own country town here. But they weren't tempered, hardened, sharpened, like the treacherous people in cities who live by grinding or cheating or poisoning their fellowmen. He had helped to bury two of his fellow-workmen in the tailoring trade, and he was distrustful of the organized industries that see one out of the world in big cities. Here, if you were sick, you had Doctor Ed to look after you; and if you died, fat Mr. Haycock, the kindest man in the world, buried you.

It seemed to Rosicky that for good, honest boys like his, the worst they could do on the farm was better than the best they would be likely to do in the city. If he'd had a mean boy, now, one who was crooked and sharp and tried to put anything over on his brothers, then town would be the place for him. But he had no such boy. As for Rudolph, the discontented one, he would give the shirt off his back to anyone who touched his heart. What Rosicky really hoped for his boys was that they could get through the world without ever knowing much about the cruelty of human beings. 'Their mother and me ain't prepared them for that,' he sometimes said to himself.

These thoughts brought him back to a grateful consideration of his own case. What an escape he had had, to be sure! He, too, in his time, had had to take money for repair work from the hand of a hungry child who let it go so wistfully; because it was money due his boss. And now, in all these years, he had never had to take a cent from anyone in bitter need,—never had to look at the face of a woman become like a wolf's from struggle and famine. When he thought of these things, Rosicky would put on his cap and jacket and slip down to the barn and give his work-horses a little extra oats, letting them eat it out of his hand in their slobbery fashion. It was his way of expressing what he felt, and made him chuckle with pleasure.

The spring came warm, with blue skies,—but dry, dry as a bone. The boys began ploughing up the wheat-fields to plant them over in corn. Rosicky would stand at the fence corner and watch them, and the earth was so dry it blew up in clouds of brown dust that hid the horses and the sulky plough and the driver. It was a bad outlook.

The big alfalfa-field that lay between the home place and Rudolph's came up green, but Rosicky was worried because during that open windy winter a great many Russian thistle plants had blown in there and lodged. He kept asking the boys to rake them out; he was afraid their seed would root and 'take the alfalfa.' Rudolph said that was nonsense. The boys were working so hard planting corn, their father felt he couldn't insist about the thistles, but he set great store by that big alfalfa field. It was a feed you could depend on,—and there was some deeper reason, vague, but strong. The peculiar green of that clover woke early memories in old Rosicky, went back to something in his childhood in the old world. When he was a little boy, he had played in fields of that strong blue-green colour.

One morning, when Rudolph had gone to town in the car, leaving a work-team idle in his barn, Rosicky went over to his son's place, put the horses to the buggy-rake, and set about quietly raking up those thistles. He behaved with guilty caution, and rather enjoyed stealing a march on Doctor Ed, who was just then taking his first vacation in seven years of practice and was attending a clinic in Chicago. Rosicky got the thistles raked up, but did not stop to burn them. That would take some time, and his breath was pretty short, so he thought he had better get the horses back to the barn.

He got them into the barn and to their stalls, but the pain had come on so sharp in his chest that he didn't try to take the harness off. He started for the house, bending lower with every step. The cramp in his chest was shutting him up like a jack-knife. When he reached the windmill, he swayed and caught at the ladder. He saw Polly coming down the hill, running with

the swiftness of a slim greyhound. In a flash she had her shoulder
under his armpit.

'Lean on me, Father, hard! Don't be afraid. We can get to the
house all right.'

Somehow they did, though Rosicky became blind with pain;
he could keep on his legs, but he couldn't steer his course. The
next thing he was conscious of was lying on Polly's bed, and
Polly bending over him wringing out bath towels in hot water
and putting them on his chest. She stopped only to throw coal
into the stove, and she kept the tea-kettle and the black pot
going. She put these hot applications on him for nearly an hour,
she told him afterwards, and all that time he was drawn up stiff
and blue, with the sweat pouring off him.

As the pain gradually loosed its grip, the stiffness went out of
his jaws, the black circles round his eyes disappeared, and a little
of his natural colour came back. When his daughter-in-law buttoned his shirt over his chest at last, he sighed.

'Da's fine, de way I feel now, Polly. It was a awful spell, an'
I was so sorry it all come on you like it did.'

Polly was flushed and excited. 'Is the pain really gone? Can I
leave you long enough to telephone over to your place?'

Rosicky's eyelids fluttered. 'Don't telephone, Polly. It ain't no
use to scare my wife. It's nice and quiet here, an' if I ain't too
much trouble to you, just let me lay still till I feel like myself.
I ain't got no pain now. It's nice here.'

Polly bent over him and wiped the moisture from his face.
'Oh, I'm so glad it's over!' she broke out impulsively. 'It just
broke my heart to see you suffer so, Father.'

Rosicky motioned her to sit down on the chair where the tea-
kettle had been, and looked up at her with that lively affectionate
gleam in his eyes. 'You was awful good to me, I won't never fer-
git dat. I hate it to be sick on you like dis. Down at de barn I
say to myself, dat young girl ain't had much experience in sick-
ness. I don't want to scare her, an' maybe she's got a baby comin'
or somet'ing.'

Polly took his hand. He was looking at her so intently and
affectionately and confidingly; his eyes seemed to caress her face,

to regard it with pleasure. She frowned with her funny streaks of eyebrows, and then smiled back at him.

'I guess maybe there is something of that kind going to happen. But I haven't told anyone yet, not my mother or Rudolph. You'll be the first to know.'

His hand pressed hers. She noticed that it was warm again. The twinkle in his yellow-brown eyes seemed to come nearer.

'I like mighty well to see dat little child, Polly,' was all he said. Then he closed his eyes and lay half-smiling. But Polly sat still, thinking hard. She had a sudden feeling that nobody in the world, not her mother, not Rudolph, or anyone, really loved her as much as old Rosicky did. It perplexed her. She sat frowning and trying to puzzle it out. It was as if Rosicky had a special gift for loving people, something that was like an ear for music or an eye for colour. It was quiet, unobtrusive; it was merely there. You saw it in his eyes,—perhaps that was why they were merry. You felt it in his hands, too. After he dropped off to sleep, she sat holding his warm, broad, flexible brown hand. She had never seen another in the least like it. She wondered if it wasn't a kind of gypsy hand, it was so alive and quick and light in its communications,—very strange in a farmer. Nearly all the farmers she knew had huge lumps of fists, like mauls, or they were knotty and bony and uncomfortable-looking, with stiff fingers. But Rosicky's was like quick-silver, flexible, muscular, about the colour of a pale cigar, with deep, deep creases across the palm. It wasn't nervous, it wasn't a stupid lump; it was a warm brown human hand, with some cleverness in it, a great deal of generosity, and something else which Polly could only call 'gypsy-like,'—something nimble and lively and sure, in the way that animals are.

Polly remembered that hour long afterwards; it had been like an awakening to her. It seemed to her that she had never learned so much about life from anything as from old Rosicky's hand. It brought her to herself; it communicated some direct and untranslatable message.

When she heard Rudolph coming in the car, she ran out to meet him.

'Oh, Rudy, your father's been awful sick! He raked up those

thistles he's been worrying about, and afterwards he could hardly get to the house. He suffered so I was afraid he was going to die.'

Rudolph jumped to the ground. 'Where is he now?'

'On the bed. He's asleep. I was terribly scared, because, you know, I'm so fond of your father.' She slipped her arm through his and they went into the house. That afternoon they took Rosicky home and put him to bed, though he protested that he was quite well again.

The next morning he got up and dressed and sat down to breakfast with his family. He told Mary that his coffee tasted better than usual to him, and he warned the boys not to bear any tales to Doctor Ed when he got home. After breakfast he sat down by his window to do some patching and asked Mary to thread several needles for him before she went to feed her chickens,—her eyes were better than his, and her hands steadier. He lit his pipe and took up John's overalls. Mary had been watching him anxiously all morning, and as she went out of the door with her bucket of scraps, she saw that he was smiling. He was thinking, indeed, about Polly, and how he might never have known what a tender heart she had if he hadn't got sick over there. Girls nowadays didn't wear their heart on their sleeve. But now he knew Polly would make a fine woman after the foolishness wore off. Either a woman had that sweetness at her heart or she hadn't. You couldn't always tell by the look of them; but if they had that, everything came out right in the end.

After he had taken a few stitches, the cramp began in his chest, like yesterday. He put his pipe cautiously down on the window-sill and bent over to ease the pull. No use,—he had better try to get to his bed if he could. He rose and groped his way across the familiar floor, which was rising and falling like the deck of a ship. At the door he fell. When Mary came in, she found him lying there, and the moment she touched him she knew that he was gone.

Doctor Ed was away when Rosicky died, and for the first few weeks after he got home he was hard driven. Every day he said to himself that he must get out to see that family that had lost their father. One soft, warm moonlight night in early summer he started for the farm. His mind was on other things, and not until his road ran by the graveyard did he realize that Rosicky wasn't over there on the hill where the red lamplight shone, but here, in the moonlight. He stopped his car, shut off the engine, and sat there for a while.

A sudden hush had fallen on his soul. Everything here seemed strangely moving and significant, though signifying what, he did not know. Close by the wire fence stood Rosicky's mowing-machine, where one of the boys had been cutting hay that afternoon; his own work-horses had been going up and down there. The new-cut hay perfumed all the night air. The moonlight silvered the long, billowy grass that grew over the graves and hid the fence; the few little evergreens stood out black in it, like shadows in a pool. The sky was very blue and soft, the stars rather faint because the moon was full.

For the first time it struck Doctor Ed that this was really a beautiful graveyard. He thought of city cemeteries; acres of shrubbery and heavy stone, so arranged and lonely and unlike anything in the living world. Cities of the dead, indeed; cities of the forgotten, of the 'put away.' But this was open and free, this little square of long grass which the wind for ever stirred. Nothing but the sky overhead, and the many-coloured fields running on until they met that sky. The horses worked here in summer; the neighbours passed on their way to town; and over yonder, in the cornfield, Rosicky's own cattle would be eating fodder as winter came on. Nothing could be more undeathlike than this place; nothing could be more right for a man who had helped to do the work of great cities and had always longed for the open country and had got to it at last. Rosicky's life seemed to him complete and beautiful.

New York, 1928

HOUSE OF THE ONE FATHER

By Mary Antin

THE Catholic priest was taking his leave when two representatives of the nearest Jewish community appeared upon the scene. All on the same errand: soliciting funds for their respective religious enterprises. The priest was building a suburban chapel, and the Jewish gentlemen were starting a Hebrew school. As I saw my civic duty, I owed support to both. When the priest departed, taking my check and leaving me his blessing, my Jewish neighbors called me to task for my unorthodox charity.

It was known, of course, that I was married to a Gentile—a Protestant. Still it was assumed there were limits to my apostasy. How came the Catholic priest to apply to me at all?

The answer was Margaret Nolan. At the deathbed request of a friend, a social worker in New York, my husband and I had taken over her best-loved protégé, a Catholic girl of twelve, who had seen too much of the gutter and too little of the schoolroom. Arrangements had to be made to take up the slack in her education, especially the religious branch. After some thoughtful discussion, my husband and I agreed that as proxies for Margaret's natural guardians we owed her the kind of training they would approve.

In the neighboring town of White Plains I found a Catholic center where the Sisters gladly undertook Margaret's religious training. Nobody questioned my informal guardianship of a Catholic child. The soft-voiced Sister only said she wouldn't have expected a Jewish woman to go out of her way to arrange for a Catholic child's religious instruction.

I was too much taken aback to enlighten the Sisterhood. I

From *Common Ground*, Spring 1941. By permission of the author and publisher.

failed to make the point that I was acting from the best Jewish
tradition. My slowness of tongue, however, did not hinder
Margaret's progress. She went faithfully for instruction until she
was ready for confirmation; and it was this episode that had left
my name on the books of the local Catholic community, with the
result that I was included in a canvass for funds for their chapel.

'Quite natural, you see,' I commented at the end of my recital.
The two men consulted by raising eyebrows. What was the
proper mode of rebuking an erring Jewish woman whose husband, though a Gentile, was a great scholar and thereby entitled
to supreme respect? Mr. Rosen cleared his throat and frown-
ingly said nothing. Mr. Garfinkle cleared his throat and assumed
the authority of the faithful in Israel before the unfaithful.

'Excuse me, Mrs. Grabau, I'll ask you a question. About the
girl, it's all right. You did right.'

'Thank you.'

'Sure. A bad home—the mother a drunk—kept her out of
school. Here you have a nice home, a—a beautiful home.'

His gesture doubled our acreage and enlarged our simple
frame house to a mansion. 'It's a *mitzvah*'—a deed of merit—'to
take the orphan into your home. She's as good as an orphan, this
Irish girl.'

'She was, yes. She's decently settled now.'

'So that's all right. So what I ask is—excuse me, Mrs. Grabau—
why do you have to be mixed up with Catholic priests now?'

'That's right,' cut in Mr. Rosen, belligerently. 'Why?'

Mr. Garfinkle frowned at the other's lack of finesse. I played
up to Mr. Garfinkle's pretense of philosophical detachment.

'The priest,' I said, 'as far as I am concerned, represents community responsibility, just as you gentlemen do.'

Mr. Rosen bristled. Mr. Garfinkle set his mouth in a line of
endurance. I firmly expounded my thesis. The beautiful homes
they so admired in our village of Scarsdale were kept up, I told
them, with the help of many hired hands—cooks and chamber-
maids and gardeners, recent immigrants, Polish and Italian,
Catholics. The Catholic contingent was swelled by construction
gangs on long-time local projects. All these workers, on whom

depended the smooth functioning of our lives, constituted a social island in the sea of American life, only scantily watered by the stream of American culture.

Scarsdale was too far from a high school—it was the pre-Fordian era—too far from the nearest Catholic church. Even if these Catholic newcomers had had any other gathering place, their lives were spiritually barren in the absence of an accessible church of their own denomination. It was a good thing they were building a chapel.

'But do you want to see the Catholic Church spread?'

'I don't want to see a group of potential American citizens left without spiritual sustenance.'

'What's that got to do with citizens? Do they make American citizens in the Catholic Church?'

'They teach them that all men have one Father, and that's the beginning of Americanism—of democracy.'

Both my visitors looked astounded. I was happy. This was my opportunity to parade a recent discovery. I tried to express myself modestly, but I was too elated.

'What is democracy,' I declaimed, 'except the ancient Hebrew idea of the Fatherhood of God, from which follows the Brotherhood of Man, here in America incorporated in a political and social system which works the principle down into daily life?'

'I don't see why that's American,' began Mr. Rosen, heavily.

Mr. Garfinkle interrupted. 'Yes, it is. She's right.'

'Well, yes, American, but—but it's Jewish, ain't it?'

'He's right, too,' confirmed Mr. Garfinkle, ever hewing to the line. 'Justice is not an American patent. We didn't have to come to America to learn justice. It's the way of our fathers, the ideas and the laws and going after anyone who's hard on the widow and the orphan or mean to the stranger and won't do his part in the community.'

'Exactly!' I took my cue with enthusiasm. 'It was the model of the Hebrew Commonwealth they had in mind, the first Americans. They were great students of the Old Testament . . .'

The intoxication of newly acquired knowledge! I had recently been presented with a stack of the Old South Historical

Leaflets. I had devoured these and other source papers of American history, I had 'discovered' the Hebrew-Christian basis of American democracy, and I found it very exciting. And integrating. During my first years in the U.S., my Russian-Jewish beginnings had figured in my consciousness as a mere jumping-off place for a new life as an American. Only later did I fully realize that the two philosophical systems, the Hebrew and the American, were essentially one.

At this time I was only beginning to read the New Testament; I was not yet aware of the supreme role of Jesus of Nazareth in mediating the Hebrew tradition to the modern world. That was to come later; but already I was a queer enough fish from the orthodox Jewish standpoint. Mr. Garfinkle challenged:

'Listen, Mrs. Grabau, I see you're a philosopher, and you got some ideas. About God and democracy, maybe so. But you don't mean you *like* the Catholic Church? What about the pogroms in Russia? What about the bloody persecution in all Christian lands since they got their Church?'

Here my glibness failed me. For a moment I was very much a Jew, in the tragic restricted sense of self-identification with the century-long sufferings of the group. I was not so long healed of the psychic wounds of terror and distrust, acquired during my Ghetto childhood, that the soreness of spirit could not be revived in me by allusions to universal Jew-baiting.

The moment sickened under a flood of recollection of an incident during my first return to Europe, after seventeen years in America. I was in Prague, sightseeing at leisure, when I came upon a Greek Orthodox church. I was thankful that I was alone; there was no witness to my painful discomfiture. It was all I could do to make myself enter the building. Like bitter blasts blowing from all quarters at once, my childhood terrors in the neighborhood of a Christian church, which stood for blood and fire and spoliation, swirled over me and choked and blinded me. The process of relaxation of age-old antipathies was under way. In America I had visited churches on occasion, Protestant churches under liberal pastors. But I had not, up to this day in Prague, entered a Catholic church, with its maximum of visible symbols of the separation between Jew and Christian. Here in an Old World setting, confronted by a church edifice recalling my native Polotzk, the old terrors revived in full. I was sucked back into the Dark Ages of intolerance. I stood defenseless in the shadow of a Cross that people who called themselves Christians had perverted into a scourge.

I went in. I moved up the aisles and down. I slid slant-eyed past images with shockingly human expressions and mesmeric gestures. There was dimness thick with color, there were fluttering candle flames, there were alien smells, there was stillness like cotton in my ears. I saw and I did not see the altar. I don't know how long I stayed. It was all a grayness and a smother. I returned to the daylight exhausted.

Mr. Garfinkle had been saying, 'You don't mean you *like* the Catholic Church?'

I answered haltingly through the confusion of my moment's immersion in the past. 'I once visited a Catholic church and I was—uncomfortable. I think if I should go again—with an open mind—with an intelligent guide, like some one of my Catholic friends—'

The discussion went on over some bumpy ground. Religion, after all, is a delicate subject, and here was I, in the name of Americanism, proposing untried expressions of goodwill which my opponents—simple men loyal to their traditions—found fantastic, not to say unholy. Exactly as two orthodox Christians would have felt in a corresponding situation.

Yes, of course, agreed my Jewish inquisitors, we mustn't bear a grudge against the mass of good Christian people because members of their churches in different times and places had persecuted our people. 'But that's not the point,' insisted Mr. Garfinkle. 'The point is: doesn't it make any difference to you about the Jewish religion?'

'But I'm subscribing to your *Talmud Torah*.'

'And that's the same to you as helping the Catholic priest?'

I had to admit it was not the same—that there was, in fact, a world of difference in my feelings for the two churches: the one a strange country with painful associations, the other, *home,*

even though I had partly grown away from it. But I managed
to save the argument by wide generalizations, with a mental
note to post myself about Catholic teachings in detail.

'But anyway,' I swung back, after much philosophical banter,
'their Church is the place where *their* people are reminded of
God and brotherhood, and that's at the bottom of Americanism.'

If my triumphal return to my starting point did not convince
my opponents, it did strengthen my own conviction. I was to
learn, with the softening of years, to deal more gently with
orthodox sentiment, whether Jewish or Christian; but in mend-
ing my manners I surrendered nothing of the principle of co-
operation. Today institutions like the inter-faith Round Table
are spreading over the country. But I had to wait a quarter century for my doctrine to catch on.

When a word becomes flesh—when a formula turns into living
drama, then is life exciting. An hour of that pure excitement
awaited me in a country town of Vermont where I arrived one
afternoon in spring, in the course of a lecture tour, a year or
two after the Scarsdale incident. As I always spoke *ex tempore*
from the barest captions, I was glad of several hours of seclusion
for concentration on the subject of the day. When my summons
came, I emerged padded with buffers of inattention to externals,
painfully tense and pretending the contrary.

There was a short ride in a twilight that rebuked my tense-
ness. We were going, I thought, to the High School—or was it
the Town Hall? The place of meeting was given on my instruction sheet for the day, from my booking agent's office, but
I had forgotten.

The car stopped at the side door of a church. That was new—
a secular meeting in a church. Always surprises in this lecture
business.

The preliminaries behind the scenes went off briskly. I was
ushered to the speaker's place with my chrysalis of absorption
almost intact.

As usual, I endured the introductory patter through the nervous tortures of stage fright. Then, in response to my name

spoken somewhere between me and the audience, I was on my feet.

What was this? Where was it I was standing, looking down into crowded rows of expectant faces shimmering in the splash and crackle of applause? With a shock I realized that I was standing in the pulpit itself, the place of authority of a Christian house of worship. I, not so long ago a fugitive from the Ghetto, had been set up there, above them all for that hour, to speak freely from my heart.

Stage fright burned off in a flame of exaltation. The audience saw and hushed. Out of the hush, a miracle! Open your eyes, America, and see a miracle! I stand before you *healed*, I sang, with a great and final healing that spreads to a whole people. Centuries of Jewish history are atoned for in this moment you have created. The dark abyss of separation between Jew and Gentile is closed by my presence in this pulpit.

Those first few minutes passed over us like the wind of Pentecost. It was not I speaking, but ancient prophecies in which we had all been nurtured, these New Englanders rooted in the American soil and I their guest from another world. Old words came to me to tell new matters. Of American history as the steady pushing back of *the rulers of the darkness of this world, of spiritual wickedness in high places,* of which things I spoke as from actual witness. I was not alone in the pulpit after all: a great host surrounded me, the oppressed of all nations, who had suffered for conscience' sake. I remembered it was written:

God is no respecter of persons, but in every nation he who feareth Him and worketh righteousness is accepted with Him.

I don't know if I was aware that I was speaking words from the New Testament. There were no dividing walls left standing. The hundreds in the pews and I in the high pulpit saw one thing: how every door in America that opened to the stranger of every race and creed—the schoolhouse door, the public library door, door of the common playground, door to any job a man was equipped to fill—each was a door to the House of the One Father, where differences shrank and sometimes fell away.

The God of their fathers was gaining ground in my heart because all doors had been left open for my fathers' God as well.

Another corner was turned one winter season when I shared
a cottage on Anastasia Island, Florida, with an amiable lady
who like myself was seeking health in the southern sun. Attracted in the first place by her genial humor and unostenta-
tious courage in the face of a disorder that threatened slow
death, I soon discovered in Lydia Sayre an admirable variety of
a type of Christian that had previously repelled me. People who
lived only, in their own phrase, to 'bring souls to Christ,' aroused
in me the antipathy of the hunted for the hunter. My dislike
for the proselytizer, though originally the inherited attitude of
a member of a hunted group, had acquired the dignity of personal judgment. Both the philosophy and the methods of the
typical missionary Christian of that time were repugnant to me,
on the same grounds they have since been challenged by leading
Christians everywhere. And here was I living in a web of domestic intimacy with a burning evangelist!

It might have been very uncomfortable—but not with Lydia
Sayre. She never once transgressed the lines of good breeding. If
I was free from fixed prejudice, she was guiltless of spiritual
arrogance. I don't know what subtle arts she may have employed that escaped my notice—probably only the art of inter-
cessory prayer—just as she did not know that at first I laid myself open to her approach partly out of chivalry. A woman like
her to be kept from the work she longed to do! Was there not
something I could do to ameliorate her frustration? I could let
her show me her spiritual treasures.

She showed me treasures in plenty from her knowledge of
the Bible. I was then a casual reader of the Bible where she
was a devoted student. Presently we were reading together and
discussing our readings without constraint. Religion had ceased
to be a delicate subject; it was a field of comradely research.

If I was not converted at that time, it was not from mental
stubbornness or emotional bias. But I was enlightened. It was
the beginning of the long process of getting to feel *at home* in
the New Testament. Lydia, on her part, acquired insight into

the singular integrity represented by Jewish monotheism, into the deeper humanistic reference of Jewish ritual and ceremonial and their creative penetration into daily life. She came to see a Jew from the inside and I began to see from the inside the type of devout Christian who is impelled by conviction and temperament to missionary activity. I then and there repented my wholesale judgment of missionaries. Thereafter I met them as individuals; and I was to meet a number of them, in later life, who sharpened my sense of kinship with all earnest seekers after God.

Once again the God of my neighbors had a chance to reach me because American life followed a democratic pattern. In those days, before our wholesale importation of un-American attitudes and rules, the same guest houses, as often as not, invited Jews and Gentiles without discrimination. Today if I look for lodging in summer or winter resort in many parts of our country, I shall be faced with no occasion to reconsider my judgments on fundamentals of Christianity. In the places where I will be admitted, there will be only Jews to talk to.

At the present moment, under the shocks of the Hitlerian object-lesson on the fruits of intolerance, we are all doing a job of reviewing our attitudes and practices. I find myself grateful that social conditions in my early years in America allowed me to follow freely an inborn drive for religious exploration without a hindering concern for the people who gave me birth—who endowed me with my basic traits—on the ground that they were in trouble. For decades I lived cut off from Jewish life and thought, heart-free and mind-free to weave other bonds. There was nothing intentional or self-conscious in this divorcement. It was simply that my path in life ran far from the currents of Jewish experience. Today I find myself pulled by old forgotten ties, through the violent projection of an immensely magnified Jewish problem. It is one thing to go your separate way, leaving friends and comrades behind in peace and prosperity; it is another thing to fail to remember them when the world is casting them out. I can no more return to the Jewish fold than I can return to my mother's womb; neither can I in decency continue to enjoy my accidental personal immunity from the penalties of being a Jew in a time of virulent anti-Semitism. The least I can do, in my need to share the sufferings of my people, is declare that I am as one of them.

Here, in my own case, is a hint of the historic tragedy of the individual Jew whose nature is to lose himself in universal relationships, but who is driven back into some Ghetto without walls by the action of anti-Semitism. God helping, I shall not let myself be stampeded. I have found my wider world of the spirit, and nothing can dislodge me though my title may be mocked. I will pray for the world's restoration to sanity sometimes in a bare New England meeting house, sometimes in a serene Jewish temple, sometimes in a glowing cathedral interior where worshippers kneel intent on rosary and crucifix, as these many years I have prayed for things worthy to mention in prayer. In all those places where race lines are drawn, I shall claim the Jewish badge; but in my Father's house of many mansions I shall continue a free spirit.

Perhaps it was for a time like this that I and others like me have been unknowingly preparing, through personal exploration in religion. In every communion with which I have had contact, I have found men and women filled with the spirit of God. No fabricated walls of separation can again divide me and my Gentile neighbors, because I have appropriated the blessed St. Francis of the Catholics, the saintly John Woolman of the Quakers, the inexhaustible Ramakrishna of the Hindus; appropriated, tardily but with homing joy, the Sought of all seekers, the One Christ of many names. Humbly respectful of those who feel called to that bitter labor, I shall no more spend myself in defense of the Jew on sectarian or folk lines, except incidentally, as my knowledge of things Jewish may illumine a given situation. Not to dissociate myself from the Jewish lot, but to establish the more unassailable bond, I here declare that the point where I come to life as a member of modern society, where my fullest sense of responsibility is kindled, is deep below the ache and horror of the Jewish dilemma, at the juncture of social forces where I see the persecution or belittlement of a group—*any* group, whether of race, creed, or color—as an attack on democracy. Let me pass in the world under any label the social vision of the time may apply, here at this point I feel alive and equipped to do my part: where the spiritual foundations of America are threatened, where God is mocked in the denial to a single individual or group of 'just and true liberty, equal and impartial liberty, in matters spiritual and temporal,' as they sharply phrased it in the days of the first making of America.

RED NECKTIE

By Jo Sinclair

On Woodland Avenue Mendel saw colored people for the first time in his life. He was afraid of them. He was afraid of all people except Joe Greenberg. Joe had brought him to America. He had drawn up a paper called an affidavit and sent it to Hungary, and by some miracle, he, Mendel Hirsh, was now in America. His cousin, Joe, had done this and was therefore to be trusted.

Nor was Mendel afraid of Molly, the nag Joe had given him. Old and bony and slow, she drew Mendel's wagonful of newspapers and old tires and furniture.

'Old clothes!' Mendel cried in his broken voice, from his high seat on the wagon. 'Paper, old rags!' To the horse, in his own language, he was saying, 'Molly, Molly, what are we doing? We are old. What do we know about paper and old clothes? I had a farm once, Molly. In Huste, in Hungary. I could dig you a garden, beautiful like a dream. Did you know a meadow when you were young, Molly?'

Woodland Avenue is a fast-flowing, dirty street, filled with the city's poor. They cluster like insects on the pavements before the clothing, furniture, and food stores. They clamber on the street-cars . . . They sold Mendel great stacks of newspapers and mattresses with bedbugs crawling in them.

'Cash,' Mendel told them. 'I give cash.' Joe had taught him the small, necessary English phrases; others he had picked up himself in the streets. 'Cash,' he said to the Negro housewives. 'Ten cents for tables, ten cents for bed springs.' And he cringed, waiting for them to curse him or lift their hands to strike.

'Listen, Mendel,' Joe explained patiently, 'I tell you nobody

From *Common Ground*, Spring 1941. By permission of the publisher.

is going to hit you. Nobody wants to kill you here. You're in America. Pretty soon I'll make you a business man, then a citizen. Come on, practice your English. Here a business man has got to know how to talk English first of all. Say, "I live in Cleveland, Ohio." *Say* it!'

'I—live in—Cleve—land, O—hi—o,' Mendel repeated in his tired, cracked voice. 'But Joe, the colored ones, they are so many. They will not beat me with sticks? They are many, and I am one. I am not like them. They do not want me. They talk to me, sharp and loud, like they would be wanting to hit me.'

'Mendel,' Joe said, 'you imagine better than a movie picture. Of all people they should hit you, Mendel? I tell you they do not know you are alive. So they should hit you yet. We are poor people here, Mendel. We live with the poor. Get it into your head: we are all alike here. The colored people are even poorer than we. Why should they want to kill their own kind?'

Mendel's voice faltered. 'Sixty-two years I lived in Huste,' he said. 'Why, all of a sudden, did the poor peasants start hitting and killing me and my kind? Because we were Jews. Do I have to tell you again, Joe?'

'Look around you,' said Joe. 'There are plenty Jews here. And plenty Gentiles. By us, here, we are Americans. You can't get it into your head? Not Jews, not Gentiles, not colored people. Just people. People—in Cleveland, and Cleveland is in America. Mendel, open your head and let in the words. You are a free man here.'

Mendel sat hunched in the slow-moving wagon, the reins slack. Old he was, and afraid. What would keep an old man safe? His beard? His Talmud? This Cleveland was a city. Where were the farms? Where were the grandchildren a man gathers about him in his late years?

He rode slowly. He sang softly and sadly the words of an old lullaby, a grandchild-song. 'To sleep, my little darling,' he sang to the squalid street. 'I will give you raisins and almonds,' he sang to the Negroes, to the long, ugly, yellow streetcars, the ruined houses.

At two o'clock he stopped in front of the People's Restaurant.

It was snowing, and his horse looked up at him, the flakes melting as they touched her. 'Soon, Molly, soon,' he promised.

Inside it was steamy and warm. Mendel smelled corned beef, saw Joe at a table eating slices of rye bread and cabbage.

'Well?' Joe said. 'You made your living today?'

Mendel sat down heavily. 'Nobody has things, not even to sell.' He sighed. 'In Europe I heard my own speech. Here I find only strangers. Who wants to be old in a strange land? Who wants to die for lack of a word?'

Joe clicked his teeth. 'Mendel, forget Europe. You are in America. Alive. Why should you talk about dying? Eat a sandwich, eat a piece of herring. Be glad.'

'So I'll have a glass of tea,' said Mendel. 'But I want to ask you: why will not the same thing happen here? So many Gentiles. And then these colored ones. They run in the street. I see them in my dreams. If I was hit in Hungary, why will I not be hit here?'

Joe finished his soup. 'Mendel,' he said harshly, 'I want you should pay me back the money you cost me. I brought you to America, I bought you a horse and wagon, I started you in business in the streets. Not by crying like a baby will you make money. I want you should start working like a man.' He did not look at Mendel as he spoke. 'Mendel, you hear me? I want you should go to Woodland Market and try there. They got old wood there, and sometimes they got furniture to throw out. You're listening?'

'I hear you,' said Mendel. The tea was bitter in his mouth. Even Joe shouted at him. So. Into the streets! Who wanted an old man?

Mendel climbed up on the wagon, and Molly began her slow-gaited passage through the dirt-poor streets. He rode through the falling snow, old and hunched upon his wagon. The Market was on the outskirts of Woodland Avenue, and he pulled Molly to a stop just before the first of the stalls reared its green stuffs out of the snow. The pavements were crowded with men and women who sniffed the fruits and touched each tomato before they bought.

He climbed from the wagon, but he was afraid to enter the world of commerce. Who would listen to him? They were so full of motion, so busy buying and selling.

Then he saw the little Negro sitting on an old apple box, warming his hands at a bucket of live coals. He was a tiny old man in a huge ragged coat, and he looked at Mendel out of small, merry eyes like shining glass. Near the bucket of coals stood a rack of cheap neckties.

'Git your tie,' the little Negro called. 'Only a dime, a brand new tie,' he piped at Mendel, but he laughed so that Mendel came close and stretched his hands toward the bucketful of warmth. 'Like an elf in the woods,' Mendel said wonderingly in Yiddish.

'What?' the little man said. His voice was like laughter. Mendel began to feel a gaiety he had not known since he left the wheat fields of Huste.

'Why do you laugh?' he went on in Yiddish. 'You are an old man. Like me. What is there to laugh at?'

'Git your tie,' the little black man said in his quavering, song-like voice. He did not understand Mendel's words, but the tone was familiar. It was a fear tone, a sound of shyness or loneliness. 'Whyn't you sit down?' he urged Mendel. 'You look cold, Mister. There's plenty of coals.'

Mendel sat, sharing the empty apple box. 'That your horse?' the little Negro said. 'It's a handsome horse.'

'Her name is Molly,' Mendel said. 'She is my only friend.'

The two old men sat, their hands out to the coals. Around them swirled the people, their gestures and movements furious with activity, and over all came the snow, softly, steadily. Mendel felt a stillness. He saw the green and red and orange foods at the stalls, clear and beautiful against the snow. Now and again, the old hunched man at his side cried gaily, 'Ties? Git your ties. Only a dime, only ten cents.' Nobody stopped to look or to buy, but the laughter gurgled in his pipe-stem throat like a secret spring, and he bent over the burning coals with pleasure.

'What are you called?' asked Mendel. 'Your name?'

'Tom's my name,' the merry-eyed man said.

'I am called Mendel.'

'Mendel,' the little man repeated. 'That's a right pretty name. That's my pawnshop man's first name. He's a Jew, by the name of Newman. He's got a beard like your'n, too—Mendel Newman.'

They could scarcely understand each other's words, but in the tones they felt like brothers. 'How is business?' Mendel asked. 'Is it hard to make a living?'

'All I need's a little snuff,' Tom said, talking to the burning coals or to himself. 'A little something to eat. I like to be warm when it's cold like this. Snow's right pretty when you got coal between your feet. The Market's nice. All these Eyetalians and Greeks give me stuff to eat; ain't very rotten stuff either. Cut off the black spots, and the cabbage and greens are good as new. This is the best place in the city to sit and watch.'

'I used to grow cabbage. And wheat.' Mendel spoke half in English and half in Yiddish, but Tom nodded his head after each sentence as if he understood.

'Pretty soon it'll be spring,' the little black man said. 'Market smells good in the spring. It's warm, and people laugh better. Lots of sun here then. You'll see. Best sun in the city, all day long.'

Mendel wanted to touch Tom's shoulder, half-buried in the great dirty coat. He was older even than Mendel. Under the pointed woollen hat his hair was gray, and his eyebrows were gray. But there he sat, like a warm word. His name was Tom.

'You're not afraid?' Mendel asked.

'I sit here and look at the people. The sights are pretty,' Tom said, not listening. 'Right now, your horse is the prettiest sight in the city. It's mighty nice to sit and look . . . *Ties!*' he cried then. 'Git your tie, a dime apiece, git your tie here!'

'Nobody hits you?' Mendel asked, trying painfully to understand the little man's wandering speeches. 'You're a black man, and you're old. Like me. Nobody swears at you? Nobody raises a hand to you?'

'Ain't nobody bothers me,' Tom said. 'I don't bother nobody, and nobody bothers me. They buys a tie now and then. They walks by here, all day long, like a parade. In the summer this

Market's the prettiest old place you ever did see. Seems like it's
the greenest and the best-smellingest place in all the city.'

The crowds moved past and were like shadows to Mendel.
Looking up, he saw Molly standing patiently in the snow, and
she was the same. But he was not the same. He was different,
beginning to draw breath easily and stroke his beard for its softness and for its being part of him.

'You sit,' he said carefully to Tom, 'you make a living. Nobody hollers, nobody lifts a hand to you. If you want to smell
the celery, you smell. If you want to look at apples, you look,
and it's the same color for you like for them?' He drew a long
breath. 'So this is what Joe meant.'

They sat, warming their hands.

'Git your ties,' Tom cried, making a song out of it. 'Big sale
on ties. One dime apiece, ten cents a tie.'

'So I'll take a tie,' Mendel said suddenly. He felt an overwhelming gladness.

'Yes, sir!' said the little man calmly, not moving. 'Pick your
tie, Mister Mendel. Pick any tie you see. It's your'n for a dime.
Man needs a new tie. Man gets a feeling from a new tie.'

'You know what I want?' said Mendel. 'That red one . . . I
never had a red tie.'

He gave the little man his ten-cent piece and put the tie
around his neck. 'How is it?' he asked anxiously.

'It looks right pretty under your beard,' Tom said. 'You're
gonna feel like a new man, Mister Mendel, with that new tie
on you.'

Mendel stood up, an awkward, fresh laughter struggling
within him. 'You should only know!' he said, leaning over the
merry eyes.

They looked at each other, not quite understanding the words,
only the smiling and the brother-brother sound of the voices.
'Sure,' Tom said. 'Now you take care of your tie, Mister.'

'Good-bye,' said Mendel. 'We will think of each other sometimes.'

'Good-bye,' said the little, wizened Negro, laughing like bells
ringing in the snow. 'You be good now.'

At the wagon, Mendel patted Molly's head. 'You like my new tie? . . . It's red and new like my blood, Molly.'

They drove off into the snowfall. 'To sleep, my little darling,' Mendel sang loudly. 'I will give you raisins and almonds. I will give you raisins and bread.'

THE EDITORS OF LIFE JOIN WITH
THE EDITORS OF TIME IN PRESENT-
ING A NEW KIND OF PICTORIAL
JOURNALISM:

THE MARCH OF TIME

1. **Title:** AMERICANS ALL!
   Statue of Liberty background
   (Scene)
2. l.s. Magistrate administering oath to aliens
3. m.s. Aliens taking oath
4. c.u. Girl same
5. c.u. Magistrate

6. c.u. Man and woman same
7. c.u. Man same
8. c.u. Magistrate

9. l.s. Magistrate and aliens

10. l.s. American Consulate
11. c.u. Consulate seal
12. l.s. Foreigners registering fo passports
13. c.u. **Insert:** American Passpo
14. m.s. Foreigners registering fo passports
15. c.u. Man and woman
16. l.s. American Export liner com ing into pier
17. l.s. People down gangway
18. l.s. Another shot same
19. c.u. Same
20. c.u. **Insert:** Hotel Wien stick on baggage
21. l.s. Vienna Boulevard
22. l.s. Schoenbrunn, statue in foreground
23. l.s. Night exterior building
24. l.s. Vienna ball
25. c.u. Same
26. l.s. Same
27. **Insert:** Sticker on baggage— Alcron, Praha
28. l.s. Bridge in Prague
29. m.s. of city
30. l.s. Street
31. l.s. Statue of John Hus and tw towers
32. l.s. Crowd in street
33. **Insert:** Sticker Le Grande Hotel, Paris
34. l.s. Champs Elysees
35. l.s. Arc de Triomphe

19

Music

Narration

Magistrate: *Do you solemnly swear, on oath, that you absolutely and entirely renounce and abjure all allegiance and fidelity to any foreign prince, potentate, state or sovereignty of whom*
or to which you have heretofore been a subject or citizen;
that you will support and defend the Constitution and laws of the United States of America
against all enemies, foreign and domestic; that you will bear
true faith and allegiance to the same:
and that you take this obligation freely without any mental reservation or purpose of evasion,
so help you, God?

All: *I do!*

Voice of Time: In the year Nineteen Hundred and Forty-one,
no privilege is more eagerly sought,
by many millions of the world's people,
than asylum in the one nation, which, for one hundred fifty

years has been the great and unfailing refuge
of the world's oppressed and persecuted peoples.

From a dozen once-free and democratic nations are

coming scholars and artists, doctors and scientists, who have found that the pursuit
of wisdom and the practice of the free arts are no longer possible
in Nazi Europe.
Men of science and men of medicine

have been driven from old Vienna—once one
of the cultural centers of the modern world.

Great men of music have been exiled from their ancient Bohemian

city, Prague—until yesterday the prospering capital of the newborn
Republic of Czechoslovakia.

Students and artists have fled from Paris,

whose long and unrivalled cultural life and freedom

40

42

58

61

f individual expression have been ended by Nazi conquest.

Fleeing imprisonment or death, stripped

of all their possessions, hundreds of Europe's men of genius and talent have come to

the New World, hoping—like other immigrants before them—to become a part of the life stream
of America; to contribute to it new blood,
new brains, and their devotion to democracy.
Nowhere in the world does the European exile find more
sympathy and help than in America, but U.S. immigration—

since 1929—has been strictly limited to some one hundred fifty thousand
admissions a year, with a definite quota allotted
to each nation.

Today, U.S. officials are investigating the background of every applicant for admission
to the United States. Those found to be
undesirable are denied entrance and forthwith deported.
With fear and suspicion of Axis agents rising
everywhere since the betrayal of Norway and the Low Countries,
into Congress have gone a score of bills aimed at dangerous aliens.

Virginia's Smith would

deport all aliens who have ever been affiliated with radical political organizations.
Most violent of all

suggested measures is that of Georgia's Stephen Pace, who would immediately bar
all further immigration, deport all aliens,
good and bad alike.
But most U.S. lawmakers and citizens feel that existing

alien legislation, which already requires
registration and fingerprinting, provides ample protection
and sets up no discrimination against the five million
law-abiding foreign-born who have not yet become
citizens.
Outstanding champion of America's foreign-born
is 42-year-old Louis Adamic, a one-time immigrant from Yugoslavia,
today, author, editor, and national defense consultant.

Adamic: *In this period of emergency we need to look upon our immigrant groups as
a source of great national strength.*
*Our American development has been, in great measure, due to the variety of talent
and forces which have come to us from every land.*
*And now more than ever before we need to avail ourselves of this backlog of energy
and courage.*

75

78

81

87

oice of Time: More than three hundred years ago, the first immigrants began
uilding in the American wilderness a new nation that was to become the creation
nd the expression not of one people, but of many
eoples, from many lands.
s pioneers came
en and women from England and Scotland, Ireland and Wales;
ith them came the Dutch, Swedes, Finns and Germans,
nd French and Spanish. And as America
ecame a nation, with land
nd work and freedom for all,
ere came others—to push back the frontiers,
 settle the West, and to open up all the treasures
 a vast continent.
'ithin the past century,

most forty million people from Europe and Asia,
exico and the West Indies, have entered
merica to begin a new life and to follow—
ich in his own way—the American dream.
to the building of
merica has gone the blood and sweat, the talent
d skill of generations of immigrants
ho paved its streets and highways, built its skyscrapers and subways,
ised its bridges and dug its tunnels,
anned the continent with a network of rails.
d today in New York, there
ists a living history of the successive waves of immigration,

ich, together, have shaped the pattern of American civilization.
r, within the five boroughs of Greater New York
contained a cross section of all the world's nationalities,
ces and creeds.

ayer: *Blessed art Thou, O Lord, our God, King of the universe, who createst the*
uit of the vine.
erged into the life of the nation

day are its Irish-Americans, descendants of the millions who came to America
 the first great wave of nineteenth-century immigration.

ce strangers in a strange land, the Irish are now

ong the nation's leaders, and they are the backbone of the Roman
tholic Church, whose many institutions they generously support.

92

93

100

105

109. c.u. Tombstone
110. c.u. Another
111. l.s. German woman spinning
112. c.u. old German man
113. l.s. Germans playing cards
114. c.u. old Germans
115. m.s. Baker
116. c.u. Watch repairer
117. c.u. Fixing watch
118. l.s. German beerhall

119. m.s. Same
120. **Insert:** Pictures of foreigners on deck
121. l.s. Foreigners off Ellis Island ferry
122. c.u. Women and child
123. m.s. Rural mailboxes
124. c.u. Same
125. pan shot farm

126. l.s. Cows in dairy
127. l.s. Scandinavian family at table
128. c.u. Girl pouring coffee
129. c.u. Father
130. l.s. Industrial district, river in foreground
131. l.s. Down street
132. c.u. Street sign Pulaski St.
133. l.s. Houses on street

134. m.s. Polish meeting hall (White Eagle)
135. l.s. People in hall
136. m.s. Women listening
137. m.s. Men listening
138. l.s. Polish girl and mother in kitchen
139. c.u. Polish girl
140. c.u. Polish boy
141. l.s. Children playing in gym
142. m.s. Same
143. l.s. Capitol dome
144. c.u. Flag on dome
145. c.u. Senator Davis
146. c.u. Senator Wagner

Second in the successive waves of immigration were
Germans, who began arriving in the eighteen-fifties,
in numbers reaching two hundred thousand a year.
Many of today's German-Americans are the descendants of Germany's first
political exiles, who fled to the New World a
century ago in search of freedom.
Industrious, well-disciplined, and highly trained,
old-line Germans found employment, not as unskilled laborers,
but as artisans in work requiring patience and precision.
With their wide technical knowledge, they brought a love of genial and comfortable
living—
gemütlichkeit—that has influenced the life of the whole nation.
Though Swedes, Danes, Norwegians and Finns were among the earliest settlers of
North America,
the high tide of Scandinavian immigration came around the turn

of the century. Within a generation
one-fifth of the entire population of Norway and Sweden migrated
to the New World. Today, most
of them and their descendants live in rural areas where they have helped raise the
standards of American agriculture, for no farms are more properous and productive
than
those worked by Scandinavians.

But today, American industry, stepping up production to meet defense

demands, is most heavily dependent upon the labor of a great army of
immigrants from Eastern Europe and the Balkans,
who have settled in the big milltowns and industrial centers of the East and Middle
West.
Coming largely from Slavic countries where

illiteracy was widespread, where only the rich landowner had a voice in
government, some of these immigrants have been slow in adapting
themselves to the standards of American life.
But today, with a whole new generation American-born,

old-country customs are fast disappearing as Poles
and Hungarians, Yugoslavs, and Rumanians,
like all other immigrants, become merged into one great people—
Americans all.
Today, high in the councils of the nation are many
men who came to the United States as immigrants:
men like Welsh-born U.S. Senator James J. Davis,
German-born Robert F. Wagner,

111

117

147. c.u. Justice Frankfurter
148. m.s. Sidney Hillman
149. c.u. William S. Knudsen
150. l.s. Boy Scout Board meeting
151. **Insert:** Boy Scout poster *Help me be prepared*
152. l.s. Japanese Boy Scouts
153. m.s. Scoutleader
154. l.s. Boy Scouts cooking at campfire
155. m.s. Boy Scouts eating
156. l.s. Boy Scouts in canoes
157. l.s. Boy Scouts putting out brushfire
158. c.u. Boy Scout at press drill
159. l.s. Boy Scouts hiking
160. Another shot Scouts hiking
161. l.s. Warren Harding High School
162. l.s. Children singing *America*

163. m.s. Boys
164. m.s. Girls
165. m.s. Boys and girls
166. **Title:** Upon the united purpose of all its many peoples—native and foreign-born alike — the United States must depend for its security and strength in the critical days ahead
167. l.s. Workers entering factory
168. c.u. Guard inspecting worker
169. l.s. Lockheed Aircraft plant
170. l.s. Interior aircraft factory
171. c.u. Men riveting
172. c.u. Men working on engine
173. l.s. Factory
174. **Insert:** *Only Native-born Americans need apply*
175. m.s. F.B.I. office
176. c.u. F.B.I. worker
177. m.s. Guard confiscating camera
178. **Insert: Sign:** *No Cameras Allowed*
179. c.u. Same as scene 177
180. l.s. Naval Intelligence office
181. c.u. **Insert:** Alien characters
182. m.s. Intelligence officer
183. c.u. Hammer and sickle

127

138

ustrian-born Justice Felix Frankfurter,
ussian-born Sidney Hillman,
anish-born William S. Knudsen.
mong the generation from whom must come the leaders of tomorrow,
ne of the most powerful influences for welding together

ll races and creeds into a single united democracy,
the nationwide Boy Scout
ovement. As Scouts, the youth of the nation learn

respect each other's beliefs and origins,
be of service to each other and to the community,
accept the responsibilities as well as the privileges of their democracy and freedom.

nd in the schools of America, new generations, composed of countless

cial and national strains, are growing up to carry on and perpetuate the American
adition
f liberty and equality.

1941 as the United States
ckles the gigantic task of arming against aggression, it is drawing heavily
on the services, resources, and loyalty of more than thirteen million
reign-born—of more than thirty million sons and daughters
the foreign-born.
t as industry, labor, and government close ranks,
nd the U.S. develops a war consciousness—there are already
anifestations of a war hysteria against whole sections of the foreign-born popu-
tion.
regional offices of the F.B.I., thousands of anxious Americans are daily
porting their suspicions of disloyal and subversive activities
the part of aliens and citizens.

ough most fears are proved groundless,
e nation's intelligence agents know that a small but dangerous U.S. Fifth Column
hard at work in an attempt to undermine democracy
d American institutions.
osely watched today are the

142

155

164

165

ctivities of the Communist party and its U.S. membership, including not only aliens but old-stock Americans. And ever since Soviet Russia became a silent partner of Nazi Germany, American

Communists have shouted loudly against any aid to Britain.

Communist: *Stop the deceitful aid to Britain policy which is leading to dictatorship and war—it's a rich man's war.*

Voice of Time: Singled out for surveillance by Army, Navy, and F.B.I. are Japanese spies, seeking to use the peaceful and loyal Japanese in the U.S. as cover for their operations. Commonly suspected by apprehensive Californians are West Coast fishing fleets, reputedly manned by Japanese naval reservists to keep tabs on the comings and goings of the U.S. Battle Fleet.

Of the nation's five million Italians and Italian-Americans, U.S. officials estimate that but two hundred thousand have Fascist leanings, and even fewer are impressed by Benito Mussolini—whose military failures have acutely embarrassed his one-time Italian-American admirers. But still outspoken and often frank in its admiration for the

Fascist regime is the biggest Italian daily in the U.S.—*Il Progresso Italo-Americano.*

Italian: *The real danger of the fifth column is among the super-patriots. America has nothing to fear and no vital interests in common with the English plutocracy which is now ready to fight—to the last American soldier.*

Voice of Time: Most openly subversive element operating in the United States today are the Nazi-ruled German-American organizations and their uniformed storm troopers.

Bundists Singing

Voice of Time: In thirty-five U.S. cities, Bunds headed by local *gruppen-fuehrers* appeal to German-Americans on the basis of Hitler's doctrine—once a German—always a German. Patterned along lines approved by Nazi Propaganda Minister Paul Joseph Goebbels are a dozen small-time Nazi newspapers in the U.S., all of them bitterly denouncing American rearmament and aid to Britain,

all of them anti-Semitic, and fiercely opposed to democracy.

German: *Mr. Roosevelt has prayed for unity. Unity for what?—To combine our blood and bodies into a military machine to rescue the bloody British Empire from chaos which she brought upon herself with perfidies and promises?*

Voice of Time: But far and away the greater part of the nation's seven

million Germans and German-Americans reject Adolf Hitler and the Nazi doctrines for which he stands,

222

226

227

230

220. m.s. Father serving dinner

221. **Insert:** *God Bless America* pennant on wall
222. c.u. Bulletin board of Adult Education class
223. l.s. Class in library
224. c.u. Alien reading
225. l.s. Instructor and class
226. l.s. Adult Education class

227. m.s. Aliens in class

228. m.s. Another angle of same
229. Same as scene 226
230. l.s. Foreign family in living room
231. c.u. Father and mother
232. c.u. on mantle piece
233. l.s. Army recruits at attention
234. c.u. Recruit
235. m.s. Same
236. l.s. Entrance Brooklyn Navy Yard
237. l.s. Loading ammunition on ship
238. l.s. Marines boarding transport
239. l.s. Naval officers at muster
240. m.s. Same

241. c.u. Naval officers

242. l.s. Fleet from deck of boat
243. l.s. Cruiser
244. l.s. Battleships

and, like the nation's other national, racial and religious groups are steadfast in their loyalty and devotion
to the American ideal.

So great is the immigrant's desire today to become a citizen

and identify himself with his adopted land, that Americanization classes
are everywhere crowded with eager men and women who
see in the United States the world's great stronghold of democracy.
Instructor: *This is a*
Class: *Telephone.*
Instructor: *The telephone rings. I answer the telephone.*
What do I say?
German: *Goodbye, please.*
Class Choruses: *No.*
German: *Oh, yah, yah—hallo, hallo, please.*
For a nation that is calling upon its foreign-born today,

in an hour of need, well knows that in the past
its immigrant sons have never failed it—that in every great crisis
those who helped to build the country have always come forward
to preserve it. And today, as
America prepares, in the face of whatever may happen,
to defend the democracy built and cherished jointly by its native and adopted

sons, it knows, that upon no men can it call with more confidence

and certainty than upon those whose fathers came from many
lands to find in the New World a better way of life.
Officer: *Scarpello?*
Reply: *Here, sir.*
Officer: *Silverman?*
Reply: *Here, sir.*
Officer: *Spaulding?*
Reply: *Here, sir.*
Officer: *Karkacian?*
Reply: *Here, sir.*

TIME MARCHES ON!

EXAMINING OUR PREJUDICES

By Mildred H. McAfee

We live in a country where all men are believed to have been created equal and to share the inalienable rights of life, liberty, and the pursuit of happiness. If we practiced what our faith preaches we should not witness the prejudice which keeps men of equal initial opportunity in a relationship of mutual antagonism and suspicion, nor would we tolerate the closing of the door of access to the expression of inalienable rights. We regret the existence of racial and religious prejudice which has made our differences divisive instead of merely differentiating. That prejudice we all deplore.

There are people who insist that religious prejudice, like any other kind, is an inevitable characteristic of human nature associated with the particular cleavages which now exist between social groups. To such people it is 'natural' and inevitable that Protestants and Catholics would be suspicious of each other, that Jews and Gentiles should fear each other, that because we differ we must dislike each other. Not long ago an editorial in the Boston *Transcript* enjoined us to 'disagree without being disagreeable.' There are people who seem to believe sincerely that friendliness cannot remain in the realm of religious differences. I protest that assumption.

Prejudice is a social habit, not a social law. It develops in the course of history in response to conditions which historians, sociologists, social psychologists can describe and analyze. We cannot turn the clock back to unmake the conditions which have given rise to twentieth-century inherited prejudices, but we can refuse to accept the false notion that hate or fear of each other is an inevitable trait of human nature. Fear and hate

By permission of the author.

are basic, elementary emotions, but the objects which excite them are culturally defined, and I protest the assumption that potentially rational human beings are incapable of re-defining groups and situations so that they will no longer incite prejudice.

In the passion of inflamed hate it is hard to conceive of new and friendly attitudes. In 1776 Americans were suspicious and fearful of the British. Have you thought how interesting it is that the city of Washington, named for a Revolutionary hero, should be the headquarters for 'all-out aid to Britain'? Attitudes do change. The longer the prejudice has been held, the harder it is to dislodge it, but to dislodge it is not impossible.

These are dogmatic assertions. The evidence on their behalf would take a long time to present. It takes three forms—the evidence of infancy, of past history, and of contemporary experience. Babies may fear the unknown but they do not exhibit spontaneously religious or race prejudice. Inherent biological reactions would presumably show themselves as soon as the situation develops which would call them forth. The evidence of students of childhood points to the conclusion that prejudice is socially acquired, taught to children by adults and by other children. The story of history reveals changes in the status of prejudice. Sometimes the Catholics persecuted the Protestants. Sometimes the Protestants tortured the Catholics. Sometimes each accepts each other without antagonism. Sometimes anti-Semitism is rampant. Sometimes Jews and Gentiles live in amity with each other.

As to contemporary evidence, Hawaii as a social phenomenon has been the challenging delight of students of prejudice. I understand that while prejudice exists there, it is of a form radically different from that in this country.

In an article in the *Survey* for May 1, 1926, William Allen White said, 'The actual government of Hawaii is in the hands of a white industrial and financial oligarchy . . . As one racial group after another has come to the Island as coolies—the Chinese, the Koreans, the Japanese, and now last of all the Filipinos —the welfare work which these benevolent oligarchs have instituted, the schools, the clinics, the hospitals, the playgrounds, the employment agencies, the churches, the fair trading at the company stores, the ideal of a decent, minimum wage, have taken one group after another out of the coolie class into a trading class! The thing that has happened in Honolulu to the Asiatics is comparable with what happened in Boston to the Irish. Coming as common laborers they have become, first, skilled laborers, then merchants, and their children are now in the professions. The fact that a fourth of the marriages of the Island cross race lines indicates how much self-respect these benevolent oligarchs have unconsciously injected by their institutions into the minds and hearts of these who were brought to the Island in another day and generation as mere hewers of wood and drawers of water.' I protest, then, the widespread assumption that prejudice is inevitable.

I further protest the assumption that the prejudice which exists is the result of deliberate and intentional meanness and lack of good-will on anyone's part. If it were, it would probably be easier to conquer. People could be preached to and told to change their ways; and a great many people would try to do it. But prejudice is a social habit, not a deliberately malicious act. We can accomplish little, therefore, by scolding people about their antagonisms. Try it some day and you will discover, of course, that your criticism will never be recognized or admitted by the prejudiced person. You know how it goes: 'Why, I don't dislike Jews, or Catholics, or Protestants. Some of my best friends are Jews [or Catholics, or Protestants]. I believe in giving everyone a chance, but you know Jews [or Catholics, or Protestants] really would like to run the whole country and I just don't believe in letting them get into control, and if you give them [Jews or Catholics or Protestants] an inch they will soon be running all the rest of us [Jews or Catholics or Protestants] out.' That isn't malice. That's acceptance of certain social attitudes toward groups other than our own which seems so self-evident to the person expressing it, be he Jew, Catholic, or Protestant, that preaching at him gets just exactly nowhere.

The third assumption which I protest is that religious prejudice is caused by mere stupidity. Sometimes those who exhibit such prejudice most strongly are not the least intelligent people in our communities. Prejudice is a social habit, not a reasoned attitude, and the most highly skilled reasoners may know all the available facts and still act habitually in an unreasonable fashion.

The word 'prejudice' means 'pre-judgment.' Learning facts *after* judgment has been passed does astonishingly little to change the judgment.

A month before my appointment as president of Wellesley College was announced, I was arguing the merits of women's colleges with an extremely interesting, distinguished, and stubborn Chinese girl who had come to this country on the same boat with President Robert Hutchins of the University of Chicago. She had evidently decided that any institution which could have such a handsome president was *ipso facto* more valuable than a woman's college, specifically Wellesley. She assured me that when Madame Chiang was here, Wellesley was a good college, but that 'everybody knew' it was rapidly degenerating. In view of its latest presidential appointment I could not deny the degeneration, but I was not willing to accept the general thesis that Wellesley had less to contribute to higher education than the University of Chicago. I argued that they were different from, but not better nor worse than, each other. I brought forward various arguments, 'facts,' which seemed relevant to me. She listened politely, but made it plain that my so-called facts proved nothing. Finally I said, 'But, Jeanette, I do know more about this than you. I spent four years at a woman's college and spent another two years on its campus as an alumnae secretary after I was graduated. I also studied at the University of Chicago off and on for years. My facts ought to carry more weight than yours, since you have worked at neither sort of institution.' Her reply is a good illustration of the point I am trying to make: that our prejudices are not dependent on factual evidence. She said she questioned my judgment on the ground that, by my own confession, I had returned to my college after my graduation and spent two years there. This action showed that I loved my college, and she asked me sweetly, 'Don't you remember that "love is blind"?'

We all argue in that way. Prejudice colors facts; destruction of prejudice by logical argument alone is quite hopeless.

Prejudice is a social habit. Like every habit, it can be unlearned, but the unlearning of it is often at the expense of severe emotional strain. Because prejudice is a social habit, individuals free themselves of it with more difficulty than if it were the result of a personal idiosyncrasy, but eradication can be achieved and must be achieved if we are to accomplish the purposes of a nation 'worthy to be free.'

Breaking a habit involves a good many elements. It usually requires conscious attention to what has become habitual. It involves frequent checks on one's actions to see whether unconsciously the old habit operated and thus grew stronger instead of weaker. Usually an old habit can be more easily broken by substituting a new habit for the old. Prejudice against other racial faiths takes the overt forms of avoidance of representatives of those faiths, of uncomplimentary remarks about them, of acquiescence in adversely critical judgments on them. Breaking that habit involves deliberate association, selection of the favorable rather than the unfavorable comment, critical analysis of the adversely critical judgment. Breaking an unconscious habit necessitates conscious attention to the habit.

Such conduct is easy to expect of the person who wants to break the habit, but how may that desire arise in a prejudice-ridden situation? Chiefly by the contagion of prejudice-free personalities, of people who have seen the stultifying effect of antagonistic divisions between groups and have freed themselves of a bad habit of animosity or assumed superiority. Contagion can be encouraged by people who want it to spread. It is easier to maintain freedom from prejudice than to create it. The person determined to increase this freedom will do all in his power to avoid its loss. Youngsters of different religious groups will be introduced to each other as potential friends rather than as menacing threats. Even more important in this land of individuality, youngsters will be taught to avoid the injustice of categories which deny individuality.

A pernicious social habit, closely allied with religious and race prejudice, is that of attributing undesirable traits to a whole group and interpreting every individual's expression of such traits as characteristic of his group. Let a blond or a brunette exhibit temper, and he has the blame for it. Let a redhead do the same thing, and we say, 'What can you expect?' Let a Protestant cheat his customer, and he bears his own blame. Let a Jew do it, and his entire race is invoked to carry the responsibility for him. The injustice of such hasty judgment is that redheads get no credit for the sunny dispositions of many of them. Jews too rarely share the merit of their many philanthropic representatives.

We who would break the social habit of prejudice must learn to shatter the stupid, irrelevant generalizations we have too easily accepted about each other. We must teach our children and ourselves to judge other individuals on their own merits and not on the basis of preconceived ideas of their group's suppositious limitations. To the extent that we can thus recognize the differences between individuals within groups, we can redefine these groups, not as units characterized by the traits of their least desirable members, and therefore feared or scorned or hated, but as units including men and women like ourselves, good, bad, indifferent, possessed of the inalienable right to claim respect as human personalities.

Prejudice is a social habit, a bad social habit. To men and women of good will the world is too full of jobs to be done, of purposes to be accomplished, to excuse them for perpetuating bad habits. May the National Conference of Christians and Jews serve an increasingly large group as an aid in freeing us from the habit of divisiveness, so that in this our good land God may, indeed, 'crown our good with brotherhood, from sea to shining sea.'

HARD-BOILED PARISH

By Stephen V. Feeley

IN 1910 the district surrounding St. John Kanty's Church in
East Side Buffalo was known widely as the 'Bloody Eighth Precinct.' It had blocks of drab houses, occupied almost exclusively
by poor immigrants and their American-born children. About
twenty years before, Buffalo had received more than 100,000 of
the same race, but those settled around St. John Kanty's were
conceded to differ from the rest. Staunchly they clung to old
country language and customs, and fiercely and literally fought
the rest of the city.

There were fifteen gangs of railroad car burglars in the area,
who fought each other for supremacy, but often they collabo-
rated in gun battles with railroad detectives and city police.
The district had the reputation of sending more men to the
electric chair than any other sector of New York State. So many
of its boys were sent to Elmira State Reformatory that local
wags dubbed the institution 'East Buffalo Prep School.'

Policemen walked the side streets in pairs, because so many
lone policemen had been mobbed. One citizen, who dared join
the hated police department, had to be rescued from angry
neighbors who hanged him from a railroad bridge in an effort
to express their attitude toward such an evidence of civic-mind-
edness and personal ambition on the part of one in their midst.

The gang leaders were undisputed neighborhood heroes and
held court in the numerous saloons. The saloons were the only
recreation centers in the area and had pool rooms for young
men and dance halls for young women. There was one large
field in the congested precinct, but it was owned by a railroad
and its 'no trespass' signs were rudely enforced.

From *The Commonweal*, 25 April 1941. By permission of the author and
publisher.

Shootings and brawls were common in the saloons on Saturday nights, when a special riot squad waited in the Eighth Precinct House. But if no call came for the squad, it raided one of the taverns anyway to avenge the recent beating of a patrolman or 'just to beat a little law into 'em.'

At least 90 per cent of the people were Catholics, but only about a third practiced their religion. Several pastors, appalled by conditions in the parish, fled as soon as they could. After one had stayed only two months, the Reverend Andrew S. Gartska was sent there. Immediately he was nicknamed 'Shorty' by the corner loungers, who insulted him as he passed. Although the church had a debt of $150,000, his first Sunday collections amounted to just $7.30.

To meet his parishioners he gave a lawn fête. This was a great social success, but St. John Kanty's parish profited nothing, because willing workers stole every cent that came into their hands.

Father Gartska came as a surprise to the few faithful parishioners. He never ascended his pulpit to complain or scold, but one Sunday he preached a sermon in which he sounded harsh because he was telling plain facts. He said he knew what was wrong with his erring flock and said he intended to do something about it.

The most valuable asset the parish had was a large school building with a hall in the basement. He began dances in the hall on Saturday evenings, with a nominal admission fee. The dances were permitted to last as long as the dancers' endurance, which usually was early Sunday morning. Some elements professed to be scandalized by these early Sabbath soirées, but they had another shock coming. Father Gartska learned that some of the poorest girls preferred to go to the dimly lit saloon dance halls, where their old and unfashionable clothes would not be as noticeable as in the parish hall.

Without more ado, he hired a dressmaker-hairdresser to give free lessons in the parochial school. Young and old women flocked to the classes and Buffalo's first free beauty culture school was established.

Early in 1911, Father Gartska broke down the hostility between the people and railroads enough to get permission to use the railroad lot as a playground. Then he organized a baseball team, deliberately selecting nine young men who were considered the toughest in a district which gloried in being the toughest in Buffalo. Six of the original nine had spent time either in Elmira State Reformatory or Auburn State Prison. To equip them he sold statues out of his church to newer parishes.

This team was what the French might term 'a success foolish.' Fortified by a frenzied neighborhood loyalty, it won consistently and by the end of its first season was well on its way to championship of the Buffalo Municipal Baseball League. As Father Gartska hoped, this quickly ousted the gang leaders as heroes for the boys and young men. At their pleading he formed ten other teams and coached them all.

Adroitly he called team meetings on Saturday evenings in the school. After the meetings the young men naturally joined the young women for the usual dance. Few except the saloonkeepers suspected that an ingenious Saint George was giving the saloon-dragon some blows. A few came to complain and were met by a sympathetic businessman, who had financial problems of his own and sincerely asked them for advice. Soon the St. John Kanty's Businessmen's Committee, named with tactful euphony, was in existence. This committee not only gave Father Gartska sterling advice, but even took some from him, for in a steady unspectacular way members dropped the more nefarious attractions which had thrived in their saloons.

It didn't take the hard-bitten and hard-pressed people of the parish long to discover that Father Gartska's rectory was the place to take their troubles. Wives thought nothing of calling him out of bed early in the morning to bring a tardy husband home from a saloon, because he always went. Women came to cry over meals ruined by the inept operation of the new-fangled gadgets which came into the neighborhood with gas and electricity, so he set up model kitchens in the school at the expense of the utility companies, who also supplied lecturers on cooking.

Classes in English, American history, and civics were begun after men complained that their poor English or lack of American citizenship held them to menial jobs. Teachers came willingly, or were worn down by Father Gartska's persistence. Parents could not afford higher education for their boys, but Father Gartska decided that some, with specialized study, might qualify for civil service posts, and men in important government positions in Buffalo gladly came to guide the studies. Good craftsmen and tradesmen in the parish were flattered by being asked to teach their vocations.

By 1915, St. John Kanty's parochial school building literally trembled with activity every night in the week and all day Sunday. The spirit of self-improvement was infectious; in time, hardly a man, woman or child in the parish but found some business to take him to the parish school several times a week.

Church attendance began a steady rise when the baseball players came to Mass on Sunday mornings to pray for victory on the diamonds that afternoon. More women began to approach the altar for communion after the grateful sewing class began to make vestments and altar linens. The first books they bought, explaining church history and liturgy to guide their sewing, have since grown into a 4,000 volume library.

St. John Kanty's Church and its kindly pastor had become such a necessity to the parishioners that support of them was a pleasure; Sunday collections by 1915 had increased to about $300.

The police were the last to appreciate what Father Gartska had accomplished in the Eighth Precinct, although records of decreasing arrests lay under their noses and they could patrol the streets singly. When a resolute Father Gartska appeared beside one of his parishioners in court any time they were arrested, police stopped exaggerating trivial offenses into great crimes before the judge. The judges sensed the great social vision of the earnest priest and before long they had made him something of a one-man probation department.

A common boyish peculation was the raiding of farmers' stalls in the Broadway Market. This stopped when Father Gartska showed mothers that their heavy, monotonous meals were driving their children to theft in order to vary them, and the cooking classes got new pupils. Shoplifting was common among young women, but this stopped when Father Gartska sent them

to the sewing classes to make their own pretty clothes. Juvenile
delinquency was vanishing in Father Gartska's district—until
automobiles became common and then it rose sharply. Police
were the first to say 'We told you they were born crooks.' But
Father Gartska bought some old automobiles, put them in the
school yard and urged the boys to tinker to their hearts' content. The auto thefts dropped and from then on police were on
Father Gartska's side. More often delinquents were rushed to
his rectory rather than to the precinct house.

From 1920 to 1930, Buffalo had more crime than at any time
in its history and East Buffalo had one of the city's most vicious
bootlegger gangs, but crime continued to decrease where Father
Gartska was an influence. He kept his people too busy to be
bad. During the decade the old school building became too
small to contain the parish social program.

Despite the growing economic depression the parishioners demanded a new building. With some misgivings, St. John Kanty's
Lyceum was built at a cost of $400,000 and was opened in Sep-
tember 1931. Built to accommodate the forty parish societies
and organizations, the building is a city block long and four
stories high, including the basement. When the WPA, New
York State, and Buffalo began their adult education programs,
they could find no better model than St. John Kanty's parish.
The agencies started twenty-seven classes in the building and at
times more than 8,000 persons were working or playing in the
Lyceum at one time.

The debt on the building is still large, but nobody is worried about it. The building could not be duplicated today for
$500,000, architects say. At the request of Buffalo authorities,
St. John Kanty's gave its educational and recreational services
to persons outside the parish free for two years, but four years
ago the city appropriated $150 a month for the parish's services.
This is a mere pittance compared to what parishioners donate
and earn for their own program. One spectacular pageant given
by parish talent brought in $15,000. Rentals of the halls, bowl-
ing alleys, cafeteria, gymnasium, classrooms, and art studio
amount to about $8,000 a year. Dramas and social affairs given
by the parish also bring in a steady income. The Holy Name

Society, one of the largest now in Buffalo, donates $1,000 every year. Recently the sewing class turned over its treasury of $4,000 to be used by Father Gartska to combat juvenile delinquency.

The Lyceum is closed only from 3 to 8 a.m. every day of the week. Rules for its use are sensible and enforced. Only one person has been excluded from the building for misconduct in nine years.

Police Commissioner Austin J. Roche was one of the policemen who used to patrol in pairs in the old 'Bloody Eighth Precinct.' 'The entire Buffalo police department could not have accomplished what Father Gartska did there,' Commissioner Roche says. 'The precinct is now one of the most law-abiding in Buffalo. If we had more Father Gartskas we might not need a Crime Prevention Bureau.'

On September 25, 1935, the late Pope Pius XI made Father Gartska a Monsignor. Pope Pius cited him as 'a priest imbued with the best spirit of religion, who exercised his parochial duties to the great benefit of needy youth and souls.'

Father Gartska is the despair of reporters who attempt to interview him. Instead of talking about himself or his work, he tries to inveigle the newspaper people into starting journalism classes for his young people.

AMERICAN MEDICINE LEADS THE WORLD

By Elsie McCormick

ONLY a generation ago Vienna was the holy Mecca of our physicians and surgeons. American doctors went there by hundreds to study under its brilliant specialists, to walk the wards of the huge Krankenhaus, one of the world's largest and most efficient hospitals, and to attend the innumerable and varied autopsies possible only in a city that drew patients from the four corners of the earth.

Today the crown for pre-eminence in healing belongs to the United States. This is all the more astonishing when one considers that thirty years ago the standards of admission to our medical schools were lower than in any civilized country, that our hospitals, on the whole, were far below Viennese standards of efficiency, and that our medical research was laughed at in every laboratory of central Europe.

Many men still in practice have lived through this dramatic transformation. They have seen Viennese leadership decline for more than twenty years and then go into complete eclipse under the oppression of a hater of scientific truth. They have seen American hospitals reach heights of efficiency undreamed of in the old Krankenhaus. They have seen the standards of American medical schools change from the lowest in the civilized world to the highest. Today they see American medical research occupying thousands of devoted workers and saving lives all over the world. Of 410 medical discoveries made from 1928 to 1938 and listed by the National Geographic Society, 17 can be credited to Germany and Austria, 35 to the British Empire, 22 to other countries, and 336 to the United States! It is our responsibility to carry on research for lands where medical science

From *The American Mercury*, November 1941. By permission of the author, publisher, and Ruth and Maxwell Aley, literary agents.

has been set back by generations, to keep alive the spirit of scientific inquiry stifled in totalitarian countries. And today we are equipped to meet this enormous responsibility. The U.S.A. has become the medical center for all mankind!

What are the factors that brought us from the rear ranks to the vanguard? One impetus toward betterment came in 1910 when Dr. Abraham Flexner visited 155 American medical schools on behalf of the Carnegie Foundation for the Advancement of Teaching. He found institutions that offered no laboratory work, autopsies, or clinical experience—nothing, in fact, except lectures unembellished by even a skeleton. One professor stated in all seriousness that it would be a good idea to have the students see at least one delivery before they graduated and began to bring babies into the world! Schools would graduate anybody who paid his bills, even if he couldn't tell an appendix from a dried angleworm. Only two demanded any college work of entering students; few required even a high-school diploma. There were practically no state board examinations; a diploma from even the feeblest medical school served as a license to practice. The ignorance of some of the professors was stupendous. In his book, *I Remember,* Dr. Flexner tells of asking the dean of an Oregon medical school if they had a physiological laboratory. 'Yes,' said the dean. 'I'll bring it down to you.' He scampered upstairs and returned with a small machine designed to register the beat of the pulse.

Dr. Flexner's report struck home with the force of a land mine. He was informed that if he ever returned to Chicago, home of fifteen medical schools, he could look forward to being shot. He visited Chicago, departed unshot, and had the satisfaction of seeing the fifteen schools reduced to three. The American Medical Association published separately a classification of the medical colleges that helped to speed reform. Today, according to a recent AMA report, instead of 155 hit-or-miss colleges we have 77 modern, splendidly equipped institutions. The medical schools of no other nation require as much of entering students or give such advanced and varied courses. More than 90 per cent of the graduates serve at least a year as hospital in-

ternes before being wafted out to try their arts on the general
public.

Just as striking has been the improvement in our hospitals.
Not long ago Americans hospitals were cordially distrusted.
Having a baby in one was considered the equivalent of a bend
sinister on the family shield. For the public's suspicions there
was ample basis. Although some institutions, like Johns Hopkins, maintained excellent standards, few states bothered to regulate their hospitals. Many houses for the ill were dirty, ill-
equipped, staffed with low-grade help and run by superintend-
ents who had never got beyond grammar school. It is chiefly
watchfulness and careful policing, on the part of the College
of Physicians, the College of Surgeons, and the AMA, that has
worked such wonders since then. Today, though state supervision of hospitals often remains negligent, the fact that sub-
standard institutions are denied AMA registration usually drives
them to close their doors quickly. There are now but 545 wild-
cat hospitals in the United States, and their combined capacities
amount to less than .7 per cent of the facilities offered by the
registered institutions.

Patients are being admitted to our hospitals at the rate of
one every 3.1 seconds! Last year 10,087,548 cases were handled,
not counting the delivery of 1,214,492 babies. Capacity increased
by 31,219 beds—which equals an 80-bed hospital arising full-
panoplied every day of the year. Personnel has continued to improve. The first two nursing schools in the United States opened
in 1873. In 1938, our 1328 schools of nursing had about 82,000
students. Our nurses' skill is not the least reason why American
hospitals are unsurpassed.

Another recent development has been the rise of the medical
center—a group of hospitals of different types clustered together
to form a city of practice and research. They offer a wealth of
clinical material undreamed of by physicians of twenty years
ago, and promote to a high degree the cause of post-graduate
education. New York's sky-towering Columbia Presbyterian Medical Center is an excellent example. No European nation boasts
such a huge and handsomely equipped city of healing.

II

The brightest star in the crown of American medicine is its record in research. The old-fashioned American doctor of only yesterday distrusted 'laboratory methods.' He preferred to rely on the look of the tongue, the rate of the pulse, and his own God-given intuition. He railed in the journals against 'laboratory scientists' who sought to throttle and regiment the beautiful art of medicine. A few doctors made research a part-time hobby, but the idea of men devoting their lives to seeking out the causes of disease was all but unknown.

The opening of the Rockefeller Institute for Medical Research in 1901 furnished an impetus still being felt in America and throughout the world. It soon became clear that, given the opportunity, Americans have a peculiar gift for research. The love for the unknown that burned in the pioneers made men equally eager to try their wits on the frontiers of science. Research in this country has been primarily a young man's game, characterized by ingenuity and daring. The typical medical research man is no longer an old doctor pottering among test tubes in his back office; he is more likely to be a youngster under thirty who approaches a medical problem from the standpoint of the chemist or physicist and gets answers undreamed of by the conservative practitioner.

Additional momentum came when the Rockefeller Foundation was established in 1909 to finance investigations in many lands. Since 1915 it has provided fellowships for 6800 research men in 74 countries. It is chiefly interested in spade work and drops a research subject when it becomes popular, to break ground in new directions. Today, for example, it makes no grants at all for cancer research. Instead, within recent years, it has devoted as much as half of its medical budget to the far less popular subjects of psychiatry and neurology. Since 1922 it has supported a study of the psychological and neurophysiological aspects of sex, a subject with dark and baffling angles. It has lately financed investigation of the elusive common cold, study of influenza, and an experiment in building up resistance against tuberculosis by inoculation with heat-killed bacilli, now being carried on with promising results among the natives of Jamaica. In 1939 the Foundation's International Health Division was conducting health projects in 47 different countries. Its men have walked the dried-up canals of Egypt, gathering the snails that cause an obscure disease, schistosomiasis. They have found hitherto unsuspected carriers of the yellow-fever virus, treated hookworm sufferers in many countries, studied the common cold under Arctic conditions and wrestled with sanitary problems arising from the flood waters of the Yangtze Kiang. The Foundation is now waging a vast anti-malaria campaign in collaboration with 17 Latin-American governments. Even in a war-battered world, its influence is not likely to die. This is the largest of the great foundations, but there are others—some 56 of them, supporting research on diseases ranging from undulant fever to whooping cough, as well as in pure science. Great numbers of expert American investigators in hospitals and clinics, university laboratories, and the research institutions of large drug firms are fighting down the common enemies of man.

So far, our achievements in medical research have been financed largely by millionaires with a bent for social service, a form of philanthropy that has not developed to any extent in Europe. But in recent years government-supported studies have come into increasing prominence. Not long ago the Federal government appropriated $1,393,000 to establish at Bethesda, Maryland, an investigation center for the United States Public Health Service which ecstatic scientists refer to as a laboratory heaven. American research cannot be judged merely by the fact that it has the world's finest laboratories. The real question is the value of the results obtained. The scientist naturally does not think in terms of national rivalries; medical research nearly always means a cross-fertilization of ideas. But although this country cannot take complete credit for all the discoveries attributed to it, there is no doubt that years before the present war we were leading the world in exploring medical frontiers. To consider even a few of them is to catch a glimpse of a time when scores of diseases will be conquered, and, barring bomb casualties and totalitarian oppression, life will be longer and happier than ever before.

III

In the foreground of current American discoveries is the work on vitamins. Some findings in this realm are not yet conclusive; but doctors already predict that better understanding of vitamins will bring the normal life span in this country up to eighty years. At the clinic of Dr. Thomas Spies in Birmingham, Alabama, mouth-breathing hill-billies with IQ's in the sixties and seventies have been turned overnight into normal human beings by dosing with nicotinic acid, a substance found in the Vitamin B complex. People are being freed of serious nervous symptoms by simple diet changes. Pellagra victims who a few years ago had only a 50-50 chance of recovery now are said to face almost complete certainty of cure if provided with certain inexpensive food elements. Drinkers who see striped elephants, we now know, may be suffering from vitamin starvation. There are indications that pure Vitamin E stops degeneration of the nerves; that at least in some cases, Vitamins E and B can restore muscles weakened by infantile paralysis; that Vitamin B_6 can greatly reduce paralysis agitans tremblings. Surgical hemorrhages and the bleeding that has taken the lives of so many new-born infants are being checked by the use of Vitamin K. Six universities are now joining with the United States Public Health Service in investigating almost every disease on the docket, in order to find out if it may not be caused by vitamin deficiency.

Amazing new cures have studded the field of chemotherapy. Not so long ago the doctor who leaned heavily on the corner drugstore was considered dated; people had more faith in the man who emphasized sun-ray lamps, Florida vacations, and other drugless and pleasant procedures. With the discovery of sulfanilamide, which has brought new hope to sufferers from thirty different diseases, drugs have returned to the scene like so many meteors. America cannot claim to have discovered sulfanilamide, but she can take credit for helping to demonstrate its value in pneumonia and for finding and using several of its chemical relatives. Recently American doctors have demonstrated that one of these, sulfaguanidine, slaughters the swarms of germs in the lower intestinal tract which have made operations in that area so perilous; that impetigo, children's skin disease, succumbs readily to sulfathiazol; that sulfathiazol is a possible cure for bubonic plague. It has been sensationally successful in the treatment of gonorrhea.

This magic chemical family conquers certain severe eye infections and forms of meningitis once nearly 100 per cent fatal. Perhaps even more important are recent American experiments showing that tuberculosis in guinea pigs can be cured by promin, another member of this versatile drug family. If promin proves effective for tuberculosis in human beings, one of the world's most serious medical problems will have been solved.

No nation has done more to shed light on the mystery of cancer. Experiments are following several different lines—the search for a virus, the study of the factor of heredity, the investigation of the relationship between hormones and malignant growths. Interesting reports have been made of the regression of cancers treated with fast neutron rays of the cyclotron; but even more striking is the discovery, by Dr. Paul E. Steiner of the University of Chicago, of a substance found in the livers of people suffering from a malignant growth elsewhere in the body. When this brown, flaky material is injected into mice, it causes cancer in what the medical journals call 'a significant number of cases.' There is at least a chance that further investigation may lead in time to the conquest of cancer.

In dealing with the various forms of allergy—hay fever, asthma, hives, migraine, etc.—American medicine has made tremendous strides. Injection tests and immunization treatments have been developed. Doctors studying the mental factors involved have found that patients frequently develop allergic symptoms when subjected to unusual emotional stress. Many sufferers, they declare, can be greatly relieved or even cured if helped to improve their emotional attitudes.

For years after European doctors began their study of syphilis, a peculiar Nice Nellie attitude over here prevented frank facing of the problem and put treatment of the disease largely into the hands of quacks. Within the last decade improved curative methods and a public education campaign have combined to fight it effectively. The United States now has about 2500 free and low-priced clinics for syphilitic patients. In 1939, 1823 state-controlled syphilis laboratories made 5,600,000 blood tests. Doctors in a New York City hospital have worked out a new therapy—a drip technique by which drugs are injected into the veins, drop by drop, ten hours a day for five consecutive days. This heroic cure is equal to eighteen months of the usual office visit routine. The artificial fever treatment developed in this country has restored the sanity of thousands of men and women in the early stages of paresis.

Almost endless is the list of American victories over disease and suffering. There is the liver treatment for pernicious anemia for which Doctors G. H. Whipple, G. R. Minot, and W. P. Murphy received the Nobel Prize. This treatment has rescued thousands of weak, paper-white victims from almost certain death. There have been the wonderful developments in surgery —the irradiation of operating rooms by germ-killing ultra-violet rays; the electric knife that has so greatly reduced mortality in surgical work; the pre-operative glucose treatment which increases powers of resistance; the recently developed methods of stomach surgery that have saved the lives of many ulcer and cancer victims; and the new, mild anaesthetics that make it possible to operate with comparative safety on old people and sufferers from heart disease.

In mental therapy we can claim credit for adapting and improving many techniques imported here from abroad. Shock treatments for schizophrenia have been greatly improved by American physicians. Dr. Walter Freeman and Dr. James W. Watts developed from a European idea the delicate operation on the pre-frontal lobes of the brain which has turned many melancholy, hag-ridden men and women into sane and contented, if somewhat sluggish, citizens. Recently a group of American doctors have been giving special attention to the influence of the mind in causing illness. They emphasize the treatment of patients as 'whole beings,' rather than as bodies divorced from minds.

New ideas and developments, indeed, are mentioned in every

issue of the medical journals and at every important medical conference. A few among the large number of discoveries reported since 1932 are vaccines for yellow fever and whooping cough; a serum for Rocky Mountain spotted fever; a nasal spray of picric acid and sodium alum which offers hope of successful prevention of infantile paralysis; a vaccine known as amniotic fluid which promises to reduce operative risk in peritonitis by 30 per cent; a device for taking infra-red ray photographs which reveals heart disease in its early stages; a vaccine for psittacosis, or parrot fever; a way of administering oxygen under the skin which may eliminate the clumsy and dangerous oxygen tents; a drug, trichlorethylene, which relieves angina pectoris suffering and in some cases cures the disease; a tiny ultraviolet ray lamp inserted into the bronchial tubes for TB treatment; a way of locating brain tumors by testing the patients' sensitivity to the odors of coffee and citral; a tiny camera that takes color photographs of the inside of the stomach; an ascorbic acid treatment for certain disfiguring skin diseases; the use of diathermy, an idea borrowed from radio, in treating rheumatism and other afflictions; a machine for studying the effects of drugs on the living brain; and a method of treating with intravenous injections of hydrochloric acid the victims of submersion, asphyxia, and electrical and surgical shock. Closely related to the needs of today is the method of immobilizing wounds and allowing them to heal untreated under a plaster cast. This idea, worked out by Dr. Hiram W. Orr, an American, was not used on a large scale until the Spanish civil war. Now it is helping badly torn air-raid victims to recover.

Not all our progress has been in the field of developing new drugs, instruments, and techniques. American public health work has undergone vast improvement. Its effectiveness today is shown by the fact that, except for tuberculosis and pneumonia, all communicable diseases have been eliminated as important factors in the death-rate. We are also making notable progress in industrial hygiene and the study of occupational diseases.

It is not in a chauvinistic spirit that we should rejoice in the pre-eminence of American medicine. We are now in a position to keep medical science alive and progressing through the twilight of the intellect that is deepening over Europe.

Abroad, university laboratories have been looted, professors killed in action or driven into concentration camps, and hospitals and colleges bombed into rubble. Upon us falls the heavy responsibility of keeping their lamps lighted as well as our own.

THE MAYO BROTHERS AND THEIR CLINIC
By Harvey Cushing

THERE was nothing mysterious or supernatural about this twentieth-century Lourdes at whose doors incredible numbers of the lame, halt, and blind have for years been daily delivered from the ends of the earth. Nothing supernatural—unless possibly the flawless, lifelong devotion of two brothers for one another be so regarded. Not since the somewhat mythical attachment of those fifth-century physicians, Cosmos and Damian, both of whom in due time came to be sanctified, has there been anything quite like it.

Rochester, Minnesota, fifty years ago, then scarcely on the map, was a prairie town near the headwaters of the Mississippi where in a humble way, at St. Mary's Hospital, the Clinic had its beginning. It was, to be sure, a Catholic foundation in which Sisters of Mercy doubtless prayed for the recovery of their patients. But it was not primarily for prayer, however efficacious, that the afflicted as by a magnet came to be drawn to that particular shrine.

It was rather the world-wide reputation of two forward-looking men whom I like to remember as they were thirty years and more ago, young and vigorous; each blessed with rare surgical judgment, each with hands which seemed possessed, in an emergency, with an uncanny ability to do, unflustered, just the right thing at the right moment.

At this shrine there was plenty of ritual, to be sure, but it was the ritual of the well-drilled, silent operating room where for every movement there is a reason; where the incense in the air is not to conceal corruption but to produce painless sleep; where

From Harvey Cushing, *The Medical Career and Other Papers*, 1940. By permission of Little, Brown & Company and the Atlantic Monthly Press.

the water in which gloved fingers are dipped is holy only because it is sterile.

Their father, the senior Dr. Mayo, pioneer and Indian fighter, was still alive when I first came to know the place in its early simplicity. There were then but two operating tables, at one of which 'Dr. Will' officiated, at the other in an adjoining room 'Dr. Charles.' They were thus affectionately differentiated by everyone—staff, patients, employees, and fellow townspeople—not to mention the countless visiting doctors who even then were wearing a path to their door.

For these also soon came from all parts of the world, often by special trains, to see for themselves what modern miracles were being performed daily in this once obscure country town. To what they could learn and carry away for their own use they were more than welcome, for our profession has no trade secrets. The more widely knowledge can be disseminated, the better for everyone.

And so, as the years slipped rapidly by, a great tower of healing, known everywhere as the Mayo Clinic, was finally erected—a living memorial to a great idea, not a mere place of worship for tradition dead and gone, like the Basilica of SS. Cosmos and Damian built some fifteen centuries ago in Rome by Pope Felix IV.

Another contemporary pair of no less self-effacing brothers—Wilbur and Orville Wright of Dayton, Ohio—were also at about the same time dreaming dreams of a different sort that in no less spectacular fashion came likewise to be fulfilled. Like the Mayos, they seem to have imbibed in their youth the flavor of the old Northwest Territory where the offspring of the early settlers were reared to think more highly of serving mankind than of helping themselves.

One is led to wonder whether imaginative visions of such kind are not more likely to occur and be more possible of realization for those who live where horizons are broad than for those cooped up in metropolitan centers where, even could the rising or the setting sun ever be seen, there would be no time to stop and commune with it.

Different as W. J. and C. H. Mayo were from each other, I have always felt that there was something Lincolnesque about them both. It was shown not only by their modesty and self-effacement, but by their shrewd appraisal of other people in whatever walk of life; and also by their quiet, dry sense of humor. About this there was nothing boisterous, but I have known them to save, with Lincoln-like readiness, many an awkward situation by an appropriate story, more often turned on themselves than otherwise.

Lincoln, of course, was pitchforked out of his native environment in the old Northwest into a position of responsibility he could not refuse. So the Mayos were ready to serve when called, as they did during the War; but they very much preferred their own countryside with its comparatively simple life, despite the ever-increasing responsibilities and laborious routine of their professional work. They felt only an amused pity for those who thought they were wasting their talents in a small town and who ventured to offer them positions elsewhere of supposedly wider influence.

W. J. once said to me, 'When Charlie gets so busy on his farm he forgets to have his shoes cleaned, he takes a night sleeper to Chicago knowing that he will find them well polished under his berth in the morning.' Had he been encountered by some traveler on the train who with Midwest informality asked his occupation, he would have replied, 'A Minnesota farmer.' Had Dr. Will been similarly asked who he might be by some chance companion, he probably would have replied: 'I'm C. H. Mayo's elder brother.'

After Charlie's death, their friends knew the separation could not be for long. There is a tradition among surgeons that they are likely to meet their end by the same malady in the treatment of which they have themselves specialized. So it was entirely consistent that 'Dr. Will' when nearly eighty should calmly submit to an operation whose difficult technique he had not only perfected, but countless times had successfully carried out on persons of younger age who still survive to bless him.

The modern world is all too accustomed to gauge success in

terms of net income, and thus measured the returns from the
Mayo Clinic exceeded the dreams of avarice; but when in 1915
the Mayo Foundation was established Dr. Will simply stated:
'We never regarded the money as ours; it came from the people
and we believe, my brother and myself, that it should go back
to the people.'

YOUTH AND CIVIC LEADERSHIP

By Murray Seasongood

IF the hopes of those who believe in democracy are to be measurably realized and the characterization by Bryce, a generation ago, of the government of cities as 'the one conspicuous failure of the United States' is to be obliterated, we must have better education, a new code of morals, new social standards, and leadership in city and county affairs.

Civic education must begin with the youngest and extend through schools and colleges. It must diffuse the truth that local government is not, as now considered by many, the least important branch of government, but the most vital. For such it surely is. The national government, in time of peace, touches the citizen but casually, indirectly, and slightly. Local government, however, affects him and those dear to him constantly, immediately, and weightily; it concerns his life, safety, and happiness. It is of far greater importance to him than state or national government. State government in Ohio in 1931 cost $79,000,000. In the same period, Ohio cities and counties spent three and a half times as much. But more important than financial considerations, the citizen judges the national government, with which he is only slightly familiar, by that government with which he is in daily contact. If he has no respect for his city and county governments and considers them undependable, corrupt, and undeserving of loyalty, his appraisal of the national government will be similar, and his resolution to support it in time of need will be weakened.

There must be discarded the prevalent opinion that city government and county government are the lowest branches of ad-

From *Local Government in the United States,* Cambridge: Harvard University Press, 1933. Reprinted by permission of the author and the President and Fellows of Harvard College.

ministration, and that the holding of state and national office constitutes advancement. There is no higher peacetime activity than creating and perpetuating good local government.

The youth of the country must be familiarized with the great names and achievements in civic endeavor, as they are now taught the names and records of the nation's warriors and statesmen. How many have ever heard of Folk in St. Louis, Clarke in Minneapolis, Kent and Fisher in Chicago, Heney in San Francisco, Jerome and Mitchell in New York, Pendleton and Hunt in Cincinnati, Tom Johnson in Cleveland, and Whitlock and Jones in Toledo? Young men and women must be made to realize that these civic knights displayed as fine a heroism as the most valiant soldiers on the field of honor. These latter risked their lives out of love for country, but they fought for a united people and against a known foe in their wager of battle. The civic warrior must needs possess moral bravery as well. His motives will be misunderstood and misinterpreted. His good name may be filched. He may be subjected to ridicule and calumny without possibility of reply. Instead of being one of a great army, all united and acclaimed, scoffed at he holds the pass or the bridge with few or alone. He must face corruption and danger as Banquo did the witches:

> Speak then to me, who neither beg nor fear
> Your favours nor your hate.

Surely it is a lame and faulty education which overlooks such effort or treats it as petty and undeserving of attention. Textbooks must include chapters on what has been done, is being done, and can be done in the cities of this urban country. Boy and girl scout manuals must be enlarged to include in the list of good turns daily devotion to the affairs of one's community. More young men and women must be taught the oath of the Athenian youth, which was as follows:

We will never bring disgrace to this, our city, by any act of dishonesty or cowardice, nor ever desert our suffering comrades in the ranks; we will fight for the ideals and sacred things of the city, both alone and with many; we will revere and obey the city's laws and do our best to incite a like respect and reverence in those above us who are prone

to annul or to set them at naught; we will strive unceasingly to quicken
the public's sense of civic duty; thus, in all these ways, we will transmit
this city not only not less, but greater, better, and more beautiful than
it was transmitted to us.

And the words of Pericles, 'We differ from other states in regarding the man who holds aloof from public life, not as quiet, but
as useless.'

The universities, also, must place more emphasis on government and modernize their political science departments. A Cambridge (England) student complained, with humorous, slight
exaggeration, that nothing was taught in his college that was not
500 years old; anything more recent was considered vulgar.
Engaging in public local administration is a new profession, especially helpful now when occupations are too few.

Four different kinds of professional career beckon to the student: he may become a city manager, connect himself with a
bureau of governmental research, serve as city, county, or regional planner, or become a municipal engineer. In the last
profession, especially, there is a surprising dearth of skilled
material. Special training is needed to develop highway, sewer,
and viaduct engineers, and good ones are difficult to obtain.

If, however, the student does not wish to make his interest
in local government more than an avocation, he can probably,
with reasonable effort, be elected to the local council, or to some
office which will not take all of his time. Local political contests
and service are not all sweat and blood, and there is a great deal
of pleasure to be gained from them by widened contacts and
relations with likable people.

If this is too much to ask, the university graduate should be
one of an honest elections committee or of a discussion group
to interest itself in the problems of local government and to
make investigations and reports in special fields. These may be
very helpful to conscientious administrators, and where officials
are not such, may serve to focus public attention on defects in
their conduct of office.

Should even that be more than he cares to do, then the young
man or woman can at least give one day a year to the service

of the community by acting as election official, witness, and challenger or by standing at the polls to distribute literature and instruct the voter regarding the ballot.

Some of the colleges have kept pace with the times. There was no course on municipal government at Harvard, if I am correctly informed, before 1904, but such courses are now given there and in 300 other colleges of the country; some institutions have city and regional planning schools, and six, notably, Syracuse University, have schools of administration and public affairs offering special preparation for the city-manager profession. Eight other universities offer courses which they consider suitable preparation for city managership. The University of Southern California at Los Angeles has a school of administration to which public officials resort for instruction. Many universities, as before stated, are headquarters for leagues of municipalities in their state, with a professor in the political science department as active secretary; some, as in Cincinnati, co-operate with the local city administration, testing materials, assisting in appraisements and valuations; and others, as in Chicago, Toledo, and Lexington, Kentucky, require students to serve at the polls as part of their work. If this can be done in Chicago without loss of the student's life or limb, it ought to be reasonably safe elsewhere. Municipal universities have a special duty and an exceptional opportunity to help the cities which maintain them.

On the other hand, many political science departments are jejune and perfunctory, and instead of inspiring pupils discourage participation in local affairs. Of 508 students who answered a questionnaire sent out by the Phillips Brooks House Association to members of the freshman class at Harvard, more than half stated their intention to enter the medical profession, law, engineering, teaching, and business; only one looked forward to politics as his life pursuit. Advisers sometimes tell young men that obstacles in the way of sound politics and good government are too great, and counsel their pupils to leave politics alone. The *Yale Daily News,* in April 1932, following an exhortation by Governor Cross of Connecticut in the *Forum* to college graduates to enter politics, assured its readers:

The best men will stay out of politics. It's just too dirty. The most serious of menaces to American principles is the increasing abhorrence of educated young men for politics. Politics is no longer a decent profession . . . When a government has fallen in the estimation of a people so that the finest and strongest people will not take part in it, that government is on the wane. The American Government is menaced by a very real, nation-wide disgust of this kind.

The reply of the *Michigan Daily* to the call was:

In general, we believe politics is too unremunerative as a profession to be a field for the college graduate. The general attitude is one of disinterestedness . . .

Would that it were!

As far back as 1867 Mr. Godkin, in a letter to the London *Daily News,* refuted the oft-repeated assertion that there is no political career open to educated Americans. He wrote:

I can honestly say that I am unable at this moment to mention a single man who, being qualified by culture or character for a political career, has been shut out from it by popular dislike of his mental, or moral, or social excellences . . . I have gone over all the men I know of . . . and I can assign in every instance a good reason for their not being in politics, apart from their culture or social position. Either they are lazy and will not work with the energy which political success as well as every other kind of success in this country requires, or they have no skill in public speaking, or they have not capacity for entertaining political ideas, or they are excessively fastidious and fond of a quiet and studious life, or else they are resolutely hostile to the principle of the government, and make no secret of it . . . In fact, I should say, as the result of my observation, that a man of culture and refinement who chooses a political career has, in this country, a great advantage, other things being equal, of a competitor who is wanting in culture and polish. I do not know of a single instance which seems to constitute an exception to this rule.

No one expressed better than did Theodore Roosevelt the duty of qualified persons to engage in local politics. His example and success stimulated tens of thousands to believe with him that 'what a man does for himself dies with him, but what he does for his community lives long after his death.'

The ermine is captured, says the naturalist in *Don Quixote,* by the hunter's spreading in front of its retreat muck through which, because unwilling to soil its white fur, it will not pass. Those who refuse to touch local politics because it is too dirty are like the ermine, and merit a similar fate.

Someone has said, 'The first thing for the reformer to cultivate is a geologic sense of time.' Mr. Godkin, in a period of discouragement, wrote to a friend: 'Nobody should have anything to do with politics who is not prepared to see all improvements postponed till after his death.'

Whether or not Godkin was right, 'God buries His workman but carries on his work.' With increasing emphasis on the importance of local government and knowledge of its possibilities, city and county governments are bound to improve and good administrations persist for longer periods. The great philanthropic and educational foundations in this country have so far not seemed to realize except dimly that in bettering local government they benefit a larger group than in aiding strictly charitable or educational projects. But the Spelman Fund has recently made a substantial contribution to the co-operative effort of county, city, and schools in the Cincinnati region, and also to the University of Cincinnati, for an enlarged teaching of municipal administration in more direct contact with the city government. The Julius Rosenwald Fund has contributed much needed support to the City Managers Association, the National Municipal League, and the American Legislators Association, and doubtless similar aids have been rendered by other foundations. The vastness of the results to be accomplished through improved local government should lead benevolent and educational agencies to increasing help or study and dissemination of facts regarding local government.

Some of the great newspapers of the country, and particularly the Scripps-Howard chain, have actively espoused the cause of improved local government. Mr. Godkin once said, in wrathful pride, that the *Nation* was 'intuitively dreaded by every charlatan and every scoundrel in the country.' In 1890, aiding his early insistence that Tammany Hall was not a political party, but an association for plunder, he published in the *New York Evening Post,* of which he had become editor, a series of biographical sketches of the leading personages of Tammany Hall, showing the criminal or semi-criminal record of many of them. He was arrested for criminal libel and had many suits brought against him. In 1890 and again in 1892 Tammany was successful, but in 1894 it was beaten, and Godkin's part in the result was fully recognized. He served without pay as Civil Service Commissioner under Mayor Strong. The recent editorial observations of the New York newspapers, together with their full reporting of the proceedings of the Hofstadter legislative committee investigating the conduct of the city government and of the governor's hearing and action on the charges presented [against Mayor James J. Walker], are worthy of imitation in other localities where the facts are not so patent. The Committee on Civic Education by Radio is now giving nationally a series of lectures on local government subjects. Lincoln Steffens and Norman Thomas in their latest writings say that there is no chance for efficient local government because privilege is too widespread and cannot be deracinated. But they are judging too much by the past, and are not sufficiently taking into account what better education in local affairs may do.

Religion has not assumed the part it should in the great community struggles for honesty and decency. Its emphasis and insistence have been more particularly upon conventional morality. But 'Thou shalt not steal' is of equal worth with the other commandments, and 'Thou shalt love thy neighbor as thyself' is also in the Bible. Some spiritual leaders have no knowledge of local political affairs, while others are timorous, fearing to divide their followers and offend powerful parishioners. Some few, on the contrary, have raised their voices powerfully against corruption in the cities.

With better education, civil and religious, influential persons will no longer be pinchbeck benefactors of their community. New social standards will compel them to adhere, as in England, to principles of absolute honesty in public affairs.

An educated and morally aroused electorate is indispensable for the success of democracy. But leaders are likewise essential. It is the duty of those who have had the best educational advantages to become such leaders for civic, as well as national, righteousness. The struggle for civic ideals put into practical operation is worthy of the greatest devotion and self-sacrifice. Let none hang back to ask, 'Am I worthy or capable of so large a task?' Let him rather inquire, 'What can I do to help?' Let youth consecrate itself before the altar of this noble cause, for 'As the judge of the people is himself so are his officers, and what manner of man the ruler of the city is, such are all they that dwell therein.'

JANUARY FIRST NINETEEN FORTY-ONE

By Edith Bjornson Surrey

JANUARY first, nineteen forty-one. On that day a blood-mad Europe paused a moment before plunging into another year of the hate and violence and sacrifice of war. The American people, sobered yet strangely exhilarated by their President's impassioned plea that the United States become an 'arsenal of democracy' against the totalitarian powers, tried to visualize the pattern of this new year of feverish building and arming against a great armed foe, and to resign themselves to the sacrifice of the liberty, comfort, and gain it would entail. And I, a little startled after years of dreaming of the romance and glamour of being a 'college girl,' actually found myself at last in the midst of my first college year.

Harold J. Laski has said: 'Our level of education is higher than in any age, yet its main result has been the intensification of our discontents.' A common cry of the last-war generation is that the youth of today is cynical, discontented, destructively critical. Perhaps they would like to hear, in brief, what one typical college undergraduate was thinking about the world as the last leaf fell from the 1940 calendar. Perhaps they may find explained in my speculations some of the beliefs and hopes of this younger generation.

Since this great new war and America's part in it is undoubtedly the uppermost question in the minds of the American people, I shall first make clear, as the starting-point of my discussion, that I do not believe this war to be entirely one of selfish European imperialism. Of course, economic and imperial-political issues admittedly are involved, but for want of knowledge I shall not even attempt to discuss them here. However, I honestly

From *Wellesley Alumnae Magazine*, 1 January 1941. By permission of the author and editor.

believe that democracy is defending itself against the threat of brutal force as the fundamental basis of human relationships, the coercion of man's natural beauty and goodness of thought into a narrow, ugly pattern. I believe that the democracies are battling for the principle of freedom against men who admit the existence of no laws or principles, and that it is the moral duty of the United States to accept its responsibility in this struggle, then to help build up after the war (if democracy is triumphant) some kind of workable world government, a true federation of nations to unite men into fellowship and peace.

I believe that there are two effective ways for our country to take her part in this war which, in spite of the disillusioned contempt in which the term has been held, I shall call 'the war to make the world safe for democracy.'

The first method has an economic basis. I believe that the first step against the United States in the world-domination which the aggressor nations are seeking will be our economic strangulation, to be followed easily by political and military domination. It is extremely important, therefore, that we have a strong economic front, to be built up, in my opinion, by the equalizing of our economic system.

In this great and beautiful nation, where all men are endowed by law with equal political rights, many of them are sick and starving, living in wretched dwellings that cannot be dignified by the name of 'home,' frightened and bewildered that they are unable to find some measure of security for themselves and their families, especially when they see the luxury and wealth of more privileged classes. And as Mr. Laski says, 'When men feel insecure, they grow afraid, and the mood of fear is unfavourable to the use of reason. But democratic institutions depend for their hold upon the power of reason over men's minds . . ."
Thus might economic slavery lead to the loss of political freedom. For it is to the little people, the bewildered, frustrated shopkeeper and unemployed laborer, that the high-sounding promises of fascist leaders must appeal. Although I personally would rather have a little less food for my stomach and a little more freedom for my mind, I think I can understand how a hungry man might lose his reasoning power in the temptation

to give up the political freedom he momentarily forgets, for even the promise of future economic security.

Not only would a more equal economic system satisfy the workers and lessen the danger of the fascist system gaining a hold in this country, but knowledge that the wealthy industrial class is willing to sacrifice would, in a more positive way, make the workers more eager to work hard to fight fascism. If public opinion demands that labor stop striking for better pay and more decent working hours during this war-emergency, why should the employers of these men not be willing to support an excess-profits tax on their war-earnings? America can surely not be making the greatest effort possible to push the war-effort if its excess-profits tax remains at an almost negligible per cent while England's is 100 per cent. And if, as is often alleged, no profit will be made from this war, then surely industrial owners would not object to bearing this tax in name only, if such a form would satisfy the working classes and give them more confidence that, after the war in which they are fighting so hard, they will have economic as well as political freedom. And with new eagerness and hope for the future, then surely the workers of America will rise to the great strength and power of labor and sacrifice to which the English people has proved itself equal in this great crisis.

Secondly, I accept rather than believe in the fact that the United States, besides making this economic adjustment, will have to build up a great militaristic system for defense against the aggressor nations. We shall have to bend all our effort to making ourselves strong in the ugliest sense of the word. We shall first have to send arms and supplies to England and our democratic allies, in an attempt to turn what may be the rising tide of German victory. In any case, whether England stands or not, we shall have to make up our minds that a German-dominated Europe will not fall in a day, and that we shall have to be strong for the military domination that may follow economic 'invasion.'

Thus my future, and that of all my contemporaries, seems far from bright in my speculations. In the next years, I shall belong to the youth of a nation on a wartime basis. The country will be in high fever, and economic and political conditions will be greatly disrupted to prepare in time for the great conflict. Taxes and the cost of living will be high. We shall have to give up many of the luxuries to which we have been accustomed; perhaps I myself may not be able to finish my four years at Wellesley. Many of our liberties will be taken from us, a sacrifice we shall cheerfully make in such a great emergency, for if we do not make some kind of effort and sacrifice we shall lose our liberties anyway, but by pressure from an outside force. Many of our finest young men, friends and brothers and cousins of all of us, will be forced to give up to compulsory military or industrial service their opportunities for education and career, or even their very lives.

But no matter. I, for one, am willing to work and sacrifice to any demand when our very freedom is at stake. I can only hope that all America will wake in time from its slumber of easy tolerance, will cease in time its questioning and quarreling over which bucket to use to put the fire out. Perhaps already it is too late . . .

The consequences of a possible German domination of America are terrible in their implications. Even if, by some miracle, we do manage to defeat these ruthless madmen, reconstruction problems will be perhaps even worse than those following 1918. I believe that in order to battle effectively, we shall have to establish some kind of industrial dictatorship greater than that ever dreamed of in the last war. Such a step would make it tremendously difficult, if not impossible, to re-establish the old capitalistic system. Therefore, it seems to me that after the war we may expect some kind of democratic socialism (democratic, that is, if any liberties remain to us from the sacrifice of wartime); and the economic and political chaos attendant upon the establishment of a new system of government will make this country, as well as the rest of a world struggling to awaken from the nightmare of totalitarian dictatorship and war, a far from easy place in which to live.

I feel it my duty as a future responsible citizen to prepare myself for these difficult years ahead of me. I hope that college will give me the knowledge and the attitudes of mind I shall need to be a positive, instead of a negative, force in society.

In the first place, I want wide learning. Although I am not scientific-minded, I wish to have some understanding of the principles and ways of thinking in a world which is making rapid scientific progress. And for several reasons, I want to know about economics, political science, and history. First, I want to have a useful career after I graduate, most probably in some branch of work in government or economics. Secondly, if I do not prove successful in this line of work, I am determined to be able at least to teach these subjects intelligently in a classroom, or to explain better to my children why this war happened, than the last war has ever been explained to me. And most important of all, I refuse to live my life in a world of whose great forces, movements, and events I am ignorant. Our time needs an alert and intelligent youth, wide-awake to its manifold responsibilities and duties, however unpleasant, and willing to face the problems of war and its aftermath clearly and intelligently. I can try at least to take my part in fighting intolerance and ignorance with knowledge and careful thinking.

I also feel deeply the essential importance, in a world greatly concerned with warfare and boundary disputes and minority questions, of keeping alive in the world the realization that truth is not merely concerned with economics and politics, that 'Beauty is truth, truth beauty.' Perhaps I and my generation will never see a time of peace and friendship between nations, a time when men have leisure from blood and hate and hunger to enjoy and create beautiful things: to listen to Mozart, to read Keats on summer afternoons, to wander through galleries of charming Renoirs and Degas, to wonder about Sir Thomas More, to discuss the elements of human happiness. But perhaps I can help keep alive in the world some conception of the beauty and fullness of man's thought. I can at least bring to a new generation of war-born children, my own or other people's, some dim conception, such as I myself am just beginning to feel, of the pleasures to be found in lovely things: joy in the beauty of painting and poetry, excitement in seeing the human body perfectly controlled in the grace of the ballet, exaltation to be found in hear-

ing great music, awe at the greatness of man's mind as it is
found in his eternal works. We are a transition generation, and
in creating a new world we must not forget the old. We must not
leave behind us Socrates, Raphael, Shakespeare, Bach, Goethe,
or Yeats. Therefore it is now my duty, as well as my delight, to
learn all I can of the beauty of the world, that through me a little of it may be preserved from the holocaust of human carnage.

I have tried to set forth in this paper some of my beliefs and
speculations about America's future, then to show the small part
I hope to play in it: in learning about great issues and events,
that I may either have a career in government or economics, or
pass on my knowledge to another generation; in learning about
the beauty of the world, that I may help keep alive its memory
for the time when this war and its terrible aftermath have passed
away. I want college to teach me to be constructively critical,
politically aware, socially responsible, tolerant and understanding of people and ideas.

Impossibly idealistic, you say? Then perhaps the youth of today is not so cynical, after all. Discontented, yes, with a social
and economic system of such great inequality and with a generation of men who would allow such an affront to human integrity
as the present war; but willing to learn to be constructive, as
well as destructive, in criticism. We will work hard to untie the
knots of our discontent, to create a new order of social and international equality in a peaceful and united world.

V

Education for Freedom

IT becomes expedient for the public happiness that those persons whom nature hath endowed with genius and virtue should be rendered by a liberal education worthy to receive and able to guard the sacred deposit of rights and liberties of their fellow citizens; and that they should be called to that charge without regard to wealth, birth, or other accidental condition or circumstance.

THOMAS JEFFERSON, *A Bill for the More General Diffusion of Knowledge,* 1776

THE children of a democratic society should be taught at school, with the utmost explicitness, and with vivid illustrations, that inequalities of condition are a necessary result of freedom; but that through all inequalities should flow the constant sense of essential unity in aim and spirit. This unity in freedom is the social goal of democracy.

CHARLES W. ELIOT, *The Function of Education in a Democratic Society,* 1897

THE DEMOCRATIC NOBILITY

THE democratic school must teach its children what the democratic nobility is. The well-trained child will read in history and poetry about patricians, nobles, aristocrats, princes, kings, and emperors, some of them truly noble, but many vile; and he will also read with admiring sympathy of the loyalty and devotion which through all the centuries have been felt by generous men and women of humbler condition toward those of higher. He will see what immense virtues these personal loyalties have developed, even when the objects of loyalty have been unworthy; and he will ask himself, 'What are to be the corresponding virtues in a democracy?' The answer is, Fidelity to all forms of duty which demand courage, self-denial, and zeal, and loyal devotion to the democratic ideals of freedom, serviceableness, unity, toleration, public justice, and public joyfulness. The children should learn that the democratic nobility exists, and must exist if democracy is to produce the highest types of character; but that it will consist only of men and women of noble character, produced under democratic conditions by the combined influences of fine inherited qualities, careful education, and rich experience. They should learn to admire and respect persons of this quality, and to support them, on occasion, in preference to the ignoble. They should learn that mere wealth has no passport to the democratic nobility, and that membership in it can be transmitted to children only through the transmission of the sound mental and moral qualities which are its sole warrant. This membership should be the rightful ambition of parents for their children, and of children for their future selves. Every person of the true quality, no matter what his station or vocation, is admitted of right to this simple democratic nobility, which home, church, and school unite in recruiting; and there are, consequently, more real nobles under the democratic form of government than under any other.

CHARLES W. ELIOT, *The Function of Education in a Democratic Society,* 1897. From William Allan Neilson, *Charles W. Eliot, the Man and His Beliefs.* By permission of Harper & Brothers, publishers.

THE EDUCATED PERSON IN AN
UNTIDY WORLD

By Horace Taylor

WHAT, you may ask, have educated people to do with an untidy world? It is my purpose to argue here that they have everything to do with it. All of us look out upon the things around us and find in them only the qualities which we are able to apprehend. Tidiness in things means simply that their arrangement and order appear to conform to our mental patterns of what they ought to be. An untidy world is one for whose specific conditions we can find no sufficient reason or no adequate justification. Those conditions which conform to our mental patterns of what they ought to be, we call reasonable, natural, just. They make a tidy world. Those conditions which do not conform to our mental patterns of what they ought to be, we call irrational, diabolical, unjust. They make an untidy world.

At this point we become involved in relativity and statistics. If 99 per cent of people were to believe that what we call white is black, that yes is no, that right is wrong, these matters would be settled in accordance with their beliefs. White *is* white, yes *is* yes, right *is* right, only because of a preponderance of opinion. People whose opinions in these matters vary widely from the accepted norm are called insane. But the variations occur. Herr Hitler, for example, appears to regard his objectives in the war in Europe as reasonable, natural, and just, and since he professes also to believe that means are justified by ends, he must regard the war itself as reasonable, natural, and just. This is essentially the reason that some people of different views have called him a dangerous maniac. And others involved in the making and the

Reprinted from Taylor, 'The Educated Person in an Untidy World,' *Columbia University Quarterly*, XXXII, December 1940, 257-68, by permission of Columbia University Press.

conduct of the same war, but whose variations from the norm of opinion are less fundamental and less violent than Herr Hitler's, have had their views characterized as idiotic, simple-minded, or merely stupid.

Enough of relativity and statistics. I have said that educated people have everything to do with the world's untidiness. Educated people have minds that are trained in orderliness and in sustained reason. When the minds of educated people can find no sufficient reason or no adequate justification for what they see going on about them, then indeed there is no true meaning for the mind and no true value for the spirit as our bodies spin aimlessly through space and time. This test by the minds and by the spirits of educated people is the ultimately convincing proof of an untidy world. It also is the prelude to the frustration and despair to which educated people always are peculiarly subject, but from which they can make their own escape by the very power of their education.

An educated person tries, by his knowledge of the past, so to understand the present that he can visualize and prepare an abundant future. In this sense he seeks a command over time. But education itself ties us strongly to the past; it is only our visions and our hopes that relate us now to the future. The education which our past offers surpasses so greatly our finite capacities that its total can be expressed only as an ideal. The ideal involves knowing, understanding, and appreciating in the full light of our critical faculties the civilization which has shaped us and which we make.

More concretely, what we mean by education consists of three great basic divisions: first, our understanding of man's relation to the universe through religion, science, mathematics, and philosophy; second, that rich endowment of the spirit in humane letters, in music, in the plastic and structural arts; third, our understanding of the relations of man to man, of tribe to tribe, of nation to nation, through history, politics, law, and economics. It is in the last of these three great divisions, the relations of man to man and of nation to nation, that the world's untidiness and the educated person's frustration most immediately lie. We will consider these in some detail, with due regard, I trust, to the way in which time bears upon both the untidiness and the frustration.

In this regard and at most times, both the past and the future appear to be more orderly and more coherent than the present. We are able to look at an epoch in the past only as a pattern held together by some internal consistency, and at a trend in the past as a series of consecutive and mutually consistent changes. Because of our predictions and our plans we usually look at the future as fulfilling our expectations or as becoming what we intend that it shall be. In both directions lie neatness and order. The bewilderment of the present comes from the double failure of the past to continue and of the future to commence.

If our bewilderment seems to us greater than any that our fathers knew, it must be because, at times now past, we misunderstood the meaning of what lay behind us, and we built on false foundations our predictions and our plans of things to come. For the devastating effects of these misapprehensions all of us bear some burden of responsibility. For the educated men among us there is the urgent obligation to acknowledge error and to seek truth.

Our education with regard to the relations of man to man and of nation to nation is shaped especially by men's ways of making a living and of living together which have developed in the past three centuries. The political and economic philosophy which accompanied the developments, and interpreted them, is called the philosophy of liberalism. The principles of thinking and acting in which all of us have been trained, and to which the faith of many of us is attached, are liberal principles. Most of us are, in some degree, liberals.

In saying that we are liberals, I am using the word in its original and only true meaning, not in the current vulgar sense which makes it synonymous with 'radical.' In this original and true sense it means simply a person who believes in and advocates liberty in thought, in speech, in action. This is the liberalism of John Locke, of David Hume, of Adam Smith, of Voltaire, of Thomas Jefferson, of Abraham Lincoln. It is the liberalism of the bold words, *Liberté, Egalité, Fraternité,* which symbolized the purpose of men in the French Revolution. It is the liberalism of the English Bill of Rights, and of the American Declaration of Independence. It is these things that I mean when I say that we are educated in the liberal tradition.

It has not been long, as history goes, since men found inspiration and hope and a sanctified purpose in the forms of thought and action that liberty made. The attitude was powerfully expressed by the great poet of evolution, of progress, in the famous lines:

Yet I doubt not thro' the ages one increasing purpose runs,
And the thoughts of men are widened with the process of the suns . . .
Not in vain the distance beacons: forward, forward let us range,
Let the great world spin forever down the ringing grooves of change.

It is exactly a century since Tennyson wrote 'Locksley Hall.' But the tidy world of which he sang seems remote and dim and unreal.

Whence comes our world's untidiness? Is it that we of this generation have been betrayed by those men called great in the history of liberal thought and action? But betrayal is a conscious act, and those men did not know either us or our times. No man can betray people of whose very existence he is not aware, in situations of which he has never even dreamed. The fidelity of these men—as well as their wisdom—must be tested in the light of their own environments and according to their attitudes toward the problems that they faced. This test shows that, by knowing their past, they understood their present so that they were able to visualize and prepare an abundant future. They were loyal to their own convictions. They were educated men.

These men did not betray us. It is we who have not been faithful to the principles for which they stood. We have sought a mastery over our times by adopting the conclusions which these men reached, and have neglected or forgotten the methods which they used. To the extent that we have done this, we do not deserve the name of educated men.

Too many of us have become addicted to those deadly narcotics of the mind, slogans, overgeneralized formulas, and too-simple explanations. These affect our understanding of the relations of man to man and of nation to nation by blinding us to the particulars which are relevant. The conclusions which were uttered by the great liberals of the past as propositions which summed up and clarified the facts and trends of their times are mouthed by men today in ways which obscure truth. Untested and unverified generalizations were abhorrent to the great minds of the liberal tradition. That is essentially the reason that the men who possessed those minds were educated men.

It is for us to examine the foundations of our beliefs. The eighteenth-century doctrine of liberalism was concerned with the liberty of individual men. Its conclusions with regard to practical action and the future of mankind were based on this conception. In this view liberty was certain to yield, in Bentham's classic expression, 'the greatest good to the greatest number, each person to count as one.' What was implicit to the liberals of that time was that this proposition was modified by the phrase, 'as long as each person thinks as one and acts as one.'

This implicit limiting phrase will not survive, without still further limitation, the test of careful scrutiny in our times. In men's ways of making a living and of living together, each person does not think as one or act as one. This is a difference of degree; in Bentham's own time, people did not think and act in strict accordance with this norm. But the deviations now are greater and are growing. Individual thought is giving way before mass programs, and individual action is being submerged in collective action. In our economic life, determining power is exerted not so much by individuals acting according to their own free choices as by entrenched organizations, such as corporations and trade unions, with which no single individual is strong enough to cope. In our political life also, the determining power is coming more and more to be exerted by organized factions and pressure groups.

Our ways of thinking about the conduct of affairs among nations also call for modification according to ascertainable facts. The liberalistic internationalism of Adam Smith, for example, was based on the conception of a nation as a free association of free men. As regards this assumption, also, there always have been deviations. But here again the deviations now are greater and are growing. Nations are coming more and more to act according to the dictates of a single directing intelligence toward the fulfillment of a single objective. When the directing intelligence gives way to fanatical fury, and the objective is distorted into sheer greed, the deviation from the liberal premise becomes a complete shift of position.

I do not ask you to accept uncritically the broad statements that I have made. I ask you only to test them by the facts that you know or that you can discover. If you find that these things are true, then we must agree that the postulates from which the generalizations of eighteenth-century liberalism arise are no longer tenable. In this case we must agree also that it is the method of the great liberals, rather than their generalized conclusions, that is most important to us and to our education.

The great French historian Fustel de Coulanges had a motto which he gave to all his students. That motto was: *quaesto*, search. That, in a word, is the method that the great liberals bequeathed to us. If we use this method diligently in our treatment of the problems that we face, if there is among us the genius to squeeze significance from the facts that we find, if we can rid our minds of slogans, of overgeneralized formulas, of too-easy explanations, then we, like the great liberals, will be educated men.

The conditions of our time do not mean that the relations of man to man and of nation to nation can never again be free. It even seems clear that there lies before us, if we seek it with sufficient purpose, a more abundant liberty than men have ever known. We have only begun to realize, for example, the great liberalizing benefits of modern science. And we also have only begun to achieve that greater liberty of the mind and the spirit which is the glory of the educated man. It is easier to mouth slogans, and to play that formulas are wisdom; we have to get our education and our liberty the hard way.

How deep runs the courage of our conviction? Or, as one of my friends recently exclaimed: 'Are we men, or are we only liberals?' Waste and war and torture to the spirit are barbarities, and detestable to the sight of educated men. Now, as always, the conflict is between people of antithetical views. As always, it is educated men who must resist and must attack barbarians. To the extent that they prove themselves not to be educated, to the extent that they lack purpose and courage and conviction, to the extent that they are indifferent or complacent, to the extent that they hold back from exacting and making material sacrifice to the end of achieving a tidier and a more humane world—to these extents our civilization will fail. It is a set of large necessities, but that which is at stake is vastly greater than them all.

It frequently has been urged that our ideal of having a large number of educated people is false, and that an insidious danger lurks in assuming that it is true or that it even is possible. How many of us but have pretended knowledge and understanding of matters which we did not know or understand? May not our established modes of education be only mechanical, and so breed pretense and dishonesty at least as often as they serve to make educated people? I believe the answer is that they may, but there is no reason that they must or should. No one can say now that our ideal of having a large number of educated people is true or that it is false. Whether it is the one or the other depends solely on those people who aspire, or who presume, to be educated. The difference that it makes is crucial: the intellectual dishonesty of those who pretend to be educated, but are not, can defeat the aspirations of those who are. Such defeat, in these times of perplexity and trial, will bring ruin upon mankind.

How perfectly the necessities of education conform to the ideal of liberty. How perfectly they accord with the ideal of individual responsibility. Masses and mobs can never be educated; only individual men can be. Nor can masses and mobs consist of educated men; mob minds and educated minds present a contradiction which no dialectic can evade and no sophistry can explain away. The greatest individualists have been those men who saw most deeply into their times and thought most clearly about them. Being great individualists, they also attained the highest rank as educated men. Thus Goethe, whose individuality lifted him high above any mass, any single race, any single nation, spoke through Faust to proclaim:

> Yes, to this thought I hold with firm persistence,
> The last result of wisdom proves it true;

He only wins his freedom and existence
Who daily conquers them anew.

The freedom and existence we aspire to gain are the freedom and existence of educated men. They can be conquered only by each person for himself. It is only through his own inner urge, under his own direction, and by virtue of his own criticism of himself, that any man ever is educated. Without the last of these, a passion for purposive self-criticism, no strength of inner urge and no astuteness in direction can yield an educated man. It is the lack of this controlling factor that makes the intellectual pretentiousness to which I referred a moment ago. It has been said that a little education is a dangerous thing. Without a large capacity for self-criticism, the extent of any man's education is less than a little, and the extent of the danger cannot be measured. He who would win the freedom and existence of an educated man cannot merely assert those things that he knows; he also must know and acknowledge what things he does not know. He cannot by these means win once for all time; he must, in Goethe's phrase, 'daily conquer them anew.'

Such energies, pursuing with such persistency the evanescent but ever expanding forms of truth, of beauty, and of love, will not be content with slogans, with overgeneralized formulas, with too-simple explanations. Yet even for those of strongest purpose, it is not easy to escape the narcotic effects of these things. It is not merely that men are susceptible to them, but also that enemies of clear perception and orderly thinking are using these drugs in their attack on educated people. The defense against them lies in even clearer perception and in even more orderly thinking.

These defenses are needed always. If our need for them is especially urgent now, it is because our situation now is more critical than any that has fallen to the lot of man in modern times. I believe that this does not overstate the seriousness of our position. Unless the defense is strong, there can no longer be the 'freedom and existence' of the educated man. He will no longer be able each day to 'conquer them anew.' Unless the defense is strong, those values which our civilization affords to the educated man, the liberty to pursue truth, beauty, and love in their particular manifestations, will disappear from the earth. Then it follows that the educated man also will be swallowed up in the disorder of an untidy world.

It follows also from what has been said that the point at which any person can start in trying to remove the untidiness from the world is with his own education. Any start that he may make that leaves out this foundation step must fail; it can result only in greater untidiness rather than in less.

It is likely that most of us, some tacitly and some unconsciously, are Platonists. It is even possible that our weaknesses and our incessant quest for certainty and faith predispose all of us to this view. We want and expect philosophers to be kings. To some minds, simply waiting for philosophers to become kings throws a mystical aura of purpose and a semblance of sanction around our imperfect behavior. It also is supposed to lighten our obligations to the future by making our responsibilities to the present only those of trusteeship. But the doctrine is false, and so is any complacent sense of a responsibility that is only tentative and incomplete. What philosopher is to be king, and what philosophy is he to espouse? Plato was not able to silence the objection of his contemporaries who simply wanted to know by whom the philosopher-king was to be chosen. Our own bafflement runs even deeper than this. We are compelled to recognize that a supremely wise earthly being must, in his wisdom, recognize us for what we are. If he assumed responsibility for us, with our imperfect ways of thinking and acting, he would thereby demonstrate a lack of the supreme wisdom required of a philosopher-king. So our wishful thinking amounts to no more than a contradiction in terms.

Our danger, however, is more concrete than a logical fallacy. We are confronted constantly with men of small soul and great ambition who offer themselves as personal embodiments of Plato's ideal. They pretend to be philosophers because they want to be kings. They set their pretensions persuasively before us, first, by denying all those generalizations from the past which no longer serve to explain or to justify the particulars of the present, and then by promising us, in a new set of generalizations, a future of peace, security, abundance, and brotherly love. Here again the educated person must seek to pierce the generalizations and to discover the relevant particulars. Some of these particulars are immediately apparent; they are detailed conditions of greed, of tyranny, of treachery, of murderousness. The generalizations which are proclaimed are seductive; the voices which proclaim them are those of baritone sirens. These men will to be kings. But if they are philosophers, then surely Circe was the goddess of virtue. And, like Circe, these would-be kings purpose for their own ends to turn men into swine. To know these pretenders in detail for what they are, to denounce them and resist them, is the most imperative moral obligation of educated people in our time.

We cannot have philosophers for kings. But we can do better than that. To do so would entail a heavy obligation of each person to himself—which is the only true liberty. If we practice the arts of education until we seek truth, beauty, and love in their particular manifestations and as ends in themselves, then we will have become philosophers in the sense of Plato's ideal. When enough citizens have become philosophers, there will be no place for kings.

Can we do this, and in so doing rid ourselves of the narcotic craving for slogans, for overgeneralized formulas, for too-simple explanations? If we can we will emerge from a past that was what it was without regard to us into the future of the only free person—the educated person. We will, that is, if our educated minds are wise and if our educated hearts are strong.

THE LIBRARY

By Chauncey Brewster Tinker

Soon after the members of the freshman class are admitted to college, they are addressed by a series of upper-classmen who represent the various activities with which the place abounds. The post of honor is usually given to the captain of the football team, who pleads for a large squad and attendance at the games. The football player is succeeded by those who advertise the other sports; and they, in turn, by the representatives of the literary world—students are not to forget the importance of the college newspaper (be it daily or weekly is a matter of no consequence). There are often social and fraternity appeals added to the confusion; and, lastly, religious and scholarly activities— the class deacon and the president of Phi Beta Kappa—are given a belated hearing. But even then, when the newly enrolled college man has been shown all the rewards that may come from giving his allegiance to the world, it is doubtful whether any of the speakers will have mentioned the college library.

This of course is because the library has no outward and visible reward to offer to its devotees. Even to many who might become devotees it seems like a cold and dusty place, where the books are locked away in distant 'stacks' which the student cannot visit, and which are too often presided over by male or female dragons whose obvious aim seems to be to protect them from those who wish to use them. There is an old story told of a triumphant librarian who, on a famous occasion, boasted that all the books save one were on the shelves, and, added he, 'I know where that is, and tomorrow the library will be complete.' In opposition to such a theory as this it would be wiser to contend that the ideal library is one in which the shelves are empty,

From *On Going to College*, Oxford University Press, 1938. Reprinted by permission of the author and publisher.

since the books are all in circulation. Between these two contrary states, the college library preserves a precarious life. The circulation of its books is like the circulation of the blood, passing constantly back and forth from the heart to the members of the body.

The frequent assertion that the library is the heart and center of the college is the simple truth. All scholarly work, and all undergraduate study as well, consists either of the reading and interpretation of the recorded thought of the past or of the setting down of new information for the guidance of posterity. This is true of science as well as of the 'humanities.' Experiments made in laboratories are recorded, first of all, in notebooks and later in the learned publications of the science concerned. The results of all such work are promptly given to the world, so that others may use and profit by them. If the power of recording thought in writing, or print, which is only another form of writing, were taken from us—by divine *fiat,* let us say—all civilization would cease at once, and we should relapse into the state of beasts.

The average devotee of a library passes, commonly, through three stages. A man's first notion regarding a public library is that it is filled with books to amuse our leisure. It is very probable that the student coming to college has been in the habit of drawing from the town library such fiction as he has read. If that library has been wisely administered, he has gradually learned that there are many other uses to which it may be put, if only he is so disposed. And this is, in general, a healthy notion at that time of life. A boy has gained a great deal if he merely realizes that sources of intellectual amusement are to be found within public library walls, and he should continue to derive such entertainment from the college library.

Meanwhile in his classes the student will have been required to purchase certain books for study, and the mastery of them will be demanded by his teachers; but, in addition to this, he will be sent to the college library to consult other books without any intimation from his instructors that he should purchase them. He is only to learn how to consult these books, how to bring the information that he will find there into relation with the subject as set forth in his textbook. He will then learn that no book can be adequately understood by itself alone, but will yield up its treasure only when its words are compared with those of other books, and its truths tested by the experience of other men. The student will find that some of the books to which his attention has been directed are to be quickly consulted and quickly laid aside, as containing but little—though that little may be of great importance—that is related to the subject which he is investigating. Others may well seem to him more important than his textbook, and he may indeed in certain cases come to realize that his textbook has been quarried out of some larger and grander treatise on the subject. Gradually he will come to understand the truth of Bacon's words, 'Some books are to be tasted, others to be swallowed, and some few to be chewed and digested: that is, some books are to be read only in parts, others to be read, but not curiously; and some few to be read wholly, and with diligence and attention.' [1] Such counsel as this of Bacon's implies the guidance of a teacher and the existence of a library to which the student may be sent. No teacher will be content if his instruction ends in his classroom, and a student will have begun the educational process only when he carries away the lessons which he has received in the classroom, not as a body of dogma, to be received as *de fide*, but as an organic and growing thing to be constantly nourished by human intercourse and by private study.

After a student has thus used the library for many months, he will discover that his work there has constituted a kind of initiation into scholarship, or what is more narrowly described as 're-search.' He will find that in his restless pursuit of elusive facts, his examination of sources, and his comparison of one man's view with another's, he has come into possession of information and of ideas which may fairly be termed *new*—in short, that he has entered the very narrow group of those who have a right to an opinion on the matter. He may even come to possess more knowledge of the subject than anybody else. His knowledge may

[1] From the 1625 edition of 'Of Studies,' which differs from the 1597 edition.

be humble and remote from human interest; it may even be trifling information which he has uncovered; but the experience of thus acquiring it is not trifling, for in it he may see reflected the whole process and progress of learning. He will come to understand why scholars enclose themselves in libraries and scientists in laboratories; why lawyers must be perpetually concerned with precedents—the history—of their profession; and why physicians who aspire to excel must be always studying the latest developments of the art of healing. For every true exponent of a profession is interested not only in learning but in the progress of learning. And the student will come to see that the library or laboratory is a temple dedicated to a faith.

When he has been fully initiated as a scholar, he will also understand why professional practitioners are always talking of documents and of 'original sources.' He will understand why a scholar is peculiarly excited by written evidence coming to him out of the remote past, in words written long ago by a hand that has now crumbled to dust. *Litera scripta manet* [The written letter remains]. Here is something that bears testimony to conditions of life which have long since passed away, and are to be rescued and made to live again only by the efforts of scholars. I cannot here do better than to quote the words of a collector of autograph letters, whose name I do not know, but who summarized very well what I am trying to put before the college student:

An autograph is not only a rarity, but it is a unique rarity. You cannot duplicate it. And it is not only a unique rarity; it is, in a real sense, the embodiment of a human personality. One touches hands, so to speak, with the writer himself; and if the writer be a famous person who, by his genius, has won our hearts, the autograph becomes a veritable living thing. It speaks for the man in a way that no printed page can.

That is, I think, a happy expression of the delight which a scholar feels when, at last, he holds in his hand the written evidence on which a recorded fact reposes. Happy is the student who, while yet in college, has such an experience. It is only in a library that he can have it.

I must not conclude these remarks without some word regarding the value of a student's *private* library. Nothing can ever take the place of that. Not the British Museum, not the Bibliothèque Nationale can take the place of the books which the student has bought and read for their own beloved sake. They are like the twenty books clad in black or red, which were prized by Chaucer's Clerk above all the pleasures of the world. To live in the daily presence of a few great books is itself an education. There is something in their very physical presence which invites us to turn and to return to them, till at last old acquaintance begets in us a likeness to our ancient associates, the worthies of the world.

No personal library can ever discharge the function of a great college library, as no college library can ever be to a man what his own humble collection of well-worn books may be; but love of one begets a love of the other, and as there is distinction in a great college library, so there may be distinction in a private assemblage of books, however small.

There is an old and perhaps foolish query about the books which one would wish to take with him if he were to sojourn upon a desert island. But like some other foolish questions, the problem which it sets us is worth pondering. Upon the voyage of life there are few books of which we may hope to make lifelong companions; and, as in the other relations of life, it behooves us, if we hope to avoid calamity on our voyage, to choose our mates with discretion.

OF THE LIBRARIAN'S PROFESSION

By Archibald MacLeish

NOTHING is more difficult for the beginning librarian than to discover in what profession he is engaged. Certain professions define themselves. Others are defined by those who practice them. The librarian's profession is of neither nature. A librarian is so called not for what he does, as the farmer who farms or the lawyer who laws, but from the place in which he does it. And the definitions of the librarians, though they are eloquent in describing the librarian's perfections, are reticent in saying what the librarian's perfections are for.

Hugo Blotius, the sixteenth-century librarian of the Hofbibliothek in Vienna, defined his profession by saying that a librarian should be learned in languages, diligent and quiet—adding, by way of reminder to his master, the Emperor, that 'if not of noble blood he should be given a title to enhance the dignity of his office.' Cotton des Houssayes told the general assembly of the Sorbonne in 1780 that when he reflected 'on the qualifications that should be united in your librarian' they presented themselves to his mind in so great a number, and in such character of perfection, that he distrusted his ability not only to enumerate but even to trace a true picture of them. Pressing himself to the point, however, the learned orator (who spoke, it should be noted, in the Latin tongue) supplied the following description of the office: 'Your librarian should be, above all, a learned and profound theologian; but to this qualification, which I shall call fundamental, should be united vast literary acquisitions, an exact and precise knowledge of all the arts and sciences, great facility of expression, and lastly, that exquisite politeness which con-

From Archibald MacLeish, *A Time to Speak,* 1941. By permission of Houghton Mifflin Company, publishers.

ciliates the affection of his visitors while his merit secures their esteem.'

One gathers that M. des Houssayes thought well of the librarian's office, but beyond that, and a certain conviction of personal inadequacy, one is little wiser than before. To be at once a profound and learned theologian, the possessor of vast literary acquisitions, the exact and precise master of all the arts and all the sciences, a facile writer and a charming gentleman possessed of that exquisite politeness which wins heads as well as hearts, is to be an unusual and admirable human being—but even to be all these things at once is scarcely a profession.

And yet it is largely in the vein of the orator of the Sorbonne and the librarian of the Hofbibliothek that the profession of the librarian is presented. Modern librarians—perhaps because they do not speak in Latin—have never been as eloquent as Cotton des Houssayes, but even modern librarians write as though the profession of the librarian had been defined when the scholarly attainments and linguistic achievements of the, perhaps, ideal librarian have been described.

The consequence is that the beginning librarian is thrown upon his own resources, upon the dictionary, and upon the familiar sentences of the great founder of the Bodleian Library at Oxford. From Sir Thomas Bodley, besides learning that a librarian should not be 'encumbered with marriage nor with a benefice of cure' and that he should be 'a personable scholler and qualified, if it may be, with a gentlemanlike speeche and carriage . . . able to interteine commers in aswel of other nations as our owne, with meete discourses for the place,' the apprentice librarian will learn that a librarian is a keeper of a library. From the dictionary he will learn that a library is 'a large collection of books, public or private.' And by his own resources he will attempt to deduce what the keeper of a large collection of books, public or private, may, in actionable and intelligible language, be. Keeper, but how a keeper? Of books—but what, then, in this context is a book?

It is not an altogether simple question, and for this reason. There are two meanings of the word 'book,' and two relations, therefore, between a book and the man entrusted with its keeping. There is one meaning which signifies a physical object made of certain physical materials in a physical shape. There is another meaning which signifies an intellectual object made of all materials or of no materials and standing in as many shapes as there are forms and balances and structures in men's minds. The two meanings overlap and are confused. Readers associate the intellectual book with the physical book, thinking of Plato's vision of the world in terms of dark green linen and a gilded name. Collectors associate the physical book with the intellectual book, imagining that because they possess a rare edition of a poet's work they somehow have possessed the poem. But the two meanings are nevertheless distinct. The physical book is never more than an ingenious and often beautiful cipher by which the intellectual book is communicated from one mind to another, and the intellectual book is always a structure in the imagination which may hang for a time above a folio page in ten-point type with a half-calf binding only to be found thereafter on a different page above a different type and even in another language.

When it is said, therefore, that a librarian is a keeper of books, it must be determined first of which of these two books he is the keeper. Is he, for one example, the keeper of the small, clothbound object of 110 pages of text and 6 of front matter manufactured by Macmillan & Co., Ltd., in London in 1928 and called *The Tower,* by W. B. Yeats? Or is he the keeper of that very different object created in many men's minds before, and now in yours, by this—these words, these symbols, images, perceptions—

> That is no country for old men. The young
> In one another's arms, birds in the trees,
> —Those dying generations—at their song,
> The salmon falls, the mackerel-crowded seas,
> Fish, flesh or fowl, commend all summer long
> Whatever is begotten born and dies.
> Caught in that sensuous music all neglect
> Monuments of unaging intellect.

It makes a difference whether the book is the cloth and paper or the intellectual image. If it is the physical book of which a librarian is keeper, then the character of his profession is obvious enough. He is a custodian as all keepers of physical objects are custodians, and his obligations are a custodian's obligations. He is a sort of check boy in the parcel room of culture. His duty is to receive the priceless packages confided to him by the past and to redeliver them to the future against the proper stub. To perform that obligation he must be reliable, orderly, industrious, and clever. He must devise infallible and complicated ticket systems to find the parcels on the shelves. He must read the notations of origin and ownership in a dozen tongues. He must guard the wrappers from the risks of time and theft and matches and men's thumbs. He must be courteous and patient with the claimants. And for the rest he has no duty but to wait. If no one comes, if no one questions, he can wait.

But if it is not the physical book but the intellectual book of which the librarian is keeper, then his profession is a profession of a very different kind. It is not the profession of the custodian, for the intellectual book is not a ticketed parcel which can be preserved by keeping it from mice and mildew on a shelf. The intellectual book is an imagined object in the mind which can be preserved only by preserving the mind's perception of its presence. Neither is the librarian's profession the profession of the check boy who receives and guards and redelivers—receives from the past, guards against the present, and redelivers to the future—for the intellectual book is not a deposit of the past which the future has a right to call and claim. The intellectual book is a construction of the spirit, and the constructions of the spirit exist in one time only—in that continuing and endless present which is now. If it is the intellectual book rather than the physical book of which the librarian is keeper, then the profession of the librarian is not and cannot be the neutral, passive, negative profession of the guardian and fiduciary, but must become instead the affirmative and advocating profession of the attorney for a cause. For the intellectual book is the word. And the keepers of the word, whether they so choose or not, must be its partisans and advocates. The word was never yet protected by keeping it in storage in a warehouse: the preservation of the word is now, as it has always been, a cause—perhaps the greatest —not, I think, the least in danger in this time.

It makes a difference, therefore—a very considerable difference in the understanding of the librarian's profession—which of these two meanings of the book is taken. Both are held. The librarian who asserts that the sole and single strength of his profession in a distracted world is its disinterested objectivity, meaning its negative and custodial detachment from the dangers which beset the Word, thinks of the book necessarily as a physical object on his shelves for which, in its intellectual aspects, he accepts no share of risk or credit. The library trustee or the moralizing editor who demands of librarians that they stick to the job of pasting on the labels and handing out the loans accepts, but with less honesty, the same assumption—less honesty because he speaks, not from love of the librarian's profession, but from hatred of the Word, and fear of its persuasions.

Those who love the power of the Word and who defend it take the opposite position. Shortly after William Dugard was released, through the efforts of John Milton, from Newgate prison, he published two letters by John Dury, deputy keeper in 1649 of the King's medals and library, which put the case with eagerness and passion: 'For if librairie-keepers did understand themselves in the nature of their work, and would make themselves, as they ought to bee, useful in their places in a publick waie; they ought to become agents for the advancement of universal learning . . . The end of that imploiment, in my conception, is to keep the publick stock of learning, which is in books and mss., to increas it, and to propose it to others in the waie which may bee most useful unto all. His work then is to bee a factor and trader for helps to learning, and a treasurer to keep them, and a dispenser to applie them to use or to see them well used, or at least not abused.'

As between these two conceptions of the profession, a man can choose only for himself and not for those who practice the profession with him. But there are, notwithstanding, certain considerations which even a novice among librarians may propose. The chief of these considerations is the nature of the times in which men live. In a different time from ours—such a time as men a generation ago considered natural and normal—it made relatively little difference whether a librarian behaved himself as a custodian of volumes or as a 'factor and trader for helps to learning, and a treasurer to keep them, and a dispenser to apply them to use.' A generation ago the word, the life of the mind, the monuments of unaging intellect, were not under attack. It was agreed by all civilized nations, by all governments in power, that the cultural tradition was a common treasure, that truth was an end to be sought equally by all men, and that the greatest glory and final justification of human life was the creativeness of the human spirit. In such a world the librarian who considered himself a custodian, who devoted himself to the perfection of his catalogue and the preservation of his bindings, and who waited for the calls of those who had business with his collections, was not only prudent but entirely wise. There was no need for him to advocate the cause of learning or to assert the supreme importance of the contents of his library, for no one doubted the one or challenged the other. The librarian who presented himself in the years before the Great War as a champion of culture would have received the ironic welcome he deserved. What was required of him then—and what he practiced—was discretion, dignity, and a judicial calm.

But the world in which we live is not that world. The world in which we live is a world that world would have believed impossible. In the world in which we live it is no longer agreed by all governments and citizens that truth is the final measure of men's acts and that the lie is shameful. There are governments abroad, and there are citizens here to whom respect for truth is naive—governments and individuals who, when it is proved they lie, have not been shamed 'either in their own or in their neighbors' eyes.' In the world in which we live it is no longer agreed that the common culture is a common treasure. There are governments abroad, and there are citizens here to whom the common culture which draws the peoples of the West together is a common evil for which each nation must now substitute a private culture, a parochial art, a local poetry, and a tribal worship. In the world in which we live it is no longer agreed that the greatest glory and final justification of human history is the life of the human mind. To many men and many governments the life of the human mind is a danger to be feared more than any other danger, and the word which cannot be purchased, cannot be falsified, and cannot be killed is the enemy most hunted for and hated. It is not necessary to name names. It is not necessary to speak of the burning of the books in Germany, or of the victorious lie in Spain, or of the terror of the creative spirit in Russia, or of the hunting and hounding of those in this country who insist that certain truths be told and who will not be silent. These things are commonplaces. They are commonplaces to such a point that they no longer shock us into anger. Indeed it is the essential character of our time that the triumph of the lie, the mutilation of culture, and the persecution of the word no longer shock us into anger.

What those who undertake to keep the libraries must consider —or so it seems to me—is whether this profound and troubling alteration of the times alters also their profession. Granted that it was not only possible but desirable for the librarian to think of his profession in negative and custodial terms in the quiet generations when the burning of books was a medieval memory, is it still possible for librarians to think of their profession in these passive terms in a time in which the burning of the books is a present fact abroad and a present possibility at home?

Granted that it was not only prudent but wise as well for the librarian to admit no positive, affirmative duty to the cause of learning in a time when learning was universally honored and the works of great art and great scholarship were admired monuments, is it still wise for librarians to admit no positive duty to learning in a time when governments abroad teach ignorance instead of knowledge to their people, and fanatical and frightened citizens at home would, if they could, obliterate all art and learning but the art and learning they consider safe?

In a division which divides all men, because it is a division drawn through everything that men believe, can those who keep the libraries—those who keep the records of belief—avoid division? In a struggle which is truly fought, whatever the economic interpreters and the dialectical materialists may say to the contrary, across the countries of the spirit, can those who hold those countries remain neutral? In an attack which is directed, as no attack in history ever was directed, against the intellectual structures of the books, can those who keep the books contend their books are only objects made of print and paper?

I can answer only for myself. To me the answer is not doubtful. To me the changes of the time change everything. The obligations of the keepers of the books in such a time as ours are positive obligations because they have no choice but to be positive. Whatever the duty of the librarian may have been in a different world and a more peaceful generation, his duty now is to defend—to say, to fight, and to defend. No one else—neither those who make the books nor those who undertake to teach them—is bound as he is bound to fight in their behalf, for no one else is charged as he is charged with their protection. No one as much as he must say, and say again, and still insist that the tradition of the written word is whole and single and entire and cannot be dismembered. No one is under obligation as he is under obligation to meet the mutilators of the word, the preachers of obscurantism, the suppressors—those who would cut off here and ink out there the texts their prejudices or their parties or their churches or their fears find hateful. And these obligations are not obligations which are satisfied by negatives. The books can be protected from the preaching demagogues and the official liars and the terrorizing mob not by waiting for attack but by forestalling it. If the cultural tradition, the ancient and ever-present structure of the mind, can still be saved, it can be saved by reconstructing its authority. And the authority of art and learning rests on knowledge of the arts and learnings. Only by affirmation, only by exhibiting to the people the nobility and beauty of their intellectual inheritance, can that inheritance be made secure.

Some years before his elevation to the bench Mr. Justice Brandeis referred to himself as 'counsel for the situation.' The librarian in our time, or so it seems to me, becomes the counsel for the situation. His client is the inherited culture entrusted to his care. He—he more than any other man—must represent this client as its advocate. Against those who would destroy the tradition he must bring the force of the tradition. Against those who would mutilate the monuments he must bring the beauty of the monuments. Against those who would limit the freedom of the inquiring mind he must bring the marvels of the mind's discoveries.

Keepers of books, keepers of print and paper on the shelves, librarians are keepers also of the records of the human spirit— the records of men's watch upon the world and on themselves. In such a time as ours, when wars are made against the spirit and its works, the keeping of these records is itself a kind of warfare. The keepers, whether they so wish or not, cannot be neutral.

June, 1940

THOREAU AT HARVARD:
SOME UNPUBLISHED RECORDS

By Raymond Adams

BIOGRAPHERS of Thoreau in describing his four college years
have come to lean heavily upon the only extended first-hand
account in print of that period of his life, an account written
by a classmate, John Weiss, in 1865.[1] The author of that essay
was a member of the Class of 1837 at Harvard and, though there
is no evidence that his relations with David Henry Thoreau between 1833 and 1837 were anything more than casual, saw the
Concord student almost daily and seems to have formed a definite opinion of him. He devoted the first quarter of his essay
to a description of Thoreau as he had known him in college.
It seems, however, to have been a peculiarity of Thoreau's temperament that those who knew him but casually often knew him
scarcely at all. Lowell knew him casually and knew so little
about him that he could declare that Thoreau had no humor.
Citizens of Concord knew him casually for a whole lifetime and
yet declared him a misanthrope even while the Concord children, sensing his friendliness, trooped after him on berrying
parties and hunts for arrowheads. His townsmen declared that
he did not earn his salt even while they were depending on him
for their surveying and might easily have seen him operating
the prosperous plumbago business his father had built up. (They
could hardly know how meticulous he was about paying his
board bill at home.) So John Weiss, acquainted with Thoreau
in college, perhaps did not know him.

Moreover, by the time Weiss wrote his recollections, Thoreau's

From *The New England Quarterly*, March 1940. By permission of the
author and publisher.
[1] 'Thoreau,' *The Christian Examiner*, LXXIX (July 1865), 96-117. The essay
is a review of Thoreau's first five books, but considers his personality and
habits as well as his writings.

reputation as a recluse and anti-social being had been well established. He had been called a 'Yankee Diogenes' [2] and a 'Rural
Humbug'; [3] he had been described as a hermit of nature by his
neighbor, Bronson Alcott; [4] and especially he had been presented
as the realization of the ideal of the poem 'Forbearance' and the
darling of nature described in 'Woodnotes' by the author of
those poems, Emerson, when he spoke at Thoreau's funeral and
enlarged his remarks for the August, 1862, *Atlantic Monthly*.

Later in 1865, Emerson would publish his austerely edited
Letters to Various Persons, which settled Thoreau's reputation
in America for half a century. But three months before this
book appeared John Weiss had plenty of warrant for thinking
that his recollection of Thoreau in college thirty years before
had been correct, for time seemed to have proved it right. So he
launched his essay with the description of Thoreau which has
served as a source for the Harvard chapter of every biography of
Thoreau from Sanborn to Canby. He inadvertently mentioned
Thoreau's 'collegiate career' and then checked himself by saying,
'He would smile to overhear that word applied to the reserve
and unaptness of his college life.' Then, as if to drive home the
fact of that reserve and unaptness, he wrote in rapid succession
sentences like the following:

> We could sympathize with his tranquil indifference to college honors
> . . . He was cold and unimpressible . . . He did not care for people;
> his classmates seemed very remote . . . This revery hung always about
> him, and not so loosely as the odd garments which the pious house-
> hold care furnished . . . He went about like a priest of Buddha who
> expects to arrive at the summit of a life of contemplation, where the
> divine absorbs the human . . . Now it is no wonder that he kept
> himself aloof from us in college; for he was already living on some
> Walden Pond, where he had run up a temporary shanty in the depths
> of his reserve . . . But he had no animal spirits for our sport or
> mischief.[5]

[2] The title of a review of *Walden* by Charles Frederick Briggs in *Putnam's
Monthly Magazine,* IV (October 1854), 443-8.

[3] *Walden* was compared with P. T. Barnum's autobiography under the
title 'Town and Rural Humbugs,' *Knickerbocker Magazine,* XLV (March
1855), 235-41.

[4] 'The Forester,' *Atlantic Monthly,* IX (April 1862), 443-5.

[5] Weiss himself had so great a share of animal spirits that in the great
'Dunkin Rebellion' of the class, when protest against the exactions of a

Since John Weiss's sketch, very little new material about Thoreau in college has been published. Two of his classmates wrote accounts in 1887 which differed in no particular from that of Weiss twenty-two years before. The first of these, that of David Greene Haskins,[6] consists of but four sentences by way of comment on the change which Haskins noticed after Thoreau came under the spell of Emerson:

In college Mr. Thoreau had made no great impression. He was far from being distinguished as a scholar. He was not known to have any literary tastes; was never a contributor to the college periodical the 'Harvardiana'; was not, I think, interested, certainly not conspicuous, in any of the literary or scientific societies of the undergraduates, and, withal, was of an unsocial disposition, and kept himself much aloof from his classmates.

The second 1887 account, that of class secretary Henry Williams,[7] is satisfied with quoting Weiss and Haskins and certainly gives one the same picture of a discontented recluse shunning his fellows. The journal of Thoreau, when it was published, added little or nothing, for it was not begun until Thoreau left Harvard, and very little of it represented the first years out of college, when recollections would have been fresh. The college essays, compositions assigned by Professor Edward Tyrrell Channing, might have been helpful but proved disappointing when they were published,[8] for it became evident that these are not essays but exercises with rigidly assigned topics and rigidly directed thinking.

Meanwhile, however, there had been one published hint that perhaps Thoreau in college was not so cold as had been supposed. In 1906 appeared a letter which Junior Sophister Thoreau

teacher of Greek went beyond the usual burning of shutters and throwing of stoves down dormitory stairs and resulted in the storming of the chapel, Weiss and one other, being ringleaders, were apprehended and rusticated. Without exception, the entire class seems to have engaged in the riot. It may be that Weiss was so far in the lead that he could not see short-legged Thoreau.

6 David Greene Haskins, *Ralph Waldo Emerson, His Maternal Ancestors* (Boston, 1887), 119-20.

7 'Henry David Thoreau,' *Memorials of the Class of 1837 of Harvard University* (Boston, 1887), 37-43.

8 F. B. Sanborn, *The Life of Henry David Thoreau* (Boston, 1917), 66-189.

had written from Concord, July 5, 1836, to his classmate Henry
Vose,[9] proposing that they room together during their senior
year 'if you will request that sage doughface of a Wheeler to
secure me one of the following rooms,' and Thoreau listed half
a dozen rooms in order of preference. The sage doughface com-
plied. The entire letter shows Thoreau as an undergraduate
who was friendly and gay toward those whom he had singled
out as friends. It is certainly not the letter of one who, in Weiss's
phrase, 'did not care for people.' A second glimpse of this other
side of Junior Sophister Thoreau came in 1916, when a letter in
similar vein was published.[10] This letter, describing a ten-minute
voyage of Thoreau's 'oblong bread-trough' boat, the *Red Jacket,*
on Sudbury River, was written to another classmate, Charles
Wyatt Rice, on August 5, 1836. In it, as in the letter to Vose
a month before, Thoreau reveals a gay humor and a warm
friendliness toward his classmates.[11]

There still remain some unpublished documents which go far
toward showing this side of Thoreau's life at college, a spright-
lier side that made him not entirely a stranger to the hobbies
of college students in the 1830's or to the society and banter of
his fellows. Of these, three especially—two letters by Thoreau
and an account of his last Sunday night at Harvard by one who
roomed with him that commencement week—go so far toward
humanizing Henry Thoreau, student at Harvard, that they
should be better known. The first of these in point of time is
an October 13, 1837, letter to Henry Vose, the correspondent
of fifteen months before, to whom Thoreau seems to have been
drawn in college because both boys had been 'nursed on the
selfsame hill,' Concord Academy, where the nutriment dished
up by Preceptor Phineas Allen seems to have been somewhat
thin. According to Henry Williams in the *Memorials of the Class
of 1837* (pages 48-51), Vose himself, because of illness and because of his residing outside the Yard in the home of Professor

---

[9] 'Early Letters of Thoreau During an Absence from College,' *Fifth Year-
book* (Boston, 1906), 53-6.
[10] *Two Thoreau Letters* (Granite Reef, Mesa, Arizona, 1916).
[11] Both letters have been printed in full in Sanborn's *Life,* 56-63. Thoreau,
Vose, and Wyatt, were grouped together in one of the discussion 'parts' at
Commencement in 1837.

Henry Ware, Jr., had but limited intercourse with his class-mates. From the letters which passed between them, however, it would seem that Thoreau and Vose struck up a real friendship; they roomed together; and, contrary to Sanborn's supposition, Vose rather than James Richardson (an earlier roommate) may have been the person whom Thoreau once referred to as his col-lege chum. Three months after graduation, months that seem to have dragged slowly for Thoreau while his classmates were find-ing niches for themselves and he was 'vegetating' in Concord, he addressed his classmate, then teaching school at Butternuts, New York, with the following letter:

CONCORD OCT. 13TH 37

FRIEND VOSE

You don't know how much I envy you your comfortable settlement —almost sine-cure—in the region of butternuts. How art thou pleased with the lay of the land and the look of the people? Do the rills tinkle and fume, and bubble and purl, and trickle and meander as thou expectedst or are the natives less absorbed in the pursuit of gain than the good clever homespun and respectable people of New England?

I presume that by this time you have commenced pedagogising in good earnest. Methinks I see thee, perched on learning's little stool thy jet black boots luxuriating upon a well polished fender while round thee are ranged some half dozen small specimens of humanity thirsting for an idea:

> Pens to mend, and hands to guide.
> O, who would a schoolmaster be?

Why I to be sure. The fact is, here I have been vegetating for the last three months. 'The clock sends to bed at ten, and calls me at eight.' Indeed, I deem conformity one of the best arts of life. Now should you hear of any situation in your neighborhood, or indeed any other, which you think would suit me, such as your own, for instance, you will much oblige me by dropping a line on the subject or, I should rather say, by making mention of it in your answer to this.

I received a catalogue from Harvard the other day, and therein found classmate Hildreth set down as assistant in elocution, Chas Dall divinity student—Clarke and Dana law do., and C. S. W. resident graduate. How we apples swim! Can you realize that we too can moral-ize about college pranks, and reflect upon the pleasures of a college

life, as among the things that are past? Mayst thou ever remember
as a fellow soldier in the campaign of 37

Your friend and classmate
THOREAU

P.S. I have no time for apologies.[12]

Surely this letter sounds like one from a recent graduate who
had known his classmates and who had an interest in what they
were doing after graduation. There is more than a suggestion in
the last two sentences that Thoreau did have his part in the college pranks and campaigns, even that great 'Dunkin Rebellion'
which ended in the state courts. It is the last paragraph of the
letter that reflects Thoreau's undergraduate life. The early part
is serious enough, for young men must eat. But even in the first
paragraph it is perhaps not too much to see in the series of verbs
describing the wandering brook some recollection of a lesson in
rhetoric over which he and Vose had had their fun.

The next document, written to a Harvard undergraduate ten
years after Thoreau was out of college and while he was living
at Walden Pond, may be chiefly interesting as a confession of
his limitations as a naturalist and of his humanitarian traits. But
it is also a very human account of one of the avocations of Harvard undergraduates in Thoreau's day which he engaged in with
the others. This ornithological interest of the undergraduates at
Harvard in the 1830's has escaped notice, just as no one has
pointed out that Thoreau as a local naturalist was but one of
hundreds of local naturalists who flourished in New England
during his lifetime. The letter, addressed to Horatio B. Storer,
14 Winter Street, Boston, follows:

CONCORD   FEB. 15TH 1847

DEAR SIR,

I have not forgotten your note which I received sometime since.
Though I live in the woods I am not so attentive an observer of
birds as I was once, but am satisfied if I get an occasional night of
sound from them. My pursuits at present are such that I am not likely
to meet with any specimens which you will not have obtained. More-

---

[12] Copied with the permission of the late W. T. H. Howe from Thoreau
manuscripts in his possession, and used with the permission of Miss Edith
Tranter, administratrix of Mr. Howe's estate. Thoreau's punctuation has been
unaltered. The full names of the classmates mentioned were Samuel Tenny
Hildreth, Manlius Stimson Clarke, Richard Henry Dana, and Charles Stearns
Wheeler.

over, I confess to a little squeamishness on the score of robbing their nests, though I could easily go to the length of abstracting an egg or two gently, now and then, and if the advancement of science obviously demanded it might be carried even to the extreme of deliberate murder.

I have no doubt that you will observe a greater number of species in or near the College yard than I can here. I have noticed that in an open country where there are but few trees, there are more attractions for many species of birds than in a wooded one. They not only find food there in greater abundance, but protection against birds of prey; and even if they are no more numerous than elsewhere, the few trees are necessarily more crowded with nests. Many of my classmates were quite successful in collecting birds nests and eggs, and they did not have to go far from the college-yard to find them—I remember a pigeon woodpecker's nest in the grove on the east side of the yard, which annually yielded a number of eggs to collectors, while the bird steadily supplied the loss like a hen, until my chum demolished the whole with a hatchet. I found another in the next field chipped nearly two feet into a solid stump. And in one of the fields near the yard I used to visit daily in the winter the dwelling of an ermine-weasel in a hollow apple tree. But of course one must be a greater traveller than this if he would make anything like a complete collection.

There are many whippoorwills & owls about my house, and perhaps with a little pains one might find their nests. I hope you have more nimble and inquisitive eyes to serve you than mine now are—However, if I should chance to stumble on any rarer nest I will not forget your request. If you do come to Concord again, as I understand you sometimes do, I shall be glad to see you at my hut—Trusting that you will feather your own nest comfortably without stripping those of the birds quite bare—I am

Yours &c

HENRY D. THOREAU [13]

The third document giving an insight into the naturalness of Thoreau's undergraduate life is a manuscript autobiography

[13] From a manuscript letter owned by the Abernethy Library of American Literature, Middlebury College Library, Middlebury, Vermont. Used with the permission of Dr. Viola C. White, Curator of the Abernethy Library. Thoreau seems to have misread the initial. Horatio R. Storer was at Harvard in 1847. There is no record of any Horatio B. Storer.

Since the present article was written, Thoreau's letter to Storer has been published, virtually without comment, on the correspondence page of *The Saturday Review of Literature* of November 11, 1939. Its value toward an understanding of Thoreau's life at Harvard is not there indicated.

of John Shepard Keyes, a graduate of Harvard in 1841.[14] Though this is undated, the internal evidence of a reference to Thoreau's part in 'the John Brown excitement of last year' indicates that it was written in 1860. Pages 39 and 40 of the manuscript book have to do with the Harvard commencement season of 1837:

The Monday before Commencement, then the last Wednesday in August, was the appointed time. To reach Cambridge in season involved then going down Sunday night, and my arrangements to spend the nights with David Henry Thoreau, as we all called him then, had all been comfortably agreed upon . . . Nothing memorous can I remember happened on that momentous ride bearing a green boy to the first of his decisive trials in real life, and I was dropped at the yard gate where Thoreau met me and took me to his room in Stoughton. I was anxious of the morrow's fate, overawed by the dull old college walls, and not a little inclined to be over-thoughtful at the sudden change it all implied. But these fancies were soon dispelled, a burst of Thoreau's classmates into his room, headed by Charles Theodore Russell, Trask [15] and others who chaffed Thoreau and his Freshman in all sorts of amusing ways, and took down some of our local pride and Concord self-conceit for which I soon found out that my host was as distinguished in college as afterwards. These roaring seniors fresh from vacation's fun and with no more college duties to worry about made a sharp contrast to a Sunday evening at home. It was seeing something of the end before even the beginning. There had been some kind of a row with the faculty and the trouble was carried into the Criminal Court and I had heard the county side of it at home and now was told the students' side by some of the actors or sympathizers and got some ideas of college discipline that varied essentially from the home notion. It was startling and novel to hear 'Old Prex' and other nicknames familiarly applied to such dignitaries as Concord had almost worshipped, and I fear that the introduction wasn't of the most useful sort to just such a boy as I was.[16]

[14] John Shepard Keyes, born in Concord in 1821, attended academy with the four Thoreau children, became a member of the State Senate eight years after his graduation from college, was a delegate to the convention that nominated Lincoln, a United States Marshal from 1861 to 1866, and a Justice of the District Court of Central Middlesex from 1874 until his death in 1910.

[15] No Trask is listed as belonging to the Class of 1837.

[16] Used with the permission of Judge Prescott Keyes, son of John Shepard Keyes.

Surely this cannot be the same Thoreau whom John Weiss remembered as avoiding his classmates, for this one is host to a group of roaring seniors on the last Sunday night of college. This Thoreau takes a chaffing not about his shrinking from view but about his 'Concord self-conceit.' This Thoreau is not averse to discussing the 'campaign of '37' any more than he was averse to mentioning it to Vose three months later. This Thoreau is the boy who graduated at Harvard in 1837, who (contrary to legend) received a diploma along with everyone else in the class that Wednesday. There was also another Thoreau at Harvard, the Thoreau made known to us by the biographers, who spent four unhappy years in a discipline that irked him and from which he escaped into the alcoves of the library where the books of seventeenth-century English poets were, who walked the yard as if looking for arrowheads in some field of Concord, who suffered poverty and had to spend one winter schoolteaching at Canton, who suffered ill health and had to spend one season at home an invalid. All of these things are true. But there was a boy named Henry Thoreau who took pleasure in college life and graduated from Harvard a happy member of the Class of 1837 on August 16 of that year.

WOMAN'S PLACE IS IN THE WORLD

By Paul Swain Havens

WITH the words 'Kirche, Küche, und Kinder'—Church, Kitchen, and Children—an unknown phrase-maker, as he thought, put woman in her place, slurring womankind and three fundamental human activities—the worship of God, the care of a household, and the rearing of children. Despite this attitude, women of many nations emancipated themselves, brought dignity to all they did, and entered every activity which talent and circumstance permitted—until now, when it is unhappily true that with the rise of the totalitarian state their gains have been seriously threatened. Today in certain countries a woman's sphere has again been reduced to the drudgeries of home and field in the narrowest sense.

It is well to recall these facts as one considers the place of woman in our own society. The contrast between her lot in a democracy and under a dictatorship is startling, and is evidence of the uncertain and varying status of woman in a 'man's world.' Those who are in any way concerned for the education of young women will do well to consider this matter in all soberness.

The ultimate aim of the education of woman is, and possibly always will be, a matter of debate. Despite differences of opinion, however, one may venture the positive assertion that the first objective of all education is to enable a person to take his place effectively in the world in which he is to live. What *is* woman's place? A woman may become a wife and mother and head of a household. She may through choice or necessity become economically independent, earn her own living, and even care for dependants. In some instances she may by reason of her special talents be called to posts of great public responsibility.

Reprinted from *Wilson College Alumnae Bulletin*, February 1940. By permission of the author.

Since we in a democracy believe no one can say what any young woman will face in life, it must be the goal of a democratic educative process to enable her to fill with the greatest intelligence, effectiveness, and satisfaction whatever place the circumstances of her life may assign her.

It follows then that a woman's education can be no narrowing process. Although a majority of college-trained women marry, establish homes, and rear children, it is not enough that a college seek to prepare its students for motherhood and homemaking. Life asks more of an educated woman than is implied in 'Kirche, Küche, und Kinder.' Nor should a college be a training school for specific vocations. Education must go beyond, far beyond, the business of training an individual merely to perform a specialized task or to fill one designated role in life. A woman's education should, in the largest sense, prepare her to live her life with distinction, to meet the problems of life, whatever they may be, with understanding and courage, to the end that she fulfill her obligations to herself and to the society of which she is a part.

It is an interesting commentary on present-day attitudes that the majority of parents sense this need of training for broad and varying responsibilities. At least three out of every four parents enrolling their daughters in Wilson College express the belief that their children should have an independent career after college, and participate, if only for a short time, in the work of the world. They are aware, as we all must be, that no person can be assured these days of economic or social security, but—perhaps for this very reason—they believe that their children ought to be ready after college to assume a degree of independence and gain the life-long confidence which comes from meeting adult responsibilities.

Now a college which seeks to equip young women for participation in life must in the truest sense be a part of life, a little segment of the world itself, and the years spent there should be looked upon as an integral part of life. It is nonsense to talk of the college years as only a preparation for life. They are *part of life,* just as much as any other four-year period. Every concept a student acquires in college, each talent she develops, becomes a part of her life pattern. As she grows in understanding and in ability, she becomes, under the influence of her teachers and advisers, her true and mature self. During four years she is guided into living in such a way as to develop fully her capacities— mental, physical, and spiritual. When she leaves college she knows how to live intelligently because she has had practice in doing so; and although she may later find herself in circumstances utterly different from those experienced in college, she will be sustained by the precepts and guided by the principles that she learned there. Thus in the real sense there is no break between the college years and those that follow.

Indeed, the integration of college and life is essential to a truly liberal education. The modern college utilizes the whole world as its classroom and laboratory. Students in the social sciences use the newspapers in their work, they observe local government as an example of democracy in action, and in the neighboring welfare agencies they actually engage in social work. Biology students find bacteriology problems in the local water and milk supply. In the near-by hills geologists learn at first hand of the ravages of the glacial age. In the same practical way, college women in their student government face and solve problems that develop their sense of justice; in their forums they debate live issues, and in the college publications exercise freedom of speech. In these and a variety of other democratic college activities, young women are brought into immediate contact with situations which are part of life. By doing they learn, and by self-discipline they become normal, controlled human beings. They are in the world: for college is part of the world.

And after college? If they become teachers, physicians, lawyers, social workers, librarians, technicians, or hold a position in business as executive or secretary, their place is in a busy world which will judge them mercilessly for what they are. If they marry and devote their time to the direction of home and children, their place is equally in a busy world. For the 'Küche' is no longer an isolated retreat. The inventions of an ingenious era have come into it, and with their coming the mistress has been freed to go outside it. Children bring the world into the home as they never did in the last century, and their welfare demands that their mother participate in activities outside the home which did not exist when someone struck off the phrase 'Kirche, Küche, und Kinder.' Whether she likes it or not, whether she earns her own living or directs the life of her family, woman's place these days is in the world. The sheltered days are gone; and it is just as well. For the American woman of 1940 is a person in her own right; she is a citizen of the world.

This being so, the college has a peculiar responsibility. The world is demanding, and its complexities grow daily. The modern woman requires many times the equipment that was needed by her grandmothers of 1500 or 1800. During the four years of her life that she spends at college, the institution must see to it that she is awakened mentally and brought to a wider understanding of herself and her world, that she is taught sound habits of health and a clear-headed knowledge of her body and its care, and that she is fortified spiritually to encounter and master the distractions of an age that is groping for its direction.

WHAT ABOUT PROGRESSIVE EDUCATION?

By Carleton Washburne

WHAT is 'progressive education' and what are its results? A few years ago only the initiated were familiar with the term. Now even people who know little or nothing about it write articles on it, blame the ill manners of youth upon it, fear that it undermines patriotism, wonder if it will prepare children for college, question whether it fits them for the rigors of real life.

In the minds of many parents, and some educators, a 'progressive' school is one where there is no discipline—the children are rude and do as they please; where the three R's are neglected and, on the higher levels, there is no scholarship; where what learning there is is so sugar-coated that children are not prepared either for higher education or the rigors of life; and where an atmosphere of radicalism prevails.

Maybe there is such a school somewhere. If so, it would be disowned by every progressive educator. Yet these misconceptions are so widespread that they must have some origin. As we discuss what progressive education really is, perhaps we shall see why otherwise intelligent people have such fears and beliefs in regard to it.

Right at the start, however, we are confronted with one cause of confusion: there is no definitive statement of exactly what progressive education is. It is elusive. This is because it is not a set method, plan, or technique, but an attitude, an implicit philosophy, a point of view. No two progressive educators describe it in the same terms; no two schools practice it in identical ways.

Yet there are certain common elements in the thought and practice of most people who consider themselves or their schools progressive. These can be very simply stated. Progressive edu-

From *The Parents' Magazine,* June 1941. By permission of the publisher.

cation is always concerned with the *whole* child—both as an individual and as a member of society. It is therefore concerned (1) with his health and his emotional adjustment; (2) with his self-fulfillment as a unique individual, having initiative and creativeness; (3) with his acquisition of whatever knowledge and skill he needs for taking his part in the world; and (4) with his development as a socially conscious, participating citizen of a democracy.

Let us look at these four aspects of education more closely.

The first evidently subdivides into two parts—physical health and emotional adjustment. The progressive school considers both as vital parts of education. On the physical side it tries to provide hygienic surroundings; an adequate physical education program; a program of physical examinations followed up by conferences with parents to see that defects are remedied; care that contagion does not spread; and adequate emphasis on health and safety in the curriculum.

This phase of modern education is characteristic not only of progressive schools but of many good schools which are in other ways traditional. The only opposition it meets is from those who want to keep taxes down and who think of education as mere book-learning.

The emotional adjustment of the child, however—mental hygiene—is much less understood, much less characteristic of even good traditional schools, but is considered basic in progressive education. The best progressive schools try to get down to the roots of behavior, to analyze the deep-seated causes of a child's lying, bullying, teasing, showing off, laziness, day dreaming, recalcitrance, over-concern with sex, or over-compliance. These forms of behavior are recognized as symptoms of something the child lacks in satisfying his basic emotional needs. The cure for these undesirable forms of behavior is obviously not in repressive discipline, or even in reasoning with the child. It lies in finding wherein the child is not getting the deep satisfactions necessary for his wholesome development, and then helping him to find acceptable ways of satisfying these needs.

And right here is a cause of one of the misconceptions regarding progressive education. The teacher who understands mental hygiene represses as little as possible, tries to give children a chance to work out their own characteristic design of growth in acceptable ways, tries to give them a sense of belonging, of being appreciated and loved, tries to help them to participate in the planning of their own lives and to co-operate with their fellows in group enterprises. This does not lead to the kind of order where you can hear the clock tick—a kind which we adults seldom have in our own lives. But, rightly conceived, it does not lead to chaos. It is not *laissez-faire*. A child's right to freedom is always limited by the equal right of his fellows. A child does not get the sense of belonging by a form of behavior that alienates him from his fellows. And co-operation with others necessarily calls for self-discipline and at times for subordination. The wise teacher leads children to see this for themselves and to behave acceptably, not through fear or because told to do so by a person in authority, but because they themselves see the desirability of such behavior. This is a slower process and requires skill, understanding, and patience. But it is a far surer, more permanent, and more socially useful type of discipline.

There are, of course, situations where one must obey a person in authority. In adult life such situations occur when we obey a traffic officer, or a superior in our work. Almost always, however, we see the reason for the obedience. And most of the time we work toward an end which we want to accomplish, and discipline ourselves. The worker who works only when the foreman's eye is on him is not worth his salt. Training in self-discipline toward ends one accepts as one's own is therefore much better training for actual life than training in blind obedience to authority.

The second aspect of progressive education is the development of the child's individuality—his self-fulfillment in accordance with his own characteristic design of growth. We have already seen that this is a basic need in his emotional life—that he must have a chance for self-expression. But it is also a necessity for his choice of wholesome use of leisure, for his choice of a vocation in which he will have both interest and skill, and for his own unique contribution to the growth of society.

The progressive school therefore encourages spontaneity, variation, initiative, creative work, and independent thinking. Many of the activities in the progressive school look to the outsider like mere play—painting, drawing, modeling, woodworking, issuing school papers, dramatizing, writing stories and verses, making and playing musical instruments, to name only a few. Yet these are among the most effective means of education. Through them the child not only gets needed emotional satisfaction, but discovers his own bents and his own limitations, which of his interests are passing impulses and which are lasting. Through them he finds where he can appreciate and enrich the culture in which he lives, and how he can best contribute to the work of society.

There is discipline, however, in each of these things. One has to learn to use tools—brush, or saw, or flute, or pen—and to use them well if one is to get satisfaction from them. The discipline of creative work is incomparable discipline which does not disappear when the eye of authority turns away, but which abides throughout life. It is this discipline toward which progressive education strives.

The third aspect of progressive education has to do with the three R's and scholarship—helping children and youth to acquire the skills and knowledge which are necessary for participation in the work and play of the world. Progressive education is very much concerned with this responsibility. But it considers it as only part of education, not as the whole. Its emphasis upon physical health and mental hygiene, upon creative self-expression, and upon learning citizenship through democratic participation in activities, makes the emphasis upon learning arithmetic, reading, spelling, history, geography, and science seem subordinate. But it is no less real. Progressive education insists, however, that learning shall be functional—not the memorizing of dry facts, or drill in little-needed skills, on the supposition that someday one might need them, but live knowledge applied to everyday problems. This is sound psychology. Such learning is much more efficient and permanent than the endless drill of the old school. But functional learning is pleasant, so some parents feel that their children are not working as hard as they once did. Many still adhere to the long discredited psychological notion of mental training through mere intellectual effort and grind. What they fail to realize is that one always works hardest on a job which is interesting. It is not the work that seems like work which is most efficient, but work that is done with the zest of play.

Does this unfit one for the drudgery of adult life? Maybe. But the converse of this is that perhaps a generation that knows work can be fun will try to make adult work more interesting.

Parents are often distressed by the tendency of progressive schools to postpone formal learning—to have children begin reading at the age of seven instead of six, or learn long division in sixth grade instead of fourth. But this, too, is sound psychology, and of proved efficiency. Learning, to be effective, must be based on experience. The progressive school seeks to give children experience first, the symbols of reading, spelling, and number only when experience has made these symbols meaningful. As will be shown later, this results in no ultimate loss in time or quality of learning, but tends rather to save time for the other aspects of education.

One other objection is raised: The children do not learn as many facts—capitals and boundaries of states, dates of battles, and so on, as did children in the old schools. No, they don't. To cram children's heads with masses of memorized material is as painful as it is futile. What they learn instead, far better than under the old system, is a general orientation in the world and skill in using libraries and books of reference to find details as they need them. This is the way of the scholar.

Finally, the fourth aspect of progressive education is education for citizenship. This includes, first of all, direct experience with democratic living. The progressive school is a democratic school in which the superintendent and principals are chairmen of teachers' groups, executive officers and stimulating leaders, but not autocrats, and in which the teacher in the classroom exerts her authority as seldom as possible and acts far more often as the wise guide and arbiter, allowing the children, as far as they are able, to think and plan co-operatively. She even lets them learn by their mistakes when this can be done without serious harm. Only so can they feel responsibility.

Besides innumerable experiences in living democratically within the school the children have much more contact with the world outside than do those who have the traditional bookish schooling. They go on many field trips to get first-hand knowledge of their community and its environs. They see the interdependence of people, they become aware of the human and material resources of their surroundings, and, as they approach and go through adolescence, they see some of the many unsolved problems of our life today. Under good teaching they reach an appreciation of the ideals and accomplishments of our society, and a keen desire to play their part, as they grow up, in helping it to realize its ideals more fully. But while they are still children they participate directly in local improvements—clean-up campaigns, wild-flower planting and preservation, safety, and the like. They must learn citizenship by practicing it.

Direct experience is extended through pictures—mounted pictures from such magazines as the *National Geographic;* stereopticon slides, and movies. The children learn to know their own country—and through knowledge come respect and devotion. And they learn to know other peoples as fellow human beings.

Discussions, talks in assembly, and radio, broaden indirect experience further. And books—many books, far more than are used in traditional schools—extend experience indefinitely.

Youngsters—particularly adolescents and post-adolescents—get a keen sense of the controversial issues of the day and awake to a determination to help right the wrongs of society. And this is why progressive education is sometimes accused of radicalism. The young people are taught to look honestly at the evils that exist—war, class struggle, slums, corruption, race prejudice—and to examine fearlessly all proposed solutions. If the parents have a strong emotional prejudice on one side of a controversial issue, their children are likely to take the opposite side in discussions at home. And parents don't like to hear their children espousing a point of view which differs from their own. Yet therein lies thought and progress.

Progressive education does not indoctrinate children with any particular solution to our problems, but instils in them a desire to examine all proposals, to get beneath propaganda and prejudice, to seek facts and reasons, and to think boldly. This is radicalism only in the best sense—getting at the roots of problems.

A patriotism based on understanding rather than shibboleths, a patriotism that is not afraid to acknowledge weaknesses in one's country and is determined to seek ways of overcoming them, is the only true patriotism.

So much for the theory and practice of progressive education. Does it work? Does it accomplish its aims?

This question cannot yet be answered categorically. We have no adequate measures for emotional adjustment, for creativeness, initiative, and development of individuality; or even for the various phases of citizenship, although some of these have been at least partially measured. But we can measure whether children educated in progressive schools do as well in the academic parts of education as do those in traditional schools, and this has been done.

For the past thirty years American schools of all kinds have been using standardized tests in reading, spelling, arithmetic, geography, history, and so on. Sheer knowledge and skill in these fields are accurately measured. Such tests have been used for comparing children's accomplishment, along academic lines, in progressive and traditional schools.

In terms of the broader objectives of progressive education, J. Wayne Wrightstone, Director of the Division of Research of the New York City Schools, has made the most extensive comparison between traditional and progressive schools. He shows that in working skills, skill in organization, ability to interpret facts, ability to apply generalizations, civic beliefs, initiative, work spirit, reliability, courtesy (yes!), co-operation, critical thinking, children in progressive schools excelled those in traditional schools.

But do progressive schools prepare children for college? This is not properly a basic objective—each school should give students the best possible education on its own level, and the school that follows should adapt its course to the students. Nevertheless to many parents the question of whether the students can fit into college is crucial. On this point we have the most thorough study yet made of the results of progressive education.

Several years ago, with grants from the Carnegie Corporation and the General Education Board, and the co-operation of most of the leading colleges and universities of the United States, a commission of the Progressive Education Association selected thirty high schools which agreed to carry out an eight-year experiment. These high schools were told that all usual examinations and requirements for college entrance would be waived for their graduates for a period of five years, beginning when they had carried out an experimental program for three years. Each school was allowed to work out its own program. Some changed little, some changed to a really progressive kind of education. The graduates entered the various colleges as had been agreed, and then were meticulously compared with students of equal intelligence and similar home and community background in the same colleges.

Taken as a whole, the students from the thirty schools were equal or slightly superior to their peers from other schools in the college grades they made in almost every subject.

But some of the schools in the thirty had made very little change from traditional methods, while others had departed widely. The graduates of the six which were most traditional were compared with their matched pairs, and those from the schools which had made fullest use of their freedom to carry out a progressive program were compared with their own pairs. The results were striking. The students from the more traditional six schools were just equal to those with whom they were compared. But the students from the six most progressive high schools got higher grades in college than their peers in every subject but one. They spent more time on study, were more critical of their educational experiences, were more active in student social life, took more part in student government, dramatics, publications, and clubs, and attended more lectures, concerts, and plays.

Progressive education appears to be the best preparation for college.

It would be strange if the results of all these studies were not what we have found them to be—better than the results of traditional schooling. For the curriculum and methods of the old-type school are based upon a tradition that had its origin before we had begun any scientific study of how children develop and it was planned, however inadequately, for a society which since then has undergone drastic changes. Progressive education, on the other hand, is simply modern psychology and social science applied to the all-round education of the child; an attempt, in the light of our best scientific findings and practical experience, to help each child to find self-fulfillment as an individual and as a participating member of a democratic society.

THE FANTASIA OF CURRENT EDUCATION

By I. L. Kandel

EVER since some educational theorists made the profound discovery that we live in a changing world, that authoritarianism began to be undermined by Galileo and that life is precarious and the future uncertain, experimentalism has run riot and education has been bombarded with a chaotic welter of theories. Some twenty years ago C. W. Bardeen wrote an article under the title, 'The Man Milliner in Education,' but the educational milliner was just beginning to be active when he wrote; since that time the milliner's energies and activities have not flagged and every year produce several crops of new plans, new projects, new theories. Educational bibliographies have to be annotated with statements that the earlier works (written as long as fifteen or twenty years ago) of some authors do not represent their present views; one educator, careful not to be left behind by the rapidity of the changing cultural stream, announced in the 1939-40 catalog of one institution two courses on the 'Psychology of American Culture'—the first semester to cover the period from 1860 to 1939, the second semester the period from 1860 to 1940, with an unfortunate gap of about two weeks unaccounted for.

Despite the widespread attacks upon it because of its traditionalism, American education has never been as rooted in its principles and practices as have the European systems. The first prize in a competition instituted by the American Philosophical Society in the early years of the Republic went to Samuel Knox for his *An Essay on the Best System of Liberal Education Adapted to the Genius of the Government of the United States* [1799]. Education since that time has been marked by constant attempts at adaptation but never with the intensity characteris-

From *The American Scholar*, Summer 1941. By permission of the author and publisher.

tic of the last two decades. There are, however, many educators who would reject the notion of adaptation as an end of education and would embark on a program of reconstructing society through the schools in an effort to meet the uncertain future.

The educator is turning his attention from the schoolroom to the community, to society, to the world at large and, discovering that everything is wrong, is ready to tear down the walls of the school so that pupils and students, seeing the ills of the world in which they live, may learn how to correct them. We have been through a World War; we are in the midst of another. We passed through a boom period; we are now in the midst of a depression. Youth has been betrayed by the older generation; it must be made wiser and be trained to solve the problems which the older generation has through complacency, indifference, or ignorance allowed to accumulate. And the older generation has failed because the traditional education it received failed to develop its social or any other kind of intelligence, and predisposed it not only to accept but to be content with the status quo. This point of view was expressed in the preliminary program of the winter meeting (1940) of the Progressive Education Association:

Schools no longer bound education. The teeming life of the community, the State and the nation are more really and vitally educative than books. In the educational experiences they give their children, how can the schools use these resources that lie all about them? And what can schools do to help children to become aware of the problems inherent in these resources, so that the children may help to solve these problems as they grow into manhood and womanhood?

The problems which experts the world over have failed to solve may now safely be left to children in the schools under the guidance of teachers who are only too ready to disprove Bernard Shaw's gibe and whose claims to expertness seem to have been overlooked in the formation of brain trusts. This is not the first time that teachers and educators, weary of the tasks they have professionally assumed, have sought new worlds to conquer. The sophists had useful recipes for the solution of the problems of their day. Comenius (whose reputation rests on the production of the first illustrated school text), when he grew weary of the *puerilia illa toties nauseata,* as he described his work as a teacher, had an ambitious plan to set the world of his day right by his pansophic scheme.

Despite the fact that educational literature is full of accounts of failures in the established routine subjects of the school, in the teaching of which teachers may be expected to have acquired some proficiency, they are now to become experts in the solution of all social problems. Despite the known fact that many college students fail because they are unable to read, despite a growing library of literature concerned with the problems of teaching reading, and despite the fact that in the field of adult education books have to be rewritten to make them readable, children in schools are to be plunged into surveys of their community, national and world resources, which 'are more really and vitally educative than books.' The reality of ideas is to be abandoned for contact with realities.

A little more than a year ago there was a conference at Teachers College, Columbia University, on 'How Can Economic Illiteracy Be Reduced?' Seminars were held to discuss what can be done in this field at different school levels. The report on the findings of the Seminar on 'What Can Be Done in Elementary Schools?' (grades six and below) contained the following statement:

It was agreed that to educate satisfactorily for economic literacy, the teacher must have a definite philosophy of life evolved from living a full life, and must have an orientation in economic theory. *Although such orientation is now generally lacking, we cannot afford to wait to re-educate teachers,* but we must proceed as that process of re-education goes on. The materials to be used in such education are to be determined in the light of the problems to be solved. They shall be decided upon by *teachers, children, specialists, and others in the situation.* It was agreed that research is needed to determine what materials are required for this type of instruction.

The italics, which are not in the original, are intended merely to draw attention to a trend which is not new—the optimistic attempt to have illiterates taught by illiterates.

If this proposal were due merely to an accident of wording or

to a chance admission that teachers are not yet economically literate it would be bad enough. It is still worse when, as in an
article in *School and Society,* October 21, 1939, it is justified as
a principle. Here the author writes:

> A teacher does not need to have studied economics in order to give
> a good course in the subject. All that is needed is a teacher (1) who is
> alert to the problems of the day, (2) who is openminded, (3) who can
> stimulate pupils to bring economic problems to class for discussion,
> (4) who permits and encourages free and open discussion of all con-
> troversial subjects, (5) who instills into the pupils a spirit of tolerance
> for all views and a respect for the opinions of others, and (6) who shows
> in all discussion that he or she has at heart the solution of the economic
> ills of the day in a way which will restore prosperity and happiness to
> the whole people.

Only the traditionally trained academician would be disposed to
criticize such frank open-mindedness.

Unfortunately the statement just quoted does not stand alone.
A report published a few years ago revealed that there were
about 150,000 high school teachers giving instruction in subjects
they themselves had never studied. To this number should be
added another large percentage of teachers who hold high school
certificates but in no specific subjects. When German was ousted
from the schools during the World War a crop of teachers blos-
somed forth overnight to teach Spanish. When the recent vogue
for 'social studies' was introduced there was no lack of teachers
ready and willing to teach them, because 'a teacher does not
need ever to have studied [any subject] to give a good course in
the subject.' Lest those in higher educational circles take too
much unction to themselves it is well to remind them of the
college president who requested the dean of a well-known graduate school to send him two Ph.D.'s. When the dean inquired
what fields the Ph.D.'s were to expound, the answer came back
that the fields did not matter; all that the president needed was
'just two Ph.D.'s.'

The harm done American education by the cult of such superficiality is incalculable. A number of explanations can be ad-
duced for this situation. The first is a somewhat widespread
contempt for knowledge and its mastery, or, as the educational

theorists put it, the important thing is not 'the what' but 'the how,' not content but method, not ideas but the thinking process. How the one is possible without the other is never explained. Hence the prevalent criticism of objective tests of scholastic attainments as measuring 'mere knowledge.' Hence the traditional emphasis on methods and pedagogy rather than content in the preparation of teachers, and the distinction between teaching 'the child' and teaching 'subjects.' Thus, also, it is claimed that a great measure of success has been achieved in a large city school system in an experiment with the activity program; the pupils in these experimental classes excel in co-operation, initiative, experimentation, critical activities and leadership; but they are at a substantial disadvantage, when compared with pupils in traditional classes, in arithmetical computation, arithmetical reasoning, reading speed, spelling, and language usage. These results are interpreted as bringing 'democracy into the classroom.' If it is objected that the pupils cannot compute, attention is directed to their initiative; the charge that they cannot spell or read is met by referring to their independence and experimentation; if inadequacy in subjects is mentioned it is countered by citing their critical activities and leadership. The new school thus becomes 'dynamic' and is to replace the obsolescent traditional school which was 'static.'

The second explanation is to be found in a certain discontent with the preparation given to meet the problems of citizenship. The school must train pupils to solve the controversial issues of the day. Education can only be made 'meaningful' as it deals with the immediate problems of the environment in which the pupils live. Whether the pupils realize the existence of these problems, whether they have any direct stake in their solution, whether the problems and the solutions will be the same when they in turn become adults is immaterial. Nor is it clear whether those who advocate the study of controversial issues at any school level are interested in fact-finding about the present or in the acquisition of methods of attack. No one could object, of course, to the development of techniques of argument and debate in the classroom; indeed a good case could be made out for teaching everything controversially. The position is different, however, with the controversial issues which it is proposed to inject into the school to develop social, political, and economic literacy. Here, for example, are two problems taken from a social studies textbook actually used in a class of fifteen-year-old girls:

(1) If you were appointed economic dictator of the United States, what steps would you take to prevent business depressions? (2) Imagine yourself a member of the Round Table Conference on India which met in England in 1931. Give arguments for Indian independence from the point of view of an Indian Nationalist. Give arguments for England's retaining control from the point of view of an English Conservative. Outline the main points of what you consider a settlement fair to all concerned.

To avoid any objection that these questions are exceptional two others from another study guide for group and class discussion at the high school level may be cited:

(1) If purchasing power were increased to the extent of providing a high standard of living could mortgaging the future be prohibited? How? By whom? (2) Does the Fascist economic system balance production and consumption? How does this planning differ from the proposals of the scientific students, or the plans for controlled private capitalism in America?

Such is the revenge of the progressive educator on the traditional academic curriculum for transmitting 'inert knowledge' and for its failure to be 'meaningful,' interesting, and realistic!

A third explanation is to be found in the theory that the process of thinking can only be stimulated by having a problem to solve when a fork in the road is reached or when the choice of a course of action has to be made. How the existence of a problem can be recognized without a background of antecedent knowledge is not explained. Here again, since next steps are always uncertain and the future is always precarious, the experimental habit of mind must be cultivated. Habits, stereotypes, and routine must be replaced by scientific methods of thinking; 'life situations' must be dealt with as the scientist deals with his material. Unfortunately a cog is always slipped in the theory; the scientist's problems arise out of a background of knowledge accumulated by his predecessors and himself and when he experiments it is with a hypothesis or a set of hypotheses which have to be proved.

There is still another reason for the demand that pupils become discoverers rather than absorbers of knowledge. This is to be found in the fear of indoctrination through handing out what is called 'knowledge fixed-in-advance.' Hence the pupil is to be constantly confronted with problems since the only knowledge which becomes enduring is that resulting from his own quest. Thinking and the discovery of knowledge thus become 'creative acts' which in turn contribute to the pupil's growth. Learning ceases to be the acquisition and becomes the discovery of knowledge to suit the particular situation in which the pupil finds himself or the problem he has to solve.

Underlying this movement is the critical attitude toward everything traditional in education and a faith that the latest is always the best. Traditional education, it is asserted, was passive; the pupil sat patiently at his desk while the teacher poured ready-made information into his unwilling mind. Traditional education did not develop the thinking powers. The traditional curriculum ignored the 'needs, urges, drives, and interests' of the pupil, was remote from the realities about him, did not train him to deal with 'life situations' and did not develop his creative abilities. Those who survived the prison walls of school, who became good and intelligent citizens and who even developed creative powers, did so in spite of their mis-education. The school must now devote itself to creative arts, creative music, creative writing, and creative building of new social orders. The French emphasis on *répétition, assimilation, et création* is, according to this theory, completely fallacious and unsound. Psychologically every individual has an urge to express himself; it is the business of the school to encourage this urge, even though the pupil has nothing to express. In no other way can an integrated personality be developed. To thwart self-expression by a program fixed-in-advance is to thwart the integration of personality and to perpetuate inhibitions, obsessions, and complexes.

And thus the next stage in the development of current theories is reached. No obstacles in the form of definite aims and purposes or of subjects must be placed in the way of the child's growth lest that growth be thwarted by the suppression of native drives, urges, needs, and interests. The tradition of education with its formal curriculum and 'subject-matter laid-out-to-be-learned' failed because it set up such obstacles. It failed for another reason; it was too intellectualistic; it sought to train the mind and failed to educate the whole person because it ignored the emotions which play such an important part in the development of attitudes. The teacher must now be not merely a psychologist but also a mental hygienist if the school is not to produce a host of misfits and mis-educated individuals. Hence instruction must concern itself with the unconscious and even the subconscious as well as with the conscious determinants of the thinking process. It is no longer the mind that is to be educated but the whole organism. Starting with an attack on 'intellectualistic' education and stressing the part played by the emotions the latter-day theorists, without realizing it, are promoting the retreat from reason.

Two ends are to be served by the new education. The first is to cultivate ability to solve the problems and issues arising out of pressing 'life situations.' The second is to develop an integrated personality. The first objective is to be achieved by what is called a 'face to face confrontation' with the environment; the second by giving free play to the urge of the whole organism for creative activity. The duty of the school is to promote the happiness of the individual which comes from the proper adjustment to all the pressures and demands of life and from direct and personal experiencing and purposing. The traditional obstacles to the development of an integrated personality have been a fixed curriculum divided into compartments known as subjects. The whole organism is affected by a whole and not a compartmentalized environment. The school must be an experiencing institution with an integrated curriculum in which elements of what used to be called subjects are drawn upon as they are needed. The traditional school was formal in its aims, formal in its methods, and formal in its organization. Form and formalism must be discarded; their place is to be taken by an integrated curriculum or what is coming to be more widely known as 'general education,' which should deal with all the major functions of human living. For subjects there are substituted 'experiences' which make for esthetic living, social living, healthy living, vocational living, and so on.

It will no doubt be objected that this description of current tendencies is overdrawn. That it does not apply to any one particular school is readily admitted; that each school seeks to interpret the tendencies in its own way is equally true. When a few years ago, the eight-year experiment was undertaken whereby thirty secondary schools, public and private, were permitted to organize their work in their own way on the understanding that their graduates would be admitted to colleges on their records, an analysis of their programs revealed that they were embarking on twenty-six different plans—which rendered the task of evaluation rather onerous if not impossible.

The tendencies are, of course, rooted in the principle that 'education is life and not a preparation for life,' a principle which is sound but for school purposes requires much closer analysis than it has received. Since no one has seriously taken the trouble to discover what aspects of life should be selected for purposes of school education, 'schools no longer bound education' and their activities are directed to the 'teeming life of the community, the State and the nation.' The new tendencies have their appeal, further, because they promise immediate returns in understanding and action; they are the educational analogies of the get-rich-quick notion.

Another explanation may be found in still another direction —the American tradition of having no traditions. It is interesting that tendencies similar to those described are found in countries without a strong social or cultural tradition or in countries where, as in Italy, Soviet Russia, and Germany, there is an effort to make a complete break with the past; in England, France, and the Scandinavian nations the new theories have their advocates but only a small body of followers. The rootlessness of American culture has been noted by many American writers. 'Ideas,' wrote Santayana, 'are abandoned in virtue of a mere change of feeling.' Van Wyck Brooks, in one of his critical essays, has dealt with the 'superficiality of rootlessness.' Rootlessness is the theme of Bromfield's *The Man Who Had Everything;* it appears again in Louis Adamic's *Grandsons.* One of the best characterizations of American education is that given by T. S. Stribling in *These Bars of Flesh:* 'American education,' he writes, 'is like a man who continuously builds himself new homes and never lives in one. He perishes running here and there with his stones and his new blueprints.'

This rootlessness has always left the door open for changes and adaptations in education. To rootlessness must be added the rapid tempo of change in the past generation, and to both of these the experimentalism which has affected all aspects of culture, not only in this country but everywhere else. The United States has undertaken a formidable task in attempting to provide an education to everybody on equal terms; the efforts have in too many cases resulted in failure; the failure has been attributed to the tradition of the so-called academic curriculum, and subjects rather than the poor preparation of teachers have been attacked; since the old curriculum has failed, new subjects or new integrations are being tried out—the teachers remain pretty much the same and their deficiencies are made up by more attractive textbooks. The venture into the new is justified on the ground that 'education is life.' There is, further, no real guidance from psychologists, who, having surrendered the mind as beyond definition, are busy developing a number of competing and conflicting theories. The American public still retains its faith if not in education at least in schooling and is willing to tolerate experimentation just as it welcomes every other new sensation. Under these conditions it is not surprising that experimentalism runs riot.

The educator will maintain that in embarking on experimentalism he is following the lead and methods of the sciences. Paradoxically enough the group sponsoring the new theories is the group most strongly arrayed against those who in the last thirty years have laid the foundations for a science of education. The experimentalism that characterizes the current trends in education is not, however, analogous to experimentalism in science. It is more similar to that in literature and art.

In its emphasis on functionalism it has some affinities with architecture. It has its parallels in the current novel which seeks to explore the hidden springs of thought and behavior, and to deal with the immediate and particular rather than with the universal and the permanent. But the closest analogies are found in music and art. An educational theory which aims at growth with nothing-fixed-in-advance is not in its organization and results unlike atonality in music. In the field of art its nearest analogies are to be found in surrealism and in Dadaism; one could even find some similarities between 'college' and the 'integrated curriculum.' Like the modernist composer and modernist artist, the modernist educator starts off with a diatribe against the traditional. He refuses to believe that the modernist in art or in music has normally had a training first in the classics of his field. He would dismiss as unsound pedagogy the story that Picasso once tore up the canvas of a 'creative' student in his atelier with the words 'To paint like Picasso you must first learn to draw.' The only criterion acceptable to the new educator is not unlike that prevalent among certain art and music critics— 'Has the pupil fulfilled to his own satisfaction the task which he has undertaken?' The emphasis again is on 'the how' and not 'the what.' Education thus has its counterparts in such current remarks as 'The music in itself was not much but it was played beautifully' or 'Of course the picture is beyond me but look at the technique' or 'The play was no good but the acting was superb.' As in other fields there has been a transition in education from classicism to romanticism to expressionism. And, finally, as in modernist music which always seems to require an enlarged orchestra and the use of every possible sound-making device that was ever created, the modern educator never has enough equipment or materials or he looks for them outside the school, so that 'the community, the State, and the nation' become his workshop.

There is, of course, another trend which merges into those preceding it: the effort to use the schools to build a new social order—for the educator, like the creative artist in art and music, does not feel he can keep aloof from the current political scene. At present there still seems to be some indecision as to whether education will become a 'Fantasia of the Unconscious' or will help to build a 'Brave New World.' In any case experimentalism is rampant. As in contemporary art and music, some contribution may survive to enrich the permanent stream. Undoubtedly much that is called traditional in education is not adapted to the vast hordes now crowding into high schools and colleges; undoubtedly many of the criticisms leveled against traditional education merit consideration. One point can be insisted upon, however: educational salvation will not come either by discarding content as traditional or by substituting the new as the best. A successful education cannot be expected from recipes and panaceas; a successful education can only be looked for as teachers become masters of what they teach, recognize the relation of what they teach to the society in which they teach, and have a sympathetic understanding of those whom they teach. Unfortunately, while buildings, equipment, textbooks, modern methods, and new curricula have been made the subjects of propaganda for the support of education, little, very little, has been done to 'sell' teachers to the American public. Before that can be done the American public needs to become more aware of what is sold to it under the guise of progress in education.

EDUCATION VS. WESTERN CIVILIZATION

By Walter Lippmann

IT was once the custom in the great universities to propound
a series of theses which, as Cotton Mather put it, the student
had to 'defend manfully.' I should like to revive this custom
by propounding a thesis about the state of education in this
troubled age.

The thesis which I venture to submit to you is as follows:

That during the past forty or fifty years those who are responsible for education have progressively removed from the curriculum of studies the Western culture which produced the modern democratic state;

That the schools and colleges have, therefore, been sending
out into the world men who no longer understand the creative
principle of the society in which they must live;

That, deprived of their cultural tradition, the newly educated
Western men no longer possess in the form and substance of
their own minds and spirits, the ideas, the premises, the ration-
ale, the logic, the method, the values or the deposited wisdom
which are the genius of the development of Western civilization;

That the prevailing education is destined, if it continues, to
destroy Western civilization and is in fact destroying it;

That our civilization cannot effectively be maintained where
it still flourishes, or be restored where it has been crushed, without the revival of the central, continuous, and perennial culture
of the Western world;

And that, therefore, what is now required in the modern
educational system is not the expansion of its facilities or the

An address delivered under the auspices of Phi Beta Kappa at the annual
meeting of the American Association for the Advancement of Science, Irvine
Auditorium, University of Pennsylvania, 29 December 1940. From *The American Scholar,* Spring 1941. By permission of the author and publisher.

specific reform of its curriculum and administration but a thorough reconsideration of its underlying assumptions and of its purposes.

I realize quite well that this thesis constitutes a sweeping indictment of modern education. But I believe that the indictment is justified and that there is a prima facie case for entertaining this indictment.

Universal and compulsory modern education was established by the emancipated democracies during the nineteenth century. 'No other sure foundation can be devised,' said Thomas Jefferson, 'for the preservation of freedom and happiness.' Yet as a matter of fact during the twentieth century the generations trained in these schools have either abandoned their liberties or they have not known, until the last desperate moment, how to defend them. The schools were to make men free. They have been in operation for some sixty or seventy years and what was expected of them they have not done. The plain fact is that the graduates of the modern schools are the actors in the catastrophe which has befallen our civilization. Those who are responsible for modern education—for its controlling philosophy—are answerable for the results.

They have determined the formation of the mind and education of modern men. As the tragic events unfold they cannot evade their responsibility by talking about the crimes and follies of politicians, businessmen, labor leaders, lawyers, editors, and generals. They have conducted the schools and colleges and they have educated the politicians, businessmen, labor leaders, lawyers, editors, and generals. What is more they have educated the educators.

They have had money, lots of it, fine buildings, big appropriations, great endowments, and the implicit faith of the people that the school was the foundation of democracy. If the results are bad, and indubitably they are, on what ground can any of us who are in any way responsible for education disclaim our responsibility or decline to undertake a profound searching of our own consciences and a deep re-examination of our philosophy?

The institutions of the Western world were formed by men who learned to regard themselves as inviolable persons because they were rational and free. They meant by rational that they were capable of comprehending the moral order of the universe and their place in this moral order. They meant when they regarded themselves as free that within that order they had a personal moral responsibility to perform their duties and to exercise their corresponding rights. From this conception of the unity of mankind in a rational order the Western world has derived its conception of law—which is that all men and all communities of men and all authority among men are subject to law, and that the character of all particular laws is to be judged by whether they conform to or violate, approach or depart from the rational order of the universe and of man's nature. From this conception of law was derived the idea of constitutional government and of the consent of the governed and of civil liberty. Upon this conception of law our own institutions were founded.

This, in barest outline, is the specific outlook of Western men. This, we may say, is the structure of the Western spirit. This is the formation which distinguishes it. The studies and the disciplines which support and form this spiritual outlook and habit are the creative cultural tradition of Europe and the Americas. In this tradition our world was made. By this tradition it must live. Without this tradition our world, like a tree cut off from its roots in the soil, must die and be replaced by alien and barbarous things.

It is necessary today in a discussion of this sort to define and identify what we mean when we speak of Western culture. This is in itself ominous evidence of what the official historian of Harvard University has called 'the greatest educational crime of the century against American youth,—depriving him of his classical heritage.' For there will be many, the victims of this educational crime, who will deny that there is such a thing as Western culture.

Yet the historic fact is that the institutions we cherish—and now know we must defend against the most determined and efficient attack ever organized against them—are the products of a culture which, as Gilson put it, is essentially the culture of Greece, inherited from the Greeks by the Romans, transfused by the Fathers of the Church with the religious teachings of Christianity, and progressively enlarged by countless numbers of artists, writers, scientists, and philosophers from the beginning of the Middle Ages up to the first third of the nineteenth century.

The men who wrote the American Constitution and the Bill of Rights were educated in schools and colleges in which the classic works of this culture were the substance of the curriculum. In these schools the transmission of this culture was held to be the end and aim of education.

Modern education, however, is based on a denial that it is necessary or useful or desirable for the schools and colleges to continue to transmit from generation to generation the religious and classical culture of the Western world. It is, therefore, much easier to say what modern education rejects than to find out what modern education teaches. Modern education rejects and excludes from the curriculum of necessary studies the whole religious tradition of the West. It abandons and neglects as no longer necessary the study of the whole classical heritage of the great works of great men.

Thus there is an enormous vacuum where until a few decades ago there was the substance of education. And with what is that vacuum filled: it is filled with the elective, eclectic, the specialized, the accidental, and incidental improvisations and spontaneous curiosities of teachers and students. There is no common faith, no common body of principle, no common body of knowledge, no common moral and intellectual discipline. Yet the graduates of these modern schools are expected to form a civilized community. They are expected to govern themselves. They are expected to have a social conscience. They are expected to arrive by discussion at common purposes. When one realizes that they have no common culture is it astounding that they have no common purpose? That they worship false gods? That only in war do they unite? That in the fierce struggle for existence they are tearing Western society to pieces? They are the graduates of an educational system in which, though attendance is compulsory, the choice of the subject matter of education is left to the imagination of college presidents, trustees and professors, or even to the whims of the pupils themselves. We have established a system of education in which we insist that while everyone must be educated, yet there is nothing in particular that an educated man must know.

For it is said that since the invention of the steam engine we live in a new era, an era so radically different from all preceding ages that the cultural tradition is no longer relevant, is in fact misleading. I submit to you that this is a rationalization, that this is a pretended reason for the educational void which we now call education. The real reason, I venture to suggest, is that we reject the religious and classical heritage, first, because to master it requires more effort than we are willing to compel ourselves to make, and, second, because it creates issues that are too deep and too contentious to be faced with equanimity. We have abolished the old curriculum because we are afraid of it, afraid to face any longer in a modern democratic society the severe discipline and the deep, disconcerting issues of the nature of the universe, and of man's place in it and of his destiny.

I recognize the practical difficulties and the political danger of raising these questions and I shall not offer you a quick and easy remedy. For the present discussion all I am concerned with is that we should begin to recognize the situation as it really is and that we should begin to search our hearts and consciences.

We must confess, I submit, that modern education has renounced the idea that the pupil must learn to understand himself, his fellow men, and the world in which he is to live as bound together in an order which transcends his immediate needs and his present desires. As a result the modern school has become bound to conceive the world as a place where the child, when he grows up, must compete with other individuals in a struggle for existence. And so the education of his reason and of his will must be designed primarily to facilitate his career.

By separating education from the classical religious tradition the school cannot train the pupil to look upon himself as an inviolable person because he is made in the image of God. These very words, though they are the noblest words in our language, now sound archaic. The school cannot look upon society as a brotherhood arising out of a conviction that men are made in a common image. The teacher has no subject matter that even pretends to deal with the elementary and universal issues of human destiny. The graduate of the modern school knows only by accident and by hearsay whatever wisdom mankind has come to in regard to the nature of men and their destiny.

For the vital core of the civilized tradition of the West is by definition excluded from the curriculum of the modern, secular, democratic school. The school must sink, therefore, into being a mere training ground for personal careers. Its object must then be to equip individual careerists and not to form fully civilized men. The utility of the schools must then be measured by their success in equipping specialists for successful rivalry in the pursuit of their separate vocations. Their cultural ideal must then be to equip the individual to deal practically with immediate and discrete difficulties, to find by trial and error immediately workable and temporarily satisfactory expedients.

For if more than this were attempted the democratic secular school would have to regard the pupil as having in him not merely an ambition but a transcendent relationship that must regulate his ambition. The schools would have to regard science as the progressive discovery of this order in the universe. They would have to cultivate Western tradition and transmit it to the young, proving to them that this tradition is no mere record of the obsolete fallacies of the dead but that it is a deposit of living wisdom.

But the emancipated democracies have renounced the idea that the purpose of education is to transmit the Western culture. Thus there is a cultural vacuum, and this cultural vacuum was bond to produce, in fact it has produced, progressive disorder. For the more men have become separated from the spiritual heritage which binds them together, the more has education become egoist, careerist, specialist, and asocial.

In abandoning the classical religious culture of the West the schools have ceased to affirm the central principle of the Western philosophy of life—that man's reason is the ruler of his appetites. They have reduced reason to the role of servant to man's appetites. The working philosophy of the emancipated democracies is, as a celebrated modern psychologist has put it, that 'the instinctive impulses determine the *end* of all activities . . . and the most highly developed mind *is but* the instrument by which those impulses seek their satisfaction.'

The logic of this conception of the human reason must lead progressively to a system of education which sharpens the acquisitive and domineering and possessive instincts. And in so far as the instincts, rather than reason, determine the ends of our activity the end of all activity must become the accumulation of power over men in the pursuit of the possession of things. So when parents and taxpayers in a democracy ask whether education is useful for life they tend by and large to mean by useful that which equips the pupil for a career which will bring him money and place and power.

The reduction of reason to an instrument of each man's personal career must mean also that education is emptied of its content. For what the careerist has to be taught are the data that he may need in order to succeed. Thus all subjects of study are in principle of equal value. There are no subjects which all men belonging to the same civilization need to study. In the realms of knowledge the student elects those subjects which will presumably equip him for success in his career; for the student there is then no such thing as a general order of knowledge which he is to possess in order that it may regulate his specialty.

And just as the personal ambition of the student rather than social tradition determines what the student shall learn, so the inquiry and the research of the scholar becomes more and more disconnected from any general and regulating body of knowledge.

It is this specialized and fundamentally disordered development of knowledge which has turned so much of man's science into the means of his own destruction. For as reason is regarded as no more than the instrument of men's desires, applied science inflates enormously the power of men's desires. Since reason is not the ruler of these desires, the power which science places in men's hands is ungoverned.

Quickly it becomes ungovernable. Science is the product of intelligence. But if the function of the intelligence is to be the instrument of the acquisitive, the possessive and the domineering impulses, then these impulses, so strong by nature, must become infinitely stronger when they are equipped with all the resources of man's intelligence.

That is why men today are appalled by the discovery that when modern man fights he is the most destructive animal ever known on this planet; that when he is acquisitive he is the most cunning and efficient; that when he dominates the weak he has engines of oppression and of calculated cruelty and deception no antique devil could have imagined.

And, at last, education founded on the secular image of man must destroy knowledge itself. For if its purpose is to train the intelligence of specialists in order that by trial and error they may find a satisfying solution of particular difficulties, then each situation and each problem has to be examined as a novelty. This is supposed to be 'scientific.' But in fact it is a denial of that very principle which has made possible the growth of science.

For what enables men to know more than their ancestors is that they start with a knowledge of what their ancestors have already learned. They are able to do advanced experiments which increase knowledge because they do not have to repeat the elementary experiments. It is tradition which brings them to the point where advanced experimentation is possible. This is the meaning of tradition. This is why a society can be progressive only if it conserves its tradition.

The notion that every problem can be studied as such with an open and empty mind, without preconception, without knowing what has already been learned about it, must condemn men to a chronic childishness. For no man, and no generation of men, is capable of inventing for itself the arts and sciences of a high civilization. No one, and no one generation, is capable of rediscovering all the truths men need, of developing sufficient knowledge by applying a mere intelligence, no matter how acute, to mere observation, no matter how accurate. The men of any generation, as Bernard of Chartres put it, are like dwarfs seated on the shoulders of giants. If we are to 'see more things than the ancients and things more distant' it is 'due neither to the sharpness of our sight nor the greatness of our stature' but 'simply because they have lent us their own.'

For individuals do not have the time, the opportunity or the energy to make all the experiments and to discern all the significance that have gone into the making of the whole heritage of civilization. In developing knowledge men must collaborate with their ancestors. Otherwise they must begin, not where their ancestors arrived but where their ancestors began. If they exclude the tradition of the past from the curricula of the schools they make it necessary for each generation to repeat the errors rather than to benefit by the successes of its predecessors.

Having cut him off from the tradition of the past, modern secular education has isolated the individual. It has made him a careerist—without social connection—who must make his way—without benefit of man's wisdom—through a struggle in which there is no principle of order. This is the uprooted and incoherent modern 'free man' that Mr. Bertrand Russell has so poignantly described, the man who sees

surrounding the narrow raft illumined by the flickering light of human comradeship, the dark ocean on whose rolling waves we toss for a brief hour; from the great night without, a chill blast breaks in upon our refuge; all the loneliness of humanity amid hostile forces is concentrated upon the individual soul, which must struggle alone, with what of courage it can command, against the whole weight of the universe that cares nothing for its hopes and fears.

This is what the free man, in reality merely the freed and uprooted and dispossessed man, has become. But he is not the stoic that Mr. Russell would have him be. To 'struggle alone' is more than the freed man can bear to do. And so he gives up his freedom and surrenders his priceless heritage, unable as he is constituted to overcome his insoluble personal difficulties and to endure his awful isolation.

PLEA FOR AN AGE MOVEMENT

By Ralph Barton Perry

> King David and King Solomon
>   Led merry, merry lives,
> With many, many lady friends
>   And many, many wives;
> But when old age crept over them—
>   With many, many qualms,
> King Solomon wrote the Proverbs
>   And King David wrote the Psalms.

I READ this selection from an unknown poet to set the key for my remarks. I need not say that I claim neither the wisdom of Solomon, nor the sweet singing of David. But I find that as the years roll by I devote less and less time to doing things and more and more time to advising other people to do them. I assume that you are having the same experience, and that you will not think it out of place if I give less place to merriment, and more to what might be called 'Reflections on Senescence.'

We have heard a good deal recently about the 'youth movement' and I think it's about time we started an 'age movement.' There was a time when old men held a good position in the world. I need not remind an audience of classical scholars that a Roman named Cicero devoted a work called *De Senectute* to this topic. I haven't the Latin handy. The translation runs as follows:

> Intelligence, and reflection, and judgment, reside in old men, and if there had been none of them, no state could exist at all. (XIX)
>
> Old age, especially an honored old age, has so great authority, that this is of more value than all the pleasures of youth. (XVII)

The theory was that although we had slowed down physically, and although our arteries had hardened a bit, and although our

From *Plea for an Age Movement* by Ralph Barton Perry, published by Vanguard Press, New York. By permission of the author and publisher.

wind was short except for talking, and although we had lost something of our sex appeal, we had more than made up for it. We were supposed to have laid by stores of wisdom so that we could offer sound advice. Our very disabilities were supposed to have given us a long view of things, and a certain elevation above passion and action.

We were supposed to dwell in the realm of ideas, and to survey all of history, so that we could speak profoundly when we condescended to advise our inferiors. We were supposed thus to be qualified to be the rulers of our wives, the mentors of our children, and the elder statesmen of the realm.

Recently we have fallen to an all-time low. We are retired at an early age from business and the professions. We are hustled by our juniors in politics. And as to the armed services, we hear it said on every side that what they need is young officers. The Joffres and Hindenburgs are regarded as accidents. The success of the Germans is attributed to the youth of their officers, the failure of the French to the age of theirs.

The most striking evidence of the downfall of the aged is to be found in the domestic circle. The authority of the father was first broken by the mother, and the children poured through the breach. The last remnant of paternal authority was the period in which the father was an ogre, who came home at the end of the day to deal with major offenses, and who could be invoked by the mother as a threat during his absence. Although he was no longer magistrate he was at least executioner.

But even this role disappeared when domestic criminology was modernized, and the child's insubordination was regarded as a personality problem to be solved by love, hygiene, and psychoanalysis. The father, knowing neither physiology nor Freud, and having been denied all natural affection in order to serve as the big stick, now played no part whatever in the civil order of the home. As head of the family he went definitely out, along with such ideas as naughtiness, punishment, discipline and obedience. He remained, of course, as bread winner, choreman, and studhorse, but these functions carried no prestige. The mother, who had conspired with the children to break down the authority of the father, lived to regret it. She suffered from the same age disability as the father and she was more continuously exposed to its consequences. The outcome was that both parents found themselves on the defensive.

Children now learned the facts of life almost at birth, and parents could no longer deny their ultimate responsibility. They were overtaken with a sense of conscious guilt and spent their domestic life apologizing to their children for having brought them into existence and for having endowed them with all their less endearing traits.

The institution of the school was originally created in order that the young might learn from the old, who had when young learned from their elders. The idea was that the infant was a vegetable, the small child an animal, the adult a human being, and the aged adult a wise human being with a touch of deity. On this theory the individual learned from a superior who had something to give.

Progressive education (though just why progressive is not clear) reversed all this. The child being a genius and the adult a fossil, nobody taught anybody anything. The child unfolded in accordance with his own creative impulses and the adult provided the tools and conveniences. Meanwhile as the child grew to manhood he himself gradually fossilized until he became a dodo in his own right.

Something of the same sort happened in the field of so-called higher education. It was once supposed that the professor derived authority from his years, from his knowledge, and from his learning. This authority began to disappear as soon as the idea got abroad that there was no such thing as knowledge and that learning embraced only the obsolete litter of the dead past.

Learning went out with the attic when the mind, like the house, became functional. So professors changed their tone, and began to use the subjunctive and interrogative instead of the indicative and affirmative. They presented so-called facts and tentative opinions and anxiously awaited the verdict of their students, promising when the verdict was unfavorable, to do better next time. They sought the guidance of 'undergraduate opinion,' deterred only by the fear of seeming to offer guidance. The students, meanwhile, tolerated the aged professor for reasons of humanity, but deprecated his large salary, encouraged his early retirement, and transferred their allegiance to the younger instructors who, being young themselves, could be counted upon to understand the young, and who, not having yet lived, could be counted upon to be in touch with the life of the times—or with the life of the times to come.

There is an application of all this to the present situation in the world at large. The young having ceased to respect their elders have banded together and become a sort of social class or political party, under their own leaders. Their opinions and sentiments are treated as touchstones of policy.

Those who are old enough to remember several wars are supposed on that account to be disqualified from judgment about this one. Those whose judgment is respected, those who are supposed to know what war is, are those who have never experienced war and who have even forgotten their history. They tell us, for example, that wars never settle anything, and they are supposed to know. The elders being rejected from military service for physical reasons, may not offer counsel lest they be suspected of a sadistic desire to sacrifice the young.

Such, in brief outline, is the story of the fall of age from its once high eminence. We have taken it. We have with pathetic eagerness tried to please our juniors and do whatever they would like to have us do, hoping to find some role, however humble, in a world of youth. But where does modesty get us? It is my mature opinion, discredited no doubt by its maturity, that it gets us nowhere. We are victims of the fallacy now known as appeasement. The more we try to please the more our opponents raise their demands. Whereas once we were feared enough to provoke rebellion, we are rapidly approaching a position in which we shall inspire only contempt. If by this procedure we could excuse ourselves and evade responsibility, that would be something.

But it hasn't worked that way. The children to whom we deferred turn upon us and say, 'Why did you spoil us?' The students to whose opinions we have modestly deferred now turn upon us and say, 'Why didn't you make us take the courses that were good for us? Why didn't you give us your solutions of the problems of life so that we would have some anchorage and landmark in a world of change?' So it appears that we are going to be blamed anyway; and if so, I say let us also enjoy the rank, the prerogatives, the esteem, and the authority.

This is a serious matter. The vital statisticians tell us that the average age of living Americans is rapidly rising. In other words, at the same time that there is an increasing number of old men in the world there is less use for them; at the same time that people live longer there is a more rapid turnover and depreciation. Either the majority of mankind are going to be kept in idleness, or liquidated; or we have got to change our ideas of the value of age.

Now I admit that it isn't easy to regain an ascendancy once lost. But let us begin by starting an age movement. Let us band together and not allow our force to be weakened by division. I do not mean that we should associate exclusively with one another. That has, as a matter of fact, been one of the sources of our weakness. We have acquired a sense of social inferiority until we hesitate to intrude upon the circles of youth, lest our accent, our manners or our clothes betray a trace of obsolescence. No, let us mingle freely with the young, with an air of confidence in ourselves and of social adequacy. With a little courage we shall in the end be accepted. But at the same time let us feel a sense of moral solidarity and encourage one another by example and by mutual understanding.

There is one idea that will, I think, carry us a long way, if we can only get it accepted. We must distinguish between deadness and length of life. After all, we don't say that a youth of eighteen is less alive than an infant of three weeks; though he is much older. Some individuals are born dead and remain dead. Some individuals are born with a low degree of vitality and grow more alive with the years.

Between physical birth and physical death there is no fixed point at which men can be said to reach the maximum of liveliness. It behooves us, then, as elders to take the view that the course of years is a passage from less to greater vitality, from inertness to activity. We can prove the idea by applying it, so that it comes back in the end to what you and I are going to do with our years.

This is only a special application of a very general idea, which I think it is now time to proclaim. Every form and every stage of life has its own gifts, and its own pride. There is a pride of youth, and I would not have it one whit abated. But there is also a pride of age, which is ours if we will only affirm it. Let us leave off apologizing. The alternative is not boasting, which is only a compensation for self-distrust. But let us have confidence in our powers, and earn our own self-respect and the respect of others by asking much of ourselves. If we expect much of ourselves we shall rise to the high level of our own expectations.

For some time I have made it a matter of principle to let no occasion pass when I am on my feet without making some allusion to the present emergency. I suppose that none of us who read and think would doubt that this is the most serious crisis in our history since at the time of the American Revolution we resolved to be a free nation, and since at the time of the Civil War we resolved to be one nation.

Within the next few years it is to be decided whether or not this is going to be a world in which free nations can continue to exist. In that decision we shall play the major part, whether by action or by default. We have already committed ourselves through a government of our own choosing. It now remains for us to make good our commitment. We cannot go back without losing the respect of the world, and without losing our own respect. I grant that we are a divided nation, but I submit that if we go back we shall be more divided, as well as isolated and friendless. For the only thing that can unite us is that allegiance to our creed of freedom which bids us go forward.

Under present conditions there is, I think, only one thing for us as a nation to do, which is forget our internal jealousies, conflicts, and suspicions, and gather ourselves and our total resources into one mighty force pledged to the victory of freedom at home and abroad. The fundamental condition of that will to victory is that we should feel a healthy pride not only in ourselves, whether old or young, and of whatever condition, but a common pride in our common country and in our common cause.

THE ANCIENT CLASSICS
IN A MODERN DEMOCRACY

By Samuel Eliot Morison

'When Youth are told, that the Great Men whose Lives and Actions they read in History, spoke two of the best Languages that ever were, the most expressive, copious, beautiful; and that the finest Writings, the most correct Compositions, the most perfect Productions of human Wit and Wisdom, are in those Languages which have endured Ages, and will endure while there are Men; that no Translation can do them justice, or give the Pleasure found in Reading the Originals . . . they may be thereby made desirous of learning those Languages, and their Industry sharpen'd in the Acquisition of them . . .'—Benjamin Franklin's 'Proposals Relating to the Education of Youth,' 1749, in T. H. Montgomery, *History of the University of Pennsylvania*, p. 499.

'Classics, in spite of our friend Rush, I must think indispensable.'— John Adams to Thomas Jefferson, 16 July 1814. *Works*, x, 105.

STYLE, defined by Whitehead as 'an aesthetic sense, based on admiration for the direct attainment of a foreseen end, simply and without waste,' is above all things the mark of an educated man or woman; and never has there been found anything equal to the literature of Rome and Greece for inculcating that sense of *style* which is one of the best things you can acquire from education. Style, whether in art, literature, science, engineering, or business, has the same qualities, attainment and restraint. And style is not only the last acquirement of the educated mind; but the most useful. It pervades the whole being. The administrator with a sense of style hates sloppy ways of doing things. The engineer with a sense of style economizes his material, and erects structures that have intrinsic beauty through their perfect adap-

From *The Ancient Classics in a Modern Democracy*. Commencement Address Delivered at the College of Wooster, 12 June 1939. New York: Oxford University Press, 1939. By permission of the publisher.

tation to the function expected of them. The writer with a sense
of style uses not a word too few or too many, and employs the
right words in the right combination, to express his thought.
'Style,' says Whitehead, 'is the ultimate morality of mind.' A
democratic society not only needs style more than does any
other, but appreciates it more, as a rare quality.

It is often said that the classics are all very well for an aristocratic society, but are not to be cultivated in a democracy, because other things are more important for the average boy, and
because their acquisition marks off those so educated as a separate caste. Now, let us admit at once that other things are more
important nowadays for the average American, who will end his
formal education at the age of sixteen or eighteen. Latin Grammar is a *pons asinorum* for certain minds, more effective than
the Fifth Proposition of Euclid; many otherwise intelligent
young people can make nothing of it. But it seems to me a perverted logic to deny the classics to *some* because they are beyond
attainment for *all*. Yet that is what many progressive educators
today advocate. They would keep school studies so easy, so elementary, that no child in full possession of his faculties would
fail; and for the morons they make a laudable provision of special
classes, so that they won't go out in life with an inferiority complex, while providing nothing to challenge the admiration and
stimulate the ability of a gifted young person. This levelling
down is the inversion of true democracy, which implies a levelling up.

Thomas Jefferson never expected education to produce equality; on the contrary: 'It becomes expedient for the publick happiness,' he wrote, 'that those persons, whom nature hath endowed with genius and virtue should be rendered by a liberal
education worthy to receive, and able to guard the sacred deposit
of the rights and liberties of their fellow citizens; and that they
should be called to that charge without regard to wealth, birth
or other accidental condition or circumstance.' In other words,
Jefferson's educational object was to create an intellectual aristocracy, by taking the most gifted young men, irrespective of
their parents' wealth or social station, and giving them a liberal
education—an education of which the classics and ancient his-

tory were the core—that they might be the more fit to govern America, to embellish her cities with beautiful buildings, and to write a national literature. And in all his schemes of education, the classics were central. He himself was an excellent classical scholar. At the age of fifty-six, when Vice-President of the United States, he wrote 'to read the Latin and Greek authors in their original, is a sublime luxury . . . I thank on my knees, Him who directed my early education, for having put into my possession this rich source of delight; and I would not exchange it for anything which I could then have acquired, and have not since acquired.' A young man who visited Jefferson at Monticello when the sage was eighty-two years old recorded that he rode horseback ten or twelve miles a day, spent several hours on the business of the University, and passed his leisure reading Greek. Jefferson is a good enough democrat for me!

Yet I am aware that if the classics are to be retained as an investment of democracy, some immediate return, some palpable dividend must be promised. If thus valued, the classics ask for no more than a fair comparison with rival subjects. Is it not a generous estimate to assume that less than five per cent of the boys and girls who are now learning algebra in school will ever find any 'use' for it? French is as much a dead language for the average high-school graduate as Latin. He will never hear it spoken or read a page of it again; but let us waive that, and apply the practical test to the ancient languages and literatures.

In several different ways, Latin and Greek are superb instruments for developing the human intellect. Latin is so concise, and the words so packed with meaning, that it cannot even be translated into another language with equal brevity. That is why the study of Latin helps one to write clear, concise, forceful English prose. And Greek is the most magnificent instrument so far invented for the precise expression of complicated thought, by the human mind. It combines simplicity with flexibility and sensitiveness—the qualities attained in the best English poetry. Both languages are organic, not slipshod like the uninflected modern languages, where so much depends on idiom, or the order of words. A Greek poem, or a passage of good Latin prose, is articulated, functional, and inevitable, like the steel skeleton of a skyscraper; everything is there that is structurally necessary, though the Alexandrian pedants might have spared us those pesky accents! One who has mastered Latin grammar can forget his vocabulary, yet see by inspection just where every word fits in a Latin sentence. This logical quality of the ancient languages is such that the very act of translation is an intellectual discipline of the highest order, helping one to counteract the tendency of English to gain emphasis by mere repetition, and to check the sloppiness in which writers not educated in the classical tradition, like Charles Dickens and Gertrude Stein, are prone to indulge. Just as musical theory and counterpoint enable a musician to compose melodies, concertos, and symphonies out of his national folk-song; so Latin and Greek enable an American to organize the common speech of his countryside into enduring literature. Of this I have an example that will surprise you. It was Ernest L. Thayer, one who took A's and B's in his classics course, a graduate *magna cum laude* of my own university, who wrote that classic on the great American game, 'Casey at the Bat'!

Latin, Greek, and Mathematics are instruments unrivalled by anything invented in twenty centuries of educational experience for the training of youthful minds in accurate and original thought. The analysis involved in translating Latin or Greek into English provides an unconscious training in logic. If in after life your job be to think, four years or more of Latin is the best training you can possibly have. You are learning logic, the art of thinking, without knowing it. And the art of thinking is the key to creative work in science and statesmanship, as in philosophy.

For understanding the best English literature and modern European literature, the classics are vital. The ancient world was implicit in the writings of Dante, of Chaucer, of Montaigne, of Milton, and of Goethe, to name only a few. They cannot become explicit to us, unless we grasp in some measure the background of their thought. How wretched are those school texts of Milton, with every god and goddess and classical allusion annotated! If we cannot teach our pupils a little Greek and Roman mythology first, better give up Milton and Dryden, Keats and Shelley, and start English poetry with Walt Whitman.

For future scientists, the ancient languages are important not merely as a mental discipline, and as a means of recreation, but as the basis of all scientific terminology. After a man has made up his mind to choose a career in medicine, engineering, or applied science, it is usually too late to get a fundamental grounding in Latin. One result of engineers and scientists' neglecting the classics is a purely parrot-knowledge of their basic terminology, and a blatant misuse of it both in speech and writing. The style of the average American scientific paper nowadays is often so bad that even specialists in the writer's own field cannot tell what he is trying to say. Indeed, the only worse English to be found nowadays is written by those 'Progressive Educators' who have done their best to kill the classics, and who write dissertations on high-school plumbing in a jargon that may best be described as Pedagese English.

Again, the ancient classics are of use as an introduction to the social sciences, and a running interpretation of them. They open a window to your mind from these times to other times, and from this place to all other places. The Roman Empire is a bottle-neck through which the vintage of the past has flowed into modern life. To comprehend in some manner the mentality of Rome is the key to medieval and modern history; and in ancient history you will find many of the current questions of today threshed out in a clean-cut fashion that will help you to comprehend your own age. What a terrible warning Thucydides gives of the consequences of war and power politics and demagogery! And it will enable you to get under the skin of American history, too. The fathers of our Revolution, the framers of our federal and state constitutions, and the great Senators (note the term) of the nineteenth century were steeped in Roman and Greek History. Antique liberty was a phrase often on their lips, and ever in their hearts. They were closer to the ancients in spirit, Americans as they were, than we are to them. Those men, the founders of our Republic, seemed to know what they were doing, and where they were going, whilst 'The *merely modern* man never knows what he is about.' Our forefathers were not *merely modern,* even in their own day. Behind them, in the backs of their minds, and before them as a goal there was always the supreme achievement of Judaea in religion, the supreme achievement of Hellas in the good life, and the supreme achievement of Rome in statecraft. They knew what they wanted, in terms of the attainable. Most of our present leaders don't know what they want, except that they want very much to get in power if they are out, or stay in power if they are in.

No generation of Americans has ever accomplished so much of permanent good for this country as the generation of 1770. Thirty years saw independence won, a colonial policy—the Northwest Ordinance—worked out, the gateways to the West opened, state constitutions adopted, the Federal Constitution drafted and ratified, federal government placed in successful operation on a scale hitherto unknown, the war debt liquidated, American credit placed higher than that of most European countries, the bases of American foreign policy laid, and finally, a peaceful revolution (the election of Jefferson) effected by the ballot. No American can look back upon the achievements of that generation without pride; and, when we contemplate the mess the world is in today, we can look back not only with pride but with wonder at those men who pledged to the cause of Independence their lives, their fortunes, and their sacred honor. Where did they acquire the political maturity that enabled them to perform so admirably these almost superhuman tasks? Partly, no doubt, from the experience in self-government that they had enjoyed as part of the great nation whose sovereign we have just been entertaining. That nation had a long tradition in self-government, from which we benefited and the ripe experience of which went into our constitutions, our bills of rights, and our political tolerance. Yet, partly, the achievement of our heroic age must be ascribed to the fact that America was a Christian nation, that far from regarding the State as the be-all and end-all of political existence, an entity that could do no wrong, its interest was the supreme good; our founders believed that citizens individually were responsible to God for the acts of the state, that righteousness exalteth a people, and sin is a reproach to any nation. And partly, too, the amazing success of the young republic was due to the classical training of her leaders. A majority of the signers of the Declaration of Independ-

ence and of the framers of the Federal Constitution were classi-
cally trained college men; and most of the remainder had studied in school more classics than most Americans nowadays
learn in college. Our Revolutionary leaders were *not* fitted for
responsibility by courses in civics, sociology, and psychology. It
was by Plutarch's Lives, the orations of Cicero and Demosthenes,
and by Thucydides that the young men of the 1760's learned the
wisdom to deal with other men and with great events in the
1770's and 80's. American Revolutionary leaders both North
and South, the Adamses and Trumbulls of New England; Hamilton, John Jay, the Morrises and Stocktons of the Middle States;
Madison, Mason, and Jefferson of Virginia; and the Rutledges
and Pinckneys of South Carolina were prepared for their unexpected tasks by a study of classical culture that broadened their
mental horizon, sharpened their intellectual powers, stressed
virtus and promoted *areté,* the civic qualities appropriate to a
Republican. It was of Greek virtue and Roman honor that
Thomas Jefferson was thinking when he concluded the immortal
Declaration, 'We mutually pledge to each other our lives, our
fortunes, and our sacred honor.'

And so I come to this final argument, that we need the classics
because our country needs the intelligent leadership and disinterested service of an intellectual aristocracy—not a plutocracy,
or a hereditary ruling caste, but an intellectual élite recruited
from the people, as Thomas Jefferson said, 'without regard to
wealth, birth or other accidental condition or circumstance.' It
was just such an aristocracy of brains and character that won the
United States independence, that secured by diplomacy our free
access to the West, that founded our colleges and universities.
And it was want of it, in business and in politics, that led to the
great depression. Now that we all know the slough in which
materialism, unrestrained greed, and untrained leaders brought
us, it would seem logical to return to the noble American tradition of Thomas Jefferson: an intellectual aristocracy in a political democracy. And it is only in liberal arts colleges like Wooster
that men and women can be trained to serve the Republic. If
educated people simply drift with the current, reject responsibility, and adopt the protective coloring of the mediocre, Amer-

ica may well drift into the gangster state of present Italy and Germany, the negation of democracy, or, at best, will aim no higher than to provide for the needs and desires of the average. Without a leadership imbued with the standards of antique virtue, and trained in the classical tradition, our civilization threatens to become the mirror where the common man contemplates himself, and is pleased at the sight of his imperfections. Now, the only base on which to rebuild an intellectual aristocracy, so far as I can see, is the civilization of the ancient world, working hand in hand with Christianity, as it has done in the universities of Europe and America these six hundred years. Let the autocracies of today, Russia and Germany, if they wish, delude themselves into believing that they can establish a completely new order divorced from the past, unblessed by God. We, I trust, are wiser than they, and will hold fast to that which is good. To cut loose from our classical background would be to sever the main nerve of modern civilization, to attenuate and impoverish life, and to leave some of man's noblest capacities unused.

NOAH WEBSTER, SCHOOLMASTER
TO AMERICA

By Harry R. Warfel

ON his seventieth birthday, October 16, 1828, Noah Webster lifted his eyes from the last proof sheet of the scholarly Introduction to his Dictionary. Slowly he wiped the ink from the quill, laid it down, and methodically capped the inkwell. His moist eyes blinked. He turned to his wife and colleague, caught her hands. Together they knelt by the desk and prayed tremblingly in giving thanks to God for His providence in sustaining them through their long labor. Since June 4, 1800, when the project was first publicly announced, Webster had dandled his book on his knee to the tune of a public lullaby of jeers, insults, and misrepresentation. Every opprobrious epithet in the vocabularies of calumny and abuse had been showered upon him. Undeterred by it, he had completed single-handed America's first monumental work of scholarship. *An American Dictionary of the English Language* was immediately acclaimed, in England and Germany as well as in America, the best work of its kind ever prepared.

Today, *Webster* and *dictionary* are synonymous terms in our language. No tribute can surpass this one.

Yet, curiously enough, although the name *Webster* is on the tip of every person's tongue who wants to consult that indispensable reference book, the dictionary, few can give the lexicographer's first name. When asked the question, the average informed person looks blank a moment, then hesitantly ventures, 'Daniel, I guess.' Thus Noah Webster, who eminently deserves a niche in the Hall of Fame, not only is not memorialized in that

From *Noah Webster: Schoolmaster to America,* 1936. By permission of the author and The Macmillan Company, publishers.

pantheon, but has suffered an even worse fate: his name has coalesced with that of the famous orator and statesman who was not even his kinsman.

Like Dr. Samuel Johnson, whose dictionary lost ground as Webster's gained, Noah Webster was more than a 'harmless drudge,' a writer of definitions. Before announcing his dictionary at the age of forty-two, Noah Webster had become the pivotal figure in American education and literature. As the author of a series of primary school textbooks and as the expounder of a nationalistic theory of education, he had become the young nation's first schoolmaster. As an itinerant propagandist for a Constitution, he had done more than any other single individual to prepare a climate of opinion in which a Constitutional Convention could be successful. As a clear-visioned economist, a humanitarian, a magazine and newspaper editor, a historical scholar, and a moralist, he ceaselessly drove his pen in furthering the best interests of his country. Although he completed the Dictionary in 1828, he never surrendered work until death called him in his eighty-fifth year, May 28, 1843.

Something of the many-sided intellectual quality of Benjamin Franklin reappeared in Webster. Both possessed astonishing versatility and delved into every area of knowledge, leaving marks of influence in almost every field of activity developed in their times. It was fitting that Franklin, in his old age, befriended the young schoolmaster and tutored him in simplified spelling. But Webster, unlike Franklin, did not permanently slough off the iron mantle of New England Calvinism. And Webster never sought or obtained high political position. Essentially a scholar and publicist, Webster wielded his pen as a weapon in the perennial warfare against social injustice, scientific error, mental torpor, and national instability. Early in life he called himself The Prompter, the man who sits behind the scenes to correct errors or assist the memory.

Webster became our greatest schoolmaster. He passed successively from the desk of a Connecticut log schoolhouse to the lecture platform, to the editorial chair, and finally to the home library table as the arbiter of every English-speaking reader's and writer's diction. His schoolbooks were carried from the hills of New England across the Alleghenies; his were among the first books printed in every new settlement. Across the prairies and over the Rocky Mountains his carefully marshaled columns of words marched like warriors against the ignorance that tended to disrupt the primitive society of thinly spread and localized culture of America. Dialect variation disappeared from our writing and spelling, and to his blue-backed Speller, of which nearly one hundred million copies were sold before it went out of general use, America owes its remarkable uniformity of language. No other book, the Bible excepted, has strained so many heads, or done so much good. It taught millions to read, and not one to sin. And today the monolithic 'Webster' on every schoolteacher's desk, on the reference tables of libraries, at the elbow of the justice, and on the study table of the scholar, bears silent testimony to Noah Webster's enduring labors and superb genius.

Patient, indefatigable laborer for American cultural advancement that Webster was, he yet never won the warm personal sympathy of his countrymen. A pugnaciousness in propagating his own strongly phrased ideas, a gesture many people considered egotistic, rendered Webster socially unattractive. His tall, spare, Yankee form stiffened under opposition. His massive head grew rigidly upright in an inflexible ambition to do good. The mountainous forehead, crowned with a forest of autumn-tinted hair, sloped to beetling crags of eyebrows. Deep set, as in a cave, small gray eyes flashed lightning warnings of intense mental operations. A massive square jaw and a jutting nose persuaded opponents that here was one endowed by nature to hold his own against any and all opposition. The narrow, thin line of lips held taut a tongue ever ready to castigate error. 'If my name is a terror to evildoers,' Webster once wrote, 'mention it.' In this respect, too, Webster was the typical schoolmaster, the man who is more concerned to have lessons well learned than to secure the adulation of shirking, fawning ignorance.

II

Dictionaries belong in a class with sacred writings, so venerated are these volumes. Disputes are settled by an appeal to their pronouncements, and fanatic devotees guard the honor

and extol the virtues of their bible. Paper wars have been fought
over the comparative merits of Johnson and Webster, and of
Worcester and Webster. Words are dynamite, and a dictionary
seems to be concentrated nitroglycerin, if one can judge by its
innate combustible power to stir controversy.

Dictionaries developed slowly through the ages. On ancient
Latin manuscripts scholars placed annotations opposite hard or
unusual words. Later these 'hard words' were collected into a
glossarium or *glossary.* The first use of the word *dictionary* occurs
in Sir Thomas Elyot's *Dictionarius Liber* or *Dictionarium*
(1538), the literal meaning being 'a repertory of *dictiones* or
sayings.' Until the end of the sixteenth century such collections
were of Latin, or another foreign language, words with English
equivalents. About 1600 Robert Cawdrey prepared *The Table
Alphabeticall of Hard Words,* in which the proper spelling and
meaning of some three thousand learned terms were given.
Henry Cockeram extended *The English Dictionarie* (1623) to
include ordinary words and a key to allusions. In the first part,
the 'hard words,' he defined 'bubulcitate' as 'to cry like a cowboy,' 'collocuplicate' as 'to enrich,' and 'garble' as 'to clense
things from dust.' The 'ordinary words' were explained by hard
equivalents; for example, 'youthful babbling' meant 'juvenile
inaniloquence,' and 'abound' meant 'exuperate.'

Nathaniel Bailey in 1721 included all words in his *Universal
Etymological English Dictionary,* ten editions of which appeared
in twenty-one years. This was the 'golden age' of literature and
dictionary-making, for it was the desire 'to fix the language by
means of a Standard Dictionary, which should register the proper
sense and use of every word and phrase, from which no polite
writer henceforth would be expected to deviate.' In 1747 Dr.
Samuel Johnson contracted with a syndicate of London booksellers to produce the desired Standard Dictionary within the
space of three years for the sum of fifteen hundred guineas. Eight
years and considerably more money were required by Johnson
and his assistants to produce two massive folios, each seventeen
inches long and three and one half inches thick. It was a marvelous achievement. Johnson elevated lexicography into a department of literature. His work had two innovations: it in-

cluded illustrative quotations drawn from the best English writers, and it delicately discriminated the senses of words . . .

Dr. Johnson's work was not allowed to stand alone. Dr. William Kenrick in 1773, William Perry in 1775, Thomas Sheridan in 1780, and John Walker in 1791 brought out competing tomes. Walker became the supreme arbiter of elegant pronunciation, just as Johnson was pre-eminent in definition and illustration. Walker's affectations won a great following in America, so much so that Webster was frequently advised to alter the pronunciation of his Spelling Book and Dictionary to conform to Walker's. A sample of the stage directions supplied in great quantity in Walker's book may illustrate why Webster went into a towering rage every time the Englishman's name was mentioned. Under *Garden* Walker wrote: 'When the *a* in this and similar words is preceded by G or K, polite speakers interpose a sound like the consonant *y* which coalesces with both, and gives a mellowness to the sound; thus *a Garden* pronounced in this manner is nearly similar to the two words *Egg* and *Yarden* united into *eggyarden,* and *a Guard* is almost like *eggyard.*'

Imagine the horror with which Anglophiles would receive a book in which the nasal twang of New England was recommended as a better pronunciation than Walker's. Imagine the consternation, too, that would greet the announcement of a spelling-book-maker that he would outdo the learned cham of literature, Samuel Johnson, LL.D., F.R.S. Imagine an American teaching the English anything!

On June 4, 1800, Webster inserted into the New Haven newspapers this indirect statement:

Mr. Webster of this city, we understand, is engaged in completing the system for the instruction of youth, which he began in the year 1783. He has in hand a Dictionary of the American Language, a work long since projected, but which other occupations have delayed till this time. The plan contemplated extends to a small Dictionary for schools, one for the counting-house, and a large one for men of science. The first is nearly ready for the press—the second and third will require the labor of some years.

It is found that a work of this kind is absolutely necessary, on account of considerable differences between the American and English language.

New circumstances, new modes of life, new laws, new ideas of various kinds give rise to new words, and have already made many material differences between the language of England and America. Some new words are introduced in America, and many more new significations are annexed to words, which it is necessary to explain. It is probable that the alterations in the tenures of land and the ecclesiastical polity, will dismiss from the language in America several hundred words which belong in the English. The differences in the language of the two countries will continue to multiply, and render it necessary that we should have *Dictionaries* of the *American language.*

Three small American dictionaries had already appeared. The first had come in 1798 from the hands of Samuel Johnson, Jr. Caleb Alexander, the Boston textbook maker, had published the *Columbian Dictionary* in 1800, and Johnson and John Elliott brought out a revised edition of the first one in 1800. Webster approved 'the general plan and execution' of this work in a testimonial. All of them were intended 'for schools and polite readers,' and each promised that 'no *low* or indecent word will therefore be found in the work.' This quotation is from the preface of William Woodbridge's *A Key to the English Language* (Middletown, Connecticut, 1801). Certainly dictionary-making must have seemed a harmless, yet useful, occupation to these men. And to Webster. But the American press thought otherwise.

Be it remembered that in 1800 Webster was the butt of ridicule for his political and medical opinions and his theories of language. The announcement of the forthcoming American Dictionary speeded the tempo of criticism . . .

Although busy with many other books and with duties as state legislator, it was to the Dictionary that Webster gave his best thought and time. Here was to be made his great gift to scholarship, a solemn declaration to this effect having given caution, if not sloth, to his progress. Where the sciolist rushed to print after a few weeks' work in compilation, Webster scanned his sources, tested etymologies, and investigated definitions. Much was wrong. Johnson, whose Dictionary had been pilfered by all successors, did not know law, medicine, and the physical sciences. His imitators knew less. Rapidly growing vocabularies in chemistry, botany, and geology found no record in the new books. Webster set out to correct this deficiency.

What qualifications did Webster have for this task of writing a new Dictionary? First, he had literally taken all knowledge for his province, and he had achieved distinction as a contributor in many departments. In law he had not only practiced before local courts, but he had served as legislator and judge, and had written essays and treatises of great merit. In medicine he had made adequate studies for the preparation of the first history of epidemic diseases. His experiments in science had kept him abreast of the developments in these fields, and his writings on scientific subjects in *Elements of Useful Knowledge* had required a complete survey of these topics. A keen student of economics, he had written wise words on American business conditions. As a New Englander he was by inheritance a theologian, a field in which he would soon distinguish himself. As an itinerant lecturer, schoolmaster, and editor, Webster had touched life at many points; his clear, gray eye missed nothing.

Second, Webster may have been 'a born definer of words,' as James A. H. Murray has said, but the fact is that he was called by his experiences to exercise and develop whatever native talent he possessed. In every essay he took time to define carefully each important term he used; by this means, as in his distinction between impost and excise, he carried conviction. Fuzzy thinking, arising from fuzzy terminology, had led astray legislators and people alike. From the day he entered the newspaper scribbling contest in 1782 until his death, he was writing definitions to help his countrymen think straight. The meaning of meaning was no idle pun with him; it was fundamental that the root meaning of every word be fixed and that all additional radiations be understood in relation to that root.

Third, Webster delighted in etymological investigations; language study afforded pleasureful relaxation from other duties. He kept his Greek fresh by comparing the English translation of the New Testament with the original. He learned German, Danish, and Anglo-Saxon in order to trace the relationship between English and its ancestors. Horne Tooke had mentioned Celtic as the parent of English; Webster studied Welsh and

Old Irish. Old Testament study required Hebrew; Webster studied it. Hebrew had connections with Persian; Webster studied it. Soon there were twenty alphabets from as many languages which had revealed their secrets to him. It became a fascinating study to put together the same root word, like *father,* in its twenty different language forms. Startling results appeared. Consonants and vowels squirmed like protean snakes. *Father* doesn't look much like Latin *pater,* or Greek *patar,* or German *vater.* But see: the *p* became *v* in German, and this in turn became *f* in English. Try it again: *foot,* Latin *pes, pedis,* German *fusz.* It doesn't always happen the same way, but still that Latin (and Greek) *p* became *f.* The labials, the letters formed by the lips, had a sequence in the progression of time. How about that *t* in *pater* becoming *th* in *father.* Let's try again: *tres* becomes *three.* And so on. There were many exceptions, many anomalous cases. But the consonants seemed to shift from language to language with a fixed regularity. Likewise the vowels, though here the problem was more complicated. It all resolved itself to consonantal groups or radicals, Webster decided, and on this ground he proceeded. It all may seem like a game, but Webster found in it guidance through the daedalian maze of etymology.

Fourth, Webster's curiosity was fortified by the scholar's greatest asset, patience. Unhurriedly, imperturbably he pushed forward on a work which would take, he thought, three to five years. Only his awareness that one is not immortal allowed him to stop investigating at the end of twenty years and bring his work to a temporary close.

By comparison with all other earlier lexicographers, even Johnson, Webster stands out the superior in qualifications. But he was wont to be touchy, arrogant if you will, about his unique possession of truth; he turned friends against him and forever alienated others by constantly harping on his discoveries and on the errors of Johnson. It was Webster's old trick, this of denouncing all competitors, but it served to get him nowhere. The more he talked, the more his opponents ridiculed him. The mocking screech of the charivari horsefiddle, scraped since 1783, continued its harassing music.

A Compendious Dictionary of the English Language, in which 'compendious' was defined as 'short, brief, concise, summary,' came from Sidney Babcock's press, New Haven, on February 11, 1806, price $1.50. The title page boasted the addition of five thousand words to the 'best English compends,' and further promised, 'for the benefit of the merchant, the student, and the traveller,' tables of moneys, tables of weights and measures, the divisions of times among all nations, an official list of post-offices in the United States, the number of inhabitants in the United States and the value of exports, and 'new and interesting chronological tables of remarkable events and discoveries.' This was not the first time a dictionary was made the bearer of useful information of this variety; but Webster's example caused other compilers to add similar encyclopedic material . . .

In December 1807, he published his second dictionary, an abridgment of the first, with the title, *A Dictionary of the English Language; compiled for the use of common schools in the United States.* In this book obsolete, improper or vulgar, and learned terms found no place, although words of everyday use in the home, factory, and farm were included. This collection of thirty thousand words and their brief definitions sold for a dollar a copy. In order to keep the price down, Webster gave John West, the Boston printer, the right to print an edition of three thousand copies in return for twenty-five copies. This book sold well, several editions being called for. But Webster's income from it, as from *A Compendious Dictionary,* was small.

On February 25, 1807, Webster mailed to all his friends and to bookstores throughout the country a circular letter, setting forth his aims, present achievement, and plans for completing the large dictionary. He asked the assistance of scholars and men of wealth, the former to give etymologies and the latter to contribute to his support during the coming years. All might help by extending the use of his schoolbooks. In England similar undertakings were supported by contributions; the plan was novel in America, and of course much ridicule was heaped on the ambitious scholar. Rufus King, John Jay, Oliver Wolcott, Chancellor James Kent, among others, sent Webster contributions, but not one of these encouraged Webster to look either for general support or public approbation. King wrote: 'I am sorry to remark that I am able to discover but little probability of your receiving adequate encouragement to continue to devote your time and talents to the important and laborious investigation in which, for so many years, you have been engaged. Neither learning, morals, nor wisdom seem any longer to be regarded as objects of public esteem and favour.' He followed these remarks with a gloomy description of American 'prejudice against learning.' Oliver Wolcott, then president of a bank in New York, wrote: 'I cannot encourage you to expect success.' These paralyzing statements came despite the fact that the circular contained an 'unqualified approbation of the design' by the faculties of Yale, Princeton, Dartmouth, Williams, and Middlebury colleges.

In his lexicographical creed, published in *The Panoplist* (July and August 1807), Webster wrote: 'The lexicographer's business is to search for truth, to proscribe error, and repress anomaly . . . The compilers of dictionaries should not be "dabblers in etymology," as many of them have been, but men of deep research and accurate philological knowledge . . . The lexicographer should not be misled by his habits, nor biased by the caprices of eminent men.' To this creed Webster remained faithful.

In 1807 Webster had mastered twelve languages. Steadily as grammars and dictionaries were made available, he penetrated the secrets of new languages or dialects. By 1813 he had learned twenty languages, seven of them being Asiatic or dialects of the Assyrian; these were: Chaldaic, Syriac, Arabic, Samaritan, Hebrew, Ethiopic, Persian, Irish (Hiberno Celtic), Armoric, Anglo-Saxon, German, Dutch, Swedish, Danish, Greek, Latin, Italian, Spanish, French, Russian, and, of course, English. Later he added Portuguese, Welsh, Gothic, and the early dialects of English and German.

As soon as *A Compendious Dictionary* was printed, Webster set to work to complete his unabridged dictionary. His ambition was merely to correct such errors as had escaped former compilers and to supply such new terms as had sprung from modern improvements in science. But in searching the originals of English words, he found that the field of etymology had been very imperfectly explored. One discovery succeeding another, his curiosity was excited to persevere in the pursuit. Finding no safe clue through the labyrinth, he wrote, 'I adopted a new plan of investigating, that of examining and comparing the primary elements, articulations or consonants of words in twenty different languages.' After completing two letters of the alphabet, he turned aside to prepare a synopsis of the affinities of these twenty languages.

The Synopsis, which never reached publication, required ten years of steady labor. Webster's method of work was this: On a semicircular table, two feet wide, he placed his books; beginning at the right end of the table, he would thumb grammars and dictionaries while tracing a given word through the twenty languages, making notes of his discoveries. Many times a day did he follow this pendulum movement. At four o'clock Mrs. Webster brought him fruit or nuts and cake, a signal that the lexicographer should remove his eyeglasses and relax. Much caustic humor has been printed about Webster's Synopsis, the manuscript of which is in the New York Public Library. An examination of it reveals a mine of philological lore. It is not mere guesswork, but a serious effort to bring together words whose form might throw light on the affinities of languages and on the primary sense in each word. In this work may be seen Webster's knowledge of the interchange of consonants, since he based all his work on consonantal radicals. Often, too, his groupings indicate a clear understanding of the vexed problems of the relationships of vowels. The results of his research were embodied in his Dictionary; the Synopsis gave him the great grasp necessary for defining well the basic meaning of each word . . .

In November 1821, Webster had reached the letter H in his Dictionary, and he correctly estimated that he would complete the whole work in four years. Since America afforded inadequate materials, he and his son William set out in June 1824 for France and England . . .

One statement of Webster shows with what excitement he, then in his sixty-seventh year with a heart that cut didoes and an over-active mind that often caused nightmares, reached the end of his gigantic research task: 'I finished writing my dictionary in January 1825, at my lodgings in Cambridge, England. When I had come to the last word, I was seized with a trembling, which made it somewhat difficult to hold my pen steady for writing. The cause seems to have been the thought that I might not then live to finish the work, or the thought that I was so near the end of my labors. But I summoned strength to finish the last word, and then walking about the room a few minutes, I recovered.'

If the European visit brought to successful completion the manuscript of the Dictionary, it failed to achieve two other goals. Just as Webster had sought to bring a degree of unanimity in the treatment of yellow fever, so he had gone to England to achieve a similar agreement in the matter of the pronunciation of the English language. Letters were dispatched to Oxford University with an invitation to members of that institution to meet with Lee and other Cambridge professors and Webster, in an effort to adjust the principles of spelling and pronunciation so that both nations might follow a single code. Here might have been founded an international academy, but Oxford, unable to endure the cool effrontery of a Yankee schoolmaster's dabbling in affairs peculiarly English, did not reply . . .

After a short tour through southern England, Webster and William embarked on May 8 on the ship *Hudson*. They landed at New York on June 18 and the next day were in New Haven.

For a time it appeared that Webster would have to finance the publication of the Dictionary himself. Early in 1826, however, Sherman Converse assumed responsibility for the publication, although Webster endorsed a large note. A prospectus was issued on March 3. James Madison, atoning for his failure to lend a friendly hand in 1809, immediately commended Webster's 'learned research, elaborate discrimination, and taste for careful definition.' In Boston, however, the old animus was revived by *The American Quarterly Review*, which denounced Webster's heretical notions about Johnson and Walker. Converse procured oriental types from Germany, but 'everything else about the work,' Webster told Madison proudly, 'will be *American*.'

When the two bulky quarto volumes of *An American Dictionary of the English Language* were delivered to the subscribers, a swelling chorus of praise greeted the ears of the seventy-year-old lexicographer. Praised were the successful etymological researches, the great vocabulary of 70,000 words (12,000 more than Todd's Johnson), the perspicuity of the definitions, and the careful distinctions in the many radiations of meaning in common words. There remained no doubt about Webster's success in surpassing Johnson. Here and there, however, especially among the English booksellers and publishers supporting Todd and Richardson, efforts were made to minimize the work. But E. H. Barker, an English scholar, promptly applied for permission to bring out an English edition. This appeared in parts between 1830 and 1832. Soon Webster became the standard in England, as he had become the standard in America by the adoption of the Dictionary in the halls of Congress and in the various American courts of law.

The nationalism of Webster appeared not only on the title page in the adjective 'American' but also at length in the Preface. 'The chief glory of a nation,' Webster quoted Dr. Johnson, 'arises from its authors'; and just as Johnson had expressed a wish to give celebrity to Bacon, Hooker, Milton, and Boyle, so Webster had the same ambition to honor Franklin, Washington, Adams, Madison, Jay, Kent, Irving, and others. 'It is with pride and satisfaction,' Webster wrote, 'that I can place them, as authorities, on the same page with those of Boyle, Hooker, Milton, Dryden, Addison.' Webster also declared that 'the genuine English idiom is as well preserved by the unmixed English of this country, as it is by the best English writers . . . I may go further and affirm with truth that our country has produced some of the best models of composition. The style of President [Samuel S.] Smith [of Princeton]; of the authors of the Federalist; . . . of Chancellor [James] Kent; the prose of Mr. [Joel] Barlow; of Dr. William [Ellery] Channing; of Washington Irving; of the legal decisions of the Supreme Court of the United States; of the reports of legal decisions in some of the particular states; and many other writings; in purity, in elegance, and in technical precision, is equalled only by that of the best British authors, and surpased by that of no English compositions of a similar kind.' This statement was literally slapped in the teeth of those Britishers and American Anglophiles who were then echoing Sydney Smith's disparaging remarks about American culture. In concluding his Preface Webster wrote: 'It satisfies my mind that I have done all that my health, my talents, and my pecuniary means, would enable me to accomplish. I present it to my fellow citizens, not with frigid indifference, but with my ardent wishes for their improvement and happiness; and for the continued increase of the wealth, the learning, the moral and religious elevation of character, and the glory, of my country.'

The edition of 2500, at twenty dollars a set, moved quite rapidly, but Converse went bankrupt as a result of speculations, and the work became tied up in litigation. A new issue became impossible, and the market really remained unsupplied. Webster made very little profit from the work, his receipts prior to Converse's failure having been barely sufficient to pay the editorial assistants.

There is much that might be said about the 1828 Dictionary to explain its lasting qualities. In the final analysis the definitions can be said to have made it supreme in its own day. After all, a dictionary is designed to give word meanings; anything else is a gift from the author or publisher. Webster had included much encyclopedic material, and the latest large Webster, in continuing the tradition, has brought within one set of covers, a vast array of reference material. But fundamentally the definitions are most important. In this department Webster was supreme and unequalled.

To Webster the Dictionary was, next to the Bible, the great schoolbook. He wanted a copy placed on the desk of every schoolmaster where students might consult it freely. Like a lodestar it might guide youth, not only to accuracy, but also to correct thoughts on the fundamentals of religion and morality. Cautiously he labored to eliminate sectarian bias, but just as actively he wrote into his illustrations such sententious wisdom as his wide experience had given him.

Webster's Dictionary was a highly personalized volume, despite the great care with which he suppressed Johnsonian prejudice and animosity. None of his own writings was drawn on for illustrative examples, and, vain though he was said to be, he frequently expressed doubts about his etymologies, about his success in linking languages, and about the exact sense of a word. Only once did Webster insert the first person:

> Witness, *v.t.* To see or know by personal experience. I *witnessed* the ceremonies in New York, with which the ratification of the constitution was celebrated in 1788.

Yes, not only did Webster *witness* the procession in New York in 1788, he also *witnessed* the procession of English words in the process of formation from the time of the dispersion to 1828. And just as he described the 1788 parade, so he described with amazing accuracy, fullness, and discrimination the marshaled columns of English and American words. The completion of the Dictionary was the feat of a pre-eminent scholar who had not forgotten his days of schoolmastering, and who therefore continued to instruct his fellow citizens through the world's most important secular book.

VI

'The Pursuit of Happiness'

EACH of us inevitable,
Each of us limitless—each of us with his or her right upon
the earth,
Each of us allow'd the eternal purports of the earth,
Each of us here as divinely as any is here.

WALT WHITMAN, *Salut au Monde*, 1856

I RAISE a voice for far superber themes for poets and for art,
To exalt the present and the real,
To teach the average man the glory of his daily walk and
trade, . . .
For every man to see to it that he really do something, for
every woman too; . . .
And hold it no disgrace to take a hand . . .

WALT WHITMAN, *Song of the Exposition*, 1871

Do you see O my brothers and sisters?
It is not chaos or death—it is form, union, plan—it is eternal
life—it is Happiness.

WALT WHITMAN, *Song of Myself*, 1856

THE DEMOCRATIC SPIRIT IN ART

WHEN I pass to and fro, different latitudes, different seasons, beholding the crowds of the great cities, New York, Boston, Philadelphia, Cincinnati, Chicago, St. Louis, San Francisco, New Orleans, Baltimore—when I mix with these interminable swarms of alert, turbulent, good-natured, independent citizens, mechanics, clerks, young persons—at the idea of this mass of men, so fresh and free, so loving and so proud, a singular awe falls upon me. I feel, with dejection and amazement, that among our geniuses and talented writers or speakers, few or none have yet really spoken to this people, created a single image-making work for them, or absorb'd the central spirit and the idiosyncrasies which are theirs—and which, thus, in highest ranges, so far remain uncelebrated, unexpress'd . . .

America demands a poetry that is bold, modern, and all-surrounding and kosmical, as she is herself. It must in no respect ignore science or the modern, but inspire itself with science and the modern. It must bend its vision toward the future, more than to the past. Like America, it must extricate itself from even the greatest models of the past, and, while courteous to them, must have entire faith in itself, and the products of its own democratic spirit only. Like her, it must place in the van, and hold up at all hazards, the banner of the divine pride of man in himself (the radical foundation of the new religion) . . . Erect, inflated, and fully self-esteeming be the chant; and then America will listen with pleas'd ears.

WALT WHITMAN, *Democratic Vistas*, 1871

FOR WHAT?

By Sherwood Anderson

THE big German man came along the river bank to where I was lying on the brown grass at the river's edge. The book I had been reading was on the grass beside me. I had been gazing across the sluggish little river at the distant horizon.

I had hoped to spend the day working. There was a story I wanted to write. This was in a low flat country southwest of the city of Chicago. I had come there that morning by train with the others, Joe and George, and Jerry, the big German.

They all wanted to be painters. They were striving. The Sundays were very precious to the others and to me. We were all working during the week and looking forward to the week ends. There were certain canvases the other wanted to paint. If one of them could get a painting hung in the Chicago Art Institute, it might be a beginning.

We used to speak of it at the lunch hours during the week.

There was a certain story that had been in my mind for weeks, even months. We were all living about in little rooming houses. We were clerks. Jerry, the big German, had been a truck driver. Now he had a job as a shipping clerk in a cold storage warehouse.

I had tried time and again to write the particular story that was in my mind. I told the others about it. I didn't tell them the story. That would bring bad luck. I spoke instead of how I wanted the words and sentences to march.

'Like soldiers marching across a field,' I said.

'Like a plow turning up its ribbon of earth across a field.'

Fine phrases about work not done. There had been too much of that. You can kill any job so. Just keep talking about the

From *The Yale Review*, Summer 1941. By permission of Mrs. Sherwood Anderson.

great thing you are to do, some time in the future. That will kill it.

'Yes, and it is so also that paint should go on a canvas.'

This would be one of the others, one of the painters speaking.

There was this big talk, plenty of that, words, too many words. Sometimes, after the day's work, in the hot Chicago summers, we all got together to dine in some cheap place. There was a chop suey joint to which we went often, soft-footed, soft-voiced China-men trotting up and down. Chop suey and then a couple of bottles of beer each. We lingered long over that. Then a walk together along the lake front on the near North Side. There was a little strip of park up there facing the lake, a bathing beach; working men with wives and children came there to es-cape the heat, newspapers spread on the grass, whole families huddled together in the heat, even the moon, looking down, seeming to give forth heat.

We would be full of literary phrases, culled out of books. Some one of us had been reading Kipling.

'City of dreadful night,' he said.

Only Jerry, the big German, was a little different. He had a wife and children.

'What's it all about? Why do I want to paint? Why can't I be satisfied driving a truck and working in my warehouse?

'Going home at night to the wife and kids.

'What is it keeps stirring in a man, making him want to do something out of just himself?'

He grew profane. He would be describing a scene. He had come to the Chinese place from his warehouse across the Chi-cago River, this before the river was beautified, in the days of the old wooden bridges over the river.

He had stood for a time on one of the bridges, seeing a lake boat pass, lake sailors standing on the deck of the boat and look-ing up at him standing there above on the moving bridge, the curiously lovely chrysoprase color of the river, the gulls floating over the river.

He would begin speaking of all that, the beauty of the smoky sky over buildings off to the west. Sometimes he pounded with his fists on the table in the chop suey joint. A string of oaths flowed from his lips. Sometimes tears came into his eyes.

He was, to be sure, ridiculous. There was in him something I knew so well later in another friend, Tom Wolfe—a determination, half physical, all his big body in it, like a man striving to push his way through a stone wall.

Out into what?

He couldn't have said what any more than I could of my own hopes, my own passionate desires, of which I was always half ashamed.

To get it in some way down, something felt.

A man was too much in a cage—in some way trapped.

A man got himself trapped. All this business of making a living. There were Jerry and Joe, both married. They both had children.

Joe had been a farmer boy, on his father's farm, somewhere in Iowa. He had come to Chicago filled with hope.

He was like Jerry, the German. He wanted to paint.

'That's what I want.

'I want something.'

And why the hell did a man get married? They spoke of that. They weren't complaining of the particular women they had married. You knew they were both fond of their children.

A man got stuck on some dame. A man was made that way. When it got him, when it gripped him, he thought, he convinced himself, that in her, in that particular one, was the thing he sought.

Then the kids coming.

They trap you that way.

Joe speaking up. He wasn't as intense as Jerry. He said we couldn't blame them, the women, his own or any other man's woman.

How'd we know they weren't trapped too? They were wanting to be beautiful in some man's eyes, that was it. They had, Joe declared, as much right to want their thing as we had to want ours.

But what was it we were all wanting, the little group of us, there in that vast Chicago, who had in some way found each other?

Comradeship in hungers we couldn't express.

Anyway it wasn't really success. We knew that. We had got that far.

George said we ought to be skunks. 'A man should be a skunk,' he said. George wasn't married but had an old mother and father he was supporting. He was laying down a law he couldn't obey.

'So I'm a clerk, eh?

'And whose fault is it?

'Mine, I tell you.

'I ought to walk out on them, on everyone, let 'em go to hell.

'What I want is to wander up and down for a long time. Look and look.

'People think of it as a virtue, a man like me, sticking to a clerk's job, supporting my old father and mother, when it's just cowardice, that's all.

'If I had the courage to walk out on them, be a skunk.'

It was something he couldn't do. We all knew that . . .

By the river bank, on the Sunday afternoon, after a morning trying to write the story I had for weeks been trying to write, I had torn up what I had written. There were the pages of meaningless words, that refused to march, thrown into the sluggish river, floating slowly away.

White patches on a background of yellow sluggish river.

'Patience, patience.'

White clouds floating in a hot sky, over a distant cornfield.

'Oh, to hell with patience.'

How many men like me, over the world, everywhere, all over America, in big towns like Chicago and New York, small towns or farms.

Trying for it.

For what?

There was something beyond money to be made, fame got, a big name. I was already past thirty. There were the others, Joe, Jerry, and George, none of them any longer young.

The World War had not yet come. It was to scatter us, shatter us.

The big German, Jerry, came down to where I lay on my back on the dry grass by the sluggish stream. He had with him the canvas on which he had been working all day. Now it was growing late. At noon, when we had together eaten our lunches he had been hopeful.

'I think I'll get something. By the gods, I think I will.'

Now he sat beside me on the grass at the stream's edge. He had thrown his wet canvas aside. Across the stream from us we could see stretched away the vast cornfields.

The corn was ripening now. The stalks grew high, the long tips hanging down. Soon it would be corn cutting time.

It was a fat rich land—the Middle West. At noon Jerry, the German, son of a German immigrant, who had been a city man all his life, had suddenly begun talking.

He had been trying to paint the cornfield. For the time he had forgotten to be profane. We others had all come from farms or from country towns of the Middle West. He had said that he wanted to paint a cornfield in such a way that everyone looking at his painting would begin at once to think of the fatness and richness of all Middle Western America.

It would be something to give men new confidence in life. He had grown serious. He was the son of a German immigrant who had fled to America to escape military service. Germany believed in the army, in the brute power of arms, but he, Jerry, wanted by his painting to make people believe in the land.

I remember that, in his earnestness, he had shaken a big finger under our noses.

'You fellows, your fathers and grandfathers were born on the land. You can't see how rich it all is, how gloriously men might live here.'

He had spoken of his father, the immigrant, now an old man. We others couldn't understand how hard and meagre life had become for the peasants in all the European lands. We didn't know our own richness—what a foundation, the land, on which to build.

But he would show them, through the richness of the fields.

The skyscrapers in the cities, money piled in banks, men owning great factories, they were not the significant things.

The real significance was in the tall corn growing. There was the real American poetry.

He'd show them . . .

He sat beside me on the grass, by the stream. We sat a long time in silence. There was a grim look on his face, and I knew that he had failed as, earlier in the day, I had. I did not want to embarrass him by speaking. I stayed silent, occasionally looking up at him.

He sat staring at the sluggish stream and looking across the stream to where the cornfields began, and I thought I saw tears in his eyes.

He didn't want me to see.

Suddenly he jumped up. Profane words flew from his lips. He began to dance up and down on the canvas lying on the grass. I remember that the sun was going down over the tops of the tall cornstalks, and he shook his fists at it. He cursed the sun, the corn, himself. What was the use? He had wanted to say something he'd never be able to say—'I'm a shipping clerk in a lousy warehouse, and I'll always be just that, nothing else.' It was a child's rage in a grown man. He picked up the canvas on which he had been at work all day and threw it far out into the stream . . .

We were on our way to the suburban station where we would get our train into the city. All the others, Joe, George, and Jerry, had their painting traps, their easels, boxes of color, palettes. They had little canvas stools on which they sat while painting, and Joe and George carried the wet canvases they had done during the day.

We went along in silence. Joe and George ahead while I walked with Jerry. Did he want me to carry some of his traps?

'Oh, to hell with them, and you, too.'

He was in this grim mood. Fighting back something in himself. We went along a dusty road beside a wood and cut across a field in which tall weeds grew. We were getting near the station where we were to take the train.

Back to the city.

To our clerkships.

To his being a shipping clerk in his warehouse.

To little hot and cold Chicago flats where some of us had wives and children waiting.

To be fed, clothed, housed.

'A man can't just live in his children. He can't, I tell you.'

Something rebellious in all of us.

What is it a man wants, to be of some account in the world, in himself, in his own manhood?

The attempts to write, to paint—these efforts only a part of something we wanted.

All of us half knowing all our efforts would end in futility.

I am very sure the same thoughts were in all our minds that evening, in the field of tall weeds, in the half darkness, as we drew near the little prairie railroad station, the lights of the train already seen far off, across the flat prairies.

And then the final explosion from Jerry. He had suddenly put his painting traps down. He began to throw his tubes of paint about, hurling them into the tall weeds in the field.

'You get out of here, damn you. Go on about your business.'

He had thrown his easel, his stool, his paintbrushes. He stood there dancing among the tall weeds.

'Go on. Go away. I'll kill you if you don't.'

I moved away from him and joined the others on the platform by the station. It was still light enough to see the man out there in the field, where the tall weeds grew waist-high. He was still dancing with rage, his hands raised, no doubt still cursing his fate.

He was expressing something for us all. He was going through something we had all been through and before we died would all go through again and again.

And then the train came and we got silently aboard, but already we could see, happening, what I think we all knew would happen. We saw Jerry, that brusque, profane German already down on his knees among the weeds in the field.

We knew what he was doing, but, when our train arrived in the city and we separated at the station, Joe and George still clinging to the canvases they both knew were no good, when the others had gone I hung about the station.

I had been a farm boy, an American small-town boy like Joe and George. I was curious. Jerry, the big German, had spoken of the land. We had, all of us, been thinking of ourselves as rather special human beings, men with a right to that curious happiness that comes sometimes, fleetingly enough, with accomplishment.

Forgetting the millions like us on farms, holding minor jobs in cities.

What old Abe Lincoln meant when he spoke of 'the people.'

I was remembering bad years when I was a small-town boy, working about on farms, farmers working all through the year, from daylight until dark.

Big Jerry wanted to express something out of the American land.

Droughts coming, hailstorms destroying crops, disease among the cattle, often a long year's work come to nothing.

Something else remembered out of my own boyhood.

Springs coming, after such disastrous years, and the farmers near my own Middle Western town out again in their fields, again plowing the land.

A kind of deep patient heroism in millions of men, on the land, in cities, too.

The government pensioning men who went out to kill other men but no pensions for men who spent long lives raising food to feed men.

Killers become heroes, the millions of others never thinking of themselves as heroes . . .

There would be another train in an hour, and I wanted to see what I did see, keeping myself unseen, the arrival of Jerry, most of his painting traps again collected.

Knowing, as I did know, that on another week end he would be trying again.

AMERICAN PAINTING TODAY

By Forbes Watson

WHOEVER understands the art of a country is at least partially equipped to understand the people of that country. Indeed, there is some question whether a people can be understood, to any enlightened degree, by those who, however informed in other fields of its activities, are ignorant of its art. Ignorance of our art may explain why America is so often misjudged by natives and foreigners alike. Not to know its derivations leads to misreading. Our art has not evolved from a primitive base, but from a series of transplantings, from the multifarious roots imported by the immigrants who were our forefathers. It is the art of a people which, until comparatively recently, has looked to Europe for guidance in matters of learning. For a considerable number of years our scholars, philosophers, and scientists looked to Germany, our artists to France, and our writers to England. Ours is the art of a country which throughout its colonial, pioneering, and industrial rise remained an intellectual province of Europe, and it is only a few years since American art has become independently conscious of itself and American artists have become concerned primarily with America.

From Mrs. Trollope to the present time a popular thought about us has been that we have no taste. In several European countries I have heard us referred to as vulgarians and dollar-chasers. Yet our art tells the opposite story. Taste is of its essence. Our reputation for boastfulness is widespread, yet our art is the expression of a modest people. We are supposed to be without tradition, and certainly without respect for tradition.

Our art, on the contrary, suggests that our respect for tradition is almost too humble. From Copley to Hawthorne, from Thoreau to Max Weber, if we may skip from writers to painters, taste has predominated. We have no Rabelais in writing. Emerson, James, and Van Wyck Brooks more nearly hit our bull's eye. We have no Rubens in painting. The slightly discredited Whistler more nearly fits the pattern of our tradition . . .

I think that the simplest way to clarify the situation so that the amazing changes now in progress can be grasped, is to point out a few of the important differences between the opportunities that faced the American artist ten years ago and those which he enjoys today. No one will deny that painters cannot, so to speak, develop in mid-air. Yet some such miracle seems to have been expected of them both here and abroad not more than a short generation ago. It was believed in America that a lonely painter from Missouri could sit in his Paris studio busily devising theoretical combinations on canvas which were determinedly too esoteric for any other citizen of Missouri to read, and that by this expatriate process he could richly and warmly express not only his own genius but the genius of his country and his time.

Looking back today upon those lonely and distracted efforts we can smile if we wish to. Yet there was a kind of pathos and an aspiration in them. The hope was to escape from the provincialism to which one had been born and find heaven in pure and unadulterated theory. Why should one attempt to evolve a language of painting which the home folks would understand since from one's earliest efforts they had mocked and laughed? Why not resort to an expression reserved for the understanding of a small group of international sophisticates? Did they not constitute the world which appreciated and supported the artist? It was not the drugstore clerk back home who cared. It was that curiously dislocated group of Rumanians, Spaniards, English, and Americans whom one was forever running into in the cafés, many of them brilliant, all of them detached. The more detached the more superior to the realities. It became possible to imagine that Giotto would have been a better painter if he had set out to execute his frescoes in Santa Croce, for example, in a painting language which no other citizen of Florence could possibly read. At this point the wiser expatriates bought their tickets back to America. Such was the inevitable impasse to which the international dealer system, through its demands for the esoteric, was bringing painters and public alike. The system reached the utmost limits of its own complexities in the last fade gasps of the School of Paris.

Fifteen years ago America was the most paying branch of this system. No system is perfectly good or perfectly bad, and considering to what a degree snobbishness, intellectualization, and unhealthy preciousness had taken possession of the world of art, some astonishingly able inventions were produced by the painters who, if not in mid-air, were certainly far removed from life. The painting communicator produced his pictorial message. Bright middlemen invented a key to the puzzle. And the public swallowed. Literally what happened was that the artist's brainchild was conveyed to the dealer who, coached by Paris, spoke his piece with convincing ability to the buyer, and sent him happily on his way not knowing whether he carried under his arm a stick of dynamite or the last rose of summer. The important matter was to have the right name attached to the article. Then if impossible to understand, it still was not impossible to market. This mocking account does not greatly exaggerate what happened to public and artist alike in the Paris mid-air period, which enjoyed its second blooming in America during the ten years of Mardi Gras extravagance immediately preceding the great depression. No one quite touched earth, not even the bankers, who harbored the imposing moneys of the rich Paris painters and the fabulous accounts of the madly speculating dealers. What were the opportunities for the American artist in this fantastic situation? He saw that picture buying in New York was dominated by Paris dealer agents, who at every turn discouraged their American clientele from buying the work of the native artist.

The ultimate artificialities of the Paris picture exchange were made marketable in America because it was from Paris also that superb examples arrived of more than a century of great French painting. These gave a new splendor to even those American collections which also accepted at the dealer's face value the small and calculating fry who followed busily in their wake. By the time our period began, America had been treated to a quarter of a century of propaganda so astute and untiring that even minor talents, if quoted on the Paris picture bourse, could sell perverse and disingenuous work more easily on the American market than American major talents could sell sincere and able pictures. What chance had the native painter against such well-organized and far-reaching rivalry? The brave answer is that his chance lay in producing better paintings than those which were imported. But when he occasionally did, he found, instead of healthy encouragement, a public which was positively flabby in its extraordinary docility to even the most extreme commands from Paris . . .

With such difficulties facing the American artist in his efforts to dispose of his pictures how could he manage to live? He could teach. He could send his work to the various exhibitions of American art. These were numerous, but in only a few of them were remunerative prizes offered and effective sales made. Once in a while he could sell a picture, and he could devote his spare time to the necessary business of making a name, for he knew that without a name he could rarely sell his paintings, no matter how often they might be placed on public view. People who purchased pictures on the basis of quality alone and without regard to the fame of the artist were exceedingly rare. Even when an artist enjoyed exceptional good fortune, knew his way about, and was lucky in his sales it took time to make a name. At best it was a long and difficult road to economic independence, and the journey was successful for only a handful, comparatively speaking, of the painters who crowded the upward path. Although measured in terms of money the amount spent on American art by private and public buyers was large, its effect on the great body of American artists was small indeed. What might have happened if we had been blessed with braver buyers in search of quality, and with museum purchasing committees composed of men more professionally equipped can only be surmised. Suffice it to say that, although the market domination of the French was finally broken by a determined effort on the part of the American artist and although scores of reviewers wrote endless columns praising the home product, more fame was won by the Americans than profit . . .

The first three years of the depression were increasingly difficult for the American artists. Outwardly the usual activities appeared to be going on in the usual way. The large national exhibitions were repeated annually. The dealers bravely held their one-man and group shows, and the various art associations and other organizations which pride themselves on their periodic efforts to 'spread culture' valiantly continued their exhibition activities. Beneath these outward goings-on, however, was a growing sense, on the part of the artists, of the futility, at least from the material point of view, of much that was being done. If we consider the immense spread of interest in art that has taken possession of America during the twentieth century it is not surprising that the patience of some artists while waiting for this interest to strike home to them has become somewhat tattered. What with increased attendances at art schools, increased art classes in colleges, and the bounding abundance of sitting lectures and ambulatory talks in museums, about the only groups left out of our all-embracing system of discussing art are the little ones in baby carriages and the inmates of the blind asylums. And at any time I expect to run into a parade of baby carriages in the Metropolitan Museum led by a motherly docent teaching the babies to googoo Rembrandt and gaga Greco. No one can deny the breadth of our interest in art. Yet a few artists churlishly do question the depth of our interest. This important debate, if continued, will bring to the surface a national idiosyncrasy.

At some time in the history of American appreciation a great confusion arose between art and virtue. I am afraid that this confusion, although diluted, still exists. It is a rather fashionable virtue, supposed to accrue to all those having a passion for culture without effort on their part. When the ladies of the art association in one of our smaller cities or larger towns not to mention our great cities, talk about the number of exhibitions that they have held during the season, they frequently have an air of wanting to show the visiting stranger what a civilized town is theirs. They like it to be known that they exhibit 'important' examples of the work of all the better known painters, that they hold lectures by the leading critics, and that they have an art school of their own. If, after listening to the glowing account which more or less innocently is offered in proof of their own appreciation and goodwill toward art, one asks them how many paintings they have bought during the year, they are apt to look upon their questioner as a vulgar materialist. There is money in the town to pay for exhibitions, lectures, and monthly luncheons, and a rather inferior brand of art instruction, but, it turns out with disquieting frequency, there is no money to pay for pictures. I am sure that I am not exaggerating when I say that similar unacquisitive activities are carried on in hundreds of the smaller cities of the United States.

Dozens upon dozens of exhibitions are held throughout the country. They are supposed to reflect some mythical virtue on the part of the people who maintain these activities. At the same time, these good people remain beamingly immune to the truth that no artist can live unless he sells his work. At least, he has to find some other way of making money if he can't make it through his art. I have often wondered how people can look at so many pictures and resist the desire to own the paintings for which they claim such an intense interest. I have noticed that men do not have to be rich in order to join the golf club on which they have set their heart, and that a great many ladies unrelated either to Mr. Morgan or to Mr. Rockefeller finally acquire the fur coats upon which they have cast an ambitious eye. Following this reasoning I find it a little difficult to believe completely in the avowed enthusiasm which a great many well-to-do men and women claim for painting and sculpture, although the thought of buying painting and sculpture never appears to enter their heads. These vulgar thoughts invite suspicion of the profundity of that interest in art which produces countless exhibitions, teas, and luncheons but comparatively few sales, so few that in one year a single painter had forty pictures on exhibition in forty different large and small shows, and that during that time he received not a nibble for one of his moderately priced works. That same year the attendance at our large museums and at the dealers' galleries in New York went into the millions.

I am not citing these facts as depression facts, but as evidence of the curious self-righteousness which to a greater or lesser degree tends to render unfruitful the ever-growing interest in contemporary American art. The conditions which I have described at such length because they seem to me to have an important bearing on the development of art in the country, were characteristic of the decade of over-sized profits that led to the depression. That being true it requires no imagination to realize how non-resisting our widespread interest in art was to the forces of the depression. For years uninformed people have thought that what the government was doing in its employment of artists amounted to large-scale charity in behalf of inept painters and sculptors. People spoke of artists on relief as if their being on relief proved their inferiority. Nothing was further from the truth. Middle-aged painters who had earned an honorable living in the honorable practice of their profession, in some cases found themselves after the years 1930, '31, and '32 without funds. Younger painters, well up on the road to success, men and women of outstanding talent, were stopped dead in their tracks by the depression. Great numbers of unknown, still younger men and women of indubitable promise were suddenly forced out of their professions as artists, and, not to be melodramatic, there were plenty of painters whose work we all respect who did not have enough to eat . . .

I hope not to be misunderstood when I say that the depression was the greatest blessing that has come to American art. I say this with full recognition of the personal hardships and sorrows that it brought to many artists. On the other hand, had it not been for these very hardships it is doubtful if the government would have established—first, the Public Works of Art Project, and after that, the Section of Fine Arts formerly in the Treasury Department and now in the Federal Works Administration. But the Section of Fine Arts in the scope of its work is much more restricted than the broad-based artist relief program directed by Holger Cahill under the Works Progress Administration formerly headed by Harry Hopkins. Since these various government art programs are what primarily differentiate the period from 1933 to the present from all other periods in the history of American art, a few words should be devoted to their general make-up.

The Public Works of Art Project employed artists at craftsmen's wages. It divided the country into sixteen regions, and selected artists in each region in proportion to the number of artists who lived there. Each region had a chairman who, with the assistance of a volunteer committee, made a complete study of the economic circumstances of the artists in his territory. Under this system more than three thousand artists and craftsmen were employed for six months. The government came into possession of a staggering amount of work. Much of it was rubbish but a surprising amount of it was excellent. Secretary Morgenthau was so impressed by what had been accomplished that he invited Edward Bruce to establish a Section of Fine Arts in the Treasury Department for the purpose of decorating with the painting and sculpture our Federal buildings. The Supervising Architect's Office was in the Treasury Department. Now, like the Section of Fine Arts, it is in the Public Buildings Administration, Federal Works Agency.

Meanwhile Harry Hopkins broadened his program and invited Holger Cahill to extend the organization established by the Public Works of Art Project. A relief program which employed artists in the same way that they were employed under the first government project, but to a much larger extent, was established under the Works Progress Administration. It grew to immense proportions. It was not limited to the productions of professional artists. Teaching, the now celebrated Index of American Design, children's classes, community art centers, and other new fields were developed. Millions of dollars were spent for the relief of an immense variety of citizens working in the arts and the crafts, or associated with such work. This is not the time or the place to attempt to estimate the value of this astonishing experiment in social and art relief.

What we can definitely say about all the work that the various government departments have done in their individual and separate programs is that they completely transformed the national interest in art from something vaguely idealistic to something much more real. Before 1933, as I have said, we had a large groping, hungry public which looked to art as a means whereby its cultivation and outlook on life could be broadened. This was a public which, thanks to its idealistic optimism, did not realize the facts about the artist. Suddenly a country which generally speaking wanted to be tenderly cultivated without buying was transformed into a country which overnight became the largest purchaser of art in the making that the world has known.

If I dwell insistently on the question of the purchase of art, at least I do so without the slightest shame. For artists to grow to their highest possible point of achievement it is absolutely necessary that they should feel that they are needed by the community. While it is a pretty saying, and one common in the earlier part of this century, that if an artist sold his work before he was forty it was proof that he was a bad artist, it is not a healthy saying. It indicates a separation between the artist and the community which is not good for the artist. It connotes preciousness, and suggests too accurately our passion for the star system, in other words for the pursuit of names. Arnold Bennett used to say that art was supported by 'the passionate few,' and many have said that 'art is not purchased, it is sold.' The depression brought about a much healthier and simpler attitude . . .

It seems natural that as long as painting is limited to a comparatively small special class of men and women who are slightly removed from the affairs of common mortals, more encouragement is given to academic, archaistic, and reminiscent styles of painting. When, on the other hand, a mass of artists is at work from end to end of a great country there are sound reasons why art should become healthier in its being and more direct and simple in its expression. Such wide productivity acts like a bomb thrown at the luxury trade. No artificially stimulated, precious, and snobbish market could possibly absorb the normal amount of worth-while art that a genuine mass movement is certain to produce. If not consciously, at least unconsciously, the artists know this. They turn away from the luxury market understanding that their very productiveness is against its luxury principles. Decentralization sets in and regional non-luxury markets come into being.

As already suggested the change is not from black to white. But the process has set in. Following the good example of Cleveland more and more centers throughout the country are finding that the pursuit of unacquisitive culture is not the solution of the artists' problems. For this development, still slow, but broadly based, and rendered necessary if the great present-day movement in American art is to fructify, we owe a debt of gratitude to the government. If the government had been satisfied to direct its program exclusively from a Washington bureau nothing like this could have happened. It has always used local juries and local committees, thereby making the various communities realize that they were directly concerned with the selection of the art which they as taxpayers have purchased.

It is obvious that with artists at work in every state and with hundreds of communities purchasing painting and sculpture a much fresher and more stimulating relationship between the artist and the public is established than that which exists between the luxury trade in art and its comparatively limited lists of buyers. It is equally clear that the artist has found an extensive and much less sophisticated audience. I am sure that this audience is not one whit less sophisticated than that which the great mural painters of Italy addressed. Giotto, Piero, Masaccio, and the others, were able to portray simply and clearly. Yet they employed the medium of art with a profound meaning which only the initiated are able fully to appreciate. We have abundant proof in the art of the past that painting can be clear to the people and also profound. So let the precious be afraid, if they wish to, lest a mural in a small town post office be superficial because it is understandable. Let them hug their Dalis to their bosoms and shudder at the new order. It is not they who will stop it. They are already swallowed up in the old order.

NEBRASKA FOLKLORE

By B. A. Botkin

STORIES belong on the frontier, where story-telling whiles away lonely hours, solves problems, and projects heroic symbols. In this way folk tales—and for that matter folk songs—have double value, as fantasy and as history; in extending life they also reflect ways of living. Nebraska folklore is thus part of the history of the Middle Western frontier. Traditions themselves are migrants and settlers, and have a way of becoming adapted to changing circumstance; but whatever survives of this heritage of fantasy and faith is valid lore of the region to which it has been transplanted.

The very place names of Nebraska have their stories, rooted in local tradition. The most obvious of these names—like Trunk Butte and Saddle Butte—merely suggest the natural formations they label. Others tell of the finding of objects that marked the spot: thousands of buffalo and cattle skeletons at Bone Creek, a relic of an Indian burial at Broken Bow. Still others are mementoes of frontier encounters. At Sowbelly Canyon a rescue party came to the aid of a band of soldiers who had run out of rations while hard-pressed by Indians—even the dry salt bacon, which was all the rescuers had, must have tasted good to the soldiers. At Rawhide Creek a white man from a wagon train was tied to a tree and skinned alive because he had kept his vow to kill the first Indian he saw. Sowbelly and Rawhide bite the tongue and the imagination. But Weeping Water Creek is one of those specious misnomers that absurdly, if sweetly, testify to the white man's ignorance of the Indian's language. A confu-

From *Nebraska, A Guide to the Cornhusker State*. (Compiled and Written by the Federal Writers' Project of the Works Progress Administration for the State of Nebraska.) Copyright 1939 by the Nebraska State Historical Society. By permission of the author and the Viking Press, Inc.

sion of two Indian words caused the creek to 'weep' instead of 'rustle,' and gave rise to a sentimental tale: A beautiful Indian maiden was abducted by a rejected suitor while she was bathing in the lake near Weeping Water village. In the bloody fight that followed the pursuit of her captor, all her father's tribesmen were slain, and the women mourning their dead wept a stream of tears.

Certain localities preserve tradition not in their names but in stories attached to the places themselves, and here local history must yield to folklore the more marvelous exploits of frontier heroes and villains. The shooting of Dave McCanles and his two companions by young William Hickok at Rock Creek Station was thereafter magnified into the 'McCanles Massacre' in order to glorify the name of 'Wild Bill.' North of the Platte was the scene of the nine months' trek of Hugh Glass after he had been mangled by a grizzly bear and left by his companions to die. Along and beyond the Missouri, Mike Fink spread his reputation as a crack shot and a 'ring-tailed roarer'—the hero of the keelboatmen.

On the model of these actual heroes the plainsman, with humorous exaggeration, invented mythical figures who did the business of pioneering as he would have liked to do it. The most recent of these, Febold Feboldson, is largely the creation of Paul R. Beath, who has assembled and edited a collection of Febold tales from material originally published by Wayne Carroll and Don Holmes in the *Independent* and the *Times* of Gothenburg, Nebraska. According to Mr. Beath, 'Year by year more and more odds and ends of narrative material have fastened themselves to the Febold legend until today his name has become a by-word with people who know of his adventures.' (*Nebraska Folklore Pamphlets, Number 5.*) While the scholars worry over the authenticity of Febold, we may enjoy his yarning from the Liars' Bench.

Reminiscent of a long line of tall men from the backwoods Davy Crockett to the superman Paul Bunyan, Febold 'liked a good big job' and, whether it was drought-busting or killing off grasshoppers and coyotes, he was generally equal to the task. It was Febold who laid a straight boundary line between Kansas and Nebraska, after Paul Bunyan with his blue ox, Babe, had failed, ridiculously, by plowing a crooked furrow (now the Republican River). Febold spent fifteen years breeding eagles with bees until he had bees as big as eagles. Then all he had to do was hitch one of his best specimens to a plow, and make a bee-line between the two States. Febold was always good at picking assistants. Before the days of machinery, he used the happy auger (cousin of the dismal sauger) to pinch hit as a digger of post holes. (This was after red cedar posts had taken the place of the posts furnished by digging post holes in the fall and letting them freeze all winter, then digging them up before the first spring thaw, varnishing them, and stringing them with wire.) The auger, a peculiar animal resembling the kangaroo, had a habit of spinning round on its heavy corkscrew tail every time it sat down, thus screwing the tail several feet into the ground. Febold then would sneak up behind the poor creature and fire a six-shooter, scaring the auger so that it jumped twenty feet into the air and left the prettiest post hole imaginable.

The appeal and the appropriateness of Febold lie in his pioneer ingenuity and inventiveness—the heritage of the modern businessman and politician with whom he has much in common. Realizing that the day of miracles was over and that the land must be conquered by science, Febold finally went off to California to study irrigation and forestry against a second coming—though some say he went to enjoy well-earned peace in his old age.

Antoine Barada, strong man of the Missouri River, played Hercules to the wily Ulysses, Febold. Between them they share legendary honors for brain and brawn. Antoine, unlike Febold, was not one to take his time and figure things out for himself; rather, with the innocence of a child and the restlessness of a tiger, he was apt to lose his patience and discover things quite by accident. That was what happened, for instance, when, tired of watching a pile-driver at work on a 40-foot hitching post for a boat, Antoine picked up the derrick and threw it over into Iowa, and then smote the post with his mighty fist. The post went so deep into the earth that it formed an artesian well that spouted 50 feet into the air, and all in the vicinity surely would have drowned had not Antoine sat upon the hole until every one had rushed to safety.

Historical foundations have been claimed for both the Febold and the Antoine legends. Bergstrom Stromsberg, Febold's nephew and chronicler, has been traced by Paul Beath to Olaf Bergstrom, a Swedish adventurer who led a party of immigrants to America and later disappeared. Antoine had a historical namesake, the son of a Parisian count and an Omaha Indian maiden, who lies buried at the little village of Barada, where tales of the mythical hero are especially persistent. Told at old settlers' picnics, during the midday meal of threshing crews, and around red-hot stoves in wintertime, his superhuman feats in wrestling, throwing, and long-distance jumping suggest the very contests in which his narrators might have engaged. So folk tales embalm not only history but folkways and fantasy.

The trials and triumphs of Nebraska pioneer life are similarly reflected and commented on with humor (but with none of the gags of Febold, which smack of literary comedy) in the homesteader and cowboy songs that are found side by side with the English and Scottish ballads and other Old World pieces. The pioneer, when he needed a song to fit an occasion, was quick to adapt words or tune. 'The Little Old Sod Shanty on the Claim' is a parody of the pseudo-Negro song, 'The Little Old Log Cabin in the Lane,' by Will S. Hays (1871), and has been attributed to or claimed by many. In Nebraska, Emery Miller is said to have written it while holding down a claim in the eighties. As in that other homesteader's complaint (also recovered in Nebraska), 'Starving to Death on a Government Claim,' the bachelor of the soddy shows true pioneer humor and independence in making the best of a bad deal—leather hinges, paneless windows, howling blizzards, hungry coyotes, and all.

> My clothes are plastered o'er with dough, I'm looking like a fright,
> And everything is scattered round the room,
> But I wouldn't give the freedom that I have out in the West
> For the table of the Eastern man's old home.

More loyalty than fortitude is displayed in 'The Kinkaider's Song,' an idyllic picture of the sandhills dedicated to Moses P.

Kinkaid, author of the Homestead Act of 1904, which cut the last of the Nebraska free land into 640-acre sections. 'The Kinkaider's Song,' still popular at sandhill picnics and reunions, is sung to the tune of 'My Maryland' and is in the tradition of State songs—strong on tribute and weak in rhyme.

> The corn we raise is our delight,
> The melons, too, are out of sight.
> Potatoes grown are extra fine
> And can't be beat in any clime.
>
> The peaceful cows in pastures dream
> And furnish us with golden cream.
> So I shall keep my Kinkaid home
> And never far away shall roam.

In parodies, however, the sandhiller spared neither truth nor feelings.

> I've reached the land of drouth and heat,
> Where nothing grows for man to eat.
> For wind that blows with burning heat,
> Nebraska land is hard to beat.
>
> Al Reneau was a ranchman's name,
> Skinning Kinkaiders was his game,
> First mortgages only, at a high per cent,
> Jew you down on your cattle to the last red cent.

The last word in and of grim realism is the rhyme carved on the door of a deserted shack in the dry-land table near Chadron in the nineties, as recorded by Mari Sandoz in *Old Jules* (1935):

> 30 miles to water
> 20 miles to wood
> 10 miles to hell
> And I gone there for good.

Hell, as painted by a 'sky pilot' at a sandhill revival, is described by the same author in 'Sandhill Sundays' (*Folk-Say, A Regional Miscellany: 1931*)—in terms of the same waterless and treeless land familiar to sandhill sinners.

You see them heat waves out there on the prairie? Them's the fires of hell, licking up round your feet, burning your feet, burning your faces red as raw meat, drying up your crops, drawing the water out of your wells! You see them thunderheads, shining like mansions in the sky but spurting fire and shaking the ground under your feet? God is mad, mad as hell!

In the sandhill country, where the going was tougher, leaner, and lonelier, and the folklore tougher, fatter, and more plentiful, history may be retraced in the amusements of the people. The 'nesters' gradually supplemented revivals with husking-bees, feather-stripping parties, socials, sings, masquerades, literaries, and dances. The literary programs in the schoolhouses featured spell-downs, songs ('Love is Such a Funny, Funny Thing,' 'Oh, Bury Me Not on the Lone Prairie'), recitations ('The Deacon's Courtship,' 'The Face on the Barroom Floor') , and debates on such questions as Popular Elections of Our Presidents and the British Colonial Policy ('Resolved, that the Irish should be free,' and 'Resolved, that Grant was a great butcher instead of a great general') . People came to the dances from as far as forty miles away in wagons or on horseback, in response to some such invitation as the following inserted in the news columns of the community paper: 'Party and dance at Cravath's December 2. Dinner from one to seven. Beds and breakfasts for all. Everybody come.' After a midnight snack of coffee and ham sandwiches, there might be a 'chapping' match, in which two swains drew lots and took turns whacking each other with half of a horsebacker's leather chaps (unlaced to allow the two legs to fall apart) , the victor being rewarded with the pick of a girl, if he had none.

With the sheepmen came coyote hunts, to round up the sheep killers. The chase was perhaps less important than the big dinner which followed, on long boards over barrels in the barn. Later the Kinkaiders, many of them Easterners, brought in Sunday schools and ladies' aids; and those who had 'Methodist feet,' or religious objections to dancing, skipped, instead, at play-parties or bounce-arounds, to vigorously rhythmic words and tunes such as 'Skip to My Lou,' 'Three Little Girls Went Skating on the Ice,' 'Old Brass Wagon.' They also ran foot races and played charades, guessing games, and children's games—Pussy Wants a Corner, Drop the Handkerchief, and All the Ones in Free. With the railroads came the combination farmer and stockman; sandhill Sundays were ranch Sundays; and the corral was the scene of informal rodeos or scratching matches, in which cowpunchers showed off before the girls by scratching (roweling or raking with the spurs) horses that were sullen and refused to pitch.

Just before the coming of the automobile, old settlers and their children were distinguished from newer settlers by annual barbecues given in their honor. After the huge dinner (served on tables made of salt barrels and planks covered with white cloths) there were contests for all—fat men's, sack, three-legged, potato, and peanut races, a wagon race for the women and, for the young cowpunchers, bucking broncho contests and wild cow, wild mule, and surcingle races.

Today modern dances have not entirely displaced the shindigs, play parties, sociables, box suppers, and community fish fries. The old co-operative entertainments also survive, in somewhat commercialized form, in the many local and seasonal festivals held annually over the State. Old-timers' reunions compete with carnival features in the King Korn carnival at Plattsmouth, the Friendly Festival at Hay Springs, the Panhandle Stampede at Alliance, the Oregon Trail Days at Gering, and the Winnebago Indian and Massacre Canyon Pow-wows at Winnebago and Trenton.

In some localities national groups have endeavored to preserve Old World customs and traditions in such community observances as Omaha's Bohemian 'Grape Harvest,' the Italian Festival of Santa Lucia, and the widespread German *Sängerfest*. But community expression is not limited to holiday celebrations or to dancing, singing, and playing together; it is found also, in rural districts, in such kindly workaday customs as husking corn, plowing for a sick neighbor, and bringing gifts of food to a house in which there has been a death.

The life of the individual is further colored by traditional belief and inherited idiom. Local influence is less palpable, however, in the proverbial signs and prophecies concerning weather, crops, cures, character, love and marriage, wishes, and dreams.

These belong rather to the universal lore of superstition, which is circulated with varying degrees of faith and skepticism. The most interesting folk beliefs have practical relation to farm life, such as the use of plants and animals in portents and remedies. For example, a severe winter is predicted by the thickness of corn husks, of the fur coats of animals, or of the houses built by muskrats. To cure warts, 'Walk in the woods until you find the bone of an animal, rub the bone carefully over the wart with the side which was next to the ground, then dig a hole in the ground and bury the bone. When it decays, the wart will be gone.' Other remedies of local interest are those of reputed Indian origin, such as the Pawnee wash for inflamed eyes made from the root of wild roses, and the Pawnee salve for burns made from the pulverized root of the cattail plant.

A stronger local color and regional flavor adhere to speech, especially to sandhill talk and Nebraska pioneer English. Through the terms and phrases that have come in with successive waves of migration, the history of Nebraska settlement may be traced.[1] Fur-traders, trappers, hunters, boatmen, soldiers, Indians, pioneers, buffalo hunters, railroaders, settlers, speculators, squatters, homesteaders, and townspeople not only opened and built up a new country but also developed a new language—a lingo of the river, the fort, the post, the trail, the farm, and the ranch. These linguistic deposits form an invaluable record of the land and the people—their food, clothes, dwellings, household articles, tools, implements, transportation, trading, and social customs. Peculiarly expressive are the terms describing the sandhill region: blow-out (hollow), whitecap (a high hill scarred with blow-outs), choppies or chop-hills (billows of hills mostly bare of grass), dune-sand (unfit for cultivation), hogback and turtleback (hills or ridges suggesting these forms), nigger-wool sod, and howler (the terrific wind that brings blizzards). And eloquent of the life of the sandhiller are: Kinkaider (settler under the act of 1904), to kinkaid, a kinkaid (640 acres), Texas gate (several bands of wire stapled to sticks attached by wire loops to the fence posts), to juice or pail a

[1] See 'Nebraska Pioneer English' by Melvin Van den Bark, *American Speech*, Vols. VI, VII, and VIII (1931-1933).

cow, cream day (Saturday, when cream and eggs are taken to the store), hangout (inland store or post office), on pump (buying necessities at the store on credit), hay burner (a boiler-like heating contrivance stuffed with twisted hay and turned face down on the open stove, bible (mail-order catalog), groan box (organ), grub-line rider (a bachelor or widower who 'makes' a good cook's home just before mealtime to get a free meal), schoolmarm chasers (eligible young men interested in teachers), and catalog woman (a wife obtained through a matrimonial bureau).

Tradition touches the lives of Nebraska folk lightly, with a guiding rather than a restraining hand—guiding them wisely and wittily into a future that has its roots in the past. 'One can go into a wild country and make it tame, but, like a coat and cap and mittens that he can never take off, he must always carry the look of the land as it was.' (*Old Jules.*)

PECOS BILL, CYCLONE BUSTER

By Irving Fiske

WHAT Paul Bunyan is to the lumberman, Pecos Bill is to the cowboy of the Southwest. Compared to Pecos Bill, however, Bunyan was a Milquetoast. The heroes of American folklore are the biggest, lustiest, most swashbuckling immortals evoked by the imagination of any people, and Bill is the most riproaring of them all—altogether a credit to the vitality of the cowboy imagination. Men of the Southwest cattle country for generations have swapped tall tales of Bill's colossal strength and superb contempt for opponents, whether men, beasts, floods, or cyclones.

Bill's career is unparalleled for versatility. As pioneer, range-rider, and cowboy supreme, he roved from Colorado south to the Rio Grande, from Texas west to the Pacific, opening up huge new stretches of territory wherever he went. He invented not only the six-shooter, but lassoing, train-robbing, highjacking, and most of the crimes popular in the old Southwest. He thought up tarantulas and centipedes as a practical joke on friends. Bill didn't invent cow-stealing—that was done by King David in the Bible—but he raised it to a fine art. His flair for the artistic even extended into more legitimate channels. He could handle a guitar as easily as a pair of six-shooters and was no mean composer. All the cowboy songs and ballads sung nowadays were written by him.

The southwestern and western landscape bears lasting marks of Bill's exploits. Once, when the cattle country was threatened by a tidal wave from the Pacific, Pecos Bill got his men together, we are told, and threw up breastworks to save the country. You may have heard about those protuberances; they're known as the Rocky Mountains.

From *The American Mercury*, December 1939. By permission of the author and publisher.

When Bill wearied of bronchobusting, he invented cyclone-busting to make life interesting, and tamed some of the ugliest cyclones that ever tried to tear a countryside apart. One of them finally managed to avenge itself on him. Bill was riding a bucking cyclone over three states on a bet, egging it on with ear-splitting whoops, pausing now and then to light a cigarette on a lightning streak. Over California the cyclone turned on Bill, and rained out from under him. Bill fell with a terrific crash into Death Valley—now 280 feet below sea level as a result.

According to cowboys, Bill was born on the banks of the Pecos River in east Texas, at about the time Sam Houston came to that state—1832. His mother, a husky pioneer lady who had once killed forty-five Indians with a broomstick, weaned him on moonshine and panther's milk. Bill made the neighborhood wild-cats his playmates, helping them track down their prey, and whenever one of them made a catch, Bill jokingly snatched it away and swallowed it. This hurt their feelings so much the wildcats didn't want to play any more and moved out of the district *en masse,* leaving Bill without playmates.

When he was a year old, another family moved in, fifty miles downstream. 'Country's gittin' so doggone overcrowded a man ain't got room to move his elbows any more,' said Bill's father. The family pulled up stakes, and struck out west. A few days later, Bill fell out of the oversize trailer that had been espe-cially built for him. There were twenty-eight other children in the family—sixteen brothers and twelve sisters—so three weeks passed before his parents missed him. Then it was too late to go back.

Bill, in the meantime, had adopted a pack of coyotes for com-pany, squatting with them on the hills at night, howling his lungs out, and regarding himself as a coyote like the rest. By the time Bill was 6, he weighed a quarter ton, being then, cattle-men observe, just about half as big as a present-day Texas ranger thinks he is.

It wasn't until Bill was 10 that he again met another human being—a rawboned Texas cowboy, who persuaded him to return to the fold of humanity. The cowboy came upon Bill as he was engaged in killing a grizzly bear by hugging it to death.

'That's uncouth,' said the cowboy, much annoyed.

'So what?' said Bill, ripping a hind leg off the bear and gnawing at it. 'I'm a coyote, ain't I?'

'No, you ain't,' said the cowboy, firmly. 'Where's your tail? You're a human.'

'I'm a coyote. I got fleas, ain't I?'

'That's nothing—all Texans got fleas.' The cowboy unlimbered his shooting-iron to lend emphasis to his remarks. 'You're a human, I said.'

'Maybe you're right,' replied Bill. 'Lead me to them humans. I'll look 'em over.'

The cowboy guided him to the nearest town. Bill visited the saloons, depleted their stock, and settled down to stay. He experimented with all the vices, improved on most of them, and decided that he was a human being, all right. He associated with bad company, sank lower and lower in the human scale, and finally became a cowboy.

He soon was a bad man and the terror of the Southwest, but he had his redeeming qualities. Though he killed men in endless numbers, he had a soft heart. He never shot women, children, or tourists out of season. He never scalped his victims, but skinned them alive, and tenderly tanned their hides.

II

When Pecos Bill had killed all the bad men, Indians, and buffalo in west Texas, he decided to go into the cattle business for himself, and struck out west. The object of his search was the hardest, toughest outfit of cowhands in the world, and the story of the obstacles he overcame to find them is a major epic. Three days out on the journey, his horse broke a leg and had to be shot. Bill slung the saddle over his shoulder and went off swearing. (Bill invented swearing.) Just then a twelve-foot rattlesnake rose in his path. Bill let the snake bite him three times first, just to fight fair, and then stepped in and punished it until it rattled for mercy. He carried the snake off with him, twirling it like a rope in his hands.

Fifty miles further on a mountain-lion twice as big as three steers lay crouching on the brow of a cliff. It saw Bill striding through the gulch below, and sprang, clawing and biting, onto his shoulders. Bill was in no mood for pleasantries. He slammed it against the ground, and gave it a real hard slapping around. Thirty seconds of that was enough for the lion, so Bill saddled the beast, mounted it, and using the snake as a quirt, went leaping off, one hundred feet at a jump. In the distance was a band of hostile bad men lying in wait for him. Bill came bounding in among them, the mountain-lion a-screechin', the snake a-rattlin', and Bill himself a-yippin' and a-howlin' like an ill-tempered nightmare. The terrified bad men broke and ran at the sight. On a clear day some of them can still be seen dashing franti cally up and down the sides of the Sierra Nevadas.

Bill spurred his mount on, and four days later ran into the cow outfit he was looking for. They stood around a campfire, whittling pieces of crowbar with their jack-knives and chewing raw cactus spikes—the orneriest, most vicious batch of hombres this side of Hades. A boilerful of beans was on the fire. Bill was hungry. He dismounted, strode in without a word, and emptied the whole boilerful down his throat. The others looked on silently. Then Bill stove in the top of a barrel of whiskey, up-ended it, and washed his meal down with twenty gallons of red-eye swallowed in twenty gulps. He was elected boss without further ceremony.

With his new outfit Bill revolutionized the cattle business. He staked out New Mexico as a cattle range, Arizona as a calf-pasture, and dug the Rio Grande to bring fresh water into his back yard. He introduced long-horn cattle, invented bulldogging, and taught his boys the use of the lariat—he himself could rope a whole herd in a single throw. When the railroads came into the Southwest, Bill contracted to supply them with wood. He got a gang of Mexicans to do it, and gave each Mexican one-fourth of the wood hauled in payment. They had no idea what to do with it. He graciously took it off their hands for them, and didn't even charge them a cent. Pecos Bill, the cowboys say, originated many of the methods later adopted by big business.

One day Bill's men caught a week-old colt so big that it was straddling a full-grown pine tree when they found it. Bill raised it on dynamite sticks and nitroglycerine, and he was the only man in the world who could ride it. This was his horse Widow-Maker, famed throughout the cattle country.

It goes without saying that Pecos Bill had innumerable gargantuan love affairs, unprintable in nature. Only the tragic story of Slue-Foot Sue, Bill's bouncing bride, may be told in detail. He fell in love with Sue at first sight one morning when he saw her riding down the Rio Grande on a whale-sized catfish. Sue fell in love not only with Bill, but with his horse as well. Her one consuming ambition was to ride Widow-Maker, but to all her pleas Bill remained adamant until their wedding day.

The minute the ceremony was over, Sue renewed her entreaties with such fervor that Bill gave in. Sue sprang upon Widow-Maker's back with a gleeful whoop. The horse bucked harder than ever, and she was thrown so high into the air she had to duck to let the moon go by. Sue was wearing a bustle made of spring steel and whalebone, and each time she hit the ground she bounced high into the air again. She bounced up and down for twenty-two days, while Bill stood by begging her to stop, but she couldn't. So he had to shoot her to keep her from starving to death. Her death left an aching void on Bill's big bosom. He unofficially married only three dozen wives after that, but none of them could take the place of Slue-Foot Sue, his bouncing bride.

Bill turned to drink for consolation. Ordinary liquor had long before lost its effect. He mixed strychnine, wolf-poison, barbed wire, and fish-hooks into his drink to get a kick out of it; but that merely gave him indigestion. From then until he died, he took to ranging up and down the Rio Grande, shooting bad men by the hundreds to relieve his feelings.

Ironically enough, Pecos Bill bit the dust through the innocent agency of a mild-mannered tourist from Boston. The tourist approached him one day, all dressed up in a mail-order cowboy suit, and asked so many fool questions about the West that Bill stretched himself out at full length upon the ground and simply laughed himself to death.

HOUSES AND CITIES

By Catherine Bauer

MOST of us have some sort of shelter with four walls, a roof and a floor, to which we repair when we need rest, privacy, refreshment, or the company of family and friends. For most of us this dwelling is closely surrounded by a great many other dwellings, by stores, factories, offices, schools, movie-palaces, railroad stations, and a hundred other kinds of building—all of them tied together by a complicated network of pavement, pipes, wires and tracks. Both houses and cities, then, are part of our daily experience.

On the other hand, 'housing' and 'city planning' have meant for most of us only the remotest sort of abstraction. If we have used the terms at all, it was only in connection with some special undertaking—philanthropic rehabilitations of an ancient slum district, for instance, or putting through a handsome and showy boulevard. 'Housing' had nothing to do with our own houses. 'City planning' was strictly limited to certain superficial aspects of city development.

The ordinary methods of constructing average human environment seemed to present no special problem. Any family of normal ambition could, it was assumed, buy a nice piece of land and erect thereon a decent home, becoming thus both respectable and secure. Houses in the future would doubtless have more and better bathrooms, newer and trickier gadgets. Skyscrapers would be taller and have faster elevators; subways would be longer and quicker; land-values higher and wider. The problem of traffic congestion would somehow be solved by double-decker streets or vertical parking elevators, or perhaps by cheap airplanes.

From *Art in Modern Times in America*, 1934, edited by Holger Cahill and Alfred H. Barr, Jr. By permission of the Museum of Modern Art, New York, N. Y.

Seldom indeed, as the houses multiplied to infinity and the cities swallowed up the countryside for miles around, did we look at these things objectively, or evaluate them in terms of real human convenience and amenity. We did not stop to question the strange fact that houses had doubled in cost while automobiles had been halved and quartered in price. If we were sometimes vaguely dissatisfied with the lack of sun or air or outlook in our home, or its distance from our work and play places, we accepted these drawbacks philosophically and hoped to get an electric refrigerator instead. High taxes we attributed, grumbling, to 'corruption.' Never did we have any fundamental doubts as to the premises and practices underlying our methods of producing human environment.

But suddenly today our indifference has been changed to a sense of urgent necessity. What happened in the realm of abstract economics is reflected even more dramatically, if that be possible, in the physical world of houses and cities. Something is vitally wrong, and something drastic must be done about it. 'Housing' and 'city planning' have become great issues which affect the life and living of every citizen.

Before we consider what should be done we must acquaint ourselves with what was done in the past. American cities have historic periods quite as clearly defined and as significant as the Romanesque-Gothic-Baroque of European towns. Let us see what these periods are and what heritage they have left us. Every layer of man-made environment crystallizes a whole set of purposes and beliefs. What forces shaped the building of Chicago and Pittsburgh, of Topeka and Tallahassee?

The majority of American towns were settled by individuals who had left the old centers of civilization, either on the Eastern seaboard or in Europe, in order to 'seek their fortunes.' Only rarely were these settlers unified by any collective purpose or common background. Virtues they had aplenty, but they were the individualistic virtues of the pioneer: initiative, personal courage and ambition, self-sufficiency, ingenuity, hardihood. As soon as a man grew restless or dissatisfied with his neighbors or his situation, he 'moved on' into the wilderness where there was more elbow-room.

But the virtues of the pioneer are not, by and large, the virtues which produce handsome, efficient, permanent centers of civilization. Such cities are necessarily the result of harmonious communal enterprise and group responsibility. Individuals must work with other individuals for a common end, subordinating thereto certain personal interests and ambitions. Whatever the political-economic framework may be, architecture is essentially a collective art.

Many mid-Western cities still have that air of impermanence, as if the citizens were just preparing to move on, that characterized all of them when first they were being worked for their gold or oil or iron. But perhaps our deepest heritage from the frontier was the ideal of 'individual' houses, designed, built and owned by the resident, and surrounded on all four sides by as large a piece of land as possible. A man's house was his fortress, his defense against all the other members of a predatory society, symbol of his success and expression of his personality. So strong is this ideal still, even in the midst of congested apartments, and mass-produced bungalows, that few Americans can realize how different it is from the ideal which produced the great city civilizations of Europe. Nor do they realize how impossible of achievement it is within the complex network of modern urban society. The pioneer who felt crowded when there was another hut within two miles of him is reflected today in the miles of deep, narrow 'individual' frame houses which dot the suburbs of any American town.

Moreover, the habit of 'mine and move,' of competitive exploitation for quick profits, was not confined to mineral wealth. From the beginning, the same practice was applied to that primary resource of the city, land itself.

Almost all American cities were 'planned,' in a very real sense. Not only were streets and lots laid out in advance of use, but they were laid out with a definite purpose in mind. That purpose had little or nothing to do with ultimate convenience, efficiency or beauty, and was modified only with great difficulty to allow for a minimum of sanitation and safety. The accepted end of all 'development,' the conscious or unconscious purpose of all 'planning,' was a maximum of quick profit for the developer.

The mechanical gridiron plan, with its hills leveled off and its valleys filled in, with its standardized blocks and lots and its undifferentiated streets without beginning or end, was the ideal pattern for this purpose. It provided a maximum of 'front feet,' easily negotiable because they were 'standard' and highly speculative because no one could possibly predict the ultimate future use.

New York City itself is one of the prime examples of this profit-planning. As early as 1807 the ambitious city fathers made a gridiron city-plan covering the whole of Manhattan (the existing town was then only a small village down around the Battery) with absolutely standardized streets and lots, regardless of topography, possible future use, or any other non-statistical consideration. The whole island became one vast parcel of speculative commodities.

The same mechanical measures and purely quantitative standards carried over into other matters. The prosperity of cities was gauged entirely by such matters as the rate of population-growth, the increase in lot prices, the mileage of paved streets and utility lines, average wealth per capita regardless of its distribution, the number of new industrial plants and stores, etc. All of these matters were thought of as statistical curves of progress, produceable to infinity.

With the appearance of enormous centralized junction-towns, in which all numerical records were broken, congestion itself became a symbol of prosperity. Small towns which had once been spacious did their best to ape the unwieldy chaos of Metropolis, skyscrapers, tenements and all. There was no sense of the city as an organism which, if it is to function efficiently, has certain inherent limitations on form and growth.

City governments themselves encouraged and speculated on their own indefinite spread. Endless paved streets and utility lines were laid out long in advance of any possible use, to facilitate lot speculation. By 1929 almost every progressive city had enough lots staked out to take care of several times its actual population. Those miles of unused concrete and rotting pipes are today among the most dramatic monuments to the New Era and one of the prime causes of municipal bankruptcy.

The houses which were built in such enormous numbers in the spreading suburbs were not, perforce, designed with much attention to real human needs or real technical or material possibilities. They had to be fitted into the rigid limitations of a completely mechanical scheme in whatever manner would bring the largest immediate profit to the builder. Land and utilities were increasingly expensive; every bit of open space was just so much 'waste.'

Land speculation (gambling, that is, on the possibilities of future congestion) was a potent factor in determining the actual form of the American home, as distinct from that vague frontier ideal of secluded individual mansions. In addition, there was a growing body of complicated 'building restrictions,' the result of sheer vital necessity, which legalized the congestion and pegged up both construction and land costs, but which did at the same time attempt to enforce crude minima of safety and sanitation.

Together, these two factors shaped the average homes of the past fifty years: 'one-family houses' four to eight feet apart; bungalows; 'duplexes'; three- and four-decker flats; tenements covering three quarters of the site or more. The majority of them were mass-produced by small speculative builders. What a far cry they were from that magazine-cover 'ideal home' which was still promoted as a real possibility!

From about the beginning of the century onward, there were signs of reaction against the barrack-towns of the nineteenth century. But this reaction did not, unfortunately, carry with it enough vitality of purpose or understanding to put through any fundamental changes.

The Great White City of the Chicago World's Fair of 1893, together with Burnham's plan for Chicago, galvanized a fairly widespread interest in the tags of Renaissance city-planning—an interest which had been more or less moribund in America since L'Enfant planned Washington. Avenues and parkways, vistas and perspectives, radicals and rond-points, duly punctuated with large white public buildings as nearly 'classic' as possible, became the objective of all civic-minded individuals. 'Civic centers' were planned, and some of them were executed. But, outside of a certain amount of admirable park-planning, perhaps the best inheritance of many American cities, most of these earnest efforts amounted to little more than surface show.

At the same time the new yearning for 'culture' (which invariably signified past European culture) had an even more obvious effect on residential exteriors. The experiments of the seventies and eighties, often crude and vulgar but lively and imaginative nevertheless, gave way to a period of worried 'good taste' which has lasted up to the present. All the literature on past 'styles' was ransacked, and the houses of the rich were faithful copies of Tudor, Italian, Norman or 'Colonial' villas. Middle-class houses were vulgarized copies of the houses of the rich. (The houses of the poor were, of course, the cast-offs of another generation and were not supposed to be tasteful.)

The net effect of the whole movement was merely, all in all, to reinforce and bedizen the earlier pattern, which underneath remained quite as chaotic and exploitive as ever. No matter what monumental effect was contrived for the center, the city continued to spread out at the edge in a rash of amorphous subdivisions over which the city-planners had no control whatsoever, and indeed, asked none. And, no matter how letter-perfect they might be individually, a street full of French, Italian and Olde Englishe houses, each competing with the other for the attention and approbation of the passer-by, is an architectural monstrosity. A congested tenement, whether it is on Chrystie Street or Park Avenue and whether it has a Gothic or baroque vestibule or merely a dingy 'hall,' is still nothing more nor less than a congested tenement . . .

If we are to build houses and cities adequate to the needs of the twentieth century, we must start all over again, from the ground up. Many of our preconceived notions as to what a house or a city should look like must be altered. We must build from a fresh set of premises. We must be prepared to scrap much of the physical, sentimental and financial heritage of the past fifty years. And finally, we must be ready to fight those forces whose vested interest in the old scheme of things makes them bitter enemies of change.

What are houses and cities made of? Physically speaking—

land, labor and materials. We have an ample supply of land. We have thousands of highly skilled building workers, most of them at present entirely without employment. Tons of materials are rotting in warehouses or being artificially kept from production. New improved processes and techniques are available but are not being used.

What are houses and cities made for? Their only real purpose, when all is said and done, ought to be human protection, convenience, comfort, health and pleasure. They must provide opportunity for privacy, and also for social intercourse. They must offer labor-saving devices, without making us slaves of machinery. They must be so arranged that all kinds of work and play can be carried on with a minimum of wasteful friction. They must be satisfactory to the eye and the other senses, both in details and in the whole.

Architects and technicians and planners have in recent years been devising methods and techniques for building just such a human environment. Much scientific knowledge, hitherto unused, can at last be put to human service. Why should not these rich resources, this new knowledge, be used to replace our obsolete equipment with houses and cities designed to meet efficiently the most complex human requirements?

Why not indeed? These premises seem very simple and obvious. And yet, outside of a few difficult experiments, they never entered into the production of nineteenth-century environment or into the houses and cities which we live in today.

The path is not entirely uncharted. In Europe much has already been achieved—several million modern dwellings built in planned communities by non-profit, non-competitive enterprise, and let at rents within reach of average citizens. Housing has become a 'public utility,' and the unit of plan, of design, of construction and of administration is the complete neighborhood, equipped from the start with all the facilities for a well-rounded social life and for productive leisure. In America there have been a few such experiments, and some of the government projects now under construction will provide a few more.

Out of the European experience has grown already a new kind of architecture. It has been called 'functionalism,' which means merely that sun and air and human convenience and modern technique become integral elements in architectural design. Forms are devised which can directly employ the most efficient modern materials and methods. Empty, pretentious, 'styled' façades are eliminated and a truly modern architecture becomes possible. Instead of the monotonous repetition of jerry-built Tudor villas, standard parts are used to build up harmonious groups. Architecture, after more than two hundred years as an expression of snobbishness and 'conspicuous waste,' comes into its own once more as the mother of the arts and a fitting expression for a working social organism.

Can we have good houses, efficient cities and modern architecture in America? There are two major conditions. We must be willing to plan for *use* and not for profit. And above all, as consumers, as workers, as individuals, as families, as citizens, as voters, we must want a better living environment enough to fight for it.

THE MOTION PICTURE

By Iris Barry

THE motion picture is unique in three important ways. First, it is the one medium of expression in which America has influenced the rest of the world. Second, it has had a marked influence on contemporary life. And third, it is such a young art that we can study it at first hand from its beginnings: the primitives among movies are only forty years old.

Though many experiments and inventions had gone before, the motion picture as we know it did not come into being until, upon Eastman's inventing film to take the place of photographic plates, Edison perfected the kinetoscope. This peep-show machine made its first appearance at Broadway and 34th Street in New York in April 1894. At first it was regarded only as a semi-scientific curiosity, even after other inventors had taken the animated pictures out of the peep-show and projected them on to a screen. For a time the public was satisfied merely to see things move. Scenic views, actual street scenes or simple actions—a woman dancing, an engine puffing towards the audience, a boy playing a prank—provided the subject-matter for these early movies. Little improvised comic or dramatic incidents were screened before the close of the nineteenth century, but very few attempts at sustained story-telling or drama were made until about 1903. In that year an Edison cameraman, Edwin S. Porter, combined several popular ingredients into a distinct plot in *The Great Train Robbery*, which was a whole reel long. Italy, France, and England contributed many of the crude one-reel historical dramas, condensed plays, and novels that followed, while America became identified with the livelier, more graphic,

From *Art in Modern Times in America*, 1934, edited by Holger Cahill and Alfred H. Barr, Jr. By permission of the Museum of Modern Art, New York, N. Y.

and more purely cinematic cowboy dramas and slapstick come-
dies. Gradually films grew longer. The most famous of the early
multi-reel movies was undoubtedly the French *Queen Elizabeth,*
with Sarah Bernhardt, made in 1911.

In 1913 Italy sent over the super-spectacle *Quo Vadis,* complete with crowds, lions, and the Colosseum in eight reels. D. W.
Griffith, an ambitious young director who had then been with
the American Biograph Co. for five years, determined to outdo
Quo Vadis. The result was *The Birth of a Nation,* the film with
which the history of the motion picture as a great popular art is
usually judged to have begun. Griffith had already realized that
the camera need not confine itself to action like that of the stage,
with the players always seen at full-length at a constant distance
from the spectator. He had already brought the camera closer
to both actors and inanimate objects, and now found how to
alternate more distant scenes of action with closer and more
intimate scenes of emotion, making the film at once more fluid
and expressive and less literal. He made dramatic use of the dissolve, the close-up, and other technical tricks, and employed the
old 'ride to the rescue' motive of the early Western films, along
with cutbacks, to achieve a contrapuntal method of pictorial
narration. *The Birth of a Nation,* because of its magnitude as
well as its subject and its treatment, and Griffith's colossal *Intolerance,* made two years later, had a lasting effect on the developing motion picture. It is noteworthy that *Intolerance,* perhaps
the most momentous of all movies, was, like most of the interesting early American pictures, based on a story written specially
for the screen and not on an adaptation of a novel or play.

From 1914 to 1918 the work of Griffith and others in America
carried the movie out of the nickelodeon stage with its exagger-
ated gestures, rapid action and psychological crudity. It was
during these years that Charlie Chaplin progressed from the
rough-and-tumble farces of his beginnings to that brilliant succession of tragi-comedies which were tender and sardonic as well
as funny, filled with a profound knowledge of human nature
and assembled with an instinctive feeling for the medium. Both
Griffith and Chaplin brought more complex situations and characters to the screen and taught it to find a purely visual expres-

sion unlike that of the drama or of fiction. Chaplin developed a sure feeling for the exact length of time each single shot should last: he, particularly, is a master of editing and of timing. Other men in this country made contributions, but many of them unhappily relied on famous stage actors, or on plots drawn unchanged from plays and novels; they too eagerly exploited sensationalism and personalities, and were more concerned with creating an impression of opulence than curious about the potentialities of the medium.

From the time film-goers acclaimed the Biograph Girl with the golden curls, long before she was known as Mary Pickford, through to the time of Rudolph Valentino and Greta Garbo, the star system has done much to injure motion pictures. The great popular favorites themselves have all been exceptionally expressive players, but their popularity was abused when motion picture companies stressed who was in a movie rather than what was in it.

The years following the armistice brought technical innovations and an added sophistication from Germany. German films from the expressionist *Cabinet of Dr. Caligari* (1919) through to Dupont's *Variety* and Murnau's *The Last Laugh* (1925) left a marked impression. The use of camera angles and of the traveling camera, the designing of scenery for pictorial rather than for theatrical effect, both came from the German studios. It was the example of the Germans which influenced Hollywood to use artificial lighting as a rule rather than as an exception, and to construct artificial 'outdoor' scenes within the studio in place of natural settings. With their slower movement, their exploration of somber moods and psychological bypaths, the beautiful German films themselves were seldom to the public taste. But they were closely studied by American directors, and the innovations they presented were incorporated into the general technique of production, again widening the film's range of expression. During this period, many German directors, actors, and cameramen were brought over to Hollywood.

The American movie on its own account had by no means stood still, despite the frankly commercial attitude of its makers. Cruze's *The Covered Wagon* (1923) was a far cry from the one-reel Westerns but was equally pure cinema. Erich von Stroheim's *Blind Husbands* (1919)—a remarkable piece—and his *Foolish Wives* (1922) were followed in 1923 by a movie which Chaplin directed but did not act in, *A Woman of Paris*. All three of these assumed a considerable degree of visual and intellectual alertness on the part of their audiences, and all of them contrived in a way, which at the time seemed startling, to suggest rather than to illustrate the finer shades of moods and of situations. Vivid and subtle as we found the American-made movies of the German director, Ernst Lubitsch—such, for instance, as *The Marriage Circle* and *Forbidden Paradise*—their sparkle and eloquence had been foreshadowed in von Stroheim's and Chaplin's pictures . . .

In 1928 with the appearance of *The Jazz Singer* every motion picture studio set about making talkies. The movies had achieved a remarkable degree of eloquence through pictures alone. There was a temporary setback with the coming of audible dialogue. Canned plays threatened to sweep away most of the advances made by the silent films. It is well to remember, however, that except in unusual productions like Chaplin's *The Woman of Paris* and Murnau's *The Last Laugh,* one third of the footage of the average silent film consisted of printed subtitles. Silent films, too, were invariably accompanied by both music and sound effects from the theater orchestra.

By 1929 talkies like Victor Fleming's outdoor *The Virginian* and von Sternberg's German-made *The Blue Angel* succeeded in shaking off the restrictions at first imposed by the mechanics of sound-recording. A French movie, René Clair's *Sous les toits de Paris,* indicated to what an extent intelligently used sound could become an asset. The screen quickly regained its range and wealth of pictorial expression, dialogue became briefer, less continuous, and more natural. In the brilliantly edited Mickey Mouse and Silly Symphonies, the animated cartoons equipped with sound have shown a new vitality and inventiveness beyond that displayed by other branches of the art.

The influence of many remarkable films made in Soviet Russia has not been very marked. The Russian directors, of whom Pudovkin and Eisenstein are best known, avowedly derive in part from D. W. Griffith. With a metronomic, machine-gun fire of rapid and realistic shots (usually close-ups) in place of the customary sustained scenes, they have achieved in almost physical intensity of expression. The present tendency to choose players physically well-suited to interpret each part rather than established favorites may well be due to them. But their influence in this country was more noticeable in an increase of productions with a sociological flavor, such as *I Am a Fugitive from the Chain Gang* and *Wild Boys of the Road*.

The many types of films—documentary, spectacular, historical, Western, comedy-drama, slapstick, animated cartoon—were established in the early days of the cinema. Not a single type has yet been fully developed, though recent years have seen considerable advances both in photography, décor, and acting and three or four notable extensions in the technical use of the medium. From the first, progress has been retarded by the necessity for producing companies to entertain their immense public, their consequent neglect to explore the innate possibilities of the film itself, and their insistence on proved ingredients and glamorous personalities. Almost all purely experimental movies have been the work of amateurs—painters like Charles Sheeler, Fernand Léger, Viking Eggeling, Salvador Dali (on whose scenario the striking surrealist movie *L'Age d'Or* was based), Jean Cocteau with his surrealist *Le Sang d'un Poète*, or Melville Webber and Dr. Watson whose *Fall of the House of Usher* and *Lot in Sodom* are among the most interesting non-commercial films made in this country. Very seldom, as with *The Cabinet of Dr. Caligari* and Chaplin's *A Woman of Paris*, and then only under special conditions have experimental films been made within the industry itself.

Another grave detriment has been the passing of almost all motion picture theaters into the hands of the producing companies, so that mass-produced films are automatically poured out through chain-store theaters. The result is necessarily mediocre, as though all book publishers and booksellers strove to issue nothing but best sellers. Good films are produced and are sometimes overwhelmingly successful, whether nationally advertised as is usual with superfilms good or bad, or whether brought back time and again by popular demand. Others however, and those often the most vital and original, are shown only in a fugitive way to small and often the wrong audiences, or cannot find an outlet at all.

Much could be done to remedy this state of affairs by organization on the part of discontented film-goers. It has been proved that active local demand can dictate what shall be shown in neighborhood houses. Much could also be done by discriminating film fans with letters written to producing companies and to cinemas. These would not be disregarded. Unfortunately, it is usually the undiscriminating and not the critical film-goers who write letters. Nevertheless, it is undoubtedly in the hands of the few creative directors and of the general public that the future of this great twentieth-century art still lies. They will determine whether it shall remain as now largely a diversion in which mere photography and second-hand theater play all too large a part, or whether it shall develop fully its unique methods of expression.

RADIO'S BIG CHANCE

By Charles Siepmann

RADIO's big chance has come. Will it take it, exploit it, or simply pass it up? After a month of war the answer is still in doubt. But a straight answer is as vital to the future of ordinary citizens in a working democracy—listeners or not—as to the future of the radio industry itself.

Radio faced up to war with all the outward signs of that alert efficiency that we associate with its services. Radio's reporters were everywhere. In some recent programs it has risen magnificently to the occasion—witness the program commemorating the Bill of Rights, an almost perfect example of what radio can do to make the life blood of our past history beat in the pulse of our contemporary veins. In that splendid hour we saw radio way out in the lead, where it belongs. So, too, with numbers of other individual programs. For a night, a week, some sponsors even retired (a little sanctimoniously) from news bulletins and conceded the full time to commentators. Networks showered on us news bulletins with the rapid succession of pattering machine guns. This is all good—in intention if not always in effect. But there are also blots on radio's copybook, enough to make us wonder whether it has in fact realized that a page has been turned. With genuine gratitude for services rendered and in full recognition of the difficulties faced, we must, therefore, inscribe on the new page the listeners' Bill of Rights. War now dictates the terms.

For one thing, mere gestures are not enough. Sponsors are back again—the same voices, the same blurbs, the same high-pitched tones of blustering persuasion or of intimate appeal. At best they are incongruous; at worst an affront to listeners. Spon-

From *The New Republic,* 12 January 1942. By permission of the author and publisher.

sorship we recognize, but not crude assaults on quickened sensibilities. Conditioned though we mostly are by what life and radio offer us, we may yet come to acknowledge taste without embarrassment. We prefer bulletins and news commentators without sponsorship. We plead that in any case sponsors shall be brief.

To announcers we say this. The war is your big chance as well. You can help make or break civilian morale. Study the good manners of communication and add a cubit to your stature. Don't shout. Don't race. This is war, not a World Series. Remember that on the air, tone and pitch are the equivalent of headlines.

A word, next, to news editors. The President's words to you were weighed and weighty. 'You have a grave responsibility.' You've risen to it in many ways, but you have overlooked two things—our dependence on you and our nerves. You lead, we follow. Put on bulletins at every quarter-hour and we'll tune in. We're suckers for silly habits. So don't encourage us. The endless repetition of the same news exasperates. Regular news at reasonable intervals will help us to sober habits. Above all, stop interrupting programs for the latest 'flash' from your newsroom. We're jumpy enough as it is, without hot bricks being set in our path. In a wartime news service, being in at the kill may be just bloody murder to the listener. Remember, too, when you quote Berlin, Tokyo, Rome, that this is a war of nerves and that the enemy invented it. 'Mental confusion, contradiction of feeling, indecision, panic, these are our weapons.' That's Hitler's and that's their game. They plant news just to provoke reaction. The President asked that you give only news that's officially confirmed. We ask it too. Save us suspense.

To commentators: Your personalities we welcome. They add humanity to much that is inhuman in what you have to tell us. Spare us, however, your prejudices; and spare us prophecy. Spare us, too, from uplift. We need morale but not moralities. The symbolism of events will prove more eloquent than tinsel phrases. Spare us excessive reference to 'the cause' and 'the task before us.' Do not pontificate.

To sponsors, advertising agents, and to program builders:

Remember that we're experiencing real emotions. At least, we ought to be. Treat us as adults, even if we're not. To invite indulgence in cheap escapism and vicarious emotion is no longer just an offense against decent taste but against morale. Morbid, credulous and indiscriminating—we're all of those. 'Radio is the preferred medium of the most suggestible.' That is a social fact. For radio it has been a source of profit, and an unrecognized responsibility. Daytime serials have long been a target of abuse, often by those who never heard one. But listen to Bill Cunningham, who did hear several. 'Try driving 400 miles, as I did yesterday, with nothing but the radio for company, and if you don't go nuts between 10 A.M. and sundown, you're tough enough to laugh off anything. In every one of these mournful instalments [of soap opera] everyone was in perfectly awful trouble. A child went blind in one. A man lay at the point of death in another . . . All that ought to be expunged in rapid order. Not even a plump housewife needs a serving of synthetic worries any more, and that mournful tripe has no place in our present picture.' There is the unrecognized responsibility. Nor are daytime serials unique. 'Good will' and other terms and pretexts have been callously exploited on the radio. Remember that you enjoy a huge prestige. You may not be your brother's keeper but you do have responsibility. Keep drugs off the market.

Remember, too, that we are serious. Not earnest, just plain serious. More of us than you think, more of us than yet know it in themselves. We have nerves and feelings, and maybe, as the war years drag on, we're likely to learn unexpected things about ourselves, untapped resources, unrealized susceptibilities, new needs. Quiet, for instance, and reflectiveness. We're not much given to either. On the whole, we have lived and thought gregariously. But at times a man has touched us to the quick, with a word or a reference that had the authentic ring, that had quality. You've done it for us—in the Treasury Hour when, in between layers of laughter and orchestration, you've slipped in the Pericles funeral oration, the Gettysburg address and Demosthenes' appeal to the Athenians. There is evidence to the point here from England. Between 1939 and 1940 the Everyman edition of great classics jumped sales from 1,000,000 to 2,300,000.

Englishmen discovered the touchstone of quality and found suddenly that it corresponded to the needs and temper of a war effort. There's more in us than you suppose. Give us the chance of self-discovery.

To the National Association of Broadcasters: You have a code manual of decent practice in broadcasting. Enforce it. The station which broadcast 'Here is a late important news bulletin: use Smith Brothers cough drops . . .' was not unique—except in its public apology after the event. Enforce that code. It bars 'continuity which describes repellently any functions or symptomatic results of disturbances, or relief granted through use of any product.' Don't let's beat about the bush. You mean laxatives. But they're on the air—one of them right alongside a patriotic song hit. Is that decent practice? Enforce that code—and extend it. It isn't very bold. Decency is more than avoidance of indecency. Your wartime circular to member stations says all the right things. Do you mean them? Will you expel a member station that won't honor the code?

But perhaps this all sounds pernickety. Let's get down to fundamentals. Beyond the war looms peace and an ever harder job to do. Are we prepared for it? This is no place for post-war prophecy, but a few certainties already stare us in the face. (1) A worldwide planned economy is a post-war imperative. That means the assumption of unprecedented powers by government and the breakdown in ourselves of some traditional adhesions. (2) The need for intelligent co-operation by the workers and the general public in realizing a planned economy is no less certain. And a third certainty links the first two. (3) If we are to preserve democracy—control over government and willing collaboration with it—interpretation to the people of what is asked of them is going to be vital.

Radio's big chance is implicit in these three certainties. Its generous service to the government in the emergency already provides a pattern for the more intricate and comprehensive design of future collaboration. For the general public (and let us remember that listening increases progressively as we descend the economic scale) radio has long been the preferred medium of communication. And of popular interpretation radio is a past master. It has understood far better than its critics the importance of adhering to the vernacular. The men who write the scripts for the Treasury Hour, 'We Hold These Truths,' and countless other programs need no instruction. They need only a more constant incentive to realize the best that is in them. The prerequisites of public service are there. All that is lacking is a policy, a strategy of action that envisages a future different from the past—in the problems it sets, the demands it makes on us, and the qualities of mind and spirit that are going to be paramount. Radio's continued independence is at stake. Will it anticipate in time the changed needs and unarticulated aspirations of a new society and its own new responsibilities?

Commercial radio will survive only if the natural and necessary incentive of profit is subordinated to the public interest as a criterion of policy. To date, radio's concern over profits has blinded it both to many profitable opportunities and to the evil social consequences of some of its commercial practices. It has, for instance, yet to realize (1) that exploitation of a credulous public, whether in advertising or in programs, is socially dangerous in a wider context than that of the specific field of exploitation. (2) That widespread ignorance in a modern society is evil, a risk that democracy cannot afford. In the race against time, therefore, to provide distraction for a weary world is not enough. (3) That profit and popular acclaim are inadequate criteria for public service. Democracy rests on belief in people. Radio must realize such belief in far more programs that have intrinsic merit. It is in the nature of private enterprise to take risks. Radio can here take risks with the prospect of rich reward. For we the people are going to need a deal more education than we have ever had, or maybe, wanted. Not schoolbook stuff, but education for living in an intricately organized worldwide community. Radio's big chance is the virtual certainty of the emergence of fresh appetite for knowledge and understanding. It has so far eschewed whole fields of opportunity in social education—on matters of material day-to-day concern to everyone. Radio, in fact, has taken no risks with the public. That is unjust, and it is going to prove unwise. Radio has done splendid things, but more in the manner of a high-spirited, resourceful playboy than of a responsible adult. It has yet to appreciate the first part of W. B. Yeats's dictum, 'Think like a wise man but communicate in the language of the people.'

NEWSPAPERS IN A DEMOCRACY

By Grove Patterson

THE institutions of democracy rest more securely upon the foundation of a free press than upon any other idea or practice known to man. We recognize five institutions for social, economic, political, and moral betterment. They are the home, the church, the school, industry, and the newspaper.

The responsible editor long ago came to the conclusion that he faced the opportunity of making a newspaper into something more than a newspaper. He faced and seized the opportunity of making it into an institution for constant service in the community.

He knows now that he faces the even greater opportunity, the profound duty, of making the newspaper the chief agent for enabling representative government to function. After traveling through 14 countries in Europe, I came home convinced that the free newspaper is the major defense that can keep one man or one group of men from stealing a government and operating it in the interest of a privileged few.

In supporting the role of the newspaper in American life, I shall submit three observations. The first has to do with the nature of democracy itself.

A great deal of misstatement is made and written about democracy. I have heard it praised as superior to all other forms of government. I question this. Autocracy is more competent. Things can be done over night in the dictatorship state that take six months or a year to do under a loose system of representative government. That is not the point. Let us not miss the essence. Let us not miss the real meaning of democracy. If God had an idea in putting life upon the earth, it was not principally

From *Editor and Publisher*, 27 December 1941. By permission of the author and the publisher.

that man might develop a gadget for government. I believe it was and remains His primary purpose to bring forth the good man and the good woman, who may some day come to live what the philosophers call the Good Life.

Democracy is immeasurably more than a form of government. Democracy is the spirit. Democracy provides an atmosphere in which man can be somebody and go somewhere under his own power. We think of it as a great inheritance which can be eternally preserved without continuing individual effort. We think of it as a gift more than we think of it as a responsibility. But I say that if man is to continue to breathe in the atmosphere which democracy provides, if under its provisions he is to continue to express himself in meaningful terms of utility and beauty, he must come to regard it as a continuing, co-operative effort in human society.

In short, he must put into the field of democracy, in sacrifice and in devotion, as much as he takes out in privilege.

Taken as a form of government, it seems to me that democracy has been superficially defined as the rule of the majority. That is not a definition. The glory of democracy is that it is the one type of government upon the earth which provides for the continuing rights of a minority not in power. What could be more despotic, more tyrannical than a majority in power, without provision for the rights of the minority? The newspaper is peculiarly the medium for the expression of the minority not in power, because it is not under the control of government.

Free expression is the most important attribute of democracy and a free newspaper is its most vital medium. For the printed word gives permanence to free expression. Unhappily the average American citizen does not think through the meaning of a free press, its significance in a representative government. It probably occurs only to a minority that the institutions of a democracy rest upon a system which opens and keeps open a channel for human expression, a channel through which flows, from the center of government, the stream of information which makes it possible for democratic organization to function over the far-flung territory of a nation. It was H. G. Wells who said that the Roman Empire could not endure because there were no news-

papers—no methods of apprising the outlying peoples of the behavior of the center.

Democracy, then, can continue to function only so long and
in so far as this channel is not tampered with or dammed or
used exclusively by the state, as in dictatorship countries—this
channel through which can flow constantly, from the center to
the border, a stream of objective information, and, from the
border to the center, a stream of analysis, of criticism, of praise
and, if necessary, condemnation.

Millions in the totalitarian countries of Europe and in all the
lands possessed by the Dictator, millions with hopes and fears
and aspirations like unto our own, are chained in the slavery of
silence, or driven under the whip of official falsehood.

Every morning at ten o'clock the jittery editors of Berlin
gather at the office of the Ministry of Propaganda and are told
not only what they shall print and not print, but are instructed
as to whether the government story for that day shall be put
under a one-column head, a two-column head, given little play
or heavy play.

Every newspaper is a design for lying . . .

My second observation is that the newspaper, not only because
of its information service, not only because of its analysis of national policies, but because of its advertising service, is vital to
the *economic* health and well-being of this country.

As Mr. Paul Garrett, vice-president and director of public relations of the General Motors, points out: 'Look back to a time
when we had no radios, no electrical household appliances, no
automobiles, no moving pictures, no plastics, no wireless communication, no telephones, no electric refrigeration, no air-condi-
tioning, no rayon, no incandescent lamps, no canned foods, no
bathtubs, no streamliners, and no air travel. We call these the
products of mass production. And so they are. But who would say
they have come to be the necessities of American life *solely* because we learned earlier than the rest of the world the art of
mass production? Of what value would mass production be without mass consumption? How could we stimulate mass consumption without mass merchandising? And how could we have mass
merchandising without mass advertising?

'May I establish in your mind the part advertising plays in this peculiar American mass production formula. Advertising *basically* is a vital part of our economy, equally important with designing, engineering, and production.'

How often does it occur to those not engaged in some form of the business, to sense the major contribution that mass advertising has made to the widening of the horizons of the average man and to the elevation of the standard of living? Mass production, mass merchandising, mass advertising, and mass consumption! The highest standard of living ever reached in this world has been built upon and stands today upon those achievements. Advertising is as fundamental to well-being as manufacture. Advertising is the inevitable concomitant of a high standard of living.

Just as democracy is inconceivable without a free press, so business, free enterprise, is inconceivable without a free press. The newspaper, unlike the radio, is so far free from government regulation. Business deserves to be immeasurably more free from bureaucratic regulation than it is. No medium is in such good position, so well equipped, as the newspaper to preach and to teach the value of free enterprise. It is not only the privilege, it is the duty of the advertiser—the duty of the business man and the professional man—to build up, to support, to strengthen this most substantial of all bulwarks against the encroachments of totalitarianism . . .

And now I want to speak for a moment somewhat critically to my colleagues in the profession of journalism and in the business of making newspapers. Daniel Burnham, the architect, once said: 'There is no magic in little thoughts.' We are called upon to have a renewed faith in the high calling upon which we are engaged, and we must, especially in this emergency, accept a greater responsibility than we have ever felt before. As Robert Quillen, able Southern editor, has said: 'The press has the right to be free, but the more free it is, the less right it has to be wrong.'

The most constructive suggestion that can come to any man is the idea of personal responsibility for corporate action. Our newspapers can rise no higher than ourselves. We must impose upon ourselves the censorship of good taste. We must be restricted—but only by truth and decency. We must serve not only our better natures, but the better natures of those who look to us for interpretation in a bewildering world. If we are to have a free press, we must furnish a responsible press.

Thus, I have devoted myself to three observations: first, that the institutions of democracy rest principally upon the foundation of an independent press; second, that the newspaper, as the chief medium of information and advertising, is vital to the economic well-being of the nation; third, that we newspaper people, desiring a free press, must accept the duty of furnishing a responsible press. We must weave for ourselves, and wear, not only in this hour of crisis, but in life's sunshine and storm, the durable fabric of character.

Our newspaper must be something greater than an information service, finer than a service of criticism and interpretation, more than a medium for the sale of goods. Those who make it must have the imagination to see it in higher terms. They must be guided, above all, by an impulse that comes from the heart and the emotions as much as from the mind.

We have been given this precious instrument to use, but we cannot use it aright unless we have love in our hearts.

We are engaged, in some fashion, in widening the horizons of men's thinking. There is surely something humanly progressive, eternally purposeful, in this effort. May we editors—indeed may we all—write over our doors, over our minds, over our hearts, those words of Thomas Jefferson, carved in stone, above the entrance to the University of Virginia: 'Enter by this gateway to seek the light of truth, the way of honor, and the will to work for men.'

A CHAMPION ALL THE WAY

By John Kieran

It seems that Joe Louis is always doing the right thing. He is simply grand, and the words 'simply grand' are used advisedly. He is simple, straightforward, honest and natural in speech and action. He is grand, whether that word is used in the colloquial English sense of 'superlatively good, admirable, really swell' or with the more scholarly implications that come with its Latin derivation, 'large, imposing, beyond ordinary dimensions.'

So with reference to Joe Louis, it goes double. By his bearing and his actions it may be that he has done more for the Negro race than any man since Booker T. Washington. And he has done plenty for the white race, too. He has shown them a boxing champion who never dodged a fight with a fit opponent, never delayed in taking one of them on, never quibbled over the rules or the referee, never took unfair advantage over a rival in the ring, didn't whimper in defeat, didn't crow in victory, and altogether was an outstanding example of the best qualities that the boxing game can produce.

Joe Louis was also the first world's heavyweight champion to put his crown on the line in a fight that, as far as he was concerned, was all for charity. When he is in uniform at Camp Upton tomorrow he will be the first heavyweight champion to wear that crown and a soldier suit at the same time.

Well, what's so great about a big fellow, a heavyweight champion fighter, going into the Army? Thousands upon thousands of skinny unknowns have gone into the Army and nobody cheered them except their families and close relatives. Why all this to-do about Joe Louis? He's just doing what's right, isn't he?

Quite so. He's just doing what's right. Don't look now, but

From *The New York Times*, 13 January 1942. By permission of the author and *The New York Times*.

how many of us always do what's right? (Stop pointing!) Most of
the misery in the world is caused by persons who don't always
do what's right. There were 35,000 deaths by auto accident in
this country in 1940, most of them caused by thoughtlessness,
selfishness and bad manners. It's as simple as that. The drivers
of so many cars didn't do the right thing as citizens of a civilized community. Joe Louis always has done the right thing
since he has been under the public eye.

It's true that Joe Louis has had wonderful opportunities for
doing the right thing. A roll-call of those who had wonderful
opportunities and made no use of them would run till the crack
of doom. The point is that Joe Louis Barrow, an unlettered
Negro up from the cotton fields, never missed a chance to make
good. He didn't wait for Opportunity to knock twice like the
postman: Joe was there at the door, in training, ready and fit
for the job.

The Shuffler is a man of few words and great deeds in his
sphere. A couple of weeks ago, in a sequestered place, this observer asked Joe what he expected to do when he went into the
Army.

'Do what they tell me,' said Joe. And not another word.

Simple, isn't it? Simple in the best sense of the word. Some
fellows—very decent chaps, too—are finicky. They want to be
in the pack artillery or the anti-aircraft or the radio section or
the aerial photographic branch. They have their prejudices or
their preferences, some of them quite logical and sensible.

But Joe Louis, a famous figure, the heavyweight champion of
the world, has no preference. He will go where they order him
to go. He will do what they tell him to do. He feels that his
superior officers will know better than he does what he should
do. So far he has done about everything he should have done.
This, above all, would be no time to stop.

Joe will know how to take orders. He has been taking them
from Trainer Jack Blackburn ever since he entered the ring.
Taking those orders and carrying them out to the best of his
ability.

There was just one time when he missed. Certainly Trainer
Blackburn didn't order him to go out there and take that fear-

ful beating in his first meeting with Max Schmeling. Something went wrong that night. But good came of it in the long run. It made Joe a better fighter. He learned something in defeat and he profited by it in later battles.

One thing learned about Joe Louis by all onlookers that evening was that he knew how to lose as well as win. He never gave up until he was knocked senseless. He climbed off the floor and fought back as long as he could wave his arms. And when he lost he made no excuse and he lodged no complaint against the weather, the ring platform, the referee, his opponent or the gods of chance. He lost; that was all. The other fellow licked him. It's too bad that his example isn't followed more often by other workers at the same trade.

The late Ring Lardner wrote a savage short story entitled 'The Champion.' It was a merciless masterpiece, a satirical exposure of what sometimes—alas, that such things should be!—occurs in the boxing game. The Lardner portrayal was of a boxing champion who was a hero in public and strictly a rat of the lowest degree in private. Any fancied resemblance to any person then living was not entirely coincidental.

There have been such champions. But here's Joe Louis. And that's another story. There have been fine fellows in the boxing game, men who were champions out of the ring as well as inside the ropes. But none with a finer record than Joe Louis. A great fighter, a thorough sportsman, a modest gentleman, a good citizen and, now, the proudest title of all, a soldier of the U.S.A.

THE AMERICA OF WILLA CATHER

SAPPHIRA AND THE SLAVE GIRL. By Willa Cather
New York: Alfred A. Knopf [1940]. *295 pp. $2.50*

Reviewed by Frederic R. Gunsky

FEW American novelists have attained the maturity of Willa Cather. In *Sapphira and the Slave Girl* she is once more concerned with realities, not absolutes; and all the co-existent, varied aspects of the ante-bellum Virginia scene are considered in the careful pattern of her story.

Here Miss Cather exhibits the mastery of style and form, the distinctive sense of social values, the qualities of mind and heart which placed her in the first rank of American creative writers on the publication of *O Pioneers!* almost thirty years ago. Again there is the thrill of the right word rightly used, of rural backgrounds limned with a painter's eye, of authentic individuals profoundly and sympathetically portrayed.

This novel of a mulatto slave, persecuted by the jealous wife of her master, and her eventual escape to Canada by way of the Underground Railroad is in the tradition of Miss Cather's books, where representative characters of nearly every major racial, national, and religious group in America have been portrayed. Sapphira Dodderidge Colbert and her husband trace their ancestry to Flanders and the English counties; their daughter Rachel had married an Irishman; and they are Virginians of at least the third generation. The Negroes in *Sapphira,* however, except for the gentle, weary maid who cares for old Mrs. Harris in *Obscure Destinies,* are the first of their people to appear in Miss Cather's fiction. In their story one perceives the essential history of chattel slavery in this country.

Old 'Aunt' Jezebel received her name from the slavers who

From *Common Ground*, Spring 1941. By permission of the publisher.

brought her from Guinea in the 1780s, a fierce creature who bit and scratched until they tamed her with sugar and respect. Jezebel had had many owners before she came to the Dodderidges, but she always retained the pride of body and spirit which enhanced her value as an item of property. Till, her daughter, was contrastingly genteel. Reared as a servant in Loudoun County, she became Sapphira's housekeeper at Mill Farm and resigned herself to a marriage of convenience with poor shuffling Jeff, the more willingly since she was allowed her affair with an itinerant Cuban painter. The issue of the latter episode is Nancy, golden yellow in complexion, gentle, sensitive, and timid in character until her escape to freedom liberates the positive qualities which give her poise and assurance.

Slaves as persons are a rarity in literature; they are usually either patronized or beatified. Miss Cather makes no accusations, calls no names, demands nothing of the reader's sympathies save an unreserved appreciation of certain qualities of character and a certain way of existence. Jezebel and Till and Nancy, unimpressive Jeff and respectable old Washington, malicious Lizzie and her casual, giggling daughter Bluebell, each according to his or her circumstances and motives exhibits the virtues and vices of a people forced into an uncongenial mold, yet irrepressibly alive and unmistakably part of the human experiment.

This attitude of acceptance is not, of course, anything new in Willa Cather. Her remarkable gallery of fictional portraits includes Bohemian and Scandinavian farm folk, French priests and French Canadian pioneers, Southwestern Indians, Mexican ne'er-do-wells, German artists and working people, Jewish merchants and dilettantes, cosmopolitan Americans and numerous figures in the more conventional Anglo-Saxon tradition, drawing their heritage from a dozen separate sources, mingling intimately on American soil, but retaining flavors of background and belief, endowing shared activities with different meanings, contributing a rich variety to a new cultural order. This is one of the author's great themes.

Consider the heroic women who are the central figures of three of Miss Cather's earliest and best novels: Alexandra Bergson in *O Pioneers!*, a more capable farmer than any man in the community, imbued with faith and strength and the simplicity, honesty, and courage which arise from a deep sense of personal truth; Thea Kronborg in *The Song of the Lark,* also of Scandinavian stock, but concerned with struggle in another world of accomplishment, the international realm of music and art which, even when she has conquered it, does not diminish the liberal Western quality of her personality; and hearty Antonia Shimerda in *My Antonia,* whose mild Czech father is driven to suicide by the cruelty of the Nebraska prairie, while Antonia, on the other hand, submits naturally to, and grows under, the hardship and rough labor of frontier existence. Through her submission she gains in strength and stature, rising finally to be a symbol of all that is vital and inspiring in the pioneer generations. 'She was a rich mine of life,' the narrator observes, 'like the founders of early races.'

Such figures are the most prominent in retrospect, but the author's study of individual character has never been narrow or conventional. From the beginning, Miss Cather has been aware of conditioning factors ignored by the majority of novelists. The literature of local color and Walt Whitman's poetic vision of a teeming, wide new land, her companionship with immigrants during a prairie girlhood and adolescence, her experience of European culture and her first preoccupation with art and artists —all have influenced her writing. Out of them she has produced a succession of works evoking the spirit of native and immigrant American communities, describing distinctive gifts often unrealized and unappreciated, suggesting the intangibles of this problem of living together, condemning the 'native' Middle West as 'a smug, domestic, self-satisfied, provincial world of utter ignorance,' and affirming the worth of vitality, honesty, and creative values wherever they appear to challenge that world.

Thus, in two of the sketches in *Obscure Destinies,* Anton Rosicky, the amiable little Czech farmer, and buxom Mrs. David Rosen, the Jewish housewife *par excellence,* share a fondness for 'order and comeliness,' a desire to live not extravagantly but expansively, loving the rich texture of common things enjoyed with perception. Rosicky's farm and Mrs. Rosen's kitchen produce genuine works of art and are centers of neighborliness. Father Latour and his Indian guide Jacinto, in *Death Comes for the Archbishop,* spend a summer night under the stars in perfect understanding; although their intellectual sources lie as far apart as Auvergne and a Southwestern pueblo, they have in common the knowledge that courage and dignity are the making of a man, and that the immensity of night on the desert is beyond knowledge. The 'florid style' of the Jewish connoisseur Louie Marsellus, in *The Professor's House,* is irritating alike to Professor St. Peter, whose tastes are French and austere, and to his son-in-law, Scott McGregor, who is modern American rather than Scottish, but too poor and too plain to admire this variety of magnificence. Krajiek, the Shimerdas' dishonest Bohemian creditor, possesses only too many of the traits which make unscrupulous Ivy Peters so detestable in *A Lost Lady.* Euclide Auclair, the 'philosopher apothecary of Quebec' in *Shadows on the Rock,* is no more conservative an Old World figure than the comfortable German Kohlers in *The Song of the Lark,* or Alexandra Bergson's homesick Norwegian mother. Rachel Blake, Sapphira's daughter, is as straightforward in her affections and her sympathies as Alexandra, who must, like Antonia, find happiness in a rather unequal marriage. Sapphira herself, proud and forceful even in her invalid's chair, frustrated but not defeated, is as much a lost lady as Captain Forrester's fascinating wife, who comes from the other side of the continent and an equally distant social milieu.

It is evident that Willa Cather, as completely as any author, has caught the vision of America as the coming together of many races, many sects, many distinctive ways of thought and behavior. In her quiet fashion, with a fine consistency, she has moved from setting to setting, absorbed in the inner realities of personality and the social and physical contexts which form them, interpreting what it has meant to be an immigrant farmer in Nebraska, a singer in flight from provincial Colorado, a professor with European inclinations on a Great Lakes campus, an apostolic bishop among the Indians, a settler of early Quebec, and now a slaveholder and a slave in Old Virginia. She has re-

gretted the disintegration of older beliefs and the resulting confusion of ideals and principles, for what she demands of life is
that it have beauty and meaning for the individual, and this is
ordinarily possible only through adherence to tradition, personal
faith, and the maintenance of a coherent social order.

THOMAS WOLFE'S SIGNIFICANCE AS A WRITER

THE WEB AND THE ROCK. By Thomas Wolfe
New York: Harper and Brothers [1939]. 695 *pp.* $3

Reviewed by Alfred Kazin

WHEN Thomas Wolfe died last September at the age of thirty-eight he was what the world calls a major novelist; but no one would have called him a prodigy. There have been writers, like the twenty-five-year-old Keats, whose last letters are moving in their very profundity, who compressed all maturity into their boyhood, and even transcended it. Thomas Wolfe was always a boy, and his significance as a writer is that he expanded his boyhood into a lifetime, made it exciting and important without touching many of the problems that give life its common savor. Naive, fantastically self-absorbed, full of home-spun mysticism and adolescent grandeur, he cut his way blindly and noisily to that achievement; yet by his passionate insistence on the importance of youth, that youth is the very center of existence, he gave its fever and uncertainty the dignity of mature understanding.

Wolfe's very innocence was his strength. Believing in nothing but his own power, he infected the world of his novels with it. He made his characters larger than life without suggesting that they were superior to it. He lived in a world in which man was forever haunted by his own promise and deflected from it. There were no half-tones in that world, only compromises with fate. He believed so completely in the possibility of happiness that he gave human ambition, human valor, human expression a rooted strength in nature.

From *New York Herald Tribune Books,* 25 June 1939. By permission of the author and the publisher.

It was not only life as an idea, but life as victory, that possessed him. In a world of endless possibilities and limitless power, every object took on a new glamour, and every function had its heroic purpose. His hero was able to bestride cities, to hear in every love affair the detonations of fate, to feel every twinge as a blow, every yawn as a snicker, to hear as from his own heart the music of multitudes, to read a hundred books and guess at the contents of a thousand, to eat like a regiment, to bellow at the universe and hear it whimper back. He proclaimed himself (as in *Of Time and the River*) Orestes and Faust, Telemachus in search of the father and Proteus in the sea-world of the city; Jason on the eternal voyage and Antaeus back to earth; Kronos dreaming of time and Faust gazing at Helen.

He was also a gangling, overgrown Carolina boy with seven brothers and sisters whose mother kept a boarding house in Asheville, and whose father was a stonecutter with a taste for rhetoric. He had been mocked as a child, had been awakened on cold winter mornings to deliver newspapers (lost, lost, forever lost), and had suffered like a million other American boys because his parents were dull, his gifts unrecognized, and his teachers stupid. The stonecutter's son had gone on to college, self-conscious before the middle-class nobility; he was no good at baseball, he had a taste for Elizabethan prose, and he was vaguely rumored to be queer. Later he went to Harvard, wrote plays, and came to New York to dazzle the stage.

Instead he became a college instructor. His classes were full of gossipy, hungry, loud and superficial children who stared at him, who did not love the best that has been thought and said in English literature, and whose greatest ambition was to become Certified Public Accountants. Wolfe raged and suffered; he was lonely, he prowled the streets of New York, hated the beast-city and the beast-people, wept, and thought himself a failure. At night he wrote savagely in old ledgers, and wrote always of himself; he would reclaim the dream of time, he would make himself a monument. 'Could I make tongue say more than tongue could utter! Could I make brain grasp more than brain could think! Could I weave into immortal denseness some small brede of words, pluck out of sunken depths the roots of living, some hundred thousand magic words that were as great as all my hunger,. and hurl the sum of all my living out upon three hundred pages . . . !'

Sitting in a Paris café, he would remember the railing on the Atlantic City boardwalk, an iron bridge across an American river, the chink of a milkman's horse going slowly up the morning street. He was in love with America, and lost from it. By scaling the walls of his memory, he hoped to reclaim his heritage and explain it. His autobiography, he said, would be history. All art was autobiography, an artist could write of no one but himself. Self-fascinated and self-tormented, he set down with agonizing precision the look on the face of an old teacher, the mountain coldness and Appalachian heights, the tone of boys playing one-o'-cat in the sleepy twilight. He dramatized himself in pride and in suffering, rose in his books above the world he was trying to discover; but he could not save himself. For at the bottom of all his frenzy, his savage misery, the thousands of words that spurted out of his pen without drawing him closer to the salvation, the answer, he needed so desperately, lay a genuine fear of himself and the world he lived in. He was proud of his passion, he even gloried in it; but it did not satisfy him.

There were two forces in Wolfe, and they were always at war with each other. One was the mountaineer's son who wrote with a hard, driving force of the people he had hated as a child, who described the death of Old Gant, the peregrinations of Bascom Hawke, his mother's haggard kitchen sourness and scolding old age—the Wolfe who poured into the first third of *The Web and the Rock* a beautiful and haunting chronicle of mountain legends and mountain life. That Wolfe was a superbly talented novelist, with an ear for dialogue, a sense of timing (consider the reproduction of the gasping, stammering Gant speech in the first chapter of *Of Time and the River*), a rich and overflowing knowledge of his people that were unsurpassed in their nervous power. The other was the ubiquitous, heavily breathing, gluttonous, silly Eugene Gant, who was so much Wolfe that he even dropped into the first person in some pages of *Of Time and the River,* and who is the character in all his work one knows least. That Wolfe was the Tarzan of rhetoric, the noble lover, the antagonist of cities, the spear of fate—the Wolfe whose rhetoric, swollen with phrases out of the English classics, hysteria, and mere sloth, is as painful to read as a child's scrawlings. Its language was pilfered recklessly from the Jacobeans and Sir Thomas Browne, for Wolfe was so enraptured with the altitudinous, swooning prose of the seventeenth century that he adopted it for his own purposes almost unconsciously. Why? He was perpetually trying to defend himself; he was lost between his grievance against and overwhelming native love for those who had bred him, and what he believed his own destination to be. He could write with remorseless, bitter certainty about his sister Helen, his pathetic brother Ben, his nagging mother; they were his people, he loved and hated them, but they were in his blood. Yet it took him, as in that uncut version of *Of Time and the River,* hundreds upon hundreds of pages to describe his trip from Asheville to Harvard. And the best scene in that monstrous cavalcade of Eugene Gant's ambitions, dreams, dislikes, hunger and thirst, has nothing to do with Eugene at all. It is the cry of one Pullman porter to another as two trains flash by each other in New York. 'Hey boy, you seen that gal from Memphis? You tell her what I said?'

II

The Web and the Rock is at once the best and the worst of Thomas Wolfe's novels. For some obscure reason he thought he could avoid the charge of excessive autobiography by changing Eugene Gant's name to George Webber. It is the same Gant career, however, and always the same Wolfe. The first three hundred pages are extraordinary. There is a perfect story in it of a Negro who deserted from the Army to the little mountain village, and in one night of ruin went mad, killed off a posse, and was fiendishly lynched. There is old Jenny, who slaved seven days a week in Mrs. Hopper's genteel boarding house, but would take two hours off on Sunday afternoon, doff her apron, and run shrieking down to the court square, 'O sinners, I'se a-comin'!' No one was in the square, but Jenny would harangue the stones and the drifting trolleys. There is a whole stalking portrait gallery of mountain people, with their wrestlin's, their ghost stories, the lusty butcher's wife assaulting her daughter's impetuous suitors.

At least half of the novel is devoted to Gant-Webber as a college instructor, of which there was more than enough in *Of Time and the River,* and his love affair. There is also a long, occasionally hilarious, and severely bitter satire on New York literati. The love affair, with its multitudinous yearnings, its scandals and alarums, his remarks on her immortal spirit and her remarks on his immortal spirit, is less interesting.

It is significant that the more Wolfe sank into the bog of 'lost, ah forever lost,' 'the fairest fame of praise,' 'a thousand barren and desolate places, a thousand lights and weathers of the soul's gray horror,' 'he was the Lord of life, the master of the earth, he was the city's conqueror,' the more did he seek refuge, not in what he felt but in celebrating his own uncertainty. He wrote himself out because he had no faith in that writing; he repeated himself, rang endless variations on the same phrase, embossed it. As he wrote on and on, he yielded to his confusion; it came to hold a music for him, for in the very statement of his wretchedness, with its emotion and nervous clamor he found the physical equivalent of his spaceless and inchoate ambition. And what was that ambition? To find America in himself, to announce, with the passion that Whitman had given to Manifest Destiny and Herman Melville to fate, that he was alone in America, and that America was alone among the nations; that it was a world in itself, different in kind and pursuing an ageless dream; that it was high, vast, beautiful and lonely; that ghosts rumbled through its present and a wild, bursting energy forced it onward to a nameless future.

'The young men of this land are not a lost race—they are a race that never yet has been discovered.' Wolfe did not know why he believed that. He knew only that as he towered over men, so there was something in America that haunted the race of man. He wanted to be its prophet, to kindle in its bones the fire that leaped in him. And in that he failed. For he was so obsessed by the spirit that he exhausted it; he confused the truth that lay everywhere about him during his lifetime with the truth that he bore in himself. Consider that all his books fall within one decade, the convulsive thirties. Who, reading his books in twenty or thirty years, would learn from them that it was a decade of war and panic, a decade that has taught men the bitterness and confusion of modern life? The tragedy in his novels flows out of individual disappointment, the absence of love and comfort; it never suggests, and is never nourished by, the common experience of dismay and insecurity that has tormented America these last few years. There are failure and triumph in Wolfe's books, much nonsense and unparalleled grandeur; but they are his alone. He went roaring through a world he had never made and which he never fully understood; a gargantuan boy (they had told him he was different, and he believed it; they told him he was a greedy child, and he affirmed it) begging, out of loneliness and defeat, 'Believe! Believe!'

RECREATION IN AMERICAN LIFE

AMERICA LEARNS TO PLAY. A History of Popular Recreation,
1607-1940. By Foster Rhea Dulles. New York: D. Appleton-
Century Company [1940]. *Illustrated.* 441 + xvii *pp.* $4

Reviewed by R. L. Duffus

THIS book might be called a history of leisure in America, popular and aristocratic, sacred and profane. Mr. Dulles begins with
the settlers at Jamestown, hungry but not bored, 'playing happily at bowls.' It ends, of course, with the radio, the movies, the
Sunday afternoon traffic jam, a vast variety of sports and hobbies, and 'countless pleasures once limited to the privileged few,'
but now open to the multitude. A good part of the story might
stir yearnings for the simpler past, but another good part might
not. Mr. Dulles thinks our ancestors and predecessors on this
continent were often oppressed by the monotony of life. He
thinks there has been progress.

The difficulty in an attempt to establish this thesis in a book
of this kind is that the author must write of pleasures because
there is almost nothing to be said about boredom. Moreover,
there is an almost uncontrollable impulse to believe that the past
was more interesting than the present. Whoever had a headache
in the golden days? In general Mr. Dulles makes an excellent
case for the virtues of the shorter working day, the decline of
the theory that tedium is an acceptable offering to God, and the
rise of new inventions for amusement and recreation. But he
fails in one thing: his book is nowhere tedious. The interest inherent in his material and his lively method of treatment overwhelm his thesis. In short, this is a fascinating book.

He makes a good deal of the Puritan attitude toward life. If

From *The New York Times Book Review,* 14 April 1940. By permission of
the author and *The New York Times.*

one wished to quibble on that point one might say that the convinced Puritans probably enjoyed their own attitude, and that this was why they clung to it. No one not brought up in a prohibition community can ever guess the satisfaction of not spending ten nights in a barroom. But Mr. Dulles himself realizes very well that the repressions of the Puritan community were also confessions. 'Much of the legislation of early New England forbidding tavern sports, card-playing and dancing,' he concedes, 'throws a penetrating light on how a very considerable number of the people were spending such free time as they had.' There had to be 'successive edicts with respect to observance of the Sabbath,' which proves that some people went right on 'shouting, hollowing, screaming, running, riding, singing, dancing, jumping, winding horns or the like' (in the words of an old blue law), in spite of hell and high water.

It was in Massachusetts in the eighteenth century that Sarah Tuttle and Jacob Murline created a scandal; 'they sat down together,' said the court record, 'his arm being about her and her arm upon his shoulder or about his neck, and hee kissed her and shee kissed him, or they kissed one another, continuing in this posture about half an hour.' Often a colonial dance lasted till dawn—the practice did not come in with the motor car. There was a game played with 'gouff clubs' in New York City before the British left. George Washington loved to dance, as did John Quincy Adams. At weddings, house-raisings and revival meetings the pioneer knew how to enjoy himself. Something called 'Spiritual Neking' was on a stage program in New York about 1847, and Walt Whitman, not yet the poet of democracy, denounced the contemporary stage as having 'hardly a pleasant point to mitigate its coarseness.' A Western cowboy ordered and got a champagne bath. Baseball is almost or quite a century old, depending on how one reckons; roller skating is more than three-quarters of a century old; college football was being damned as professional forty-five years ago; Summer resorts were in full swing early in the history of the Republic; Chautauqua and the bicycle antedated the present century, as did the trolley and the public amusement park which was often to be found at the end of the line.

Youth would be served. This is one conclusion at which one arrives as one peruses these entertaining pages. Human nature has changed little, though its facilities for amusing itself have multiplied and its leisure for using them has increased. Yet there has been a constant development, interrupted only once—by the return to Puritanic customs and attitudes which came after the Revolutionary War and lasted into what ought to be called, in America, something besides the Victorian Age. Mr. Dulles makes a good point of this lapse, though he does not fully explain it. Perhaps it was partly an illusion, due to the rise in social status of a class which had previously lived plain lives because nothing else could be afforded. At any rate, the period passed. This is not the Victorian Age.

There is so much in Mr. Dulles's book that it is hard to make a satisfactory inventory. The theatre runs through many pages, first frowned upon ('Othello' was banned in Newport, R. I., in spite of being advertised as a 'moral dialogue,' in the year 1772); then given over to an odd mixture of rowdies and people of fashion; then, divorced from vaudeville and variety, attaining maturity in almost our own generation. The sports and amusements of cities, towns and country are separately discussed as we approach modern times. It may seem to some that Mr. Dulles exaggerates the monotony of farm existence before good roads, the motor car, and the radio opened it up to the outside world. When one looks closely at the small town or farming community of a generation ago it is seen to lack most of the modern amusements, as well as most of the urban amusements of its own day. Mr. Dulles thinks this lack 'played no small part in stirring up the discontent that led to agricultural revolt and to the Populist movement of the Eighteen Nineties.' Yet it is impossible to describe the lighter side of rural life without making it at least interesting, and in some degree attractive. County fairs, Fourth of July parades, church socials, picnics, singing schools, the Grange, barn dances, corn huskings, sleigh rides and hay rides, all sound like fun now, though they certainly weren't enough to halt the rush from the country to the city. But machinery which enabled fewer farmers to raise more crops had something to do with this migration—the boys did not merely leave, they were pushed out.

The most obvious gain would appear to this reviewer to have taken place among the populations that were being crowded more and more compactly into the growing cities. They couldn't live entirely on the thrills of Barnum's Museum and its successors, nor go every night to the theatre. The spectator sports came to them slowly; organized participation sports even more belatedly. No Robert Moses had yet appeared to lead them out of the Egypt of stifling tenements and streets into the Canaan of parks and playgrounds. They could not afford bicycles during the craze of the Eighteen Nineties. The trolley of about the same period, or a little later, gave them their first real chance to breathe, though steamboats and railroads had offered excursion opportunities on a more limited scale much earlier. There were 'special trolley carnivals in the evening—the cars gayly illuminated with multi-colored lights and boasting even a number of musicians to provide popular band music.'

Then amusements and leisure came with a rush. There can be no doubt that Americans became physically and mentally a healthier race than they were during the doldrums of the nineteenth century. With the depression 'the "challenge of the new leisure" became a vital issue.' Psychologists even had to explain and justify leisure-time activities; their value, said one writer, lies 'in the nervous release which they afford from the customary and coercive activities which the social order imposes upon us.' In Puritan New England play was 'mispense of time.' Much later it had to be justified as having a beneficial effect on work— the chief end of man. Now it is a 'release' and tomorrow, perhaps, a duty. Do we enjoy life more than our ancestors did? Mr. Dulles appears to be convinced that we do, but it is probably too late to be sure. At least we spend about $4,000,000,000 a year trying to enjoy it, which is something.

The book is profusely illustrated with reproductions of old prints, paintings, play-bills, and so on. It can be fairly described as a source of very agreeable recreation for those who like to read. Yet, curiously enough, Mr. Dulles does not list reading as an important American recreation.

SANDBURG'S *ABRAHAM LINCOLN*

ABRAHAM LINCOLN: THE WAR YEARS. 4 vols. By Carl Sand-
burg. New York: Harcourt, Brace and Company [1939]. *2503 pp. $20.*

Reviewed by Robert E. Sherwood

TWENTY years ago Carl Sandburg of Illinois started to write the
fullest, richest, most understanding of all the Lincoln biographies. His work is now complete. *The War Years* follows *The
Prairie Years* into the treasure house which belongs, like Lincoln
himself, to the whole human family. It has been a monumental
undertaking; it is grandly realized.

The War Years begins where *The Prairie Years* ended, with
Lincoln's departure from Springfield—an unknown, threatened,
doubted man. It ends with the return of his body to the soil on
which it grew. Mr. Sandburg's finest passages are those describing his final journey, and all the immediate aftermaths of the
assassination, the shocking effect on men everywhere. Even the
wild tribesmen in the Caucasus were asking a traveler, Leo
Tolstoy, to tell them of this Western man who was 'so great that
he even forgave the crimes of his greatest enemies.' And Tolstoy
told them, 'Lincoln was a humanitarian as broad as the world.'

The War Years is compounded of such quotations. We are enabled to look at Lincoln through thousands of contemporary
eyes, including those of Tolstoy, and Jefferson Davis, and John
Bright, M.P., and Hendrik Ibsen, and Nathaniel Hawthorne,
and a South Carolina lady named Mary Chesnut. Mr. Sandburg
gives us his own estimates of many other figures, big and little,
of the period, but not of Abraham Lincoln. He indulges in no
speculation as to what was going on within the heart and soul
and mind of this peculiar man. If there is anything lacking in

From *The New York Times Book Review*, 3 December 1939. By permission
of the author and *The New York Times*.

The War Years, it is the presence of two men of the prairie years, Joshua Speed and William H. Herndon, who saw more deeply into Lincoln than did any others who ever knew him. When Lincoln stepped into the White House he stepped into a great isolation which no one—not even his old friends, Browning and Lamon, nor his secretaries, Nicolay and Hay—seems to have penetrated. In the analyses of his character provided by those who observed him at closest range the word 'unfathomable' recurs again and again.

In *The Prairie Years,* with fewer documents and many more myths at his disposal, Mr. Sandburg gave greater play to his own lyrical imagination. Any one can indulge in guesswork about the raw young giant who emerged from the mists of Kentucky, and Indiana, and Sangamon County, Illinois, and Mr. Sandburg's guesses were far better than most. But in *The War Years* he sticks to the documentary evidence, gathered from a fabulous number of sources. He indulges in one superb lyrical outburst at the conclusion of the chapter in which is described the dedication of the cemetery at Gettysburg; and, in the last volume, after John Wilkes Booth has fired the one bullet in his brass derringer pistol, Mr. Sandburg writes with the poetic passion and the somber eloquence of the great masters of tragedy.

Mr. Sandburg's method is unlike that of any biographer since Homer. He starts *The War Years* with the usual appreciative Foreword surveying his source material—and this Foreword provides an excellent survey of Lincolniana—but he reveals the odd nature of his essential research when he says, 'Taking my guitar and a program of songs and readings and traveling from coast to coast a dozen times in the last twenty years, in a wide variety of audiences I have met sons and daughters of many of the leading players in the terrific drama of the Eighteen Sixties.' From these sons and daughters he obtained old letters and pictures and clippings, and reminiscences and rumors which led him to upper shelves in remote libraries. Thus, his 'program of songs' (like Homer's) brought him into the very spirit of the people, the same people of whom—and by whom, and for whom—was Abraham Lincoln. Quite properly, Mr. Sandburg's great work is not the story of the one man's life. It is a folk biography. The hopes and apprehensions of millions, their loves and hates, their exultation and despair, were reflected truthfully in the deep waters of Lincoln's being, and so they are reflected truthfully in these volumes.

It is less the events than the men and women who made them that concern Mr. Sandburg. He gives relatively scant attention to the tactical, strategic course of Bull Run, the Peninsula, Antietam, Vicksburg and Gettysburg, but he is tireless in his telling of all that can be told of the generals and the privates who fought these battles of victory or defeat. Similarly, he provides many clear portraits of the men who formed the Congress during the Civil War, but leaves the reader in considerable confusion as to just what the Congress *did*. The reader's confusion on this point, however, is no greater than was that of the Congressmen themselves; the fact is that they accomplished next to nothing in the historic task of saving the Union; save as a persistent cause of irritation to Lincoln, they were little more potent than the members of the present Reichstag.

The first volume of *The War Years* contains the dramatis personae of *the terrific drama* and the dismal events of the years 1861-2. Lincoln began his Presidency by sneaking furtively into Washington, disguised, said his many enemies, in an absurdly long military cloak and a Scotch plaid cap. Confronted immediately with the crisis of Fort Sumter, he acted with arbitrary forcefulness, brusquely dismissing the generous offer of the more experienced Seward to run the country from the State Department. Having grimly assumed leadership and accepted war, Lincoln then proceeded to display weakness and temporizing indecision, which earned for him the contempt of friend and foe. At the end of 1862, he said, beautifully but helplessly, 'Fellow-citizens, we cannot escape history. We of this Congress and this Administration will be remembered in spite of ourselves.' Had his life then come to an end, he would have been remembered only as one who had haplessly fumbled great responsibility, as one of noble words and feeble deeds. A California Abolitionist newspaper described him as 'a driveling, idiotic, imbecile creature.' To a disgruntled officeseeker who snorted, 'Why, I am one of those who made you President!' Lincoln wearily said, 'Yes, and it's a pretty mess you got me into.' The whole country was indeed a pretty mess of corruption, equivocation, hypocrisy, incompetence, treachery, disunion.

In the second volume, which covers 1863 and the beginning of 1864, we see the great turning point in Lincoln's public life and, consequently, in the course of the Civil War. Mr. Sandburg calls this phase 'Storm Center.' Out of it comes the Emancipation Proclamation, the first Northern victory at Gettysburg, the assignment of the high command to U. S. Grant, and the Gettysburg Address. In 1864 Lincoln was to face the ordeal of a campaign for re-election. He turned just in time.

The third volume tells of the campaign—Lincoln against George B. McClellan, the arrogant soldier who had been for so long the undeserving beneficiary of Lincoln's incredible patience, at whose hands the President of the United States had accepted humiliation. August 1864 was 'the darkest month of the war,' and so low was Lincoln's stock that his party moved to replace him with another candidate. Quoting from a Miss Wentworth, who described a visit to Lincoln's office at this time and saw the hordes of petitioners and protesters who were forever surging in, Mr. Sandburg tells a poignant, revealing story. A Catholic priest said to the President, 'I should like a private interview.' 'I do nothing privately,' was the calm answer. 'All I do is public.' Could the bitterness of loneliness in high station be better expressed? Mr. Sandburg quotes the dying Hawthorne, and his words have a strange significance for bewildered people of today:

The Present, the Immediate, the Actual, has proved too potent for me. It takes away not only my scanty faculty, but even my desire for imaginative composition, and leaves me sadly content to scatter a thousand peaceful fantasies upon the hurricane that is sweeping us all along with it, possibly, into a limbo where our nation and its polity may be as literally the fragments of a shattered dream as my unwritten romance.

After Lincoln's re-election, which occasioned great astonishment among British Tories, who assumed that this vulgar fellow would be buried by hostile ballots, *The London Spectator* uttered this remarkably sage observation: 'This journal alone in

England has pointed out steadily, not as an argument, but as the one necessary datum for argument, that *the American Republic is not in times of excitement governed by its talking class.*' (The italics are this reviewer's.) Mr. Sandburg quotes *The Spectator* frequently and gives it a high rating among the world's journals in its power to estimate Lincoln.

The fourth volume of *The War Years* begins with Lincoln's political triumph, the passage of the Thirteenth Amendment, covers the second inaugural, Sherman's march to the sea, Grant's final victory at Richmond, the performance at Ford's Theatre on the evening of Good Friday, the funeral, of which Mr. Sandburg says:

The line of march ran seventeen hundred miles. It was garish, vulgar, massive, bewildering, chaotic. Also it was simple, final, majestic, august. In spite of some of its mawkish excess of show and various maudlin proceedings, it gave solemn, unforgettable moments to millions of people who had counted him great, warm and lovable. The people, the masses, nameless and anonymous numbers of persons not listed nor published among those present—these redeemed it.

In this last volume of his mighty work, Mr. Sandburg does not forget Mrs. Chesnut, who was writing, down in Lincolnton, N. C., 'Shame, disgrace, beggary, all have come at once, and are hard to bear—the grand smash! Rain, rain, outside, and naught but drowning floods of tears inside.'

Any review of *The War Years* at this time can be no more than a smattering report of quickly remembered fragments. It is so great a work that it will require great reading and great reflection before any true appreciation of its permanent value can be formed. It will beget many other books. But, in the meantime, the people of this nation and this human race may well salute and thank Carl Sandburg for the magnitude of his contribution to our common heritage.

A DRAMA ABOUT THE LEAGUE OF NATIONS AND WOODROW WILSON

By Brooks Atkinson

No doubt the gravity of this hour contributes something to a playgoer's appreciation of Howard Koch's and John Huston's 'In Time to Come,' which was acted at the Mansfield last evening. But even in the ambiguous period that preceded our going to war, this drama about Woodrow Wilson and the League of Nations would have been profoundly sobering and impressive.

For Mr. Koch and Mr. Huston, authors of 'Sergeant York,' have written the record of the greatest of the world's lost causes without rhetoric or recrimination. There, by the grace of God, went a chance to prevent the scourge of warfare that is now beating the aching back of the world. Although Woodrow Wilson is their hero, they have not averted their eyes from his defects of personality, his sharp temper and high-handed use of men. They have unfolded a great tragedy of ideals and the hero who stood for them, and they have not cheapened it. When Woodrow Wilson goes down in the last scene, you know that the ancient blackness is settling down over the world again.

Dramas populated by public men of current or recent memory are usually painful to watch in the theatre. Impersonation is likely to be the grotesque side of acting. But most of the acting in 'In Time to Come' is of a high order. And Richard Gaines, who acts Woodrow Wilson, gives a remarkable performance. His make-up is plausible enough, although the resemblance is not striking. But he admirably conveys the intellectual alertness and the moral tenacity of a great leader. Nor does he evade the cold personal pride of a man who cannot deal with those who are not with him in everything. Mr. Gaines's portrait is full of interior passion. Reticent externally, it is flaming inside. Even-

From *The New York Times*, 29 December 1941. By permission of the author and *The New York Times*.

tually it burns out a human soul and leaves the pitiable derelict of an old man stumping around in the White House. For the authors of 'In Time to Come' know that the tragedy of the League of Nations is the tragedy of Woodrow Wilson, and Mr. Gaines is able to convey their central idea.

The play chronicles the League of Nations from the moment in September, 1918, when Wilson is thinking of attending the prospective peace conference in person, to March 4, 1921, when, a broken chief, he is preparing to leave the White House with the ashes of his great idea. It gives a glimpse of him on the steamship George Washington when he has just learned by wireless that his fourteen points are being reduced to thirteen. It shows him surrounded with enemies in a conference room in Paris where cynicism and the greed of his allies are whittling down his expectations of a peace that will endure. In a stormy, bitter-tongued interview with Lodge it moves a little nearer to tragedy, and the last scene completes his undoing.

Otto Preminger has directed a neat and illuminating performance. As Colonel House, Russell Collins, in an obvious wig, startles this column's preconceptions of that shadowy figure. Was he so facile and chipper? But all the other parts are well played despite some very gauche wigs. Guy Sorel's portrait of Clemenceau is extraordinarily good—tired, scornful and vindictive. There is an uncommonly good sketch of Judge Brandeis by Bernard Randall. John M. Kline's Henry White is skillfully drawn, and House Jameson's Senator Lodge is short on resemblance but long on vitality and hatred. As Mrs. Wilson, Nedda Harrigan is alive and affectionate. And William Harrigan is at his best in the part of the loyal Tumulty.

In designing the four sets, Harry Horner has had some difficulty with their mobility. The waits between scenes are obviously too long. But the sets are excellent in themselves and they help in the projection of an honest high-minded drama about a great subject. Mr. Koch and Mr. Huston have not overwritten it. They have let the facts speak for themselves. In our hearts we know what they mean. And now that we are drawn once more into a world calamity we know that peace must not be slain again.

MACBETH: A SLAUGHTERHOUSE SYMPHONY

By John Mason Brown

WHEN Malcolm at the evening's end refers to Macbeth and Lady Macbeth as 'this dead butcher and his fiendlike queen,' one understands what he means. For Shakespeare's tragedy is a bloody, brutal, and horrendous affair. Its violence is what contemporary scholars, who forget the age in which they live, are fond of referring to as Elizabethan.

No police commissioner could ever hope to find a more lurid illustration of the fact that crime does not pay than can be encountered in this chronicle of ambition soaked in gore, of ever-mounting murders and ever-increasing misery. It is a slaughter-house symphony; terrible in the swift onrush of its misdeeds, yet wonderful in its melody; a melodrama in which the forces of evil, both mortal and supernatural, possess and stain the action.

A tragedy in the manner of Shakespeare's other major tragedies, the play is not. For when, in the over-turbulent sweep of the final act, Macbeth at last meets his death, he does not die as Shakespeare's other tragic heroes do. He has waded far too deep in murder for that. There is only deep damnation in his taking off. No one can salute him, at the moment of his passing, as the noblest Roman of them all. Or accuse him of having been great of heart. Or feel that death will boast because of its possession of him. Or lament that he is not stretched out longer on the rack of this tough world. Or trust that flights of angels will sing him to his rest.

After his lady dies—she who should indeed have died hereafter—there is no ecstasy, no glorious moment of self-realization, in Macbeth's dying. There is only the prideless misery of a cor-

From *The New York World-Telegram,* 15 November 1941. By permission of the author and *The New York World-Telegram.*

nered rat. Macduff's 'Turn, hellhound, turn!' contains the perfect description of all that his crimes have left Macbeth of what was once sensitive in his poetic nature. He dies no hero, but a 'coward,' a 'tyrant,' a 'rare monster,' a bloodier villain than terms can give him out.

What is thrilling in the play is not the dull beast that Macbeth becomes in the final breathless scenes, but the shared agony of those pointless butcheries which lead to his undoing. It is this dark excitement, this awful sense of crimes in the making, which Margaret Webster in her direction, and Judith Anderson and Maurice Evans in their acting have admirably projected at the National. Although often attempted, *Macbeth,* which is so easy to read and so difficult to act, has never in our times swept across a stage with its terrible tension, its shuddery horrors and the full impact of its butcheries so completely communicated as they are in this production.

It has its scraggy moments; its interludes of straight Equity make-believe; its scenes and readings which leave much to be desired. But it can boast its glories, too—its sequences of crimson horror, its outbursts of vocal beauty, a tension which remains unbroken, and its touches of sheer genius. It is these that count; count so much, in fact, that with this revival *Macbeth* can be safely said to have been set upon a local stage for the first time in our day.

It is Miss Webster who must accept a large share of the thanks for this. Hers is an amazing touch when it comes to blowing the cobwebs off Shakespeare. She approaches the Bard unafraid, without artyness, without stunts, and with a palpable love for both his poetry and his drama. Moreover, she does not kill the thing she loves. She brings it glowingly to life. She reads the text creatively, permitting its imagination to set her own imagination free. More than any contemporary director, she can ferret out unsuspected clews in this speech or in that, or even between lines, for characterizing and theatrical values which intensify and reveal.

Only Miss Webster, I suspect, would have thought of the wonderful business in which Macbeth burns his letter to Lady Macbeth. Only she would have dreamed of giving the implication of carnal enslavement to the 'So, prithee, go with me' which Macbeth speaks to his lady. Only she would have dared to turn the King's second meeting with the witches into a dream dreamed within the palace. And only she has thought of having Macduff, in the frenzy of his fight with Macbeth, force the cornered tyrant over the parapet.

Almost all of her actors speak Shakespearean verse extremely well. If they are less bewhiskered and less venerable than the Scots seen in most revivals, their youth only adds to the melodrama's torrential pace. So does the beat of Lehman Engel's incidental music. And so do Samuel Leve's undistinguished but quick-moving settings.

If Mr. Evans' Macbeth comes across less clearly than his Richard II, his Falstaff or his Hamlet, blame Shakespeare as much as Mr. Evans for this. Macbeth is blurred in the text; blurred by those contradictions in his nature which have created difficulties for most actors, including Edmund Kean, who have tried to play him. Mr. Evans, however, is interesting throughout and has his unforgettable moments. His Macbeth is the finest our modern stage has seen; commendable in many of its details if not fully realized. It is at its best—and a remarkable best it is—in its moments of self-torture and disillusionment; and at its least effective in its earlier scenes as a warrior. In the murder of Duncan, in the dream scene with the witches, in the sense it gives of lustful subordination to Lady Macbeth, in its speaking of 'Tomorrow and Tomorrow,' and at the moment when Macduff robs him of his final hope, it is especially moving.

Judith Anderson's Lady Macbeth is one of the outstanding Shakespearean characterizations of our time. Miss Anderson creates a haunting figure, villainous, heartless, iron-strong, voluptuous and, yet, masking a concealed tenderness. For sheer brilliance our contemporary stage has seldom equalled anything like the vibrancy, intelligence and spine-twisting terror of her Sleep-Walking scene. Her desperate rubbing of her hands, her vocal changes, her dazed, dragging walk, and the implications raised by her creative 'business,' have upon them all the marks of great acting.

Indeed, this production is not to be missed. Some of us who, when its bloody hurly-burly was excitingly done, would have liked to blame a distant age for its cruelties, were properly humbled when we heard Malcolm, speaking the tragedy's valedictory, say, 'calling home our exiled friends abroad that fled the snares of watchful tyranny.'

FORWARD WITH WALT DISNEY

By Bosley Crowther

IT was just about this time last year, when Walt Disney's *Fantasia* was popping hereabouts, that Mr. Disney quite casually let drop a most revealing remark. 'Don't get the idea,' said he, 'that we are completely satisfied. This film, like everything we do, is another experiment. Gosh, you would be surprised at the problems we've yet to lick.' Coming from Mr. Disney, that remark was surprise enough. For there he was, sitting back calmly with shouts of praise ringing in his ears—shouts of praise to which only the music critics and Dorothy Thompson raised a strident discord—and telling whoever chose to listen that he wasn't satisfied. Right then we got the happy assurance that Mr. Disney is harder to please than we are.

By us that is hunky-dory, and we aren't the least bit abashed. For whenever a picture producer is more critical of his works than the critics—whenever he is not content to let well enough alone, but endeavors to make improvements and profit by previous mistakes—he is giving tremendous encouragement to every one who hopes to see better films. And that, we are glad to report, is what Mr. Disney's latest feature, *Dumbo*, is—a better cartoon, in many ways, than any of his previous master works, and one which definitely shows that he is profiting by experience. Give him another three years and his perfection will probably have us all punchy. We'll be hanging ga-ga on the ropes without a single superlative left to throw.

Let's face the facts here and now: both *Snow White* and *Pinocchio*—and, yes, *Fantasia* too, in its own unique domain—had many obvious flaws which we preferred, in our delight, to play down. (*The Reluctant Dragon* we'll politely overlook as a badly

From *The New York Times*, 26 October 1941. By permission of the author and *The New York Times*.

embarrassing by-blow.) Some of the flaws were in conception, some in artistry. *Snow White* was a first attempt at a full-length animated cartoon, and it consequently stumbled several times because it didn't know the pitfalls in its path. The audience, of course, didn't know them either, so no one was immediately upset. Mr. Disney and his staff of artists caught them, and ironed some out in *Pinocchio.* Further improvements were made— mostly technical—in *Fantasia.* And each of these films was thus a feeler through which the Disney artists reached for firmer ground.

Of course, there are no set rules for making the perfect cartoon—and Heaven help Mr. Disney if he ever gets the notion that there are. But certainly he and his boys have grasped some basic principles in *Dumbo,* which, we should state for the record, is showing at the Broadway Theatre. Perhaps the most essential is the preservation of simplicity—and in this respect, for one, his latest effort is superior. *Dumbo* is as simple as a primer; it is the childishly innocent fairy tale of a tiny baby elephant, born to Mrs. Jumbo of the circus, whose poor little life is made miserable by the fact that he has mammoth ears. All the other elephants laugh at him; he is the object of cruel ridicule. His one big chance to shine in the elephant act ends in miserable failure. And it looks as though he is doomed to lasting misery as a gaudy buffoon when suddenly, through a bit of guiltless tippling, he discovers that he can fly! That's it—those out-sized ears are a couple of practical wings. And Dumbo thereby becomes the most extraordinary elephant in the world.

Thus, you see, the story is kept well within simple, familiar bounds. Like Cinderella and the Ugly Duckling, the little hero blossoms forth to boundless fame. It is, you may say, the formula for virtually all nursery tales, but it has the great literary advantage of being universally understandable. In a film which is aimed to appeal to children every bit as much as to grown-ups, this is a consideration that cannot be overlooked.

Also, Mr. Disney has kept it uncomplicated. *Snow White* and *Pinocchio* became involved. They each contained minor digressions which broke the story line. *Dumbo* sticks close to one point straight from beginning to end. As a consequence, it has the unity of a well-constructed Disney short, elaborated only by incidents and not by projections of plot. And it runs for just a shade over a hour, which is a delightfully propitious length. If this means that Mr. Disney has discovered the monotony in too long a cartoon, especially for younger patrons, it is a matter for rejoicing, indeed.

And considering the tastes of children further, we are very happy to note that no such fearful 'menace' as the howling forest and the Old Witch in *Snow White* or Stromboli in *Pinocchio* have been slipped into this affectionate fable of Dumbo. As a matter of fact, the Disney artists have never been very good at that sort of thing. Their natures are not sufficiently evil, or else they get too much fun out of their work. Anyhow, they have kept the heavy business discreetly subdued in *Dumbo*—except for a dance of pink elephants after the tippling, and that is really fun. You'll be amazed at the difference it makes.

Finally, the boys have preserved what an artist would probably call the integrity of caricature. They have not mixed up intended human characters with out-and-out make-believe. There are no imitations of mortality, except in so far as the animals satirize human affectations. The ringmaster and the clowns are the only suggestions of real people in the picture, and they are highly burlesqued. From first to last it is an animal story, and the animals are the miraculous Disney types.

One wouldn't say, of course, that *Dumbo* is without a flaw. For one thing, it does betray a sly tendency on the part of the artists to crib from themselves. They like to repeat certain gags which have been good in previous films. But it moves in the right direction. Mr. Disney is getting better all the time. Whatever problems he has yet to lick we confidently leave to him.

KERN'S 'SHOWBOAT' SYMPHONY

By Olin Downes

THE audience which packed Carnegie Hall last night at the concert given by Artur Rodzinski, conductor, and the New York Philharmonic-Symphony Orchestra, listened to the piece which culminated the program with a degree of excitement and an obvious joy in the music which testified more strongly than any words could to the nature of its experience.

The music that created this pleasurable emotion was not Beethoven's First Symphony, or Paul Hindemith's ultra-modern 'symphony,' 'Matthis der Mahler,' after the painting of Gruenwald, or even the exquisite music that the youthful Mendelssohn composed for Shakespeare's *Midsummer Night's Dream*. No! The piece that created the commotion was the composition of an American musician who had long since won a lasting place in the hearts of his countrymen with a creation which is an enduring 'classic' and masterpiece of its kind in its popular field. No one could hear that music, those glorious tunes, without an answering grin, or surreptitious tap of the heel, or even leap of the heart. For the composer was Jerome Kern, and the music, in a new orchestral version created by him on the invitation of Dr. Rodzinski, was based upon the score of *Showboat*.

When it was agreed last Spring that at least one composition by an American composer should figure on each of the Philharmonic-Symphony programs of this season in New York, Dr. Rodzinski, with a quality of appreciation and a degree of imagination that becomes him well, thought immediately of Mr. Kern as one of the most representative popular American composers of this period. He considers *Showboat* a very typically American masterpiece, in its field. Dr. Rodzinski also asked himself why, if waltzes by Johann Strauss are considered legitimate entertain-

From *The New York Times,* 20 November 1941. By permission of the author and *The New York Times.*

ment at a symphony concert, the fascinating melodic invention of a leading American who long since had gained a permanent place in his particular domain should not have at least the same rating and the same opportunity for a hearing. The result was the 'scenario,' as Mr. Kern entitles it, on themes from *Showboat*.

They—the themes—were enormously successful with the audience. It need not be claimed that they are combined in what one could call a truly symphonic style, or developed, either, after the symphonic manner of acknowledged masters of orchestral composition. There is a simplicity and directness of procedure in this 'scenario' as sincere, simple, direct, as Mr. Kern himself, and so remote from the standpoint of the sophisticated symphonic craftsman as to be rather deliciously naive.

But the melodies themselves! The audience sat intent from the opening, which is like that of the overture to the operetta and leads after reference to several themes into the first announcement of 'Ol' Man River,' to the end. The tunes come in a succession which generally follows the course of the opera. One was impressed with the instantaneous flash of understanding and fellow-feeling, as you might say, which traversed the atmosphere from the audience to the stage.

For this is music, of course, in the popular vein, but in its most representative pages, as native as Mark Twain or Edna Ferber's novel. Some melodies are not as good as others. Some fall into operetta routine. At least half a dozen are irresistible and unforgettable. Distinguished listeners were humming them as they went home.

There are those who sniff at music of this kind, given this kind of a reception. The writer is not of them. It is a native idiom, and it is excellent melodic invention. It smacks, with sheer direct inspiration and without any pose, of an American period and an American scene—if you like, of an American romanticism. It is infinitely farther toward a native form than the vast majority of our cerebral and imitative American symphonies.

And that is the explanation of its reception. With the last chord the applause almost impinged upon the sound of the orchestra, and Dr. Rodzinski, turning to bow, quickly dived into the wings to get Mr. Kern. He appeared and was given an ovation, repeatedly called back to the stage, applauded, cheered, welcomed as only an artist is welcomed for whom the public of his countrymen feel the affection and esteem that this sincere and modest man of native genius has long since earned in this land.

Saying which, let us consider this score for a moment from the symphonic standpoint. It is not symphonic at all in the sense of development and interweaving of the musical ideas. This lack of the customary symphonic procedure is deliberate with Mr. Kern and probably well advised. He has written for the popular lyric stage. He does not exaggerate his own powers or technical resource in the symphonic field. He thought it would be better, safer, and more characteristic of his own methods of expression if he used what he called a melodic 'scenario' of his operatic score.

This score is actually a potpourri, a selection, rather too generous and extended for its own good, of themes from the show. Too many themes are employed. Five or six of them, with some pruning of connecting passages, which in instances are none too adroit or effective without the accompanying stage spectacle, would make the piece more concise, pull it together, and centralize its architecture. It might be well if 'Ol' Man River' were held in reserve for a more lengthy final peroration and many other passages shortened or cut out.

Per contra, one place that wasn't long enough for our personal wishes was the comparatively brief mention given 'Why Do I Love You' and the omission of its dance variation, as in the opera score. But that is personal. The orchestration has excellent passages, the presence of 'saxes' and various percussive auxiliaries, including sets of bells, would be all right, if there was not rather too much attempt to make every kind of an effect that one can with these various instruments, and work it in before the end is reached. In a word, it is overorchestrated, and the melodic continuity is not of the best. Here is the nucleus of a better piece, and one that would be more effective than what was heard last night, greatly as it pleased, and much reason as Mr. Kern has to be gratified with his reception.

VII

Times That Try Men's Souls

THESE are the times that try men's souls. The summer
soldier and the sunshine patriot will, in this crisis, shrink
from the service of their country; but he that stands it *now*
deserves the love and thanks of man and woman. Tyranny,
like Hell, is not easily conquered; yet we have this consolation with us that the harder the conflict, the more glorious
the triumph. What we obtain too cheap, we esteem too
lightly; it is dearness only that gives every thing its value.
Heaven knows how to put a proper price upon its goods;
and it would be strange indeed if so celestial an article as
FREEDOM should not be highly rated.

THOMAS PAINE, *The American Crisis,* 1776

THE brave old strife the fathers saw
    For Freedom calls for men again
    Like those who battled not in vain
For England's Charter, Alfred's law;
    And right of speech and trial just
Wage in your name their ancient war
    With venal courts and perjured trust.

God's ways seem dark, but, soon or late,
    They touch the shining hills of day;
    The evil cannot brook delay,
The good can well afford to wait.
    Give ermined knaves their hour of crime;
Ye have the future grand and great,
    The safe appeal of Truth to Time!

JOHN GREENLEAF WHITTIER
For Righteousness' Sake, 1856

THEN to side with Truth is noble when we share her wretched crust,
Ere her cause bring fame and profit, and 'tis prosperous to be just;
Then it is the brave man chooses, while the coward stands aside,
Doubting in his abject spirit, till his Lord is crucified,
And the multitude make virtue of the faith they had denied.

'Tis as easy to be heroes as to sit the idle slaves
Of a legendary virtue carved upon our fathers' graves
Worshippers of light ancestral make the present light a crime;—
Was the Mayflower launched by cowards, steered by men behind the
     time?
Turn those tracks toward Past or Future, that make Plymouth Rock
     sublime?

They have rights who dare maintain them; we are traitors to our sires,
Smothering in their holy ashes Freedom's new-lit altar-fires;
Shall we make their creed our jailer? Shall we, in our haste to slay,
From the tombs of the old prophets steal the funeral lamps away
To light up the martyr-fagots round the prophets of today?

New occasions teach new duties; Time makes ancient good uncouth;
They must upward still, and onward, who would keep abreast of Truth;
Lo, before us gleam her camp fires! we ourselves must Pilgrims be,
Launch our Mayflower, and steer boldly through the desperate winter
     sea,
Nor attempt the Future's portal with the Past's blood-rusted key.

JAMES RUSSELL LOWELL, *The Present Crisis*, 1844

WHAT IS AT STAKE?

By John Coleman Bennett

WHEN the claim is made that this is a war to preserve democracy, it is always possible to find plausible arguments which cast doubt upon the claim. President Hutchins thinks that he has scored a victory when he shows how undemocratic America is and when he quotes Anthony Eden to the effect that England is not a democracy and never will be a democracy. We suggest that one way of expressing what is at stake in this war is to say that upon the outcome depends the existence of an 'open society,' to use Bergson's phrase. This way of putting the matter undercuts the verbal arguments about democracy. An open society is a society which permits and even encourages criticism of itself in the light of universal standards. Such a society has at hand the means of peaceful self-correction. Such a society keeps alive the concern for objective truth and it can never be deceived into substituting the fiat of the state for objective truth. Such a society enables persons to keep their integrity as persons without constant fear of the secret police. Such a society permits minorities to organize for the purpose of changing its policies and even its structure. Such a society is uncorrupted by officially planned terror against its most independent minds and its bravest spirits. Such a society provides a framework in which the Church can preach the Gospel and keep civilization under Christian judgment. But it is not a perfect society. On the contrary it allows its imperfections to be published abroad.

An open society exists in the United States and in the British Commonwealth and it did exist in the democracies which have lost their freedom. President Hutchins is right in calling attention to the fact that all classes do not share freedom equally in

From *Christianity and Crisis, A Bi-Weekly Journal of Christian Opinion*, 19 May 1941. By permission of the publisher.

America. It is true that American democracy permits shocking inequalities of security and opportunity. The unemployed may seem to have little actual freedom. They risk the loss of relief and they may forfeit the chance for re-employment if they speak as freely as those who have economic security. In the midst of labor conflicts the ordinary forms of freedom are often the first casualties. These things are true and important. But it is also true that it is usually possible to put those who interfere with freedom on the defensive before the law. Also, where freedom is denied locally, it is possible to bring criticism to bear on that situation from outside. In many communities the migrant workers may have little freedom but their condition is kept before the entire nation by indictments such as *Grapes of Wrath;* and the LaFollette Committee is able to lay the facts before the public. In our society, when situations arise in which criticism is prevented by those who locally and for the moment exercise power, attempted suppression of criticism will itself be criticized.

One of the chief points of those who try to make us believe that there is no clear issue in this war is the experience of India. In common with a large section of British opinion we deeply regret the fact that the government of India has been characterized by such widespread repression. But even in this connection it is fair to recognize that the repression in India has not been carried on with the ultimate ruthlessness that is the mark of Nazi tyranny. Perhaps more important is the fact that the repression in India is under severe criticism in England. It is significant that Nehru was able to write his great book, *Toward Freedom,* while in prison and that the book, a persuasive indictment of British policy, is published freely throughout the English-speaking world.

A similar argument is that Britain has been allied with dictatorships in Poland, Turkey, and Greece. It is also said that America is committed to the protection of Latin American dictatorships. President Hutchins even includes China in the list of dictatorships with which we are allied, thus showing a strange blindness to the extraordinary development of the democratic spirit in China, whatever may be said about its form of government under the stress of invasion.

None of these dictatorships is as dynamic as National Socialism; none of them threatens the security and freedom of their neighbors or is as consistent in destroying freedom at home. The fact is that none of them is 'totalitarian' in the Nazi sense. There are many kinds and degrees of non-democratic governments, as there are many degrees of democratic achievement. A too simple distinction between democracy and dictatorship obscures important distinctions within each general category, and it certainly tends to obscure the dynamic intensity of the collective self-worship upon which the Nazis are embarked. Here the self-criticism of an 'open society' has been replaced by self-glorification as a basic principle.

DEFENDING JUSTICE DESPITE OUR OWN INJUSTICE

By Lynn Harold Hough

MEN have a way of becoming morally modest when this modesty decreases the pressure of responsibility. They have a way of becoming morally arrogant when their privileges are at stake. They are ready to shout all the watchwords about the rights of men when these rights may be used to buttress their own claims. They are ready to talk vaguely about the difficulty of applying moral principles, the complexity of society, and the relativity of all human judgments, when the principles in question might be used to buttress the rights of others. They are ready to call in dreams of a perfect society for the dislocation of the relationships of an order where they have what they consider an inadequate share of the goods of life. They suddenly remember the universal and inevitable distribution of evil when they are asked to go forth in battle array for the sake of giving justice to others. They do not doubt their worthiness when they are about to make demands for themselves. They have sudden compunctions about their worthiness to do battle for the sake of giving justice to others.

For this reason it becomes necessary to inspect with complete candor the motives which lie behind moral scruples of all kinds which emerge at the moment when some sort of action is demanded. A survey of the whole field where this variety of casuistry appears is a matter of real importance when we live in the sort of world which conditions our present activities.

Admittedly perfect beings could apply perfect standards with complete and immediate effectiveness in a world where no im-

From *Christianity and Crisis, A Bi-Weekly Journal of Christian Opinion,* 21 April 1941. By permission of the author and the publisher.

perfect beings had appeared. But we do not live in such a world. At some points every human being is soiled by the evil of life. At some points every human institution reflects evil qualities. In no end of ways society is corrupted by the cumulative evils which have been flourishing through the centuries of man's life on this planet. From unsuspected dark corners evil is always arising to turn to frustration the purposes which are good. So deeply true is this that the man who sets about standing for justice is always plagued by injustices of his own. The institution which lifts the flag of righteousness is always shamed by unrighteousness inherent in its own life. The nation which goes forth to fight in the name of some sort of moral order is always plagued by some of the pages of its own history. If we have to wait for completely immaculate men before we make any demand in the name of justice, we will have to wait forever. If we have to wait for perfect institutions to be the instruments of moral values, all hope of moral advance is completely lost. If we have to wait for nations with a perfect past before we make any attempt to secure civilized decency in the present, we might as well give up the whole endeavor once for all.

But this very putting of the question makes clear the way we must take. Since we cannot wait for stainless men to fight the evil in the world, we must use such men as we have. Weatherbeaten men upon whom many a storm of evil has blown, bearing the marks of much failure in the storms of life, must go forth in spite of their own imperfection to fight against the lies which destroy the soul and the actions which degrade and disintegrate the good life of man. Institutions which have made their own compromises with evil must yet come to the place where they say, 'Thus far, and no farther,' to evils both within and without their own corporate life. Nations which look back upon many a sorry tale in their own past must come upon days of stern resolution to resist the evil which presses upon them from without even as they must resist the evil which presses outward from within. Only so is some sort of justice and decency achieved in the individual life. Only so is some sort of honor and nobility given a place in the structure of corporate life. And only so do nations set themselves to move from the jungle toward the goals of truly civilized life.

When once we persuade ourselves to think of the matter honestly we see that such soundness and such justice as have become a part of human life have been achieved in just this fashion. The apostle Paul was very proud of his Roman citizenship. He understood perfectly the relative good—and a very high and commanding good it was—which the Pax Romana had given to the world. But he was able to write with stinging satire of the dark evils which belonged to that same structure of life. He was ready to perceive and appreciate and appropriate and co-operate with the good of the structure. He was also ready to draw the sharp arrows in his great bow for the piercing of the evils in that very structure. And both in his hearty appreciation and in his deadly criticism he was ready to recognize that he himself was a man with evil fibers in the very structure of his own life, safe to think and safe to act only through the great grace of God.

Feudalism achieved very great things, not only in the region of justice, but in respect of the graces which appear only when golden thoughts command the minds of men. But the feudal societies had their own evils, their own dark disloyalties to the very standards by which they lived. When the tale of chivalry was put into lovely poetry we find that imperfect men with a shining dream made up the knighthood of King Arthur's Round Table. Here was the glory and the tragedy of chivalry both as history and as poetry. But if imperfect men had not dreamed the dream, there would have been no beginnings of more gracious life. All would have been the black plight of ugly brutality.

From this standpoint we can understand the grim and hostile criticism and the glowing and tender appreciation of the same institutions by different students. One student sees the idea of justice and fine living which fires the best spirits. So he writes in glowing appreciation. Another student sees the betrayal of this ideal and watches the decaying processes which rot the ripening fruit. He writes with something like irritated scorn. Our own period has produced a vast quantity of fierce young scholars so occupied with the fashion in which human evil has betrayed man's passion for justice that they have become completely unable to see how genuine good is ever attained in a society in which dark evils flourish.

If we accept the leadership of these men whose eyes are simply eyes of gloom, we travel straight toward complete paralysis and final frustration. Unable to see the gallant fight of justice in evil hearts and in evil societies, hope dies out of their eyes and finally perishes in their hearts. It is a curious situation when a man's passion for perfection produces the complete breakdown of his will in the presence of the evils which characterize the world in which he lives. He has become so color-blind that he cannot see the good which exists, because of his preoccupation with the evils which betray that good. A man determines wrathfully that he will not tell himself lies in order to make himself comfortable in an evil world. And straightway he begins to tell himself lies by misreading the good in front of his own eyes. If it is both stupid and evil to call wrong right or black white, what shall we say of the man whose passion for a destructive interpretation of all existing human life and all historic human orders leads him to use every ingenuity to find evil motives for good deeds and dark purposes back of fair action?

The truth is that only the man who sees the good in the midst of evil and the evil coiling its dark way toward the heart of good is a safe guide. He knows how precarious is our fight for goodness in an evil world. He also knows how glorious are the achievements of good in spite of all the insistent and pervasive evil.

The peril of psychopathic judgments is one of the most sinister of the dangers confronted by men of our time. In the period between the conclusion of the first World War and the outbreak of the present cataclysm, untold millions of young people were brought up to look for a worm in every apple in the tree of life, and to go shouting with strange glee at the discovery of each new worm. The leaders and teachers of youth were so much engrossed by their own psychopathic glooms that it did not occur to them that man cannot live by the discovery of worms alone. And so a generation was produced which ceased to believe in any sort of goodness in the fruit hanging on the tree of life. Even their poetry became a dark and slimy poetry of worms. They had become so passionately engrossed with the presence of evil in the world that they became unable to see the perpetual and dauntless battle of good with evil in every human heart and in every human institution. This power to see the actual good in a world where there is so much evil is a necessity, if we are not all to come to a state of complete incapacity for action. The attack on the sources of belief in life is the most deadly of all attacks upon man's heritage. The one central insight a man must have if he is to be of any sort of worth in a world like ours is just the insight that, soiled though your life may be, you can yet give yourself to the fight against some intolerable evil and the battle for the securing of some good necessary for a decent life for men. And this insight is secured as we insistently tell the truth about the good which has been actually achieved in an evil world by men whose lives were stained by the evil of this grim world and yet had capacity for deathless loyalty to some clearly seen good and deathless hostility to some clearly understood evil.

There is no more fascinating or sardonic sport than the indoor analysis of the failure of democracy. If it merely consists of an honest criticism of a form of life which must perpetually be held up to standards from which it is perpetually tempted to fall away, this is very good indeed. But all too easily it becomes a cynical delight in the failure of democracy and at last an unhesitating condemnation of democracy itself. The democrat, because he is a creature whose loyalty to good fights its way through compromises with evil, carries his treasure in an earthen vessel. But it is a treasure. And it represents something which once and again has become very glorious on the highways of mankind. We must be honest about its failures. But in God's name we must be honest about its successes. We must tell the truth about its evil alliances. But at the peril of the very integrity of our own minds we must tell the tale of its refusal to make compromises and its spurning of alliances which were evil. It is possible for imperfect creatures to achieve a certain standard of decency and freedom in the world. And it is so not as a matter of faith, but of any honest interpretation of history.

The preoccupation with man's tendency to injustice leads to the confusion of the understanding at every point where a decision must be made. When there is a great war in the world, it enables you to claim that both sides are equally evil and so you are saved from moral judgment and from moral responsibility. Sometimes in the process you are reduced to a state of intellectual dishonesty which is enough to make angels weep. It seems beyond belief that any sincere man could follow the tale of Hitler's activities in Poland, Denmark, Norway, Holland, Belgium, and France, every step a movement in treachery and faithlessness to the plighted word, every step accompanied by remorseless barbarity and cruelty, every step a new slaughter of freedom in the name of conscienceless power—it seems impossible that any sincere man could follow this tale of complete and unabashed evil and then turn to the British Empire, with its tale of democracy increasing century by century until it holds a supreme hope for the good life for men, without feeling a contrast so complete that the very facts themselves carry the necessity for the decision that in this war the cause of Britain is the very cause of mankind. To any one capable of straight thinking in the light of the facts, the situation is clear enough. Something utterly disintegrating and uncivilized has been let loose in the world. It has won dangerous victories. Britain stands between the rest of the world and incalculable tragedy.

But the thinker, with a passion for perfection, sometimes especially alive when that passion can be used to show a way to escape responsibility, now begins to speak. He reminds us of every evil thing he can find in the history of England since the Norman Conquest. He makes a very brave attempt to blacken England in order to be able to say that since both contestants are equally evil, we can just stand aside and watch. He uses every strategy for the misinterpretation of England. He overestimates the evil. He ignores the good. And even so, after his best efforts, Britain remains a dull gray against the bitter black of Hitler's Germany. The history of parliamentary democracy is ignored. The broadening liberties of the British Empire are forgotten. The word *imperial* is used in such a fashion as to black out intelligence and to set every fact in a false perspective.

Nobody—least of all the British—would deny the dark spots in British history. But they do not represent the defining matters in the British tradition. The British Navy has been the protector of the liberties of the world. It has not been a menace to the freedom of man. The three thousand miles of unfortified boundary between the United States and Canada is itself a symbol. The British Commonwealth of Nations has been made up of very human beings; sometimes evil leaders have lifted false flags, and sometimes popular demand has involved moral compromise. But on the whole, what a splendid achievement in freedom and law is represented by the British flag! Men with all their injustice can achieve extraordinary results in maintaining justice. The British Empire is proof of it.

But that is not the whole story. The dark evils will go to incredible lengths if they are not resisted by men who care for some sort of freedom and decency, imperfect though these men may be. The two outstanding characteristics necessary for the meeting of such a crisis as the one in which the world finds itself are, first, a sense of the significant facts, and second, unhesitating courage in dealing with the facts. Dr. Van Loon has used the phrase 'fact blindness' to describe the quality which has led to the fall of many nations. The perpetual tendency of corpulent and intellectually dull men and nations is to treat wolves as if they were pleasant domestic animals. And when it is too late, the dull men and the dull nations awake to the nature of what they have done. There is no excuse for mental bewilderment in the United States since the fall of France. The evil which has been set loose upon the world must be crushed. And we cannot wait for perfect men or perfect nations to crush it.

If intellectual acuteness is necessary, the courage to act is also necessary. And in every age many men have been ready to make themselves a human wall against a threat to any sort of just life for man, even though they knew that they were themselves men whose lives needed much moral surgery. Indeed, the moment when an imperfect man gives himself to a necessary fight for the maintaining of a decent life for the world, he takes another step toward the triumph of justice in his own life. And the nation which like Britain becomes the fortress of the human cause achieves in that hour a justice and a nobility greater than any it has known before.

The first step toward moral achievement for the individual

and for the nation is the hour of commitment to something more perfect than the individual or the nation has yet achieved. Jesus put the heart of the matter into an immortal epigram when he spoke of those who were evil and yet could give and would give good gifts. We, though evil, may give the good gift of a great loyalty to the cause of man. We can achieve some sort of justice in spite of the injustice in our hearts and in our national life.

STILL 'THE HOPE OF THE HUMAN RACE'

By Henry Steele Commager

'THIS people,' wrote Turgot of Americans in 1778, 'is the hope of the human race.' It was a note that had been sounded before —from the very beginning, indeed, of settlement in the New World; it was a note that was to be sounded again and again in the years to come, by Europeans and Americans alike, by statesmen and by poets and by the plain people who sailed hopefully to the Promised Land or who followed 'fair freedom's star' over the mountains and across the plains and prairie lands of the West. We hear it in Jefferson's celebration of this Republic as 'the world's best hope,' in Lincoln's appeal for the maintenance of 'the last best hope of earth'; we hear it in those lines of Longfellow—'Sail on, O Ship of State'—which Winston Churchill read to us so dramatically, or better yet in the proud boast of Walt Whitman—

Thou holdest not the venture of thyself alone, not of the Western
    Continent alone;
With thee Time voyages in trust, the antecedent nations sink or swim
    with thee,
Theirs, theirs as much as thine, the destination-port triumphant.

What was the hope to be fulfilled, what was it the Old World expected from the New? It was, of course, what we have recently come to speak of as the Four Freedoms. It was liberty, democracy, equality, economic opportunity and security. It was the right of men to live their own lives, in peace and in comfort, to worship as they would, to marry whom they would, to follow such careers as their talents permitted, to make and unmake their own governments, to be subject to equal laws.

From *The New York Times Magazine,* 20 July 1941. By permission of the author and *The New York Times.*

That this hope has been in large part fulfilled is clear. It is well for us to remember that it was not fulfilled without effort and struggle. The United States has faced, from its beginning, many dangers; has survived many and serious threats. It won independence against overwhelming odds and against odds defended it; it maintained national integrity only at the cost of the greatest war of the nineteenth century. For two centuries, and more, Americans faced the test of the frontier—of a wilderness which might have barbarized men if men did not first tame it, of continuous uprooting and transplanting, continuous accommodation of men to environment and adaptation of environment to men. They faced, for an equally long period, the test of the melting pot—of the assimilation of millions of newcomers with different and often discordant backgrounds, cultures, faiths, and they fused out of these varied elements a unified people. They faced the test of continuous economic readjustments—the abrupt impact of the industrial revolution, the shift from a national to a world agricultural economy, the swift rise of the cities, successive depressions. All of these dangers the nation has surmounted, all of these tests—the military, the social, the economic —it has survived, preserving the essentials of liberty, democracy, and security.

Now, at the height of our power, we are confronted with a new threat—one more ominous than any we have yet known. That threat was vaguely foreshadowed a quarter-century ago, but victory then lulled us into the belief that we could retain our own liberty and democracy and security regardless of what occurred elsewhere in the world. During the decade of the thirties that illusion was gradually exposed; within the last three years it has been shattered. It is clear now that our whole way of life has been challenged, and that if we fail to respond to that challenge it will be destroyed. It is equally clear that many of us are not yet alive to the gravity of the danger that confronts us.

What is the nature of that danger? It is no mere military threat; those who talk of the possibility, or of the impossibility, of invasion delude themselves. We may have to fight, but if we recognize that fact and have the will to fight we cannot be conquered by arms. But there are graver perils than the military, more insidious forms of conquest; as the Knights of Aristophanes proclaimed many centuries ago,

There are things, then, hotter than fire, there are speeches more shame-
    less still
Than the shameless speeches of those who rule the City at will.

What is at stake now is the vindication of that hope which we had thought fulfilled—the maintenance, for ourselves and for the peoples of the world, of liberty, democracy, and security. Our ideal of democracy is condemned now by those who announce that democracy is the weakest of all systems of government and who oppose it for systems that appear far more effective. Our economic individualism is threatened by economic collectivism or by the complete subordination of economy to political purposes. Our traditional ethics is confronted by a new ethical system which denies in large part the values which we have always cherished and always taken for granted. Our faith in man is challenged by a new faith—a faith in the organic state or in the party or in a collective humanity.

It is difficult for the average American to grasp the nature of this challenge, for it is a new thing to us—new and for the most part incomprehensible. We are an easy-going people, we have never really known defeat, we have never known disillusionment—as Santayana observed, the notion of evil is foreign to our minds. Yet we must come to recognize that what we are in the midst of now is not just another imperialist war, not just a continuation of the scramble for natural resources, not just the violent expression of the megalomania of one man, but a death-struggle between two philosophies of government.

The core of the American philosophy of government is the individual. The individual is the source of government, he makes government, he can unmake government. The individual has rights and liberties—rights and liberties in society, to be sure, but nevertheless individual rights: the right to worship, to speak, to write, to go about his own affairs undisturbed by the State. No matter how socialized our thinking, our administration, our business, has become, it is still true that the ultimate objective of our government is the creation and protection of the free man.

To this philosophy Nazism and Communism oppose a diametrically different one. The totalitarian philosophy, differing in many things, agree in subordinating the individual to something larger—in one case the state, in the other society as organized in the Soviet. In these philosophies the individual is unimportant, his liberties, his property, his ambitions and hopes, his social and family relationships, negligible. And this profound difference in the point of departure of the democratic and the totalitarian philosophies has affected the whole system of values which they cherish. It is because we have failed to realize this that we are so naively shocked by what has occurred on the Continent of Europe in the last three years: by broken promises, by ruthless invasion and conquest, by religious and racial persecution, by the regimentation of life, by Fifth Column activities, by the whole strategy of terror.

By our standard of values these things are wicked, and we wonder how they could come to pass. To the totalitarians, who repudiate our standard of values and subscribe to a very different standard, they are not wicked at all; they are logical. For in that philosophy the end inevitably justifies the means, and because the practitioners are without experience and without wisdom, the justification is a short-range one.

The means are different, that much is clear, and the democracies have not yet schooled themselves to imitate them; it is a sorry joke that this war is being lost on the playing fields of Eton. Democracy appeals to reason, Nazism to authority; democracy depends on co-operation, Nazism exacts obedience; democracy has faith in education, Nazism perverts emotions through propaganda; democracy exalts tolerance, Nazism exploits intolerance—racial, religious, political.

But let it be emphasized, too, that the ends are different. The ends are not, as with us, the liberty and the happiness of the individual. The ends are the power and the wealth and the glory of the state or the party, or of some abstract and distant humanity. The means reject the age-long habits of society; the ends repudiate human values and life itself. The Nazi embraces the fallacious concept of the superman and the slave; it rests on the brutalizing pseudo-scientific notion of the survival of the fittest.

It is a negation rather than an assertion of philosophy: it is anti-liberal, anti-democratic, anti-Semitic, anti-capitalist, anti-rational, anti-Christian, anti-human. It is, in short, as Rauschning has pointed out, a philosophy of nihilism.

If these new philosophies are successful in the present conflict, their success will give them immense prestige and power. They have already spread to the Far East; they have taken root in some parts of Latin America, they are not without adherents even in this country. They are, in their very nature, progressive and aggressive. They are, by their nature, totalitarian. They are at war not only with democratic politics but with democratic economy, society, and morals. If they succeed, then indeed that danger which Woodrow Wilson saw—and fought—will have materialized: the world will no longer be safe for our democracy, not in our time.

This, then, is the challenge which confronts us, the challenge of vindicating everything that we have stood for for three centuries. To those for whom the history of mankind has meaning, America is once more the hope of the human race. If we stand by now, or if we aid timidly and foolishly, Britain will fall and Nazism will triumph—not only in Europe but everywhere.

Everywhere in the world—everywhere but in the United States, it would seem—plain men and women recognize this. They know it in the concentration camps of Germany, in the devastated towns of Poland, in anguished France, in occupied Denmark and Norway, in bleeding Finland, in war-torn China, in the frightened States of South America, in England, embattled and heroic. When we come to realize the nature of the conflict and the issues that are at stake, we too will know that we have still to fulfill our promise to mankind. We will know that now, more truly than when Lincoln spoke, 'we shall nobly save or meanly lose the last, best hope of earth.'

THE TOTALITARIAN WAR AND THE
FATE OF DEMOCRACY

By Carlo Sforza

THERE are no more tight compartments left in the world; there is no European problem which may not become an American problem. But when one has been long in public life, one is wise to make it a constant rule not to interfere in the political issues of other nations. It is my rule. When a great national issue is at stake, it is for the country involved to decide, and the duty of a foreigner is to be discreet, not to offer advice . . .

But on the other hand, I do feel that it may be useful that I give you my personal experiences. What one reads in books is not exactly the same thing as that which is seen and felt. That is why we Europeans who read about American political life while we are still in Europe do not understand very much about it. We begin to understand it only after a number of visits to your shores. I might say that the more clearly we understand your political problems, the more hesitant we are to speak of them. A great English publisher asked me three years ago to write a book about America. He said that he knew I had paid ten extended visits to the United States and that now I ought to be able to write about America. I told him that I must refuse, and that he should have asked me to write the book in 1928, after I had come here for the first time. At that time I was so sure I knew everything that I would have written a book with alacrity. After my tenth visit I knew enough to know that I did not know enough.

Just because I admit that intellectual isolation exists everywhere, I think I may contribute a few observations on points

From *The Annals of The American Academy of Political and Social Science,* July 1941. By permission of the publisher.

from which Americans may draw their own conclusions and form their own philosophy. Recently at the University of Virginia, where I am now staying during a delightful semester, we had as a visitor a very important and intelligent Latin American, who one evening complained to me that people in the United States, even in a place like the University of Virginia, know very little about Latin America. 'The North Americans,' he said, 'don't even know the names of our capitals. They don't know that Buenos Aires is the capital of Argentina or that Rio is the capital of Brazil. But in Latin America we know, all of us, even the taxi drivers, that the capital of the United States is New York City.'

I must confess that utterances I have heard from certain distinguished persons in this country have revealed to me the dangerous position which may be taken by those who are intelligent, honest, and cultured, who have the best of intentions coupled with a belief in what may be called a scientific religion, but who refuse to look at realities. That is the reason why I feel that I must submit some evidence on the opposite side, for when I hear such opinions expressed I seem to see beyond the speakers the shadows of Socialist friends of mine in Italy, in France, and in Germany, who had all the same hopes, said all the same things, declared the same antipathies, and expressed the same conviction—a conviction that the future of humanity and of social justice was a divine certainty according to the doctrines of Karl Marx. All of these men were friends of mine. They have all been murdered or are starving to death in concentration camps.

One of the most intelligent of the Italian Socialists was Turati, leader of the Marxist Socialist party. During the first years of the Fascist regime, before it became a complete regime of violence and a general reign of terror, I was leader of the Democratic party in the Senate. All Italy was sick of Fascism and of Mussolini. In the deep emotion which pervaded the country after the murder of my friend Matteotti, an important member of the opposition to Fascism, Italy seemed decided to oust Mussolini. I went to Turati and said: 'I am only a liberal, an individualist. I have no blind masses behind me, but you have. Do you not see that Fascism is going to bring Italy to ruin and, with it, Europe and the rest of the world? Do you not see that it is necessary to use force now, to destroy Mussolini's power now, and to oust him from his palace where he is trembling and in hiding?'

Turati's timid answer, and the answer of his Socialist friends, came back to my memory when I heard here certain remarks full of fatalistic confidence in the future. Turati answered me: 'We understand, but we are against violence, against risks, and against romantic adventures. Karl Marx tells us that the better society is certain to come, and we are waiting for the sunrise of the future which he promised.'

They did not know, those poor fellows, and the Americans who speak like them do not yet know, that history is made not by social fatalities, not by class organization, but by passions, by feelings, by men. That is why the same sensations of fear, the same hesitation that I felt so strongly years ago in Italy, I feel now in America.

When I was in France I saw clearly the approach of her tragedy, not because I was more intelligent, more farseeing than the French, but because this clear sight is the sad gift of a stranger—a stranger who lives in a country and loves it. To have this gift he must love the country in which he lives, because only through love can come understanding. It can never come through hatred. While a stranger who loves a country not his own may ignore many circumstances which its citizens know, he has a sort of gift of understanding and can see in the very distant landscape the danger facing the nation.

I see no reason why I should not tell the American people to-day, as I told my French friends at that time, facts which I have always refused to tell to newspapers or put into books and reviews. After all, there is a limit to modesty; and since everyone who has stayed for three months in France comes to America and writes volumes of revelations about France, I thought that I might make an exception—and remain silent. I have been Italian Ambassador to France; I have been on equal footing with, and have intimate knowledge of, five or six of the greatest leaders of France; that is why I cannot write a book like one of the many volumes written about France. There is another reason: I know too much. Some of the old leaders are now in mortal danger, and while the writings of the average newspaperman might not make a great deal of difference, something written by me might get into the documents which are collected against these poor men who are now, like Daladier, Reynaud, Léon Blum, and Gamelin, prisoners of the Vichy government, which means prisoners of the Germans.

But well may I mention two or three things which, after all, might be considered from the point of view of the Vichy men as a justification for their prisoners. For instance, I went to Daladier two or three days before the invasion of Poland caused the outbreak of the second World War. I said: 'I am constantly receiving information—feverish information—from Italy. Men from many classes, from the very highest in the land to the very humblest, tell me that they feel that Mussolini is bringing Italy into the war on the side of Germany. They say that forty-four million Italians hate the idea of fighting France, and particularly of fighting France in the service of Germany, which, if victorious, would make of Italy the most enslaved of its colonies. But to revolt against Mussolini, to create again a free Italy, we must have word from France to show that she understands what Italy wants, why Italy wants it—to show us that France understands and admits certain national rights of ours.'

Daladier answered me: 'My dear friend, you are right. But now we have the German menace. Can we not hope that Mussolini will turn to us as to a friend? After all, our Ambassador at Rome tells us that the Duce's son-in-law is rather friendly toward us. We may hope that, with some skillful handling, Mussolini may become our friend. And, above all, we have one dictator as enemy; our upper classes would not like to have two. It might appear as an ideologic war.'

I smiled sadly. I knew at once that Daladier was lost and that France was lost. She was lost if she refused to admit that the dictators were waging an 'ideologic war.' She was destroying her best trump card.

Why may I tell this now? Because the men of Vichy, on orders from Berlin, are trying to make us believe that Daladier wanted war. Daladier wanted peace to such an extent that he refused help in winning the war.

Three years before, I was in France after having lived for a time in Belgium. Up to that time I had not felt, although I soon did feel, that Belgium might become a dangerous trap. I went to Léon Blum, who had just been chosen as the first Socialist Prime Minister of France, and I talked to him frankly, because he is an honest man, an intelligent Frenchman with a deep devotion for his country. But—like my dear old friend Turati— he believes that the writings of Karl Marx are Gospel truth, and therefore he is lost. I said to him: 'Hitler and Mussolini are going to try to invade Spain on the pretext of destroying Spanish Bolshevism. In reality they want to encircle France, and when that is accomplished they will have won the first battle of their future war, and, on that day, they will despise you and the English so much that they will believe that they are going to become the masters of Europe. You cannot ask from the British Tories much power of intelligence. The British have many fine qualities, but their Tories have a complete lack of historical imagination and vision. It is for *you* to decide; it is for *you* to understand.'

Blum understood, but he did not decide. He did not decide because he lacked the courage, and, being a Socialist Prime Minister, he did as MacDonald had done in England. When the Socialists come to power they are apt to obey—out of diplomatic timidity—those who belong to the most blind and conservative parties. Blum made the Foreign Office policy the policies of reactionary France, which believed that Mussolini and Hitler were not invading Spain for the sake of destroying France, but because there was a certain danger from Bolshevism.

To advance this theory was one of the strangest phenomena of reactionary blindness. I know Spain. I like the Spaniards, although I know their faults, as I know the faults of my own country; if there is one thing that is impossible in Spain, it is Bolshevism. To me, Bolshevism is one of the four terrors of Europe. One of these is Hitler; another is his former master and present slave, Mussolini; the third is Bolshevism; and the fourth is the fear of Bolshevism. The one thing I want is to be free, knowing that only in freedom are the peace and the beauty of life. I would rather die than live in Bolshevist Russia; but the one outstanding fact about Russia is that its regime is a sort of gigantic, gloomy order. Now the beauty, the charm, the poetry of Spain is that there is no order, and there never will be order in Spain.

When I was a young man I was Counselor of the Italian Embassy in Madrid. Madrid was an old Royal Court of the eighteenth-century type, with everything turning around the king. At that time I happened to be one of the rather good polo players of Europe. The king of Spain was a very bad player, but, being a king, he was said by everyone to be a very good player. We played polo together two or three times a week for six months, which means a good deal of intimacy. Just like all kings, he was always complaining of his people. One day he said: 'Tell me, are the Italians absolutely without any discipline, also? You know that in your country, or in Germany, or in England, a baby's first word is "Mama," or, if he is a very intelligent baby, he may say "Papa"; but a Spanish boy's first word is "No." '

For once King Alfonso said the truth. And yet Spain was supposed to be the country of Bolshevism. How was it that so many people in the world, even here in this country, believed in the gigantic danger of Bolshevism?

This is the result, I think—and I say it with a certain amount of national vanity—of a marvelous invention of this fellow Mussolini, whom I knew quite well in the Italian Parliament. For years he sent emissaries to me asking what I wanted to induce me to become friends with him. This shows the low quality of his mind, because, knowing me, he should have known what my answer would be. It was always 'I want only to be free,' and freedom was the only thing he could not give me. But Mussolini has some outstanding qualities. If he were to come to Hollywood, he would outshine all the motion picture stars. He has also been a very able demagogic yellow-newspaperman.

Mussolini made a discovery which he passed on to his pupil Hitler, and it is the key to all the psychology of recent events in Europe. He discovered that a lie remains a lie if it be repeated ten times or even a hundred times, but when it is repeated twenty thousand times it becomes Gospel truth and is believed.

In New York I am constantly meeting American friends of mine, intelligent people, who believe that they are 'liberals.' They hate Fascism and they say to me that it is such a pity about Mussolini: 'How right you were! Yes, he is a criminal—but he did so many wonderful things during the first years of his regime.'

I know that this is a lie. I know that it is a libel on Italy. We Italians are the most hard-working race in the world. No other people in Europe work as hard as we do. Just because Italy is a poor country, and because he hated Italy and the Italians, Mussolini invented the slogan: 'The Italians need castor oil in order to learn how to work!'

However, my liberal friends in New York believe this lie, and, as I am not of a missionary spirit, I acquiesce. There are a great many other people in America who talk like this. I do not like to mention names of societies or groups, but as an example, there is the 'America First' Committee. These people say, or if they do not dare to say it they imply, that, after all, this new order which Hitler wants to impose on Europe is, perhaps, a lesser evil. Europe has been so divided that if some sort of new order comes, even through Hitler, who knows—perhaps it will be for the best.

This brings us to the idea that Hitler will leave so little after taking Poland, Norway, the Netherlands, Belgium, and the other small countries that it would be an advantage to have his new order. But while we are told that the silence of European populations subject to Hitler may be interpreted as a sort of assent to his domination, we must remember that it is a question of psychological intimidation.

Consider this fact: How is it that the Yugoslavs alone in Europe, with the exception of the Greeks, have defied Hitler, have thrown away a government of cowards and traitors and have willingly accepted the idea of death rather than domination, knowing the while that their little country was four-fifths encircled by the German troops? We have seen so many things and the headlines have been so dramatic for so many months that I think we have not yet realized that in hundreds of years there has not been such a heroic decision as this decision of the Yugoslavs.

As a representative of a great nation, Italy, I negotiated with Yugoslavia. I did so because, not being a fool as Mussolini is, I knew that Italy needed colonies, and I knew that the colonies Italy needed were invisible colonies—the neighboring nations which were agricultural while we were industrial. We needed to have these nations friendly toward us and desirous of having our products. These are the colonies Italy needs, and not the empty desert colonies of Africa which never pay anything. Colonies may have been a paying affair in the nineteenth century, but if an excuse must be found for Mussolini, it is the fact of his stupidity in trying to make a colonial adventure in the twentieth century, as if it were 1850. He is really a poor fellow. Dante, in the 'Inferno' of his *Divine Comedy,* shows fellows with their faces turned behind. Mussolini is just like them; his face is turned to the back.

I made a series of agreements with Czechoslovakia and with Yugoslavia and later with Turkey. In that way I secured for Italy a large number of markets, with an unprecedented flow of our exports into central Europe and the Balkans. May I here in parenthesis reveal to you that when I negotiated a peace treaty with the Yugoslavs in 1920, they were afraid to leave to Italy a certain section of Slavs whom I needed because it was not my fault that they were on our side of the Alps, the Alps being the most perfect geographic frontier in the world. When the negotiations were on the point of breaking, I told them: 'Here we are fighting for a few villages and a few valleys. You seem to forget that Italian Trieste and Yugoslav Zagreb will, in twenty years, be under German domination if we are not friends. We must be friends because the German imperialist madness may revive, and if we make a chain of free democracies, perhaps the Germans will think twice—but not if we are not united.' The Yugoslavs understood and yielded.

But this is in parenthesis, to indicate how deep is my sympathy for the Yugoslavs. In a few days Belgrade may be in ruins, just like Coventry in England or Louvain in Belgium; in a few days Croatia may be easily invaded, because it is only a vast plain. In spite of that, the Yugoslavs resisted the Axis and refused to give way. Why were they so daring? Because they have this great blessing—a country where no one is very rich and no one is very poor. Everyone is just a little fortunate. That is why they laughed at Bolshevism. When one is not afraid of that, he is bomb-proof against Fascist propaganda.

The tragic death of my old friend Count Teleki, the Prime Minister of Hungary, has brought me much sorrow. I remained in touch with him in spite of the great divergence in our political stand. I told Teleki to beware if he wanted to avoid a German invasion. I said: 'If they see that you are afraid, that you are going to make concessions to them, they will first take your fingers off, and then take all of your body.' The last time Teleki was able to send me a confidential message, he told me that on two points he would stand without possibility of compromise. First, the entire territory of Hungary must be independent; and second, Hungary must retain at least a little of that liberty which, in his mind, was the product of the liberal spirit of the Hungary of 1848.

Why did Teleki commit suicide? Knowing what he told me and knowing him, I understand. At the last moment he felt that he had gone too far along the way toward the crimes which Hitler wanted him to commit. One cannot go halfway with crime and then tell crime, 'Now I go my way.' That is why Teleki's suicide is a great moral lesson.

In Germany at the present time they know that the systems of propaganda which succeeded so well in all Europe are perhaps a little worn for America. Hitler does not believe very wholeheartedly that certain systems which were a success in France would be successful in America. France was beaten even before the German invasion of the Meuse in May 1940, for France was a house divided, and a house divided is doomed to defeat. Do you know to what extent German propaganda was successful even in France at war? (It is often said that one must not be personal, but is it strange if we most remember certain personal episodes?) Only a few weeks before the invasion of France, an organ of the navy, of the upper classes, of the aristoc-

racy, carried a long article with headlines in five columns, saying: 'We know at last who are the worst enemies of France. The
enemies of France are Churchill, Beneš, and Sforza.' Is it surprising that France was beaten?

But this type of propaganda will not be used here in America,
where the Nazi propaganda machine, which is very skillful, has
invented another system, much safer. Knowing the courage, the
spirit of independence, and the real patriotism of the American
people, the Nazis try to create evil out of good. In France it has
been discovered that many of the great speeches and articles
which were shouting that France had the best army in the world
were written by German agents. In the same way, they know
that the best means of helping Nazism in America, and an invasion—which would never be direct but, instead, invisible and indirect—is to make you believe that you are invincible.

I admit that this is offering advice, which I said at the beginning I wished to avoid. But I should be a coward if I used my
neutrality as a shield. I must warn you that the worst enemy of
America is already at work, and his name is Complacency. When
honest men like those who spoke here yesterday say that, after
all, if Germany does become the master of Europe, you still have
completely at your disposal this hemisphere, surrounded as it is
by two oceans, do you not feel that these speakers are making,
only on a larger scale, the same terrific, tragic mistake made by
the French, who said, 'We are safe behind the Maginot Line'?

And you say, 'this hemisphere.' It seems to me that the tragic
side of things is always mixed with the comic side. Do you know
whence the phrase 'this hemisphere' comes? It comes from the
fact that at school we learned geography from maps, where North
America and Latin America were united and distant from the
other map. But if we look at the world as it is, in a sphere, we
see at once that all the important places of Latin America are
much closer to Europe and Africa than to North America.

Perhaps the greatest manifestation of respect that one can
give is to tell what he believes to be the truth. Do not believe
for one minute that on the day that the German Reich becomes
master of Europe you Americans will have an ounce of prestige

in Latin America. It would be better to go there with a Portuguese or Bulgarian passport.

I speak to you truthfully, as a painful duty because of the admiration and friendship I have for your country, even though I know it is not for me, perhaps, to say certain things. What is my excuse? It is this: I am an Italian. I will die an Italian, because I am more faithful to my country in her hour of sorrow than in her hours of joy and glory. I know and feel that the United States, your country, is something of a growing miracle. It is a marvelous hope which offers itself to the world as the last hope for a trembling, suffering humanity. In the Middle Ages, writers and theologians sometimes tried to build what they called 'The City of God.' But you Americans, you alone can provide this marvelous building of tomorrow which may be called 'The City of Man,' where all the ideals, all the beauty, all the best in the world can find realization and crystallization in your America—even the best of Italian ideals. It is because I hope that America is going to become 'The City of Man' for the free men of all the world that I dare to tell you what I deeply feel to be the truth.

NIGHTMARE AT NOON

By Stephen Vincent Benét

THERE are no trenches dug in the park, not yet.
There are no soldiers falling out of the sky.

It's a fine, clear day, in the park. It is bright and hot.
The trees are in full, green, summer-heavy leaf.
An airplane drones overhead but no one's afraid.
There's no reason to be afraid, in a fine, big city
That was not built for a war. There is time and time.

There was time in Norway and time, and the thing fell.
When they woke, they saw the planes with the black crosses.
When they woke, they heard the guns rolling in the street.
They could not believe, at first. It was hard to believe.
They had been friendly and thriving and inventive.
They had had good arts, decent living, peace for years.
Those were not enough, it seems.
There were people there who wrote books and painted pictures,
Worked, came home tired, like to be let alone.
They made fun of the strut and the stamp and the strained
    salute,
They made fun of the would-be Caesars who howl and foam.
That was not enough, it seems. It was not enough.
When they woke, they saw the planes with the black crosses.
There is grass in the park. There are children on the long
    meadow
Watched by some hot, peaceful nuns. Where the ducks are fed
There are black children and white and the anxious teachers

Who keep counting them like chickens. It's quite a job
To take so many school-kids out to the park,
But when they've eaten their picnic, they'll go home.
(And they could have better homes, in a rich city.)
But they won't be sent to Kansas or Michigan
At twenty-four hours' notice,
Dazed, bewildered, clutching their broken toys,
Hundreds on hundreds filling the blacked-out trains.
Just to keep them safe, just so they may live not die.
Just so there's one chance that they may not die but live.
That does not enter our thoughts. There is plenty of time.

In Holland, one hears, some children were less lucky.
It was hard to send them anywhere in Holland.
It is a small country, you see. The thing happened quickly.
The bombs from the sky are quite indifferent to children.
The machine-gunners do not distinguish. In Rotterdam
One quarter of the city was blown to bits.
That included, naturally, ordinary buildings
With the usual furnishings, such as cats and children.
It was an old, peaceful city, Rotterdam,
Clean, tidy, full of flowers.
But that was not enough, it seems.
It was not enough to keep all the children safe.
It was ended in a week, and the freedom ended.
There is no air-raid siren yet, in the park.
All the glass still stands, in the windows around the park.
The man on the bench is reading a Yiddish paper.
He will not be shot because of that, oddly enough.
He will not even be beaten or imprisoned.
Not yet, not yet.

You can be a Finn or a Dane and an American.
You can be German or French and an American,
Jew, Bohunk, Nigger, Mick—all the dirty names
We call each other—and yet American.
We've stuck to that quite a while.
Go into Joe's Diner and try to tell the truckers

You belong to a Master Race and you'll get a laugh.
What's that, brother? Double-talk?
I'm a stranger here myself but it's a free country.
It's a free country . . .
Oh yes, I know the faults and the other side,
The lyncher's rope, the bought justice, the wasted land,
The scale on the leaf, the borers in the corn,
The finks with their clubs, the gray sky of relief,
All the long shame of our hearts and the long disunion.
I am merely remarking—as a country, we try.
As a country, I think we try.

They tried in Spain but the tanks and the planes won out.
They fought very well and long.
They fought to be free but it seems that was not enough.
They did not have the equipment. So they lost.
They tried in Finland. The resistance was shrewd,
Skillful, intelligent, waged by a free folk.
They tried in Greece, and they threw them back for a while
By the soul and the spirit and passion of common men.

Call the roll of fourteen nations. Call the roll
Of the blacked-out lands, the lands that used to be free.
But do not call too loud. There is plenty of time.
There is plenty of time, while the bombs on London fall
And turn the world to wind and water and fire.
There is time to sleep while the fire-bombs fall on London.
They are stubborn people in London.

We are slow to wake, good-natured as a country.
(It is our fault and our virtue.) We like to raise
A man to the highest power and then throw bricks at him.
We don't like war and we like to speak our minds.
We're used to speaking our minds.
                                        There are certain words,
Our own and others', we're used to—words we've used,
Heard, had to recite, forgotten,
Rubbed shiny in the pocket, left home for keepsakes,

Inherited, stuck away in the back-drawer,
In the locked trunk, at the back of the quiet mind.

Liberty, equality, fraternity.
To none will we sell, refuse or deny, right or justice.
We hold these truths to be self-evident.

I am merely saying—what if these words pass?
What if they pass and are gone and are no more,
Eviscerated, blotted out of the world?
We're used to them, so used that we half-forget,
The way you forget the looks of your own house
And yet you can walk around it, in the darkness.
You can't put a price on sunlight or the air,
You can't put a price on these, so they must be easy.
They were bought with belief and passion, at great cost.
They were bought with the bitter and anonymous blood
Of farmers, teachers, shoemakers and fools
Who broke the old rule and the pride of kings.
And some never saw the end and many were weary,
Some doubtful, many confused.
They were bought by the ragged boys at Valmy mill,
The yokels at Lexington with the long light guns
And the dry, New England faces,
The iron barons, writing a charter out
For their own iron advantage, not the people,
And yet the people got it into their hands
And marked it with their own sweat.
It took long to buy these words.
It took a long time to buy them and much pain.

Thenceforward and forever free.
Thenceforward and forever free.
No man may be bound or fined or slain till he has been judged
    by his peers.
To form a more perfect Union.

The others have their words too, and strong words,
Strong as the tanks, explosive as the bombs.

The State is all, worship the State!
The Leader is all, worship the Leader!
Strength is all, worship strength!
Worship, bow down or die!

I shall go back through the park to my safe house,
This is not London or Paris.
This is the high, bright city, the lucky place,
The place that always had time.
The boys in their shirtsleeves here, the big, flowering girls,
The bicycle-riders, the kids with the model planes,
The lovers who lie on the grass, uncaring of eyes,
As if they lay on an island out of time,
The tough kids, squirting the water at the fountain,
Whistled at by the cop.
The dopes who write 'Jimmy's a dope' on the tunnel walls.
These are all quite safe and nothing will happen to them.
Nothing will happen, of course.
Go tell Frank the Yanks aren't coming, in Union Square.

Go tell the new brokers' story about the President.
Whatever it is. That's going to help a lot.
There's time to drink your highball—plenty of time.
Go tell fire it only burns in another country,
Go tell the bombers this is the wrong address,
The hurricane to pass on the other side.
Go tell the earthquake it must not shake the ground.

The bell has rung in the night and the air quakes with it.

I shall not sleep tonight when I hear the plane.

NOT BY WORDS ALONE

By Albert Carr

I STOOD in a crowd where men and women with fervid voices and shining eyes were singing in praise of America, and even as we sang, a disturbing thought came to me. Does not patriotism begin and end for some Americans with the thrill of the national anthem? Have we not relied too much on words to prove our love for the land of the free? Are we forgetting the Biblical warning, as true today as 2,000 years ago, that 'faith without works is dead'?

Too many, I suspect, think of serving America only in terms of romantic martyrdom. They are willing to die for their country, but they do not know how to go about living for it. I know a hard-working, married businessman, an infantry captain in the last war, who, inflamed with zeal, recently took a trip to Washington to offer his services to the War Department. When the offer was courteously refused, he was indignant. It did not occur to him that heroic gestures that cause businesses to be neglected and families to be stranded are of doubtful value to a careworn government.

For most of us the real test of patriotism lies not in dramatic sacrifice but in the simple things we do—or fail to do—each day. Few have shown a deeper love of country than a certain successful lawyer of whom I have heard. Unfailingly this busy man gives an evening every week to teach a class of immigrants the meaning of Americanism. Surely the hero whose name is splashed in headlines for some single spectacular deed of valor is not more a patriot than the unknown, steadfast citizen who year after year quietly and unselfishly benefits his nation.

From *This Week Magazine*, 4 May 1941. Copyright 1941 by the United Newspapers Magazine Corporation. By permission of the author and publisher.

There is probably not one of us who, if he tried, could not find some small way to serve the cause of national defense, without breaking the normal pattern of his life. I saw the mechanic at the corner garage eating his lunch with an aviation engine chart spread out before him. 'I hear they'll be needing more men at the airplane plant,' he explained. 'It will save time if I know my stuff beforehand.' A young engineer of my acquaintance has been forcing himself to take systematic exercise and to study military-engineering problems in his spare time. 'Just common sense,' he says. Yes, but beneath that common sense one feels the glow of a patriotism more genuine than a hundred fiery Fourth of July orations. These are men of the same staunch breed that squinted down musket barrels from behind the stone walls of Lexington and Concord, when our nation was born.

Recently a manufacturer engaged in producing parts for boat engines told me a significant little story. He noticed a marked improvement in the quality of work done by his stenographer, and complimented her. Her reply startled him. 'To tell the truth,' she said, 'it never seemed worth while to push myself before. But with everybody working so hard on government production, it would have been mean not to contribute my two cents' worth.'

In factories, offices and shops throughout the land there must be many unsung patriots who sense that this is no time to be niggardly of effort. Employer and employee share responsibility for making America strong by producing more goods and services and taxable wealth. We are all in the same boat, all manning the oars; what sort of patriotism is it that refuses to pull in stroke, and a little harder, so that the race may be won?

The home, too, offers rich opportunity for practical patriotism. A friend once showed me a letter, a matter-of-fact little scrawl, written in 1917 by an American housewife who did not content herself with words. 'We feel that we must do something more to help. As Harry says, it isn't enough for our spines to tingle when the flag goes by—that's our pleasure, not our country's gain. The best thing seems to be to buy more Liberty Bonds, so we're cutting out every personal extravagance and budgeting far more carefully in the house. I was shocked when

I realized how much food we'd been wasting.' No medals of valor, no fanfare of trumpets rewarded this woman and the millions like her. Yet in their own way they fought bravely for their country, a secret army of patriots intent on victory, their weapons self-discipline and seriousness of purpose.

To prevent waste is important; but the moral force of American women can do much more. In a small town, after the last presidential election, a minister was deeply troubled by the unchecked rancors, prejudices, and hatreds that he could detect on all sides. He appealed to two prominent women who had publicly quarreled and urged them to set an example by heading a drive for better personal relations. They were reluctant, indifferent. Finally the minister burst out in wrath. 'You give lip service to your country,' he said hotly. 'I've heard you speak glibly of "the need for national unity." Yet you are unwilling to make even a gesture toward unity in your own town. Every American woman has a responsibility for the nation's morale. In these times of stress, unless you use your influence to promote good will, you are deliberately shirking your patriotic duty.' The accusation struck home. Swallowing their pride, the women made their peace and worked together to heal the psychological wounds of the community—not because they disliked each other less but because they loved their country more.

The truth is that we, the ordinary people of America, are shaping the destiny of America. The airplanes and tanks, the guns and shells, the ships and the marching men—these are only expressions of our will to be strong. The democratic spirit of America is like some mighty tree, rooted in the hearts of all of us, nourished by the vital faith that expresses itself in action. So long as we give our country something more than words, something of ourselves, American democracy will continue to grow and bear rich fruit, and our future will be bright with promise.

YOUTH, WAR, AND FREEDOM

By Raymond Gram Swing

A FEW weeks ago Dr. Robert Ley, chief of the German Labor Front, in the course of a broadcast gave this definition of freedom. 'A man is free,' he declared, 'first, when he can eat, drink, dress, and live as and where he pleases or finds necessary; second, when he can wander out into the world whenever and however he pleases; and, third, when others honor and esteem his labors. That is the true meaning of freedom.' I am not going to criticize this definition at length for what it says, though it is worth pointing out that it does not define such freedom as exists in a totalitarian state, where there is a distinct limitation on earning power; so that a man has to eat, drink, dress, and live according to an income set by the state, and not according to his pleasure or ability. In the Germany of today all young men and women, as labor conscripts, have to give outright of their services to the state, and later in life they are subject to the state's dictated rules as to how long and under what conditions they shall work, and as to the prices at which they must buy their food, clothing, lodging, and travel. But this freedom, Dr. Ley may say, if it does not now exist in practice, will be put into practice as Germany prospers. It is the Germans' ideal. It is what they are striving for. And I want to examine it first of all as an ideal.

The world, at this hour, is in dreadful chaos. It is in the grip of a conflict which bespeaks more than a competition for political power, more than a shift of world markets. Also at stake, besides political and economic power, is a concept of life, its establishment not for this year and next but for many years to come. For this reason, because the concept of life on which our

From *The Nation*, 22 June 1940. By permission of the author, publisher, and Olivet College.

nation was founded is the one that is being challenged, *we* are involved in this conflict, no matter how much or how little we may decide to do in defense of our concept. Even if the war in Europe ends in the defeat of the democracies, our concept of life will be still intact. But the challenge to it will continue, and either our concept of life or the challenging concept of the totalitarian order will prevail in the end.

Dr. Ley has defined freedom as Germany intends to establish it. It consists of economic security, the ability to travel, and the respect of the community. These are worthy objectives. But they are not the American concept of freedom, not because of what Dr. Ley says, but because of what he omits. For in his doctrine of freedom the individual is not free to think, free to speak, free to read, free to formulate his own experience of truth, free to contribute responsibility to the community, to help shape its life and direct its affairs. His freedom gives man an economic minimum and a sense of satisfaction in his labor, which surely is good. But it disregards his individual spiritual life, and the co-operation of men's individual spiritual lives for the benefit of the community and of the state. To put it bluntly, man is economically free but politically and spiritually enslaved. And there is the conflict of concepts.

A great many persons in this country have tried to evade facing the choice. They have told themselves that they were not involved in the struggle in Europe. They have ascribed other issues to the war. They have said it was a war between imperialisms, and so in a sense it is. They have said it was a war brought on by a peace treaty after the last war which did injustice to Germany, and so in a sense it is. They have said it was a war being fought a long way off. But what no one can deny truthfully is that the outcome of the war, whatever its origins, will be to establish or destroy in Europe a concept of individual and political freedom. And if it is destroyed there, it already is partly destroyed in all the world. For unless all civilized countries are free, no one country, nor even a single continent, can progress in freedom. It will be on the defensive. It will go into a stage of striving to preserve freedom which is on the wane, which has lost its appeal to modern men.

I think all of us are reluctant to admit to ourselves just how much we care about certain values in life. It is a deep process to square away to certain truths and to know that in necessity one would not flinch in defending them. Life is precious to us. Anyone who says light-heartedly that he would be ready to die for something can't be very sensitive or very honest with himself. We hope that when a test comes of our courage and our loyalty we shall not fail, but we don't go about advertising the aching conquest of ourselves. I believe that most enlightened men and women, young and old, when the emergency arises would make any sacrifice, even of life itself, to preserve a right to freedom. I believe this because it is the revelation of the ages. Many men have died to attain freedom, and to many men in the long past the necessity of freedom was the necessity of life itself.

There is a great deal of talk these days, particularly among young people, about what they are not willing to die for. I cannot criticize the younger generation for saying that they have no intention of dying for the contribution made to civilization by the older generation. As I look back upon that contribution I can well understand and respect their attitude. The generation to which I belong has done some splendid things. It has mechanized life, which is not to be sneered at. It has reduced space. The airplanes which are dropping bombs in Europe mustn't obscure our vision of the airplanes that are making the unification of China possible, that are bringing Latin America into close neighborhood with us, that have reduced the Atlantic ocean to one-fifth its breadth, that are making all men close to all men, as few men who lived in the same province a century ago were close to one another. Modern communications systems have pulled us still closer together; news, music, discussion draws every home into the vortex of art and current thought. Our newspapers and periodicals, our radios and television have annihilated the sense of separation. We all have access to the same things. We have untold opportunities of participation. The world has been given the physical integration which had to come before the development of the still more important spiritual integration.

This has been a contribution, made with initiative, resource, devotion, with an abounding energy and optimism rarely if ever duplicated by any generation. But I admit as I survey these achievements that young people who fall heir to them should not be expected to feel like dying for them. They are resplendent, but they do not evoke the deepest sense of need and gratitude. One would not die for a newspaper, not willingly, or for an automobile plant, or an airplane design, or for the stark beauty of that monument of a prosperous, mechanized America, the buildings that make up Rockefeller Center in New York. Nor have the other works of beauty of my generation been inspiring and enlisting. We have our literature, our painting, our contemporary music and verse, but we could, in necessity, dispense with them, as some men in times past could *not* dispense with their Scriptures and their psalms. The older generation has also spread before the new generation the riches of education, and done it lavishly, as in no other time in the long history of human society. Millions today have the equipment to understand the intricate complexities of this mechanized society. I do not say the education has been available to all, or has been always wise. The educational process is slow, but it is the only known process by which man does finally pull himself up by his bootstraps. Thus in appraising the older generation one must admit that it was not concerned wholly with mechanism. It had reverence for learning and beauty. It strove to make them accessible to all young people as their common right.

But the devotion and loyalty of young people to the world handed on to them has been weakened by two tremendous factors. One of these is the World War and its consequences. The other is our loss of our sense of personal validity. The second point I shall come back to later. The World War should have been the last great war and it wasn't. If the generation that fought it couldn't learn the lesson of that war, it was far too innocent and timid to deserve devotion and respect. The very first opportunity to organize peace that ever presented itself to a modern, almost integrated world came as the result of the World War. My generation botched the job. It not only botched it badly, but did it with sublime indifference, letting the strands

of a golden opportunity slip through its hands without clutching at a single thread. But it was not an experienced world.
Never had the organization of peace in a democratic civilization
been faced, thought through, and understood. People had gone
through a war, had detested it, had suffered death, desolation,
poverty, and they believed that to resolve not to fight another
war would be enough. They put war down as an evil in individual and national thought. They did not understand that war,
whatever it may be in terms of evil, is simply the consequence
of the breakdown of peace, and that peace is something that
must be built, understood, practiced every day, wisely cultivated,
constantly and consciously nourished.

It is the fashion today to decry the Treaty of Versailles and
find in it the root of the present war. But that is superficial
thinking. A treaty does not produce a war in a democratic
world. There can be no great war in a democratic world in
which peace is maintained with the same scrupulous opposition
to lawlessness and the same devotion to justice as in the domestic
life of a democratic nation. Peace is an international responsibility. Its maintenance is a function of a modern society. One cannot enjoy the fruits of freedom in a world made safe for democracy unless there is social organization to dispense justice and
to curb lawlessness. The failure after the World War was not the
Treaty of Versailles but the inadequacy of the organization of
peace. That inadequacy was in the League of Nations, both in
its constitution and in its membership. Before the League could
work—and it was man's first experiment with an organized peace
—old nations, with long memories of wars, had to be certain of
their security. Lloyd George and Wilson undertook to guarantee
France's security, as the precondition to the launching of the
League. But Wilson's pledge was repudiated by the United States
Senate, and this country was kept from membership in the
League by a minority of the Senate. So the French entered the
League determined to make it, not a new experiment in organized peace, but an instrument of security. Through the League
the French nation of forty millions was to be kept as strong
as the German nation of sixty-five millions. If the United States
had joined the League, even with the reservations worked out in

the Senate, France would have been secure, and the League might have grown from its imperfect beginnings into a workable system of peace. The origins of this war include the failure of the United States to understand that you can't have a democratic world unless you have organized a peace in which every free nation assumes its share of the responsibility.

I think the people of this country were ready to join the League. It is a myth that they weren't. If four men in the Senate had changed their votes, we should have entered, for those four men would have completed the two-thirds majority needed. I don't think the people of this country realized in the election of 1920 that they were voting on the League. Harding promised them a society of nations, and the leading Republicans of the day—among them, Root, Hughes, Hoover—gave their indorsement to the Harding pledge. Only after the election was won was the public told that the League had been repudiated. And having been told so, it didn't stop to read the record and check the facts. Somehow membership in the League, and with it organized service for peace, eluded the people of this country.

The breakdown of peace didn't begin at once, not till 1931, when Japan invaded Manchuria. If we had been in the League, this hardly would have been dared. If Japan had not demonstrated that peace *could* be broken down in safety, Mussolini would not have dared the theft of Ethiopia, Hitler would not have dared the militarization of the Rhineland, the disarmament conferences would not have collapsed because of the growing sense of national insecurity. And the world would still be enjoying the blessings of peace. I say that the older generation fought the war and lost the peace. And the new generation must either fight the war now, as it is doing in Europe, or stand to fight it later. For there is no organization of peace today, no democratic world, no system of society where power is diffused so that no single man and no little oligarchy can drive men into conquest. Unless the Allies win, peace and freedom will be on the defensive in this nation for as long as the mind can foresee. There can be only two kinds of peace—the one imposed by concentrated power, the peace of tyranny, and the peace of a free society where power is vested in free individuals, and where justice and the observance of law are organized as a social function in which all bear their responsibility. Only if the younger generation has learned that, and will set out to find the peace that alone can be tolerable—peace in a free world—can it scorn the older generation for failing to find it.

I said above that there are two factors which make it hard for young people to treasure their immediate heritage. The loss of the peace is one of them. The other is the loss of the sense of personal validity. I suggest that more destructive than the mechanized equipment of the modern army have been certain branches of the modern so-called sciences of psychology and economics. They have produced a revolution in man's attitude to himself, and it has not been, like some revolutions, a constructive influence, though I think it will be in time. Fifty years ago it was fairly easy for a person to think things through and reach a conclusion that rang as clearly as a bell. Those were the days of intellectual security. And they are gone. In their place we have the overwhelming sense that nothing is what it seems to be. We distrust all outward evidences; we look in all corners for hidden motives; we know that nothing that man tells himself is quite so, nothing that he tells others is really dependable. We have found out that the human mind works in layers, that man's thought is molded by inscrutable influences of which he himself is unaware. The modern psychologist can demonstrate that one's subconscious life is the product of emotional influences, of patterns out of childhood or infancy, and that one's conscious thought is a counterfeit, which one tries to pass off on a suspicious world. The psychologist has destroyed man's faith in the other fellow's sincerity, and to some extent man's faith in his own sincerity.

The branch of economics in which the term economic determinism was developed has done for social thinking what psychology has done for individual thinking. We are told that society never acts as it does for the reasons it gives itself. History is just the result of economic motives which men have not recognized, and history is what it is, not because of these and those individual actions, but because vast impersonal forces have played upon men. Thus there can be no national policies; there are only sinister conspiracies working beneath the surface, against which the educated person can defend himself only by utter skepticism and indefatigable suspicion. Now I think that this conception has finished off everything handed on to the new generation by the old. Why should young men revere the values of such a world, acknowledge to their depths the dignity and beauty of individual life, and be grateful for that world, if need be to the point of sublime sacrifice?

But here again, the young have no right to scorn the confusion of the old unless they are keen and talented in rediscovering the validity of the individual. If they must question all outer semblances, have they learned to trust the *processes* of establishing truth, which can be demonstrated in the research laboratory and in the recesses of their own souls: trial and error, the humility to be wrong and the greatness to learn from being wrong, the faith *in there being truth?* Do they know that the truth lies within them or does not exist for them? That for each there is no truth save that of his own experience? And can they have faith in the process of their own lives by which they steadily become more free as they become more wise? And can they have faith in the process which makes society free, the democratic process, the process of social trial and error, in which all individuals share in the trials and errors and the accruing social insight?

To come back to Dr. Robert Ley and his definition of freedom in a totalitarian state. It will be recalled that this definition omitted the freedom to think and speak and to participate in the process of government. Only individuals who have lost faith in themselves and in their individual validity would accept such a disguised enslavement. If a man does not believe in the godhood that is in him, he is going to believe there is godhood in the dictator. If he is confused and suspicious, if he can't trust the processes of experience, if he can't rely on his own judgments, in humility but always in fervent faith, he is going to give himself up, abandon himself as a worth-while possession, give himself by default to a national leader. Not having cared for responsibility, which is the other meaning of freedom, he will have thrown all the responsibility on the leader. And he will be secure, he will have no responsibility, but he will not be free. That is what it means to be a man or woman in a totalitarian state. It is a police state. You either believe what you are told to believe or you are purged.

In conclusion I would ask young people not to form a judgment of the times by looking too closely at what has been given them by the preceding generation. It is true that generation has not added much to freedom and has prepared people poorly to have faith in themselves. But we have a longer heritage. And the freedom that we possess and that young persons exercise with all the unconsciousness of good health came, not with the wind and rainfall, but out of human effort and anguish, out of great striving, great believing, and great sacrifice. Man was not always free. He did not always have the right to say, think, read what he pleased, or to have a responsible part in making and enforcing the laws to which he is subject. Men died for these things. And the soldiers of George Washington who went through the winter of Valley Forge liked the idea of dying, just as dying, no more than young men do today. They, and the men who founded this Republic, prized some things more than life itself. We are their heirs; they have no other heirs but ourselves. And if we can't be proud to be the heirs of our immediate parents, we can look farther back along the line of human endeavor and find cause to be grateful that we are free and that there were those willing to pay for that freedom. The ancestry is long, and men strove to be free, died to be free, long before Karl Marx depersonalized history with his partly true aphorisms about economic determinism, and long before Sigmund Freud made us aware of the complexities of thought processes. No label that can be glued over the freedom for which men have died can hide the reality of it. It *is* freedom. And it is *individual* freedom. They cared for it, and unless we care for it we are going to lose it.

A SOLDIER

By Robert Frost

He is that fallen lance that lies as hurled,
That lies unlifted now, come dew, come rust,
But still lies pointed as it plowed the dust.
If we who sight along it round the world,
See nothing worthy to have been its mark,
It is because like men we look too near,
Forgetting that as fitted to the sphere,
Our missiles always make too short an arc.
They fall, they rip the grass, they intersect
The curve of earth, and striking, break their own;
They make us cringe for metal-point on stone.
But this we know, the obstacle that checked
And tripped the body, shot the spirit on
Further than target ever showed or shone.

From *The Collected Poems of Robert Frost*, 1939. By permission of the author and Henry Holt & Company, publisher.

THE SOLDIER'S FAITH

By Oliver Wendell Holmes, Jr.

I ONCE heard a man say, 'Where Vanderbilt sits, there is the head of the table. I teach my son to be rich.' He said what many think. For although the generation born about 1840, and now governing the world, has fought two at least of the greatest wars in history, and has witnessed others, war is out of fashion, and the man who commands the attention of his fellows is the man of wealth. Commerce is the great power. The aspirations of the world are those of commerce. Moralists and philosophers, following its lead, declare that war is wicked, foolish, and soon to disappear.

The society for which many philanthropists, labor reformers, and men of fashion unite in longing is one in which they may be comfortable and may shine without much trouble or any danger. The unfortunately growing hatred of the poor for the rich seems to me to rest on the belief that money is the main thing (a belief in which the poor have been encouraged by the rich), more than on any grievance. Most of my hearers would rather that their daughters or their sisters should marry a son of one of the great rich families than a regular army officer, were he as beautiful, brave, and gifted as Sir William Napier. I have heard the question asked whether our war was worth fighting, after all. There are many, poor and rich, who think that love of country is an old wives' tale, to be replaced by interest in a labor union, or, under the name of cosmopolitanism, by a rootless self-seeking search for a place where the most enjoyment may be had at the least cost.

Meantime we have learned the doctrine that evil means pain, and the revolt against pain in all its forms has grown more and

From Oliver Wendell Holmes, *Speeches*, 1913. By permission of Little, Brown & Company, publishers.

more marked. From societies for the prevention of cruelty to animals up to socialism, we express in numberless ways the notion that suffering is a wrong which can be and ought to be prevented, and a whole literature of sympathy has sprung into being which points out in story and in verse how hard it is to be wounded in the battle of life, how terrible, how unjust it is that any one should fail.

Even science has had its part in the tendencies which we observe. It has shaken established religion in the minds of very many. It has pursued analysis until at last this thrilling world of colors and sounds and passions has seemed fatally to resolve itself into one vast network of vibrations endlessly weaving an aimless web, and the rainbow flush of cathedral windows, which once to enraptured eyes appeared the very smile of God, fades slowly out into the pale irony of the void.

And yet from vast orchestras still comes the music of mighty symphonies. Our painters even now are spreading along the walls of our Library glowing symbols of mysteries still real, and the hardly silenced cannon of the East proclaim once more that combat and pain still are the portion of man. For my own part, I believe that the struggle for life is the order of the world, at which it is vain to repine. I can imagine the burden changed in the way in which it is to be borne, but I cannot imagine that it will ever be lifted from men's backs. I can imagine a future in which science shall have passed from the combative to the dogmatic stage, and shall have gained such catholic acceptance that it shall take control of life, and condemn at once with instant execution what now is left for nature to destroy. But we are far from such a future, and we cannot stop to amuse or to terrify ourselves with dreams. Now, at least, and perhaps as long as man dwells upon the globe, his destiny is battle, and he has to take the chances of war. If it is our business to fight, the book for the army is a war song, not a hospital sketch. It is not well for soldiers to think much about wounds. Sooner or later we shall fall; but meantime it is for us to fix our eyes upon the point to be stormed, and to get there if we can.

Behind every scheme to make the world over lies the question, What kind of a world do you want? The ideals of the past for men have been drawn from war, as those for women have been drawn from motherhood. For all our prophecies, I doubt if we are ready to give up our inheritance. Who is there who would not like to be thought a gentleman? Yet what has that name been built on but the soldier's choice of honor rather than life? To be a soldier or descended from soldiers, in time of peace to be ready to give one's life rather than to suffer disgrace, that is what the word has meant; and if we try to claim it at less cost than a splendid carelessness for life, we are trying to steal the good will without the responsibilities of the place. We will not dispute about tastes. The man of the future may want something different. But who of us could endure a world, although cut up into five-acre lots and having no man upon it who was not well fed and well housed, without the divine folly of honor, without the senseless passion for knowledge outreaching the flaming bounds of the possible, without ideals the essence of which is that they never can be achieved? I do not know what is true. I do not know the meaning of the universe. But in the midst of doubt, in the collapse of creeds, there is one thing I do not doubt, that no man who lives in the same world with most of us can doubt, and that is that the faith is true and adorable which leads a soldier to throw away his life in obedience to a blindly accepted duty, in a cause which he little understands, in a plan of campaign of which he has no notion, under tactics of which he does not see the use.

Most men who know battle know the cynic force with which the thoughts of common sense will assail them in times of stress; but they know that in their greatest moments faith has trampled those thoughts under foot. If you have been in line, suppose on Tremont Street Mall, ordered simply to wait and to do nothing, and have watched the enemy bring their guns to bear upon you down a gentle slope like that from Beacon Street, have seen the puff of the firing, have felt the burst of the spherical case shot as it came toward you, have heard and seen the shrieking fragments go tearing through your company, and have known that the next or the next shot carries your fate; if you have advanced in line and have seen ahead of you the spot which you must pass where the rifle bullets are striking; if you have ridden by night at a walk toward the blue line of fire at the dead angle of Spotsylvania, where for twenty-four hours the soldiers were fighting on the two sides of an earthwork, and in the morning the dead and dying lay piled in a row six deep, and as you rode have heard the bullets splashing in the mud and earth about you; if you have been on the picket line at night in a black and unknown wood, have heard the spat of the bullets upon the trees, and as you move have felt your foot slip upon a dead man's body; if you have had a blind fierce gallop against the enemy, with your blood up and a pace that left no time for fear,—if, in short, as some, I hope many, who hear me, have known, you have known the vicissitudes of terror and of triumph in war, you know that there is such a thing as the faith I spoke of. You know your own weakness and are modest; but you know that man has in him that unspeakable somewhat which makes him capable of miracle, able to lift himself by the might of his own soul, unaided, able to face annihilation for a blind belief.

From the beginning, to us, children of the North, life has seemed a place hung about by dark mists, out of which come the pale shine of dragon's scales, and the cry of fighting men, and the sound of swords. Beowulf, Milton, Dürer, Rembrandt, Schopenhauer, Turner, Tennyson, from the first war song of our race to the stall-fed poetry of modern English drawing-rooms, all have had the same vision, and all have had a glimpse of a light to be followed. 'The end of worldly life awaits us all. Let him who may, gain honor ere death. That is best for a warrior when he is dead.' So spoke Beowulf a thousand years ago.

> Not of the sunlight,
> Not of the moonlight,
> Not of the starlight!
> O young Mariner,
> Down to the haven,
> Call your companions,
> Launch your vessel,
> And crowd your canvas,
> And, ere it vanishes

> Over the margin,
> After it, follow it,
> Follow The Gleam.

So sang Tennyson in the voice of the dying Merlin.

When I went to the war I thought that soldiers were old men. I remembered a picture of the revolutionary soldier which some of you may have seen, representing a white-haired man with his flintlock slung across his back. I remembered one or two living examples of revolutionary soldiers whom I had met, and I took no account of the lapse of time. It was not until long after, in winter quarters, as I was listening to some of the sentimental songs in vogue, such as—

> Farewell, Mother, you may never
> See your darling boy again,

that it came over me that the army was made up of what I now should call very young men. I dare say that my illusion has been shared by some of those now present, as they have looked at us upon whose heads the white shadows have begun to fall. But the truth is that war is the business of youth and early middle age. You who called this assemblage together, not we, would be the soldiers of another war, if we should have one, and we speak to you as the dying Merlin did in the verse which I just quoted. Would that the blind man's pipe might be transfigured by Merlin's magic, to make you hear the bugles as once we heard them beneath the morning stars! For you it is that now is sung the Song of the Sword:

> The War-Thing, the Comrade,
> Father of honor
> And giver of kingship,
> The fame-smith, the song master.
>
>   .   .   .
>
> *Priest* (saith the Lord)
> *Of his marriage with victory.*
>
>   .   .   .
>
> Clear singing, clean slicing;
> Sweet spoken, soft finishing;
> Making death beautiful,

Life but a coin
To be staked in the pastime
Whose playing is more
Than the transfer of being;
Arch-anarch, chief builder,
Prince and evangelist,
I am the Will of God:
I am the Sword.

War, when you are at it, is horrible and dull. It is only when time has passed that you see that its message was divine. I hope it may be long before we are called again to sit at that master's feet. But some teacher of the kind we all need. In this snug, oversafe corner of the world we need it, that we may realize that our comfortable routine is no eternal necessity of things, but merely a little space of calm in the midst of the tempestuous untamed streaming of the world, and in order that we may be ready for danger. We need it in this time of individualist negations, with its literature of French and American humor, revolting at discipline, loving fleshpots, and denying that anything is worthy of reverence,—in order that we may remember all that buffoons forget. We need it everywhere and at all times. For high and dangerous action teaches us to believe as right beyond dispute things for which our doubting minds are slow to find words of proof. Out of heroism grows faith in the worth of heroism. The proof comes later, and even may never come. Therefore I rejoice at every dangerous spot which I see pursued. The students at Heidelberg, with their sword-slashed faces, inspire me with sincere respect. I gaze with delight upon our polo players. If once in a while in our rough riding a neck is broken, I regard it, not as a waste, but as a price well paid for the breeding of a race fit for headship and command.

We do not save our traditions, in this country. The regiments whose battle flags were not large enough to hold the names of the battles they had fought, vanished with the surrender of Lee, although their memories inherited would have made heroes for a century. It is the more necessary to learn the lesson afresh from perils newly sought, and perhaps it is not vain for us to tell the new generation what we learned in our day, and what we still believe. That the joy of life is living, is to put out all one's powers as far as they will go; that the measurer of power is obstacles overcome; to ride boldly at what is in front of you, be it fence or enemy; to pray, not for comfort, but for combat; to keep the soldier's faith against the doubts of civil life, more besetting and harder to overcome than all the misgivings of the battle field, and to remember that duty is not to be proved in the evil day, but then to be obeyed unquestioning; to love glory more than the temptations of wallowing ease, but to know that one's final judge and only rival is oneself: with all our failures in act and thought, these things we learned from noble enemies in Virginia or Georgia or on the Mississippi, thirty years ago; these things we believe to be true.

'Life is not lost,' said she, 'for which is bought Endless renown.'

We learned also, and we still believe, that love of country is not yet an idle name.

> Deare countrey! O how dearely deare
> Ought thy remembraunce, and perpetuall band
> Be to thy foster-child, that from thy hand
> Did commun breath and nouriture receave!
> How brutish is it not to understand
> How much to her we owe, that all us gave;
> That gave unto us all, whatever good we have!

As for us, our days of combat are over. Our swords are rust. Our guns will thunder no more. The vultures that once wheeled over our heads are buried with their prey. Whatever of glory yet remains for us to win must be won in the council or the closet, never again in the field. I do not repine. We have shared the incommunicable experience of war; we have felt, we still feel, the passion of life to its top.

Three years ago died the old colonel of my regiment, the Twentieth Massachusetts. He gave our regiment its soul. No man could falter who heard his 'Forward, Twentieth!' I went to his funeral. From a side door of the church a body of little choir boys came in like a flight of careless doves. At the same time the doors opened at the front, and up the main aisle advanced his

coffin, followed by the few gray heads who stood for the men of
the Twentieth, the rank and file whom he had loved, and whom
he led for the last time. The church was empty. No one remembered the old man whom we were burying, no one save those
next to him, and us. And I said to myself, the Twentieth has
shrunk to a skeleton, a ghost, a memory, a forgotten name which
we other old men alone keep in our hearts. And then I thought:
It is right. It is as the colonel would have had it. This also is
part of the soldier's faith: Having known great things, to be
content with silence. Just then there fell into my hands a little
song sung by a warlike people on the Danube, which seemed to
me fit for a soldier's last word, another song of the sword, but a
song of the sword in its scabbard, a song of oblivion and peace.

A soldier has been buried on the battle field.

> And when the wind in the tree tops roared,
> The soldier asked from the deep dark grave:
>   'Did the banner flutter then?'
> 'Not so, my hero,' the wind replied,
> 'The fight is done, but the banner won,
> Thy comrades of old have borne it hence,
>   Have borne it in triumph hence.'
> Then the soldier spake from the deep dark grave:
>   'I am content.'
>
>   . . .
>
> Then he heareth the lovers laughing pass,
>   And the soldier asks once more:
> 'Are these not the voices of them that love,
>   That love—and remember me?'
> 'Not so, my hero,' the lovers say,
> 'We are those that remember not;
> For the spring has come and the earth has smiled,
>   And the dead must be forgot.'
> Then the soldier spake from the deep dark grave:
>   'I am content.'

ADDRESS TO THE NATION

9 December 1941

By Franklin D. Roosevelt

THE sudden criminal attacks perpetrated by the Japanese in the Pacific provide the climax of a decade of international immorality.

Powerful and resourceful gangsters have banded together to make war upon the whole human race. Their challenge has now been flung at the United States of America. The Japanese have treacherously violated the long-standing peace between us. Many American soldiers and sailors have been killed by enemy action. American ships have been sunk; American airplanes have been destroyed.

The Congress and the people of the United States have accepted that challenge.

Together with other free peoples, we are now fighting to maintain our right to live among our world-neighbors in freedom and in common decency, without fear of assault.

I have prepared the full record of our past relations with Japan, and it will be submitted to the Congress. It begins with the visit of Commodore Perry to Japan eighty-eight years ago. It ends with the visit of two Japanese emissaries to the Secretary of State last Sunday, an hour after Japanese forces had loosed their bombs and machine guns against our flag, our forces, and our citizens.

I can say with utmost confidence that no Americans, today or a thousand years hence, need feel anything but pride in our patience and our efforts through all the years toward achieving a peace in the Pacific which would be fair and honorable to every nation, large or small. And no honest person, today or a thousand years hence, will be able to suppress a sense of indignation and horror at the treachery committed by the military dictators of Japan, under the very shadow of the flag of peace borne by their special envoys in our midst.

The course that Japan has followed for the past ten years in Asia has paralleled the course of Hitler and Mussolini in Europe and Africa. Today, it has become far more than a parallel. It is collaboration so well calculated that all the contingents of the world, and all the oceans, are now considered by the Axis strategists as one gigantic battlefield.

In 1931, Japan invaded Manchukuo—without warning.

In 1935, Italy invaded Ethiopia—without warning.

In 1938, Hitler occupied Austria—without warning.

In 1939, Hitler invaded Czecho-Slovakia—without warning.

Later in 1939, Hitler invaded Poland—without warning.

In 1940, Hitler invaded Norway, Denmark, Holland, Belgium, and Luxembourg—without warning.

In 1940, Italy attacked France and later Greece—without warning.

In 1941, the Axis Powers attacked Jugoslavia and Greece and they dominated the Balkans—without warning.

In 1941, Hitler invaded Russia—without warning.

And now Japan has attacked Malaya and Thailand—and the United States—without warning.

It is all of one pattern.

We are now in this war. We are in it—all the way. Every single man, woman, and child is a partner in the most tremendous undertaking of our American history. We must share together the bad news and the good news, the defeats and the victories—the changing fortunes of war.

So far, the news has all been bad. We have suffered a serious set-back in Hawaii. Our forces in the Philippines, which include the brave people of that commonwealth, are taking punishment, but are defending themselves vigorously. The reports from Guam and Wake and Midway Islands are still confused, but we must be prepared for the announcement that all these three outposts have been seized.

The casualty lists of these first few days will undoubtedly be large. I deeply feel the anxiety of all families of the men in our armed forces and the relatives of people in cities which have been bombed. I can only give them my solemn promise that they will get news just as quickly as possible.

This government will put its trust in the stamina of the American people and will give the facts to the public as soon as two conditions have been fulfilled; first, that the information has been definitely and officially confirmed; and, second, that the release of the information at the time it is received will not prove valuable to the enemy directly or indirectly.

Most earnestly I urge my countrymen to reject all rumors. These ugly little hints of complete disaster fly thick and fast in wartime. They have to be examined and appraised.

As an example, I can tell you frankly that until further surveys are made, I have not sufficient information to state the exact damage which has been done to our naval vessels at Pearl Harbor. Admittedly the damage is serious. But no one can say how serious until we know how much of this damage can be repaired and how quickly the necessary repairs can be made.

I cite as another example a statement made on Sunday night that a Japanese carrier had been located and sunk off the Canal Zone. And when your hear statements that are attributed to what they call 'an authoritative source,' you can be reasonably sure that under these war circumstances the 'authoritative source' was not any person in authority.

Many rumors and reports which we now hear originate with enemy sources. For instance, today the Japanese are claiming that as a result of their one action against Hawaii they have gained naval supremacy in the Pacific. This is an old trick of propaganda which has been used innumerable times by the Nazis. The purposes of such fantastic claims are, of course, to spread fear and confusion among us, and to goad us into revealing military information which our enemies are desperately anxious to obtain.

Our government will not be caught in this obvious trap—and neither will our people.

It must be remembered by each and every one of us that our free and rapid communication must be greatly restricted in wartime. It is not possible to receive full, speedy, accurate reports from distant areas of combat. This is particularly true where naval operations are concerned. For in these days of the marvels of radio it is often impossible for the commanders of various units to report their activities by radio, for the very simple reason that this information would become available to the enemy, and would disclose their position and their plan of defense or attack.

Of necessity there will be delays in officially confirming or denying reports of operations, but we will not hide facts from the country if we know the facts and if the enemy will not be aided by their disclosure.

To all newspapers and radio stations—all those who reach the eyes and ears of the American people—I say this: You have a most grave responsibility to the nation now and for the duration of this war.

If you feel that our government is not disclosing enough of the truth, you have every right to say so. But—in the absence of all the facts, as revealed by official sources—you have no right to deal out unconfirmed reports in such a way as to make people believe they are Gospel truth.

Every citizen, in every walk of life, shares this same responsibility. The lives of our soldiers and sailors—the whole future of this nation—depend upon the manner in which each and every one of us fulfills his obligation to our country.

Now a word about the recent past—and the future. A year and a half has elapsed since the fall of France, when the whole world first realized the mechanized might which the Axis nations had been building for so many years. America has used that year and a half to great advantage. Knowing that the attack might reach us in all too short a time, we immediately began greatly to increase our industrial strength and our capacity to meet the demands of modern warfare.

Precious months were gained by sending vast quantities of our war material to the nations of the world still able to resist Axis aggression. Our policy rested on the fundamental truth that the defense of any country resisting Hitler or Japan was in the long run the defense of our own country. That policy has been justified. It has given us time, invaluable time, to build our American assembly lines of production.

Assembly lines are now in operation. Others are being rushed to completion. A steady stream of tanks and planes, of guns and ships, of shells and equipment—that is what these eighteen months have given us.

But it is all only a beginning of what has to be done. We must be set to face a long war against crafty and powerful bandits. The attack at Pearl Harbor can be repeated at any one of many points in both oceans and along both our coast lines and against all the rest of the hemisphere.

It will not only be a long war, it will be a hard war. That is the basis on which we now lay all our plans. That is the yardstick by which we measure what we shall need and demand: money, materials, doubled and quadrupled production—ever increasing. The production must be not only for our own Army and Navy and air forces. It must reinforce the other armies and navies and air forces fighting the Nazis and the war lords of Japan throughout the Americas and the world.

I have been working today on the subject of production. Your government has decided on two broad policies.

The first is to speed up all existing production by working on a seven-day-week basis in every war industry, including the production of essential raw materials.

The second policy, now being put into form, is to rush additions to the capacity of production by building more new plants, by adding to old plants, and by using the many smaller plants for war needs.

Over the hard road of the past months we have at times met obstacles and difficulties, divisions and disputes, indifference and callousness. That is now all past—and, I am sure, forgotten.

The fact is that the country now has an organization in Washington built around men and women who are recognized experts in their own fields. I think the country knows that the people who are actually responsible in each and every one of these many fields are pulling together with a teamwork that has never before been excelled.

On the road ahead there lies hard work—gruelling work—day and night, every hour and every minute.

I was about to add that ahead there lies sacrifice for all of us.

But it is not correct to use that word. The United States does not consider it a sacrifice to do all one can, to give one's best to our nation, when the nation is fighting for its existence and its future life.

It is not a sacrifice for any man, old or young, to be in the Army or the Navy of the United States. Rather is it a privilege.

It is not a sacrifice for the industrialist or the wage-earner, the farmer or the shopkeeper, the trainman or the doctor, to pay more taxes, to buy more bonds, to forego extra profits, to work longer or harder at the task for which he is best fitted. Rather, it is a privilege.

It is not a sacrifice to do without many things to which we are accustomed if the national defense calls for doing without.

A review this morning leads me to the conclusion that at present we shall not have to curtail the normal articles of food. There is enough food for all of us and enough left over to send to those who are fighting on the same side with us.

There will be a clear and definite shortage of metals of many kinds for civilian use for the very good reason that in our increased program we shall need for war purposes more than half of that portion of the principal metals which during the past year have gone into articles for civilian use. We shall have to give up many things entirely.

I am sure that the people in every part of the nation are prepared in their individual living to win this war. I am sure they will cheerfully help to pay a large part of its financial cost while it goes on. I am sure they will cheerfully give up those material things they are asked to give up.

I am sure that they will retain all those great spiritual things without which we cannot win through.

I repeat that the United States can accept no result save victory, final and complete. Not only must the shame of Japanese treachery be wiped out, but the sources of international brutality, wherever they exist, must be absolutely and finally broken.

In my message to the Congress yesterday I said that we 'will make very certain that this form of treachery shall never endanger us again.' In order to achieve that certainty, we must begin the great task that is before us by abandoning once and for all the illusion that we can ever again isolate ourselves from the rest of humanity.

In these past few years—and, most violently, in the past few days—we have learned a terrible lesson.

It is our obligation to our dead—it is our sacred obligation to their children and our children—that we must never forget what we have learned.

And what we all have learned is this:

There is no such thing as security for any nation—or any individual—in a world ruled by the principles of gangsterism.

There is no such thing as impregnable defense against powerful aggressors who sneak up in the dark and strike without warning.

We have learned that our ocean-girt hemisphere is not immune from severe attack—that we cannot measure our safety in terms of miles on any map.

We may acknowledge that our enemies have performed a brilliant feat of deception, perfectly timed and executed with great skill. It was a thoroughly dishonorable deed, but we must face the fact that modern warfare as conducted in the Nazi manner is a dirty business. We don't like it—we didn't want to get in it—but we are in it and we're going to fight it with everything we've got.

I do not think any American has any doubt of our ability to administer proper punishment to the perpetrators of these crimes.

Your government knows that for weeks Germany has been telling Japan that if Japan did not attack the United States, Japan would not share in dividing the spoils with Germany when peace came. She was promised by Germany that if she came in she would receive the complete and perpetual control of the whole of the Pacific area—and that means not only the Far East, not only all of the islands in the Pacific, but also a stranglehold on the west coast of North, Central and South America.

We also know that Germany and Japan are conducting their

military and naval operations in accordance with a joint plan. That plan considers all peoples and nations which are not helping the Axis powers as common enemies of each and every one of the Axis powers.

That is their simple and obvious grand strategy. That is why the American people must realize that it can be matched only with similar grand strategy.

We must realize, for example, that Japanese successes against the United States in the Pacific are helpful to German operations in Libya; that any German success against the Caucasus is inevitably an assistance to Japan in her operations against the Dutch East Indies; that a German attack against Algiers or Morocco opens the way to a German attack against South America.

On the other side of the picture, we must learn to know that guerilla warfare against the Germans in Serbia helps us; that a successful Russian offensive against the Germans helps us; and that British successes on land or sea in any part of the world strengthen our hands.

Remember always that Germany and Italy, regardless of any formal declaration of war, consider themselves at war with the United States at this moment just as much as they consider themselves at war with Britain and Russia. And Germany puts all the other republics of the Americas into the category of enemies. The people of the hemisphere can be honored by that.

The true goal we seek is far above and beyond the ugly field of battle. When we resort to force, as now we must, we are determined that this force shall be directed toward ultimate good as well as against immediate evil. We Americans are not destroyers—we are builders.

We are now in the midst of a war, not for conquest, not for vengeance, but for a world in which this nation, and all that this nation represents, will be safe for our children. We expect to eliminate the danger from Japan, but it would serve us ill if we accomplished that and found that the rest of the world was dominated by Hitler and Mussolini.

We are going to win the war and we are going to win the peace that follows.

And in the dark hours of this day—and through dark days that may be yet to come—we will know that the vast majority of the members of the human race are on our side. Many of them are fighting with us. All of them are praying for us. For, in representing our cause, we represent theirs as well—our hope and their hope for liberty under God.

A BRAVE DELIGHT

By Walt Whitman

POLITICAL democracy, as it exists and practically works in America, with all its threatening evils, supplies a training school for making first-class men. It is life's gymnasium, not of good only, but of all. We try often, though we fall back often. A brave delight, fit for freedom's athletes, fills these arenas . . . Whatever we do not attain, we at any rate attain the experiences of the fight, the hardening of the strong campaign, and throb with currents of attempt at least. Time is ample. Let the victors come after us. Not for nothing does evil play its part among us. Judging from the main portions of the history of the world, so far, justice is always in jeopardy, peace walks amid hourly pitfalls, and of slavery, misery, meanness, the craft of tyrants and the credulity of the populace, in some of their protean forms, no voice can at any time say . . . The clouds break a little, and the sun shines out—but soon and certain the lowering darkness falls again, as if to last forever. Yet there is an immortal courage and prophecy in every sane soul that cannot, must not, under any circumstances, capitulate. *Vive,* the attack—the perennial assault! *Vive,* the unpopular cause—the spirit that audaciously aims—the never-abandon'd efforts, pursued the same amid opposing proofs and precedents.

Democratic Vistas, 1871

SAIL ON, O UNION

By Henry Wadsworth Longfellow

THOU, too, sail on, O Ship of State!
Sail on, O UNION, strong and great!
Humanity with all its fears,
With all its hopes of future years,
Is hanging breathless on thy fate! . . .
In spite of rock and tempest's roar,
In spite of false lights on the shore,
Sail on, nor fear to breast the sea!
Our hearts, our hopes, are all with thee,
Our hearts, our hopes, our prayers, our tears,
Our faith triumphant o'er our fears,
Are all with thee,—are all with thee!

'The Building of the Ship,' 1849

NOTES, QUESTIONS, AND EXERCISES

'Few probably are the minds,' says Walt Whitman, 'that fully comprehend the aptness of the phrase, "the government of the People, by the People, for the People," which we inherit from the lips of Abraham Lincoln; a formula whose verbal shape is homely wit, but whose scope includes both the totality and all minutiæ of the lesson.' The definition of democracy given by Lincoln remains one of the best, because it is one of the simplest to grasp. Yet the term has implications in social, religious, artistic, and industrial areas as well as in politics. The national Pan-Hellenic Council recently decided to formulate rules to make fraternities more democratic. Labor unions insist that democracy is not fully achieved until workers have a voice in the management of industry. The W.P.A. art program is said to have democratized art in America. Democracy, therefore, is a word used in many ways and in many places. The selections in Part I of *Of the People* afford an opportunity to understand the term in its larger, all-inclusive significance. In the remaining six parts of the book the selections will illustrate or define specific aspects in the operation of the democratic concept in the United States. It is as if, having understood the word *automobile*, we were then going to examine all its parts, their function, and all the uses to which a motor vehicle can be put.

THE GETTYSBURG ADDRESS

Note that the key phrase of the Address is 'all men are created equal,' and that Lincoln develops his speech to insist upon the necessity of making this ideal an actuality. Note how the famous phrase concluding the speech follows the word 'freedom.' Note how the occasion, the dedication of a cemetery, is employed to give pertinence to a plea for equality and freedom.

THE AMERICAN'S CREED

The Latin word *credo* means 'I believe.' A creed, therefore, is a statement of belief. Usually the word is associated with religious faith, as in the Apostles' Creed, the Nicene Creed, or the Athanasian Creed.

If you are not familiar with these creeds, consult dictionaries and encyclopedias, especially *The Catholic Encyclopedia*. 'The American's Creed is a summing up, in 100 words,' says Mr. Page, 'of the basic principles of American political faith. It is not an expression of an individual's opinion upon the obligations and duties of American citizenship or with respect to its rights and privileges. It is a summary of the fundamental principles of American political faith as set forth in its greatest documents, its worthiest traditions, and by its greatest leaders.' The idea of laying special emphasis upon the duties and obligations of citizenship in the form of a national creed originated in 1916 with Henry S. Chapin. The City of Baltimore offered a prize of $1000 for the best statement.

The sources of The American's Creed are as follows:

'The United States of America.'
—*Preamble, Constitution of the United States.*

'A government of the people, by the people, for the people.'
—*Preamble, Constitution of the United States; Daniel Webster's speech in the Senate, January 26, 1830; Abraham Lincoln's Gettysburg speech.*

'Whose just powers are derived from the consent of the governed.'
—*Thomas Jefferson, in Declaration of Independence.*

'A democracy in a republic.'
—*James Madison, in The Federalist, No. 10; Article X of the amendments to the Constitution.*

'A sovereign Nation of many sovereign States.'
—*'E pluribus unum,' great seal of the United States; Article IV of the Constitution.*

'A perfect Union.'
—*Preamble to the Constitution.*

'One and inseparable.'
—*Webster's speech in the Senate, January 26, 1830.*

'Established upon those principles of freedom, equality, justice, and humanity for which American patriots sacrificed their lives and fortunes.'
—*Declaration of Independence.*

'I therefore believe it is my duty to my country to love it.'
—*In substance from Edward Everett Hale's 'The Man Without a Country.'*

'To support its Constitution.'
—*Oath of allegiance, section 1757, Revised Statutes of the United States.*

'To obey its laws.'
—*Washington's Farewell Address; Article VI, Constitution of the United States.*

'To respect its flag.'

—*National anthem, 'The Star-Spangled Banner'; Army and Navy Regulations; War Department circular on flag etiquette, April 14, 1917.*

'And to defend it against all enemies.'

—*Oath of allegiance, section 1757, Revised Statutes of the United States.*

PART I

THE VOICE OF THE PEOPLE

Often a student is asked, 'What is your philosophy?' This question sometimes merely means, What is your attitude toward a given principle, event, or person? A person's philosophy is the sum of all his attitudes toward God, nature, and man. Each one of us has some notions or beliefs which form a 'philosophy of life.' If we were to begin anew to form a philosophy, our activity might embrace the following steps. First of all our attitude must be determined toward the problem of deity and the creation of the universe. When these religious problems are settled, then an approach to the relation between the individual and the universe can be made. The natural sciences codify our learning related to the universe. Man associates with his fellows, and thus the whole realm of human relations must be accounted for. The social sciences study these areas of relationships. The department of studies called Philosophy is, in its various branches, concerned with the manner of learning truth, or *logic;* with the attainment of good conduct, or *ethics;* and with the achievement of beauty in all artistic forms, or *esthetics.* Each individual's philosophy, therefore, embraces many varied realms of activity and knowledge; his creed or possibly his set of creeds must be comprehensive, indeed, to express adequately his attitude toward the fullness of life. Sometimes we sum up our philosophy with a qualitative judgment: we say we are an optimist or a pessimist, a sentimentalist or a cynic, an idealist or a materialist.

Exercises:

1. Write a creed in which you state what you believe about your duty to your fellow men.
2. After the preceding exercise has been carried out, let a committee of students take these creeds and arrive at a composite statement. Before a final embodiment of the views of the class is prepared, the likenesses and differences among all the students' creeds should be presented for class discussion. A consensus should be achieved on major principles.

YOUNG MAN IN SEARCH OF A FAITH

It has been said that America is different things to different people. In this radio script, first used over WOR and the Mutual Network on 4 August 1941, Alvin M. Josephy, Jr., shows that America may seem to be geography and production, or it may seem to be a series of historical events, or it may be the people, 'each himself a part of the nation' blessed with freedom and opportunity.

Notice the technique here employed; examine especially the parts played by the Narrator, the Voice, and the music. Since radio appeals only to the ear, the ear must differentiate between speakers; and since silence is not a desirable mode of accentuation on a radio, music has been substituted.

Exercises:

1. Write a radio script based upon one of the following topics:
   a. The founding of a college, society, church, colony, or town.
   b. John Smith rescued by Pocahontas (or any incident from history).
   c. Johnny Appleseed at Natchez (or an incident from folklore or legend).
   d. Hester Prynne and Roger Dimmesdale on the pillory (or an incident from fiction, drama, or poetry).
2. Write an expository essay or prepare a talk explaining how Young Man reached his faith; be sure to use specific data from the script to support your statements.
3. Write an essay or prepare a talk on a topic similar to one of the following:
   a. My favorite radio artists. (Give specific instances from programs to illustrate your remarks.)
   b. The techniques of radio drama as contrasted with those of stage plays.
   c. The place of music in radio drama.
   d. Television and the radio. (A famous poet whose radio dramas have been particularly effective says that he dreads the day when television will be fully mastered, since the imagination, he believes, is better stimulated by ear than by eye. Test this assertion by a good radio program or spot news report, and present grounds for agreeing or disagreeing with the poet.)
   e. Advertising and radio. (Is it fortunate or unfortunate that American radio programs are mainly dependent on advertising for support? Find out how the British Broadcasting Corporation is maintained, and how the radio programs it offers compare in quality with American programs. If you can listen to the BBC over a short-wave receiver, present specific comparisons gained by your study of programs.)
   f. Radio in education.

AMERICA THE BEAUTIFUL

'*America the Beautiful* was written in its original form, more literary and ornate than the present version, in the summer of 1893,' Miss Bates, then professor of English at Wellesley College, stated in a note on the poem. 'I was making my first trip west. After visiting at Chicago the World's Fair, where I was naturally impressed by the symbolic beauty of the White City, I went on to Colorado Springs. Here I spent three weeks or so under the purple range of the Rockies, which looked down with surprise on a summer school. This had called to its faculty several instructors from the east, Dr. Rolfe coming from Cambridge to teach Shakespeare, Professor Todd from Amherst for lectures on Astronomy, Professor Katherine Coman from Wellesley for a course in Economics. My own subject, which seemed incongruous enough under that new and glowing sky, was English Religious Drama.

'We strangers celebrated the close of the session by a merry expedition to the top of Pikes Peak, making the ascent by the only method then available for people not vigorous enough to achieve the climb on foot nor adventurous enough for burro-riding. Prairie wagons, their tail-boards emblazoned with the traditional slogan, "Pikes Peak or Bust," were pulled by horses up to the half-way house, where the horses were relieved by mules. We were hoping for half an hour on the summit, but two of our party became so faint in the rarefied air that we were bundled into the wagons again and started on our downward plunge so speedily that our sojourn on the peak remains in memory hardly more than one ecstatic gaze. It was then and there, as I was looking out over the sea-like expanse of fertile country spreading away so far under those ample skies, that the opening lines of the hymn floated into my mind. When we left Colorado Springs the four stanzas were pencilled in my notebook, together with other memoranda, in verse and prose, of the trip. The Wellesley work soon absorbed time and attention again, the notebook was laid aside, and I do not remember paying heed to these verses until the second summer following, when I copied them out and sent them to *The Congregationalist*, where they first appeared in print July 4, 1895. The hymn attracted an unexpected amount of attention. It was almost at once set to music by that eminent composer, Silas G. Pratt, and re-published, with his setting, in *Famous Songs*, issued in 1895 by the Baker and Taylor Company. Other tunes were written for the words and so many requests came to me, with still increasing frequency, to permit its use in various publications and for special services that, in 1904, I re-wrote it, trying to make the phraseology more simple and direct.

'The new form first appeared in the *Evening Transcript* of Boston, November 19, 1904. After the lapse of a few years, during which the hymn had run the gauntlet of criticism, I changed the wording of the opening quatrain of the third stanza. The hymn as printed above is the final version . . . That the hymn has gained such a hold as it has upon our people, is clearly due to the fact that Americans are at heart idealists, with a fundamental faith in human brotherhood.' Mrs. George Sargent Burgess has given permission to reprint the poem and the foregoing note.

Study the adjectives and figures of speech in this famous song. Note the rhyme scheme and the use of internal rhyme in the seventh line of each stanza. Test this lyric against the three unmistakable characteristics of poetry: condensation (the greatest amount of meaning in the smallest number of words), figures of speech, and musical rhythm.

U.S.A.: THE LAND, THE PEOPLE, AND THE GOVERNMENT

This essay, written by a prominent English political scientist and historian for British consumption, looks at our country's totality much as we look at a foreign nation. In this statement there are some exaggerations and some statements that do not apply to your particular locality. Look for statements to which you can take exception. Can you write a detailed statement covering your area to present a correct view? How valid are generalizations about a whole country, a state, or a city? Does the exception always prove the rule?

Mr. Brogan's close-packed account is admirably clear and well put together. A study of the construction of his paragraphs may help you build your own. He makes use of various kinds of development: comparison, contrast, enumeration of particulars or instances, enumeration of divisions of the subject, effect and its causes, reasons, and developed definition. Find instances of all these. Note that all his paragraphs, except a few that are short because of some special function, are substantial. Count the number of words in three paragraphs. Count the number of sentences. Compare these statistics with three paragraphs from a letter or essay of yours. Mr. Brogan has *deductive* paragraphs, which state the topic at the beginning and then develop this topic sentence; he also has, less often, *inductive* paragraphs, which arrive at a topic sentence at the end of a chain of reasoning. Note the first and last paragraphs in Section III as instances of the inductive method of paragraph construction. Look up 'deductive' and 'inductive' in an unabridged dictionary.

A good way to improve your own paragraphs—if you can write good paragraphs, you have gone a long way toward mastery of effective writing—is to make an outline of one of these paragraphs that impresses you as well built. Set down beside each topic the words that act as cement between the thoughts; if the connection is made by parallel structure or some other non-verbal method, mention that method. Then take a topic on which you have something definite to say; try to develop it in the same way as nearly as is convenient for your material, and try to keep the same linking of thought. Make your paragraph sound as if it were completely independent of your model. If your attempt seems stiff, lay it aside for a day to see if you can find the reason. The blame may rest on its language, construction, or word order. Remember Franklin's efforts to master a good prose style by imitating Addison's essays. The exercise, to be sure, is artificial, and it does not work for everyone, but Franklin got something out of it.

Exercises:

1. Study Mr. Brogan's vocabulary, his sentences, and his wit.
2. Write an essay or prepare a talk on one of the following topics:
   a. The geographical (industrial or agricultural) uniqueness of my home community.
   b. Immigrants in my home community.
   c. My family's experiences over there and over here.
   d. Town rivalry (athletics, civic endeavor, etc.).
   e. Labor conditions in my home community.
   f. Why I work during the summer.
   g. Politics and political parties in my home community.

DEFINITIONS OF DEMOCRACY

Good writing and clear speaking demand that words be used accurately. The dictionary is an indispensable tool, even if it is not always a final authority. Only by increasing one's vocabulary can one's range of thought be widened. For more than eight out of ten people, the size of vocabulary determines the speed of comprehension of the written page; the more words you know correctly, the more able you are to grasp meanings quickly and correctly. Often the commonest words in our vocabulary may have a personal or local rather than a national meaning. A dictionary should frequently be consulted to test the correctness of the meanings and pronunciations of old and new words.

The method of definition is not difficult. For example, a chair is a *seat* with *four legs* and a *back,* and sometimes with *arms.* A stool is a single *seat* without a *back.* A chaise longue is an *elongated seat* or *couch,* having usually a support for the *back* at one end only and often having *eight legs.* The term to be defined is placed in relation to the class in which it belongs, and then the term is differentiated from all other members of the class. Thus *chair, stool,* and *chaise longue* are all *seats,* but they are differentiated one from another by peculiar qualities in each.

Exercises:

1. Define the terms *couch, sofa, cot, bed.*
2. Define the terms *mop, broom, feather duster, whisk broom.* Do these terms all belong to the same class?
3. Define the terms *rug, braided rug, hooked rug, Persian rug, Oriental rug, runner, Axminster, Wilton, Brussels.* Can you distinguish types of form, types of use, and types of weave?
4. Define *run, crawl, amble, trot, pace* as verbs.
5. Define *fraternity, sorority, sodality, club, league, guild.*
6. Define *faith, hope, charity, love, brotherhood, sincerity.*

DEMOCRACY

Democracy is a form of government; the dictionary definition supplies differentiæ by emphasizing the role played by the people, and it also emphasizes the variety of the forms of democracy.

Exercise:

1. Define other forms of government, such as *monarchy, tyranny, oligarchy, dictatorship, theocracy, aristocracy, plutocracy, matriarchy.*

DEMOCRACY AS DEFINED BY HISTORY

Carl Becker shows that a word can be stretched to mean almost anything; even the word *democracy* can be enlarged in spite of the breadth of definition given by the dictionary. His statement, rich in imaginative expression, bears close study. The following helps may be useful. *Semantics* is a branch of linguistics concerned with the science of meanings, as contrasted with *phonetics,* the science of word sounds. Words should *denote* the same meaning to all; thus a *thread* is a very thin continuous filament. Words often are used figuratively, as in 'silver threads among the gold.' Here 'threads' means hair, and the silver represents gray or old age as contrasted with the gold of youth. The connotation in this statement is pleasant, cheerful; growing old is symbolized as a beautiful event. Thus words *connote* meanings. *High hat* is a phrase meaning pride or snobbery; in some communities *blue* and *pink* when used with baby garments connote girl and boy respectively; a *black* border or armband symbolizes grief; *yellow* is used to characterize cowardice; 'take your coat off' is an invitation to fight; *tyranny* evokes pictures of terror, and so on. Connotations vary, since people have different experiences. Hence Mr. Becker says that an expansible suitcase, a Gladstone bag, may be necessary to hold the many interpretations or concepts of democracy. The term *Gladstone bag* has been used as a metaphor.

Exercises:

1. Write a 500-word definition of a term such as *loyalty, faith, love, generosity,* or *friendship*. Note that Mr. Becker has used specific examples in his third paragraph. Be sure to use similar concrete data in your definition.
2. Give the connotations of the following colors: red, pink, white, green. Name other colors and their connotations.
3. Give the connotations of the following: *hats off, sleeves rolled up, hold my glasses, heads up*. Name other phrases and their connotations.

ESSENTIALS OF DEMOCRACY

Professor Beard's statement enlarges the preceding two definitions by tracing the historical development of democracy in the United States; thus he arrives at a meaning of the word in relation to our needs today. What are the six enduring elements of democracy? Does the neglect of one imperil the fortunes of all? How so? Note that Mr. Beard does not construe the word *democracy* in a narrow sense; does he try to embrace too much within the meaning of the term? Is he erring by making the word 'a conceptual Gladstone bag'? Is governmental efficiency an important test of the success of democracy? Can we have a real democracy if one third of the population is ill-fed, ill-clad, and ill-housed? Must everybody have the right to a college education in a true democracy? Must there be absolute freedom of expression, or should the radio and newspapers have a self-imposed censorship? Should the spirit of brotherhood, of comradely fellowship, dominate a true democracy?

Exercises:

1. Study the vocabulary and sentence structure in this essay.
2. Study the paragraph structure and transition devices. Do you think that Mr. Beard could clarify his statements by further explanations? Where?

3. Write an essay or prepare a talk in support of, or in rebuttal to, one of Mr. Beard's main points.

THE BLACK COTTAGE

The minister and the poet have come to the black cottage where a lady recently died. The minister talks about the house and its furnishings. He lingers before a picture of her husband, and then he recurs to the loneliness of the cottage. The men sit on the porch; the minister tells of the lady's acquaintance with William Lloyd Garrison, the abolitionist, and John Greenleaf Whittier, the Quaker abolitionist poet; of her husband's death in battle, and of her interpretation of the War between the States on 'the principle that all men are created free and equal.' In what ways is Jefferson's sentence not 'true'? Was it more true in his own time? Does the minister think that we dispose of the meaning of Jefferson's 'mystery' by bringing such proofs against it? If you think the lady was wrong in her innocent belief, present your argument against it as if you were trying to convince such a person as she was. The minister is deterred from changing the wording of the Apostles' Creed by that bonnet in the pew. Why? Find out if you can (perhaps by questioning a minister) whether many or few churches which keep the Apostles' Creed have changed the wording of it. Lines 104-10 express a generalization about the cycle of ideas as affected by fashion, and the minister wishes for a land dedicated to truths which are abandoned for a time by men and then revived. The poem closes with a characteristically Frostian bit of drama. Just as the men entered the scene, so they depart, the conclusion being motivated by the sound of bees in the wall of the house. Are the bees a symbol or merely a dramatic device to end the minister's thinking aloud? If there is symbolism, what do the black cottage and the bees represent? What effect has the background of the black cottage upon the validity of the minister's statements? In what way, as judged by this poem, is Frost a poet of freedom and democracy? Is Frost saying that the lady's faith in human equality is temporarily outmoded, but that this idea will again 'prevail'? (Look up the various meanings of *prevail*.)

Frost uses everyday northern New England speech; note the rhythms. When lines seem irregular in meter, look for an idea that needs special attention; the speaker has hesitated or drawled, Yankee fashion, to make more emphatic what is not uttered explicitly. Note the characteristic New Hampshire touches: the shape and color of the little cottage, inside and out; the horsehair sofa; the warping boards; the bees in the clapboards; the sunlight blazing on the windows—life and light still in the dark cottage, from which the sons have gone away, 'out west,' but which they refuse to give up, even though the mother who valued their 'considerate neglect' no longer shows in the church pew her bonneted figure, half asleep in serene confidence that the eternal verities she holds to are continuing.

Why is the village minister chosen as the speaker? What sort of a man is he? Why does it make a difference whether her husband died at Gettysburg or Fredericksburg? What experience have you had with the phrase, 'created free and equal'? Have you seen more denials of it than the lady heard of?

PART II

'THAT ALL MEN ARE CREATED FREE'

'Give me liberty or give me death,' cried Patrick Henry in the Virginia House of Delegates in 1775. The essential quality of life in the United States has been its freedom; we are free to move from place to place without police registration, we are free to worship as our consciences dictate, we are free to express our opinions, and we are free in a multitude of ways unknown to people in some other lands. This great heritage of freedom we often take for granted; we assume wrongly that 'it has always been like this.' In this section is defined with greater fullness than in 'The Voice of the People' the nature and extent of freedom in the United States of America.

The symbol of American freedom is the Bill of Rights, the first ten amendments to the Constitution of the United States. These were not the first expressions of the idea of freedom in the United States or in the world; their origins lie as far back as 1215, when England's Magna Charta provided that 'no free man shall be taken or imprisoned or dispossessed, or outlawed, or banished, or in any way destroyed, nor will we go upon him, nor send upon him, except by the legal judgment of his peers or by the law of the land.' Familiar to Americans were the Petition of Right (1628) and the Bill of Rights emanating from the 'glorious revolution' of 1689. In the course of the following century it was apparent to Americans that these rights of Englishmen were endangered by two defects: there was no court of appeal in which to argue decisions made in England; and the rights had been granted by the grace of the king and not as a matter of natural right. The Declaration of Independence stated that the laws of Nature and of

Nature's God supported self-evident truths concerning certain unalienable rights granted to all men. Our Revolution was fought to attain
these rights. On 7 December 1941 Japan declared war upon the United
States by treacherously attacking our island possessions in the Pacific
Ocean at the very moment Nipponese ambassadors in Washington were
talking about peace. Sharply the fact was brought home that the issue
in the world was clarified. Two modes of thought, two philosophies
were in conflict. The Axis powers again were demonstrating their theory
that men have no rights that governments need respect; we took up
the challenge wholeheartedly to reiterate our faith in the right of every
individual.

The Bill of Rights was ratified in Congress on 25 September 1789.
Eleven state legislatures approved ten of twelve proposed amendments;
those that were not approved concerned governmental operation rather
than principle: one provided a method of Congressional reapportion-
ment, and the other pertained to compensation of members of Congress.

WHAT IS FREEDOM?

David Cushman Coyle achieves a definition of freedom by examining
the actual status of America today. Likes Charles A. Beard he finds
that new conditions create new problems and new attitudes; there has
been a growth in our idea of freedom. What is a 'democracy of responsibility'? What are the differences between a dictatorship and a
democracy? Is it proper to criticize a high official of the government?
How can elections bring about a better government? Are people always
good sports about elections; on what specific observations do you base
your conclusion? Why did the depression cause democracy to be concerned with economic freedom? What events have caused Americans
to shift emphasis from economic freedom of ourselves to political freedom for all people? Give an example of freedom of worship in this
country by naming the different churches in your community. Have
you knowledge of religious persecution in this country? Contrast the
modes of law trials in Italy and the United States. Define the following
terms: *open trial, trial by jury, a jury of one's peers, habeas corpus,
third degree, gestapo.*

Exercises:

1. Examine Mr. Coyle's vocabulary; is it more or less formal than Mr.
   Beard's? Do you approve of the use of colloquialisms in writing?
   Point out five colloquialisms.

2. Write an essay or prepare a talk on one of the following topics:
   a. If I could not speak without fear of arrest.
   b. Should the Church be under the control of the State?
   c. How the police force helps maintain freedom.

THE TRADITION OF LIBERTY IN ENGLAND AND AMERICA

Where does liberty begin? What is liberty as defined in biological terms? Is liberty one thing or many things? Is liberty a static matter? In what way has liberty been a driving force in history? What are the four liberties handed down from the seventeenth century? Do these four liberties say anything about choosing well? Are these four liberties man-made? What happened in the 1620's in Old England and in New England, and how did these events bring about a clearer definition of liberties? What limitations still existed at the end of the seventeenth century? Who urged that consideration be given to the universals of religious toleration, the rights of all men to share in government, and in freedom of speech? How has each of the four liberties broadened since 1689? What is the origin of the term Liberals? What conflicting sentiments marked recent thinking about liberty? Why do the four fundamental liberties serve as a basis for compromise between one freedom and another?

THE GRAY CHAMPION

This short story, in addition to giving stirring patriotic expression to America's will to be free, is interesting for the way in which it reveals Hawthorne's technique as a romancer; here are the use of colonial history as a theme, the Scott-like spotlighting of a few scenes, the opposition of two groups, the picturing of a procession, the creation of a twilight zone of the supernatural, the trick of multiple explanation of strange appearances, the use of symbols and allegory with moral and didactic aim, and a general expository tendency wherein abstract definitions are substituted for concrete descriptions. Hawthorne's language is strikingly poetic; note the condensation of utterance and the use of figures of speech. Examine the history of Governor Andros's rule to see whether Hawthorne has followed the facts. How has he heightened the incidents? Should a story be a transcript of actual events or an emotionally colored account? Compare Hawthorne's statement about the deformity of government and the Declaration of Independence.

Exercises:

1. Prepare a radio version of 'The Gray Champion.' Use a Narrator to set the scene, and let a Voice speak the moral interpretations.
2. Write a story based upon an historical incident in such a way as to enforce a similar patriotic lesson. Incidents from local legend or family history often are best.
3. Write into story or radio form the narrative of Barbara Frietchie as told by Whittier, or 'Paul Revere's Ride' by Longfellow; or use another poem.

THE SOURCES OF 'THE GRAY CHAMPION'

G. Harrison Orians, Professor of American Literature at the University of Toledo, has made extensive studies of the sources of Hawthorne's tales and of the influence of Sir Walter Scott's writings upon Americans. Hawthorne's reading and the part this reading played in the creation of 'The Gray Champion' are set forth to show how an incident in New England history has been altered to symbolize American patriotic feeling. What was the attitude of Bostonians in 1689 toward Andros? Who were the regicide judges? Who was the Angel of Hadley? What was the influence of Sir Walter Scott's version of the Angel of Hadley upon 'The Gray Champion'? What alterations of actual events did Hawthorne make?

Exercises:

1. Examine the footnotes to see the variety of notes used; some are footnotes of citation and some are footnotes of explanation.
2. Note the abbreviations. Some magazines and publishers italicize ibid., op. cit., and other Latin abbreviations. Each publisher has his own style; the rule to be remembered is that, whatever the style, consistency in its use must be maintained.

CONCORD HYMN

In the first stanza Emerson describes the scene and the event to be memorialized; in the second he tells what has happened to the contending forces; in the third he tells where and why the monument is being erected; and in the fourth he hopes the Spirit which animated the Revolutionary fathers will ask Time and Nature to guard the stone. To what event does Emerson refer? Poetry often implies more than the words actually denote; what is the full meaning of 'embattled farmers,' 'shot heard round the world,' 'slept' and 'sleep,' 'the dark stream which seaward creeps,' 'votive stone,' 'That memory may their deed redeem,' and 'leave their children free'? Study Emerson's verbs; why is 'arched the flood' better than 'crossed the creek'; why is 'We set today a votive stone' better than 'We erect a monument'?

Exercises:

1. Compile from Haydn's *Dictionary of Dates,* or a similar reference work, a list of the revolutions that took place in Europe between 1776 and 1850.
2. Read carefully one of Emerson's essays or a portion of his Journals. Either from a biography of Emerson or from *The Dictionary of American Biography* discover the circumstances under which he wrote the article you have read. Among Emerson's essays the following are recommended: 'The American Scholar,' 'Character,' 'Aristocracy,' 'Civilization,' 'Self-Reliance,' and 'The Young American.' It should be noted that Emerson always insisted that self-reliance is God-reliance, that man has within him latently the full creative capacity of deity.
3. Write a paraphrase of 'Concord Hymn.' Be sure that your prose statement has the effect of being a complete essay; it should not be a series of disconnected and jerky statements. Emerson's own plan is clearly worked out; yours should follow his. Because of the compact, figurative quality of Emerson's poem, your paraphrase should contain many more words than the poem.

LIBERTY AND GOVERNMENT

Because we are organized into civil society, we have civil rights guarded by law. Rousseau and Thoreau wanted to return to a state of nature, where natural rights would never be infringed upon. In a state of nature, such as that of Robinson Crusoe on the island before meeting Friday, no human restrictions are put upon us except by our own limitations, but in a civil society we are limited in our actions. We are told not to exceed a certain speed limit in an automobile; a red light at an intersection means 'stop.' These restraints are designed for the safety of all members of society. Law is the agency through which the common will is defined, and the courts of law interpret the common will. Mr. Justice Cardozo discusses the relationship between liberty and law or government with admirable simplicity, in spite of the abstract nature of the problem.

Exercises:

1. The four main divisions of Mr. Justice Cardozo's essay may be summarized by these topic sentences: (1) Liberty as a legal concept contains an underlying paradox; (2) Courts have attempted a practical solution of the problem of liberty; (3) Statutes must not be permitted to impair the liberty of mind or spirit; and (4) The

acceptance of the principle that courts define liberty does not mean that errors and injustices may not occur.

 a. Prepare a précis of the essay; write four paragraphs with the foregoing sentences as topic sentences.

 b. Prepare an outline of the essay.

2. Write an essay or prepare a talk outlining the difficulty that arises when there is a conflict between freedom and responsibility. For example, students are given great freedom with respect to their conduct off campus and on; whose responsibility is it when a student absents himself wilfully from class, or fails to prepare his lessons, or turns in reports after they are due? With what examples are you familiar, and what general principles are involved in such cases?

EMBATTLED FARMERS

Walter A. Dyer is the author of numerous excellent boys' books; one of these is *Sprigs of Hemlock: Tales of the Shays Rebellion.* 'Embattled Farmers' is an essay of historical research covering all available sources of factual information concerning Daniel Shays. In many ways it is a model research paper. The author has not merely exhibited a series of quotations from his sources; he mastered the factual information and then characterized Shays.

Exercises:

1. Outline the essay, 'Embattled Farmers.'
2. Prepare a research essay on a topic similar to one of the following:
 a. The background of the Bill of Rights.
 b. A day at the Constitutional Convention.
 c. The leadership of an individual at some moment of historical importance: John Smith at Jamestown, Col. Custer or Laughing Horse at Little Big Horn, Admiral Dewey at Manila, Kit Carson as General Frémont's guide.
3. Excellent research results have been gained from a concerted investigation of a limited area and time. Let each member of the class leaf through five or ten volumes of *The Atlantic Monthly* or some other magazine for a decade to discover what information can be gleaned of interest to him. One student may be concerned with medical progress, another with invention and engineering, another with economic problems, another with the problem of woman's rights, another with educational theory and practice, another with dress or art or architecture or music. The materials in the magazine may require further investigation, either in other periodicals or in books and encyclopedias. Enthusiastic research can produce class versions of books similar to Meade Minnegerode's *The Fabulous Forties,* Don Seitz's *Dreadful Decade,* or Frederick Lewis Allen's *Only Yesterday.*

COLONEL SHAYS

Mrs. Fisher, the famous novelist who resides in Vermont, has recounted a legend of Shays's end. Compare this fiction with the facts as presented by Mr. Dyer. What do you learn in this comparison about the techniques of research and of fiction, of objectivity and subjectivity in authorship, of intellectual and of emotional appeal in writing?

FREE

Jack Yeaman Bryan, who teaches creative writing at the University of Maryland, has published stories in *The Atlantic Monthly, Story,* and other magazines. Of 'Free' he has said: 'What set this tale going was the feeling aroused by noticing how little the word *free* really means to many a youth in this "land of the free." An evocative feeling of that kind is pulse and nerve in any tale, but the techniques by which the people in it are brought to life may have some significance. Here the principal characters emerge solely in action, for we know people best by what they do and say, rather than by what is said about them. Only the minor characters are described, and then because a quick, memorable picture is necessary for those who appear briefly. And why avoid dialect spelling? The effect of dialect is usually humorous, or at least condescending. It shows the author looking in from the outside. The people themselves would not suppose they were saying things wrong. In "Free" the regional flavor was sought through native word order rather than tricky spelling.

'Usually the brevity of a short story makes the writer confine himself to a single interpretation of his material, a single theme. He may, however, find his real purpose somehow opposed to this limitation, for as an artist his intent may be *not* to beat a drum for one belief but simply to create a sympathetic acquaintance with men and women who live the kind of life he knows. I regularly support the main theme of a story with at least one minor theme. The result is that the tale obviously does not look in only one direction. Thus in "Free" the main theme (highlighted by the title) is attended by a secondary theme which implies that the Southerner only blinds himself when he blames the "damyankees" for all his troubles. This, like the main theme, is told through irony. One justification for using irony instead of direct statement is that the purpose of the story goes beyond the ideas, and so do the beliefs behind it.'

Exercises:

1. Define *irony*. In what sense is the last sentence of 'Free' ironical?
2. Compare the symbolism in Hawthorne's 'The Gray Champion' with the apparent yet unticketed symbolism in 'Free.'
3. Compare Hawthorne's technique of expository description with Bryan's direct reporting. Which method makes for 'sympathetic acquaintance with men and women'?
4. Poe says that a short story should aim at singleness of effect. In view of Bryan's statement about a multiple purpose, test the technique of 'Free' in contrast with that of Poe's 'The Cask of Amontillado.' Can one find in this contrast the difference between the English and the French approach to fiction? The French seek unity and limitation. The English tradition has stressed the many-meaninged quality of life itself. Bryan's story leans, therefore, to suggestion; it teases the mind rather than informs it. Some authors like Bryan reject the Poe influence because it tends to put a fence around fictional reports of life.
5. The following hints might be useful in developing a story:
   a. A boy runs away from home to become free; he discovers responsibilities he had never dreamed of.
   b. A man buys a house to be free of landlords; in taxes and repairs he finds unexpected claims to restrict his dreams.
   c. A lad who says 'I am self-made' realizes through one incident his dependence on country or family.
   d. Impoverished mother gives baby for adoption, but later requests its return.
   e. Old man walks restlessly during blizzard at night; storm-stayed in young manhood, he soothed infant in need of medical aid.

THE PRICE OF YOUR FREEDOM

The seven duties set forth in this essay summarize the activities in which a good citizen will engage. Are there still further duties for us to perform?

Suggested Topics for Essays and Talks:

1. How much (or little) I know about my country.
2. My plans to learn about the whole United States.
3. Summer jobs and new ideas on America.
4. College and the cosmopolitan spirit.
5. A test of the operation of the Bill of Rights in my fraternity or dormitory.
6. Life requires 'not freedom from what, but freedom to what.'
7. The Church and one's duty.
8. The place of the labor union in economic democracy.
9. How we can give food to the ill-fed, shelter to the ill-housed, and clothing to the ill-clad.
10. Ways in which I can serve the general welfare.

LIGHT AROUND THE CORNER

The postulate of science is that man wishes to control nature; science therefore is an ally of law and order, because control involves a surrender of one freedom for another freedom. The electric stove, electric toaster, automatic refrigerator, electrically controlled oil-burning furnace, and many other inventions have freed housekeepers from drudgery. The automobile has brought freedom to travel; we forget that many Europeans in peacetime never traveled more than a few miles from their homes in a life of seventy years, while most Americans manage to travel at least a hundred miles from home once a month. Science thus demonstrates the paradox of freedom in control; Mr. Curtis concludes with a profound remark to the effect that the exercise of this control is a great problem.

Suggested Topics for Essays and Talks:
1. I am dependent on gadgets.
2. Grandmother's kitchen and mother's.
3. The old workshop and the new.
4. Botanical research and better vegetables.
5. The improvement of apples in the last fifty years.
6. Cattle breeding moves ahead.
7. Aviation is in its infancy.
8. Soon everything will be standardized, and we shall all look alike.

A BROADER BASE FOR SCIENCE

Dr. Anton J. Carlson, professor of physiology at the University of Chicago, demonstrates in this essay the ideal of a 'controlling purpose' in an essay. His purpose is to insist that 'science must descend from its ivory tower and reach the understanding of the common man.' Note how he reveals the failure of primitive scientists to make their learning available and note how this information on primitive progress startles us with the realization that mankind waited five to eight thousand years to rediscover inoculation for smallpox. The essay is clearly organized and lends itself admirably to outlining.

Exercises:
1. Prepare an outline of the essay, 'A Broader Base for Science.'
2. Note the vocabulary of Professor Carlson; he uses slang, 'our leaders would not get to first base'; he uses literary quotations, including one from the Latin; and he uses precise technical words, such as *thalamus, cerebral cortex, myopia.*

3. Compare the statement about truth's being in and out of favor in 'The Black Cottage' with the ideas in 'A Broader Base for Science.'
4. Write an essay or prepare a talk on one of the following topics:
   a. Medical superstitions.
   b. The place of the physician in community welfare.
   c. Science and human progress.
   d. Ways to popularize chemistry or physics or geology or botany.
   e. Should newspapers publish medical or legal advice?
   f. Progress doesn't come from telling people about science; it comes from lonely workers diligently pursuing research.
   g. The work of 'Science Service' in popularizing scientific knowledge.
   h. Boy Scout and Girl Scout scientific activities.
   i. Why every student should take at least a minor in natural science.
   j. Scientists forget scientific method outside their own fields of learning.
   k. What working in the laboratory has taught me about method, precision, neatness, and order.

PART III

'From an Unchallengeable Eminence'

Every boy in the United States is told that some day he may be President. The American spirit of equality is symbolized by this statement. The statement also is a tacit recognition that the President is the hero, the culture leader, the pathfinder for millions of people needing guidance. Among Presidents, a few have towered above their fellows; they are as beacons guiding the national ship of state safely to a noble destiny. Leadership is an indefinable quality; something there is which causes one person to emerge in a crisis and to exalt his people. Washington, Jefferson, Lincoln, and Wilson radiated lofty courage and gave voice to the idealism of their critical eras. We turn to them instinctively for guidance in every dark hour, for we find in their words and deeds inspiration to meet similar difficulties with similar brave spiritual force.

HOW AMERICANS CHOOSE THEIR HEROES

Dixon Wecter, a professor of English in the University of California at Los Angeles, contrasts the rootless, nomadic life in contemporary United States, the lack of any tie to place, with the people's abiding love of heroes. This symbolic devotion to our past is one of our strongest traits. Yet Dr. Wecter carefully points out that the people reverence enduringly good qualities, even though standards of heroism change from age to age.

Why is hero-worship an urgent American need? What part does hero-worship play in patriotism? Do you keep an autograph book or collect letters of famous people? What changes have marked social life in the United States in the past 120 years? What are the most precious symbols of American patriotism? Why has the people's choice of heroes been sound? What qualities must a hero have? What qualities are disliked? Is liberalism an essential quality of a hero? Is unselfish patriotism a necessary quality? When are heroes finally acclaimed? What shift in the opinion of the public has been noted with respect to Woodrow Wilson, Charles A. Lindbergh, George Herman 'Babe' Ruth, and Christy Mathewson? What was the Silver Age of our patriotism? How were our heroes debunked? How have the children of immigrants helped to bring about a new hero-worship? What is the new phase of the cycle of hero-worship?

Exercises:

1. Write an essay or prepare a talk on one of the following topics:
   a. My favorite American symbols (flag, United States Capitol, Bill of Rights, Fourth of July, Memorial Day, Armistice Day, Thanksgiving Day, Christmas, Founder's Day, Declaration of Independence, Constitution, Supreme Court, one-room schoolhouse, a farmer plowing, a mother singing a lullaby at a cradle, a postmaster reading your postcard, an airplane, a parachute, an independent mechanic, the American eagle; use these or any others that impress you).
   b. Symbolism on American money (pictures of Presidents, truncated pyramid, buffalo, Indian, olive branch, fasces, Lincoln Memorial, etc. Choose one or two coins or pieces of paper money.)
   c. Phrases used on American money, such as 'In God We Trust,' 'E pluribus unum,' 'Annuit coeptis novus ordo seclorum, MDCCLXXVI.' Explain the origin of the terms, their literal meaning, and their meaning to the United States.
   d. Symbolism in athletic trophies: cups, medals, shields, banners.
   e. Symbolism in college nomenclature: Gophers, Mustangs, Hornets, Owls, Terrapins, Bisons, etc.
   f. Symbolism in academic dress.
   g. Symbolism in clerical dress.
   h. The symbolism of the White House.
   i. Why the Secret Service guards the President.
   j. Symbolism in American church edifices.
   k. Symbolism in the classical architecture of bank buildings.
   l. Symbolism in workmen's clothes: leather apron, diving helmet, safety belt, goggles, overalls, etc.
2. Characterize your hero, whether real or imaginary.

WASHINGTON

Lowell's characterization of Washington is among the best in American poetry. List Washington's qualities, and see whether you are familiar enough with his career to give a specific instance to illustrate each of Lowell's generalizations.

THE YOUNG MAN WASHINGTON

Samuel Eliot Morison is Professor of American History at Harvard University. His characterization of Washington's youth correctly humanizes the early years of the hero. Why do we think of Washington as an old man? What qualities were balanced in Washington? How did Washington discipline himself? What was Washington's mother's character? Was Washington a religious man? Did Washington prefer books to an outdoor life? What education did Washington enjoy? When and how did Lawrence take George in hand? What part did surveying play in Washington's advancement? If Washington had gone to London, what might have occurred? Define *stoic,* and tell why Washington was a stoic. What books did Washington read? How does classical literature afford an interpretation of Washington's qualities?

LETTERS OF JOHN AND ABIGAIL ADAMS

Note the simplicity of these letters. Try your hand at a few letters giving your report on events occurring on the campus or in the newspapers. Have you begun a correspondence with a distant friend? Is it progressing pleasantly? Do you feel that you express yourself freely and easily? Do you prefer letters to themes? What differences do you discover between these letters and your themes?

HE DEDICATED US TO LIBERTY

Dumas Malone, an editor of the *Dictionary of American Biography* and director of the Harvard University Press, is preparing a biography of Jefferson.

Explain the symbolic meaning of Jefferson, Washington, Jackson, Lincoln, and Robert E. Lee to citizens of the United States. What differentiates Hitler from Jefferson? Did Jefferson prize peace or liberty? Why have the dead no rights? When and under what circumstances did Jefferson value national power? Would Jefferson take a stand for freedom today?

FAITH IN THE PEOPLE

Define *entails, primogeniture, pseudo-aristocracy.* What was Jefferson's plan for an educational system? What reform would this plan have aimed at? What contrast does Jefferson make between the people of Europe and those of America? *Canaille* is a French word meaning *rabble, riff-raff, scum. Science* in the eighteenth and early nineteenth centuries meant *knowledge* or *learning.* What effect did the diffusion of learning have upon Europe? Jefferson and Adams had been estranged from 1801 until 1813; the reference to their disagreements over principles shows how generous these two mighty leaders could be to each other. Here is the ideal of free thought and free discussion admirably illustrated.

Exercise:

1. Discuss the ideas in the correspondence of Jefferson and Adams.

LINCOLN

Lowell's poem on Lincoln, written some months after the assassination in Ford's Theatre, Washington, D. C., differs markedly from the lines on Washington. Few figures of speech give surge to the rather heavy literal exposition of Washington's traits, but the description of Lincoln is enriched with strong figures, such as 'mountain-peak of mind,' 'broad prairie,' and 'tower.' What is the value of figures of speech? Do they lend themselves to a restricted or to an enlarged meaning? Why is Lowell's description of Lincoln as a prairie rather than a mountain peak doubly appropriate?

AUTOBIOGRAPHY

Lincoln's modest statement of his ancestry and career is more than a mere catalogue of dates and places. Note how he brings a smile with his last remark, and note how imaginatively he views his experiences.

Exercise:

1. Write an autobiography around a central theme, such as: 'I am a lucky person'; 'Black cats always sneak across my path'; 'If music were love, I'd have to remain single'; 'Courage always gets there'; 'Self-help has increased my strength'; 'Misfortune cannot keep a good man down'; 'Ambition always finds a way'; or on a theme phrased by yourself.

THE NEW AMERICAN SYMBOLISM

Ralph Henry Gabriel is Larned Professor of American History at Yale University, editor of *The Pageant of America,* and author of several books, the most famous of which is *The Course of American Democratic Thought* (1940)..

In the past year has your community given most emphasis to the Fourth of July, Memorial Day, or Armistice Day? Why? In what way are America's older symbols associated with the eighteenth century? What happened to Washington as a symbol after Appomattox? What has the United States Supreme Court in its new building come to symbolize? What basis is there for Mr. Gabriel's statement that the Supreme Court has replaced the Church as a symbol? What is a cult? Why does Mr. Gabriel speak of a 'Lincoln cult'? Trace the rise of the importance of Lincoln as a symbol. Tell the story of the last days of Lincoln's life. Can you bring to class other poems about Lincoln? Have you read all or part of Carl Sandburg's six-volume biography of Lincoln? Where are shrines dedicated to Lincoln? What justification is there for Mr. Gabriel's remark that the Lincoln Memorial in Washington enshrines our first folk hero?

Exercises:

1. Write a radio play embodying Lincoln's 'Gettysburg Address' or some other statement by him; plan the play as a broadcast on the twelfth of February.
2. Read Mary Raymond Shipman Andrews's 'The Perfect Tribute.' Plan a similar short story based upon a portion of an American hero's career.
3. Write an essay or prepare a talk on one of the following topics:
   a. The meaning of Lincoln's birthday (or Jackson's birthday or any great man's birthday).
   b. Why it is proper to celebrate heroes' achievements and virtues.
   c. The part played by the flag in the United States. Using personal experience and observation, tell what the flag means to an audience at a theater, to a group watching a parade, to children at school, to immigrants, to soldiers.
   d. The history of the flag of the United States.
   e. Legal and formal codes respecting the display of the flag of the United States.
   f. The symbolism in 'The Star-Spangled Banner' and 'America.'
   g. Lincoln's 'Second Inaugural Address' is often described as the most magnanimous utterance ever pronounced by a victorious leader; define *magnanimity,* and explain how the address reveals this quality.

THE FAITH OF WOODROW WILSON

William Langer, Coolidge Professor of History in Harvard University, wrote about Wilson in the light of an international crisis similar to that faced by the United States in 1917-1918. What was Wilson's reply to ruthlessness and autocracy? What were the items in Wilson's faith? According to Wilson, what was America's mission to mankind? What was the purpose of the League of Nations? Why was participation in the League defeated in the United States? Why do events today make a return to Wilson's words seem wise?

PART IV

DEMOCRACY IN ACTION

A nation is a people in action. The qualities that seem 'democratic' emerge, in part, in the words and deeds of heroic Presidents and leaders; the people supply the conclusive evidence. We have been accustomed to speak of ourselves in the United States as a different people. Nearly all of our ancestors came here because there were opportunities for life, liberty, and the pursuit of happiness. The history of the family progress of each one of us indicates the measure to which these opportunities have yielded fruit under cultivation. The selections in this section are designed to show the average American, at home, at worship, at play. If there is present a note of hope, of sentiment, of aspiration, it is because the United States has been more than a government, more than a land in which to live; it has been a mission to carry to the world ideals of liberty, equality, brotherhood, toleration, and idealism. That we fall short in many areas is readily admitted; that we succeed so admirably in others is inspiration to lift our total life to a lofty plane.

GLAD AND PROUD TO BE AN AMERICAN

The author of this letter is an unknown American who gave thanks for the blessings afforded each person in the United States. His spontaneous letter helps explain the gifts of the American democratic way of life. Do you want to write a letter telling why you are grateful for being in college, or in a particular organization, or in the United States?

AN AMERICAN HOME

Mrs. Della T. Lutes in essays, books, and stories has pictured the daily life of the average Middlewestern American. In what ways do you find the Mason family typical of America? What differences from the home pictured here would now be noted in a Michigan parlor? Is school-teaching the only occupation open to young women today? Is matrimony the inevitable goal of every woman today? What was expected of a father of marriageable daughters forty years ago? What were women's activities then? Describe the food and its service. What happened after dinner? Section IV introduces a contrast between the Masons of a former generation and a farm family of this era. What changes have occurred in the size of the family, the size of the house, the welcome of guests? Have these changes improved American life?

The informal essay is a mixed form of composition, in which narration and description of individuals and of particular persons and events may be combined with the purpose of informing or of stimulating reflection on larger meanings underlying the particular instances. Mrs. Lutes's account of old ways is partly of the nature of the informal essay, although it leans more toward social history than toward the informal essay popularized by Charles Lamb. Compare Mrs. Lutes's essay with Lamb's famous 'A Dissertation upon Roast Pig' to find similarities of tone, method, and matter. The informal essay may vary all the way from such trivial and lightly humorous brief diversions as Lamb's 'Roast Pig,' to such serious and moving themes as his 'Dream Children' or William Hazlitt's 'On the Fear of Death.' Hazlitt's essay 'On Great and Little Things' is an excellent example of essay style and subject. 'The Contributors' Club' in *The Atlantic Monthly* and 'The Lion's Mouth' in *Harper's Magazine* provide good examples of the informal essay. The following subjects, suggested by Mrs. Lutes's account, are of various degrees of significance. Which subjects would require only two or three paragraphs of humorous comment, which might properly lead to informational essays rather than informal essays, and which might be developed into reflections on significant areas of human life and character? Try planning one of the last sort by setting down the possible topic sentences of each main division of your plan. Write the essay, bearing in mind that it is to be agreeable in style, rich in examples, and possibly indicative of your literary background.

Suggested Topics for Essays and Talks:

1. Grandmother's way and mine.
2. Grandfather at market and mother on the telephone.

3. Who holds the purse strings?
4. Does radio replace adequately the home-played musical instrument?
5. Interior decoration then and now.
6. Braided and hooked rugs versus store rugs.
7. Friendly entertaining is rare today.

THE FOURTH OF JULY

The mountaineer has been described humorously in comic strips and moving pictures, partly because he is our sole survival of primitive colonial days and partly because he insists on his rights. Traditionally these people have engaged in feuds as a result of long-standing quarrels. Newcomers, aided by a wise grandfather, brought peace to The Forks in this episode from *The Quare Women* (1923) by Lucy Furman.

Exercises:

1. Characterize each of the persons in the story.
2. Analyze the plot structure.
3. Is dialect desirable in fiction? What are the advantages and disadvantages of dialect?
4. Study the punctuation and paragraphing of 'The Fourth of July.'
5. Write a short story based upon an incident like one of the following:
   a. An ill recluse who refuses to see a physician is won over.
   b. A man in a mink coat says he is penniless.
   c. The mail must go through, flood or no flood.
   d. A boy with wayward tendencies is befriended.
   e. The man with the astronomical instrument on Broadway meets a long-lost brother.

AMERICA IN MY BLOOD

Leon Z. Surmelian, a graduate of Kansas State College of Agriculture and Applied Science, is an Armenian, who in this autobiographical sketch relates part of his experiences in this country. Do his physical experiences prepare the reader for the emotional responses that come at the end? To have America in the blood, must one own things or have certain feelings? What are Surmelian's feelings?

FOREIGNER

A one-time law student and bank clerk in Berlin, and traveling salesman through Belgium, France, and Spain, Fred D. Wieck emigrated to the United States from Germany in 1935. He joined the United States Army in November 1940, and was stationed at Fort Jay, New York. How does he first become aware of the meaning of the word *foreigner?* Describe his experience in France with Tinel-Haese. What were his experiences in the United States? What contrast between Europe and America can you make on the basis of this essay?

NEIGHBOUR ROSICKY

The foremost living American artist in fiction is Willa Cather. Her work represents more than successful picturing of a locality and its people; she reflects an insistence that life must be lived with 'disciplined endeavor' close to the soil. Vital spiritual nourishment alone can come from the earth. Show how these qualities are emphasized in this story. Examine Miss Cather's technique throughout the story. Note the opening statements; what is the effect of this beginning? How much dialect is employed? Why so little? Note the extent to which description is added to the conversation. Why does the conversation with the physician about the heart ailment come first? Note how frequently the story moves backward and forward in time; the technique of the 'backward loop' is well employed here. Characterize each of the persons in the story. What event forms the climax? Although the story has a tragic ending, why does the death of Rosicky leave us with a feeling of completeness to his life and, therefore, with a sense of resignation to his fate? What qualities make life on a farm better than life in a city? Most people are like children: they need not so much to be whipped as to be understood; explain Rosicky's view of this matter.

Suggested Topics for Stories, Radio Plays, and Talks:

1. Repressed girl wants to leave home.
2. Boy with ambition thinks his family misunderstands him.
3. The joy of winning the prize at the State Fair, with an animal or an article.
4. The struggle to bring a prize animal to the State Fair.
5. Life is good in the city, too.
6. A foreigner becomes part of his community.

HOUSE OF THE ONE FATHER

Mary Antin is the author of *The Promised Land* and *They Who Knock at Our Gates,* books that dramatize for Americans the spiritual meaning of the United States from the point of view of an immigrant.

In this article Mrs. Grabau, to use her married name, shows how she came to understand the relationship between democracy and fundamental religious faith as found in almost identical patterns in Judaism, Roman Catholicism, and Protestantism. Note the dramatic opening of the essay, the use of conversation and description. 'Their Church is the place where *their* people are reminded of God and brotherhood, and that's at the bottom of Americanism'; is this statement supported by earlier selections in *Of the People?* Why is Miss Antin's hesitation about entering a Catholic church in Prague preparatory for the second main section of this essay? How did the visit to Vermont affect Miss Antin's thinking? What was the effect of living with the evangelist, Lydia Sayre? For what is Miss Antin grateful now? What is her feeling toward sectarianism?

Exercises:

1. Define the following words: *apostasy, proselytizer, monotheism, humanism, ritual, ceremonial, sectarianism.*
2. If you have recently visited a church other than one of your sect, describe the differences in ritual.
3. Listen to the radio broadcasts of Roman Catholic, Protestant, and Jewish services; what similarities or differences do you find in the prayers, hymns, and sermons?
4. Write an essay on the topic: 'We are all brothers and sisters, because we are children of God.'

AMERICANS ALL!

This film was issued in January 1941, by RKO Radio Pictures, distributors, and was prepared by the editors of *Life* and of *Time* to present 'a new kind of pictorial journalism.' Technically it is Vol. vii, No. 7, Production #13107. It contains one reel, two sections, 1670 feet of photophone footage, and requires a running time of 18 minutes and 33 seconds. Through the courtesy of The March of Time we are permitted to present the script and a series of pictures taken from the film. The script is divided into four columns: in the first, each 'shot' is numbered successively; the second briefly describes the 'shot'; and the third contains the material, music and narration, on the sound track. The abbreviations are of photographic terms: l.s. is long shot, m.s. is medium shot, c.u. is close up, pan shot is panoramic shot.

Exercise:

1. Prepare a newsreel script illustrative of a popular extracurricular activity, or of a series of such activities. A group of still photographs might be used, as in this book, to illustrate the script.

RED NECKTIE

Jo Sinclair, who was born in Brooklyn of parents from Brest-Litovsk, has been engaged as an editor of W.P.A.'s Foreign Language Newspaper Digest in Cleveland, Ohio. Her brilliant sketch reveals both the physical and psychological aspects of Mendel Hirsh's recovery of his self-respect. Examine every detail of the story to see how Miss Sinclair gained these effects.

Suggested Topics for Essays, Sketches, Stories, or Radio Plays:

1. The rag picker comes home at night.
2. The refugee boy finds a buddy.
3. Refugee lads at school try to play baseball or basketball or another American game.
4. The old man or old lady with the vegetable cart.
5. A visit to a tenement area.
6. The attitude of children toward their foreign-born parents.

EXAMINING OUR PREJUDICES

Miss Mildred H. McAfee, President of Wellesley College, gave this address before a Conference of Christians and Jews at Boston, 27 March 1941. Why is religious and racial prejudice not necessary? Is prejudice a social habit? Can prejudice be overcome? Is the example of Hawaii a good one to illustrate the point being made? Are people intentionally mean? Is prejudice caused by stupidity? Define *prejudice*. How did prejudice color the Chinese girl's facts? How can prejudice be unlearned? How can we foster a contagious spirit of freedom from prejudice? Is it fair to attribute socially unfavorable traits to a whole group or race?

Suggested Topics for Essays and Talks:

1. Prejudices against fraternities and sororities on our campus.
2. Most people do not think; they rearrange their prejudices.
3. Prejudices against certain teachers or administrators or athletes.
4. Hatred is the world's greatest waste of talents.
5. Prejudices against political parties or labor unions.
6. Things I do not like, but I am not prejudiced!
7. Prejudice against jazz, three o'clock dances, house parties.

HARD-BOILED PARISH

In almost every community there is a man or woman whose friendly help has brightened dark places and turned downward-going youth into upward-striving adults. Mr. Feeley tells about a priest's success. Do you know of similar services? Note the structure of this essay: first is given the background, then the arrival of Gartska and his unceasing efforts to improve the neighborhood of his parish. What qualities of leadership and manhood does Father Gartska demonstrate?

Exercises:

1. Write an account of the work of a leader familiar to you; he may be a Boy Scout or Girl Scout executive, a Sunday School teacher, a newspaper editor, a fireman, a policeman, a boys' club director, banker, postmaster, grocer, clerk, preacher, physician, or lawyer.
2. Father Gartska is difficult to interview because he will not talk about his own work. Find an active person who will talk about his work, and write an article embodying the vital part of his remarks. A postman, banker, or grocer who takes an interest in the different types of people he serves can supply much material in an unannounced interview. The best interviews are often achieved by casual questions, because most people hesitate to be quoted. Be sure to add characterization and interpretation.

AMERICAN MEDICINE LEADS THE WORLD

Elsie McCormick (Mrs. Marshall Dunn), one of the foremost newspaper writers in the United States, turned her research eyes on the subject of medicine. Her report differs from a research essay only in the absence of footnotes. What has happened to Vienna's medical reputation? In what country have the great discoveries in medicine recently been made? How did Dr. Abraham Flexner alter shameful conditions in the United States? What improvements have been made in American hospitals? Is medical research fostered in the United States? What are the foremost medical discoveries of recent years? Define *vitamins, chemotherapy, allergy, schizophrenia.*

Miss McCormick's essay mentions briefly many medical topics which might be pursued profitably in a research paper.

Suggested Topics for Essays and Talks:

1. How hospitals keep clean.
2. What is pasteurized milk?
3. Recent progress in research on cancer (or another disease).
4. Why the dentist should be consulted twice a year.
5. Why everyone should have a family physician to consult.
6. Epidemics we no longer have.
7. Qualifications of a nurse.
8. Mental hospitals are necessary because of the fast intellectual pace of modern life.

9. Most accidents occur in the home.
10. Everybody should have a course in first aid.

THE MAYO BROTHERS AND THEIR CLINIC

Dr. Harvey Cushing, probably the most famous brain surgeon of recent times, compares the Mayo Brothers' clinic with the shrine at Lourdes, France, where miraculous healings have occurred. This characterization reveals some of the qualities for which the Mayo Brothers are remembered. Recent years have produced many fascinating accounts by physicians of their medical careers. In fact, doctors have for centuries shown skill in literary expression. Some notable recent books are Hans Zinsser's *Rats, Lice and History* and *As I Remember Him,* Victor Heiser's *A Doctor's Odyssey,* and Arthur E. Hertzler's *The Horse and Buggy Doctor.* Dr. Cushing's own works of general interest include a diary of the World War I, *From a Surgeon's Journal;* two books of essays and addresses, *Consecratio Medici* and *The Medical Career and Other Papers;* and the great *Life of Sir William Osler.* Dr. Osler was one of the chief persons to establish the medical reputation of The Johns Hopkins University Medical School. More information about the Mayo Brothers may be found in the biography by Helen Clapesattle, *The Doctors Mayo.*

YOUTH AND CIVIC LEADERSHIP

This article is part of one of the Godkin Lectures delivered by Mr. Seasongood at Harvard University in 1932. Why do we need a new attitude toward local and county government? What is the cost of local government? Is participation in local government less worth while than in national government? Are you familiar with the achievements of great city administrations? What is the oath of the Athenian youth? Why is local public administration a new field of activity? What are the four fields of endeavor? Why should every college graduate take part in local government? Do colleges give courses in local government? What are some typical attitudes toward participation in local government? What part do newspapers play in furthering a fuller participation by the public in civic affairs? What can the Church do to increase interest in civic affairs?

Suggested Topics for Essays and Talks:

1. Should college graduates be policemen?
2. The character of our councilmen.

3. The difference between a politician and a statesman.
4. Needed improvements in our community: parks, sewers, lights, highways, playgrounds.
5. College as a training ground for social work.
6. A Junior Chamber of Commerce aids youth to discover its place in business and in community activities.
7. Reasons for juvenile delinquency.

JANUARY FIRST NINETEEN FORTY-ONE

Edith Bjornson Surrey, formerly of Wellesley College, now is a member of the Class of 1944 in the University of Chicago. In this essay she speaks as a student about our nation, the impending crisis, and our duties. What is your response to the need of the hour? Write your sentiments in a 1000-word essay.

PART V

EDUCATION FOR FREEDOM

Education in the United States has two great objectives. The first is to inspire youth with an interest in himself and with a curiosity touching his own nature, to acquaint him with the resources of his mind, and to give him skills for pursuit of a useful and happy life. The second aim is to bring this self-disciplined and self-reliant individual into harmonious relationship with his fellows, both as individuals and as members of civil society. In a democracy the individual is of prime worth; yet since the individual draws support from society as a whole, he is expected to make his proper contribution in repayment. Education in state-wide school systems, therefore, emphasizes practicality, vocational success, and social adjustment; yet not forgotten is the ideal of a 'liberal education.' *Liberal* is derived from the Latin *liber,* meaning *free.* The ideal of liberal education arose as a means of enhancing an individual's sense of freedom; the studies were cultural not practical, and aimed to give through history, mathematics, music, philosophy, and literature an awareness of man's varied emotional and intellectual responses. Wise educators today attempt to reconcile the so-called liberal and practical curricula: engineering students are asked to pay more attention to the liberal arts, and academic students are advised to familiarize themselves with practical problems in offices, mills, social work, and governmental bureaus. Right education leads to the development of people of character, people who cherish truth, beauty, freedom, and brotherhood.

THE EDUCATED PERSON IN AN UNTIDY WORLD

Horace Taylor, a professor of Economics at Columbia University, raises in a striking way the old question whether the educated person should be concerned with making the world a better place in which to live. There are those who argue that things will run of their own momentum, that interference is unwise, and that an educated person should not soil his hands with the dirt of life. What is tidiness and a tidy world? Explain the contrast between 'reasonable, natural, just' and 'irrational, diabolical, unjust.' Why are some people called insane? Define *relativity*. What training have the minds of educated people? How does the educated mind prepare for the future? What are the three great basic divisions of education? Why does it seem easier to see a clear pattern in the past than in the present? Why does man's way of making a living and of living in society affect his interpretation of events? What kind of liberalism does Mr. Taylor support? Where did men .find inspiration and hope and sanctified purpose? What is the source of untidiness? What are slogans, over-generalized formulas, and too-simple explanations? What is the eighteenth-century foundation of our belief? How has life changed to make it difficult for the individual to remain strong enough to cope with groups or organizations? How have nations come to follow one man's will? Do you agree that the eighteenth-century postulates are no longer tenable? Is there a greater liberty possible? Can science help? Can we end barbarities? Must we change our educational procedure? What is intellectual honesty? How do the necessities of education conform to the ideal of education? How can freedom be attained? Where must each educated man begin to remove untidiness? What is a Platonist? Why are men of small soul and great ambition dangerous? Do you agree that tidiness begins at oneself?

Suggested Topics for Essays or Talks:

1. How the college student can help tidy the campus.
2. Cutting campus is a kind of untidiness.
3. Breaking campus rules and breaking state laws.
4. Campus politics and national politics.
5. Self-control begins at home.

THE LIBRARY

As Keeper of Rare Books and Professor of English at Yale University, Chauncey Brewster Tinker has experienced the pleasures available to all lovers of books and seekers of truth through the printed page. He speaks first of the appeals made to freshmen and of the absence of an appeal on behalf of the library; is there a reason for this condition? What are the two extreme theories about library management? Why is the library the heart and center of the college? What are the three stages of a student's interest in a library? How can students find leisure-time amusement in the library? In writing a research paper did you discover that Bacon's statement was correct? How is new truth gained by reading old books? Why do scholars look for documents and original sources? What constitutes the preciousness of an autograph letter of a famous person? What is the value of a private library? Do books bear any relationship to the problem of keeping the world tidy?

Exercises:

1. Prepare a radio broadcast in which the library is made to reveal its resources.
2. Prepare a class talk on classification systems used in libraries, with particular emphasis on the system in your own college library.
3. Write an essay or prepare a talk on a topic similar to one of the following:
   a. Treasures in our college library.
   b. The library is the heart of a college.
   c. The inter-library loan system.
   d. Jefferson and the Library of Congress.
   e. The private libraries of American Presidents.
   f. My favorite books.
   g. The place of books in a democracy.

OF THE LIBRARIAN'S PROFESSION

Archibald MacLeish, poet and Librarian of Congress, smiles at the inadequate description of a librarian's attainments and duties. What notions had earlier writers on the subject? What is a keeper of books? Why does *book* have two meanings? Is a librarian 'a check boy in the parcel room of culture'? Should the librarian be a partisan and advocate? Should the librarian be an agent 'for the advancement of universal learning'? Why should the librarian not adopt the custodian attitude today? Do changing times alter professional duties? What is a 'counsel for a situation'? What was the 'burning of the books' that inspired MacLeish's article?

Exercises:

1. Write an essay or prepare a talk on one of the following topics:
   a. What materials should be saved so that future generations can understand our culture?

b. How can a library be made more attractive to readers?

c. 'Silence is the golden rule of libraries.'

d. Only the dead speak in libraries.

2. If you are interested in the archaic spellings of the quoted words, look these words up in the *Oxford English Dictionary,* a twelve-volume work containing the histories of English words.

3. Are you familiar with the departments of a library? What is the function of the purchasing department, the accessions department, the catalog department, the reference department, the circulation department, rare book room, periodical department, bindery?

4. Define *stacks, carrell, stall, alcove, tier, shelf, card file.*

5. Define *broadside, folio, quarto, octavo, duodecimo.*

6. How many encyclopedias are in your college library? Are encyclopedias compiled in languages other than English?

7. What is the difference between a shelf list and a dictionary catalog?

8. Why does a book have a Table of Contents, an Introduction, a Preface, an Index?

9. Have you examined this book as a book? It is composed of a series of signatures (define the word). Page i is the half title, page ii is a frontispiece, page iii is the title page, page iv is the copyright page; what other parts of the book remain to be labeled thus?

THOREAU AT HARVARD

Raymond Adams, Professor of English at the University of North Carolina, Chapel Hill, has specialized in the study of Thoreau. This essay illustrates the manner of preparing a research paper on a biographical subject. Notice how the author presents the evidence or testimony concerning Thoreau's character; then he brings forward new manuscript material to refute the earlier opinions.

Exercises:

1. Write a biographical essay based upon available books; limit the topic severely to one episode. Examine the various biographies to see how they differ in details and in interpretations. The following topics may suggest an incident in the life of a character in whom you are interested:

a. The death of Cicero, or Socrates, or Stonewall Jackson, or Lincoln.

b. Poe in Fordham, or at the University of Virginia, or at West Point.

c. Walt Whitman in New Orleans.

d. Robert Burns as a public official.

e. Shakespeare's position as an actor.

f. Chaucer's Italian journey.

g. Dolly Madison's manners.

h. Lincoln as a lawyer on the circuit.

2. If you or your library possesses printed collections of letters by famous people, use two or three of these letters to amplify or correct an impression given by biographers. Remember that you are not concerned with the whole life story of the person; you seek merely to present a valid statement concerning the moment or period mentioned in the letters.

WOMAN'S PLACE IS IN THE WORLD

The gains made by women in recent years are in danger of being lost, says Dr. Paul Swain Havens, President of Wilson College, Chambersburg, Pennsylvania. What is the difference between woman's place in a totalitarian country and in a democracy? Why must a woman's education not be a narrowing process? How shall college and life be integrated? What particular responsibility has a college to a woman student?

Exercises:

1. Prepare a radio play based upon the achievements of a great woman, such as Jane Addams, Elizabeth Barrett Browning, George Eliot, or Margaret Fuller.
2. Write an essay upon a theme similar to one of these:
   a. Women in one of the professions: medicine, law, dentistry, engineering, journalism.
   b. Women must darn their own socks.
   c. Clothes don't make the man, but nine-tenths of what we see are clothes.
   d. Are women's fashions a confession of weakness?

WHAT ABOUT PROGRESSIVE EDUCATION?

In this analysis of what progressive schools are accomplishing, Carleton Washburne, President of the Progressive Education Association and Superintendent of Schools, Winnetka, Illinois, says that progressive education is concerned with the whole child. What four aspects of education are stressed by Progressive Education? In what ways must the schools look into every child's health and teach mental hygiene? How does the progressive school foster individuality? How does progressive education supply skills and knowledge for success in work and play? How does progressive education prepare a child for citizenship? Does progressive education indoctrinate children? Has progressive education worked successfully?

Exercises:

1. Because every child must attend school in the United States, controversy over educational theory never ceases. Since there are many points of view, a good way to examine the subject is by means of a panel discussion. Several speakers are chosen to examine a given topic from distinct points of view. After they have spoken, the audience submits questions. A chairman acts as moderator in an effort to achieve some balance of opinion; in a panel discussion it is not so important that one speaker be declared the winner as that all the points of view shall have been fairly presented. Intelligent discussion should help the audience achieve principles upon which to act. Panels on the following topics might be arranged:

   a. Should schools be open six days a week? Speakers might represent the teachers, parents, taxpayers, and children.

   b. Shall we abandon required courses for degrees in college? Speakers might represent the point of view of graduate schools, the regional association of colleges, the college administration, the parents, and the students.

   c. Shall extra-curricular activity be given credit toward graduation? Students who oppose and students who favor the grant might be represented.

   d. Should every student be required to study surveys of history, social science, natural science, and fine arts?

2. President Robert M. Hutchins of the University of Chicago has said that a poor boy should not work his way through college. If you work your way through college, speak on the question from your own experience. Do you get enough time to study adequately? Do you attempt merely to slide by in your work or studies? Do you give up activities you would like to engage in?

3. College is a training ground for life, it is said. What portion of a student's time should be spent in social activity, athletics, and other extra-curricular activity? How much time should be devoted to study?

4. Some students are quicker than others; is there any way to adjust the pace of the group to that of the speedy or the slow?

5. Write an essay or prepare a talk on one of the following topics:

   a. Better a dishwasher than not to have been in college at all.

   b. Social contacts mean more than books.

   c. It doesn't pay to be too bright.

   d. I want a Phi Beta Kappa key.

   e. College replaces the apprentice system of former generations; youth has a chance to find itself in a new environment.

   f. Seventy per cent is not passing.

THE FANTASIA OF CURRENT EDUCATION

I. L. Kandel, Professor of Education in Teachers College, Columbia University, has made profound studies of educational practice in this and other countries. His good-humored criticism of educational follies bears thoughtful analysis. Have the educators introduced many new ideas into education? Is the quotation from the Progressive Education Association meant to be an example of *reductio ad absurdum*? Does Mr. Kandel approve of having school children make community surveys? Can illiterates teach illiterates? What is 'the cult of superficiality'? Should the schools discuss controversial issues of the day? Is the problem-solving method of teaching sound? Should pupils be discoverers or absorbers of knowledge? What is the French theory of education? Should pupils be required to meet standards and fulfil aims? Does Mr. Kandel make the same interpretation of progressive education as Mr. Washburne? Is the rootlessness of American life responsible for fadism in American education? How can successful education be achieved?

Exercises:

1. 'What about Progressive Education?' and 'The Fantasia of Current Education' present opposite interpretations of progressive education. A panel discussion might be arranged to present more evidence on the subject.
2. Write an essay or prepare a talk on a subject similar to one of these:
   a. The one-room school had some advantages.
   b. Consolidated schools with gymnasiums and assemblies afford rural children the advantages of large cities.
   c. Education is chiefly a relationship between teacher and pupil.
   d. It's what we learn that matters, not whether we enjoy learning it.
   e. Qualities of a good teacher.
3. Excellent research papers can be written on topics drawn from the history and theory of education. Some topics are:
   a. Colonial schools and school masters.
   b. The reasons for creating the junior high school as a separate unit.
   c. The beginnings of teacher education in the United States.
   d. McGuffey's readers and their influence.
   e. The influence of Webster's blue-backed speller.
   f. Horace Mann's contribution to educational progress.
   g. The beginnings of state-wide education.
   h. The Morrill Act of 1862 and land-grant colleges.

EDUCATION VS. WESTERN CIVILIZATION

Walter Lippmann, noted editor and political analyst, turns to educational procedure in the United States to discover whether our schools buttress the theory of democracy. His thesis is stated in vigorous language at the beginning of the essay. Why was universal, compulsory education established in America? What part did the ideal of freedom play in the establishment of our schools? Why is a creative cultural tradition needed? What subjects replace the cultural subjects in some curricula? Do we reject classical culture because we are lazy and because questions arouse quarrels? What attitude toward the individual does Mr. Lippmann say the schools now take? Is this view in accord with Mr. Washburne's statement? Why has the removal of the classical religious tradition weakened man's feeling of brotherhood? Has the school sunk to the level of a mere training ground? Is the central principle of the Western philosophy of life the principle that 'man's reason is the ruler of his appetites'? If this ideal is lost, will materialism and a search for personal success destroy mankind? Has man become the most cunning and destructive animal on earth? Why must we fasten ourselves to a good tradition? Reread the thesis at the beginning of the essay.

Exercises:

1. Test the thesis by the essay. Has Mr. Lippmann supported each point adequately?
2. This essay lends itself admirably to outlining. Prepare an outline.
3. Write an essay or prepare a talk on a subject similar to one of these:
   a. Man does not live unto himself alone.
   b. Each of us grows up in a tradition; we either remain in it, or we find a new tradition.
   c. The tradition of the past is outmoded.
   d. Grandfather had the right idea.
   e. Neighbour Rosicky [see Willa Cather's story] learned what makes a good tradition.

PLEA FOR AN AGE MOVEMENT

Ralph Barton Perry, distinguished philosopher and biographer of William James, teaches at Harvard University. So much attention has been paid to youth, says Professor Perry, that age has lost leadership in this momentous era in history.

Exercises:

1. Write an essay or prepare a talk on a subject like one of the following:
   a. The world belongs to youth.
   b. Without the guidance of age, youth must fail.
   c. Do we need more machinery or more wisdom?
   d. King Lear had his chance.
   e. Should professors be retired at fifty?
   f. A wise old man is the best friend a youth can have.
   g. 'Grow old along with me, the best is yet to be.'

2. Write a radio script memorializing the contribution to your college or fraternity of a beloved professor or alumnus.

THE ANCIENT CLASSICS IN A MODERN DEMOCRACY

Professor Samuel Eliot Morison of Harvard University says that style is the most useful acquirement of an educated mind. Define style as Mr. Morison uses the term. Define style in baseball pitching or batting, or in women's clothes. Why are the classics suitable to a democracy? What is an intellectual aristocracy? In what ways are Latin and Greek valuable instruments for developing the human intellect? Can we understand modern literature without knowing the classics? 'Pedagese' English is English as written by pedagogues. How does the study of the classics introduce students to the social sciences? Will the study of the classics help to give the United States intelligent leadership?

Exercises:

1. Write an essay or prepare a talk on a topic similar to one of the following:
   a. Some common words derived from Latin or Greek.
   b. We use Latin and Greek every time we speak.
   c. Life moves too fast; we do not have time for the past.
   d. He is happiest who thinks the most and best thoughts.
2. Compare this essay with Mr. Lippmann's. In what ways are the statements complementary?

NOAH WEBSTER, SCHOOLMASTER TO AMERICA

This essay forms the Prologue and portions of a book so entitled. What relation does Daniel Webster bear to Noah Webster? Why is Noah Webster called America's greatest schoolmaster? Did Webster prepare the first American dictionary? What qualifications did Noah Webster have for compiling a dictionary? How many years elapsed between Webster's first dictionary and *The American Dictionary?* Did Webster reveal patriotic ardor in his big dictionary? Why is the dictionary called 'the world's most important secular book'?

PART VI

'THE PURSUIT OF HAPPINESS'

The universe exists as a playground for man. Some people prefer to work and others to play. Some cannot distinguish between work or

)lay, and philosophers have told us that happiness depends upon a
wise intermingling of the two. As civilization has advanced, man has
found new outlets for his ingenuity, more means for his pleasure. Every
primitive skill has been developed into an art. As a result, the world is
full of pleasant activities to beguile us all. Whether we seek artistry or
prefer to be a spectator, hundreds of modes of pleasure are at our disposal. In athletic games, in handicrafts, in musical performance upon
dozens of instruments, in musical composition, in painting or sculpture
or dancing or architecture, in creating new machines and inventing
new processes, in doing one's daily tasks with enthusiasm—in these and
innumerable other ways men and women are engaged in 'the pursuit
of happiness.' As long as they have a sense of fairly permanent pleasure
arising from their activities, or as long as they find their mode of life
agreeable, they admit to being happy. An ancient witticism declares
that 'some people enjoy ill health.' The whole meaning of happiness
can never be told.

One purpose of a liberal education is to lead people to a delight in,
and an understanding of, beauty. All nature is beautiful all the time,
say the philosophers. Hence there are people who hike through hills in
sunshine, rain, or snow, in calm or turbulent storm. Some seek rare
flowers or shrubs or leaves or grasses, while others never weary of gazing
at familiar scenes and the commonest plants. Some people prefer to see
nature as portrayed by the artist; they study the theory and practice
of the masters, and they themselves may paint or cut marble or compose music. Some people find beauty in mechanical organization and
construction; they tinker or experiment. Some people hook rugs, knit
sweaters, carve wood, hammer silver, or turn pottery. Some people
swim, ride, climb mountains, or play games to demonstrate the beauty
of the human body when trained to perfect co-ordination. Some people
write poetry or novels or drama. Some collect folklore and legends. In
all minds engaged in seeking beauty there must be cheerful thoughts;
he is happiest who has the companionship of interesting thoughts, for
he has plans for each waking moment.

In this section of *Of the People* some of the diversions of Americans
are represented. Emphasis is placed upon 'communication,' because
man is differentiated from the other animals by this power of recording, preserving, and transmitting his thoughts and emotions. Language
is man's greatest invention, for by means of it he has been able to
codify his skills, regularize his actions, and give some sort of logical
pattern to his endeavors. Professor Carlson has told us that knowledge
of inoculation was lost for six or seven thousand years. Other skills

similarly have been lost. The fine arts have survived holocausts, it is true, but survival of these skills will be more certain if a knowledge of them is current among all people. For this reason we introduce a number of essays and reviews on topics associated with the fine arts. Every new pattern seems strange at first sight; examine it patiently and it will yield its secret. The beauties of art seem often apparent at first glance; meditation will bring new and more beauties. The reviews of books, dramas, motion pictures, and musical performances are designed not only to help interpret these specific works, but to help develop powers of critical analysis.

FOR WHAT?

Sherwood Anderson (1876-1941) left his paint factory one day and never returned. He had decided to be a writer. After years of struggle, he found a medium to report the yearning of most men and women for expression. People want to tell their stories or paint pictures or get things straightened out. Few other authors have ever succeeded as well as Sherwood Anderson in putting in words what so many people find incommunicable.

What was the Sunday occupation of the four men? How did Anderson want his words to march? How can you kill any job? What was Jerry trying to get expressed? Why did Jerry feel himself trapped? What was Joe ambitious to do? Did Joe say women are trapped? What does George want to do? Did Jerry succeed in painting the cornfield? What meaning did Jerry want to put into his picture of the cornfield? What childlike tantrum did Jerry engage in? What was their mood on returning to the station? What did Jerry do? How did he speak for all of them? Why did the author remain at the station after Joe and George went home?

Exercises:

1. Study the emotional quality of 'For What?' How does Anderson achieve his effects? Does he splash lengthy descriptions on a page, or does he give a few details of action involving frustration and then press home the burden and pain of life?
2. In the average person are many significant stories. Try to reflect a mood of gladness or frustration or resignation or another mood in a story based on one of these situations:
   a. Late at night an elderly couple review the death of an only child, or speak of childlessness. Try for atmosphere: quiet background, possibly a fireplace scene, with occasional noises.
   b. A local demented person. Possibly a fire or accident or tragic

family occurrence brought on mental illness. View the person sympathetically.

c. The bachelor or spinster who teaches a Sunday School class. Although no mention is made of a tragic separation, such an incident or another may have occurred.

d. The man who wanted to be a preacher or physician and always talks about his failure.

e. A man who wants to write a book but cannot get started.

AMERICAN PAINTING TODAY

How does art help us understand a people? Why has American art been misjudged? What are artistic derivations? Can you tell about literary derivations, such as Hawthorne's use of Scott-like technique, the borrowings of the local colorists from Dickens and Hardy, Dreiser's early dependence upon Balzac, Bryant's imitation of Southey, or Emerson's parallels with Wordsworth? What does our art tell about America: are we vulgarians? What false notions did American artists have before 1929? Should an artist live in the area he wishes to picture? Why was the international dealer system emanating from Paris fatal to American art? What dishonest practices marked the dealer system then? How could an American artist live who did not sell to the dealer system? If Americans spent vast sums for art, why did not the American artist benefit? Explain why museum attendance leaped to new bounds between 1900 and 1930. Why is the purchase of pictures more important than teas for artists? What are the prices of prints, paintings, and sculptures; are these articles within the reach of almost everyone? Why was the W.P.A. Art Project not mere charity? How did the W.P.A. Art Project function? Is there a painting in your post office? Have you seen paintings in governmental buildings? How has the W.P.A. Art Project satisfied the hunger of millions for fine art? Should there be one or more oil paintings by living artists in every home? Dali is a Spanish abstractionist painter; he is used here as a symbol of unintelligibility.

Exercises:

1. Investigate the lives of one or more most famous artists and tell about their work. Better still, buy or borrow at the library a copy of a book containing reproductions of an artist's work.

2. Examine the reproductions in Forbes Watson's *American Painting Today* (New York: Oxford University Press, 1939) and tell the class what painters are trying to accomplish today.

3. Write an essay on one of the following topics:
   a. Artists also eat.
   b. Does art belong in museums or in the parlor?
   c. Fifty dollars for a party or for a painting?

    d. Sculpture in my neighborhood.
    e. My visit to a museum.
    f. W.P.A. art in our neighborhood.
    g. Ancient civilizations survive largely through their art.

NEBRASKA FOLKLORE

B. A. Botkin, Senior Information Specialist and Fellow in Folklore, Library of Congress, Washington, D. C., emphasizes the importance of the people's daily action, thought, and beliefs in the creation of art and culture. Although Forbes Watson emphasized the transplanting of foreign arts into America, it must not be forgotten that a native force always has been at work striving to create satisfying patterns of beauty from the materials of our environment. Our colonial ancestors wove beautiful bedspreads, etched copper bedwarmers, ornamented stoves with lacy ironwork, hammered the weathervane into the form of a bird or animal, carved beautiful wooden images to grace the bows of ships, and performed miracles of artistry in many pieces of furniture. The covered wagon, a kind of prairie ship, reflected excellent designing skill. Even pats of butter were ornamentally embossed. Thus the folk arts lent beauty to every commonplace act of living. Inevitably this attitude was carried over into machine design. Foreigners expressed admiration and astonishment at the variety and beauty of American tools and machines at the Philadelphia Centennial Exhibition in 1876. A correspondent of the London *Times* wrote: 'The American invents as the Greek sculptured and the Italian painted; it is genius.'

In music and literature a similar native force has operated. From the farm, the country store, and the frontier, places where people spoke or sang from the heart without a knowledge of art productions, there arose folk songs and folk tales. The Negroes and the mountain people reworked hymns into spirituals; they also created new songs out of their joy and pain. They created legends like those recorded by Joel Chandler Harris in *Uncle Remus*. Every trade or occupation told tales of superior achievements by one of its journeymen. A vast literature of this type arose. In Tennessee David Crockett became the type of ringtail roarer who could whip his weight in wildcats. In the cowboy country Pecos Bill became the hero about whom all legends centered; in the forests the hero was Paul Bunyan; and on the Mississippi the great keelboatman was Mike Fink. Although Mr. Botkin has written only about Nebraska, the principles which underlie his discussion apply equally well to other areas.

Do stories belong primarily on the frontier? Are traditions and legls migrants? Is Irving's 'Rip Van Winkle' a transplanted legend? place names tell stories? Are legends attached to the names of some wns? How was Febold Feboldson created? What are the characteristics f Feboldson? Why does the character of Feboldson seem appropriate? Who is Antoine Barada? What historical foundations exist for the Febold and Antoine legends? Folk tales embalm or contain what three elements? How is pioneer life reflected in songs? Where did the pioneer often get a tune for his words? Did the quality of folklore parallel the quality of pioneer experience? What social functions were held on the frontier? What is a coyote hunt? What are charades? Is any attempt being made in your community to preserve Old World customs? How is the life of an individual colored by traditional belief and inherited idiom?

Exercises:

1. Are there legends or folk tales or folklore survivals in your area? If so, the recording of such information directly from the lips of the people who can sing or relate is of great community value. Write down the songs or tales familiar in your household, or gather this material from friends or neighbors. A folklore program for a class might be developed in this way.
2. Prepare a radio script of a local legend.
3. Write an essay or prepare a talk on one of the following topics:
    a. Place names in my community.
    b. A legendary character in my community.
    c. Folk superstitions about the moon, or medical treatment, or love.
    d. The beauty of American tools. Examine your fountain pen and mechanical pencil, or the automobile and electric refrigerator.
    e. Stephen Foster as a recorder of American folk beliefs.
    f. The qualities of spirituals, or blues, or work songs.
    g. Strange idioms in my community.
    h. College slang or college superstitions or college customs.
    i. Popular superstitions in Mark Twain's *The Adventures of Huckleberry Finn.*
    j. Tall tale humor in American folklore.
    k. David Crockett as a folk hero.
    l. Paul Bunyan, the hero of the lumber camps.

PECOS BILL, CYCLONE BUSTER

Irving Fiske has told with admirable skill the story of Pecos Bill, a hero of the Southwest. In what ways does Pecos Bill reflect American or Southwestern attitudes? How does his character fulfil the requirements of a folk creation?

HOUSES AND CITIES

In what ways do we take houses and communities for granted? Why did houses go up in price while other articles came down? Is something wrong? How were towns created in America? What signs of impermanence are there in the buildings in your community? What planning marked American city development? How did land speculation and building restrictions affect house construction? What events in and after 1893 gave promise of new thought on housing? What was the effect of a 'yearning for culture' on architecture in the seventies and eighties? What attitude is necessary to create good, efficient housing?

Exercises:

1. Write an essay or prepare a talk on local architectural styles, on the style of the college buildings, or on some aspect of housing.
2. Read several issues of two or three magazines devoted to housing and city planning. Give a report on contemporary theories of design and structure.

THE MOTION PICTURE

When did the motion picture first appear? When was sustained story-telling first employed? How did *The Birth of a Nation* come into being? What were the faults of early pictures? Who were the great popular favorites before 1919? Who are the popular favorites today? What technical innovations came after 1919? When did talkies begin? What foreign influences helped shape American pictures? Have motion pictures been developed to their fullest? Are experimental pictures produced by professionals or amateurs? In whose hands does the future of the cinema lie?

Exercises:

1. Write an essay on a topic similar to one of the following:
   a. Movies I have enjoyed. (Be specific in supporting your reasons.)
   b. New movie techniques.
   c. What's wrong with color movies?

RADIO'S BIG CHANCE

What is radio's big chance? How should a radio station handle spot news? What advice is given to announcers, news editors, sponsors, and the National Association of Broadcasters? Can commercial radio survive?

Suggested Topics for Essays or Talks:

1. News items should not interrupt classical music.
2. Advertising consumes too much radio time.
3. Without advertising, independent radio stations could not exist.
4. Soap operas.
5. The radio and morale.

NEWSPAPERS IN A DEMOCRACY

Grove Patterson, editor of the Toledo *Blade*, delivered this address to his fellow editors in New York City on 15 December 1941. Why are the institutions of democracy founded upon a free press? What is the relationship between a free press and advertising? How is the press kept responsible to the people?

Suggested Topics for Essays or Talks:

1. The variety of contents in a daily newspaper.
2. The Sunday edition of a large city newspaper: its many features.
3. Should newspapers own radio stations?
4. Should the funnies be eliminated?
5. The editorial page with its variety of items.
6. The difference between news items and editorials.

A CHAMPION ALL THE WAY

John Kieran, sports columnist for *The New York Times* and member of the radio quiz program, Information Please, characterizes Joe Louis as an athlete, a gentleman, and a potential soldier. Examine the details used to round out the picture.

Suggested Topics for Essays or Talks:

1. The policeman or postman or preacher or teacher in our neighborhood.
2. Character comes from what we put into our life.
3. Horace Mann said, 'Be ashamed to die until you have done some service for humanity.'

REVIEWS

Modern life affords so many opportunities for pleasure through books, plays, movies, art exhibitions, music, and the dance that we need competent guides to assist us. Such persons are named critics or reviewers; their comments are published in books, magazines, and newspapers, or are broadcast over the radio. *Criticism* is 'the art of judging or evaluating with knowledge and propriety the beauties and faults of works of art or literature.' Critics also give consideration to moral values, soundness of thinking, and social utility. A *review* is that type of criticism which seeks first to explain the nature or content of a work of art or exhibition and then to pass judgment. In determining which moving picture to attend, for example, a person may go to his 'guide' for information. A summary is not so desirable as a classification which immediately shows the relevance or irrelevance of the current pictures to one's tastes and interests; a schoolboy may want to see a 'Western' or an aviation picture, while the college student may wish to supplement his literary experience with attendance at *How Green Was My Valley* or *Jane Eyre* or *The Scarlet Letter*. After the classification there usually follows a commentary to explain attractive and unattractive features, whether of movie, book, music, dance, or work of art. A brief review cannot discuss every point of interest; yet a good review brings to focus the main items likely to please or displease the audience.

Literary criticism once was largely concerned with style, with choice of words, with grammar, syntax, and prosody. Such questions were asked as these: Are the words used accurately? Is a proper decorum maintained? Are the words euphonious? Are the sentences of proper length? Are the clauses disposed properly? Does the sentence structure conduce to clarity? Later in the history of criticism emphasis was placed upon the differences between prose and verse, among the different types of literature, and among the different forms within a type. In the eighteenth century Shakespeare was called a barbarian because he mixed comedy and tragedy in such a play as *Romeo and Juliet*. Although these formal distinctions remain a matter of critical consideration today, reviewers tend to place chief emphasis upon the evocation of moods and the presentation of ideas. *Mood* is the state or temper of mind as affected by the emotions; Hamlet is melancholy and hesitating, while Fortinbras is rashly active. Just as each character in a play displays his mood, so a whole composition, whatever its form, reflects the mood of the author or composer or director. *Tone* is the accent or inflection or modulation of voice, as adapted to the emotion, by which authors and composers achieve a unified mood in a composition. Compare the short stories in this textbook to discover the different 'voices' with which Willa Cather, Jack Yeaman Bryan, and Jo Sinclair speak about people in similar circumstances.

There exists a school of criticism which insists that literature and art have a function apart from the turmoil of daily life. Such critics believe that form is more important than substance, and that mannered style gives evidence of sophistication. In opposition to this point of view, other critics and artists hold that literature and art must serve to help the human race improve ethically, politically, economically, and spiritually. Willa Cather, for example, pleads for 'a disciplined endeavor' and illustrates her ideas in Rosicky's tender watchfulness over his daughter-in-law. Upton Sinclair has written more than sixty books to show that intrenched privilege tends to defeat democratic processes. The reviews in this textbook demonstrate the concern which the authors feel for one or another aspect of American life. It should be apparent that each person sees a work of art from the peculiar angle of his own training and experience. There is no final judgment possible on any work of art. Each of us, recognizing our limitations, has a perfect right to express our opinion in the same way as do the critics. By writing reviews and by comparing our opinions with those of more practiced critics, we increase our stature by improving our command over our experience.

A DRAMA ABOUT THE LEAGUE OF NATIONS

A review of a drama must account for the play as the author wrote it, the stage setting as designed by an artist and executed by workmen under his supervision, the direction or staging whereby the actors achieve a unified interpretation, and the acting by the individual performers. Brooks Atkinson of *The New York Times* has taken all these matters into account with sharp, deft sentences. Each item might be enlarged upon by giving more particulars; yet the principles of drama reviewing are well illustrated by this brief statement.

MACBETH, A SLAUGHTERHOUSE SYMPHONY

Since *The Tragedy of Macbeth* is familiar to all theater-goers, John Mason Brown, drama critic of the New York *World-Telegram,* emphasizes those aspects of the drama and its production which impressed him as he watched the play in November, 1941. Yet it will be noted that he brings all the vital topics related to the drama under discussion.

Exercise:

1. Collect from newspapers and magazines five or more reviews of a book or movie or play. Compare your review with these.

PART VII

TIMES THAT TRY MEN'S SOULS

In 'The Gray Champion' Nathaniel Hawthorne symbolized the readiness of the hereditary spirit of Americans to march in vindication of our ancestry against every new foe. The ideal of freedom has its last sure defense in our hemisphere. What the events of the past few years and the new World War portend, none of us can fully foresee. The daily newspapers bring new, startling challenges. The selections in Section VII survey our national duty in terms of our country's ideals.

WHAT IS AT STAKE?

John Coleman Bennett, Professor of Systematic Theology at the Pacific School of Religion, analyzes the term 'open society' and shows that the present conflict is one which places this ideal in jeopardy. What is an open society? Has the United States always been free from criticism? Is England's treatment of India as ruthless as Germany's treatment of conquered nations? How have the Nazis replaced self-criticism with self-glorification?

Suggested Topics for Essays and Talks:
1. The proper attitude of a conqueror toward his victim.
2. Might is right.
3. Might is not right.
4. Hitler's self-glorification. (Use *Mein Kampf* as a source.)
5. Hitler's broken promises.

DEFENDING JUSTICE DESPITE OUR OWN INJUSTICE

Lynn Harold Hough, Dean of Drew Theological Seminary, Madison, New Jersey, is the author of many books and essays interpreting the spiritual ideals of the United States. Dr. Hough's initial sentence bears rereading; he says that men become gentle in enforcing their standards when they can thus shift responsibility away from themselves. Have you ever seen a referee make a decision and then back down and lose the courage of his convictions as pressure was brought against him? On the other hand, when a man wants something, he is likely to insist that right and justice and morality are on his side. Do you agree with Dean Hough on these points? Is evil always present in life? In the fight against evil must we use stainless men or such men as we have? In what way is the Apostle Paul an example? Is feudalism an example? What two points of view may historians use in viewing a social condition? What will result from viewing a problem through gloomy eyes? Who is the safe guide? What is the definition of *psychopathic?* What errors of thought followed World War I? What is the definition of *sardonic?* Must we talk only about the successes or the failures of democracy? Why does a preoccupation with injustice omit a most important consideration? Why is there no excuse for mental bewilderment in the United States? Is the courage to act necessary? What is the first step?

Suggested Topics for Essays and Talks:

1. An analysis of Edwin Arlington Robinson's 'Flammonde.'
2. The fallacy of a gloomy view of life.
3. Seeing both sides (of a specific case or two).

STILL 'THE HOPE OF THE HUMAN RACE'

Henry Steele Commager, Professor of History at Columbia University, is the biographer of Theodore Parker and co-author with Samuel E. Morison of *The Growth of the American Republic* (Oxford University Press, 1930). In incisive style he phrases the American ideal, the challenge to America, and the alternative. What is the hope of the human race? What is the threat? Is it a mere military threat? Why is it difficult for us to comprehend the danger? What is the core of American philosophy of government? What treatment is accorded the individual by totalitarian philosophy? State the contrast between Nazism and democracy. If the totalitarian philosophies succeed, what may happen to America? What is our duty in this crisis?

Suggested Topics for Essays and Talks:

1. Whitman's dream of American leadership.
2. Creating friendly relations with Latin American nations.
3. Should a New League of Nations be organized?

THE TOTALITARIAN WAR AND THE FATE OF DEMOCRACY

Count Carlo Sforza, a refugee from Italy where he had a long diplomatic career, has devoted much energy in speaking and writing to oppose the doctrines of Fascism and Nazism, and to indicate the true status of America in the present world conflict. Are there tight compartments of isolation left in the world? What was the Italian mistake? What was the French mistake? Did Daladier want peace? What was

Léon Blum's error? What are the four terrors of Europe? Why is Bolshevism unlikely in Spain? What was Mussolini's attitude toward Count Sforza? What was Mussolini's discovery about a lie? What mistake do 'liberals' make about Mussolini? What mistake is made about Hitler? Why did the Jugoslavs risk death? Why was Mussolini behind the times in his colonization moves? What was Count Sforza's attitude toward colonization and conquest? What was the Hungarian mistake? What is the moral of Count Teleki's suicide? How did propaganda undermine France? Why is complacency the worst enemy of America? Does the map assure us of safety? What hope does Count Sforza hold of America?

Suggested Topics for Essays and Talks:
1. Individual freedom is at stake.
2. Mistakes we must not make.
3. America's duty to the world.

NIGHTMARE AT NOON

Stephen Vincent Benét, author of *John Brown's Body,* 'The Devil and Daniel Webster,' and many other poems and stories, has phrased in poetry better than most of his contemporaries the dangers facing America.

Exercises:
1. Analyze the ideas of 'Nightmare at Noon.' What incidents from recent experience are presented? Does Benét speak frankly?
2. Examine Benét's language? Should a poet write about 'Joe's diner'?
3. Write an essay in which you imagine the scene on the campus or in the city if a bomb were dropped.
4. Prepare a radio script of 'Nightmare at Noon.'

NOT BY WORDS ALONE

Albert Carr shows that by the simple everyday acts of our lives we demonstrate our faith in America. Can you add further examples to those which he here gives?

YOUTH, WAR, AND FREEDOM

Raymond Gram Swing, distinguished news analyst for the Mutual Broadcasting System, delivered this address at the Commencement of Olivet College, Olivet, Michigan, on 16 June 1940. Long before many other people sensed the danger to us, Mr. Swing cautioned American youth to be on the alert. Why is Dr. Ley's statement unrepresentative of Germany's actual freedom? Why is Dr. Ley's statement not the American ideal? What will be the outcome of the war in Europe with respect to individual freedom? Are we reluctant to express our concern over certain values? What contribution has Mr. Swing's generation made to American life? What two tremendous factors have weakened youth's loyalty? Was the job botched after World War I? Is the Treaty of Versailles to blame for the present war? Did the United States err in not entering the League of Nations? When did the breakdown begin? Next to the loss of the peace, says Mr. Swing, the loss of the sense of personal validity has weakened youth's loyalty; how so? What about the new psychology, the new economics? Why is Dr. Ley's omission of freedom to think and speak a key to the difference between Germany and the United States? Why must we care for freedom today?

A SOLDIER

In this sonnet Robert Frost denies that a soldier's life in behalf of an ideal is wasted. Notice the poetic treatment of the topic; instead of giving literal statements, Frost always makes indirect ones. Through the poem the figure of a thrown missile is sustained. Instead of speaking about a dead soldier the poet tells of a fallen lance. If men fail to see a worthy mark at which the soldier aimed, it is because men see but a short distance. Notice the geometric figure which now follows. The arc of the earth is large; man's lance traverses a shorter, sharper arc, and hence it cuts athwart the greater arc. As these two arcs intersect at the curve of earth, the thrown missiles fall and break; that is, lives come to an end. But, says Frost, we know that the soldier has gained immortality, because the earth that stopped the flight of the body has sped the soul onward farther than the earthly goal or its far-distant reflection. Notice the compact utterance, and the tight, formal speech replacing the cadence of familiar speech in Frost's dramatic narratives.

THE SOLDIER'S FAITH

Oliver Wendell Holmes, Jr., was wounded in the War between the States. Some thirty years later, on Memorial Day, 30 May 1895, he delivered this address to the graduating class of Harvard University. At this time he was a distinguished judge in Boston; later he was appointed a justice of the Supreme Court of the United States. Does Holmes think the acquisition of wealth a worthy goal? Has the revolt against pain brought results? Is the struggle for life the order of the world? Must we worry about falling? What is 'a splendid carelessness of life'? Are cynical thoughts trampled under foot in times of stress? Why is life like a place hung about with dark mists? Is war the business of young men? Why is war needed as a teacher? Is the experience of war pleasant? What is the product of heroism? How do we get leadership? What carelessness is ours toward our traditions? What is the soldier's faith?

ADDRESS TO THE NATION

Two days after the treacherous Japanese attack upon Pearl Harbor, President Franklin D. Roosevelt addressed the nation by radio. He summarizes the history of the relations between Japan and the United States, he urges disbelief in rumors, he reports on our rearmament program, he speaks of the privilege of self-sacrifice for our country, he hints at the strategy to be employed, and he assures us that our democratic ideals of freedom and individuality will survive a victorious war.

INDEX BY TYPES OF WRITING

INDEX OF AUTHORS AND SELECTIONS

Titles of essays, poems, scripts, and stories are in italic type; names of authors are in Roman; and section headings are in capitals. Notes to the selections are indicated by numbers within parentheses.

The text of this book has been set in 10 point Linotype Baskerville with 2 points leading. The display type used for the part titles is Bulmer, a modern version of a face which was cut for the English printer, Bulmer, by William Martin. Martin apparently learned his trade in Baskerville's foundry and based his design on Baskerville's type.

The 16-page *March of Time* insert was printed in gravure by Photogravure & Color Company. The text composition, printing, and binding were done by Quinn & Boden Company, Inc. The format was designed by John Begg.